Critical Thinking

Eighth Edition

Critical Thinking

Brooke Noel Moore
Richard Parker
California State University, Chico

Chapter 12
with Nina Rosenstand and Anita Silvers

Boston Burr Ridge, IL Dubuque, IA Madison, WI New York
San Francisco St. Louis Bangkok Bogotá Caracas Kuala Lumpur
Lisbon London Madrid Mexico City Milan Montreal New Delhi
Santiago Seoul Singapore Sydney Taipei Toronto

Higher Education

Published by McGraw-Hill, an imprint of The McGraw-Hill Companies, Inc., 1221 Avenue of the Americas, New York, NY 10020.

This book is printed on acid-free paper.

2 3 4 5 6 7 8 9 0 VNH/VNH 0 9 8 7

ISBN-13: 978-0-07-312625-8
ISBN-10: 0-07-312625-X

Editor in Chief: *Emily Barrosse*
Publisher: *Lyn Uhl*
Sponsoring Editor: *Jon-David Hague*
Marketing Manager: *Suzanna Ellison*
Director of Development: *Lisa Pinto*
Developmental Editor: *Angela Kao*
Editorial Coordinator: *Nicole Caddigan*
Production Editor: *Chanda Feldman*
Manuscript Editor: *Patricia Ohlenroth*
Art Director: *Jeanne Schreiber*
Design Manager: *Violeta Diaz*
Text and Cover Designer: *Amanda Kavanaugh*
Art Editor: *Ayelet Arbel*
Illustrators: *Lotus Art*
Photo Research: *Brian J. Pecko*
Supplements Producer: *Louis Swaim*
Production Supervisor: *Tandra Jorgensen*
Composition: *10/12 Trump Medieval by Thompson Type*
Printing: *45# Pub Matte Plus, Von Hoffmann*

Cover: *Another Dimension.*
© Bill Binzen/Corbis

Credits: The credits section for this book begins on page 533 and is considered an extension of the copyright page.

Library of Congress Cataloging-in-Publication Data
Moore, Brooke Noel.
Critical thinking / Brooke Noel Moore, Richard Parker. — 8th ed.
p. cm.
"Chapter 12 with Nina Rosenstand and Anita Silvers."
Includes index.
ISBN-13: 978-0-07-312625-8 (alk. paper)
ISBN-10: 0-07-312625-X (alk. paper)
1. Critical thinking. I. Parker, Richard. II. Title.
B105.T54M66 2007
160—dc22 2005054389

www.mhhe.com

To Alexander, Bill, and Sherry,
and also to Sydney, Darby,
Peyton Elizabeth, and Griffin

Brief Table of Contents

Table of Contents

Box List

Preface

Readers of our last edition may recall Dr. Hague, the hard-boiled philosophy editor at McGraw-Hill. Dr. Hague is the perfect New York editor, tight-lipped and taciturn. When he attempts to smile, which happens occasionally, the natural contours of his face tend toward sneering. Thus, when we announced we had an unusual idea for a new edition, Dr. Hague looked up from his work and sneered politely.

We viewed this as encouraging. "Based on our experience," we said, "we have concluded that university professors face a new challenge. Students no longer actually read."

"Books," Moore explained. "They don't like to read books. They read monitors and such. Also, they like pictures."

"So," Parker concluded, "we thought it would be good to shade the edges of each page to resemble a TV screen."

Dr. Hague's expression darkened. He did not seem impressed. "You wish to disguise the fact that your book contains words?" he asked.

"Well," Parker began, thinking how to respond.

Hague cut him off. "If today's students like pictures, give them the means to think critically about them," he advised and turned back to work.

This is why they pay Hague the big money. We had to admit, he was on to something. In fact, it became the seminal idea for the eighth installment of this text.

CHANGES TO THE EIGHTH EDITION

But did we say the *eighth* installment? Is this necessary? Have the principles of logic and the standards of clear thinking even *changed?* Well, while the standards and principles of logic and good thinking don't change, various improvements in coverage and presentation and other innovations do call for new editions from time to time. This edition in particular contains several important revisions and one major change. The latter relates to Hague's idea about critical thinking and pictures: In this edition we expand coverage to full-color images.

Images

Loaded images have always been employed by those who seek to influence beliefs and attitudes; such images are a vital component of advertising and propaganda. Indeed, pictures may be more effective than words as instruments of persuasion. Plus, in these days of digital photography it is a snap to edit and circulate images. Watch *The Daily Show* (with Jon Stewart), for example, and you will see "news photos" of important people, photos that may encourage a certain point of view. For instance, there is a still of Hillary Clinton grinning happily; or the president appearing slightly cross-eyed; or Dick Cheney leering menacingly. Students are bombarded daily by these images, and something needs to be said about this kind of thing—and in this edition we say it. For good measure, we also provide extra visuals for analysis at the back of the book.

Applying Your Feedback

We also have rethought some of the key concepts of the book. Dr. Hague cautions us not to overly stress this point because, to the extent we change our minds about things, it might be thought that our earlier work contained mistakes. Well, let's just say we listen to your feedback and our thinking on important topics evolves. In this edition there are philosophical adjustments that are rather significant; we won't go into details here, but you will find changes pertaining to the objective/subjective distinction, the question about whether value judgments can be objective, the nature of deduction and induction, and the differences between inductive generalizations and arguments by analogy.

Our Teaching Experience

Another source of revisions comes from our experience in the classroom. We both still are "in the saddle" teaching critical thinking skills, and we learn constantly from experience. (As you can see from the photo at the end of the preface, we are not quite masters of the spellbinding lecture.) Plus, we receive many suggestions from other instructors who use this book. These revisions are the pedagogical enhancements of the new edition. They include such things as relabeling "rhetorical comparisons" as "rhetorical analogies," treating inductive arguments as predictions, and explaining the "cautiousness" of the conclusion of an inductive argument in terms of the implied "level of confidence."

What works best in our own classes is to illustrate principles rather than explain them. In the past, both in our classes and in this book, we had a tendency to lecture. In this edition you will find more reliance on examples and illustrations, especially real-life examples, and less space devoted to boring explanations. This technique works for us, and we hope it will work for you as well.

Keeping up with Current Events

Another set of revisions has to do with our constantly changing culture. A student who is eighteen years old midway through George W. Bush's second term was only twelve when the Supreme Court ruled in Bush's favor in the 2000 Florida vote and may scarcely even remember who Al Gore was. He or she was only ten when Bill Clinton was impeached and only four when Clinton was first elected. He or she probably has only a vague recollection of the Clinton presidency. Some of our students were not alive when the Willie Horton ad aired, and most seem not to have heard of George Dukakis. "Dan Quayle?" "Potato?" Huh? We had a photo of Jimmy Carter in the last edition; kids didn't know who he was. (He's still in this edition, but at least we explain.) Not every student nowadays knows the individual names of the Beatles; few know who Robert Blake was. Throughout the book we have updated the examples to include individuals and events familiar to today's students. If you are like us, you may feel sufficiently challenged teaching the art of critical thinking without having to teach history as well.

FEATURES

Critical thinking includes a variety of deliberative processes aimed at making wise decisions about what to believe and do, processes that center on evaluation of arguments but include much more. We believe the best way to teach critical thinking is to integrate logic, both formal and informal, with a variety of skills and topics useful in making sound decisions about claims, actions, and practices—and to make it all palatable by presenting it in real-life contexts. This book is chatty in tone but it doesn't duck important issues, and we are gratified by its popularity. All of the features that may have something to do with its success have been retained and we've added a few new features as well.

- Thinking Critically About Images
  We incorporate discussion of images from the very beginning, and say something about them in most chapters. There are now around 130 color photographs included in this book. If one wants to talk about photographs and other images, it's nice to have examples of the real thing. This edition is like *The Wizard of Oz* after Dorothy leaves Kansas and we think it will be easier for you to use.
- Newly Organized Box Program
  The boxes in this book have always served educational purposes, though we admit that a few of them are mainly just for fun. In this edition we categorize the boxes as falling under one of these headings:

In Depth: These boxes take the important concepts of a chapter to a deeper level. They contain important rules, definitions, or guidelines that are central to the chapter topic.

In Depth

Innocent Until Proved Guilty

We must point out that sometimes there are specific reasons why the burden of proof is placed entirely on one side. The obvious case in point is in criminal court, where it is the prosecution's job to prove guilt. The defense is not required to prove innocence; it must only try to keep the prosecution from succeeding in its attempt to prove guilt. We are, as we say, "innocent until proved guilty." As a matter of fact, it's possible that more trials might come to a correct conclusion (i.e., the guilty get convicted and the innocent acquitted) if the burden of proof were equally shared between prosecution and defense. But we have wisely decided that if we are to make a mistake, we would rather it be one of letting a guilty person go free than one of convicting an innocent person. Rather than being a fallacy, then, this lopsided placement of the burden of proof is how we guarantee a fundamental right: the presumption of innocence.

I'm not?" Well, it may be possible to prove he's not a student, but it's no easy chore, and it would be unreasonable to require it.

Incidentally, some people say it's *impossible* to "prove a negative." But difficult is not the same as impossible. And some "negatives" are even easy to prove. For example, "There are no elephants in this classroom."

3. *Special circumstances.* Sometimes getting at the truth is not the only thing we want to accomplish, and on such occasions we may purposely place the burden of proof on a particular side. Courts of law provide us with the most obvious example. Specific agreements can also move the burden of proof from where it would ordinarily fall. A contract might specify, "It will be presumed that you receive the information by the tenth of each month unless

Real Life

When Is an Ad Not an Ad? When It's a Product Placement!

Coca Cola cups prominently displayed on the television show "American Idol."

When Katherine Hepburn threw all of Humphrey Bogart's Gordon's Gin overboard in the *African Queen,* it was an early example of product placement, since the makers of Gordon's paid to have their product tossed in the drink, as it were. Readers of a certain age may remember the 1960s television show *Route 66,* which starred not just Martin Milner and George Maharis, but also a new Chevrolet Corvette and probably contributed to more than a few Corvette sales. Reese's Pieces were centrally placed in the movie *ET,* and the sales of Red Stripe beer jumped 50 percent after it appeared prominently in the movie *The Firm.*

These days, the paid placement of products in both movies and television (and possibly even in novels) is a serious alternative to traditional commercials and it has the advantage of overcoming the Tivo effect: recording programs and watching them while skipping over the commercials.

Real Life: These boxes contain honest-to-goodness examples of critical thinking—and lack of it—in real life.

In the Media: These boxes are comprised of quotations from print, television, radio, and the Internet, covering a wide variety of topics, many of which are political in nature.

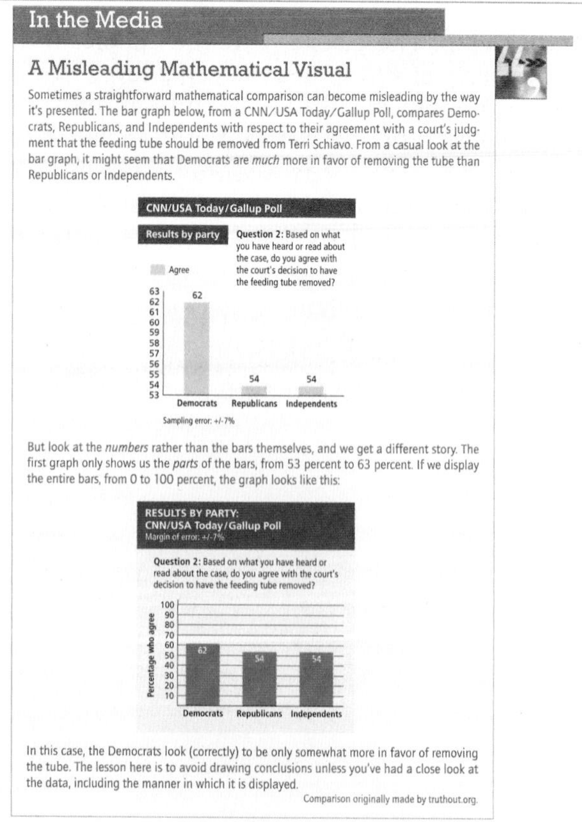

In the Media

A Misleading Mathematical Visual

Sometimes a straightforward mathematical comparison can become misleading by the way it's presented. The bar graph below, from a CNN/USA Today/Gallup Poll, compares Democrats, Republicans, and Independents with respect to their agreement with a court's judgment that the feeding tube should be removed from Terri Schiavo. From a casual look at the bar graph, it might seem that Democrats are *much* more in favor of removing the tube than Republicans or Independents.

But look at the *numbers* rather than the bars themselves, and we get a different story. The first graph only shows us the *parts* of the bars, from 53 percent to 63 percent. If we display the entire bars, from 0 to 100 percent, the graph looks like this:

In this case, the Democrats look (correctly) to be only somewhat more in favor of removing the tube. The lesson here is to avoid drawing conclusions unless you've had a close look at the data, including the manner in which it is displayed.

Comparison originally made by truthout.org.

On Language

Legislative Misnomers

Several polls have reported that voters sometimes indicate approval of a measure when they hear its title, but indicate disapproval once they've heard an explanation of what the measure actually proposes. This isn't surprising given the misleading proposal titles assigned by members of Congress and state legislatures, and by authors of ballot measures. Here are a few examples of recent laws, initiatives, etc., the names of which don't exactly tell the whole story:

Healthy Forests Initiative (federal)—Reduces public involvement in decision-making regarding logging, reduces environmental protection requirements, and provides timber companies greater access to National Forests

Clear Skies Act (federal)—Loosens regulation of mercury, nitrous oxide, and sulphur dioxide, and puts off required reductions of these substances for several years beyond the limits of the current Clean Air Act; allows companies to trade off "pollution credits" so that some communities would get cleaner air and others dirtier air

Limitations on Enforcement of Unfair Business Competition Laws (California)—Makes it impossible for consumer groups of all types to sue corporations and businesses to prevent fraud, false advertising, and other deceptions before they take place

Payroll Protection Plan (many states)—Prevents any part of a union member's dues from being used for political purposes without his or her written consent

Right to Work (many states)—Prevents unions from collecting fees from nonmembers of bargaining units

Prohibition of Discrimination and Preferential Treatment (California)—Weakens or eliminates affirmative action programs

Earth? Judging from realistic simulations involving a sledge hammer and a common laboratory frog, we can assume it will be pretty bad."* The last examples are, of course, intended to be humorous, but they illustrate the concept.

A similar rhetorical device is the rhetorical definition, which we encountered in Chapter 2. "Real" definitions are primarily used to clarify meaning; **rhetorical definitions** use emotively charged language to express or elicit an attitude about something. Defining abortion as "the murder of an unborn child" does this—and stacks the deck against those who think abortion is morally defensible. Likewise, "human being" could be restricted in its meaning to an organism that a human gives birth to. Under this definition, abor-

Looks like two different engineers started work[ing at] opposite ends and cou[ldn't] look at what the other [was] doing until they met at center post.

—Click and Clack, usin[g an] analogy to describe th[e] Pontiac Aztec

On Language: These boxes highlight the power of language in action when it comes to critical thinking.

Exercises

The exercises give guided practice in applying important critical thinking skills. As much as possible, we try to involve students actively in the learning process. Several exercises require students to collaborate with one another, and in our experience these exercises work pretty well. Sometimes we even use these exercises *before* explaining the material in the chapter for which they are relevant. There are numerous exercises contained here in the text, and for instructors, many more in *The Logical Accessory* (The Instructor's Resource CD-ROM).

5. The ocean on the central coast is the most beautiful shade of sky blue. It's more green as you go north.
6. Her favorite color is yellow because it is the color of the sun.
7. Pooh is my favorite cartoon character because he has lots of personality.
8. You must turn off the lights when you leave the room. They cost a lot of money to run and you don't need them on during the day.
9. Television programs have too much violence and immoral behavior. Hundreds of killings are portrayed every month.
10. You'll be able to find a calendar on sale after the first of the year, so it is a good idea to wait until then to buy one.

Exercise 1-3

Some of these items are arguments and some are not. Can you divide them up correctly?

▲ 1. Roddick is unlikely to win the U.S. Open this year. He has a nagging leg injury, plus he just doesn't seem to have the drive he once had.

2. Hey there, Marco!—don't go giving that cat top sirloin. What's the matter with you, you got no brains at all?

3. If you've ever met a pet bird, then you know they are very busy creatures.

▲ 4. Everybody is saying the president has made us the laughingstock of the world. What a stupid idea! He hasn't made us a laughingstock at all. There's not a bit of truth in that notion.

5. "Is the author really entitled to assert that there is a degree of unity among these essays which makes this a book rather than a congeries? I am inclined to say that he is justified in this claim, but articulating this justification is a somewhat complex task."
From a book review by Stanley Bates

6. As a long-time customer, you're already taking advantage of our money management expertise and variety of investment choices. That's a good reason for consolidating your other eligible assets into an IRA with us.

7. PROFESSOR X: Well, I see where the new chancellor wants to increase class sizes.
PROFESSOR Y: Yeah, another of his bright ideas.
PROFESSOR X: Actually, I don't think it hurts to have one or two extra people in class.
PROFESSOR Y: What? Of course it hurts. What are you thinking, anyway?
PROFESSOR X: Well, I just think there is good reason for increasing the class size a bit.

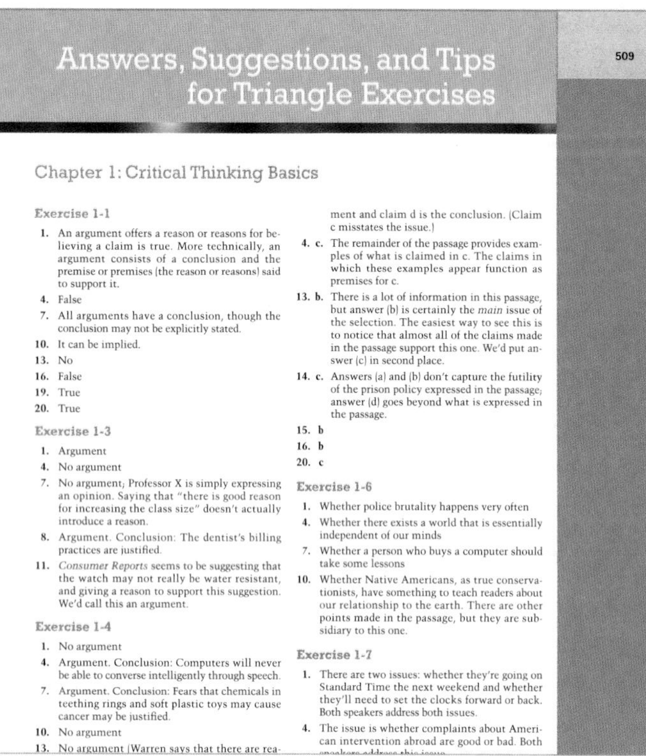

509

Answers, Suggestions, and Tips for Triangle Exercises

Chapter 1: Critical Thinking Basics

Exercise 1-1

1. An argument offers a reason or reasons for believing a claim is true. More technically, an argument consists of a conclusion and the premise or premises (the reason or reasons) said to support it.
4. False
7. All arguments have a conclusion, though the conclusion may not be explicitly stated.
10. It can be implied.
13. No
16. False
19. True
20. True

Exercise 1-3

1. Argument
4. No argument
7. No argument; Professor X is simply expressing an opinion. Saying that "there is good reason for increasing the class size" doesn't actually introduce a reason.
8. Argument. Conclusion: The dentist's billing practices are justified.
11. *Consumer Reports* seems to be suggesting that the watch may not really be water resistant, and giving a reason to support this suggestion. We'd call this an argument.

Exercise 1-4

1. No argument
4. Argument. Conclusion: Computers will never be able to converse intelligently through speech.
7. Argument. Conclusion: Fears that chemicals in teething rings and soft plastic toys may cause cancer may be justified.
10. No argument
13. No argument (Warren says that there are rea-

ment and claim d is the conclusion. (Claim c misstates the issue.)

4. c. The remainder of the passage provides examples of what is claimed in c. The claims in which these examples appear function as premises for c.
13. b. There is a lot of information in this passage, but answer (b) is certainly the *main* issue of the selection. The easiest way to see this is to notice that almost all of the claims made in the passage support this one. We'd put answer (c) in second place.
14. c. Answers (a) and (b) don't capture the futility of the prison policy expressed in the passage; answer (d) goes beyond what is expressed in the passage.
15. b
16. b
20. c

Exercise 1-6

1. Whether police brutality happens very often
4. Whether there exists a world that is essentially independent of our minds
7. Whether a person who buys a computer should take some lessons
10. Whether Native Americans, as true conservationists, have something to teach readers about our relationship to the earth. There are other points made in the passage, but they are subsidiary to this one.

Exercise 1-7

1. There are two issues: whether they're going on Standard Time the next weekend and whether they'll need to set the clocks forward or back. Both speakers address both issues.
4. The issue is whether complaints about American intervention abroad are good or bad. Both

Answers, Suggestions, and Tips

Questions marked with a triangle in each chapter are answered in the "Answers, Suggestions, and Tips" section in the back (look for the colored pages) along with some discussions that expand upon other text material. Students may use this section to check themselves before a test and instructors may find the answer section to be a useful teaching aid or a foil for their own explanations and comments.

Glossary

The glossary at the end of the book defines important terms, usually correctly.

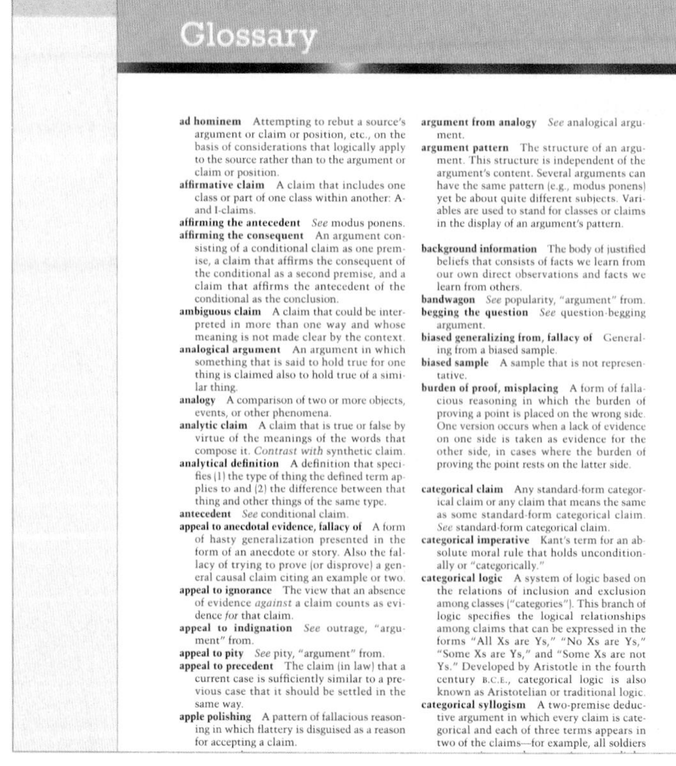

502

Glossary

ad hominem Attempting to rebut a source's argument or claim or position, etc., on the basis of considerations that logically apply to the source rather than to the argument or claim or position.

affirmative claim A claim that includes one class or part of one class within another: A- and I-claims.

affirming the antecedent *See* modus ponens.

affirming the consequent An argument consisting of a conditional claim as one premise, a claim that affirms the consequent of the conditional as a second premise, and a claim that affirms the antecedent of the conditional as the conclusion.

ambiguous claim A claim that could be interpreted in more than one way and whose meaning is not made clear by the context.

analogical argument An argument in which something that is said to hold true for one thing is claimed also to hold true of a similar thing.

analogy A comparison of two or more objects, events, or other phenomena.

analytic claim A claim that is true or false by virtue of the meanings of the words that compose it. *Contrast with* synthetic claim.

analytical definition A definition that specifies (1) the type of thing the defined term applies to and (2) the difference between that thing and other things of the same type.

antecedent *See* conditional claim.

appeal to anecdotal evidence, fallacy of A form of hasty generalization presented in the form of an anecdote or story. Also the fallacy of trying to prove (or disprove) a general causal claim citing an example or two.

appeal to ignorance The view that an absence of evidence *against* a claim counts as evidence *for* that claim.

appeal to indignation *See* outrage, "argument" from.

appeal to pity *See* pity, "argument" from.

appeal to precedent The claim (in law) that a current case is sufficiently similar to a previous case that it should be settled in the same way.

apple polishing A pattern of fallacious reasoning in which flattery is disguised as a reason for accepting a claim.

argument from analogy *See* analogical argument.

argument pattern The structure of an argument. This structure is independent of the argument's content. Several arguments can have the same pattern (e.g., modus ponens) yet be about quite different subjects. Variables are used to stand for classes or claims in the display of an argument's pattern.

background information The body of justified beliefs that consists of facts we learn from our own direct observations and facts we learn from others.

bandwagon *See* popularity, "argument" from.

begging the question *See* question-begging argument.

biased generalizing from, fallacy of Generalizing from a biased sample.

biased sample A sample that is not representative.

burden of proof, misplacing A form of fallacious reasoning in which the burden of proving a point is placed on the wrong side. One version occurs when a lack of evidence on one side is taken as evidence for the other side, in cases where the burden of proving the point rests on the latter side.

categorical claim Any standard-form categorical claim or any claim that means the same as some standard-form categorical claim. *See* standard-form categorical claim.

categorical imperative Kant's term for an absolute moral rule that holds unconditionally or "categorically."

categorical logic A system of logic based on the relations of inclusion and exclusion among classes ("categories"). This branch of logic specifies the logical relationships among claims that can be expressed in the forms "All Xs are Ys," "No Xs are Ys," "Some Xs are Ys," and "Some Xs are not Ys." Developed by Aristotle in the fourth century B.C.E., categorical logic is also known as Aristotelian or traditional logic.

categorical syllogism A two-premise deductive argument in which every claim is categorical and each of three terms appears in two of the claims—for example, all soldiers

Appendix 1: Essays for Analysis, Now with Images

These essays and images can be used in various ways: They are excellent topics for analysis, in-class discussion, or out-of-class writing exercises.

- Appendix 1 begins with an essay that we call "The Whole Enchilada." In this selection, we illustrate how many different critical thinking skills are brought to bear on a serious real-life issue. It serves as a good review for many of the chapters in the book.
- The next selection in Appendix 1 is the "model essay." We've taken an essay that deals with a controversial topic that we found in a moderately obscure magazine and edited it down to manageable length. We offer this example as a fairly well-reasoned series of arguments designed to support a conclusion (that is probably not too popular) about the September 11, 2001, terrorist attacks. You can use it as an example of how to adduce arguments to a conclusion, or if you disagree, challenge it with rebuttals.
- New to this edition, we've also added examples of advertisements to Appendix 1. While images are not essays, they still convey ideas and associations in their own ways. You might consider such questions as "What is the target audience of each ad?" or "How does this ad appeal to a particular audience?"

Appendix 2: The Top Ten Fallacies of All Time

Here is our list, based on our experience gathering real-life examples of fallacies to use for text illustrations and exercises. The list isn't scientifically derived, but we have a pretty good idea of which fallacies occur most often.

Appendix 3: The Scrapbook of Unusual Ideas

A compendium of topics to generate discussion or to adapt for homework assignments or in-class material. Don't have time to prepare a lecture? Here's your answer: Turn to this section, pull out an interesting issue or two and have people take positions and defend them with arguments.

Front and Back Covers

A streamlined list of the "Top Ten Fallacies of All Time" appears inside the front cover; "Common Categorical Argument Patterns" and "Common Truth-Functional Argument Patterns" appear inside the back cover.

NEW CONTENT

In addition to enhancing all of the above material, we've made the following alterations in this edition:

Chapter 1, *Critical Thinking Basics*

We drove this one into the shop for a tune-up. We now offer what we think is an improved definition of critical thinking, and we explore the nature of argument in more depth. We even explain the difference between induction and deduction right here at the outset, so adopters who want to move directly to

Part 3, Arguments, will find it easy to do so. Induction and deduction are depicted differently from earlier editions, as well.

Another important change: We tend now to think that our earlier distinction between "factual claims" and "nonfactual" claims was confusing, and somewhat tangential to the ultimate objectives of critical thinking. The distinction that matters, we think, is that between objective and subjective claims (and other expressions). It is a mistake, we explicitly argue in this chapter, to think that all value judgments are expressions of subjective taste.

Chapter 2, *Clear Thinking, Critical Thinking, and Clear Writing*

This chapter, too, has seen major alterations. In previous editions, we made this basically a chapter on writing and brought in critical thinking as instrumental to good writing. In this edition, we continue where we left off in Chapter 1 about the importance of clear thinking to critical thinking, and then bring in the argumentative essay as an application of critical thinking to paper. This makes the transition from Chapter 1 much smoother.

Chapter 3, *Credibility*

In many cases, we must assess the credibility of sources as well as inherent believability of what they assert. This entire chapter is devoted to credibility, authority, and expertise. New to this edition, we include a different and somewhat more skeptical slant on the news media, and this includes more attention to news sources that are *not* ABC, CBS, NBC, the *New York Times* or the *Washington Post.* New influences on the news (including completely fake news) are noted.

Chapter 4, *Persuasion Through Rhetoric*

Starting here, we deal with a large and diversified inventory of persuasive devices, emotional appeals, and irrelevancies that we all use to add psychological power to our assertions. This part of the book helps students distinguish weak reasons from irrelevant considerations, a subtle but important distinction. New to this edition, we include more detail about photographs and other images as potential pieces of nonverbal "rhetoric."

Chapter 5, *More Rhetorical Devices;* and Chapter 6, *Ad Hominem and More Fallacies*

Here we expand the coverage of the most important fallacies to include their photographic analogues.

Chapter 7, *The Anatomy and Varieties of Arguments*

In this chapter we delve into the basics of argument, using a new, improved depiction of the difference between deductive and inductive argument. The idea, basically, is that a valid deductive argument *demonstrates* or *proves* the conclusion, while a strong inductive argument *supports* the conclusion. (These concepts are explained.) Adopters who were uncomfortable with our defining induction and deduction with reference to someone's intentions, should be happy with the new treatment. And those instructors who wish to transition directly from Chapter 1 to Part 3 will find it easier to make the move.

Chapter 8, *Deductive Arguments I: Categorical Logic*

Here you will find colorized Venn diagrams, a nice pedagogical addition.

Chapter 9, *Deductive Arguments II: Truth-Functional Logic*

Here we make the biggest (and best) change to Chapter 9 yet: The linkage of truth-functional logic with electrical circuits.

Chapter 10, *Inductive Arguments*

This time we emphasize the predictive nature of inductive arguments. Also, we provide better separation between inductive generalizations and analogical arguments. We also better clarify the distinction between "hasty generalizing" and "biased generalizing," and treat them separately from "poor analogy," a term we use for the first time.

Chapter 11, *Causal Arguments*

We've taken the opportunity offered by having a new edition to more fully illustrate the principal types of causal arguments, using real-life examples.

Chapter 12, *Moral, Legal, and Aesthetic Reasoning*

There are important changes in the section of this chapter that pertains to moral reasoning. Again, heavy lifting in this edition is done by the distinction between objective and subjective expressions rather than by the distinction between factual and nonfactual claims. This shift in perspective is carried forward in Chapter 12.

BEYOND THE BOOK: SUPPLEMENTS

Online Learning Center

Go to www.mhhe.com/criticalthinking8 for interactive exercises and resources for students and instructors. It is compatible with McGraw-Hill's free PageOut course management system as well as WebCT and Blackboard, allowing instructors to create customized course Web sites.

The Logical Accessory (Instructor's Resource CD-ROM)

Available to instructors who teach with this book, this CD-ROM contains an Instructor's Manual, Test Bank, PowerPoint Presentations, and Classroom Performance System. The Instructor's Manual provides additional answers to many exercises not answered in the book. It also provides many more examples, exercises, and test questions. Here and there we include hints, strategies, lecture topics, tangents, and flights of fancy.

Essay Grading Rubric

Grading rubrics are widely used in schools, and are found increasingly on the college scene as well. Students like rubric-based grading. They think it reduces the subjectivity involved in evaluating essays. Our rubric is tucked into *The Logical Accessory.*

Students responding enthusiastically to a Moore/Parker lecture.

Photo Credit: Bill Husa, Chico Enterprise Record.

Acknowledgements

If you find mistakes in this edition, don't blame our gifted editorial and production team, which includes Dr. Hague; Angela Kao, who was our well-organized and innovative development editor; Chanda Feldman, who oversaw the production process; Patricia Ohlenroth, our copyeditor—who gave us seven packs of sticky notes worth of great improvements; and Brian Pecko, who helped us find photographs for this edition.

We are grateful to those who advised us in preparing for this edition.

K.D. Borcoman, Coastline College/CSUDH
Sandra Dwyer, Georgia State University
Ellery Eells, University of Wisconsin–Madison
Geoffrey B. Frasz, Community College of Southern Nevada
Judith M. Hill, Saginaw Valley State University
William Krieger, California State University–Pomona
Jamie L. Phillips, Clarion University
Mehul Shah, Bergen Community College
Matt Schulte, Montgomery College
Richard Sneed, University of Central Oklahoma
Marie G. Zaccaria, Georgia Perimeter College

We continue to be grateful for the thoughtfulness and insight of previous reviewers and others who have contacted us about the book.

Charles Blatz, University of Toledo
Dabney Gray, Stillman College
Steven Hoeltzel, James Madison University
Eric Parkinson, Syracuse University
James Stump, Bethel College

We give special thanks to James Anderson of San Diego State University. An extended correspondence with Jim convinced us we needed to rethink some of our positions in Chapters 1 and 10. He hasn't seen the new material, and it may turn out not to his liking, but he was the one who started our engines.

We also want to give special thanks to Dan Barnett, who teaches philosophy at Butte College and who provided careful critiques of our new material and revised the selected answers to chapter exercises; Anne Morrissey at Chico State, who tries to keep us supplied with good material; and Curtis Peldo of Chico State and Butte College, who gave us nice ideas and good examples.

Thanks are due as well to other colleagues at Chico State: Greg Tropea, Marcel Daguerre, Wai-hung Wong, Randy Larsen, Becky White, and Ron Hirschbein.

Finally, we add special thanks to Alicia Alvarez Parker and Marianne Larson for their affection, patience, and support in ways that really count.

About the Authors

Both Moore and Parker have taught philosophy at California State University, Chico, for more years than they care to count. Aside from courses in logic and critical thinking, Moore also tries to teach epistemology and analytic philosophy. He is also chair of the department and once was selected as the university's Outstanding Professor. Parker's other teaching duties include courses in the history of modern philosophy and philosophy of law; he has chaired the academic senate and once upon a time was dean of undergraduate education.

Brooke Noel Moore and Richard Parker, not necessarily in the order pictured above.

Moore majored in music at Antioch College; his Ph.D. is from the University of Cincinnati. For a time he held the position of the world's most serious amateur volleyball player. He and Marianne currently share their house with three large dogs. Moore has never sold an automobile.

Parker's undergraduate career was committed at the University of Arkansas; his doctorate is from the University of Washington. He drives a '62 MG, rides a motorcycle, plays golf for fun, shoots pool for money, and is a serious amateur flamenco guitarist. He and Alicia live part of the year in southern Spain.

Moore and Parker have been steadfast friends through it all.

This is not entirely a work of non-fiction.

Chapter 1

Critical Thinking Basics

Johnnie Cochran (1946–2005), for years one of America's best-known defense attorneys, represented O.J. Simpson, Michael Jackson, and Puff Daddy (Sean Combs), among many others. In the Simpson trial, Cochran's blend of logic, rhetoric, and explanation—these concepts are all examined in this book—resulted in an acquittal for his client. His closing statement, "If it doesn't fit, you must acquit," refers to the gloves used as evidence against Simpson in the trial. The statement is a good example of deductive logic, examined in detail in Chapters 7, 8, and 9.

Butte City, California, is located in the Sacramento Valley between Princeton and Ord Bend. You won't find buttes there, or bluffs, or even mounds. It is also not a city. The state highway sign lists the population at 291 and even that may be generous.

The few people who do live in Butte City are mostly connected one way or another to agriculture. Butte City has a gas station, now closed, a saloon, and what looks like a place for people to discard farming equipment parts. Recently, however, someone opened another business, a tanning salon.

The prospects for a tanning business in Butte City do not seem bright. In the Sacramento Valley clouds are scarce, and the people who live there tend to look for ways to get out of the sun. Deepening their tans seems an unlikely priority.

We humans are clever enough to land spacecraft on a moon of Jupiter, combine genetic material to alter life forms, and build computers that outplay grand masters at chess, yet we sometimes make unwise decisions like opening a tanning salon in a tiny sun-baked farming community. Despite the impressive accomplishments of the human intellect, one frequently comes face to face with examples of faulty reasoning, error, and misjudgment. Back when one of us lived in Cincinnati, he knew someone named Ross, who used Vick's VapoRub.

"About a tablespoon," Ross would say. "It works. Eat that, your cold disappears."

Ross didn't hold this theory up to rational scrutiny. The "Rub" part of the name does not suggest an internal use, and when the container warns against putting the product in your mouth, you can bet there is a reason for it. Besides, colds eventually disappear on their own accord. Eat anything and your cold disappears. Eat dirt and your cold disappears.

We humans are unique among animals in our ability to subject our thoughts to rational scrutiny, and we would do well to take advantage of that gift. Other animals don't really have the knack, as far as we know. To offer one example, in the height of the 2004 camping season, a black bear broke into coolers belonging to campers at Baker Lake Resort in Washington. The bear punctured and drank three dozen cans of Rainier beer, and then passed out on the lawn. If a human had done this (one of our students, for example), we'd cite it as an example of failing to think critically. But bears, as far as anyone knows, are unable to think critically, so they can't be faulted for not doing so.*

This bear story illustrates other aspects of critical thinking. According to the news reports, the bear first tried a can of Busch but drank less than half the can and threw it away. It then ignored the remaining supply of Busch and commenced on the available Rainier. This bear, in other words, was thinking, making decisions, and even making discriminations worthy of a beer connoisseur—it was exercising a preference. But it wasn't acting either wisely or unwisely. It wasn't thinking critically or failing to think critically. It was just thinking. Critical thinking is more than just thinking or making decisions or acting selectively.

Above all else, thinking critically means screening your ideas to see if they really make sense. We shall be more precise about this in a moment, but the thing about critical thinking that distinguishes it from other forms of thinking is that if you aren't doing it, you may end up wishing you had. Not long ago we read about one Patrick Lawler, 23, a construction worker from Littleton, Colorado, who accidentally shot himself in the head with his nail gun. Although he said he felt like he had been hit with a bat, he didn't realize the gun had fired a 4-inch nail into his brain, a fact that came clear only when an X-ray was taken several days later after he went to the dentist complaining about a world-class toothache. Surgeons removed the nail, and Mr. Lawler apparently is okay. Unfortunately, Lawler had decided not to buy medical insurance, though he made enough to do so. This was very unwise, given the kind of work he did. From time to time, all of us make poorly thought out decisions like this—and not infrequently we regret it. Lawler's medical bills top $100,000, and he has no way to pay for them.**

If you are reading this book for a course, chances are you will be expected to critique others' ideas, and they will be asked to critique yours. Everyone understands the importance of screening one's own ideas for defects and defi-

*Wildlife agent Bill Heinck and other agents awakened the bear and tried to chase it from the campground, but the animal climbed a tree and slept for four more hours. At that point, the agents managed to awaken the animal again and shoo it away. Unfortunately, the next morning it returned. The agents then baited a large trap with doughnuts and open cans of beer (Rainier), and captured the bear for relocation. Associated Press report, August 18, 2004.

**Associated Press report by Caroline Liss, January 21, 2005.

■ Thinking critically, the photographer used remote control to shoot this gem.

ciencies (although we do not always do so), but many people draw a line when it comes to subjecting the views of others to scrutiny. Doing this is sometimes seen as a kind of personal attack. "Everyone is entitled to his or her opinion," you often hear it said. But critiquing another person's ideas does not mean you are attacking that person. It's not a put-down. Pointing out reasons for not eating VapoRub isn't insulting Ross; if anything it is trying to help him. Cases arise in which it would be dead wrong *not* to criticize another person's ideas. Not long ago, we read about some teenagers who thought it would be neat to wind a rope around a merry-go-round, then attach the other end to a pickup truck and drive off at high speed while someone tried to hang on. They tried it, and one person was hurled from the merry-go-round; afterward the driver of the pickup faced a manslaughter charge. Was he entitled to his opinion that this was a good idea? Of course not. Every one of us makes mistakes, and sometimes we need others to help us see them. We don't do a friend a favor by pretending his idea to open a tanning salon in Butte City is a good one. And we don't do ourselves any favors by not listening to others or by refusing to think critically about our own ideas.

CLAIMS

At this point, we need to introduce vocabulary. When you state a belief or opinion (same thing), you are making a **claim.** When you present a reason for thinking a claim is true, you are giving an **argument.** We'll provide a more technical definition in a moment, but an argument is what a prosecutor gives a judge or jury to show that the defendant is guilty. It is what a parent gives you when he or she tells you why you should do something, or if you are a parent, what you give your own children. It is what a scientist says to support a theoretical finding. It is what you give yourself when you justify taking some course of action, or not taking it. An argument against opening a tanning salon in Butte City is what the people who opened one may eventually wish they'd considered. *Whenever* there is a breakdown in critical thinking, there is an argument someone should have paid more attention to. Critical thinking requires evaluating arguments that support the claims we are considering, and weighing them against those that support alternative or contrary views.

One can critically examine (or fail to examine) claims about anything, from how best to train a puppy to what type of gasoline to buy. You can critically examine claims about silly little issues, like which potato chip brand is the best, to claims about very important things, like whether to invade another country. Any claim you make, or are thinking of making, or are merely considering, or someone else has made or wants you to make, is fair game. Critical thinking consists of the rational evaluation of specific claims, including weighing the arguments for and against them.

Some claims do not require much by way of critical evaluation; they may be self-evident or indisputable on the face of things, or just plainly false. Extended investigation or deliberation isn't required to determine if your throat is sore or if Costco is still open; there is no need there to weigh arguments. But other claims aren't quite so tractable. You can provide your own examples, but claims about what you should major in, how you should vote, whether a practice is likely to have health consequences, and what to do in personal relationships are all candidates for careful screening and critical evaluation, and they represent only a handful of the many claims that require critical attention. Some people occupy offices where their decisions deeply affect others; decisions of that sort perhaps require more scrutiny than any other.

ARGUMENTS

As we said, when you present a reason for thinking a claim is true, you give an argument. Recently a student named Kevin asked one of us if we thought brushing your teeth could really help you lose weight. Kevin had heard a report about a study published in a Japanese scientific journal that said that encouraging people to brush more frequently could help prevent obesity. Japanese researchers had studied almost 4,000 people and found that people who brushed three times a day were much more likely to be slender; and the student concluded from this that brushing your teeth could help you lose weight. When we looked up the media report of the Japanese study that's what it had concluded, too.

Now, you may not think of scientific data such as those contained in the Japanese study as an "argument," but here the data were given as a reason for thinking that brushing could help you lose weight, so they count as an argument. As arguments go, this one actually is poor, but it is an argument nevertheless.* It is an argument because it is a reason for thinking some claim is true. As you can see, an argument can be long and involved. Einstein didn't

*We'll get back to this very argument in Chapter 11, if we don't forget. One obvious problem with this argument is that people who brush frequently may be more health savvy or more concerned about their appearance and eat moderately for those reasons.

When you think critically, you weigh the pros and cons of an idea, which this person clearly didn't.

just pull "$E = mc^2$" out of his hat; he had complex theoretical reasons that require a lot of mathematics and physics to comprehend, and together they amounted to an argument that $E = mc^2$.

At the other extreme, every professor has heard: "My grandmother just died," offered as an excuse for having missed class. Here again, something is used as a reason for thinking something else is true, and that makes it an argument. My grandmother just died; therefore I should be excused for missing class, is the reasoning. Arguments can be short and simple like this one, or long and involved like Einstein's, or anywhere in between. It's not word count that determines whether something is an argument, but function. If one claim is given as a reason for thinking another claim is true, you have an argument; if it isn't, you don't.

An unfortunage minor complication must be mentioned at this point. Logicians think of an argument as including not merely the reason for thinking a claim is true, but also the claim itself. From this perspective an argument has two parts: the supported part, which is called the **conclusion,** and the supporting part, which is called the **premise.** The premise of an argument, in other words, specifies the reason (or reasons) for accepting the conclusion. The statement "I should be excused because my grandmother just died" has the required two-part structure. "My grandmother just died" is the premise, and "I should be excused" is the conclusion.

And thus we arrive, finally, at a technical definition of the most important ingredient in critical thinking. An argument consists of two parts, and one part (the premise or premises) is supposedly a reason for thinking that the other (the conclusion) is true. Critically thinking about a *claim* that is not self-evidently or obviously true or false requires evaluating the arguments both for and against it.

Does this mean this book is going to be about arguments? The answer is yes; but there are numerous parameters, as you might guess from seeing how big the book is.

OTHER CONCEPTS AND TERMS

Many bedrock concepts in this book use a vocabulary straight from ordinary English. People have *opinions, views, thoughts, beliefs, convictions,* and *ideas;* for our purposes these are the same. People may also express these opinions and the like in *statements, judgments, assertions,* or—to use our preferred word—*claims.* "Statement," "judgment," "assertion," and "claim" all mean the same thing for our purposes.

Whenever a claim is called into question or its truth or falsity becomes the subject of consideration or judgment, an *issue* or *question* has been raised. We use the terms "issue" and "question" interchangeably. For example, recently the Virginia Senate considered making it illegal for kids (or maybe anyone) to wear clothes that expose underwear. In other words, the claim "It should be illegal to wear clothes that expose underwear" was under consideration; whether it should become illegal to do that was the issue or question. When you think critically about a claim, you call it into question, thus making it an issue, and you weigh the arguments for and against, which is exactly what the Virginia lawmakers did.* As we shall see, in many real-life situations it is an important and sometimes difficult task to identify the claim that is in question.

Next, about *truth:* You may well wonder what sort of thing truth is, and what sort of things facts are. We must leave these mysteries for your next philosophy course. In a real-life situation, when people say a claim is true, they are often just agreeing with it. Likewise, when they say a claim states a fact, they are often just employing an alternative method of agreeing with it. Thus, in real-life conversations, these four claims often serve the same purpose:

A book is on the table.

It is true that a book is on the table.

It is a fact that a book is on the table.

I agree; a book is on the table.

Knowledge is another important concept. We have to admit we don't know what knowledge is. However, you are entitled to *say* you know that a claim, such as "There is a book on the table" is true, if (1) you believe there is a book on the table, (2) you have an argument beyond a reasonable doubt for thinking there is, and (3) you have no reason to think you are mistaken, such as might be the case if you hadn't slept for several nights or had recently taken a large dose of some hallucinogenic drug.

SUBJECTIVISM

Right here at the start we need to discuss an idea that could puncture the hull before the ship leaves port. This is the idea that one opinion is as good as the

*The bill passed the state House, but was dropped in the Senate. The argument deemed to carry the most weight was that the bill made the legislature look silly. *USA Today,* February 11, 2005.

next, or that what is true is what you think is true. This concept is known as **subjectivism.** If you have never heard anyone say "One opinion is as good as the next," or "It may not be true for you, but it's true for me," or "What is true is what you think is true," then it is only because you never took a philosophy class and listened to your peers. Such assertions are quite common in that setting—until the instructor explains what is wrong with them, as we shall be doing shortly.

Obviously, if it is true that one opinion is as good as the next, there isn't much point in thinking critically about any opinion, since it already is as good as any alternative. No need to go to school either since your opinion is already as good as Einstein's.

In fact, nobody is a subjectivist about *everything,* at least nobody is who goes to the doctor. What would be the point in going to the doctor, if your opinion is already as good as the doctor's? Of course, you may not have an opinion and are only going to the doctor to get one. But then why go to the doctor and not a fortune teller or a friend, who will probably give you an opinion for free? It's also worth noting that if one opinion is as good as the next, then the opinion that subjectivism is silly is as good as any contrary view.

At the same time, it's quite right to be a subjectivist about certain matters. For example, does Miller Lite taste great? Well, one opinion about that *is* as good as the next. If you think Miller tastes great, then that is true for you, and there is no other truth to be considered. This is quite unlike "You have Type A influenza," which if you don't have Type A influenza, is false no matter what you think. Somewhere in between "Miller tastes great" and "You have Type A influenza" is where the controversy lies.

What is it that makes a concept subjective? The answer is that there are expressions which we generally let people apply as they see fit. Countless adjectives and adjectival phrases, adverbs and adverbial phrases, as well as nouns, fall into this category. The category includes "soothing," "cuddly," "terrifying" "great tasting" (and "great taste"), "super," "slowly," "carefully," "happy," "happiness," and so forth. Even here, it's not the case that *anything* goes: People would look at you oddly if you called the sound made by a jackhammer "soothing" or "sublime." But some expressions obviously do not work this way. You can't call just anything a "car," and you can't use "weighs more than one hundred pounds" according to your own private rules, and if you are of the opinion that your Grand Marquis does not weigh more than one hundred pounds, your opinion is incorrect.

Most everyone agrees that "tastes great" is purely subjective and that "weighs more than one hundred pounds" is not subjective in the least. But there are concepts that fall between these extremes. For example, consider the concept of beauty and of being beautiful. You may have heard the expression that beauty is in the eyes of the beholder. This statement expresses the idea that beauty is subjective, that the beauty in an object is what the viewer finds there; that if the mother finds her baby beautiful then she isn't wrong even if nobody agrees with her, and if nobody at all finds an object beautiful, or if nobody at all has seen it, then it just isn't beautiful. There are those, in fact, who think that "art" is itself a subjective concept. However, while probably many lay people are subjectivists about beauty and art, many philosophers of art (aestheticians) believe some aesthetic judgments are not subjective. For example, when the children of one of the authors were in second grade, they joined the school "orchestra." It was a memorable event for the author;

there were all the sons and daughters of whom the parents were so proud with their trumpets and flutes and so on, but the sound produced by the group was remarkably unpleasant. This aesthetic judgment seems not entirely subjective.

A rough rule of thumb for telling if a claim is subjective is the *"contradiction test."* If Sarah says "A" and Stanley says "Not-A," must one of them be mistaken? If not, that means the opposed claims are subjective. If Sarah says Miller tastes great, and Stanley says "No, it doesn't," then you wouldn't say one must be mistaken. If Mom says the baby is gorgeous and another nods and smiles while saying to himself, "Gad, what an ugly kid," then you allow them both to have their opinion. In these examples, "tastes great" as applied to beer and "is gorgeous" as applied to the baby are subjective concepts.

If a claim is entirely subjective, it doesn't require critical scrutiny to determine if it is true. If you think "Miller tastes great," then Miller tastes great to you, end of discussion. There is a minor complication in the fact that there is such a thing as a cultivated taste, and beer connoisseurs may well have standards to which they agree concerning what counts as a great taste in a beer. But speaking broadly, most English speakers agree to let people apply "tastes great" to beer as they think appropriate, which is to say that for most speakers of English the concept is subjective.

Unfortunately, there is an important group of statements, called "value judgments," that many people assume are subjective. However, not every value judgment is subjective, as we explain next.

VALUE JUDGMENTS

Recently, Paul Mitchell Systems, the largest privately owned shampoo company, launched a line of pet-grooming products. Each product is said to be "tested on humans, so it's safe for your pets." One of us tried one of the shampoos on his dogs and it did work well. "It worked well" is what is called a "value judgment." The term is a widely used, nontechnical name for a statement that expresses an evaluation of something. This particular value judgment expresses a positive evaluation of the pet shampoo. "Tastes great" is a favorable evaluation of Miller beer. "We should open a tanning business in Butte City" is a value judgment that expresses a favorable evaluation of opening a tanning business in Butte City. "George W. Bush is a better president than even George Washington" is a positive value judgment about the president.

There are different kinds of value judgments, because we evaluate different sorts of things. "That is a beautiful painting" is a positive aesthetic value judgment. "Pea soup is best served cold" is a culinary value judgment that expresses a positive evaluation of serving pea soup cold. "You should not invest in real estate until after the bubble bursts" is a practical value judgment.

There are also value judgments that assign ethical/moral values to objects and actions. "Thou shalt not steal," for example, is a *moral value judgment;* it evaluates stealing as not a good thing, morally speaking. "Good for you for helping that person to get across the street!" is a positive moral judgment. Though the values expressed in these examples may seem obvious, it can sometimes be difficult to determine what kind of value is expressed in a particular value judgment.

Value judgments obviously include decisions that are among *the* most important we make. Deciding how much support to contribute to an aging parent, for example, is no trivial matter. Unfortunately, many people, including many beginners in critical thinking, make a fundamental mistake about value judgments: They uncritically assume that *all* value judgments are purely subjective. For this reason, they are disinclined to subject any value judgment to critical examination, believing that the value judgment is just a matter of opinion, or that one opinion is as good as the next.

From an abstract point of view, it is easy to understand why people might have the idea that morality is purely subjective. But when we are confronted with a clear and real-life moral transgression, we instantly see a difference between moral value judgments and such judgments as "this beer tastes great." When Bill Clinton was president, three men who were members of an antigovernment "militia" debated whether to fire rounds from high-powered rifles into a huge propane tank south of Sacramento, California. The idea, as reported in the press, was to cause death and destruction sufficient to start a "revolution." One of the men, thank goodness, balked at the idea and eventually prevailed on the others not to proceed with the plan.* Many things could be said about this, but one thing you would *not* say is that the men who favored the plan and the man who didn't were equally correct. The claim fails the "contradiction test" we mentioned in the previous section.

To take another example, recently one John Russell Reed thought it would be nice to shoot a 1,000 pound elk who was a descendant of a herd of Rocky Mountain elk brought from Yellowstone to California in the 1960s. The elk, named Big Daddy, spent most of its time grazing and sleeping in and around the town of Bear Valley Springs in the Tehachapi Mountains and was, apparently, as tame and sweet as an elk is ever likely to be. Reed simply walked up to the harmless beast, which had no reason to be afraid, and shot it between the eyes.** Was this wrong? Of course, it was wrong. There is a huge difference between the value judgments "It was wrong to shoot Big Daddy" and "Miller tastes great." There are commonly accepted standards of sportsmanship and humane treatment of animals, but there are no common standards set for great taste in beer. What qualifies as humane treatment of animals is not as sharply defined or as universally accepted as what qualifies as a house or car, but whatever the standards are, shooting Big Daddy doesn't measure up.

Now, in fact there seem to be commonly accepted standards not merely of such things as sportsmanship and humane treatment of animals, but of moral right and wrong and good and bad in general. It is true these standards, though commonly accepted, are perhaps not universally accepted. Apparently, there are people who think it is a mark of virtue to blow up propane tanks in densely populated areas, but this doesn't mean that whether or not it would be good to do so is just a matter of opinion. In Chapter 12, we explain these commonly accepted criteria of moral good and bad and right and wrong, and discuss criteria that apply to aesthetic judgments as well. Meanwhile, you should not reflexively dismiss a judgment as subjective or not worth serious debate just because it is a value judgment.

---

*See the Anti-Defamation League's Law Enforcement Agency Resource Network's Web site at <www.adl.org/learn/criminal_activity/Nov_01.asp>.

**Reported by Steve Hymon in the *Los Angeles Times*, February 11, 2005. See also One Bakersfield, December 16, 2004 <www.1bakersfield.com/news/read/2/10628>.

■ This is Owen, a baby hippo. When Owen's mother washed out to sea, Owen glommed on to this giant turtle. Now Owen and his foster parent are inseparable.

Do hippos think? Probably. Do they think critically? Probably not. The difference is explained in this chapter.

BASIC CRITICAL THINKING SKILLS

When you think critically about a belief/opinion, or more precisely about the claim used to state it, the first order of business is to pinpoint *what* claim is under consideration. Sounds easy, but we guarantee this can be tough sledding. Claims can be vague, ambiguous, and obscure in other ways. In his inaugural address, President Warren G. Harding stated elegantly:

> We have mistaken unpreparedness to embrace it to be a challenge of the reality and due concern for making all citizens fit for participation will give added strength of citizenship and magnify our achievement.

This is formidable. It is also meaningless. (American satirist H.L. Mencken described it as a "sonorous nonsense driven home with gestures."*) Understanding what is meant by a claim has so many aspects we are obliged to devote an entire chapter to the subject. Socrates, the ancient Greek philosopher hailed by the Delphic Oracle as the wisest of humans, said defining terms is the first step toward wisdom. You will understand the truth in this when you read Chapter 2.**

Then, there are different kinds of claims, and you must know what kind of claim you are considering. "We should go to Ogata's for dinner" looks a lot like "We should bomb Iran" in that both are value judgments, but they are different kinds of remarks, demanding different sorts of support. Merely identifying arguments poses its own special set of difficulties, because arguments bear a superficial resemblance to other things; we'll begin discussing this later in this chapter. Many times when you might think a claim has been supported by an argument, it hasn't been supported at all. A goofy photo of the president is not an argument, but if an opponent of the president pastes it in an article about one of the president's proposals, it might dispose a reader unfavorably toward the proposal.

A lot of extraneous stuff—rhetorical flourishes, asides, tangents, and other things—gets mixed in with arguments, and you need to sort through all of this to find an actual argument. Once you find the argument, you then have to iden-

*Reported on NBC News "Meet the Press," January 16, 2005.

**It isn't that much of a stretch to say that ancient Greek philosophy generally boils down to defining terms.

In the Media

The Talk-Show Syndrome

> Those of us in the lay community don't reason that way; we don't think in those terms of logic; it doesn't compute with us, that type of philosophical reasoning; we don't care.
>
> – Radio talk-show host BRUCE SESSIONS, summarizing his reaction to a logician giving examples of illogical arguments from Rush Limbaugh

Our suspicions are confirmed.

tify the premises and conclusion. In addition, you need to recognize that there are different kinds of arguments, and they involve different principles of evaluation. We cover all these angles in this text, so this is not a short book.

Of course, there is no point in considering arguments for and against a claim if you have no idea what would count toward its being true or false. Take, for example, the claim "There is an identical you who lives in a different dimension." We have no idea at all what sort of evidence would count as supporting this claim, and what sort of evidence would support saying the claim is false. (Almost any claim about different "dimensions" or "planes" or "parallel universes" is apt to suffer from the same problem.) "All is one" would qualify as well. Philosopher Adolf Grunbaum's famous example, "Everything doubled in size last night" illustrates the point nicely too, as does "There is an invisible gremlin in my watch."

Claims problematic in this regard needn't be so metaphysical, either. You don't know where to begin looking, for example, for evidence either for or against "Americans aren't thinking seriously these days." Recently, we heard Senator Charles Grassley of Iowa declare emphatically, "It is human nature to desire freedom." People do talk a lot about freedom and human nature, but it is hard to know what kind of data would support or undermine Grassley's claim.

This is not to imply that only claims subject to scientific test or the experimental method are worth discussing. Sometimes claims are made in contexts in which it is not important they be true, as for example when one is telling a joke. Even when truth is paramount, a scientific test may not be necessary. Mathematical theorems aren't confirmed via experimentation but rather as deductions from other mathematical propositions. Appearing in the Bible would count as proof of a statement if you believe the Bible is the revealed word of God, though doubters might press you on that. The point is that *you* need to have some idea about what counts for or against a claim's truth if *you* are to entertain it seriously, or if you expect others to take it seriously.

TWO KINDS OF GOOD ARGUMENT

Logicians recognize two kinds of good argument: A good "deductive" argument and a good "inductive" argument. Before we explain these arguments, we should point out that the distinction between the two is second nature to instructors of critical thinking, and it is easy for them (and for us) to sometimes forget that it is new to many people. In addition, within just a few pages we have already brought up several new ideas, including "critical thinking," "claim," "argument," "premise," "conclusion," "value judgment," "subjective claim," "issue," and more. This is quite a load, so don't worry if you don't understand the distinction immediately. In Chapter 7 we will go into more detail about arguments, and will return to the distinction we are about to present. Your instructor may even wish to wait until then to go into the matter in depth.

Deductive Arguments

The first type of good argument, a good **deductive** argument, is said to be "valid." That's an argument whose premises being true would mean *necessarily* that the conclusion is true. For example, our student, Josh Fulcher, lives in Alaska; that means necessarily that Josh Fulcher lives in the United States. "Josh Fulcher lives in Alaska; therefore Josh Fulcher lives in the United States" is an example of a deductive argument. "Josh Fulcher is taller than his wife, and his wife is taller than his son; therefore Josh Fulcher is taller than his son" is another example.

Inductive Arguments

The second type of good argument, a good **inductive** argument, is said to be "strong." That's an argument whose premises being true would mean that *probably* the conclusions are true. "Josh Fulcher lives in Alaska; therefore he buys a lot of mosquito repellant." That's a strong inductive argument. Living in Alaska makes it probable that he buys lots of mosquito repellant, but it doesn't mean that necessarily he does so. "Not many people live in Butte City and those who do already spend a lot of time in the sun; therefore a tanning business won't do well there" is also a strong inductive argument: The premises being true make it probable that the conclusions are true, but certainly don't mean necessarily that it is true.

As you can see, valid deductive arguments *prove* or *demonstrate* their conclusion; strong inductive arguments merely *support* their conclusion. That's as deep as we need to go at this point; determining whether a deductive argument is valid and whether an inductive argument is strong will take up separate chapters later in the book.

RECOGNIZING ARGUMENTS

Critical thinking requires evaluating arguments for and against a claim, but, as we said above, it isn't always easy to recognize an argument as such. Extraneous elements frequently work their way into arguments, confusing matters. Plus, other things can be mistaken for arguments. Not every sequence of statements is an argument.

The Two Parts of an Argument

As we said, an argument, whether deductive or inductive, has two parts, and one part is presented as a reason for believing the other part is true. The cardinal rule of *argument identification* is, therefore, elementary. You need at least two claims, and the word "therefore" or an equivalent must stand, either explicitly or implicitly, before one of them. "He said and she said and then I said and he goes and I am like, etc., etc." is *not* an argument, or not usually so; the support/demonstration relationship is lacking. "This happened and that happened and that other thing happened," might be an argument, but only if it really means "This happened and that happened; therefore that other thing happened." For example, "The murder happened in the sitting room and Colonel Mustard was not in the sitting room at the time; therefore, Colonel Mustard did not commit the murder" is an argument.

Unfortunately, often the word "therefore" is left unstated, as in "Miller tastes great; we should get some." Also, unfortunately, a premise or even the conclusion can be left unstated. You will get much practice later identifying arguments, so we won't labor things here. The all-important point is: An argument consists of *two* parts, one of which (the premise or premises) demonstrates or supports the other part (the conclusion). If you are using a yellow highlighter to mark sentences in this book, you should already have highlighted a sentence to this effect.

The Language of Arguments

What are the other words and phrases that work like "therefore" to indicate a conclusion is about to be expressed? They include:

- It follows that . . .
- This shows that . . .
- Thus . . .
- Hence . . .
- Consequently . . .
- Accordingly . . .
- So . . .
- My conclusion is . . .

Unfortunately, some of these phrases have other uses than as conclusion indicators, but one can usually assume that what follows them is the conclusion of an argument.

In addition to conclusion-indicating words are premise-indicators, words that often indicate a premise is about to be stated:

- Since . . .
- For . . .
- Because . . .
- In view of . . .
- This is implied by . . .
- Given . . .

For example, the premise of "We shouldn't open a tanning salon because people in Butte City already get more sun than they want" is the phrase that follows the word "because."

Critical thinking often requires careful reading—of situations as well as signs.

On Language

Doing Things with Words

You should not get the idea from this chapter that the only important thing you can do with words is make claims or take positions on issues. You can do lots of other important things: You can hypothesize, conjecture, suppose, and propose. You can amuse or entertain. You can try to persuade others (or yourself) of something or attempt to get them (or you) to do something. We use words to pray, promise, praise, and promote; to lie, deceive, insult, and humiliate; to excuse, comfort, and let off steam; and so on indefinitely. (Sometimes we don't know *what* we are up to when we use words.) All these things are subject to critical thinking as to success, efficacy, completeness, legitimacy, authenticity, originality, clarity, and many other qualities. In this book, however, we focus primarily on claim-making and argument-presenting functions of discourse and, to a lesser extent, on hypothesizing and conjecturing functions.

Here are some examples of a few of the many different things people do with words:

Red meat is not bad for you. Now blue-green meat, that's bad for you.

— Tommy Smothers, amusing us

I want to rush for 1,000 or 1,500 yards, whichever comes first.

— New Orleans Saints running back George Rogers, expressing a desire

I enjoyed reading your book and would look forward to reading something else you wrote if required to do so.

— E-mail from one of our students; we'd like to think this is praise, but . . .

Do not take this medication within two hours of eating.

— Caution note on some gunk one of us had to drink. It's warning us, but notice that you can't tell if you're not supposed to take the medication within two hours before eating or within two hours after eating or both.

Whenever I watch TV and see those poor starving kids all over the world, I can't help but cry. I mean, I'd love to be skinny like that but not with all those flies and death and stuff.

— Mariah Carey, expressing compassion

They know so little science that they don't realize how ridiculous they look to others.

— Marilyn Vos Savant, offering her explanation of why people claim to be psychic

It's due to the country's mixed ethnicity.

— National Rifle Association president Charlton Heston, explaining the country's high murder rate and making it clear he may not know too much about the subject

I did not have sexual relations with that woman.

— Bill Clinton, telling a fib

Osama bin Laden is either alive and well or alive and not too well or not alive.

— Defense Secretary Donald Rumsfeld; beats us

Again, to repeat, many arguments don't contain indicator words; you just have to pay attention to whether a passage is an attempt to support or demonstrate something. We provide several exercises at the end of this chapter to help you learn to identify arguments.

TWO CONFUSIONS ABOUT ARGUMENTS

Difficulties in identifying arguments are compounded by two important confusions: (1) that arguments are the same as explanations, and (2) that arguments are attempts to persuade someone of something.

Arguments and Explanations

You are sure to remember that Patrick Lawler had a world-class toothache because he had a 4-inch nail in his brain. This is an explanation of why he had a toothache; it gives the cause of the problem. By contrast, "Patrick Lawler should have carried insurance because now he can't pay his bills" is an argument, not an explanation. For various reasons, people often confuse arguments and explanations. Let's put the two sentences about Patrick Lawler side by side, and compare them again.

"Patrick Lawler had a toothache because he had a nail in his head"	"Patrick Lawler should have carried medical insurance because now he can't pay his medical bills."

Both statements say, "X because Y." But remember, an argument has two parts, and one part (the premise) provides a reason for thinking the other part (the conclusion) is true. The sentence on the right above is indeed an argument, because "he can't pay his medical bills" provides a reason for thinking it is true that Patrick Lawler should have had medical insurance. By contrast, in the sentence on the left, the part that says "he had a nail in his head" is *not* given as a reason for thinking that "Patrick Lawler had a toothache." Patrick Lawler doesn't need a reason for thinking he had a toothache, and neither do we, if he tells us he has one. "He had a nail in his head" states the *cause* of the headache, and is not offered as proof that Patrick Lawler had one.

Basically, an argument attempts to support or prove a conclusion, while an explanation specifies what caused something or how it works or what it is made out of and so forth. Arguing *that* a dog has fleas is quite different from explaining what *caused* the fleas. Arguing that violent crime has increased is different from explaining what caused it to increase. Offering an explanation of Dutch elm disease is entirely different from trying to prove that your explanation is correct. Explanations and arguments are different things. However, they are easily confused, and we include an exercise that will help you keep them straight.

Arguments and Persuasion

"The environment needs George W. Bush like farmers need drought." We heard somebody say this who was trying to persuade an audience that George W. Bush had a bad environmental record. The remark, however, is not an argument; it's just a statement that portrays Bush in a bad light. Now, some writers define an argument as an attempt to persuade somebody of something. This is not correct. An argument attempts to prove or support a conclusion. When you attempt to persuade someone, you attempt to win him or her to your point of view; trying to persuade and trying to argue are logically distinct enterprises. True, when you want to persuade somebody of something, you might use an argument. But not all arguments attempt to persuade, and many attempts to persuade do not involve arguments. In fact, giving people an argument is often one of the least effective methods of persuading many people—which, of course, is why so few advertisers bother with arguments. People notoriously are persuaded by the flimsiest of arguments and sometimes are unfazed by even quite good arguments. Propaganda, for example, is an effective means of persuasion. Flattery has been known to work, too.

Real Life

The Greatest President?

According to a CNN poll, 66 percent of registered Republicans think George W. Bush is a greater president than George Washington.

We have two purposes in this box. The first is to call your attention once again to the way images can affect people. A photo is not an argument; it is not even a statement. Nevertheless, coupling a goofy photo of George W. Bush with a stately photograph of George Washington serves to ridicule the idea that Bush could be considered as great as Washington.

The second is to call attention to this: For some reason, "The greatest president" doesn't feel quite as subjective as "The greatest beer." If one person says Bush is the greatest president and another person says Washington is, we are not entirely comfortable saying "They both can be correct." The difference is that "the greatest" when applied to beer has fewer restrictions on its use than does "the greatest" when applied to U.S. presidents. We allow people to apply "the greatest" to beer almost entirely as they see fit. However, there are at least a few commonly accepted standards of presidential greatness.

RELEVANCE, RHETORIC, AND KEEPING A CLEAR HEAD

Another difficult aspect to thinking critically about claims and arguments is the need to identify and weed out *extraneous considerations*. Mom's opinions are bound to carry extra weight just because she is Mom. They may even carry more weight than the opinions of experts in the subject. It is a fact of life that we are influenced in our thinking by considerations that, logically, are beside the point; a speaker's relationship to us is just one example.

There is, for another example, our friend and former colleague Professor B., who spoke with a fine English accent and wore woolens and tweed and smoked a pipe. No matter what Professor B. talked about, he sounded authoritative; when he spoke, you tended to take notes. Now, it is easy to base estimates of expertise on factors like accent or dress that usually are irrelevant, and to transform a favorable opinion about a person into a positive judgment about what he or she says. This, of course, is exactly why advertisers show people you admire or like using their products, so you will transfer the feeling to the product. So you have to be careful to evaluate claims, just as you would products, on their merits and not on the merits of the person advocating for it.

Obviously, it's not just positive feelings about people that may be transferred to their claims and arguments. It is very easy to downgrade what someone says if he or she seems nervous or shifty or stumbles over words. We know two sisters; one smiles and makes eye contact, and the other tends to not look you in the face and doesn't smile as much. Both sisters are honest and intelligent, and probably both are equally knowledgeable about things. We might expect the first sister to be the more successful salesperson, and it wouldn't be surprising if people tended to take her claims more seriously, too. After all, there is a reason speaking coaches encourage eye contact and smooth delivery. We remember a recent TV ad for a deodorant, in which a football coach warns against "letting them see you sweat," the point apparently being that looking self-confident helps keep the troops from doubting you.

Comparing claims with consumer items leads us to another type of extraneous consideration that has to be identified and weeded out when you evaluate claims and arguments. Advertisers sell products not only by having them used or endorsed by people you like or who look authoritative, but also by describing the products in language that enhances their attractiveness. Dog food manufacturers lately are covering bags with mouth-watering assertions about natural ingredients, whole grains, freshness, and so forth, along with pictures of fresh lean meat and vegetables, as if dogs even liked carrots. As it is with dog food, so it is with claims and arguments. People dress up what they say with *rhetoric*—language that has psychological force but carries no extra weight logically. A president, for example, may support a call to arms with stirring "arguments" about freedom and democracy and saving the world from Armageddon. John Kennedy's famous line, "Ask not what your country can do for you, ask rather what you can do for your country" is really just "Do volunteer work" in a rhetorically pretty package.

One must be especially alert to negative rhetoric. Newt Gingrich, a former Republican Congressperson and Speaker of the House, advised Republicans to use the words "extreme," "traitor," and "treasonous" when referring to Democrats or their proposals. Words can inflame passions, and make it difficult to evaluate ideas on their merits. The emotional associations of words is a constant obstacle to an objective and neutral assessment of ideas; it is difficult to see beyond the rhetoric to the core idea being stated. Negative political advertising is very common, presumably because it is effective.

Although psychological and emotional coloration is the staple of demagoguery, it is present as well when good and decent people honestly state their opinions. After all, there is nothing wrong with presenting your views in the best light or in trying to be as persuasive as possible. But as consumers of thoughts and ideas, we must refine our ability to distinguish between the thought itself and the psychological packing in which it is given to us. Because of the difficulties here, we devote three full chapters to this and closely related topics.

One also must be wary of claims that are accompanied by photographs and other images, because images, just like rhetoric, can elicit powerful emotions. Political advertising, for example, basically boils down to images and rhetoric, and the two can make a witches' brew of persuasion. We will have an opportunity to comment more on this in later chapters.

A WORD ABOUT THE EXERCISES

For some reason, tennis doesn't seem as popular as it once did. Nevertheless, ace tennis players probably are every bit as good as they once were. To get good at tennis, or any other skill, you have to practice, practice, and practice more. It's the same way with critical thinking, and that's why we provide so many exercises. For some of the exercises, there is no such thing as only one correct answer, just as there is no such thing as only one correct way to serve a tennis ball. Some answers, however—just like tennis serves—are better than others, and that is where your instructor comes in. In many exercises, answers you give that are different from your instructor's are not necessarily incorrect. Still, your instructor's answers most likely will be well thought out, reliable, and worth your attention. We recommend you take advantage of your instructor's experience to improve your ability to think critically.

By the way, answers to the exercise items marked with a triangle are found in the answer section (look for the colored edges) at the back of the book. You'll also find an occasional comment, tip, suggestion, joke, or buried treasure map back there.

Recap

According to a recent news report, one Emerson Moore, no relation to the author, was arrested for drunk driving in Muhlenberg Township, Pennsylvania, and then was released on bail. Later, when he returned for his court hearing, he got into a heated discussion with an officer outside the courtroom. The officer perceived that Moore was again under the influence and arrested him for being intoxicated in public. "Whatever were you thinking, showing up here like that?" asked Justice Dean R. Patton.*

Whatever Moore was thinking, he wasn't thinking critically. Thinking critically means screening your beliefs to see if they really make sense, and instead of doing that, Moore reminded the judge that when the judge released Moore on bail he had told Moore "You can drink at home."

Beliefs are expressed in claims, and critical thinking, a bit more precisely expressed, requires evaluating and weighing the arguments for and against the claims that express our beliefs. Moore's argument for showing up drunk at his hearing for drunk driving (i.e., for the claim that there was nothing wrong with his doing so) was that the judge had told him he could drink at home, by which

*Associated Press report, September 15, 2004.

the judge meant, be intoxicated only at home. The argument against showing up drunk (i.e., for the claim that there was something wrong with his doing so) is what happened when Moore tried his argument out on the judge. Justice Patton waived Moore's bail, had him incarcerated, and Moore now faces a charge of public intoxication to go along with the drunk driving charge.

In addition to "critical thinking" and "claim," the important terminology in the chapter includes:

- Argument: a two-part structure of claims, one part of which (the premise or premises) is given as a reason for thinking the other part (the conclusion) is true
- Issue/Question: what is raised when a claim is called into question
- Valid deductive argument: an argument whose premises being true means that necessarily the conclusion is true
- Strong inductive argument: an argument whose premises being true means that probably the conclusion is true
- Subjective expression: an expression which by common agreement is left up to the individual to apply as he or she thinks is appropriate, within certain broad constraints
- Subjectivism: the idea that any opinion is as good as the next, or that what is true is what you believe is true
- Value judgment: a claim that expresses an evaluation of something
- Moral value judgment: a claim that expresses a moral or ethical evaluation of something
- Rhetoric: language that is psychologically persuasive but does not have extra logical force

In addition, we mentioned important mistakes that can be obstacles to thinking critically.

- To reflexively suppose that all value judgments are subjective
- To confuse arguments with explanations
- To confuse argument with persuasion
- To confuse rhetorical or psychological force with logical force, and to think that a psychologically more persuasive argument must be a better argument logically

Exercises

Exercise 1-1

Answer the questions based on your reading of Chapter 1, including the boxes.

▲ 1. What is an argument?

2. T or F: A claim is what you use to state an opinion or a belief.

3. T or F: Critical thinking involves attacking other people.

▲ 4. T or F: Whether a passage contains an argument depends on how long it is.

5. T or F: When a claim has been questioned, an issue has been raised.
6. Do all arguments have a premise?
▲ 7. Do all arguments have a conclusion?
8. T or F: If the premises being true means necessarily that the conclusion is true, the argument is deductively valid.
9. T or F: If the premises being true means that probably the conclusion is true, the argument is inductively strong.
▲ 10. Can a conclusion be implied, or must it always be explicitly stated?
11. Explain the connection between an argument and an issue.
12. T or F: "Miller Lite tastes great" is a value judgment.
▲ 13. Are all value judgments subjective?
14. T or F: If one of two people disagreeing on an issue must be mistaken, then the issue is not subjective.
15. T or F: Only claims subject to scientific testing are worth discussing.
▲ 16. T or F: All arguments are used to try to persuade someone of something.
17. T or F: All attempts to persuade someone of something are arguments.
18. T or F: Whenever a claim is called into question, an issue has been raised.
▲ 19. T or F: Subjectivism is the idea that one opinion is as good as the next.
▲ 20. T or F: Sometimes we transfer a favorable or unfavorable opinion of a speaker to what the speaker says.
21. T or F: Explanations and arguments serve the same purpose.
22. "Therefore" and "consequently" are conclusion-indicators.
23. T or F: "Rhetorical" or "emotive force" refers to the emotional content or associations of a word or phrase.
24. T or F: The rhetorical force of language can get in the way of clear and critical thinking.
25. T or F: We should not try to put our own position on any issue in the most favorable light.

Exercise 1-2

This exercise is designed to be done as an in-class group assignment. Your instructor will indicate how he or she wants it done. On the basis of a distinction covered in this chapter, divide these items into two groups of five items each such that all the items in one group have a feature that none of the items in the second group have. Describe the feature upon which you based your classifications. Compare your results with those of a neighboring group.

1. You shouldn't buy that car because it is ugly.
2. That car is ugly, and it costs over $25,000, too.
3. Rainbows have seven different colors in them, although it's not always easy to see them all.
4. Walking is the best exercise. After all, it is less stressful on the joints than other aerobic exercises.

5. The ocean on the central coast is the most beautiful shade of sky blue. It's more green as you go north.
6. Her favorite color is yellow because it is the color of the sun.
7. Pooh is my favorite cartoon character because he has lots of personality.
8. You must turn off the lights when you leave the room. They cost a lot of money to run and you don't need them on during the day.
9. Television programs have too much violence and immoral behavior. Hundreds of killings are portrayed every month.
10. You'll be able to find a calendar on sale after the first of the year, so it is a good idea to wait until then to buy one.

Exercise 1-3

Some of these items are arguments and some are not. Can you divide them up correctly?

▲ 1. Roddick is unlikely to win the U.S. Open this year. He has a nagging leg injury, plus he just doesn't seem to have the drive he once had.

2. Hey there, Marco!—don't go giving that cat top sirloin. What's the matter with you, you got no brains at all?

3. If you've ever met a pet bird, then you know they are very busy creatures.

▲ 4. Everybody is saying the president has made us the laughingstock of the world. What a stupid idea! He hasn't made us a laughingstock at all. There's not a bit of truth in that notion.

5. "Is the author really entitled to assert that there is a degree of unity among these essays which makes this a book rather than a congeries? I am inclined to say that he is justified in this claim, but articulating this justification is a somewhat complex task."

   From a book review by Stanley Bates

6. As a long-time customer, you're already taking advantage of our money management expertise and variety of investment choices. That's a good reason for consolidating your other eligible assets into an IRA with us.

7. PROFESSOR X: Well, I see where the new chancellor wants to increase class sizes.
   PROFESSOR Y: Yeah, another of his bright ideas.
   PROFESSOR X: Actually, I don't think it hurts to have one or two extra people in class.
   PROFESSOR Y: What? Of course it hurts. What are you thinking, anyway?
   PROFESSOR X: Well, I just think there is good reason for increasing the class size a bit.

▲ 8. Yes, I charge a little more than other dentists. But I feel I give better service. So I think my billing practices are justified.

9. If you want to purchase the house, you must exercise your option before June 30, 2003. Otherwise, you will forfeit the option price.

10. John Montgomery has been the Eastern Baseball League's best closer this season. Unfortunately, when a closer fails, as Montgomery did last night, there's usually not much chance to recover.

▲ **11.** "'Water resistant to 100 feet,' says the front of this package for an Aqualite watch, but the fine-print warranty on the back doesn't cover 'any failure to function properly due to misuse such as water immersion.'"

Consumer Reports

Exercise 1-4

Determine which of the following passages contain arguments, and, for any that do, identify the argument's conclusion. Remember that an argument occurs when one or more claims (the premises) are offered as a reason for believing that another claim (the conclusion) is true. There aren't many hard-and-fast rules for identifying arguments, so you'll have to read closely and think carefully about some of these.

▲ **1.** The *Directory of Intentional Communities* lists more than two hundred groups across the country organized around a wide variety of purposes, including environmentally aware living.

2. Carl would like to help out, but he won't be in town. So we'll have to find someone else who owns a truck.

3. In 1976, Washington, D.C., passed an ordinance prohibiting private ownership of firearms. Since then, Washington's murder rate has shot up 121 percent. Bans on firearms are clearly counterproductive.

▲ **4.** Computers will never be able to converse intelligently through speech. A simple example proves that this is so. The sentences "How do you recognize speech?" and "How do you wreck a nice beach?" have entirely different meanings, but they sound similar enough that a computer could not distinguish the two.

5. Recent surveys for the National Science Foundation report that two of three adult Americans believe that alien spaceships account for UFO reports. It therefore seems likely that several million Americans may have been predisposed to accept the report on NBC's *Unsolved Mysteries* that the U.S. military recovered a UFO with alien markings.

6. "Like short-term memory, long-term memory retains information that is encoded in terms of sense modality and in terms of links with information that was learned earlier (that is, *meaning*)."

Neil R. Carlson

▲ **7.** Fears that chemicals in teething rings and soft plastic toys may cause cancer may be justified. Last week, the Consumer Product Safety Commission issued a report confirming that low amounts of DEHP, known to cause liver cancer in lab animals, may be absorbed from certain infant products.

8. "It may be true that people, not guns, kill people. But people with guns kill more people than people without guns. As long as the number of lethal weapons in the hands of the American people continues to grow, so will the murder rate."

Susan Mish'alani

9. June 1970: A Miami man gets thirty days in the stockade for wearing a flag patch on the seat of his trousers. March 2004: Miami department stores are selling boxer trunks made up to look like an American flag. Times have changed.

▲ **10.** Levi's Dockers are still in style, but pleats are out.

11. There is trouble in the Middle East, there is a recession under way at home, and all the economic indicators have turned downward. It seems likely, then, that the only way the stock market can go is down.

12. Lucy is too short to reach the bottom of the sign.

▲ **13.** "Can it be established that genetic humanity is sufficient for moral humanity? I think that there are very good reasons for not defining the moral community in this way."

Mary Anne Warren

14. Pornography often depicts women as servants or slaves, or as otherwise inferior to men. In light of that, it seems reasonable to expect to find more women than men who are upset by pornography.

15. "My folks, who were Russian immigrants, loved the chance to vote. That's probably why I decided that I was going to vote whenever I got the chance. I'm not sure [whom I'll vote for], but I am going to vote. And I don't understand people who don't."

Mike Wallace

▲ **16.** "President Clinton's request for $1 billion to create summer jobs for low-income young people was killed in the Senate, forcing him to settle for $166.5 million. Jobs would help make them part of the real community and would represent a beacon of hope—the first step out of poverty and despair."

Christian Science Monitor

17. "Hayek argues that we cannot know enough about each person's situation to distribute to each according to his moral merit (but would justice demand we do so if we did have the knowledge?)."

Robert Nozick

18. The Great Lakes Coastal Commission should prepare regulations that are consistent with the law, obviously. We admit that isn't always easy. But there's no reason for the commission to substitute its judgment for that of the people.

▲ **19.** We need to make clear that sexual preference, whether chosen or genetically determined, is a private matter. It has nothing to do with an individual's ability to make a positive contribution to society.

20. "Cinema rarely rises from a craft to an art. Usually it just manufactures sensory blizzards for persons too passive to manage the active engagement of mind that even light reading requires."

George Will

Exercise 1-5

For each passage in this exercise, identify which of the items that follow best states the primary issue discussed in the passage. Be prepared to say why you think your choice is the correct one.

▲ **1.** Let me tell you why Hank ought not to take that math course. First, it's too hard, and he'll probably flunk it. Second, he's going to spend the whole term in a state of frustration. Third, he'll probably get depressed and do poorly in all the rest of his courses.

a. Whether Hank ought to take the math course
b. Whether Hank would flunk the math course
c. Whether Hank will spend the whole term in a state of frustration
d. Whether Hank will get depressed and do poorly in all the rest of his courses

2. The county has cut the library budget for salaried library workers, and there will not be enough volunteers to make up for the lack of paid workers. Therefore, the library will have to be open fewer hours next year.

a. Whether the library will have to be open fewer hours next year
b. Whether there will be enough volunteers to make up for the lack of paid workers

▲ **3.** Pollution of the waters of the Everglades and of Florida Bay is due to multiple causes. These include cattle farming, dairy farming, industry, tourism, and urban development. So it is simply not so that the sugar industry is completely responsible for the pollution of these waters.

a. Whether pollution of the waters of the Everglades and Florida Bay is due to multiple causes
b. Whether pollution is caused by cattle farming, dairy farming, industry, tourism, and urban development
c. Whether the sugar industry is partly responsible for the pollution of these waters
d. Whether the sugar industry is completely responsible for the pollution of these waters

▲ **4.** It's clear that the mainstream media have lost interest in classical music. For example, the NBC network used to have its own classical orchestra conducted by Arturo Toscanini, but no such orchestra exists now. One newspaper, the no-longer-existent *Washington Star,* used to have thirteen classical music reviewers—that's more than twice as many as the *New York Times* has now. H.L. Mencken and other columnists used to devote considerable space to classical music; nowadays, you almost never see it mentioned in a major column.

a. Whether popular taste has turned away from classical music
b. Whether newspapers are employing fewer writers on classical music
c. Whether the mainstream media have lost interest in classical music

5. This year's National Football League draft lists a large number of quarterbacks among its highest-ranking candidates. Furthermore, quite a number of teams do not have a first-class quarterback. It's therefore likely that there will be an unusually large number of quarterbacks drafted early in this year's draft.

a. Whether teams without first-class quarterbacks will choose quarterbacks in the draft
b. Whether there is a large number of quarterbacks in this year's NFL draft
c. Whether an unusually large number of quarterbacks will be drafted early in this year's draft

6. An animal that will walk out into a rainstorm and stare up at the clouds until water runs into its nostrils and it drowns—well, that's what I call the world's dumbest animal. And that's exactly what young domestic turkeys do.
   a. Whether young domestic turkeys will drown themselves in the rain
   b. Whether any animal is dumb enough to drown itself in the rain
   c. Whether young domestic turkeys are the world's dumbest animal
7. The defeat of the school voucher initiative was a bad thing for the country because now there won't be any incentive for public schools to clean up their act. Furthermore, the defeat perpetuates the private-school-for-the-rich, public-school-for-the-poor syndrome.
   a. Whether there is now any incentive for public schools to clean up their act
   b. Whether the defeat of the school voucher initiative was bad for the country
   c. Two issues are equally stressed in the passage: whether there is now any incentive for public schools to clean up their act and whether the private-school-for-the-rich, public-school-for-the-poor syndrome will be perpetuated
8. From an editorial in a newspaper outside southern California: "The people in southern California who lost a fortune in the wildfires last year could have bought insurance that would have covered their houses and practically everything in them. And anybody with any foresight would have made sure there were no brush and no trees near the houses so that there would be a buffer zone between the house and any fire, as the Forest Service recommends. Finally, anybody living in a fire danger zone ought to know enough to have a fireproof or fire-resistant roof on the house. So, you see, most of the losses those people suffered were simply their own fault."
   a. Whether there were things the fire victims could have done to prevent their losses
   b. Whether insurance, fire buffer zones, and fire-resistant roofs could have prevented much of the loss
   c. Whether the losses suffered by people in the fires were their own fault
9. "Whatever we believe, we think agreeable to reason, and, on that account, yield our assent to it. Whatever we disbelieve, we think contrary to reason, and, on that account, dissent from it. Reason, therefore, is allowed to be the principle by which our belief and opinions ought to be regulated."

   Thomas Reid, Essays on the Active Powers of Man

   a. Whether reason is the principle by which our beliefs and opinions ought to be regulated
   b. Whether what we believe is agreeable to reason
   c. Whether what we disbelieve is contrary to reason
   d. Both b and c
10. Most people you find on university faculties are people who are interested in ideas. And the most interesting ideas are usually new ideas. So most people you find on university faculties are interested in new ideas.

Therefore, you are not going to find many conservatives on university faculties, because conservatives are not usually interested in new ideas.

a. Whether conservatives are interested in new ideas
b. Whether you'll find many conservatives on university faculties
c. Whether people on university faculties are interested more in new ideas than in other ideas
d. Whether most people are correct

11. In pre–civil war Spain, the influence of the Catholic Church must have been much stronger on women than on men. You can determine this by looking at the number of religious communities, such as monasteries, nunneries, and so forth. A total of about 5,000 such communities existed in 1931; 4,000 of them were female, whereas only 1,000 of them were male. Seems to me that proves my point about the Church's influence on the sexes.

a. Whether the Catholic Church's influence was greater on women than on men in pre–civil war Spain
b. Whether the speaker's statistics really prove his point about the Church's influence
c. Whether the figures about religious communities really have anything to do with the overall influence of the Catholic Church in Spain

12. The movie *Pulp Fiction* might have been a pretty good movie without the profanity that occurred all the way through it. But without the profanity, it would not have been a believable movie. The people this movie was about just talk that way, you see. If you have them speaking Shakespearean English or middle-class suburban English, then nobody is going to pay any attention to the message of the movie because nobody will see it as realistic. It's true, of course, that, like many other movies with some offensive feature—whether it's bad language, sex, or whatever—it will never appeal to a mass audience.

a. Whether movies with offensive features can appeal to a mass audience
b. Whether *Pulp Fiction* would have been a good movie without the bad language
c. Whether *Pulp Fiction* would have been a believable movie without the bad language
d. Whether believable movies must always have an offensive feature of one kind or another

▲ **13.** "From information gathered in the last three years, it has become clear that the single biggest environmental problem in the former Soviet Union—many times bigger than anything we have to contend with in the United States—is radioactive pollution from nuclear energy plants and nuclear weapons testing and production. Soviet communist leaders seemed to believe they could do anything to hasten the industrialization process and compete with Western countries, and that the land and natural resources they controlled were vast enough to suffer any abuse without serious consequence. The arrogance of the communist leaders produced a burden of misery and death that fell on the people of the region, and the scale of that burden has only recently become clear. Nuclear waste was dumped into rivers from which downstream villages drew their drinking water; the landscape is dotted with nuclear dumps which now threaten to leak into the environment; and the seas around Russia are littered with decaying hulks of nuclear submarines and rusting metal containers with tens of millions of tons of nuclear waste. The result has been radiation poisoning and its awful effects on a grand scale.

"A science advisor to former Russian President Boris Yeltsin said, 'The way we have dealt with the whole issue of nuclear power, and particularly the problem of nuclear waste, was irresponsible and immoral.'"

Adapted from the Washington Post

a. Whether communism failed to protect people from nuclear contamination as well as capitalism did
b. Whether nuclear waste problems in the former Soviet Union are much worse than had been realized until just recently
c. Whether former leaders of the Soviet Union made large-scale sacrifice of the lives and health of their people in their nuclear competition with the West
d. Whether communism, in the long run, is a much worse system than capitalism when it comes to protecting the population from harm

▲ **14.** "The United States puts a greater percentage of its population in prison than any other developed country in the world. We persist in locking more and more people up despite the obvious fact that it doesn't work. Even as we build more prisons and stuff them ever more tightly, the crime rate goes up and up. But we respond: 'Since it isn't working, let's do more of it'!

"It's about time we learned that fighting criminals is not the same thing as fighting crime."

Richard Parker, radio commentary on CalNet, California Public Radio

a. Whether we build more prisons than any other country
b. Whether we imprison more people than do other countries
c. Whether reliance on imprisonment is an effective method of reducing crime
d. Whether attacking the sources of crime (poverty, lack of education, and so on) will reduce crime more than just imprisoning people who commit crimes

▲ **15.** In Miami–Dade County, Florida, schools superintendent Rudy Crew was inundated with complaints after a police officer used a stun gun on a six-year-old student. As a result, Crew asked the Miami–Dade police to ban the use of stun guns on elementary school children. Crew did the right thing. More than 100 deaths have been linked to tasers.

a. Whether a police officer used a stun gun on a six-year-old student
b. Whether the superintendent did the right thing by asking the police to ban the use of stun guns on elementary school children
c. Whether 100 deaths have been linked to tasers
d. Whether the fact that 100 deaths have been linked to tasers shows that the superintendent did the right thing when he asked the police not to use tasers on children

▲ **16.** Letting your children surf the Net is like dropping them off downtown to spend the day doing whatever they want. They'll get in trouble.

a. Whether letting your children off downtown to spend the day doing whatever they want will lead them into trouble

b. Whether letting your children surf the Net will lead them into trouble
c. Whether restrictions should be placed on children's activities

17. The winner of this year's spelling bee is a straight-A student whose favorite subject is science, which isn't surprising, since students interested in science learn to pay attention to details.

a. Whether the winner of this year's spelling bee is a straight-A student
b. Whether science students learn to pay attention to detail
c. Whether learning science will improve a student's ability to spell
d. Whether learning science teaches a student to pay attention to details
e. None of the above

18. Illinois state employees, both uniformed and non-uniformed, have been loyally, faithfully, honorably, and patiently serving the state without a contract or cost-of-living pay increase for years, despite the fact that legislators and governor have accepted hefty pay increases. All public employee unions should launch a signature-gathering initiative to place on the ballot a proposition that the Illinois constitution be amended to provide for compulsory binding arbitration for all uniformed and non-uniformed public employees, under the supervision of the state supreme court.

a. Whether Illinois state employees have been loyally, faithfully, honorably, and patiently serving the state without a contract or cost-of-living pay increase for years
b. Whether public employee unions should launch a signature-gathering initiative to place on the ballot a proposition that the Illinois constitution be amended to provide for compulsory binding arbitration for all uniformed and non-uniformed public employees, under the supervision of the Illinois Supreme Court
c. Neither of the above

19. That Japan needs reform of its political institutions is hardly in doubt. The country is experiencing the worst recession since the Second World War, with forecasts of up to minus 3 percent growth this year. Japan is not only the world's largest economy, but it also dominates the East Asian economic zone, so recovery through that region depends directly on Japan. Reforms are urgently needed to ensure this recovery will happen.

a. Whether Japan needs reforms of its political institutions
b. Whether Japan is experiencing its worst recession since the Second World War
c. Whether Japan is the world's second largest economy
d. Whether reforms will ensure that recovery will happen

▲ **20.** YOU: So, what do you think of the governor?
YOUR FRIEND: Not much, actually.
YOU: What do you mean? Don't you think she's been pretty good?
YOUR FRIEND: Are you serious?
YOU: Well, yes. I think she's been doing a fine job.
YOUR FRIEND: Oh, come on. Weren't you complaining about her just a few days ago?

a. Whether your friend thinks the governor has been a good governor.
b. Whether you think the governor has been a good governor.

c. Whether the governor has been a good governor
d. Whether you have a good argument for thinking the governor has been a good governor

Exercise 1-6

Identify the main issue in each of the following passages.

▲ **1.** Police brutality does not happen very often. Otherwise, it would not make headlines when it does happen.

2. We have little choice but to concentrate our crime-fighting efforts on enforcement because we don't have any idea what to do about the underlying causes of crime.

3. A lot of people think that the gender of a Supreme Court justice doesn't make any difference. But with two women on the bench, cases dealing with women's issues are being handled differently.

▲ **4.** "The point is that the existence of an independent world explains our experiences better than any known alternative. We thus have good reason to believe that the world—which seems independent of our minds—really is essentially independent of our minds."

Theodore W. Schick, Jr., and Lewis Vaughn, How to Think About Weird Things

5. Sure, some of the hotdoggers get good grades in Professor Bubacz's class. But my guess is that if Algernon takes it, all it'll get him is flunked out!

6. It is dumb to claim that sales taxes hit poor people harder than rich people. After all, the more money you have, the more you spend; and the more you spend, the more sales taxes you pay. So people with more money are always going to be paying more in sales tax than poor people.

▲ **7.** If you're going to buy a computer, you might as well also sign up for some lessons on how to use the thing. After all, no computer ever did any work for its owner until its owner found out how to make it work.

8. Intravenous drug use with nonsterile needles has become one of the leading causes of the spread of AIDS. Many states passed legislation allowing officials to distribute clean needles in an effort to combat this method of infection. But in eleven states, including some of the most populous, possession of hypodermic syringes without a prescription is illegal. The laws in these foot-dragging states have to be changed if we ever hope to bring this awful epidemic to an end.

9. The best way to avoid error—that is, belief in something false—is to suspend judgment about everything except that which is absolutely certain. Because error usually leads to trouble, this shows that suspension of judgment is usually the right thing to do.

▲ **10.** "[Readers] may learn something about their own relationship to the earth from a people who were true conservationists. The Indians knew that life was equated with the earth and its resources, that America was a paradise, and they could not comprehend why the intruders from the East were determined to destroy all that was Indian as well as America itself."

Dee Brown, Bury My Heart at Wounded Knee

Exercise 1-7

For each item, identify the issue that the first speaker is addressing. Are the two speakers addressing the same issue?

Example

THERESA: I think toilet paper looks better if it unwinds from the back side of the spool.

DANIEL: No way! It looks stupid that way. It should unwind from the front side of the spool.

Analysis

The issue for both Theresa and Daniel is whether the toilet paper looks better if it unwinds from the front of the spool.

▲ **1.** MR.: Next weekend we go on Standard Time again. We'll have to set the clocks ahead.
MRS.: It isn't next weekend; it's the weekend after. And you set the clocks back one hour, not ahead.

2. BELIEVER: Ghosts exist. People everywhere in all cultures have believed in them. All those people couldn't be wrong.
SKEPTIC: If ghosts exist, it's not for that reason. People once believed Earth was flat, too.

3. SHE: You don't give me enough help around the house; you hardly ever do anything.
HE: That's not true. I mowed the lawn on Saturday and I washed both of the cars on Sunday. What's more, I've been cleaning up after dinner almost every night and I've hauled all that stuff from the garden to the dump. So I don't see how you can say I hardly ever do anything.
SHE: Well, you don't want to hear all that *I* do around here; your efforts are pretty puny compared to mine!

▲ **4.** HEEDLESS: When people complain about American intervention in places like Iraq, they tell every tinhorn dictator to go ahead and take over because America will just stand by and watch. I, for one, think people who complain like that ought to just shut up.
CAUTIOUS: Not me. Complaining like that reminds everyone that it isn't in our best interest to get involved in extended wars abroad.

5. ONE SPEAKER: Nothing beats summertime. It's sunny and warm, and you can wear shorts, go on picnics, take hikes, and, best of all, take in a ball game.
ANOTHER SPEAKER: Naw, summer's hot and sticky, and there's no skiing or skating or getting warm 'round a nice cozy fire. Summer's okay—if you're a mosquito.

6. FITNESS BUFF ONE: Look here, the speedometer cable on this exercise bike is starting to squeak. If we don't fix it, the speedometer is going to stop working.
FITNESS BUFF TWO: What we need to do is get a new bike. This old thing is more trouble than it's worth.

7. YOUNG GUY: Baseball players are much better now than they were forty years ago. They eat better, have better coaching, you name it.
   OLD GUY: They aren't any better at all. They just seem better because they get more publicity and play with a livelier ball.
8. STUDENT ONE: Studying is a waste of time. Half the time, I get better grades if I don't study.
   STUDENT TWO: I'd like to hear you say that in front of your parents!
9. PHILATELIST: Did you know that U.S. postage stamps are now being printed in Canada?
   PATRIOT: What an outrage! If there is one thing that ought to be made in the United States, it's U.S. postage stamps!
   PHILATELIST: Oh, I disagree. If American printing companies can't do the work, let the Canadians have it.
10. FIRST NEIGHBOR: Look here. You have no right to make so much noise at night. I have to get up early to get to work.
    SECOND NEIGHBOR: Yeah? Well, you have no right to let your idiot dog run around loose all day long.
11. STUDY PARTNER ONE: Let's knock off for a while and go get some pizza. We'll be able to function better if we have something to eat.
    STUDY PARTNER TWO: Not one of those pizzas you like! I can't stand anchovies.
12. FEMALE STUDENT: The Internet is totally overrated. It takes forever to find something you can actually use in an assignment.
    MALE STUDENT: Listen, it takes a lot longer to drive over to the library and find a place to park.
13. CITIZEN ONE: In 2008 it's going to be Condi Rice for the Republicans and Hillary for the Democrats, what do you want to bet?
    CITIZEN TWO: I doubt it. Hillary has too many enemies. The Democrats will find someone else.
14. CULTURALLY CHALLENGED PERSON: A concert! You think I'm gonna go to a concert when I could be home watching Monday Night Football?
    CULTURALLY CHALLENGED PERSON'S SPOUSE: Yes, if you want dinner this week.
15. DEMOCRAT: I don't think the President's budget requests make a lot of sense.
    REPUBLICAN: That's because you can't stand to cut taxes.

Exercise 1-8

For each of the brief conversations that follow, identify the issue the first speaker is addressing. To what extent does the second speaker address the same issue? Does he or she miss the point? If so, might the misdirection be intentional? Some of these are best suited to class discussion.

Example

MOORE: I've seen the work of both Thomas Brothers and Vernon Construction, and I tell you Thomas Brothers does a better job.

PARKER: Listen, Thomas Brothers is the highest-priced company in the whole blasted state. If you hire them, you'll pay double for every part of the job.

Analysis

Moore thinks Thomas Brothers does better work than Vernon Construction; Parker thinks Thomas Brothers' work is overpriced. Moore's view is quite compatible with Parker's view: Thomas Brothers may indeed do the best work (i.e., Moore is right) *and* charge wildly excessive prices (i.e., Parker is right, too). However, there is an underlying issue on which Moore and Parker will almost certainly disagree: whether Thomas Brothers should be hired. They have not made this disagreement explicit yet, however.

▲ **1.** URBANITE: The new requirements will force people off septic tanks and make them hook up to the city sewer. That's the only way we'll ever get the nitrates and other pollutants out of the ground water.
SUBURBANITE: You call it a requirement, but I call it an outrage! They're going to charge us from five to fifteen thousand dollars each to make the hookups! That's more than anybody in my neighborhood can afford.

2. CRITIC: I don't think it's morally proper to sell junk bonds to anybody without emphasizing the risk involved, but it's especially bad to sell them to older people who are investing their entire savings.
ENTREPRENEUR: Oh, come on. There's nothing the matter with making money.

▲ **3.** ONE HAND: What with the number of handguns and armed robberies these days, it's hard to feel safe in your own home.
THE OTHER HAND: The reason you don't feel safe is that you don't have a handgun yourself. It's well known that a criminal would rather hit a house where there's no gun than a house where there is one.

4. ONE GUY: Would you look at the price they want for these recordable DVD machines? They're making a fortune in profit on every one of these things!
ANOTHER: Don't give me that. I know how big a raise you got last year—you can afford *two* of those players if you want!

▲ **5.** FED-UP: This city is too cold in the winter, too hot in the summer, and too dangerous all the time. I'll be happier if I exercise my early retirement option and move to my place in Arkansas.
FRIEND: You're nuts. You've worked here so long you'll be miserable if you retire, and if you move, you'll be back in six months.

Exercise 1-9

On the basis of a concept or distinction discussed in this chapter, divide the following issues into two groups, and identify the concept or distinction you used.

▲ **1.** Whether George Pataki was as old when he became governor as Mario Cuomo was when he became governor.

2. Whether George Pataki is kinder than Mario Cuomo was when Mario Cuomo was governor.

3. Whether Willie Mays hit more home runs than Mark McGwire.
▲ 4. Whether Leno told better jokes than Letterman.
5. Whether your teacher will complain if you wear a baseball cap in class.
6. Whether your teacher should complain if you wear a baseball cap in class.
▲ 7. Whether there has ever been life on Mars.
8. Whether golf is more challenging than tennis.
9. Whether the movie scared me.
▲ 10. Whether I said the movie scared me.
11. Whether the movie is scary to a majority of people.

Exercise 1-10

Which of the following raises a subjective question? If some items are difficult to decide, explain why you think this is so.

▲ 1. How much does Manuel weigh?
2. Does diet soda taste more bland than regular soda?
3. Does diet soda contain less sugar than regular soda?
▲ 4. Does replacing regular soda with diet soda cause you to lose weight?
5. Is it more fun to sail on a cruise ship than to lie on the beach at Hilton Head?
6. Is it expensive to sail on a cruise ship?
▲ 7. Is there life on another planet somewhere in the universe?
8. Would most people find this bath water uncomfortably hot?
9. Is the lake frozen?
▲ 10. Is Conan O'Brien better looking than Jon Stewart?
11. Is Tiger Woods a better golfer than Jack Nicklaus was?
12. Is Al Sharpton smarter than George W. Bush?
▲ 13. Is abortion immoral?
14. Is Elvis still alive?

Exercise 1-11

▲ Some of the following are subjective claims, and some are not. Can you identify them correctly?

1. Rice vinegar tastes a darn sight better than white vinegar.
2. White vinegar removes lipstick stains; rice vinegar doesn't.
3. None of the Supreme Court justices view the Constitution objectively.
4. Nine authors collaborated on that article.
5. Microsoft shares are significantly overpriced.
6. People who go to church regularly live longer than people who don't.
7. The FBI and CIA don't share information as often as they should.

8. The report stated that the FBI and CIA don't share information as often as they should.
9. Okay—enough of this logic stuff. It's Miller Time!
10. That last item is too challenging for this text.

Exercise 1-12

Rewrite any of the following sentences that contain subjective expressions.

▲ 1. The house, an imposing two-story colonial-style building, burned to the ground.
2. Assad, who was reluctant to do so, attended the summit that took place in Qatar last March.
3. Hurricane Fran stranded 175 devastated homeowners on barrier islands.
▲ 4. The Coors Brewing Company, long a supporter of a right-wing agenda, began offering gay partners the same benefits as spouses in 1995.
5. Castellanos attended the University of North Carolina but dropped out in disgust during his final semester.
6. On August 22, the leader of a Kurdish faction wrote a desperate plea to Saddam Hussein.
▲ 7. McCovey, who at the time was overwhelmed with grief, was able to finish the assignment on time.
8. In his question, Larry King, the best interviewer in the business, probed Mr. Cheney's business contacts.
9. Senator Byrd announced his proposal to protect the pension funds of struggling workers.
▲ 10. The Reverend Jesse Jackson's provocative visit to Pakistan has been delayed due to lack of support from the Bush administration.
11. Senator Clinton gave a sharp and vigorous response to the Republican challenger.
12. This Sunday, as prescribed by the barely functioning peace accords, Bosnians are to go to the polls to elect a president.
▲ 13. For two years the rapidly expanding global computer matrix had nagged at Gates like a low-level headache.
14. Creative policies have stopped the declining enrollments at Chaffey College.
15. In early 2004 the U.S. Senate tried to reach agreement on the perplexing question of how to rescue Medicare.

Exercise 1-13

Revise each of these press reports to exclude any subjective elements. If no such elements appear, leave the original as is.

▲ 1. OROVILLE—A judge Friday ordered an accused gunman held for trial on a felony assault charge stemming from an aborted residential robbery last month during which an Oroville bank executive was wounded.

2. WASHINGTON—As details of a remarkable week of grand jury testimony by the senator filter into the public domain, his apologists are unwinding a fragile string of explanations to protect him against charges of perjury and obstruction of justice.
3. LHOK SUKON, Indonesia (AP)—Human rights workers on Saturday dug up the skeletons of people whom activists believe were killed by the Indonesian military. Villagers looking on shouted slogans against former President Suharto.
4. ▲ Gunshots were fired at an apartment complex off 10th Street Friday during a "gang bang," which, according to witnesses, may have been contrived to intimidate or retaliate against rival gang members.
5. WASHINGTON—From hideouts in Afghanistan's rugged mountains, Osama bin Laden used his wealth to create cells of Muslim fighters to cleanse the country of its Soviet occupiers. Now bin Laden, who became the most significant sponsor of Islamic extremist activities in the world, is still using his wealth in his war on the United States.
6. HARRISBURG, PA. (AP)—With no bathrooms or portable potties in space, NASA has relied on a brand of inexpensive, compressed adult diapers to let astronauts take care of business while they work.
7. ▲ WASHINGTON—The attorney general has launched a 90-day investigation to see if she should seek still another independent counsel, this time to check into the truthfulness of the vice president. On the face of it, suspicion arises that the investigation might be more a means of dealing with political pressure—another stalling tactic—than of enforcing the law, since the probe won't be finished until after the November elections.
8. SACRAMENTO (AP)—State senators on Thursday approved a bill by Assemblywoman Debra Bowen, D–Marina del Rey, that would give computer owners a way to block unwanted commercial electronic mail, which is commonly known as spam.
9. Radio shock jock Eric "Mancow" Muller hasn't exactly turned into a choirboy, but the irreverent host has toned down his notoriously risqué morning show on Q101 in Chicago, a program that used to be filled with sexual banter.
10. ▲ Prior to the election, President George W. Bush asked whether character counts. Those who felt character was important went on to elect the feeblest intellect this nation was ever to suffer under as president.

Exercise 1-14

Which of the lettered options serves the same kind of purpose as the original remark?

Example

Be careful! This plate is hot.

a. Watch out. The roads are icy.

b. Say—why don't you get lost?

Answer

The purpose of (a) is most like the purpose of the original remark. Both are warnings.

▲ **1.** I'd expect that zipper to last about a week; it's made of cheap plastic.

a. The wrinkles on that dog make me think of an old man.
b. Given Sydney's spending habits, I doubt Adolphus will stick with her for long.

2. If you recharge your battery, sir, it will be almost as good as new.

a. Purchasing one CD at the regular price would entitle you to buy an unlimited number of CDs at only $4.99.
b. I shall now serve dinner, after which you can play if you want.

3. To put out a really creative newsletter, you should get in touch with our technology people.

a. Do unto others as you would have them do unto you.
b. To put an end to this discussion, I'll concede your point.
c. You'd better cut down on your smoking if you want to live longer.

▲ **4.** GE's profits during the first quarter were short of GE's projections. Therefore, we can expect GE stock to fall sharply in the next day or so.

a. Senator Torricelli apparently thinks what he does in private is nobody's business but his own.
b. The dog is very hot. Probably he would appreciate a drink of water.
c. The dog's coat is unusually thick. No wonder he is hot.

5. How was my date with your brother? Well . . . he has a great personality.

a. How do I like my steak? Well, not dripping blood like this thing you just served me.
b. How do I like the dress? Say, did you know that black is more slimming than white?

6. The wind is coming up. We'd better head for shore.

a. They finally arrived. I guess they will order soon.
b. We shouldn't leave yet. We just got here.

▲ **7.** Ties are as wide as handkerchiefs, these days. That's why they cost so much.

a. Belts are like suspenders. They both serve to keep your pants up.
b. Football is like rugby. Given that, it is easy to understand why so many people get injured.

8. Daphne owns an expensive car. She must be rich.

a. This dog has fleas. I'll bet it itches a lot.
b. This dog has fleas. That explains why it scratches a lot.

9. Dennis's salary is going to go up. After all, he just got a promotion.

a. Dennis's salary went up after he got a promotion.
b. Dennis's salary won't be going up. After all, he didn't get a promotion.

▲ **10.** Outlawing adult Web sites may hamper free speech, but pornography must be curbed.

a. The grass must be mowed, even though it is hot.
b. The grass is much too long; that means it must be mowed.

Exercise 1-15

Five of the following questions call for an explanation; five call for an argument. Identify which call for which. (It may be possible to imagine strange situations in which all ten questions call for explanations and possible to imagine other strange situations in which all ten questions might call for arguments. Don't try to imagine far-out situations like that. Try to imagine normal, everyday situations in which somebody might ask these questions.)

▲ 1. YOU TO A FRIEND: You really think the dog is overweight? What makes you so sure?

2. YOU TO A FRIEND: Hey! The dang dog got out again! How do you suppose that happened?

3. YOU TO YOUR DENTIST: Yes, yes, I know I have another cavity, but what I don't understand is why. How did I get it—too many Jolly Ranchers?

▲ 4. YOU TO YOUR DENTIST: You're saying I have another cavity? Are you certain?

5. YOU TO YOUR DOCTOR: I haven't been sleeping very well, and I wondered what might account for that.

6. YOU TO YOUR DOCTOR: Doc, I've heard really bad things about that medication. Should I be taking it?

▲ 7. YOU TO A MECHANIC: This Hyundai is always giving me problems. Half the time I can't even get it in gear! What causes something like that?

8. YOU TO A MECHANIC: Well, I certainly don't dispute what you are saying, but can you tell me again why you think I need a new transmission?

9. YOU TO YOUR TEACHER: I don't understand this grade! Are you sure you didn't make a mistake?

▲ 10. YOU TO YOUR TEACHER: I understand this grade; but can you tell me how I can do better next time?

Writing Exercises

1. Turn to the "Essays for Analysis" in Appendix 1. Identify and write in your own words the principal issues in the selections identified by your instructor.
2. Do people choose which sex they are attracted to? Write a one-page answer to this question, defending your answer with at least one supporting reason. Take about ten minutes to write your answer. Do not put your name on your paper. When everyone is finished, your instructor will collect the papers and redistribute them to the class. In groups of four or five, read the papers that have been given to your group. Divide the drafts into two batches, those that contain an argument and those that do not. Your instructor will ask each group to read to the class a paper that contains an argument and a paper that does not contain an argument (assuming that each group has at least one of each). The group should be prepared to explain why they feel each paper contains or fails to contain an argument.
3. Using the issues you identified in Exercise 1 for each of the selections, choose a side on one of the issues and write a short paper supporting it.

Chapter 2

Clear Thinking, Critical Thinking, and Clear Writing

This chapter is about things that aren't quite as clear as these signs.

Kraft Foods, Inc., makers of Oscar Meyer franks, Velveeta, and other gourmet items, recently faced a dilemma with their new candy line. The candies were selling well, but a few consumers, including the New Jersey Society for the Prevention of Cruelty to Animals, were not pleased with Trolli Road Kill Gummi Candy, which had been made to look like flattened chickens and squirrels with tire treads across the carcasses. Kraft promptly discontinued the line, because "we take comments from our consumers really seriously and in hindsight we understand that this product could be misunderstood."*

Anyone can understand Kraft's reason for discontinuing the candies. Frequently, however, we are confronted with arguments that are more difficult. Not long ago, Fort Irwin Elementary, a California public school, extended its kindergarten hours in order to provide, according to a newsletter from the principal, "a thinking meaning appropriately centered-based academic/social program to meet the diverse needs of the kindergarten students." Was this a good reason for extending the kindergarten hours? It is difficult to say even what the reason is, it is so confusing.

*Associated Press report, March 4, 2005

Still, the claim this argument tried to support is clear enough. The kindergarten hours should be extended. Unfortunately, however, often even the claim is unclear. For example, Allan Bloom, the famous American educator who authored *The Closing of the American Mind,* which was read (or at least purchased) by millions, wrote in that book:

> If openness means to "go with the flow," it is necessarily an accommodation to the present. That present is so closed to doubt about so many things impeding the progress of its principles that unqualified openness to it would mean forgetting the despised alternative to it, knowledge of which makes us aware of what is doubtful in it.

Is this true? Well—that's really hard to say. The problem is, you don't know exactly what Professor Bloom is asserting in this passage.

Those who survived the San Francisco earthquake said, "Thank God, I'm still alive." But, of course, those who died—their lives will never be the same again.

— U.S. SENATOR BARBARA BOXER (D), California

If I said anything which implies that I think that we didn't do what we should have done given the choices we faced at the time, I shouldn't have said that.

— BILL CLINTON (reported by Larry Engelmann)

The President will keep the promises he meant to keep.

— Bill Clinton's White House senior adviser, GEORGE STEPHANOPOULOS

Lack of clarity in a statement derives from various causes. President George W. Bush once reportedly said, "We'll be a great country where the fabrics are made up of groups and loving centers."* This sentence demonstrates what can happen if you string words together in random order. One of our former students wrote in an essay that "Legal laws are fine, but illegal ones should be changed." This is what philosophers call confusing categories; you can ask whether your teacher is old, but you can't ask whether being old is old. Or take this remark from a newspaper call-in column:

> I am glad to be an American, and I appreciate our system of government. Also, I am for a very strong defense. However, the people protesting the war on all sides are out there because they care about life. Now we are in an awful mess. Why? We need to put ourselves in the other guy's shoes. Going out and killing the other guy may be the way to preserve your own.

Here, the problem is not that words were assembled randomly, but that sentences were.

So any number of problems may make a statement unclear. Not infrequently, people just don't say what they mean. On the television program 60 Minutes II, George W. Bush said "We want anybody who can find work to be able to find work."* This is something like wanting anyone taller than 6 feet to be over 6 feet tall. What's unclear is why anyone would want something that couldn't *not* happen. The President misspoke. He probably intended to say there should be jobs available for people who want them, and it just came out funny. We once read in a letter to the editor the statement, "When I was in the Marine Corps, I was plainly told that many good men died in the uniform that was issued to me." Here, too, the writer probably just wanted to say something simple, probably that good men die serving as Marines, but he lost control of his sentence.

Although obscurity can issue from various causes, three sources of confusion stand out as paramount: excessive vagueness, ambiguity, and terms

---

*From *George W. Bushisms* by Jacob Weisberg.

*December 5, 2000. Reported in *George W. Bushisms* by Jacob Weisberg.

Real Life

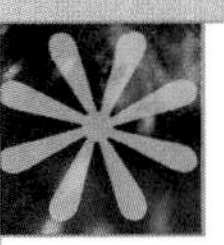

Who Said What?

Can you tell which of these quotations are from students in community college and which are from the forty-third president of the United States, who happens to be a Yale graduate?

1. "Sometimes the standards of society causes people to wear a mask."
2. "Reading is the basics for all learning."
3. "I played all types of sports that was offered to children then."
4. "More and more, our imports come from overseas."
5. "Children are born as a ball of clay; to mold into what we are able, good or bad. To enhance who we are and to carry on the person we are known to be."
6. "Drug therapies are replacing a lot of medicines as we used to know it."
7. "You teach a child to read and he or her will be able to pass a literacy test."
8. "He uses an abundance of words and phrases both of which I don't believe should have."
9. ". . . if you say you're going to do something and you don't do it, that's trustworthiness."
10. "Male dominance has long been a factor in human existence since our existence."
11. "My pro-life position is I believe there's life. It's not necessarily based in religion. I think there's life there, therefore the notion of life, liberty and pursuit of happiness."

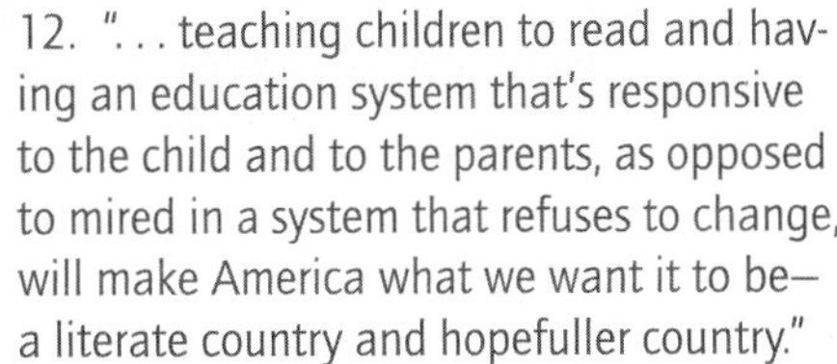

12. ". . . teaching children to read and having an education system that's responsive to the child and to the parents, as opposed to mired in a system that refuses to change, will make America what we want it to be—a literate country and hopefuller country."
13. "Men love women who can cook good."
14. "I have never really thought of myself to be very interesting as a human being or as anything else."

1, 3, 5, 8, 10, 13, and 14—Community college student; 2, 4, 6, 7, 9, 11, 12—Yale graduate

From an article by Jaime O'Neill, a member of the English faculty at Butte Community College, in *San Francisco Chronicle,* September 2, 2001.

that need defining. In this chapter, we shall consider vagueness and ambiguity in detail, and then talk in detail about definitions.

Also, from time to time situations arise in which we need to think critically in writing, in the form of what is called an argumentative essay. In this

In the Media

Say What?? . . .

You don't have to be a national political figure to put your foot in your mouth. Ordinary folks can do it too!

> The President's energy tax won't even be noticed. Besides, it will discourage consumption.
>
> *[Hey, if it won't be noticed, it won't discourage consumption.]*
>
> Females score lower on the SAT than males, which right there proves the tests don't show anything. They also demonstrate that teachers do a better job of teaching male students, which is just what you'd expect given the sexual bias that exists in the classroom.
>
> *[If the SATs don't show anything, then they don't show that teachers do a better job teaching males.]*
>
> We have to liberate discussion on this campus and not be so restrained by the First Amendment.
>
> *[Right. And we can make people free by sticking them in jail.]*
>
> Once your body gets cold, the rest of you will get cold, too.
>
> *[On the other hand, if you can keep your body warm, the rest of you will stay warm, too.]*
>
> It's hard to support the President's invasion of Haiti when the American public is so strongly against it. And besides, he's just doing it to raise his standings in the polls.
>
> *[Hmmm. How's it going to raise his standings if the public is so strongly against it?]*
>
> Has anyone put anything in your baggage without your knowledge?
>
> *[Asked of our colleague Becky White by an airport security employee]*

type of writing enterprise, one takes a position on an issue and supports it with argument. A good argumentative essay consists of four parts: a statement of the issue, a statement of one's position on that issue, arguments that support one's position, and rebuttals of arguments that support contrary positions. Obviously, an argumentative essay is weakened by statements that are obscure, and what we say in this chapter has direct application to writing clear argumentative essays. We shall return to this subject after we discuss vagueness, ambiguity, and definitions.

VAGUENESS

The single most common form of unclear thinking or writing is excessive vagueness. The concept of vagueness is pretty easy to grasp. A vague statement is one whose meaning is indistinct, imprecise, or lacks details. Vagueness is what elevates your blood pressure when you are trying to find someone's house and it is late and the directions you have been given include something like "Go down the road a ways to the turn and you'll be there." Vagueness is what annoys students when the teacher says the term paper "should be long enough to get the job done." When candidates for public office say they want to reduce crime, are for fairness in taxation, and favor a healthy environment, it sounds grand, but you generally have no real idea what they have in mind because they are speaking vaguely. If your boyfriend or girlfriend is vague when you ask if he or she loves you, you may well press for clarification.

For how long?

For more than almost half a century, the Humane Society has led the fight to protect animals.

— Humane Society solicitation sent to one of us

The first thing to notice about vagueness is that it is not all or nothing. Vagueness comes in degrees. "My house payments are higher than they used to be" is vaguer than "My house payments went up 30 percent beginning last month." "The New Jersey SPCA sent a written request to Kraft asking that Trolli Road Kill candy not be sold" is less vague than "Animals rights activities griped about a new line of candy." "Norman is nice" is vaguer than "Norman has good manners," and the last assertion is vaguer than "Norman always holds the door open for you."

Generally speaking, what is to be avoided is not vagueness per se, but an undesirable degree of vagueness. Even though a claim may be less precise than it could be, that doesn't mean it should be more precise. If you tell your friend you expect higher house payments, your friend doesn't necessarily expect you to be more precise. But if your mortgage lender tells you to expect higher house payments, you want details because the lender's degree of vagueness is unacceptable. Recently, we were behind a van that said: "PRISONER TRANSPORT. STAND BACK." The second sentence is vague, but we got the idea.*

Sometimes you want to be vague. If your friend asks you for your opinion of her mother, you might temper an unfavorable reply with a certain amount of vagueness. When Oscar Goodman, the mayor of Las Vegas, was asked by a class of elementary school students what he would want most if he were stranded on an island, he said, "a bottle of gin."** Some parents complained; and we think perhaps he should have been more vague.

Although you may sometimes want to be vague, there is a point at which a claim is so vague it is impossible to determine if it is true or false. Obviously, before one can even begin to consider whether or not such a claim is true, one must attempt to clarify it. For example, we recently heard people on National Public Radio discussing whether "three servings of dairy a day will help you lose weight." Is this claim true? Well, that's not the right question to ask at this point. The appropriate questions are, what is meant by a serving, what is included as "dairy," and what counts as helping you lose weight. What is called for is what logicians call *precising definitions,* definitions that spell out in more detail what is meant by a vague concept. We shall say more about precising definitions in a moment; for now, the point is the obvious one that vague statements may require preliminary sharpening before one can consider whether they are true or false. If someone says, "Women can tolerate more stress than men," the best place to begin would *not* be by saying, "Prove it," or "How interesting," or "I agree," but by attempting to clarify what was meant by "tolerate," by "stress," and by "more." Of course, some claims may be so vague that it would be best just to move on to another topic. "This country is morally bankrupt" might fall in this category.

*Come to think of it, perhaps the last two words were not even necessary.

**Associated Press report, March 4, 2005.

On Language

A "Weakest Link" Quiz

Here is a "Weakest Link" quiz that was circulating on the Net a while back. It's a good test of your ability to read carefully and think clearly, two key components of critical thinking.

1. You are competing in a race and overtake the runner in second place. In which position are you now?
   Answer: If you said "first," then you aren't reading carefully (or aren't thinking clearly). The correct answer, of course, is "second."
2. If you overtake the last runner, what position are you in now?
   Answer: Second to the last? Hardly. The question doesn't make sense.
3. Take 1,000. Add 40. Add another 1,000. Add 30. Add 1,000 again. Plus 20. Plus 1,000. And plus 10. What is the total?
   Answer: If you said 5,000 you weren't reading carefully. The correct answer is 4,100.
4. Marie's father has five daughters:
   1. Cha Cha
   2. Che Che
   3. Chi Chi
   4. Cho Cho
   5. ??

   What is the fifth daughter's name?
   Answer: Chu Chu? Wrong, wrong, wrong. It's Marie!

Thanks to Anne Morrissey.

The vagueness of some claims is due to the use of relative words, such as "old," "bald," and "wealthy," that have borderline cases. Bill Gates, for instance, clearly is wealthy and clearly is not bald. But is a person who makes over $150,000 a year wealthy? Is Bruce Willis bald? It's hard to say in borderline cases. But if a candidate for governor says, "We should raise taxes on the wealthy," time is well spent trying to pin down what he or she has in mind by "wealthy." Thus, claims with relative terms are not always too vague; it just depends on the situation.

Further, the absence of relative words does not automatically immunize a claim from undesirable vagueness. "Maria is bringing her sibling to class on Friday" is probably precise enough, depending on the kind of class we are talking about. But "Maria plans to bring her sibling to the slumber party Friday night" may not be precise enough if your own daughter is going to the slumber party and Maria's siblings include brothers. Neither statement about Maria contains vague relative terms, but the context of the second one may make it unduly vague.

As should be clear by now, it makes little sense to insist that a claim be totally free of vagueness. If we had to be absolutely precise whenever we made a statement, we would say and write little. That being said, it is probably true that most people err more on the side of being too vague rather than the opposite.

VAGUE AND MISLEADING COMPARISONS

Comparisons deserve to be singled out for special mention in a discussion of clarity, since they so often are vague or lack important details. Here are a number of comparisons often seen in advertisements:

- Cut by up to half
- Now 25 percent larger
- Quietest by far
- New and improved
- Now better than ever
- More than 20 percent richer

Such claims cry out for clarification. What does "up to half" include? Twenty-five percent larger than what? How far is "by far"? New and improved over what? Better in what way? How much more than 20 percent? And you can ask other questions, too. Remember, though, that the amount of vagueness you can tolerate in a comparative claim depends on your interest and purposes. For example, knowing that attic insulation will reduce your utility bill "by 15 to 45 percent" may be all it takes for you to know that you should insulate.

Some comparisons may be too vague even to be meaningful. Consider the statements "Have more fun in Arizona," "Gets clothes whiter than white," "Delivers more honest flavor." These phrases simply mean have fun in Arizona, gets clothes white, and can be tasted. There are no meaningful comparisons among them. On the other hand, "Nothing else is a Pepsi" isn't too vague; taken literally, it's necessarily true. Nothing else is a turkey, either. What the claim means, of course, is that no other soft drink tastes as good as Pepsi.

Questions to keep in mind when you are considering comparisons include the following:

1. *Is important information missing?* It is nice to hear that the unemployment rate has gone down, but not if you learn the reason is that a larger percent of the workforce has given up looking for work. Or, suppose someone says that 90 percent of heroin addicts once smoked marijuana. Without other information, the comparison is meaningless, since 90 percent of heroin addicts no doubt listened to the Beatles, too. Our local U.S. Congressional representative Wally Herger recently warned his constituents that Social Security is in dire straits. At one time, he said, there were 42 workers to support a single retiree and now there are only three. This does indeed sound ominous, except Representative Herger didn't mention that the 42 to 1 ratio was at the startup of Social Security before many had retired; he also failed to mention that the 3 to 1 ratio has been around for the past 25 years, during which period Social Security accumulated a surplus.*

*Statistics from our colleague, Professor (of American History) Carl Peterson.

Real Life

Misleading Comparisons in Medical Studies

Ever wonder why so many medical studies discover spectacular benefits from new drugs? Maybe it's because researchers report the numbers in a way that makes them sound better than they should.

That's the concern of Dr. Jim Nuovo, professor of family and community medicine at the University of California at Davis. In a study published in the June 5 [2002] *Journal of the American Medical Assn.*, Nuovo looked at 359 studies from leading medical journals and found that only 18 of them reported results in terms of absolute risk reduction. The rest reported only relative risk reduction—which can sound far more substantial.

Here's an example from Nuovo to explain the difference: Suppose an existing drug cuts the rate of heart attacks in men to 5%. A new drug cuts that risk to 4%. In terms of relative risk that's an impressive-sounding 20% improvement. In absolute terms, however, there's only a one-percentage-point difference. The risk has gone from low to slightly lower—which doesn't sound very impressive, especially if the new drug costs 10 times as much as the existing drug.

Nuovo's point is that all of these numbers, and more, ought to be reported in every study. "There's no one number that explains everything in an article," he says. "Once you start putting things into context, you start getting a better picture." Proposed guidelines for clinical trials call for researchers to report absolute risk reduction along with relative risks, Nuovo says, but those guidelines are often ignored. Editors should require authors to follow them, he says.

Business Week, June 17, 2002, p. 85.

Real Life

Cause for Alarm?

According to the National Household Survey on Drug Abuse, cocaine use among Americans twelve to seventeen years of age increased by a whopping 166 percent between 1992 and 1995. Wow, right?

Except that the increase *in absolute terms* was a little less spectacular: In 1992, 0.3 percent of Americans aged twelve to seventeen had used cocaine; in 1995, the percentage was 0.8 percent of that population.

Be wary of comparisons expressed as percentage changes.

2. *Is the same standard of comparison being used?* Are the same reporting and recording practices being used? A change in the jobless rate doesn't mean much if the government changes the way it calculates joblessness, as sometimes happen. In 1993, the number of people in the United States with AIDS suddenly increased dramatically. Had a new form of the AIDS virus appeared? No, the federal government had expanded the definition of

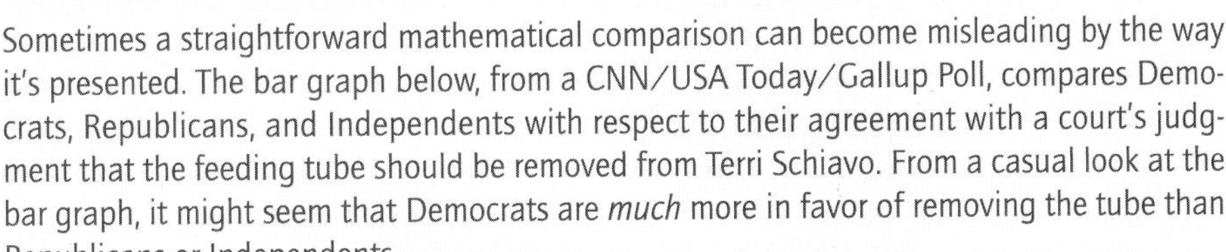

In the Media

A Misleading Mathematical Visual

Sometimes a straightforward mathematical comparison can become misleading by the way it's presented. The bar graph below, from a CNN/USA Today/Gallup Poll, compares Democrats, Republicans, and Independents with respect to their agreement with a court's judgment that the feeding tube should be removed from Terri Schiavo. From a casual look at the bar graph, it might seem that Democrats are *much* more in favor of removing the tube than Republicans or Independents.

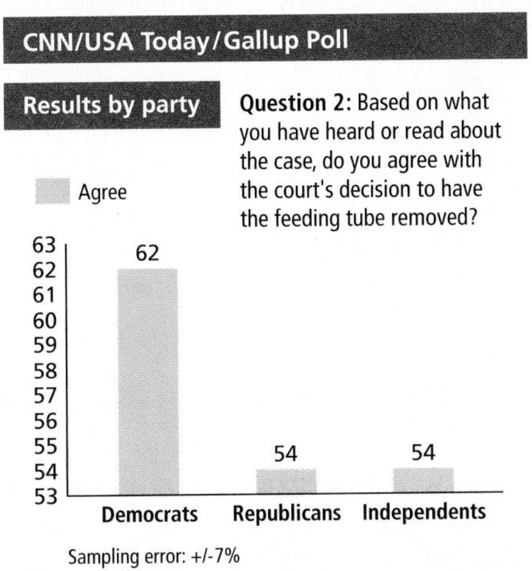

But look at the *numbers* rather than the bars themselves, and we get a different story. The first graph only shows us the *parts* of the bars, from 53 percent to 63 percent. If we display the entire bars, from 0 to 100 percent, the graph looks like this:

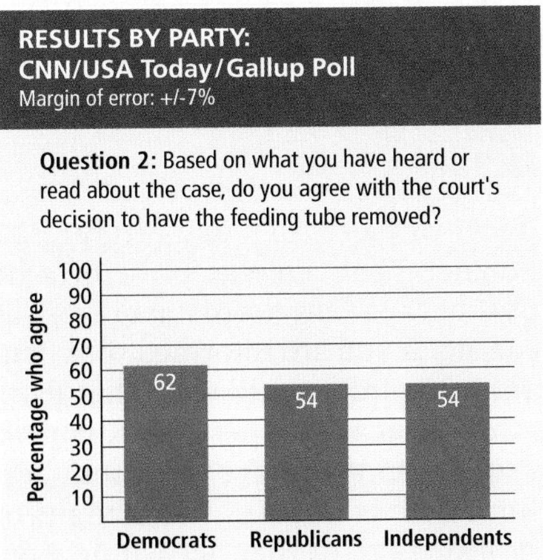

In this case, the Democrats look (correctly) to be only somewhat more in favor of removing the tube. The lesson here is to avoid drawing conclusions unless you've had a close look at the data, including the manner in which it is displayed.

Comparison originally made by truthout.org.

There is no excuse for passing children through schools who can't read.

— GEORGE W. BUSH

AIDS to include several new indicator conditions. As a result, overnight, 50,000 people were considered to have AIDS who had not been so considered the day before.

3. *Are the items comparable?* It is hard to compare baseball sluggers Barry Bonds with Willie Mays if one but not the other used steroids, or if one had the benefit of improved equipment. It's hard to derive a conclusion from the fact that this April's retail business activity is way down as compared with last April's, if Easter fell in March this year and the weather was especially cold. That more male than female drivers are involved in traffic fatalities doesn't mean much by itself, since male drivers collectively drive more miles than do female drivers. Comparing share values of two mutual funds over the last ten years won't be useful to an investor if the comparison doesn't take into account a difference in fees.
4. *Is the comparison expressed as an average?* The average rainfall in Seattle is about the same as that in Kansas City. But you'll spend more time in the rain in Seattle because it rains there twice as often as in Kansas City. If Central Valley Components, Inc. (CVC), reports that average salaries of a majority of its employees have more than doubled over the past ten years, it sounds good, but CVC still may not be a great place to work. Perhaps the increases were due to converting the majority of employees, who worked half-time, to full-time and firing the rest. Comparisons that involve averages omit details that can be important, simply because they involve averages.

   Averages are measures of central tendency, and there are different kinds of measures or averages. Consider, for instance, the average cost of a new house in your area, which may be $150,000. If that is the *mean,* it is the total of the sales prices divided by the number of houses sold, and it may be quite different from the *median,* which is an average that is the halfway figure (half the houses cost more and half cost less). The *mode,* the most common sales price, may be different yet. If there are likely to be large or dramatic variations in whatever it is that is being measured, one must be cautious of figures that represent an unspecific "average."

The wrong average can put you under.

Never try to wade a river just because it has an average depth of four feet.

— MARTIN FRIEDMAN

Misleading Averages

In 2003, George W. Bush proposed a tax cut that he said would give the average taxpayer $1,083.

The "average" here is the mean average. However, before you start dreaming about how to spend your $1,083, you might want to check on the modal average. Most taxpayers, according to the Urban Institute–Brookings Institution Tax Policy Center, would receive less than $100 under the Bush proposal.

AMBIGUOUS CLAIMS

A sentence that is subject to more than one interpretation is said to be ambiguous rather than vague. "The average price of a house in Monterey is $995,000" is ambiguous, because the word "average," as we just mentioned, has more than one meaning. If you are informed that Paul cashed a check, you won't be able to tell from that information whether Paul took in cash or gave it out; and if you hear that Jessica rents her house, you don't know if she rents it to someone or from someone. If Jennifer rises from her desk on Friday afternoon and says, "My work here is finished," she might mean she has finished the account she was working on, or that her whole week's work is done and she's leaving for the weekend, or that she is fed up with her job and is leaving the company. You can have a lot of fun finding online collections of "ambiguous headlines" with such examples as "Farmer Bill Dies in Senate."

But ambiguities can be quite subtle. People hooted when Bill Clinton maintained that the word "is" is ambiguous, but in fact sentences which use

What *do* they promote it for?

The World Health Organization does not promote a drink a day for health reasons.

— Chico Enterprise-Record

I am a marvelous housekeeper. Every time I leave a man I keep his house.

— ZSA ZSA GABOR

■ The Fantastic Four are not pleased by this book.
Of course, they aren't displeased either. Note the ambiguity in the original statement.

that word are subject to more than one interpretation. If you say, "Howard is fighting with Susan" you might mean that Howard is fighting with Susan at this very moment. But then again, you might not mean they are fighting at this very moment, but that their relationship currently is acrimonious. Bill Clinton was impeached for providing false information to a grand jury, but whether or not some of the information was false indeed "depends," just as Clinton said it did, "on what the meaning of 'is' is." Ambiguity is not necessarily obvious, and it may not be a triviality.

A problem related to ambiguity crops up when various parties to a dispute mean something different by a key claim. For example, there are those who think the "War on Terror" is a real war and there are those who do not; the two sides evidently do not have the same thing in mind by "war." Does abortion involve killing a human being? Well, some use the word in such a way that a pregnant woman is two human beings; others use it in such a way that a pregnant woman is one human being. We recently heard a debate between a supporter and an opponent of gay rights. The supporter seemed to have a different meaning for the term "rights" than his opponent had, or at least different from what the opponent said the supporter meant by the term. The supporter said he wanted gays to have the right to be treated equally under the law; the opponent said the supporter wanted additional or special rights not accorded to others. Much wasted breath and misunderstanding can result if the two sides in questions like these fail to sort out definitions of key terms.

Now, it certainly is true that often one is clear in one's own mind which of two meanings is meant. If you say "Horatio plays the trumpet by ear," you probably know whether you mean that Horatio doesn't use music or that

On Language

Making Ambiguity Work for You

Were you ever asked to write a letter of recommendation for a friend who is, well, incompetent? If you don't want to hurt his or her feelings but also don't want to lie, Robert Thornton of Lehigh University has some ambiguous statements you can use. Here are some examples:

> I most enthusiastically recommend this candidate with no qualifications whatsoever.
>
> I am pleased to say that this candidate is a former colleague of mine.
>
> I can assure you that no person would be better for the job.
>
> I would urge you to waste no time in making this candidate an offer of employment.
>
> All in all, I cannot say enough good things about this candidate or recommend the candidate too highly.
>
> In my opinion, you will be very fortunate to get this person to work for you.

Horatio uses his ear the way other trumpet players use their embouchure. But, unfortunately, sometimes people are confused about which of two meanings they have in mind, and they vacillate between meanings. For example, you sometimes hear beginning students in philosophy maintaining that every voluntary action is a selfish action, done to benefit oneself. This is a striking idea, and the student typically is quite impressed by the finding. Unfortunately, the argument given for this idea invariably utilizes a *different* concept of "selfish action," according to which, if you are doing something because you desire to do it, you are acting selfishly. And the confused argument goes something like this: All voluntary acts are done to satisfy one's own desire to do them; thus, all voluntary acts are selfish acts; thus, all voluntary acts are done for self benefit. The argument is confused, because it switches to a new concept of selfishness midstream.

Semantic Ambiguity

We want to tell you now about three different types of ambiguity. First, if a claim is ambiguous because it contains an ambiguous word or phrase, it is said to be a **semantic ambiguity.** Consider the following examples:

1. The *average* price of a house in Monterey is $995,000.
2. Calhoun always lines up on the *right* side.
3. Jessica is *cold.*
4. I know a little *Italian.*
5. Terry disputed their *claim.*
6. Aunt Amy does not use *glasses.*

Semantic ambiguity can be eliminated by substituting an unambiguous word or phrase, such as "eyeglasses" for "glasses" in the last item, or adding a clarifying phrase, such as "of the room" to the end of the second item.

On Language

Check Your Chart

The following are alleged to be actual notations in patients' records. Each has a flagrant ambiguity or other problem. Sometimes the problem interferes with clarity; other times it only produces amusement. Describe what is going on in each case.

- Patient has chest pain if she lies on her left side for over a year.
- She has had no rigors or shaking chills, but her husband states she was very hot in bed last night.
- The patient has been depressed ever since she began seeing me in 1983.
- I will be happy to go into her GI system; she seems ready and anxious.
- The patient is tearful and crying constantly. She also appears to be depressed.
- Discharge status: Alive but without permission. The patient will need disposition, and therefore we will get Dr. Blank to dispose of him.
- Healthy-appearing decrepit 69-year-old male, mentally alert but forgetful.
- The patient refused an autopsy.
- The patient has no past history of suicides.
- The patient expired on the floor uneventfully.
- Patient has left his white blood cells at another hospital.
- Patient was becoming more demented with urinary frequency.
- The patient's past medical history has been remarkably insignificant with only a 40-pound weight gain in the past three days.
- She slipped on the ice and apparently her legs went in separate directions in early December.
- The patient experienced sudden onset of severe shortness of breath with a picture of acute pulmonary edema at home while having sex which gradually deteriorated in the emergency room.
- The patient left the hospital feeling much better except for her original complaints.
- The patient states there is a burning pain in his penis which goes to his feet.

(These were sent around the Internet after they appeared in a column written by RICHARD LEDERER in the *Journal of Court Reporting*. Lederer is famous for his collections of remarks taken from student papers, especially papers on historical subjects.)

Syntactic Ambiguity

Recently, one of us obtained information from the American Automobile Association prior to driving to British Columbia. "To travel to Canada," the brochure stated, "you will need a birth certificate or a driver's license and other photo ID."

This is ambiguous. One way of looking at it means you have to take a photo ID other than a birth certificate or a driver's license, and another way doesn't mean that. Using parentheses will make these alternatives clear, we hope:

(1) (You will need a birth certificate or a driver's license) *and* (other photo ID)
(2) (You will need a birth certificate) *or* (a driver's license and other photo ID)

This is an example of what is known as **syntactic ambiguity,** a statement that is ambiguous because of its grammar or the way it has been structured or put together. Here are a few other examples:

But, then, old women filled sandbags with eight-year-old boys, too.

It's wonderful that we have eight-year-old boys filling sandbags with old women.

— Larry King, on attempts to stem Mississippi floods (reported by Larry Engelmann)

Players with beginners' skills only may use court 1.
Susan saw the farmer with binoculars.
People who protest often get arrested.
He chased the girl in his car.
There's somebody in the bed next to me.

As you can see, the cause of the ambiguity here isn't that they contain an ambiguous word. The problem is syntax. For example, in the first sentence the problem is that we don't know what "only" applies to. Does the sentence mean, players with beginners' skills may use *only court 1*? Or does it mean players with *only beginners' skills* may use court 1? Or does it mean *only players with beginners' skills* may use court 1?

The way to eliminate syntactic ambiguity is to alter punctuation or rewrite the claims. For example, you might rewrite 5 as "There's somebody next to me in the bed," to make it clear that "next to me" refers to a person and not to a bed.

Often syntactic ambiguity results when we do not show clearly what a pronoun references. "The boys chased the girls, and they giggled a lot" is ambiguous because we don't know whether "they" refers to the boys or the girls. A similar example is: "After he removed the trash from the pool, the children played in it."

A big skillet, perhaps?

I wrote a story about a girl making lunch in a skillet.

— Garrison Keillor

Modifying phrases can create syntactic ambiguities if one is careless with them: "He brushed his teeth on the carpet," will serve as an example, as will "She wiped up the water with her younger brother." "He was bitten while walking by a dog" is yet another.

Grouping Ambiguity

The third kind of ambiguity, which is really a type of semantic ambiguity, is called grouping ambiguity. Here is an example of grouping ambiguity:

Secretaries make more money than physicians.

Makes sense, sort of, if you view the boys collectively.

If you are wondering about the boys, they both got gangrene and lost some legs.

— CNN anchor Anderson Cooper

Is this claim true or false? That's the wrong question to ask, because you don't know what *the* claim is. Secretaries as a group make more money than physicians make as a group, but secretaries individually don't make more money than physicians individually. The problem, as you can see, is that "secretaries" and "physicians" are ambiguous: Are you referring to secretaries and physicians individually or collectively?

"Lawnmowers create more air pollution than dirt bikes" is a similarly ambiguous statement. We imagine lawnmowers collectively create more air pollution than dirt bikes because there are so many more lawnmowers, but on an individual basis, we aren't sure. Certainly they do not individually make as much *noise* as dirt bikes, which are among the loudest and most annoying noisemakers around.

As with the other types of ambiguities, grouping ambiguity can interfere with clear thinking. The last time a president and the Congress raised taxes, it was called the biggest tax increase in history by those who didn't like it. That particular tax increase, which happened under Bill Clinton, was indeed the biggest tax increase in terms of collective tax revenues, but it was not the biggest tax increase in the percentage of an individual's income that he or she paid to taxes. In other words, the phrase "the biggest tax increase in history" suffers from grouping ambiguity: The individual tax increases were not the biggest, the collective tax increase was.

The Fallacies of Composition and Division

In June 2005, the San Antonio Spurs won the National Basketball Association (NBA) championship, demonstrating they were the best team in the NBA. Does it follow that the players on the Spurs were the best players in the NBA? If you think it does, you have made a mistake: What's true of an entire team is not necessarily true of the players on the team.

People sometimes make this type of mistake. They think that what is true of a group of things taken collectively or as a group is automatically true of the same things taken individually. As the above example shows, this is a confusion, and this type of confusion is so common logicians have a name for it: the **fallacy of division.** (A fallacy is a mistake in reasoning.)

After the 2002 election, in which the Republicans won a majority of the seats in the U.S. Senate, George W. Bush stated that "the people voted for a Republican Senate." In one sense, this statement is true: Voters *collectively* did elect a Republican Senate. But in another sense, the statement is false: Voters *individually* did not elect a Republican Senate. Indeed, no person *anywhere* voted for a Republican Senate, because the question, "Do you want a Republican Senate" was not on any ballot. If you were to conclude that because people collectively preferred a Republican Senate, individually they did so as well, that would be the fallacy of division.

Further examples of this fallacy include:

- Congress is incompetent. Therefore, Congressman Cox is incompetent.
- The Eastman School of Music has an outstanding international reputation. Therefore, Vladimir Peronepky, who is on the faculty of Eastman, has an outstanding international reputation.

Running this reasoning in reverse is also a fallacy. What holds for a group of things individually doesn't automatically hold for the things collectively or as a group. Just because the best basketball players in the NBA are on the same team, you can't conclude that team is the best in the NBA. If you think what holds true of a group of things individually must also hold true of the same things collectively or of the group as a whole, that's the fallacy of composition. Here are other examples:

> We will briefly discuss the history of American Indians on this campus.
>
> — From a flyer advertising "Conversations on Diversity" at the authors' university

> Somewhere on this globe, every ten seconds, there is a woman giving birth to a child. She must be found and stopped.
>
> — SAM LEVENSON (1911–1980)

In Depth

More Examples of Composition and Division

Fallacy of Division

A balanced daily diet consists of the right proportion of protein, carbohydrates, and fat. Therefore, each meal should consist of the same proportion of protein, carbohydrates, and fat.

— DR. NICHOLAS PERRICONE, author of the best-selling book, *The Wrinkle Cure*

Fallacy of Composition

The Kings don't have a chance against the Lakers. The Lakers are better at every position except power forward.

— CHARLES BARKLEY

Fallacy of Division

Men are more likely than women to be involved in fatal automobile accidents. So if you are a man, you are more likely than the next woman you see to be involved in a fatal automobile accident.

— Overheard

- Roger Federer and Svetlana Kuznetsova are the two best tennis players in the world. Therefore, they'd make the best mixed doubles team.
- No member of faculty at the University of Cincinnati makes a lot of money; therefore, faculty salaries don't cost the University of Cincinnati a lot.

Recognizing and Deciphering Ambiguity

Some claims, such as "I will put the sauce on myself," might perhaps reasonably be diagnosed as either semantic or syntactic ambiguities. We advise not spending forever arguing over to which category this or that claim belongs. More important is to recognize ambiguities when you encounter them and to avoid them in your own thinking.

Some ambiguous claims don't fall into the categories we have mentioned. "The fastest woman on the squad" is ambiguous if two or more women on the squad are equally fast and faster than anyone else. "I cannot recommend him highly enough" might mean he is even better than my highest recommendation, or it might mean I cannot recommend him highly enough for you to consider him. The ambiguity is not clearly semantic or syntactic.

Often, the context of a claim will show which possible meaning a speaker or writer intends. If a mechanic says, "Your trouble is in a cylinder," it might be unclear at first whether a wheel cylinder or an engine cylinder is at fault, but the correct meaning will probably become clear in due course from the rest of what gets said. Also, common sense often dictates which of two possible meanings a person has in mind. For example, "He brushed his teeth on the carpet" would most likely not refer to an unusual technique of dental hygiene.

■ Facial expressions can't be vague, though they might perhaps be said to be ambiguous. Svetlana Kuznetsova's expression, however, is indecipherable.

That being said, ambiguous sentences are a fact of life, and how we understand them can have serious implications. For example, the Second Amendment to the Constitution states, "A well-regulated Militia, being necessary to the security of a free State, the right of the people to keep and bear Arms, shall not be infringed." This sentence suffers from more than one type of ambiguity, and among them is a grouping ambiguity. Historically, courts have tended to interpret the right to bear arms as a collective right of citizens. Under this interpretation, citizens are bearing arms if they serve in, say, a National Guard unit that has cannons and such. Recently, however, former Attorney General John Ashcroft supported an interpretation of the Second Amendment that would give citizens taken individually the right to bear arms. Under the Ashcroft interpretation, each individual has the right to bear *his or her own* weapons. Other provisions of the U.S. Constitution are equally ambiguous or vague, but terribly important nonetheless.

DEFINING TERMS

Back when the authors were young, there were no such things as Handi-Wipes, apart from the jeans we had on. When Handi-Wipes came out, it was pretty self-explanatory what they were, but at some point someone probably explained to us what exactly a Handi-Wipe is. That is, they defined the term "Handi-Wipe."

Handi-Wipes don't have much to do with critical thinking, but definitions do. Any serious attempt to think critically about a claim requires having a clear idea of what the claim actually is. If there are unfamiliar or unusual words in it, you need to know what they mean. Or, if there are familiar words used in an unfamiliar way, you need to know what they mean. For example, take "mouse." When the authors were young, this was what Mickey was. Now "mouse" has a whole different meaning to most people.

There are other reasons for defining terms related to critical thinking. Most important of these is to reduce vagueness or eliminate ambiguity. After all, if you have an ambiguous claim, you don't know *what* the claim is. And if you have a claim that is excessively vague, you may need to tighten it up before you get to work evaluating it. If someone is discussing the right to "bear arms," for example, you might want to define "bear" and define "arms." Does "bearing arms" include taking a surface-to-air missile to the movies?

The Purpose of Definitions

To summarize these two main purposes of definitions:

- Others may use terms we don't understand, and we may use terms they don't understand. One may even use terms one doesn't fully understand oneself. In all three cases, the meaning of the term needs to be spelled out. Definitions used for this purpose often are called **stipulating definitions.** A stipulating definition is called for if an unusual or unfamiliar word is used, or if a brand new word is coined, or if a familiar word is being used in a new way.
- Sometimes you need to reduce vagueness or eliminate ambiguity; you need to make things more precise. Definitions used for this purpose are called **precising definitions.**

Types of Definitions

At this point, we must make a distinction between the *purpose* a definition serves and the *type* of definition it is. A purpose and a type are different things. The purpose of food, for example, is to satisfy nutritional and caloric needs and to please the palette; the types of food include meat, vegetables, Pringles, and so forth.

Whatever purpose is served by defining a term, most definitions are of one or another of the following three types:

1. Definition by example: pointing to, naming, or describing one or more examples of something to which the defined term applies. "By 'scripture,' I mean books like the Bible or the Koran." "By 'temperate climate,' I mean weather in an area like the mid-Atlantic states." "A mouse is this thing here, see?"

2. Definition by synonym: giving another word or phrase that means the same thing. "'Fastidious' means the same as 'fussy.'" "'Prating' is the same as 'chattering.'" "'Pulsatile' means the same as 'throbbing'"; "To be 'lubricous' is to be 'slippery.'"

3. Analytical definition: specifying (a) the type of thing the term applies to and (b) the difference between the things the term applies to and other things of the same type. "A mongoose is a ferret-sized mammal native to India that eats snakes and is related to civets." "A samovar is an urn with a spigot, used especially in Russia to boil water for tea." "A mouse is a piece of computer equipment used to place the position of a cursor."

Unfortunately, the word "kill" could stand a little defining. If taken literally and followed consistently, the First Commandment would prohibit capital punishment, war, and killing in self-defense.

Thou Shalt Not Kill

Those being the classic three definition types, it must be said that what counts in the real world of critical thinking is clarifying a term by whatever method works, including combinations. A real-world definition of "mouse" in an office would probably run something like this: "Well, grandma, a mouse is part of the hardware of a computer. You see that thing there on the desk? And you see that little flashing thing on the screen? You want to be able to move that little flashing thing—like this, see? That's what the mouse does."

In real life, we sometimes need to critically evaluate claims that include big league abstractions like friendship, loyalty, fair play, war, rights, freedom, and so forth. If you had to define "loyalty" or "fair play," you might never get the boat out of the dock. Such concepts have subtle and complex parameters that might take a lifetime to pin down. For practical purposes, what is usually needed for words like these is not a complete definition but a precising definition that focuses on one aspect of the concept and provides sufficient guidance for the purposes at hand. "To me, 'justice' does not include giving a person extra opportunities just because he is a white male."

Rhetorical Definitions

If a liberal friend "defines" a conservative as "a hide-bound, narrow-minded hypocrite who thinks the point to life is to make money and rip off poor people," you have been given an analytic definition. But, you know the definition wasn't offered to clarify the meaning of "conservative." It was just a way of trashing conservatives. Definitions like this, whose purpose is to express or influence attitudes rather than to clarify, are called **rhetorical definitions.** We shall be examining this type of definition in a later chapter, but it is worth mentioning the category here, to see how they work.

Many terms convey a meaning other than their literal meaning. This "meaning" is a term's "connotation" or **emotive meaning** or **rhetorical force** (these being the same)—that is, its tendency to elicit certain feelings or attitudes. "Dog" has the same literal meaning as "pooch," "mutt," and "cur," but these words vary in the attitudes they convey. "Elderly lady" and "old bag" have the same literal meaning, but differ considerably in rhetorical force. When people use a "definition" to express their own attitude about something or to manipulate someone else's attitude, they invariably utilize the rhetorical force of the words in the definition. This means that if a definition utilizes words with strong positive or negative associations, we can be pretty sure it is a rhetorical definition, not a definition intended to clarify meaning. The words "hide-bound," "narrow," "hypocrite," and "rip off" all are rhetorically charged words; their occurrence in the definition above is what makes it rhetorical. Where thinking critically about a claim requires defining key terms, those terms should be defined as much as possible using neutral terminology.

WRITING ARGUMENTATIVE ESSAYS

Recently the Educational Testing Service revamped the infamous Scholastic Aptitude Test (SAT), which many universities use when determining whether to admit an applicant. The most significant change was to have test takers write an argumentative essay. This change in the SAT shows how important educators think the ability to write this type of essay. That's because writing an argumentative essay is doing nothing other than thinking critically—and leaving a paper trail for others to follow. This isn't a book on writing, but writing an argumentative essay is so closely related to thinking critically we would like to take the opportunity to offer our recommendations. We know professors who have retired because they could not bear reading another student essay. As a result, we offer our two-bits worth here, in hopes of continuing to see familiar faces.

As we said earlier, an argumentative essay generally has four components:

1. **A statement of the issue**
2. **A statement of one's position on that issue**
3. **Arguments that support one's position**
4. **Rebuttals of arguments that support contrary positions**

Obviously, the key terms in an argumentative essay should be free from ambiguity, vagueness, and other sources of confusion, and that in turn may require definitions. However, there is another source of obscurity in an essay, and that is faulty organization. Every now and then, we encounter pieces of writing in which words, statements, and arguments are so strangely assembled that the result is unintelligible. If you come across an argumentative essay that suffers from such serious organizational defects that it cannot be fully understood, then your only option is to suspend judgment on the unintelligible aspects. If, however, your own writing suffers from these defects, then you might benefit from a few principles of good organization.

Principles of Organization and Focus

In an argumentative essay, the most natural and common organizational pattern is to follow the four points listed above in that order: State what you are trying to establish and then proceed to establish it by setting out the considerations that support your position—adding explanations, illustrations, or other elaboration as needed—followed by a rebuttal of the arguments that run counter to your position. You don't have to adhere to this order, but if you are one who has trouble organizing your writing or don't know how to present your ideas, you can do much worse than by just following the four steps listed above in that order. Beyond that, here are four more recommendations on how to write an argumentative essay:

1. *Focus.* Make clear at the outset what issue you intend to address and what your position on the issue will be. That said, nothing is quite so boring as starting off with the words, "In this essay, I shall argue that X, Y, and Z," and then going on to itemize everything you are about to say, and at the end concluding with the words, "In this essay, I argued that X, Y, and Z." As a matter of style, you should let the reader know what to expect without using trite phrases and without going on at length. However, you should try to find an engaging way to state your position. For example, instead of "In this essay, I shall discuss whether alcoholic beverages can hurt animals," you could say: "Give your cat wine? You'd better think twice about that one. . . ."
2. *Stick to the issue:* All points you make in an essay should be connected to the issue under discussion and should always either (a) support, illustrate, explain, clarify, elaborate on, or emphasize your position on the issue, or (b) serve as responses to anticipated objections. Rid the essay of irrelevancies and dangling thoughts.

3. *Arrange the components of the essay in a logical sequence.* This is just common sense. Make a point before you clarify it, for example, not the other way around. Place support item B next to item B, not next to item F or G. For example, this makes sense:

   We should go ahead with the picnic; after all, we went to a lot of trouble. Plus, it isn't going to rain.

   This, however, does not:

   We should go ahead with the picnic. Plus, it isn't going to rain; after all, we went to a lot of trouble.

   When supporting your points, bring in examples, clarification, and the like in such a way that a reader knows what in the world you are doing. A reader should be able to discern the relationship between any given sentence and your ultimate objective, and they should be able to move from sentence to sentence and from paragraph to paragraph without getting lost or confused. If a reader cannot outline your essay with ease, you have not properly sequenced your material. Your essay might be fine as a piece of French philosophy, but it would not pass as an argumentative essay.

4. *Be complete.* Accomplish what you set out to accomplish, support your position adequately, and anticipate and respond to possible objections. Keep in mind that many issues are too large to be treated exhaustively in a single essay. The key to being complete is to define the issue sharply enough that you can be complete. Thus, the more limited your topic, the easier it is to be complete in covering it.

   Also, be sure there is closure at every level. Sentences should be complete, paragraphs should be unified as wholes (and usually each should stick to a single point), and the essay should reach a conclusion. Incidentally, reaching a conclusion and summarizing are not the same thing. Short essays do not require summaries.

Good Writing Practices

Understanding the four principles mentioned above is one thing, but actually employing them may be more difficult. Fortunately, there are five practices that a writer can follow to improve the organization of an essay and to help avoid other problems. We offer the following merely as a set of recommendations within the broader scope of thinking critically in writing.

1. At some stage *after* the first draft, outline what you have written. Then, make certain the outline is logical and that every sentence in the essay fits into the outline as it should. Some writers create an informal outline before they begin, but many do not. Our advice: Just identify the issue and your position on it, and start writing by stating them both.

2. Revise your work. Revising is the secret to good writing. Even major league writers revise what they write, and they revise continuously. Unless you are more gifted than the very best professional writers, then revise, revise, revise. Don't think in terms of two or three drafts. Think in terms of *innumerable* drafts.

3. Have someone else read your essay and offer criticisms of it. Revise as required.

We ourselves are also for that too.

I'm for abolishing and doing away with redundancy.

– J. Curtis McKay, of the Wisconsin State Elections Board (reported by Ross and Petras)

Autobiography Skewers Kansas' Sen. Bob Dole

– Headline in the *Boulder* (Colo.) *Sunday Camera* (reported by Larry Engelmann)

On Language

And While We're on the Subject of Writing

Don't forget these rules of good style:

1. Avoid clichés like the plague.
2. Be more or less specific.
3. NEVER generalize.
4. The passive voice is to be ignored.
5. Never ever be redundant.
6. Exaggeration is a billion times worse than understatement.
7. Make sure verbs agrees with their subjects.
8. Why use rhetorical questions?
9. Parenthetical remarks (however relevant) are (usually) unnecessary.
10. Proofread carefully to see if you any words out.
11. And it's usually a bad idea to start a sentence with a conjunction.

This list has been making rounds on the Internet.

4. If you have trouble with grammar or punctuation, reading your essay out loud may help you detect problems your eyes have missed.

5. After you are completely satisfied with the essay, put it aside. Then, come back to it later for still further revisions.

Essay Types to Avoid

Seasoned instructors know the first batch of essays they get from a class will include samples of each of the following types. We recommend avoiding these mistakes:

- **The Windy Preamble.** Writers of this type of essay avoid getting to the issue and instead go on at length with introductory remarks, often about how important the issue is, how it has troubled thinkers for centuries, how opinions on the issue are many and various, and so on, and so on. Anything you write that smacks of "When in the course of human events . . ." should go into the trash can immediately.
- **The Stream-of-Consciousness Ramble.** This type essay results when writers make no attempt to organize their thoughts and simply spew them out in the order they come to mind.
- **The Knee-Jerk Reaction.** In this type essay, writers record their first reaction to an issue without considering the issue in any depth or detail. It always shows.
- **The Glancing Blow.** In this type of essay, writers address an issue obliquely. If they are supposed to evaluate the health benefits of bicycl-

ing, they will bury the topic in an essay on the history of cycling; if they are supposed to address the history of cycling, they will talk about the benefits of riding bicycles throughout history.

- **Let the Reader Do the Work.** Writers of this type essay expect the reader to follow them through non sequiturs, abrupt shifts in direction, and irrelevant sidetracks.

Persuasive Writing

The primary aim of argumentation and an argumentative essay is to support a position on an issue. Good writers, however, write for an audience and hope their audience will find what they write persuasive. If you are writing for an audience of people who think critically, it is helpful to adhere to these principles:

1. Confine your discussion of an opponent's point of view to issues rather than personal considerations.

2. When rebutting an opposing viewpoint, avoid being strident or insulting. Don't call opposing arguments absurd or ridiculous.

3. If an opponent's argument is good, concede that it is good.

4. If space or time is limited, be sure to concentrate on the most important considerations. Don't become obsessive about refuting every last criticism of your position.

5. Present your strongest arguments first.

There is nothing wrong with trying to make a persuasive case for your position. However, in this book, we place more emphasis on making and recognizing good arguments than simply on devising effective techniques of persuasion. Some people can be persuaded by poor arguments and doubtful claims, and an argumentative essay can be effective as a piece of propaganda even when it is a rational and critical failure. One of the most difficult things you are called upon to do as a critical thinker is to construct and evaluate claims and arguments independently of their power to win a following. The remainder of this book—after a section on writing and diversity—is devoted to this task.

Writing in a Diverse Society

In closing, it seems appropriate to mention how important it is to avoid writing in a manner that reinforces questionable assumptions and attitudes about people's gender, ethnic background, religion, sexual orientation, physical ability or disability, or other characteristics. This isn't just a matter of ethics; it is a matter of clarity and good sense. Careless word choices relative to such characteristics not only are imprecise and inaccurate but also may be viewed as biased even if they were not intended to be, and thus they may diminish the writer's credibility. Worse, using sexist or racist language may distort the writer's own perspective and keep him or her from viewing social issues clearly and objectively.

But language isn't entirely *not* a matter of ethics, either. We are a society that aspires to be just, a society that strives not to withhold its benefits from individuals on the basis of their ethnic or racial background, skin color, religion, gender, or disability. As a people, we try to end practices and change or

Another tip on writing.

"Always" and "never" are two words you should always remember never to use.

— Wendell Johnson

On Language

Avoiding Sexist Language

Use the suggestions below to help keep your writing free of sexist language.

Instead of	Use
actress	actor
congressman	congressional representative, member of Congress
fathers (of industry, and so on)	founders, innovators, pioneers, trailblazers
housewife	woman
man (verb)	operate, serve, staff, tend, work
man (noun)	human beings, individuals, people
man and wife	husband and wife
mankind	human beings, humanity, humankind
manmade	artificial, fabricated, manufactured, synthetic, human-made
policeman	police officer
repairman	repairer
spokesman	representative, spokesperson
statesmanlike	diplomatic, tactful
stewardess	flight attendant
waitress	server, waiter
weatherman	weather reporter, weathercaster
craftsman	artisan
deliveryman	courier
foreman	supervisor; lead juror
freshman	first-year student
heroine	hero
layman	layperson

You can also refer to any of numerous reference works on bias-free language. See, for example, Marilyn Schwartz, *Guidelines for Bias-Free Writing* (Bloomington: Indiana University Press, 1995).

Complicated, but neither vague nor ambiguous

What day is the day after three days before the day after tomorrow?

remove institutions that are unjustly discriminatory. Some of these unfair practices and institutions are, unfortunately, embedded in our language.

Some common ways of speaking and writing, for example, assume that "normal" people are all white males. It is still not uncommon, for instance, to mention a person's race, gender, or ethnic background if the person is *not* a white male, and *not* to do so if the person *is.* Of course, it may be relevant to whatever you are writing about to state that this particular individual is a male of Irish descent, or whatever, and, if so, there is absolutely nothing wrong with saying so.

Some language practices are particularly unfair to women. Imagine a conversation among three people, you being one of them. Imagine that the other two talk only to each other. When you speak, they listen politely; but when you are finished, they continue as though you had never spoken. Even though what you say is true and relevant to the discussion, the other two proceed as though you are invisible. Because you are not being taken seriously, you are at a considerable disadvantage. You would have reason to be unhappy.

In an analogous way, women have been far less visible in language than men and have thus been at a disadvantage. Another word for the human race is not "woman," but "man" or "mankind." The generic human has often been referred to as "he." How do you run a project? You *man* it. Who supervises the department or runs the meeting? The chair*man*. Who heads the crew? The fore*man*. Picture a research scientist to yourself. Got the picture? Is it a picture of a *woman*? No? That's because the standard picture, or stereotype, of a research scientist is a picture of a man. Or, read this sentence: "Research scientists often put their work before their personal lives and neglect their husbands." Were you surprised by the last word? Again, the stereotypical picture of a research scientist is a picture of a man.

A careful and precise writer finds little need to converse in the lazy language of stereotypes, especially those that perpetuate prejudice. As long as the idea prevails that the "normal" research scientist is a man, women who are or who wish to become research scientists will tend to be thought of as out of place. So they must carry an *extra* burden, the burden of showing that they are *not* out of place. That's unfair. If you unthinkingly always write "The research scientist . . . he," you are perpetuating an image that places women at a disadvantage. Some research scientists are men, and some are women. If you wish to make a claim about male research scientists, do so. But if you wish to make a claim about research scientists in general, don't write as though they were all males.

The rule to follow in all cases is this: Keep writing free of *irrelevant implied evaluation* of gender, race, ethnic background, religion, or any other human attribute.

Recap

This list summarizes the topics covered in this chapter:

- If you want to think critically, think clearly.
- Claims and arguments suffer from confusion as a result of multiple causes, including, importantly, ambiguity and vagueness.
- Vagueness is a matter of degree; what matters is not being too vague for the purposes at hand.
- A statement is ambiguous when it is subject to more than one interpretation, and which interpretation is the correct one isn't clear.
- Three main types of ambiguity are semantic ambiguity, syntax ambiguity, and grouping ambiguity.
- To reduce vagueness or eliminate ambiguity, or when new or unfamiliar words are brought into play, or familiar words are used in an unusual way, definitions come in handy.

- The most common types of definitions are definition by synonym, definition by example, and analytical definition.
- Some "definitions" are intended not to clarify meaning but to express or influence attitude. These are known as rhetorical definitions.
- Rhetorical definitions accomplish their ends by means of the rhetorical force (emotive meaning) of terms.
- Critical thinking done on paper is known as an argumentative essay, a type of writing worth mastering, perhaps by following our suggestions.

Exercises

Exercise 2-1

The lettered words and phrases that follow each of the following fragments vary in their precision. In each instance, determine which is the most vague and which is the most precise; then rank the remainder in order of vagueness between the two extremes. You will discover when you discuss these exercises in class that they leave some room for disagreement. Further class discussion with input from your instructor will help you and your classmates reach closer agreement about items that prove especially difficult to rank.

Example

Over the past ten years, the median income of wage earners in St. Paul

a. nearly doubled
b. increased substantially
c. increased by 85.5 percent
d. increased by more than 85 percent

Answer

Choice (b) is the most vague because it provides the least information; (c) is the most precise because it provides the most detailed figure. In between, (a) is the second most vague, followed by (d).

1. Eli and Sarah

▲ a. decided to sell their house and move
b. made plans for the future
c. considered moving
d. talked
e. discussed their future
f. discussed selling their house

2. Manuel

a. worked in the yard all afternoon
b. spent the afternoon planting flowers in the yard
c. was outside all afternoon
d. spent the afternoon planting salvia alongside his front sidewalk
e. spent the afternoon in the yard

3. The hurricane that struck South Carolina

a. caused more than $20 million in property damage
b. destroyed dozens of structures
c. was severe and unfortunate
d. produced no fatalities but caused $25 million in property damage

▲ **4.** The recent changes in the tax code

a. will substantially increase taxes paid by those making more than $200,000 per year
b. will increase by 4 percent the tax rate for those making more than $200,000 per year; will leave unchanged the tax rate for people making between $40,000 and $200,000; and will decrease by 2 percent the tax rate for those making less than $40,000
c. will make some important changes in who pays what in taxes
d. are tougher on the rich than the provisions in the previous tax law
e. raise rates for the wealthy and reduce them for those in the lowest brackets

5. Smedley is absent because

a. he's not feeling well
b. he's under the weather
c. he has an upset stomach and a fever
d. he's nauseated and has a fever of more than 103°
e. he has flulike symptoms

Exercise 2-2

Which of each set of claims is vaguer, if either?

Example

a. The trees served to make shade for the patio.
b. He served his country proudly.

Answer

The use of "served" in (b) is more vague than that in (a). We know exactly what the trees did; we don't know what he did.

▲ **1.** a. Rooney served the church his entire life.
b. Rooney's tennis serve is impossible to return.

2. a. The window served its purpose.
b. The window served as an escape hatch.

3. a. Throughout their marriage, Alfredo served her dinner.
b. Throughout their marriage, Alfredo served her well.

▲ **4.** a. Minta turned her ankle.
b. Minta turned to religion.

5. a. These scales will turn on the weight of a hair.
b. This car will turn on a dime.

6. a. Fenner's boss turned vicious.
b. Fenner's boss turned out to be forty-seven.

▲ 7. a. Time to turn the garden.
   b. Time to turn off the sprinkler.

8. a. The wine turned to vinegar.
   b. The wine turned out to be vinegar.

9. a. Harper flew around the world.
   b. Harper departed around 3:00 A.M.

▲ 10. a. Clifton turned out the light.
   b. Clifton turned out the vote.

11. a. The glass is full to the brim.
   b. Mrs. Couch has a rather full figure.

12. a. Kathy gave him a full report.
   b. "Oh, no, thank you! I am full."

13. a. Oswald was dealt a full house.
   b. Oswald is not playing with a full deck.

14. a. The pudding sat heavily on Professor Grantley's stomach.
   b. "Set the table, please."

▲ 15. a. Porker set a good example.
   b. Porker set the world record for the 100-meter dash.

Exercise 2-3

Are the italicized words or phrases in each of the following too vague given the implied context? Explain.

▲ 1. Please cook this steak *longer.* It's too rare.

2. If you get ready for bed quickly, Mommy has a *surprise* for you.

3. This program contains language that some viewers may find offensive. It is recommended for *mature* audiences only.

▲ 4. *Turn down the damned noise!* Some people around here want to sleep!

5. Based on our analysis of your eating habits, we recommend that you *lower* your consumption of saturated fat.

6. NOTICE: Hazard Zone. *Small* children not permitted beyond this sign.

▲ 7. SOFAS CLEANED: $48 & *up.* MUST SEE TO GIVE *EXACT* PRICES.

8. And remember, all our mufflers come with a *lifetime guarantee.*

9. CAUTION: *To avoid* unsafe levels of carbon monoxide, do not set the wick on your kerosene stove *too high.*

▲ 10. Uncooked Frosting: Combine 1 unbeaten egg white, ½ cup corn syrup, ½ teaspoon vanilla, and dash salt. Beat with electric mixer until of fluffy spreading consistency. Frost cake. Serve *within a few hours,* or refrigerate.

Exercise 2-4

Read the following passage, paying particular attention to the italicized words and phrases. Determine whether any of these expressions are too vague in the context in which you find them here.

Term paper assignment: "Your paper *should be* typed, *between eight and twelve pages in length,* and double-spaced. You should *make use of* at least three *sources.* Grading will be based on *organization, use of sources, clarity of expression, quality of reasoning,* and *grammar.*

A *rough draft* is due *before Thanksgiving.* The final version is due *at the end of the semester.*

Exercise 2-5

▲ Read the following passage, paying particular attention to the italicized words and phrases. All of these expressions would be too vague for use in *some* contexts; determine which are and which are not too vague in *this* context.

In view of what can happen in twelve months to the fertilizer you apply at any one time, you can see why just one annual application may not be adequate. Here is a guide to timing the *feeding* of some of the more common types of garden flowers.

Feed begonias and fuchsias *frequently* with label-recommended amounts or less frequently with *no more than half* the recommended amount. Feed roses with *label-recommended amounts* as a *new year's growth begins* and as *each bloom period ends.* Feed azaleas, camellias, rhododendrons, and *similar* plants *immediately after bloom* and again *when the nights begin cooling off.* Following these simple instructions can help your flower garden to be as attractive as it can be.

Exercise 2-6

Critique these comparisons, using the questions about comparisons discussed in the text as guides.

Example

You get much better service on Air Atlantic.

Answer

Better than on what? (One term of the comparison is not clear.)

In what way better? (The claim is much too vague to be of much use.)

▲ **1.** New improved Morning Muffins! Now with 20 percent more real dairy butter!

2. The average concert musician makes less than a plumber.

3. Major league ballplayers are much better than they were thirty years ago.

▲ **4.** What an arid place to live. Why, they had less rain here than in the desert.

5. On the whole, the mood of the country is more conservative than it was in the nineties.

6. Which is better for a person, coffee or tea?

▲ **7.** The average GPA of graduating seniors at Georgia State is 3.25, as compared with 2.75 twenty years ago.

8. Women can tolerate more pain than men.
9. Try Duraglow with new sunscreening polymers. Reduces the harmful effect of sun on your car's finish by up to 50 percent.
▲ 10. What a brilliant season! Attendance was up 25 percent over last year.

Exercise 2-7

Critique these comparisons, using the questions discussed in the text as guides.

▲ 1. You've got to be kidding. Paltrow is much superior to Blanchett as an actor.
2. Blondes have more fun.
3. The average chimp is smarter than the average monkey.
▲ 4. The average grade given by Professor Smith is a C. So is the average grade given by Professor Algers.
5. Crime is on the increase. It's up by 160 percent over last year.
6. Classical musicians, on the average, are far more talented than rock musicians.
▲ 7. Long-distance swimming requires much more endurance than long-distance running.
8. "During the monitoring period, the amount of profanity on the networks increased by 45–47 percent over a comparable period from the preceding year. A clear trend toward hard profanity is evident."
— *Don Wildmon, founder of the National Federation for Decency*
9. "Organizations such as EMILY's List and the Women's Campaign Fund encourage thousands of small contributors to participate, helping to offset the economic power of the special interests. The political system works better when individuals are encouraged to give to campaigns."
— *Adapted from the* Los Angeles Times
▲ 10. Which is more popular, the movie *Gone With the Wind* or Bing Crosby's version of the song "White Christmas"?

Exercise 2-8

In groups, or individually if your instructor prefers, critique these comparisons, using the questions discussed in the text as guides.

▲ 1. If you worry about the stock market, you have reason. The average stock now has a price-to-earnings ratio of around 25:1.
2. Students are much less motivated than they were when I first began teaching at this university.
3. Offhand, I would say the country is considerably more religious than it was twenty years ago.
▲ 4. In addition, for the first time since 1960, a majority of Americans now attend church regularly.
5. You really should switch to a high-fiber diet.

6. Hire Ricardo. He's more knowledgeable than Annette.

▲ 7. Why did I give you a lower grade than your roommate? Her paper contained more insights than yours, that's why.

8. Golf is a considerably more demanding sport than tennis.

9. Yes, our prices are higher than they were last year, but you get more value for your dollar.

▲ 10. So, tell me, which do you like more, fried chicken or Volkswagens?

Exercise 2-9

Find two examples of faulty comparisons, and read them to your class. Your instructor may ask other members of the class to critique them.

Exercise 2-10

Rewrite the following claims to remedy problems of ambiguity. Do *not* assume that common sense by itself solves the problem. If the ambiguity is intentional, note this fact, and do not rewrite.

Example

Former professional football player Jim Brown was accused of assaulting a thirty-three-year-old woman with a female accomplice.

Answer

This claim is syntactically ambiguous because it isn't clear what the phrase "with a female accomplice" modifies—Brown, the woman who was attacked, or, however bizarre it might be, the attack itself (he might have thrown the accomplice at the woman). To make it clear that Brown had the accomplice, the phrase "with a female accomplice" should have come right after the word "Brown" in the original claim.

▲ 1. The Raider tackle threw a block at the Giants linebacker.

2. Please close the door behind you.

3. We heard that he informed you of what he said in his letter.

▲ 4. "How Therapy Can Help Torture Victims"

— *Headline in newspaper*

5. Charles drew his gun.

6. They were both exposed to someone who was ill a week ago.

▲ 7. Susan has Hillary Clinton's nose.

8. I flush the cooling system regularly and just put in new thermostats.

9. "Tuxedos Cut Ridiculously!"

— *An ad for formal wear, quoted by Herb Caen*

▲ 10. "Police Kill 6 Coyotes After Mauling of Girl"

— *Headline in newspaper*

11. "We promise nothing"

— *Aquafina advertisement*

12. Former governor Pat Brown of California, viewing an area struck by a flood, is said to have remarked, "This is the greatest disaster since I was elected governor."

— *Quoted by Lou Cannon in the* Washington Post

▲ 13. "Besides Lyme disease, two other tick-borne diseases, babesiosis and HGE, are infecting Americans in 30 states, according to recent studies. A single tick can infect people with more than one disease."

— Self *magazine*

14. "Don't freeze your can at the game."

— *Commercial for Miller beer*

15. Volunteer help requested: Come prepared to lift heavy equipment with construction helmet and work overalls.

▲ 16. "GE: We bring good things to life."

— *Television commercial*

17. "Tropicana 100% Pure Florida Squeezed Orange Juice. You can't pick a better juice."

— *Magazine advertisement*

18. "It's biodegradable! So remember, Arm and Hammer laundry detergent gets your wash as clean as can be [pause] without polluting our waters."

— *Television commercial*

▲ 19. If you crave the taste of a real German beer, nothing is better than Dunkelbrau.

20. Independent laboratory tests prove that Houndstooth cleanser gets your bathroom cleaner than any other product.

21. We're going to look at lots this afternoon.

▲ 22. Jordan could write more profound essays.

23. "Two million times a day Americans love to eat, Rice-a-Roni—the San Francisco treat."

— *Advertisement*

24. "New York's first commercial human sperm-bank opened Friday with semen samples from 18 men frozen in a stainless steel tank."

— *Strunk and White,* Elements of Style

▲ 25. She was disturbed when she lay down to nap by a noisy cow.

26. "More than half of expectant mothers suffer heartburn. To minimize symptoms, suggests Donald O. Castell, M.D., of the Graduate Hospital in Philadelphia, avoid big, high-fat meals and don't lie down for three hours after eating."

— Self *magazine*

27. "Abraham Lincoln wrote the Gettysburg address while traveling from Washington to Gettysburg on the back of an envelope."

— *Richard Lederer*

▲ 28. "When Queen Elizabeth exposed herself before her troops, they all shouted 'harrah.'"

— *Richard Lederer*

29. "In one of Shakespeare's famous plays, Hamlet relieves himself in a long soliloquy."

— *Richard Lederer*

30. The two suspects fled the area before the officers' arrival in a white Ford Mustang, being driven by a third male.

▲ 31. "AT&T, for the life of your business."

▲ 32. The teacher of this class might have been a member of the opposite sex.

▲ 33. "Woman gets 9 years for killing 11th husband."

— *Headline in newspaper*

34. "Average hospital costs are now an unprecedented $2,063.04 per day in California. Many primary plans don't pay 20% of that amount."

— *AARP Group Health Insurance Program advertisement*

35. "I am a huge Mustang fan."

— *Ford Mustang advertisement*

36. "Visitors are expected to complain at the office between the hours of 9 and 11 A.M. daily."

— *Sign in an Athens hotel*

37. "Order your summers suit. Because is big rush we will execute customers in strict rotation."

— *Sign in a Rhodes tailor shop*

38. "Please do not feed the animals. If you have any suitable food, give it to the guard on duty."

— *Sign at a Budapest zoo*

39. "Our wines leave you with nothing to hope for."

— *From a Swiss menu*

40. "Our Promise—Good for life."

— *Cheerios*

41. Thinking clearly involves hard work.

42. "Cadillac—Break Through"

Exercise 2-11

Determine which of the italicized expressions are ambiguous, which are more likely to refer to the members of the class taken as a group, and which are more likely to refer to the members of the class taken individually.

Example

Narcotics are habit-forming.

Answer

In this claim, *narcotics* refers to individual members of the class because it is specific narcotics that are habit-forming. (One does not ordinarily become addicted to the entire class of narcotics.)

▲ 1. *Swedes* eat millions of quarts of yogurt every day.

2. *College professors* make millions of dollars a year.

3. *Our CB radios* can be heard all across the country.

▲ 4. *Students at Pleasant Valley High School* enroll in hundreds of courses each year.

5. *Cowboys* die with their boots on.

6. The *angles of a triangle* add up to 180 degrees.
▲ 7. *The New York Giants* played mediocre football last year.
8. On our airline, *passengers* have their choice of three different meals.
9. On our airline, *passengers* flew fourteen million miles last month without incident.
▲ 10. *Hundreds of people* have ridden in that taxi.
11. *All our cars* are on sale for two hundred dollars over factory invoice.
▲ 12. *Chicagoans* drink more beer than *New Yorkers.*
13. *Power lawn mowers* produce more pollution than *motorcycles.*
14. *The Baltimore Orioles* may make it to the World Series by the year 2010.
▲ 15. *People* are getting older.

Exercise 2-12

In groups (or individually if your instructor prefers), determine what term in each of the following is being defined and whether the definition is by example or by synonym or an analytical definition. If it is difficult to tell which kind of definition is present, describe the difficulty.

▲ 1. A piano is a stringed instrument in which felt hammers are made to strike the strings by an arrangement of keys and levers.
2. "Decaffeinated" means without caffeine.
3. Steve Martin is my idea of a successful philosophy major.
▲ 4. The red planet is Mars.
5. "UV" refers to ultraviolet light.
6. The Cheyenne perfectly illustrate the sort of Native Americans who were plains Indians.
7. Data, in our case, is raw information collected from survey forms which is then put in tabular form and analyzed.
▲ 8. "Chiaroscuro" is just a fancy word for shading.
9. Bifocals are glasses with two different prescriptions ground into each lens, making it possible to focus at two different distances from the wearer.
10. Red is the color that we perceive when our eyes are struck by light waves of approximately seven angstroms.
▲ 11. A significant other can be taken to be a person's spouse, lover, long-term companion, or just girlfriend or boyfriend.
12. "Assessment" means evaluation.
13. A blackout is "a period of total memory loss, as one induced by an accident or prolonged alcoholic drinking." When your buddies tell you they loved your rendition of the Lambada on Madison's pool table the other night and you don't even remember being at Madison's, that is a blackout.

— *Adapted from the CalPoly, San Luis Obispo,* Mustang Daily

14. A pearl, which is the only animal-produced gem, begins as an irritant inside an oyster. The oyster then secretes a coating of nacre around the

irritating object. The result is a pearl, the size of which is determined by the number of layers with which the oyster coats the object.

15. According to my cousin, who lives in Tulsa, the phrase "bored person" refers to anybody who is between the ages of sixteen and twenty-five and lives in eastern Oklahoma.

Exercise 2-13

The sentences in this Associated Press health report have been scrambled. Rearrange them so that the report makes sense.

1. The men, usually strong with no known vices or ailments, die suddenly, uttering an agonizing groan, writhing and gasping before succumbing to the mysterious affliction.
2. Scores of cases have been reported in the United States during the past decade.
3. In the United States, health authorities call it "Sudden Unexplained Death Syndrome," or "SUDS."
4. Hundreds of similar deaths have been noted worldwide.
5. The phenomenon is known as "lai tai," or "nightmare death," in Thailand.
6. In the Philippines, it is called "bangungut," meaning "to rise and moan in sleep."
7. Health officials are baffled by a syndrome that typically strikes Asian men in their 30s while they sleep.
8. Researchers cannot say what is killing SUDS victims.

Exercise 2-14

▲ The sentences in the following passages have been scrambled. Rearrange them so that the passage makes sense. You'll find an answer in the answer section.

1. Weintraub's findings were based on a computer test of 1,101 doctors twenty-eight to ninety-two years old.
2. She and her colleagues found that the top ten scorers aged seventy-five to ninety-two did as well as the average of men under thirty-five.
3. "The test measures memory, attention, visual perception, calculation, and reasoning," she said.
4. "The studies also provide intriguing clues to how that happens," said Sandra Weintraub, a neuropsychologist at Harvard Medical School in Boston.
5. "The ability of some men to retain mental function might be related to their ability to produce a certain type of brain cell not present at birth," she said.
6. The studies show that some men manage to escape the trend of declining mental ability with age.
7. Many elderly men are at least as mentally able as the average young adult, according to recent studies.

Exercise 2-15

Rewrite each of the following claims in gender-neutral language.

Example

We have insufficient manpower to complete the task.

Answer

We have insufficient personnel to complete the task.

▲ **1.** A student should choose his major with considerable care.

2. When a student chooses his major, he must do so carefully.

3. The true citizen understands his debt to his country.

▲ **4.** If a nurse can find nothing wrong with you in her preliminary examination, she will recommend a physician to you. However, in this city the physician will wish to protect himself by having you sign a waiver.

5. You should expect to be interviewed by a personnel director. You should be cautious when talking to him.

6. The entrant must indicate that he has read the rules, that he understands them, and that he is willing to abide by them. If he has questions, then he should bring them to the attention of an official, and he will answer them.

▲ **7.** A soldier should be prepared to sacrifice his life for his comrades.

8. If anyone wants a refund, he should apply at the main office and have his identification with him.

9. The person who has tried our tea knows that it will neither keep him awake nor make him jittery.

▲ **10.** If any petitioner is over sixty, he (she) should have completed form E-7.

11. Not everyone has the same beliefs. One person may not wish to put himself on the line, whereas another may welcome the chance to make his view known to his friends.

12. God created man in his own image.

▲ **13.** Language is nature's greatest gift to mankind.

14. Of all the animals, the most intelligent is man.

15. The common man prefers peace to war.

▲ **16.** The proof must be acceptable to the rational man.

▲ **17.** The Founding Fathers believed that all men are created equal.

18. Man's pursuit of happiness has led him to prefer leisure to work.

19. When the individual reaches manhood, he is able to make such decisions for himself.

▲ **20.** If an athlete wants to play for the National Football League, he should have a good work ethic.

21. The new city bus service has hired several women drivers.

22. The city is also hiring firemen, policemen, and mailmen; and the city council is planning to elect a new chairman.

23. Harold Vasquez worked for City Hospital as a male nurse.

▲ 24. Most U.S. senators are men.

25. Mr. and Mrs. Macleod joined a club for men and their wives.

26. Mr. Macleod lets his wife work for the city.

▲ 27. Macleod doesn't know it, but Mrs. Macleod is a women's libber.

28. Several coeds have signed up for the seminar.

29. A judge must be sensitive to the atmosphere in his courtroom.

▲ 30. To be a good politician, you have to be a good salesman.

Exercise 2-16

▲ A riddle: A man is walking down the street one day when he suddenly recognizes an old friend whom he has not seen in years walking in his direction with a little girl. They greet each other warmly, and the friend says, "I married since I last saw you, to someone you never met, and this is my daughter, Ellen." The man says to Ellen, "You look just like your mother." How did he know that?

This riddle comes from Janice Moulton's article, "The Myth of the Neutral Man." Discuss why so many people don't get the answer to this riddle straight off.

Writing Exercises

Everyone, no matter how well he or she writes, can improve. And the best way to improve is to practice. Since finding a topic to write about is often the hardest part of a writing assignment, we're supplying three subjects for you to write about. For each—or whichever your instructor might assign—write a one- to two-page essay in which you clearly identify the issue (or issues), state your position on the issue (a hypothetical position if you don't have one), and give at least one good reason in support of your position. Try also to give at least one reason why the opposing position is wrong.

1. The exchange of dirty hypodermic needles for clean ones, or the sale of clean ones, is legal in many states. In such states, the transmission of HIV and hepatitis from dirty needles is down dramatically. But bills [in the California legislature] to legalize clean-needle exchanges have been stymied by the last two governors, who earnestly but incorrectly believed that the availability of clean needles would increase drug abuse. Our state, like every other state that has not yet done it, should immediately approve legislation to make clean needles available.

   — Adapted from an editorial by Marsha N. Cohen, professor of law at Hastings College of Law

2. On February 11, 2003, the Eighth Circuit Court of Appeals ruled that the state of Arkansas could force death-row prisoner Charles Laverne Singleton to take antipsychotic drugs to make him sane enough to execute. Singleton was to be executed for felony capital murder but became insane while in prison. "Medicine is supposed to heal people, not prepare them

for execution. A law that asks doctors to make people well so that the government can kill them is an absurd law," said David Kaczynski, the executive director of New Yorkers Against the Death Penalty.

3. Some politicians make a lot of noise about how Canadians and others pay much less for prescription drugs than Americans do. Those who are constantly pointing to the prices and the practices of other nations when it comes to pharmaceutical drugs ignore the fact that those other nations lag far behind the United States when it comes to creating new medicines. Canada, Germany, and other countries get the benefits of American research but contribute much less than the United States does to the creation of drugs. On the surface, these countries have a good deal, but in reality everyone is worse off, because the development of new medicines is slower than it would be if worldwide prices were high enough to cover research costs.

—Adapted from an editorial by Thomas Sowell, senior fellow at the Hoover Institution

Chapter 3

Credibility

Like the JFK assassination, 9/11 is surrounded by conspiracy theories that would have us believe the incredible. Credibility is what this chapter is about.

In 2004, a fellow we know—his name is Dave, embarrassing him a little—received an e-mail from Citibank. It notified him that there may be a problem with his credit card account and asked him to visit the bank's Web site to straighten things out. A link was provided to the Web site. When he visited the site, he was asked to confirm details of his personal information, including account numbers, Social Security number, and his mother's maiden name. The Web site looked exactly like the Citibank Web site he had visited before, with the bank's logo and other authentic-appearing details. But very shortly after this episode, he discovered that his card had paid for a plasma television, a home theater set, and a couple of expensive car stereos, none of which he had ordered or received.

Dave was a victim of "phishing," a ploy to identify victims for identity theft and credit card fraud. As this edition goes to press, the number of phishing scams continues to rise, with millions of people receiving phony e-mails alleging to be from eBay, PayPal, and other Internet companies as well as an assortment of banks and credit card companies. Some of these phishing expeditions threaten to suspend or close the individual's account if no response is made. Needless to say, a person should give *no credibility* to an e-mail that purports to be from a bank or other company and asks for personal identifying information via e-mail or a Web site.

Real Life

The Nigerian Advance Fee 4-1-9 Fraud: The Internet's Longest-Running Scam

If you have an e-mail account, chances are you've received an offer from someone in Nigeria, probably claiming to be a Nigerian civil servant, who is looking for someone just like you who has a bank account to which several millions of dollars can be sent—money that results from "overinvoicing" or "double invoicing" oil purchases or otherwise needs laundering outside the country. You will receive a generous percentage of the money for your assistance, but you will have to help a bit at the outset by sending some amount of money to facilitate the transactions, or to show *your* good faith!

This scam, sometimes called "4-1-9 Fraud," after the relevant section of Nigeria's criminal code, is now celebrating a quarter century of existence. (It operated by telephone and FAX before the Web was up and running.) Its variations are creative and numerous. Critical thinkers immediately recognize the failure of credibility such offers have, but thousands of people have not, and from a lack of critical thinking skills or from simple greed, hundreds of millions of dollars have been lost to the perpetrators of this fraud.

To read more about this scam, check out these Web sites: <http://www.secretservice.gov/alert419.shtml> and <http://home.rica.net/alphae/419coal/>.

There are two grounds for suspicion in cases where credibility is the issue. The first ground is the claim itself. Dave should have asked himself just how likely it is that Citibank would notify him of a problem with his account by e-mail and would ask him for his personal, identifying information. (Hint: *No* bank will approach its customers for such information by e-mail or telephone.) The second ground for suspicion is the source of the claim. In this case, Dave believed the source was legitimate. But here's the point, one that critical thinkers are well aware of these days: On the Internet, whether by Web site or e-mail, the average person has no idea where the stuff on the computer screen comes from. Computer experts have methods that can sometimes identify the source of an e-mail, but most of us are very easy to mislead.

Dave is no dummy; being fooled by such scams is not a sign of a lack of intelligence. His concern that his account might be suspended caused him to overlook the ominous possibility that the original request might be a fake. In other cases, such as the one described in the "4-1-9 Fraud" box, it may be wishful thinking or a touch of simple greed that causes a person to lower his credibility guard.

THE CLAIM AND ITS SOURCE

As indicated in the phishing story, there are two arenas in which we assess credibility: the first is that of *claims* themselves; the second is the claims' *sources*. If we're told that ducks can communicate by quacking in Morse code, we dismiss the claim immediately. Such claims lack credibility no matter where they come from. (They have no initial plausibility, a notion that will be explained later). But the claim that ducks mate for life is not at all out-

Real Life

Could He Be an Interested Party?

"(W)e do not think it rises to the level of a safety defect." These were the words of Chrysler spokesman Max Gates in December 2004, fighting a threatened recall of 600,000 Dodge Durango and Dakota trucks. Gates acknowledged that "upper ball joint separation" might make the trucks' wheels fall off.

Morning Call (Allentown, Pa.), December 17, 2004; Chuck Shepard, *News of the Weird*, January 30, 2005.

rageous—it's a credible claim. Whether we should believe it depends on its source; if we read it in a bird book or hear it from a bird expert, we are much more likely to believe it than if we hear it from our editor, for example.

There are degrees of credibility; it's not an all-or-nothing kind of thing, whether we're talking about claims or sources. If someone claimed that the president of the United States has been secretly abducted and replaced by an actor whose plastic surgery makes him an exact copy, we'd find this very unlikely. But however unlikely, it's still more credible than the claim that the president is in reality a robot programmed by shadowy figures in his administration or that he is actually an alien from a distant galaxy. Sources (i.e., people) vary in their credibility just as do the claims they offer. If the next-door neighbor you've always liked is arrested for bank robbery, his denials will probably seem credible to you. But he loses credibility if it turns out he owns a silencer and a .45 automatic with the serial numbers removed. Similarly, a knowledgeable friend who tells us about an investment opportunity has a bit more credibility if we learn he has invested his own money in the idea. (At least we could be assured he believed the information himself.) On the other hand, he has less credibility if we learn he will make a substantial commission from our investment in it. A person who stands to gain from our belief in a claim becomes an *interested party,* and interested parties must be viewed with more suspicion than *disinterested parties,* who have no stake in our belief one way or the other.

Although, as we've just indicated, there are all kinds of things we should take into consideration when we judge a person's credibility, unfortunately we often base our judgments on *irrelevant considerations.* Physical characteristics, for instance, are poor indicators of credibility or its lack. Does a person maintain eye contact? Is he perspiring? Does he laugh nervously? These characteristics are widely used in sizing up a person's credibility, despite the fact that they are generally worthless in this regard. A practiced con artist can imitate a confident teller of the truth just as an experienced hacker can cobble up a genuine-appearing Web site. (The word "con," after all, is short for "confidence.")

Other irrelevant features we sometimes use to judge a person's credibility include gender, height, age, ethnicity, accent, and mannerisms. People also make credibility judgments on the basis of the clothes a person wears. A friend told one of us that one's sunglasses "make a statement"; maybe so, but that

Real Life

Whom Do You Trust?

We often make too much of outward appearances when it comes to believing what someone tells us. Would you be more inclined to believe one of the individuals above than the other? As a matter of fact, we can think of at least as many reasons for the man on the left telling us something that isn't true as for the man on the right.

The "blink" method of judging credibility.

I looked the man in the eye. I found him to be very straightforward and trustworthy. We had a very good dialogue. I was able to sense his soul.

— George W. Bush, commenting on his first meeting with Russian president Vladimir Putin

statement doesn't say much about credibility. A person's occupation certainly bears a relationship to his or her knowledge or abilities, but as a guide to moral character or truthfulness, it is less reliable.

Which considerations are relevant to judging someone's credibility? We shall get to these in a moment, but appearance isn't one of them. You may have the idea that you can size up a person just by looking into his or her eyes. This is a mistake. Just by looking at someone we cannot ascertain that person's truthfulness, knowledge, or character. (Although this is generally true, there are exceptions. See the Fib Wizards box on p. 87.)

Of course, we sometimes get in trouble even when we accept credible claims from credible sources. Many of us rely, for example, on credible advice from qualified and honest professionals in preparing our tax returns. But qualified and honest professionals can make honest mistakes, and we can suffer the consequences. In general, however, trouble is much more likely if we accept either doubtful claims from credible sources or credible claims from doubtful sources (not to mention doubtful claims from doubtful sources). If a mechanic says we need a new transmission, the claim itself may not be suspicious—maybe the car we drive has many miles on it; maybe we neglected routine maintenance; maybe it isn't shifting smoothly. But remember that the mechanic is an interested party; if there's any reason to suspect he would exaggerate the problem to get work for himself, we'd get a second opinion about our transmission.

In light of these considerations a general principle emerges, to this effect:

> It is reasonable to be suspicious if a claim either lacks credibility inherently or comes from a source that lacks credibility.

Thus, we need to ask two questions: When does a *claim* lack credibility inherently—in other words, when does its content lack credibility? And when does a *source* lack credibility?

To begin with claims, the general answer is

> A claim lacks inherent credibility to the extent it conflicts with what we have observed or what we think we know—our background information—or with other credible claims.

Just what this answer means will be explained in the section that follows. After that, we'll turn our attention to the second question we asked above, about the credibility of sources.

ASSESSING THE CONTENT OF THE CLAIM

So, some claims stand up on their own; they tend to be acceptable regardless of from whom we hear them. But when they fail on their own, as we've said, it's because they come into conflict with either our own observations or with what we call our "background knowledge." We'll discuss each of these in turn.

Does the Claim Conflict with Our Personal Observations?

Our own observations provide the most reliable source of information about the world. It is therefore only reasonable to be suspicious of any claim that comes into conflict with what we've observed. Imagine that Moore has just come from the home of Mr. Marquis, a mutual friend of his and Parker's, and has seen his new red Mini Cooper automobile. He meets Parker, who tells him, "I heard that Marquis has bought a new Mini Cooper, a bright blue one." Moore does not need critical thinking training to reject Parker's claim about the color of the car, because of the obvious conflict with his earlier observation.

But observations and short-term memory are far from infallible, or professional dancer Douglas Hall would not have been awarded $450,000 in damages by a New York jury in January 2005.* It seems Dr. Vincent Feldman, twenty minutes after having placed a large "X" on the dancer's right knee, where the latter had complained of pain, sliced open the patient's *left* knee, which had been perfectly healthy up until that moment, and effectively ended

---

**New York Post,* January 29, 2005

his dancing career in the process. Although he had just *seen* where he was to operate and had marked the spot, he nonetheless managed to confuse the location and the result may have put a serious wrinkle in his own career as well as that of the dancer.

There are all kinds of factors that influence our observations and our recollections of them, and Dr. Feldman may have been affected by one or more of them: Being tired, distracted, worried about an unrelated matter, or emotionally upset could easily account for such mistakes. There are also physical conditions that often affect our observations: bad lighting, lots of noise, the speed of events, etc. We are also sometimes prey to measuring instruments that are inexact, temperamental, or inaccurate. Parker once blew out a tire at high speed as a result of a faulty tire-pressure gauge (he now carries two gauges).

It's also important to remember that people are not all created equal when it comes to making observations. We hate to say it, dear reader, but there are lots of people who see better, hear better, and remember better than you. Of course, that goes for us as well.

Our beliefs, hopes, fears, and expectations affect our observations. Tell someone that a house is infested with rats, and he is likely to believe he sees evidence of rats. Inform someone who believes in ghosts that a house is haunted, and she may well believe she sees evidence of ghosts. At séances staged by the Society for Psychical Research to test the observational powers of people under séance conditions, some observers insist that they see numerous phenomena that simply do not exist. Teachers who are told that the students in a particular class are brighter than usual are very likely to believe that the work those students produce is better than average, even when it is not.

In Chapter 5, we cover a fallacy (a fallacy is a mistake in reasoning) called *wishful thinking,* which occurs when we allow hopes and desires to influence our judgment and color our beliefs. Most of the people who fall for the 419 Fraud Internet scam (see box, p. 78) are almost surely victims of wishful thinking as much as the perpetrators of the fraud. It is very unlikely that somebody, somewhere, wants to send you millions of dollars just because you have a bank account and that the money they ask for really is just to facilitate the transaction. The most gullible victim, with no stake in the matter, would probably realize this. But the idea of getting one's hands on a great pile of money can blind a person to even the most obvious facts.

Our personal interests and biases affect our perceptions and the judgments we base on them. We overlook many of the mean and selfish actions of the people we like or love—and when we are infatuated with someone, everything that person does seems wonderful. By contrast, people we detest can hardly do anything that we don't perceive as mean and selfish. If we desperately wish for the success of a project, we are apt to see more evidence for that success than is actually present. On the other hand, if we wish for a project to fail, we are apt to exaggerate flaws that we see in it or imagine flaws that are not there at all. If a job, chore, or decision is one that we wish to avoid, we tend to draw worst-case implications from it and thus come up with reasons for not doing it. However, if we are predisposed to want to do the job or make the decision, we are more likely to focus on whatever positive consequences it might have.

Finally, as we hinted above, the reliability of our observations is no better than the reliability of our memories, except in those cases where we have the means at our disposal to record our observations. And memory, as most of

In the Media

The Lake Wobegon Effect (Sometimes practically *none* of us is credible!)

In radio humorist and author Garrison Keillor's fictitious town of Lake Wobegon, "the women are strong, the men are good-looking, and all the children are above average." Thus, the town lends its name to the utterly reliable tendency of people to believe that they are better than average in a host of different ways. A large majority of the population believe that they are more intelligent than average, more fair-minded, less prejudiced, and better automobile drivers.

A huge study was done not long ago by the Higher Education Research Institute at UCLA on high school seniors, with a million respondents to the survey. Seventy percent of them believed they were above average in leadership ability and only 2 percent thought they were below average. In the category of getting along with others, *fully 100 percent* of those seniors believed they were above average. What's more, in this same category 60 percent believed they were in the top 10 percent, and 25 percent believed they were in the top 1 percent!

People are more than willing to believe—it is probably safe to say *anxious* to believe—that they are better in lots of ways than the objective evidence would indicate. This tendency can make us susceptible to all kinds of trouble, from falling victim to con artists to overestimating our abilities in areas that can cost us our fortunes.

Adapted from THOMAS GILOVICH, *How We Know What Isn't So*

us know, can be deceptive. Critical thinkers are always alert to the possibility that what they remember having observed may not be what they did observe.

But even though firsthand observations are not infallible, they are still the best source of information we have. Any report that conflicts with our own direct observations is subject to serious doubt.

Does the Claim Conflict with Our Background Information?

Reports must always be evaluated against our **background information**—that immense body of justified beliefs that consists of facts we learn from our own direct observations and facts we learn from others. Such information is "background" because we may not be able to specify where we learned it, unlike something we know because we witnessed it this morning. Much of our background information is well confirmed by a variety of sources. Reports that conflict with this store of information are usually quite properly dismissed, even if we cannot disprove them through direct observation. We immediately reject the claim "Palm trees grow in abundance near the North Pole," even though we are not in a position to confirm or disprove the statement by direct observation.

Indeed, this is an example of how we usually treat claims when we first encounter them: We begin by assigning them a certain *initial plausibility,* a rough assessment of how credible a claim seems to us. This assessment

Real Life

"Eyewitness" Accounts

Associated Press/Rob Ostermaier

A Fairfax, Virginia, police officer signals cars after a man was shot to death October 11, 2002, at a gas station near Fredericksburg, Va. Police were looking for a white van.

When the series of sniper shootings occurred in the Washington, D.C., area during the fall of 2002, there were eyewitness reports that the perpetrators were two white men traveling in a white enclosed truck. In fact, two men who fit that description were detained and investigated by authorities. But when those doing the shootings were caught, they turned out to be two black men in a blue Chevrolet Caprice.

This is further evidence that we must be careful when deciding how much credence to put in eyewitness testimony, especially when the stakes are high. An appalling number of people have been convicted of heinous crimes by eyewitness accounts, only later to be freed from prison by conclusive DNA evidence.

depends on how consistent the claim is with our background information—how well it "fits" with that information. If it fits very well, we give the claim a high degree of initial plausibility; we lean toward accepting it. If, however, the claim conflicts with our background information, we give it low initial plausibility and lean toward rejecting it unless very strong evidence can be produced on its behalf. The claim "More guitars were sold in the United States last year than saxophones" fits very well with the background information most of us share, and we would hardly require detailed evidence before accepting it. However, the claim "Charlie's eighty-seven-year-old grandmother

Real Life

When Is a Scam Not a Scam?

There's a peculiar Web site–<www.savetoby.com>–on which a fellow has posted photos and stories of a bunny named Toby. He has also promised to have Toby butchered and to have him for dinner if he doesn't receive $50,000 in donations by a certain date. The response seems to have been a combination of donations (partly in response to the fact that the site, notwithstanding its gruesome premise, does possess a certain gallows humor) and of hate mail, to which the author responds in kind.

This is not a scam of the usual sort, and if the site author intends to carry through on his threat, it isn't a scam at all. But it is scare tactics, as described in Chapter 5. (We'll not have time to let you know whether the threat got carried out; the site may still be there when you read this.)

Real Life

The Boeing 757 Conspiracy

Conspiracy theories often involve startling claims that gain credibility through endless recycling on the Internet. As an example, we offer the claim, perhaps widely believed, that it wasn't a passenger airliner that crashed into the Pentagon on 9/11/01 but something else, such as a guided missile. Those who have been proffering this theory present apparently convincing arguments that it was physically impossible for a Boeing 757 to have caused the destruction at the Pentagon, eyewitness reports that buttress this finding, statements by engineers and scientists that add further support, reports of a suspicious absence of the right engine parts, and on and on in great detail. Only examination of the various claims could refute the entire business; but what looks to us like a pretty complete rebuttal is available at <http://www.abovetopsecret.com/pages/911_pentagon_757_plane_evidence.html>.

swam across Lake Michigan in the middle of winter" cannot command much initial plausibility because of the obvious way it conflicts with our background information about eighty-seven-year-old people, about Lake Michigan, about swimming in cold water, and so on. In fact, short of observing the swim ourselves, it isn't clear just what *could* persuade us to accept such a claim. And even *then* we should consider the likelihood that we're being tricked or fooled by an illusion.

Obviously not every oddball claim is as outrageous as the one about Charlie's grandmother. Recently, we read a report about a house being stolen in Lindale, Texas—a brick house. This certainly is implausible—how could anyone steal a home? Yet there is credible documentation that it happened,*

The authority of experience.

There are three types of men in the world. One type learns from books. One type learns from observation. And one type just has to urinate on the electric fence.

– Dr. Laura Schlessinger (reported by Larry Englemann)

*Associated Press report, March 25, 2005.

Real Life

Do Your Ears Stick Straight Out? Do You Have a Short Neck?

According to Bill Cordingley, an expert in psychographicology—that's face-reading, in case you didn't know (and we certainly didn't)—a person's facial features reveal "the whole rainbow collection" of a person's needs and abilities. Mr. Cordingley *(In Your Face: What Facial Features Reveal About People You Know and Love)* doesn't mean merely that you can infer moods from smiles and frowns. No, he means that your basic personality traits are readable from facial structures you were born with.

Do your ears stick out? You have a need to perform in public. The more they stick out, the greater the need. Is your neck short and thin? You are stubborn and dominate conversations. Large lips? You love attention. The length of your chin, location of your eyebrows, size of your ears, length of your neck, are such reliable predictors of personality that an expert can tell by looking at two people whether their relationship will succeed.

Former President Carter, shown here, apparently loves attention. President Bush is an introvert (thin lips) and a control freak (small eyelids—Hey! At least they cover his eyes.)

We leave it to you to determine how credible this is. Cordingley is the former mayor of San Anselmo, California. Does that fact make this more credible?

and even stranger things occasionally turn out to be true. That, of course, means that it can be worthwhile to check out implausible claims if their being true might be of benefit to you.

Unfortunately, there are no neat formulas that can resolve conflicts between what you already believe and new information. Your job as a critical thinker is to trust your background information when considering claims that conflict with that information—that is, claims with low initial plausibility—but at the same time to keep an open mind and realize that further information may cause you to give up a claim you had thought was true. It's a difficult balance, but it's worth getting right. For example, let's say you've been suffering from headaches and have tried all the usual methods of relief: aspirin, antihistamines, whatever your physician has recommended, and so on. Finally, a friend tells you that she had headaches that were very similar to yours, and nothing worked for her either until she had an aromatherapy treatment. Then, just a few minutes into her aromatherapy session, her headaches went away. Now, we (Moore and Parker) are not much inclined to believe that smelling

Real Life

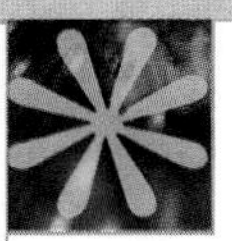

Fib Wizards

After testing 13,000 people for their ability to detect deception, Professor Maureen O'Sullivan of the University of San Francisco identified thirty-one who have an unusual ability to tell when someone is lying to them. These "wizards," as she calls them, are especially sensitive to body language, facial expressions that come and go in less than a second, hesitations in speech, slips of the tongue, and similar clues that a person may not be telling the truth. The wizards are much better than the average person at noticing these clues and inferring the presence of a fib from them.

Professor O'Sullivan, who teaches psychology, hopes that by studying the wizards she and her colleagues can learn more about behaviors that can betray a liar. She presented her findings to the American Medical Association's 23rd Annual Science Reporters Conference.

Maybe a few people can reliably tell when someone is lying. But we'd bet there are many more who *think* they can do this—and if they are poker players they probably have empty bank accounts as a result.

From an Associated Press report.

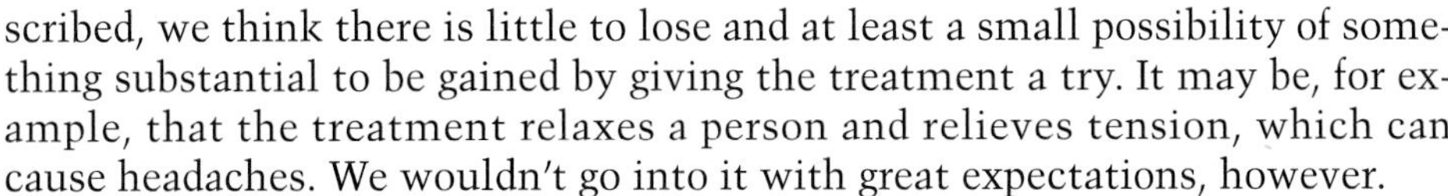

scribed, we think there is little to lose and at least a small possibility of something substantial to be gained by giving the treatment a try. It may be, for example, that the treatment relaxes a person and relieves tension, which can cause headaches. We wouldn't go into it with great expectations, however.

The point is that there is a scale of initial plausibility ranging from plausible to only slightly so. Our aromatherapy example would fall somewhere between the plausible (and in fact true) claim that Parker went to high school with Bill Clinton and the rather implausible claim that Paris Hilton has a Ph.D. in physics.

As mentioned, background information is essential to adequately assess a claim. It is pretty difficult to evaluate a report if you have no background information relative to the topic. This means the broader your background information, the more likely you are to be able to evaluate any given report effectively. You'd have to know a little economics to evaluate assertions about the dangers of a large federal deficit, and knowing how Social Security works can help you know what's misleading about calling it a savings account. Read widely, converse freely, and develop an inquiring attitude; there's no substitute for broad, general knowledge.

CREDIBILITY OF A SOURCE

In order to bolster support for the invasion of Iraq in the spring of 2003, President Bush made quite a number of claims about how dangerous the regime of Saddam Hussein had become. The Bush administration had a number of sources for their information about the situation in Iraq, but one of the most important was Ahmad Chalabi. Had any influential member of the administration followed the advice that's given in this chapter, they would have been very, very suspicious of *any* information they got from such a source. Mr. Chalabi

Real Life

Fool Me Once

In 2003, Annie Robinson, an 86-year-old woman from Sacramento, California, was the victim of a scam that fooled her into withdrawing $7,000 from her savings account and giving it to two con artists. Three months later, two more men showed up at Annie's house flashing badges and pretending to be police detectives investigating the earlier crime. They told her she would have to withdraw more money from her account as part of the investigation. This time her son learned what was going on and called the police. When Annie and the two "detectives" arrived at the bank, they were met by real police with drawn guns.

After Annie testified about the case in court, one of the pretend detectives was sentenced to twenty-three years and the other to seven in the state prison.

Fool me once, shame on you. Fool me twice, shame on me.

came from a wealthy banking family that made millions before Saddam Hussein's Baath party took over in 1968. Known in the West for his opposition to Saddam Hussein, Chalabi had tried to organize an uprising in Iraq in the mid-1990s. Supported by members of Congress, the Pentagon, the CIA, and two successive presidents (Clinton and Bush), Chalabi had reason to believe that the U.S. might support him in becoming Iraq's next ruler. Earlier (see p. 79), we referred to such a person as an interested party—a person who has a substantial stake in the outcome of the issue. And we noted that interested parties are *not* trustworthy and their opinions should always be viewed with skepticism if they cannot be corroborated by *dis*interested parties or other independent evidence. As it turns out, a lot of Mr. Chalabi's claims about Saddam's Iraq were either exaggerated or proven false by independent sources.

Would (and should) the United States have invaded Iraq had the administration not believed what Mr. Chalabi said about the situation there? It's beyond our scope to answer such questions here, but we can say without any doubt that the Bush administration gave much more credibility to this source than it deserved. While it's true that an interested party *can* provide true, accurate, useful information, it is almost always a mistake to simply *assume* that what one learns from such a source is true and accurate. (To automatically reject claims from interested parties is to commit a fallacy that we'll discuss in Chapter 6.) The proper course of action would have been to *suspend or reserve judgment* about the information received from the source.

The doubts we can have about the credibility of a source can be of two kinds: (1) We can doubt whether the source has real knowledge about the issue in question; and (2) we can doubt the person's truthfulness, objectivity, or accuracy. It is doubts of the second type that should have sprung up immediately in the case of Mr. Chalabi's advice regarding Iraq. We are not in a position to judge whether he had access to good information about Iraq, but he had at least spent much time there and can be presumed to have had connections within the country at the time he was advising the American government. But it was clear that doubts of type (2) should have been in order and those alone would have been enough to warrant suspending judgment about the information from this source.

Much of our information comes from people about whom we have no reason to suspect prejudice, bias, or any of the other features that make interested parties such bad sources. However, we might still have the kind of doubts we classified as type (1) above. The state of a person's knowledge depends on a number of factors, especially including their level of expertise and their experience, either direct (through personal observation) or indirect (through study), with the subject at hand.

Just as you generally cannot tell merely by looking at someone whether he or she is speaking truthfully, objectively, and accurately, you can't judge his or her knowledge or expertise by looking at mere surface features. A British-sounding scientist may appear more knowledgeable than a scientist who speaks, say, with a Texas drawl, but a person's accent, height, gender, ethnicity, or clothing doesn't have much to do with a person's knowledge. In the municipal park in our town, it can be difficult to distinguish the people who teach at the university from the people who live in the park, based on physical appearance.

So then how do you judge a person's **expertise?** Education and experience are often the most important factors, followed by accomplishments, reputation, and position, in no particular order. It is not always easy to evaluate the credentials of an expert, and credentials vary considerably from one field to another. Still, there are some useful guidelines worth mentioning.

Education includes but is not strictly limited to formal education—the possession of degrees from established institutions of learning. (Some "doctors" of this and that received their diplomas from mail-order houses that advertise on matchbook covers. The title "doctor" is not automatically a qualification.)

Experience—both the kind and the amount—is an important factor in expertise. Experience is important if it is relevant to the issue at hand, but the mere fact that someone has been on the job for a long time does not automatically make him or her good at it.

Accomplishments are an important indicator of someone's expertise but, once again, only when those accomplishments are directly related to the question at hand. A Nobel Prize winner in physics is not necessarily qualified to speak publicly about toy safety, public school education (even in science), or nuclear proliferation. The last issue may involve physics, it's true, but the political issues are the crucial ones, and they are not taught in physics labs.

A person's reputation is obviously very important as a criterion of his or her expertise. But reputations must be seen in a context; how much importance we should attach to somebody's reputation depends on the people among whom the person has that reputation. You may have a strong reputation as a pool player among the denizens of your local pool hall, but that doesn't necessarily put you in the same league with Minnesota Fats. Among a group of people who know nothing about investments, someone who knows the difference between a 401(k) plan and a Roth IRA may seem like quite an expert. But you certainly wouldn't want to take investment advice from somebody simply on that basis.

Most of us have met people who were recommended as experts in some field but who turned out to know little more about that field than we ourselves knew. (Presumably in such cases those doing the recommending knew even less about the subject, or they would not have been so quickly impressed.) By and large, the kind of reputation that counts most is the one a person has among other experts in his or her field of endeavor.

The positions people hold provide an indication of how well *somebody* thinks of them. The director of an important scientific laboratory, the head of an academic department at Harvard, the author of a work consulted by other experts—in each case the position itself is substantial evidence that the individual's opinion on a relevant subject warrants serious attention.

But expertise can be bought. Recall that the last part of our principle cautions us against sources who may be biased on the subject of whatever claim we may be considering. Sometimes a person's position is an indication of what his or her opinion, expert or not, is likely to be. The opinion of a lawyer retained by the National Rifle Association, offered at a hearing on firearms and urban violence, should be scrutinized much more carefully (or at least viewed with more skepticism) than that of a witness from an independent firm or agency that has no stake in the outcome of the hearings. The former can be assumed to be an interested party, the latter not. It is too easy to lose objectivity where one's interests and concerns are at stake, even if one is *trying* to be objective.

Experts sometimes disagree, especially when the issue is complicated and many different interests are at stake. In these cases, a critical thinker is obliged to suspend judgment about which expert to endorse, unless one expert clearly represents a majority viewpoint among experts in the field or unless one expert can be established as more authoritative or less biased than the others.

Of course, majority opinions sometimes turn out to be incorrect, and even the most authoritative experts occasionally make mistakes. For example, various economics experts predicted good times ahead just before the Great Depression. Jim Denny, the manager of the Grand Ole Opry, fired Elvis Presley after one performance, stating that Presley wasn't going anywhere and ought to go back to driving a truck. A claim you accept because it represents the majority viewpoint or comes from the most authoritative expert may turn out to be thoroughly wrong. Nevertheless, take heart: At the time, you were rationally justified in accepting the majority viewpoint as the most authoritative claim. The reasonable position is the one that agrees with the most authoritative opinion but allows for enough open-mindedness to change if the evidence changes.

Finally, we sometimes make the mistake of thinking that whatever qualifies someone as an expert in one field automatically qualifies that person in other areas. Lots of people thought Ross Perot would have been good at running the country because he was good at running EDS, and maybe he would have. But having a lot of business savvy doesn't automatically translate into having good ideas for public policy. Even if the intelligence and skill required to become an expert in one field could enable someone to become an expert in any field—which is doubtful—having the ability to become an expert is not the same as actually being an expert. Claims put forth by experts about subjects outside their fields are not automatically more acceptable than claims put forth by nonexperts.

CREDIBILITY AND THE NEWS MEDIA

Many Americans still read newspapers. But most get their news about what's happening in the world from people who wear suits and sit behind desks in a television studio. Every time we come to write about the news media in a new

"Those are the headlines, and we'll be back in a moment to blow them out of proportion."

edition of this book, we are a little more skeptical about what we read in the papers and a lot more skeptical about what we see on the television screen. There are several reasons for this. One general reason is that the news media in the United States are controlled by fewer and fewer corporations, the result of many mergers and buyouts over the last few years. Since 2001, when the Federal Communications Commission loosened the regulations regarding ownership of newspapers, radio stations, and television stations, the concentration of media in fewer hands has been accelerating. From thousands of independent media outlets in midtwentieth century, media ownership dropped to only fifty companies by 1983. By late 2004, the majority of all media companies in the United States were controlled by just five companies.* In 2005, there is great pressure from media conglomerates to further loosen the regulations governing ownership. We hope it's clear that the fewer hands that control the media, the easier it is for the news we get to be "managed"—that is, slanted—by either the owners or by government itself.

Government Management of the News

Speaking of government slanting, here's a recent wrinkle: phony news. Jon Stewart has said that his *Daily Show* on Comedy Central is "the most trusted name in fake news," but now he has competition: the governments of the United States and at least one state—California. Our administration in Washington wanted to convince the public that it's doing a great job in improving air travel security. So it made a video that looks just like a typical news report, except it uses a public relations employee from the Transportation Security Administration (the people with the "TSA" badges in airports) who uses a false name and poses as a reporter. The "reporter" then says nothing but

*Frank Blethen, in the *Washington Post,* September 19, 2004

wonderful things about the administration's new efforts at improving security, calling them "one of the most remarkable campaigns in aviation history." Next, these videotapes (or VNRs, for "Video News Releases") are sent to television stations complete with written introductions for the local anchor to read (e.g., "With more on the story, here's Brooke Moore.") Typically, at the end of the phony news piece, the PR person will finish with a news-report ending, e.g., "This is Brooke Moore, reporting." Some of them were even customized to fit major market news programs' anchor person: "Back to you, Richard," the "reporter" would finish.

The Clinton administration indulged in this practice as well, spending almost half as much as the current administration has spent to date. (We have not been able to determine if earlier administrations engaged in such behavior.) But the current Bush administration has pushed the practice to new heights, spending over a quarter billion dollars on it during its first four years. The videos have done cheerleading for the administration's policies in Iraq, on the Medicare drug benefit, on Social Security, and for the No Child Left Behind program, among many others. No criticism or negative aspects of these programs are ever mentioned.

As noted, here where your authors live in California, the state government is up to the same tricks. (See box, "Schwarzenegger's News.")

While we're inspecting government meddling in the news, we should mention a couple of other items that have come to light recently. First, there was Jeff Gannon, who somehow obtained hard-to-get passes to the White House press room despite the fact that he had no journalist credentials and was employed only by "Talon News," a Texas-based Web site run by a Republican activist named Bobby Eberle. Gannon, whose real name turned out to be James Guckert and who ran a sexually-explicit Web site on the side, drew the attention of other journalists by asking "softball" questions of Press Secretary Scott McClellan and President Bush. (One example: "How can you work with these people [Senate Democrats] who are so divorced from reality?") McClellan regularly passed over veteran White House reporters to call on Guckert/Gannon. The practice stopped and Guckert/Gannon was barred from the press room after he was "outed" by Americablog.*

We generally expect to find the independent opinions of the authors in opinion columns and editorials, and in their corresponding versions of television. But three "editorialists" turned up in 2004 and 2005 who had taken money directly or indirectly from the administration to promote its policies and programs. Armstrong Williams received over $200,000 from the Department of Education, and the Department of Health and Human Services gave money to syndicated columnists Maggie Gallagher ($41,500) and Michael McManus ($10,000) for writing in support of one of its proposals. Neither mentioned in their columns that they were being paid.**

Another indication of how news coverage has changed can be seen in the difference between news coverage of the Vietnam War in the 1960s and 70s and the Iraq War that began in March 2003. In the earlier conflict, there were regular photos and film footage of wounded American soldiers and of coffins containing bodies being sent back to the States. Dead and wounded Viet-

---

*More about blogs later.

**Interestingly, McManus' column is entitled "Ethics & Religion."

In the Media

Schwarzenegger's News

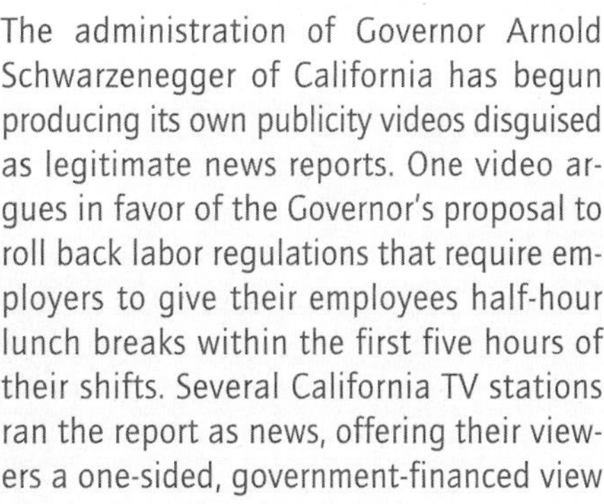

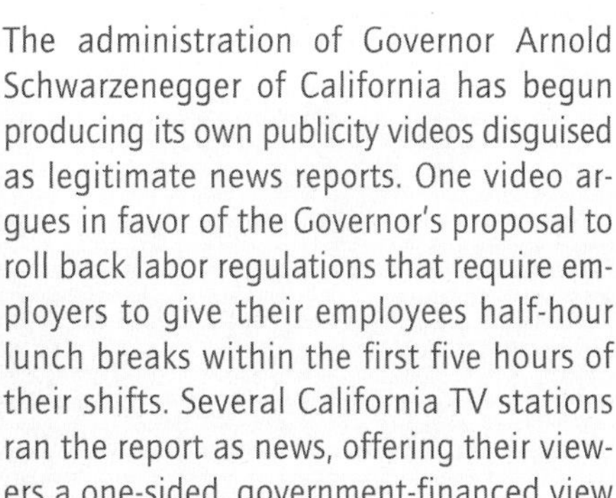

The administration of Governor Arnold Schwarzenegger of California has begun producing its own publicity videos disguised as legitimate news reports. One video argues in favor of the Governor's proposal to roll back labor regulations that require employers to give their employees half-hour lunch breaks within the first five hours of their shifts. Several California TV stations ran the report as news, offering their viewers a one-sided, government-financed view of Schwarzenegger's proposal.

namese civilians were also regularly portrayed on television and in newspapers and newsmagazines. It is widely believed—and we think it's a reasonable suspicion—that this news coverage had a lot to do with the eventual turning of public opinion against that war. In contrast, the photos and videotape that reach the United States from the conflict in Iraq have shown much less of the gruesome results of the violence there. During the invasion itself, reporters were "embedded" in military units so they could see the war more or less from the soldier's perspective. But this may also have had the effect of causing the reporters to identify with the soldiers surrounding them, thus preventing them from developing any other perspective. At least, this is the conclusion of Jim Kuypers, a professor at Dartmouth College, from a study he did on reports from both "embedded" reporters for the *New York Times* and the *Washington Post.* Here is a brief excerpt from *The Dartmouth* (October 22, 2003):

> Troops embedded in Iraq had tendencies to report more optimistic conditions than reporters in the U.S., Kuypers said. Their reports cited the weakness of Iraqi resistance, frequent Iraqi deserters and the welcome U.S. troops received from civilians.
>
> Non-embedded reporters highlighted the ferocity of Iraqi irregulars, the vulnerability of Allied supply lines and civilian mistrust of American intentions.

Although Kuypers's findings make a certain amount of sense to us, we would still be cautious about drawing any conclusions until more study is done on this matter. However, for a more straightforward example of "news management" by the military, see the box on p. 95, "Saving Private Lynch."

Media Foul-Ups

Of course, the government is not responsible for all the errors and distortions we find in the news media. The press is quite capable of fouling things up on its own. Surely the best known recent example occurred in September 2004,

In the Media

Fox News, PBS, and Misperceptions of the Iraq War

Brit Hume (third from left) from Fox News

Gwen Ifill of PBS

A study conducted by the Program on International Policy Attitudes (University of Maryland) and the Center on Policy Attitudes found that people whose primary source of news is Fox News were much more likely to hold three demonstrably false misperceptions about the war in Iraq than those who got their news from any other network, and those whose primary source of news was NPR or PBS were far less likely to hold any of the misperceptions. The differences cannot be explained as a result of differences in the demographic characteristics of each audience, because the variations were also found when comparing the demographic subgroup of each audience. See <http://www.pipa.org/OnlineReports/Iraq/Media_10_02_03_Report.pdf>.

when CBS News told of a memorandum from President Bush's former National Guard Commander that said the president had received preferential treatment while he was in the Air National Guard. While it is clear that CBS believed the memorandum was legitimate, they failed to check out their sources sufficiently and were embarrassed to learn that the person from whom they received it, William Burkett, a former lieutenant colonel in the Guard, lied to them about where he obtained it. The alleged author of the memo died in 1984, and there is now no way to determine its legitimacy. CBS News was forced to retract their story and Dan Rather, the anchor for the CBS Evening News for 24 years, retired a year earlier than planned as a result of the flap over the issue.

> Democrats have to overcome a new reality: conservative bias in the media.
>
> – *Time* magazine, commenting on obstacles the Democratic Party faced in the 2004 election

Bias Within the Media

It is commonly said that the media is biased politically. Conservatives are convinced that it has a liberal bias and liberals are convinced the bias favors conservatives. Since at least the 1970s, the cry of liberal bias has been

In the Media

Saving Private Lynch

Just after midnight on April 2, 2003, a battle group of Marine Rangers and Navy SEALs descended in helicopters on the Iraqi town of Nasiriyah. With shouts of "Go, go, go!" and rifle fire, they charged the hospital where Private Jessica Lynch was being held. The 19-year-old supply clerk was put on a stretcher and carried from the hospital to the choppers and the unit was up and away as quickly as it had come. The entire scene was captured by military cameramen using night-vision cameras.

Eight days earlier when Private Lynch's unit had taken a wrong turn and become separated from its convoy, it was apparently attacked by Iraqi fighters. According to the story in the *Washington Post,* Lynch put up a defiant stand against the attackers and "sustained multiple gunshot wounds" and was stabbed while she "fought fiercely and shot several enemy soldiers . . . firing her weapon until she ran out of ammunition." The paper cited a U.S. military official as saying "she was fighting to the death." This story was picked up by news outlets all over the world.

The ambush and the rescue sound like something out of *Black Hawk Down,* or maybe a Bruce Willis movie. It also came at a time when the military was looking for some good press out of the Iraq invasion. Like many stories that seem too good to be true, this one was too good to be true.

At the hospital in Germany to which Private Lynch was flown, a doctor said her injuries included a head wound, a spinal injury, fractures in both legs and one arm, and an ankle injury. Apparently, none of her injuries were caused by bullets or shrapnel, according to the medical reports. A doctor at the Nasiriyah hospital where she was initially treated said Lynch suffered injuries consistent with an automobile wreck. Reports that she had been ill-treated at the hospital were disputed by Dr. Harith Houssona, who was the doctor on the scene. He reported that she was given the best care they could provide, including one of the two nurses that were available. Reports that she had been raped and slapped around were also denied. Private Lynch herself suffers from amnesia regarding her treatment; it is said she remembers nothing of her treatment from the time of the wreck until she was rescued.

The rescue itself may have been rather seriously overdone. Quoted in the BBC News World Edition, Dr. Anmar Uday, who worked at the hospital, said, "We were surprised. Why do this? There was no military, there were no soldiers in the hospital. It was like a Hollywood film. They cried 'go, go, go,' with guns and blanks without bullets, blanks and the sound of explosions. They made a show for the American attack on the hospital—action movies like Sylvester Stallone or Jackie Chan."

The BBC referred to the "Saving Private Lynch" story as "one of the most stunning pieces of news management ever conceived." We shall probably never know the truth of the details, but it seems clear that the episode was stage-managed to some extent: It isn't likely an accident that the Special Forces just "happened to have" an American flag to drape over Ms. Lynch as she was carried to the helicopter on her stretcher.

the one most frequently heard. By our recollection, the first politician to attack the media directly for a liberal bias was Spiro Agnew, the first vice president under Richard Nixon. But the complaint has been heard from a parade of conservative voices from the Reagan administration, Republicans in Congress (especially Newt Gingrich in the mid-1990s) and in both father and son Bush administrations. For a contemporary update on the view that the media has a liberal bias, you can check the Mediaresearch.org Web site.

The usual basis for the conservative assessment is that, generally speaking, reporters and editors are more liberal than the general population. Indeed, a few polls have indicated that this is the case. A Roper/Freedom Forum Poll in 1992 found that a preponderance of the Capitol press corps voted for Bill Clinton rather than George Bush, for example. On the other hand, the publishers and owners of media outlets tend to be conservative—not surprisingly, since they have an orientation that places a higher value on the bottom line: They are in business to make a profit. A recent book by Eric Alterman* argues that the "liberal media" has always been a myth and that, at least in private, well-known conservatives like Patrick Buchanan and William Kristol are willing to admit it. On the other hand, Bernard Goldberg, formerly of CBS, argues that the liberal bias of the press is a fact.**

Making an assessment on this score is several miles beyond our scope here. But it is important to be aware that a reporter or a columnist or a broadcaster who draws conclusions without sufficient evidence is no more to be believed than some guy from down the street, even if the conclusions happen to correspond nicely to your own bias—indeed, *especially* if they correspond to your own bias!

Bias in the universities? According to CNN news anchor Lou Dobbs, citing a *Washington Post* survey, 72 percent of collegiate faculty across the country say they are liberal; 15 percent say they are conservative. At elite universities, 87 percent say they are liberal, and 3 percent say they are conservative.

What is important to remember is that there are many forces at work in the preparation of news besides a desire to publish or broadcast the whole truth. That said, we remind you that in previous editions we've said that the major network news organizations are generally credible, and, exceptions like those noted above notwithstanding, we think this is still true. ABC, CBS, and NBC do a generally credible job, and the Public Broadcasting System and National Public Radio are generally excellent. Among the printed media, the *New York Times, Washington Post, Los Angeles Times* and other major newspapers are generally credible, even though mistakes are sometimes made here as well. News magazines fall in the same category: usually credible but with occasional flaws.

It would be difficult to boil down our advice regarding accepting claims from the news media, but it would certainly include keeping the following points in mind:

1. Like the rest of us, people in the news media sometimes make mistakes; they sometimes accept claims with insufficient evidence or without confirming the credibility of a source.

2. The media are subject to pressure and sometimes to manipulation from government and other news sources.

3. The media, with few exceptions, is driven in part by the necessity to make a profit, and this can bring pressure from advertisers, owners, and managers.

Finally, we might remember that the news media is to a great extent a reflection of the society at large. If we the public are willing to get by with

* *What Liberal Bias?* Basic Books, New York: 2003.

** *Bias,* Regnery Publishing, Washington, D.C.: 2001.

In the Media

The Public Agony over Terri Schiavo

(*USA Today*, March 25, 2005)

The Terri Schiavo case raised strong emotions. Can you guess which people support which side of the Schiavo case in this photograph? Chris Dillard (left) supports Terri Schiavo's parents; Sean Smith (right) backs her husband.

In Chapter 2, we referred to Terri Schiavo, about whom a controversy raged over whether to withdraw life support. The Florida Supreme Court, the governor of that state (the President's brother), the Congress of the United States, the President, and the U.S. Supreme Court all involved themselves in the controversy. As critical thinkers, we have to remind ourselves that trials in which people's very lives are at stake happen all over the country every day. It is interesting to note how publicity can incite thousands of people to a high emotional state about a case involving a woman whose "persistent vegetative state" had lasted nearly a decade when other cases draw practically no attention at all.

superficial, sensationalist or manipulated news, then we can rest assured that, eventually, that's all the news we'll get.

Talk Radio

On the surface talk radio seems to offer a wealth of information not available in news reports from conventional sources. And many talk radio hosts scour traditional legitimate news sources for information relevant to their political agenda, and to the extent they document the source, which they often do, they provide listeners with many interesting and important facts. But blended in with all this, especially when callers weigh in, is much rumor, hearsay, and gossip from biased and opinionated sources, and it becomes difficult to determine which items, if any, are legitimate. A further defect in talk radio as a source of news is that the information is presented from—and colored by—a political perspective. And finally, the strident tones give us a headache.

The Internet

An important source of information is the Internet—that amalgamation of electronic lines and connections that allows nearly anyone with a computer and a modem to link up with nearly any other similarly equipped person on the planet. Although the Internet offers great benefits, the information it provides must be evaluated with even *more* caution than information from the print media, radio, or television.

There are basically two kinds of information sources on the Internet. The first consists of commercial and institutional sources; the second, of individual and group sites on the World Wide Web. In the first category we include sources like the Lexis-Nexis facility, as well as the online services provided by newsmagazines, large electronic news organizations, and government institutions. The second category includes everything else you'll find on the Web—an amazing assortment of good information, entertainment of widely varying quality, hot tips, advertisements, come-ons, fraudulent offers, outright lies, and even the opportunity to meet the person of your dreams (or your nightmares)! (Rush Limbaugh met his current wife online, and they corresponded via e-mail for a time before meeting in person. On the other hand, in October 1996, a North Carolina man described online to a Pennsylvania woman how, if she would visit him, he would sexually torture her and then kill her. She went, and he did.)

Just as the fact that a claim appears in print or on television doesn't make it true, so it is for claims you run across online. Keep in mind that the information you get from a source is only as good as that source. The Lexis-Nexis information collection is an excellent asset for medium-depth investigation of a topic; it includes information gathered from a wide range of print sources, especially newspapers and magazines, with special collections in areas like the law. But the editorials you turn up there are no more likely to be accurate, fair-minded, or objective than the ones you read in the newspapers—which is where they first appeared anyhow.

One new addition to the Internet mix is that of the blog. In case there are some of you who are unfamiliar with the term, "blog" is short for "WeB LOG." A blog is a journal kept open to the public on a Web site. Blogs began as personal journals but quickly grew to include many different specialties. As we write these words, there are over 42,000 blogs in the United States, and they are increasing at a rate of about 900 per week—and these are just the ones that are being tracked by a blog-tracking blog (Blogwise.com).

We admit it: Blogs can be a fascinating source of information. As noted earlier, the fake reporter in the White House press room was investigated not by the "real" journalists who surrounded him there on a regular basis, but by a blogger on a site called "Americablog.com." This blog and several others (Daily KOS, for example) are listed in at least one newsmagazine as standard reading. On the other hand, you can find blogs that specialize in satire, parody, and outright fabrication. They represent all sides of the political spectrum, including some sides that we wouldn't have thought existed at all. On a blog site, like any other Web site that isn't run by a responsible organization such as those indicated above, you can find *anything that a person wants to*

In the Media

Bloggers on Prime Time

You have to be wary of Internet bloggers as sources of news, because blogger reporting is not subject to source checking. However, if you want to find out what at least some bloggers are talking about, you could turn to CNN's new daily "Inside the Blogs" (a segment on Inside Politics).

put there, including all kinds of bad information. You can take advantage of these sources, but you should always exercise caution, and if you're looking for information, always consult another source, but *not* one that is linked to your first source!

Remember, when you take keyboard and mouse in hand, be on guard. You have about as much reason to believe the claims you find on most sites as you would if they came from any other stranger, except you can't look this one in the eye.

ADVERTISING

> Advertising [is] the science of arresting the human intelligence long enough to get money from it.
>
> — Stephen Leacock

In 2003, the last year for which statistics are available, $246 *billion* dollars were spent on advertising in America. Somebody really wants to sell us something!

If there is anything in modern society that truly puts our sense of what is credible to the test, it's advertising. As we hope you'll agree after reading this section, skepticism is almost always the best policy when considering any kind of advertising or promotion.

Ads are used to sell many products other than toasters, television sets, and toilet tissue. They can encourage us to vote for a candidate, agree with a political proposal, take a tour, give up a bad habit, or join the army. They can also be used to make announcements (for instance, about job openings, lectures, concerts, or the recall of defective automobiles) or to create favorable climates of opinion (for example, toward labor unions or offshore oil drilling).

Advertising firms understand our fears and desires at least as well as we understand them ourselves, and they have at their disposal the expertise to exploit them.* Such firms employ trained psychologists and some of the world's most creative artists and use the most sophisticated and well-researched theories about the motivation of human behavior. Maybe most important, they can afford to spend whatever is necessary to get each detail of an advertisement exactly right. (On a per-minute basis, television ads are the most expensively produced pieces that appear on your tube.) A good ad is a work of art, a masterful blend of word and image often composed in accordance with the exacting standards of artistic and scientific genius (some ads, of course, are just plain silly). Can untrained laypeople even hope to evaluate such psychological and artistic masterpieces intelligently?

People watching a sexual program are thinking about sex, not soda pop. Violence and sex elicit very strong emotions and can interfere with memory for other things.

— Brad Bushman of Iowa State University, whose research indicated that people tend to forget the names of sponsors of violent or sexual TV shows (reported by Ellen Goodman)

Fortunately, it is not necessary to understand the deep psychology of an advertisement to evaluate it in the way that's most important to us. When confronted with an ad, we should ask simply: Does this ad give us a good reason to buy this product? And the answer, in general terms, can be simply put: Because the only good reason to buy anything in the first place is to improve our lives, the ad justifies a purchase only if it establishes that we'd be better off with the product than without it (or that we'd be better off with the product than with the money we would trade for it).

However, do we always know when we'll be better off with a product than without it? Do we really want, or need, a bagel splitter or an exercise bike? Do people even recognize "better taste" in a cigarette? Advertisers spend vast sums creating within us new desires and fears—and hence a need to improve our lives by satisfying those desires or eliminating those fears through the purchase of advertised products. They are often successful, and we find ourselves needing something we might not have known existed before. That others can instill in us through word and image, a desire for something we did not previously desire may be a lamentable fact, but it *is* clearly a fact. Still, *we* decide what would make us better off, and *we* decide to part with our money. So it is only with reference to what in *our* view would make life better for us that we properly evaluate advertisements.

There are basically two kinds of ads: those that offer reasons and those that do not. Those that offer reasons for buying the advertised product always promise that certain hopes will be satisfied, certain needs met, or certain fears eliminated. (You'll be more accepted, have a better image, be a better parent, and so on.)

This ambiguous ad slogan creates an illusion that many doctors, or doctors in general, recommend the product. However, a recommendation from a single doctor is all it takes to make the statement true.

"Doctor recommended."

Those ads that do not rely on reasons fall mainly into three categories: (1) those that bring out *feelings* in us (e.g., through humor, pretty images, scary images, beautiful music, heartwarming scenes); (2) those that depict the product being used or endorsed by *people* we admire or think of ourselves as being like (sometimes these people are depicted by actors, sometimes not); and (3) those that depict the product being used in *situations* in which we would like to find ourselves. Of course, some ads go all out and incorporate elements

*For an excellent treatment of this and related subjects, we recommend *Age of Propaganda: The Everyday Use and Abuse of Persuasion*, rev. ed., by Anthony R. Pratkanis and Elliot Aronson (New York: W. H. Freeman and Co., 1998).

■ Do celebrity faces sell products:? What product would this face help to sell?

from all three categories—and for good measure also state a reason or two why we should buy the advertised product.

Buying a product (which includes joining a group, deciding how to vote, and so forth) on the basis of reasonless ads is, with one minor exception that we'll explain shortly, never justified. Such ads tell you only that the product exists and what it looks like (and sometimes where it is available and how much it costs); if an ad tells you much more than this, then it begins to qualify as an ad that gives reasons for buying the product. Reasonless ads do tell us what the advertisers think of our values and sense of humor (not always a pleasant thing to notice, given that they have us pegged so well), but this information is irrelevant to the question of whether we should buy the product.

Ads that submit reasons for buying the product, or "promise ads," as they have been called, usually tell us more than that a certain product exists—but not much more. The promise, with rare exception, comes with no guarantees and is usually extremely vague (Gilbey's gin promises "more gin taste," Kleenex is "softer").

Such ads are a source of information about what the *sellers* of the product are willing to claim about what the product will do, how well it will do it, how it works, what it contains, how well it compares with similar products, and how much more wonderful your life will be once you've got one. However, to make an informed decision on a purchase, you almost always need to know more than the seller is willing to claim, particularly because no sellers

Real Life

When Is an Ad Not an Ad? When It's a Product Placement!

Coca Cola cups prominently displayed on the television show "American Idol."

When Katherine Hepburn threw all of Humphrey Bogart's Gordon's Gin overboard in the *African Queen*, it was an early example of product placement, since the makers of Gordon's paid to have their product tossed in the drink, as it were. Readers of a certain age may remember the 1960s television show *Route 66*, which starred not just Martin Milner and George Maharis, but also a new Chevrolet Corvette and probably contributed to more than a few Corvette sales. Reese's Pieces were centrally placed in the movie *ET*, and the sales of Red Stripe beer jumped 50 percent after it appeared prominently in the movie *The Firm*.

These days, the paid placement of products in both movies and television (and possibly even in novels) is a serious alternative to traditional commercials and it has the advantage of overcoming the Tivo effect: recording programs and watching them while skipping over the commercials.

Meaningless but catchy slogan for GMC trucks. (We are professional grade, too.)

We are professional grade.

will tell you what's wrong with their products or what's right with those of their competitors. Remember that they are perfect examples of *interested parties.*

Further, the claims of advertisers are notorious for not only being vague but also for being ambiguous, misleading, exaggerated, and sometimes just plain false. Even if a product existed that was so good that an honest, unexaggerated, and fair description of it would justify our buying it without considering competing items (or other reports on the same item), and even if an

On Language

Celebrity Endorsements We Can Live With

One of America's greatest humorists was once asked to write an endorsement for a certain brand of piano. Because he would not speak on behalf of a product he had not tried, he wrote the following:

> Dear Sirs,
>
> I guess your pianos are the best I have ever leaned against.
>
> Yours truly,
>
> Will Rogers

Opera singer Giovanni Martinelli, when questioned by a reporter about cigarette smoking, replied, "Tobacco, cigarettes, bah! I would not think of it!" The reporter reminded Martinelli that he had appeared in an advertisement for a particular brand of cigarette and had said that those cigarettes did not irritate his throat. "Yes, yes, of course I gave that endorsement," Martinelli said impatiently. "How could they irritate my throat? I have never smoked."

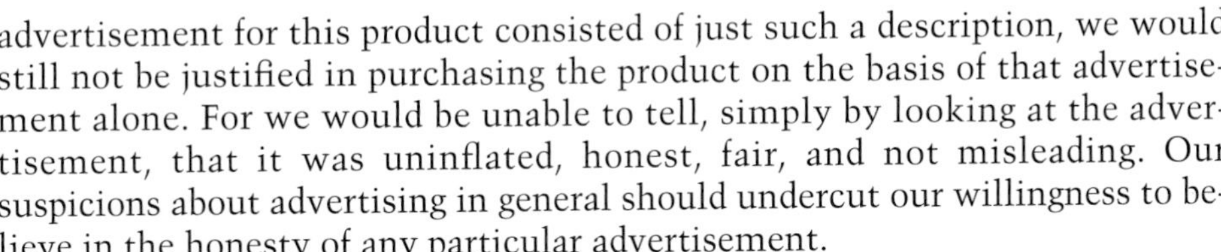

advertisement for this product consisted of just such a description, we would still not be justified in purchasing the product on the basis of that advertisement alone. For we would be unable to tell, simply by looking at the advertisement, that it was uninflated, honest, fair, and not misleading. Our suspicions about advertising in general should undercut our willingness to believe in the honesty of any particular advertisement.

Thus, even advertisements that present reasons for buying an item do not by themselves justify our purchase of the item. This is worth repeating, in stronger language: An advertisement *never justifies* purchasing something. Advertisements are written to *sell something*; they are not designed to be informative except insofar as it will help with the sales job. Sometimes, of course, an advertisement can provide you with information that can clinch your decision to make a purchase. Sometimes the mere existence, availability, or affordability of a product—all information that an ad can convey—is all you need to make a decision to buy. But if the purchase is justifiable, you must have some reasons apart from those offered in the ad for making it. If, for some reason, you already know that you want or need and can afford a car with an electric motor, then an ad that informs you that a firm has begun marketing such a thing would supply you with the information you need to buy one. If you can already justify purchasing a particular brand of microwave oven but cannot find one anywhere in town, then an advertisement informing you that the local department store stocks them can clinch your decision to make the purchase.

For people on whom good fortune has smiled, those who don't care what kind of whatsit they buy, or those to whom mistaken purchases simply don't matter, all that is important is knowing that a product is available. Most of us, however, need more information than ads provide to make reasoned purchasing decisions. Of course, we all occasionally make purchases solely on the basis of advertisements, and sometimes we don't come to regret them. In such cases, though, the happy result is due as much to good luck as to the ad.

Recap

This list summarizes the topics covered in this chapter.

- Claims lack credibility to the extent they conflict with our observations or experience or our background information, or come from sources that lack credibility.
- The less initial plausibility a claim has, the more extraordinary it seems, and the less it fits with our background information, the more suspicious we should be.
- Doubts about sources generally fall into two categories, doubts about the source's knowledge or expertise and doubts about the source's veracity, objectivity, and accuracy.
- We can form reasonably reliable judgments about a person's knowledge by considering his or her education, experience, accomplishments, reputation, and position.
- Claims made by experts, those with special knowledge in a subject, are the most reliable, but the claims must pertain to the area of expertise and not conflict with claims made by other experts in the same area.
- Major metropolitan newspapers, national newsmagazines, and network news shows are generally credible sources of news, but it is necessary to keep an open mind about what we learn from them.
- Government influence on (and even manipulation of) the news continues to increase.
- Skepticism is even more appropriate when we obtain information from unknown Internet sources or talk radio.
- Advertising assaults us at every turn, attempting to sell us goods, services, beliefs, and attitudes. Because substantial talent and resources are employed in this effort, we need to ask ourselves constantly whether the products in question will really make the differences in our lives that their advertising claims or hints they will make. Advertisers are more concerned with selling you something than with improving your life. They are concerned with improving their own lives.

Exercises

Exercise 3-1

1. The text points out that physical conditions around us can affect our observations. List at least four such conditions.
2. Our own mental state can affect our observations as well. Describe at least three of the ways this can happen, as mentioned in the text.
3. According to the text, there are two ways credibility should enter into our evaluation of a claim. What are they?
4. A claim lacks inherent credibility, according to the text, when it conflicts with what?
5. Our most reliable source of information about the world is ________.
6. The reliability of our observations is not better than the reliability of ________.

Exercise 3-2

List as many irrelevant factors as you can think of that people often mistake for signs of a person's truthfulness (for example, the firmness of a handshake).

Exercise 3-3

List as many irrelevant factors as you can think of that people often mistake for signs of expertise on the part of an individual (for example, appearing self-confident).

Exercise 3-4

Expertise doesn't transfer automatically from one field to another: Being an expert in one does not automatically qualify one as an expert (or even as competent) in other areas. Is it the same with dishonesty? Many people think dishonesty does transfer, that being dishonest in one area automatically discredits that person in all areas. For example, when Bill Clinton lied about having sexual encounters with his intern, some said he couldn't be trusted about anything.

If someone is known to have been dishonest about one thing, should we automatically be suspicious of his honesty regarding other things? Discuss.

Exercise 3-5

▲ In your judgment, are any of these claims less credible than others? Discuss your opinions with others in the class to see if any interesting differences in background information emerge.

1. They've taught crows how to play poker.
2. The center of Earth consists of water.
3. Ray Charles was just faking his blindness.
4. The car manufacturers already can build cars that get over 100 miles per gallon; they just won't do it because they're in cahoots with the oil industry.
5. If you force yourself to go for five days and nights without any sleep, you'll be able to get by on less than five hours of sleep a night for the rest of your life.
6. It is possible to read other people's minds through mental telepathy.
7. A diet of mushrooms and pecans supplies all necessary nutrients and will help you lose weight. Scientists don't understand why.
8. Somewhere on the planet is a person who looks exactly like you.
9. The combined wealth of the world's 225 richest people equals the total annual income of the poorest 2.5 billion people, which is nearly half the world's total population.
10. George W. Bush arranged to have the World Trade Center attacked so he could invade Afghanistan. He wants to build an oil pipeline across Afghanistan.

11. Daddy longlegs are the world's most poisonous spider, but their mouths are too small to bite.
12. Static electricity from your body can cause your gas tank to explode if you slide across your seat while fueling and then touch the gas nozzle.
13. Japanese scientists have created a device that measures the tone of a dog's bark to determine what the dog's mood is.

Exercise 3-6

See who in the class can find the strangest news report from a credible source. Send it to us at McGraw-Hill. If your entry is selected for printing in our next edition, Parker will send you $100. (Who do you suppose wrote this exercise?)

Exercise 3-7

In groups, decide which is the best answer to each question. Compare your answers with those of other groups and your instructor.

1. "SPACE ALIEN GRAVEYARD FOUND! Scientists who found an extra-terrestrial cemetery in central Africa say the graveyard is at least 500 years old! 'There must be 200 bodies buried there and not a single one of them is human,' Dr. Hugo Schild, the Swiss anthropologist, told reporters." What is the appropriate reaction to this report in the *Weekly World News*?
   a. It's probably true.
   b. It almost certainly is true.
   c. We really need more information to form any judgment at all.
   d. None of these.
2. Is Elvis really dead? Howie thinks not. Reason: He knows three people who claim to have seen Elvis recently. They are certain that it is not a mere Elvis look-alike they have seen. Howie reasons that, since he has absolutely no reason to think the three would lie to him, they must be telling the truth. Elvis must really be alive, he concludes!

   Is Howie's reasoning sound? Explain.
3. VOICE ON TELEPHONE: Mr. Roberts, this is SBC calling. Have you recently placed several long-distance calls to Lisbon, Portugal?
   MR. ROBERTS: Why, no . . .
   VOICE: This is what we expected. Mr. Roberts, I'm sorry to report that apparently someone has been using your calling card number. However, we are prepared to give you a new number, effective immediately, at no charge to you.
   MR. ROBERTS: Well, fine, I guess . . .
   VOICE: Again let me emphasize that there will be no charge for this service. Now, for authorization, just to make sure that we are calling Mr. Roberts, Mr. Roberts, please state the last four digits of your calling card number, your PIN number, please.

   Question: What should Mr. Roberts, as a critical thinker, do?
4. On Thanksgiving Day 1990, an image said by some to resemble the Virgin Mary was observed in a stained glass window of St. Dominic's Church in

Colfax, California. A physicist asked to investigate said the image was caused by sunlight shining through the window and reflecting from a newly installed hanging light fixture. Others said the image was a miracle. Whose explanation is more likely true?

a. The physicist's
b. The others'
c. More information is needed before we can decide which explanation is more likely.

5. It is late at night around the campfire when the campers hear the awful grunting noises in the woods around. They run for their lives! Two campers, after returning the next day, tell others they found huge footprints around the campfire. They are convinced they were attacked by Bigfoot. Which explanation is more likely true?

   a. The campers heard Bigfoot.
   b. The campers heard some animal and are pushing the Bigfoot explanation to avoid being thought of as chickens, or are just making the story up for unknown reasons.
   c. Given this information, we can't tell which explanation is more likely.

6. Megan's aunt says she saw a flying saucer. "I don't tell people about this," Auntie says, "because they'll think I'm making it up. But this really happened. I saw this strange light, and this, well, it wasn't a saucer, exactly, but it was round and big, and it came down and hovered just over my back fence, and my two dogs began whimpering. And then it just, whoosh! It just vanished."

   Megan knows her aunt, and Megan knows she doesn't make up stories.

   a. She should believe her aunt saw a flying saucer.
   b. She should believe her aunt was making the story up.
   c. She should believe that her aunt may well have had some unusual experience, but it was probably not a visitation by extraterrestrial beings.

7. According to Dr. Edith Fiore, author of *The Unquiet Dead,* many of your personal problems are really the miseries of a dead soul who has possessed you sometime during your life. "Many people are possessed by earthbound spirits. These are people who have lived and died, but did not go into the afterworld at death. Instead they stayed on Earth and remained just like they were before death, with the fears, pains, weaknesses and other problems that they had when they were alive." She estimates that about 80 percent of her more than 1,000 patients are suffering from the problems brought on by being possessed by spirits of the dead. To tell if you are among the possessed, she advises that you look for such telltale symptoms as low energy levels, character shifts or mood swings, memory problems, poor concentration, weight gain with no obvious cause, and bouts of depression (especially after hospitalization). Which of these reactions is best?

   a. Wow! I bet I'm possessed!
   b. Well, if a doctor says it's so, it must be so.
   c. If these are signs of being possessed, how come she thinks that only 80 percent of her patients are?
   d. Too bad there isn't more information available, so we could form a reasonable judgment.

8. **EOC—ENGINE OVERHAUL IN A CAN**

Developed by skilled automotive scientists after years of research and laboratory and road tests! Simply pour one can of EOC into the oil in your crankcase. EOC contains long-chain molecules and special thermo-active metallic alloys that bond with worn engine parts. NO tools needed! NO need to disassemble engine.

Question: Reading this ad, what should you believe?

9. ANCHORAGE, Alaska (AP)—Roped to her twin sons for safety, Joni Phelps inched her way to the top of Mount McKinley. The National Park Service says Phelps, 54, apparently is the first blind woman to scale the 20,300-foot peak.

This report is

a. Probably true
b. Probably false
c. Too sketchy; more information is needed before we can judge

Exercise 3-8

Within each group of observers, are some especially credible or especially not so?

▲ 1. Judging the relative performances of the fighters in a heavyweight boxing match.

a. the father of one of the fighters
b. a sportswriter for *Sports Illustrated* magazine
c. the coach of the American Olympic boxing team
d. the referee of the fight
e. a professor of physical education

2. You (or your family or your class) are trying to decide whether you should buy an Apple Macintosh computer or a Windows model. You might consult

a. a friend who owns either a Macintosh or a Windows machine
b. a friend who now owns one of the machines but used to own the other
c. a dealer for either Macintosh or Windows computers
d. a computer column in a big-city newspaper
e. reviews in computer magazines

▲ 3. The Surgical Practices Committee of Grantville Hospital has documented an unusually high number of problems in connection with tonsillectomies performed by a Dr. Choker. The committee is reviewing her surgical practices. Those present during a tonsillectomy are

a. Dr. Choker
b. the surgical proctor from the Surgical Practices Committee
c. an anesthesiologist
d. a nurse
e. a technician

4. The mechanical condition of the used car you are thinking of buying.

a. the used-car salesperson
b. the former owner (who we assume is different from the salesperson)

c. the former owner's mechanic
d. you
e. a mechanic from an independent garage

5. A demonstration of psychokinesis (the ability to move objects at a distance by nonphysical means).

a. a newspaper reporter
b. a psychologist
c. a police detective
d. another psychic
e. a physicist
f. a customs agent
g. a magician

Exercise 3-9

For each of the items below, discuss the credibility and authority of each source relative to the issue in question. Whom would you trust as most reliable on the subject?

▲ 1. Issue: Is Crixivan an effective HIV/AIDS medication?

a. *Consumer Reports*
b. Stadtlander Drug Company (the company that makes Crixivan)
c. the owner of your local health food store
d. the U.S. Food and Drug Administration
e. your local pharmacist

▲ 2. Issue: Should possession of handguns be outlawed?

a. a police chief
b. a representative of the National Rifle Association
c. a U.S. senator
d. the father of a murder victim

▲ 3. Issue: What was the original intent of the Second Amendment to the U.S. Constitution, and does it include permission for every citizen to possess handguns?

a. a representative of the National Rifle Association
b. a justice of the U.S. Supreme Court
c. a Constitutional historian
d. a U.S. senator
e. the President of the United States

4. Issue: Is decreasing your intake of dietary fat and cholesterol likely to reduce the level of cholesterol in your blood?

a. *Time* magazine
b. *Runner's World* magazine
c. your physician
d. the National Institutes of Health
e. the *New England Journal of Medicine*

5. Issue: When does a human life begin?

a. a lawyer
b. a physician

c. a philosopher
d. a minister
e. you

Exercise 3-10

Each of these items consists of a brief biography of a real or imagined person followed by a list of topics. On the basis of the information in the biography, discuss the credibility and authority of the person described on each of the topics listed.

▲ 1. Alan Jensen teaches sociology at the University of Illinois and is the director of its Population Studies Center. He is a graduate of Harvard College, where he received a B.A. in 1975, and of Harvard University, which granted him a Ph.D. in economics in 1978. He taught courses in demography as an assistant professor at UCLA until 1982; then he moved to the sociology department of the University of Nebraska, where he was associate professor and then professor. From 1987 through 1989 he served as acting chief of the Population Trends and Structure Section of the United Nations Population Division. He joined the faculty at the University of Illinois in 1989. He has written books on patterns of world urbanization, the effects of cigarette smoking on international mortality, and demographic trends in India. He is president of the Population Association of America.

Topics

a. The effects of acid rain on humans
b. The possible beneficial effects of requiring sociology courses for all students at the University of Illinois
c. The possible effects of nuclear war on global climate patterns
d. The incidence of poverty among various ethnic groups in the United States
e. The effects of the melting of glaciers on global sea levels
f. The change in death rate for various age groups in all Third World countries between 1970 and 1990
g. The feasibility of a laser-based nuclear defense system
h. Voter participation among religious sects in India
i. Whether the winters are worse in Illinois than in Nebraska

2. Tom Pierce graduated cum laude from Cornell University with a B.S. in biology in 1973. After two years in the Peace Corps, during which he worked on public health projects in Venezuela, he joined Jeffrey Ridenour, a mechanical engineer, and the pair developed a water pump and purification system that is now used in many parts of the world for both regular water supplies and emergency use in disaster-struck areas. Pierce and Ridenour formed a company to manufacture the water systems, and it prospered as they developed smaller versions of the system for private use on boats and motor homes. In 1981, Pierce bought out his partner and expanded research and development in hydraulic systems for forcing oil out of old wells. Under contract with the federal government and several oil firms, Pierce's company was a principal designer and contractor for

the Alaskan oil pipeline. He is now a consultant in numerous developing countries as well as chief executive officer and chairman of the board of his own company, and he sits on the boards of directors of several other companies.

Topics

a. The image of the United States in Latin America
b. The long-range effects of the Cuban revolution on South America
c. Fixing a leaky faucet
d. Technology in Third World countries
e. The ecological effects of the Alaskan pipeline
f. Negotiating a contract with the federal government
g. Careers in biology

Exercise 3-11

According to certain pollsters, a number of people voted for George W. Bush not because they especially liked his policies and programs or his idea of where the country should be going, but because they liked him personally. Discuss what features Mr. Bush may have that may have caused these people to vote for him. Which of these features might be relevant to how good a job he would do as president?

Exercise 3-12

From what you know about the nature of each of the following claims and its source, and given your general knowledge, assess whether the claim is one you should accept, reject, or suspend judgment on due to ambiguity, insufficient documentation, vagueness, or subjectivity (e.g., "Tom Cruise is cute"). Compare your judgment with that of your instructor.

▲ 1. "Campbell Soup is hot—and some are getting burned. Just one day after the behemoth of broth reported record profits, Campbell said it would lay off 650 U.S. workers, including 175—or 11% of the work force—at its headquarters in Camden, New Jersey."

— Time

2. [The claim to evaluate is the first one in this passage.] Jackie Haskew taught paganism and devil worship in her fourth-grade classroom in Grand Saline, Texas, at least until she was pressured into resigning by parents of her students. (According to syndicated columnist Nat Hentoff, "At the town meeting on her case, a parent said firmly that she did not want her daughter to read anything that dealt with 'death, abuse, divorce, religion, or any other issue.'")

3. "By 1893 there were only between 300 and 1,000 buffaloes remaining in the entire country. A few years later, President Theodore Roosevelt persuaded Congress to establish a number of wildlife preserves in which the remaining buffaloes could live without danger. The numbers have increased since, nearly doubling over the past 10 years to 130,000."

— *Clifford May, in the* New York Times Magazine

4. Lee Harvey Oswald, acting alone, was responsible for the death of President John F. Kennedy.

   — *Conclusion of the Warren Commission on the Assassination of President Kennedy*

5. "[N]ewly released documents, including the transcripts of telephone conversations recorded by President Lyndon B. Johnson in November and December 1963, provide for the first time a detailed . . . look at why and how the seven-member Warren [Commission] was put together. Those documents, along with a review of previously released material . . . describe a process designed more to control information than to elicit and expose it."

   — *"The Truth Was Secondary,"* Washington Post National Weekly Edition

6. "Short-sighted developers are determined to transform Choco [a large region of northwestern Colombia] from an undisturbed natural treasure to a polluted, industrialized growth center."

   — *Solicitation letter from the World Wildlife Fund*

7. "Frantic parents tell shocked TV audience: space aliens stole our son."

   — Weekly World News

▲ 8. "The manufacturer of Sudafed 12-hour capsules issued a nationwide recall of the product Sunday after two people in the state of Washington who had taken the medication died of cyanide poisoning and a third became seriously ill."

   — Los Angeles Times

9. "In Canada, smoking in public places, trains, planes or even automobiles is now prohibited by law or by convention. The federal government has banned smoking in all its buildings."

   — *Reuters*

10. "The list of vanishing commodities in Moscow now includes not only sausage and vodka, long rationed, but also potatoes, eggs, bread, and cigarettes."

    — National Geographic

11. "Maps, files and compasses were hidden in Monopoly sets and smuggled into World War II German prison camps by MI-5, Britain's counter-intelligence agency, to help British prisoners escape, according to the British manufacturer of the game."

    — *Associated Press*

▲ 12. "Cats that live indoors and use a litter box can live four to five years longer."

    — *From an advertisement for Jonny Cat litter*

13. "A case reported by Borderland Sciences Research Foundation, Vista, California, tells of a man who had attended many of the meetings where a great variety of 'dead' people came and spoke through the body mechanism of Mark Probert to the group of interested persons on a great variety of subjects with questions and answers from 'both sides.' Then this man who had attended meetings while he was in a body, did what is called 'die.' Presumably he had learned 'while in the body' what he might

expect at the change of awareness called death, about which organized religion seems to know little or nothing."

— *George Robinson,* Exploring the Riddle of Reincarnation, *undated, no publisher cited*

14. "Because of cartilage that begins to accumulate after age thirty, by the time . . . [a] man is seventy his nose has grown a half inch wider and another half inch longer, his earlobes have fattened, and his ears themselves have grown a quarter inch longer. Overall, his head's circumference increases a quarter inch every decade, and not because of his brain, which is shrinking. His head is fatter apparently because, unlike most other bones in the body, the skull seems to thicken with age."

— *John Tierney (a staff writer for Esquire)*

15. "Gardenias . . . need ample warmth, ample water, and steady feeding. Though hardy to 20°F or even lower, plants fail to grow and bloom well without summer heat."

— The Sunset New Western Garden Book *(a best-selling gardening reference in the West)*

16. "Exercise will make you feel fitter, but there's no good evidence that it will make you live longer."

— *Dr. Jordan Tobin, National Institute on Aging*

17. "Your bones are still growing until you're 35."

— *From a national milk ad by the National Fluid Milk Processor Promotion Board*

18. "*E. coli* 0157:H7 has become common enough to be the current major cause of acute kidney failure in children." [*E. coli* is a food-borne toxin originally found in the intestines of cows.]

— *Robin Cook, a physician-turned-novelist. This claim was made by a fictional expert on food-borne illnesses in the novel* Toxin.

19. "A woman employed as a Santa Claus at a Wal-Mart in Kentucky was fired by Wal-Mart when a child pinched her breast and complained to his mother that Santa was a woman. The woman complained to store managers."

— *Associated Press*

▲ 20. Paris Hilton has requested a trademark for the phrase "That's hot" from the U.S. Office of Trademarks and Patents.

— *Defamer blog*

Exercise 3-13

Identify at least three factors that can cause inaccuracies or a distortion of reports in the news media.

Exercise 3-14

Find five advertisements that give no reasons for purchasing the products they are selling. Explain how each ad attempts to make the product seem attractive.

Exercise 3-15

Find five advertisements that give reasons for purchasing the products they are selling. Which of the reasons are promises to the purchaser? Exactly what is being promised? What is the likelihood that the product will fulfill that promise?

Exercise 3-16

Watch Fox News and CNN news programs on the same day. Compare the two on the basis of (1) the news stories covered, (2) the amount of air time given to two or three of the major stories, and (3) any difference in the slant of the presentations of a controversial story. From your reading of the chapter, how would you account for the similarities between the two in both selection and content of the stories?

Writing Exercises

1. Although millions of people have seen professional magicians like David Copperfield and Siegfried and Roy perform in person or on television, it's probably a safe assumption that almost nobody believes they accomplish their feats by means of real magical or supernatural powers—that is, that they somehow "defy" the laws of nature. But even though they've never had a personal demonstration, a significant portion of the population believe that certain psychics are able to accomplish apparent miracles by exactly such means. How might you explain this difference in belief?
2. In the text, you were asked to consider the claim "Charlie's eighty-seven-year-old grandmother swam across Lake Michigan in the middle of winter." Because of the implausibility of such a claim—that is, because it conflicts with our background information—it is reasonable to reject it. Suppose, however, that instead of just telling us about his grandmother, Charlie brings us a photocopy depicting a page of a Chicago newspaper with a photograph of a person in a wetsuit walking up onto a beach. The caption underneath reads, "Eighty-seven-year-old Grandmother Swims Lake Michigan in January!" Based on this piece of evidence, should a critical thinker decide that the original claim is significantly more likely to be true than if it were backed up only by Charlie's word? Defend your answer.
3. Turn to the "Essays for Analysis" in Appendix 1 and assess the credibility of an author in a selection identified by your instructor. Based on the blurb about the author, say what you can about the author's likely expertise and susceptibility to bias on the subject of the essay.
4. Are our schools doing a bad job educating our kids? Do research in the library or on the Internet to answer this question. Make a list (no more than one page long) of facts that support the claim that our schools are not doing as good a job as they should. Then list facts that support the opposite view (or that rebut the claims of those who say our schools aren't doing a good job). Again, limit yourself to one page. Cite your sources.

Now think critically about your sources. Are any stronger or weaker than the others? Explain why on a single sheet of paper. Come prepared to read your explanation, along with your list of facts and sources, to the class.

5. Jackson says you should be skeptical of the opinion of someone who stands to profit from your accepting that opinion. Smith disagrees, pointing out that salespeople are apt to know a lot more about products of the type they sell than do most people.

   "Most salespeople are honest, and you can trust them," Smith argues. "Those who aren't don't stay in business long."

   Take about fifteen minutes to defend either Smith or Jackson in a short essay. When everyone is finished, your instructor will collect the essays and read three or more to the class to stimulate a brief discussion. After discussion, can the class come to any agreement about who is correct, Jackson or Smith?

6. Your instructor will survey the class to see how many agree with this claim: The media are biased. Then he or she will ask you to list your reasons for thinking that this claim is true. (If you do not think it is true, list reasons people might have for believing it.) After ten minutes your instructor will collect the lists of reasons and read from several of the lists. Then he or she will give you twenty minutes to defend one of these claims:

   a. The media are biased.
   b. Some of the reasons people have for believing the media are biased are not very good reasons.
   c. It is difficult to say whether the media are biased.

   At the end of the period your instructor may survey the class again to see if anyone's mind has changed, and why.

7. If you haven't done Exercise 6, your instructor will give you twenty minutes to defend an answer to the question, Are the media biased? Put your name on the back of your paper. When everyone is finished, your instructor will collect the papers and redistribute them to the class. In groups of four or five, read the papers that have been given to your group, and decide if any of them are convincing. Do not look at the names of the authors. Your instructor will ask each group to read to the class any essay that the group thinks is convincing.

Chapter 4

Persuasion Through Rhetoric: Common Devices and Techniques

During the 2004 presidential campaign, opponents of John Kerry spliced two photos to produce what you see here. This photographic version of innuendo makes it appear as though there is a connection between Kerry (left) and Jane Fonda, whose patriotism was questioned because of her antiwar activities during the Vietnam War.

In the late 1990s, tobacco companies spent millions trying to defeat Proposition 10, an antismoking ballot initiative in California. Calling themselves "The Committee Against Unfair Taxes," they mailed out expensive glossy brochures warning voters of the perils of the initiative. They were especially anxious to inform everyone that

> The sponsors of ill-conceived Proposition 10 are perennial political activist millionaire Rob Reiner and four other Hollywood/Los Angeles millionaire social engineers who believe they know more about raising your children than you do.

This warning was accompanied by a grainy black-and-white photograph of Reiner (whom you may remember from reruns of the popular 1960s TV show *All in the Family*) that brought to mind a police mug shot.

Now, when others want us to do something or want to influence our attitudes or beliefs, they may use an argument. That is, they may offer a reason why we should or shouldn't do or believe or not believe whatever it is. They might also use threats, bribery, or even more extreme measures. But the passage quoted above illustrates a technique that is used much more frequently: the persuasive power of words, or what we have called their rhetorical force or emotive meaning—their power to express and elicit images, feelings, and emotional associations. In the next few chapters, we examine some of the most common rhetorical techniques used to affect people's attitudes, opinions, and behavior.

Rhetoric refers to the study of persuasive writing. As we use the term, it denotes a broad category of linguistic techniques people use when their primary objective is to influence beliefs and attitudes and behavior. Is Rob Reiner "a perennial political activist millionaire"? Or is he an "untiring advocate of social reform willing to spend his considerable fortune for just causes"? The different impressions these two descriptions create is largely due to their differing rhetorical meaning. Does Juanita "still owe over $1,000 on her credit card"? Or does Juanita "owe only a little over $1,000 on her credit card"? There's no factual difference between the two questions—only a difference in their rhetorical force. The thing to remember through these next few chapters is that rhetorical force may be psychologically effective, but by itself it establishes nothing. If we allow our attitudes and beliefs to be affected by sheer rhetoric, we fall short as critical thinkers.

Political language is designed to make lies sound truthful . . . and to give the appearance of solidity to pure wind.

— George Orwell

Now before we get in trouble with your English teacher, let's make it clear that there is nothing wrong with trying to make your case as persuasive as possible by using well-chosen, rhetorically effective words and phrases. Good writers always do this. But we, as critical thinkers, must be able to distinguish the *argument* (if any) contained in what someone says or writes from the *rhetoric;* we must be able to distinguish the *logical* force of a set of remarks from their *psychological* force. The statement above from the tobacco companies about Rob Reiner, for example, contains *no argument whatsoever;* it just uses inflammatory rhetorical techniques aimed at getting us to vote against the antismoking initiative.

One of the things you will become aware of—as you read these pages and do the exercises and apply what you have learned to what you read and write—is that rhetoric is often mixed right in with argument. The message isn't that you should *deduct* points from an argument if it is presented in rhetorically charged language, and it isn't that you should try to get all the rhetoric out of your own writing. The message is simply that you shouldn't *add* points for rhetoric. You don't make an argument stronger by screaming it at the top of your lungs. Likewise, you don't make it stronger by adding **rhetorical devices.**

Many of these rhetorical bells and whistles have names because they are so common and so well understood. Because they are used primarily to give a statement a positive or negative slant regarding a subject, they are sometimes called **slanters.** We'll describe some of the more widely used specimens.

EUPHEMISMS AND DYSPHEMISMS

Language usually offers us a choice of words when we want to say something. Until recently, the term "used car" referred to an automobile that wasn't new, but the trend nowadays is to refer to such a car as "pre-owned." The people who sell such cars, of course, hope that the different terminology will keep potential buyers from thinking about *how* "used" the car might be—maybe it's *used up*! The car dealer's replacement term, "pre-owned," is a **euphemism**—a neutral or positive expression instead of one that carries negative associations. Euphemisms play an important role in affecting our attitudes. People may be less likely to disapprove of an assassination attempt on a foreign leader, for example, if it is referred to as "neutralization." People fighting

Real Life

The Death Tax

Here is Grover Norquist, who is the head of Americans for Tax Reform in Washington, D.C., in a press release from that organization:

> Over seventy percent of Americans oppose the Death Tax, and with good reason. It is the worst form of double-taxation, where, after taxing you all your life, the government decides to take even more when you die.

"Death Tax" is a dysphemism, of course. The estate tax is not a tax on death, but on inherited wealth, imposed on the occasion of a person's death. And the person paying the tax is not the deceased, but the inheritors, who have never paid tax on the money.

against the government of a country can be referred to neutrally as "rebels" or "guerrillas," but a person who wants to build support for them may refer to them by the euphemism "freedom fighters." A government is likely to pay a price for initiating a "revenue enhancement," but voters will be even quicker to respond negatively to a "tax hike." The U.S. Department of Defense performs the same function it did when it was called the Department of War, but the current name makes for much better public relations.

The opposite of a euphemism is a **dysphemism.** Dysphemisms are used to produce a negative effect on a listener's or reader's attitude toward something or to tone down the positive associations it may have. Whereas "freedom fighter" is a euphemism for "guerrilla" or "rebel," "terrorist" is a dysphemism.

The University of Washington admits that many of its faculty members suffer from what it calls "salary compression." The faculty themselves have a different word for it: "underpaid."

Euphemisms and dysphemisms are often used in deceptive ways or ways that at least hint at deception. All of the examples in the preceding paragraphs are examples of such uses. But euphemisms can at times be helpful and constructive. By allowing us to approach a sensitive subject indirectly—or by skirting it entirely—euphemisms can sometimes prevent hostility from bringing rational discussion to a halt. They can also be a matter of good manners: "Passed on" may be much more appropriate than "dead" if the person to whom you're speaking is recently widowed. Hence, our *purpose* for using euphemisms and dysphemisms determines whether or not those uses are legitimate.

It bears mentioning that some facts just are repellent, and for that reason even neutral reports of them sound horrible. "Lizzy killed her father with an ax" reports a horrible fact about Lizzy, but it does so using neutral language. Neutral reports of unpleasant, evil, or repellent facts do not automatically count as dysphemistic rhetoric.

RHETORICAL ANALOGIES, RHETORICAL DEFINITIONS, AND RHETORICAL EXPLANATIONS

Not long ago, we heard Robert Kittle, the editorial page editor of the *San Diego Union-Tribune,* refer to the Social Security program as a Ponzi scheme. (A Ponzi scheme is a pyramid scheme; Carlo Ponzi was responsible for a couple of the more famous examples.) People use analogies for various explanatory purposes; if a friend doesn't know what rugby is, you might bring partial

On Language

Don't Think of an Elephant

If you're told not to think of an elephant, you can't help thinking of one, according to linguist George Lakoff. In his book, Lakoff argues that the success of the Republican Party in recent years is due largely to their superiority in choosing the most effective words to frame issues. Persuasive terms like "Partial-birth abortion," "Tax relief," "No Child Left Behind,"* "Clear Skies,"* "Healthy Forests,"* "Personal Savings Accounts," help do the job. Republicans, says Lakoff, have succeeded in making the word "liberal" a dirty word in many circles, framing it around bloated bureaucracies, ill-advised social programs, and tolerance of crime. When Republicans emphasize "strong defense," "free markets," and "smaller government," he says Democrats should counter with "stronger America," "broad prosperity," and "effective government."

*These are nicknames for pieces of legislation; some people regard them as very misleading with respect to the legislation's actual content. (See box titled "Legislative Misnomers" on the next page.)

> Whether you wish to admit it or not, when you approve, morally, of the bombing of foreign targets by U.S. military, you are approving of acts morally equivalent to the bombing in Oklahoma City.
>
> – A rhetorical analogy by Timothy McVeigh, Oklahoma City bomber (reported by Larry Englemann)

enlightenment by comparing the sport to football. However, when editor Kittle likened Social Security to a Ponzi scheme, he wasn't trying to enlighten; he was trying to persuade. "Ponzi scheme" has a strong negative connotation, and calling something a Ponzi scheme portrays it in a very bad light.

Likening one thing to another thing in order to convey a negative— or positive—feeling about it is a **rhetorical analogy.** Sometimes rhetorical analogies are used as substitutes for arguments, and it is easy to see why. Facts are required to show that Social Security is financially unsustainable; it's less work and probably just as effective to call it a Ponzi scheme, which conveys the same idea and may produce conviction even without the proof.

Rhetorical analogies include both metaphors and similes. "Hillary's eyes are somewhat bulgy, like a Chihuahua's" is a simile; "Dick Cheney has steel in his backbone" is a metaphor. "Social Security is a Ponzi scheme" is, of course, a metaphor.

Rhetorical analogies also include comparisons: "You have a better chance of being struck by lightning than winning the lottery." "The environment needs George W. Bush like farmers need drought." "What do I think of her boyfriend? Silly Putty has more sex appeal." "Having kids is like having a bowling alley installed in your brain."* "What happens if a big asteroid hits

*Martin Mull

On Language

Legislative Misnomers

Several polls have reported that voters sometimes indicate approval of a measure when they hear its title, but indicate disapproval once they've heard an explanation of what the measure actually proposes. This isn't surprising given the misleading proposal titles assigned by members of Congress and state legislatures, and by authors of ballot measures. Here are a few examples of recent laws, initiatives, etc., the names of which don't exactly tell the whole story:

Healthy Forests Initiative (federal)—Reduces public involvement in decision-making regarding logging, reduces environmental protection requirements, and provides timber companies greater access to National Forests

Clear Skies Act (federal)—Loosens regulation of mercury, nitrous oxide, and sulphur dioxide, and puts off required reductions of these substances for several years beyond the limits of the current Clean Air Act; allows companies to trade off "pollution credits" so that some communities would get cleaner air and others dirtier air

Limitations on Enforcement of Unfair Business Competition Laws (California)—Makes it impossible for consumer groups of all types to sue corporations and businesses to prevent fraud, false advertising, and other deceptions before they take place

Payroll Protection Plan (many states)—Prevents any part of a union member's dues from being used for political purposes without his or her written consent

Right to Work (many states)—Prevents unions from collecting fees from nonmembers of bargaining units

Prohibition of Discrimination and Preferential Treatment (California)—Weakens or eliminates affirmative action programs

Earth? Judging from realistic simulations involving a sledge hammer and a common laboratory frog, we can assume it will be pretty bad."* The last examples are, of course, intended to be humorous, but they illustrate the concept.

A similar rhetorical device is the rhetorical definition, which we encountered in Chapter 2. "Real" definitions are primarily used to clarify meaning; **rhetorical definitions** use emotively charged language to express or elicit an attitude about something. Defining abortion as "the murder of an unborn child" does this—and stacks the deck against those who think abortion is morally defensible. Likewise, "human being" could be restricted in its meaning to an organism that a human gives birth to. Under this definition, abortion could not be classified as homicide.

In Chapter 2, we explained three forms definitions typically take. It's worth noting here that even definitions by example can slant a discussion if the examples are prejudicially chosen. Defining "conservative" by pointing to a white supremacist would be a case in point. Bill Maher once defined a conservative as one who thinks all problems can be solved either by more guns or more Jesus. If one wants to see all sides of an issue, one must avoid definitions and examples that slant a discussion.

> Looks like two different sets of engineers started working at opposite ends and couldn't look at what the other was doing until they met at the center post.
>
> – Click and Clack, using an analogy to describe the Pontiac Aztec

*Dave Barry

■ **Stereotypes.**

A pessimist is a man who looks both ways before crossing a one-way street.

— Laurence J. Peter

Rhetorical explanations are the same kind of slanting device, this time clothed as explanations. "He lost the fight because he's lost his nerve." Is this different from saying that he lost because he was too cautious? Maybe, but maybe not. What isn't in doubt is that the explanation is certainly more unflattering when it's put the former way.

We recently saw a good example of a rhetorical explanation in a letter to an editor:

> I am a traditional liberal who keeps asking himself, why has there been such a seismic shift in affirmative action? It used to be affirmative action stood for equal opportunity; now it means preferences and quotas. Why the change? It's because the people behind affirmative action aren't for equal rights anymore; they're for handouts.

This isn't a dispassionate scholarly explanation but a way of expressing an opinion on and trying to evoke anger at affirmative action policies.

STEREOTYPES

Houston? Are you hearing this, Houston?

The ventilation fans will be taken care of in a more timely manner because we know that women love to clean.

— General Yuri Glazkov, expressing the hope that U.S. astronaut Shannon Lucid would clean the fans when she joined the Russians on their space station.

When a writer or speaker lumps a group of individuals together under one name or description, especially one that begins with the word "the" (the liberal, the Communist, the right-winger, the Jew, the Catholic, and so on), such labeling generally results in stereotyping. A **stereotype** is a thought or image about a group of people based on little or no evidence. Thinking that women are emotional, that men are insensitive, that lesbians are man haters, that southerners are bigoted, that gay men are effeminate—all count as stereotypes. Language that reduces people or things to categories can induce an audience to accept a claim unthinkingly or to make snap judgments concerning groups of individuals about whom they know little.

Some of the slanters we've already talked about can involve stereotypes. For example, if we use the dysphemism "right-wing extremist" to defame a political candidate, we are utilizing a negative stereotype. Commonly, if we link a candidate with a stereotype we like or venerate, we can create a favorable impression of the individual. "Senator McCain addressed his opponent

with all the civility of a gentleman" employs a favorable stereotype, that of a gentleman, in a rhetorical comparison.

Our stereotypes come from a great many sources, many from popular literature, and are often supported by a variety of prejudices and group interests. The Native American tribes of the Great Plains were considered noble people by most whites until just before the mid–nineteenth century. But as white people grew more interested in moving them off their lands and as conflicts between the two escalated, popular literature increasingly described Native Americans as subhuman creatures. This stereotype supported the group interests of whites. Conflicts between nations usually produce derogatory stereotypes of the opposition; it is easier to destroy enemies without pangs of conscience if we think of them as less "human" than ourselves. Stereotyping becomes even easier when there are racial differences to exploit.

Mention the *strict regulations*—not protocols or rules—governing nuclear power plants.

—Republican pollster Frank Luntz, in "An Energy Policy for the 21st Century," advising Republicans how to sell nuclear energy.

INNUENDO

The next batch of slanting devices doesn't depend as much on emotional associations as on the manipulation of other features of language. When we communicate with one another, we automatically have certain expectations and make certain assumptions. (For example, when your instructor says, "Everybody passed the exam," she doesn't mean that everybody *in the world* passed the exam. We assume that the scope of the pronoun extends to include only those who took the exam.) These expectations and assumptions help fill in the gaps in our conversations so that we don't have to explain everything we say in minute detail. Because providing such details would be a tedious and probably impossible chore, these underlying conversational factors are crucial to the success of communication.

Consider this statement:

> Ladies and gentlemen, I am proof that there is at least one candidate in this race who does not have a drinking problem.

Notice that this remark does *not* say that any opponent of the speaker *does* have a drinking problem. In fact, the speaker is even allowing for the fact that other candidates may have no such problem by using the words "at least one candidate." But he has still managed to get the idea across that some

The opponents neglected to mention that the law *required* the city to assume the costs. This bit of innuendo on the part of the opponents suggested, of course, that the city was in bed with the developers.

The city voluntarily assumed the costs of cleaning up the landfill to make it safe for developers.

—Opponents of a local housing development

… Media

…graphic Innuendo

The photograph on the left appeared in *USA Today* under the headline "DeLay Under Fire." The two photos of Tom Delay are similar, but the left one is more suggestive of being "under fire." The suggestive power of photos can be deployed like the rhetorical devices mentioned in this chapter.

As another example, in the 2002 U.S. Senate race in Montana, Republican Mike Taylor dropped out of the race at the last minute, blaming a thirty-second TV ad sponsored by the Montana Democratic Party. The Democrats, he asserted, were using a stereotype to make him look gay.

In the ad, clips show Taylor dressed in a leisure suit, rubbing lotion on another man's temples, his white shirt unbuttoned to his chest, gold necklaces dangling. (Back in the 1980s, Taylor ran a beauty salon and haircare school; the clips are from a TV show he hosted.)

Democrats denied that they were implying anything about Taylor's sexuality. The ad focused on charges that Taylor diverted federal student loans when he ran the beauty salon.

Taylor had been marketing himself as a tough Montana rancher. "The ad has destroyed the campaign," said a spokesperson for Taylor.

opponent in the race *may* have a drinking problem. This is an example of **innuendo,** a form of suggestion.

Another example, maybe our all-time favorite, is this remark:

> I didn't say the meat was tough. I said I didn't see the horse that is usually outside.
>
> — *W. C. Fields*

As you can see, the use of innuendo enables us to insinuate something deprecatory about something or someone without actually saying it. For example, if someone asks you whether Ralph is telling the truth, you may reply, "Yes, this time," which would suggest that maybe Ralph doesn't *usually* tell the truth. Or you might say of someone, "She is competent—in many regards," which would insinuate that in some ways she is *not* competent.

Sometimes we condemn somebody with faint praise—that is, by praising a person a small amount when grander praise might be expected, we hint that praise may not really be due at all. This is a kind of innuendo. Imagine, for example, reading a letter of recommendation that says, "Ms. Flotsam has done good work for us, I suppose." Such a letter does not inspire one to want to hire Ms. Flotsam on the spot. Likewise, "She's proved to be useful so far" and "Surprisingly, she seems very astute" manage to speak more evil than good of Ms. Flotsam. Notice, though, that the literal information contained in these remarks is not negative in the least. Innuendo lies between the lines, so to speak.

As discussed in the text, the power of photographs and other images to convey emotions is somewhat analogous to the rhetorical force of language. For example, what emotion is elicited by this image?

LOADED QUESTIONS

If you overheard someone ask, "Have you always loved to gamble?" you would naturally assume that the person being questioned did in fact love to gamble. This assumption is independent of whether the person answered yes or no, for it underlies the question itself. Every question rests on assumptions. Even an innocent question like "What time is it?" depends on the assumptions that the hearer speaks English and has some means of finding out the time, for instance. A **loaded question** is less innocent, however. It rests on one or more *unwarranted* or *unjustified* assumptions. The world's oldest example, "Have you stopped beating your wife?" rests on the assumption that the person asked has in the past beaten his wife. If there is no reason to think that this assumption is true, then the question is a loaded one.

The loaded question is technically a form of innuendo, because it permits us to insinuate the assumption that underlies a question without coming right out and stating that assumption.

WEASELERS

Weaselers are linguistic methods of hedging a bet. When inserted into a claim, they help protect it from criticism by watering it down somewhat, weakening it, and giving the claim's author a way out in case the claim is challenged.

Overall? What does this weaseler mean?

Overall, Dodge trucks are the most powerful.

— Ad for Dodge

There used to be an advertisement for a brand of sugarless gum that claimed, "Three out of four dentists surveyed recommend sugarless gum for their patients who chew gum." This claim contains two weaseling expressions. The first is the word "surveyed." Notice that the ad does not tell us the criteria for choosing the dentists who were surveyed. Were they picked at random, or were only dentists who might not be unfavorably disposed toward gum chewing surveyed? Nothing indicates that the sample of dentists surveyed even remotely represents the general population of dentists. If

In the Media

Innuendo with Statistics

> Taxpayers with incomes over $200,000 could expect on average to pay about $99,000 in taxes under Mr. Bush's plan.
>
> – *Wall Street Journal*

Wow! Pity the poor taxpayer who makes over $200,000! Apparently, he or she will pay almost half of that amount in taxes.

But think again: In the words of the *New Republic* (February 3, 2003), "The *Journal*'s statistic is about as meaningful as asserting that males over the age of six have had an average of three sexual partners." Bill Gates and many others like him are among those who make over $200,000.

99 percent of the dentists in the country disagree with the ad's claim, its authors could still say truthfully that they spoke only about those dentists surveyed, not all dentists.

The second weaseler in the advertisement appears in the last phrase of the claim: "for their patients who chew gum." Notice the ad does not claim that *any* dentist believes sugarless-gum chewing is as good for a patient's teeth as no gum chewing at all. Imagine that the actual question posed to the dentists was something like this: "If a patient of yours insisted on chewing gum, would you prefer that he or she chew sugarless gum or gum with sugar in it?" If dentists had to answer that question, they would almost certainly be in favor of sugarless gum. But this is a far cry from recommending that any person chew any kind of gum at all. The weaselers allow the advertisement to get away with what *sounds* like an unqualified recommendation for sugarless gum, when in fact nothing in the ad supports such a recommendation.

Let's make up a statistic. Let's say that 98 percent of American doctors believe that aspirin is a contributing cause of Reye's syndrome in children and that the other 2 percent are unconvinced. If we then claim that "some doctors are unconvinced that aspirin is related to Reye's syndrome," we cannot be held accountable for having said something false, even though our claim might be misleading to someone who did not know the complete story. The word "some" has allowed us to weasel the point.

Even aside from the "up to" weaseler, this ad can be deceptive about what interest rate it's promising. Unless you listen carefully, you might think Great Western is paying 12 percent on checking accounts. The presence of the word "more" changes all that, of course. If you're getting 3 percent now and Great Western gives you "up to 12 percent more" than that, they'll be giving you about 3⅓ percent—hardly the fortune the ad seems to promise.

> Great Western pays up to 12 percent *more interest on checking accounts.*
>
> – Radio advertisement

Words that sometimes weasel—such as "perhaps," "possibly," "maybe," and "may be," among others—can be used to produce innuendo, to plant a *suggestion* without actually making a claim that a person can be held to. We can suggest that Berriault is a liar without actually saying so (and thus without making a claim that might be hard to defend) by saying that Berriault *may be* a liar. Or we can say that it is *possible* that Berriault is a liar (which is true of all of us, after all). "*Perhaps* Berriault is a liar" works nicely too. All of these are examples of weaselers used to create innuendo.

Not every use of words and phrases like these is a weaseling one, of course. Words that can weasel can also bring very important qualifications to bear on a claim. The very same word that weasels in one context may not weasel at all in another. For example, a detective considering all the possible angles on a crime who has just heard Smith's account of events may say to an associate, "Of course, it is *possible* that Smith is lying." This need not be a case of weaseling. The detective may simply be exercising due care. Other words and phrases that are sometimes used to weasel can also be used legitimately. Qualifying phrases such as "it is arguable that," "it may well be that," and so on have at least as many appropriate uses as weaseling ones. Others, such as "some would say that," are likely to be weaseling more often than not, but even they can serve an honest purpose in the right context. Our warning, then, is to be watchful when qualifying phrases turn up. Is the speaker or writer adding a reasonable qualification, insinuating a bit of innuendo, or preparing a way out? We can only warn; you need to assess the speaker, the context, and the subject to establish the grounds for the right judgment.

DOWNPLAYERS

Downplaying is an attempt to make someone or something look less important or significant. Stereotypes, rhetorical comparisons, rhetorical explanations, and innuendo can all be used to downplay something. Consider this statement, for example: "Don't mind what Mr. Pierce says in class; he's a liberal." This attempt to downplay Mr. Pierce and whatever views he expresses in class makes use of a stereotype. We can also downplay by careful insertion of certain words or other devices. Let's amend the preceding example like this: "Don't mind what Mr. Pierce says in class; he's just another liberal." Notice how the phrase "just another" denigrates Mr. Pierce's status still further. Words and other devices that serve this function are known as **downplayers.**

Perhaps the words most often used as downplayers are "mere" and "merely." If Kim tells you that she has a yellow belt in the Tibetan martial art of Pujo and that her sister has a mere green belt, you would quite naturally make the assumption that a yellow belt ranks higher than a green belt. We'd probably say that Kim's use of the word "mere" gives you the *right* to make that assumption. Kim has used the word to downplay the significance of her sister's accomplishment. But notice this: It could still be that Kim's sister's belt signifies the higher rank. If called on the matter, Kim might claim that she said "mere" simply because her sister has been practicing the art for much longer and is, after all, not *that* far ahead. Whether Kim has such an out or not, she has used a downplayer to try to diminish her sister's accomplishment.

The term "so-called" is another standard downplayer. We might say, for example, that the woman who made the diagnosis is a "so-called doctor," which downplays her credentials as a physician. Quotation marks can be used to accomplish the same thing:

> She got her "degree" from a correspondence school.

Use of quotation marks as a downplayer is somewhat different from their use to indicate irony, as in this remark:

> John "borrowed" Hank's umbrella, and Hank hasn't seen it since.

The idea in the latter example isn't to downplay John's borrowing the umbrella; it's to indicate that it wasn't really a case of borrowing at all. But the use of quotation marks around the word "degree" and the use of "so-called"

■ We find this both funny and sad. Do you? Why is this?

in the earlier examples are designed to play down the importance of their subjects. And, like "mere" and "merely," they do it in a fairly unsubtle way.

Many conjunctions—such as "nevertheless," "however," "still," and "but"—can be used to downplay claims that precede them. Such uses are more subtle than the first group of downplayers. Compare the following two versions of what is essentially the same pair of claims:

> (1) The leak at the plant was a terrible tragedy, all right; however, we must remember that such pesticide plants are an integral part of the "green revolution" that has helped to feed millions of people.
>
> (2) Although it's true that pesticide plants are an integral part of the "green revolution" that has helped to feed millions of people, it was just such a plant that developed a leak and produced a terrible tragedy.

The differences may not be as obvious as those in the cases of "mere" and "so-called," but the two versions give an indication of where their authors' sympathies lie.

The context of a claim can determine whether it downplays or not. Consider the remark "Chavez won by only six votes." The word "only" may or may not downplay Chavez's victory, depending on how thin a six-vote margin is. If ten thousand people voted and Chavez won by six, then the word "only" seems perfectly appropriate: Chavez just won by the skin of his teeth. But if the vote was in a committee of, say, twenty, then six is quite a substantial margin (it would be thirteen votes to seven, if everybody voted—almost two-

■ **John Edwards, the 2004 Democratic vice-presidential candidate.** During the campaign, humorists and some Republican Web sites referred to Edwards as the Breck Girl, because of his youthful, freshly scrubbed looks. This, of course, is a stereotype, ridicule, and, to the extent it was used to suggest Edwards was just a pretty face with no substance, an ad hominem attack, discussed in chapter 6.

to-one), and applying the word "only" to the result is clearly a slanting device designed to give Chavez's margin of victory less importance than it deserves.

As mentioned earlier, slanters really can't—and shouldn't—be avoided altogether. They can give our writing flair and interest. What *can* be avoided is being unduly swayed by slanters. Learn to appreciate the effects that subtle and not-so-subtle manipulations of language can have on you. By being aware, you decrease your chances of being taken in unwittingly by a clever writer or speaker.

HORSE LAUGH/RIDICULE/SARCASM

The kind of rhetorical device we call the **horse laugh** includes the use of ridicule of all kinds. Ridicule is a powerful rhetorical tool—most of us really hate being laughed at. So it's important to remember that somebody who simply gets a laugh at the expense of another person's position has not raised any objection to that position.

One may simply laugh outright at a claim ("Send aid to Russia? Har, har, har!"), laugh at another claim that reminds us of the first ("Support the Equal Rights Amendment? Sure, when the ladies start buying the drinks! Ho, ho, ho!"), tell an unrelated joke, use sarcastic language, or simply laugh at the person who is trying to make the point.

The next time you watch a debate, remember that the person who has the funniest lines and who gets the most laughs may be the person who *seems* to win the debate, but critical thinkers should be able to see the difference between argumentation on one hand and entertainment on the other. (Notice that we didn't say there's anything *wrong* with entertainment; just like most of you, we wouldn't like to spend *all* of our time watching people be serious, even if they *were* making good arguments.)

HYPERBOLE

Hyperbole is extravagant overstatement. A claim that exaggerates for effect is on its way to becoming hyperbole, depending on the strength of its language and the point being made. To describe a hangnail as a serious injury is hyperbole; so is using the word "fascist" to describe parents who insist that their teenager be home by midnight. Not all strong or colorful language is hyperbole, of course. "Oscar Peterson is an unbelievably inventive pianist" is a strong claim, but it is not hyperbolic—it isn't really extravagant. However, "Oscar Peterson is the most inventive musician who ever lived" goes beyond emphasis and crosses over the line into hyperbole. (How could one know that Oscar Peterson is more inventive than, say, Mozart?)

Dysphemisms often involve hyperbole. So do rhetorical comparisons. When we use the dysphemisms "traitorous" or "extremist" to describe the views of a member of an opposing political party, we are indulging in hyperbole. If we say that the secretary of state is less well informed than a beet, that's hyperbole in a rhetorical comparison. In similar ways, rhetorical explanations and definitions can utilize hyperbole.

A rhetorical definition with hyperbole. (A straw man, too, but that's for a later chapter.)

A feminazi is a woman to whom the most important thing in life is seeing to it that as many abortions as possible are performed.

— Rush Limbaugh

Hyperbole is also frequently used in ridicule. If it involves exaggeration, a piece of ridicule counts as hyperbole. The example above, saying that the secretary of state is less well informed than a beet, is hyperbole in a rhetorical comparison used to ridicule that official.

A claim can be hyperbolic without containing excessively emotive words or phrases. Neither the hangnail nor the Oscar Peterson examples contain such language; in fact, the word "unbelievably" is probably the most emotive word in the two claims about Peterson, and it occurs in the nonhyperbolic claim. But a claim can also be hyperbole as a result of the use of such language. "Parents who are strict about a curfew are fascists" is an example. If the word "mean" were substituted for "fascists," we might find the claim strong or somewhat exaggerated, but we would not call it hyperbole. It's when the colorfulness of language becomes *excessive*—a matter of judgment—that the claim is likely to turn into hyperbole.

Hyperbole is an obvious slanting device, but it can also have more subtle—perhaps unconscious—effects. Even if you reject the exaggeration, you may be moved in the direction of the basic claim. For example, you may reject the claim that Oscar Peterson is the most inventive musician who ever lived, but you may now believe that Oscar Peterson must certainly be an extraordinary musician—otherwise, why would someone make that exaggerated claim about him? Or suppose someone says, "Charlotte Church has the most fabulous voice of any singer around today." Even if you reject the "fabulous" part of the claim, you may still end up thinking Charlotte Church must have a pretty good voice. But be careful: Without support, you have no more reason to accept the milder claims than the wilder ones. Hyperbole can add a persuasive edge to a claim that it doesn't deserve. A hyperbolic claim is pure persuasion.

PROOF SURROGATES

An expression used to suggest that there is evidence or authority for a claim without actually citing such evidence or authority is a **proof surrogate.** Sometimes we can't *prove* the claim we're asserting, but we can hint that there *is* proof available, or at least evidence or authority for the claim, without committing ourselves to what that proof, evidence, or authority is. Using "informed sources say" is a favorite way of making a claim more authoritative. Who are the sources? How do we know they're informed? How does the person making the claim know they're informed? "It's obvious that" sometimes precedes a claim that isn't obvious at all. But we may keep our objections to ourselves in the belief that it's obvious to everybody but us, and we don't want to appear more dense than the next guy. "Studies show" crops up in advertising a lot. Note that this phrase tells us nothing about how many studies are involved, how good they are, who did them, or any other important information.

Proof surrogates often take the form of questions. This strategy can also be analyzed as switching the burden of proof (see Chapter 6).

There is no other country in the Middle East except Israel that can be considered to have a stable government. . . . Is Saudi Arabia more stable? Egypt? Jordan? Kuwait? Judge for yourself!

– "Facts and Logic About the Middle East"

Here's a good example of a proof surrogate from the *Wall Street Journal:*

> We hope politicians on this side of the border are paying close attention to Canada's referendum on Quebec. . . .
>
> Canadians turned out en masse to reject the referendum. There's every reason to believe that voters in the U.S. are just as fed up with the social engineering that lumps people together as groups rather than treating them as individuals.

There *may* be "every reason to believe" that U.S. voters are fed up, but nobody has yet told us what any of those reasons are. Until we hear more evidence, our best bet is to figure that the quotation mainly reflects what the writer at the *Journal* thinks is the proper attitude for U.S. voters. Without a context, such assertions are meaningless.

Remember: Proof surrogates are just that—surrogates. They are not real proof or evidence. Such proof or evidence may exist, but until it has been presented, the claim at issue remains unsupported. At best, proof surrogates suggest sloppy research; at worst, they suggest propaganda.

PERSUASIVE "RHETORIC" IN PHOTOGRAPHS AND OTHER IMAGES

In the previous chapter, you probably noticed the box about Terri Schiavo, the 41-year-old woman whose much-publicized death in March 2005 resulted from the removal of the tubes that provided her with food and water. Ms. Schiavo's heart stopped beating briefly in 1990 as the result of an eating disorder and potassium imbalance. Her brain was deprived of oxygen long enough to cause massive damage to her cerebral cortex. She failed to respond to therapy, but she was kept alive for fifteen years in a "persistent vegetative state" by means of a feeding and hydration tube. Though a tangle of legal and ethical questions have surrounded her story, we have no intention of dealing with these questions here. Instead, our purpose is a more general one.

It was difficult to read about Terri Schiavo and not feel powerful emotions. It was especially difficult for many people not to feel such emotions when seeing photographs or video images of her. This brings us to our subject: the persuasive use of visual imagery. You may have already noticed that some of the concepts we talk about in this chapter have visual analogs and we must not overlook the crucial role these visuals play in influencing people to adopt or modify beliefs and attitudes.

To start, we must note that photographs and other images are not claims, nor are they arguments. Very simply, claims are true or false. And while images may be blurry, out-of-focus, garish, inappropriate, misleading, etc, they can be seen from different perspectives and they can be given different interpretations; they can be emotionally neutral or they can cause powerful emotional responses. But they are not true or false.

That being said, it is obviously true that images can serve as the *basis* for claims. Based on a videotape of Terri Schiavo, Senate Majority Leader Bill Frist, who is also a physician, declared that there was a substantial likelihood that she was not in a persistent vegetative state. A video also served as the basis for claims in the early 1990s Rodney King case. The video showed Los Angeles police officers beating Rodney King with nightsticks. It was good evidence that the officers applied substantial force in King's arrest; however, the question in court was whether that application constituted excessive force. A video, in and of itself, cannot be an answer to the question of whether Terri Schiavo exhibited responsive behavior or whether the force was excessive in Rodney King's arrest. Video or other images can only serve as the basis for *claims* that answer those questions. That, of course, is exactly what they often do (although in a court of law one can usually expect to encounter alternative interpretations.

So, photographs and other images are not claims or arguments; instead, they provide reasons for making claims about events. Those claims can then be used in arguments.

Note, however, that images provide the basis for more than just neat, neutral statements of fact. They can produce powerful emotional impacts, as was the case in both the Terri Schiavo and Rodney King cases. Thus, visual images can function in the same way as rhetoric of the linguistic variety. Further, just like when powerful rhetorical language is used, the emotions stirred by visual imagery can impede our ability to weigh issues objectively. This doesn't mean, of course, that there is something wrong with feeling emotions in cases like our examples; on the contrary, it would be pretty weird to feel no emotion in such circumstances. But there are issues surrounding the Schiavo case, for example, that need to be decided independently of emotions felt toward her, her husband, her parents, or other principals in the case, issues such as who has legal authority to make decisions for her and the Constitutional question of jurisdiction between state and federal authorities and between the Congress and the courts. It may be said that complete objectivity is seldom found, but nonetheless we must do the best we can if we're to arrive at the best decisions we can. And the first step toward being objective is to be aware of the vehicles that transport emotion, feeling, and sentiment.

Because of their power to evoke strong emotions, imagery and rhetoric are both primary techniques used by demagogues to manipulate feelings and emotions. But, though critical thinking requires us to guard against being manipulated in this way, it is also true that both rhetoric and imagery can serve laudable purposes.

In Depth

Don't Get Carried Away!

Once you're familiar with the ways slanting devices are used to try to influence us, you may be tempted to dismiss a claim or argument *just because it contains strongly slanted language*. But true claims as well as false ones, good reasoning as well as bad, can be couched in such language. Remember that the slanting *itself* gives us no reason to accept a position on an issue; that doesn't mean that there *are* no such reasons. Consider this example, written by someone opposed to using animals for laboratory research:

> It's morally wrong for a person to inflict awful pain on another sensitive creature, one that has done the first no harm. Therefore, the so-called scientists who perform their hideous and sadistic experiments on innocent animals are moral criminals just as were Hitler and his Nazi torturers.

Before we dismiss this passage as shrill or hysterical, it behooves us as critical thinkers to notice that it contains a piece of reasoning that may shed light on the issue.

Recap

This list summarizes the topics covered in this chapter:

- When we try to persuade, we try to win someone to our point of view.
- Rhetoric seeks to persuade through use of the emotive power of language.
- Though it can exert a profound psychological influence, rhetoric has no logical force. Only an argument has logical force; i.e., can prove or support a claim.
- Euphemisms seek to mute the disagreeable aspects of something.
- Dysphemisms are used to emphasize the disagreeable aspects of something.
- Rhetorical analogies, definitions, and explanations are used to create both favorable and unfavorable attitudes about something.
- Stereotypes are unwarranted and oversimplified generalizations about the members of a class.
- Innuendo uses words with neutral or positive associations to insinuate something deprecatory.
- Loaded questions rest on unwarranted assumptions.
- Weaselers protect a claim from criticism by weakening it.
- Downplayers tone down the importance of something.
- Ridicule and sarcasm are used widely.
- Hyperbole is exaggeration.
- Proof surrogates suggest there is evidence or authority for a claim without actually saying what the evidence or authority is.
- These devices can affect our thinking in subtle ways, even when we believe we are being objective.

- Some of these devices, especially euphemisms and weaselers, have valuable, nonprejudicial uses as well as a slanting one. Only if we are speaking, writing, listening, and reading carefully can we distinguish prejudicial uses of these devices.
- Although photographs and other images are not claims or arguments, they can enter into critical thinking by offering evidence of the truth or falsity of claims. They can also affect us psychologically in a manner analogous to that by which the emotive meaning of language affects us.

Exercises

Exercise 4-1

You will want to recognize when someone is using rhetorical slanting devices to influence your attitudes and beliefs. Let's see if you can identify some of the more common devices. Select the *best* answer.

1. "His nose, however, is his redeeming feature: It is pronounced straight and well-formed; though I myself should have liked it better if it did not possess a somewhat spongy, porous appearance, as though it had been cleverly formed out of a red coloured cork."

— *Anthony Trollope,* Barchester Towers

a. rhetorical analogy
b. rhetorical definition
c. rhetorical explantion
d. loaded question
e. not a slanter

▲ **2.** Larry Kudlow, of *Kudlow and Cramer* on CNBC (in an *American Spectator* interview): "[Former Treasury Secretary] Bob Rubin's a smart guy, a nice man, but he hates tax cuts. To listen to Rubin on domestic issues, you could just die. He's a free-spending left-winger." Which category applies best to the last phrase of the quotation?

a. rhetorical analogy
b. stereotype
c. downplayer
d. loaded question
e. not a slanter

3. "Making a former corporate CEO the head of the Securities and Exchange Commission is like putting a fox in charge of the henhouse." This is best seen as an example of

a. rhetorical analogy
b. rhetorical explanation
c. innuendo
d. dysphemism
e. not a slanter

▲ **4.** "The key principle is "responsible energy exploration." And remember, it's NOT drilling for oil. It's responsible energy exploration."

— *Republican Pollster Frank Luntz, "Eight Energy Communications Guidelines for 2005"*

a. dysphemism
b. euphemism
c. innuendo
d. hyperbole
e. loaded question

5. "Right. George Bush 'won' the election in 2000, didn't he?" The use of quotation marks around "won" has the effect of a

a. weaseler
b. dysphemism
c. downplayer
d. rhetorical explanation
e. not a slanter

6. "'Democrat' equals 'ideologically homeless ex-communist.'"

— *Linda Bowles*

a. hyperbole
b. stereotype
c. rhetorical explanation
d. rhetorical definition
e. not a slanter

▲ **7.** The obvious truth is bilingual education has been a failure." In this statement, "the obvious truth" might best be viewed as

a. proof surrogate
b. weaseler
c. innuendo
d. dysphemism
e. not a slanter

8. After George W. Bush announced he wanted to turn a substantial portion of the federal government operation over to private companies, Bobby L. Harnage, Sr., president of the American Federation of Government Employees, said Bush had "declared all-out war on federal employees." Would you say that the quoted passage is

a. a rhetorical explanation
b. a euphemism
c. a weaseler
d. hyperbole/rhetorical anthology
e. not a slanter

9. "You say you are in love with Oscar but are you sure he's right for you? Isn't he a little too . . . uh, 'mature' for you?" This statement contains

a. loaded question
b. a euphemism
c. both a and b
d. neither a nor b

▲ **10.** "Before any more of my tax dollars go to the military, I'd like answers to some questions, such as why are we spending billions of dollars on weapons programs that don't work?" This statement contains an example of

a. a downplayer
b. a dysphemism

c. a proof surrogate
d. a loaded question
e. hyperbole and a loaded question

11. "Can Governor Evans be believed when he says he will fight for the death penalty? You be the judge." This statement contains

a. dysphemism
b. proof surrogate
c. innuendo
d. hyperbole
e. no slanters

▲ **12.** "Which is it George W. Bush lied about, whether he used cocaine, when he used cocaine, or how much cocaine he used?" This statement contains

a. hyperbole
b. dysphemism
c. loaded question
d. proof surrogate
e. no slanter

13. "Studies confirm what everyone knows: smaller classes make kids better learners."

— *Bill Clinton*

This statement contains:

a. proof surrogate
b. weaseler
c. hyperbole
d. innuendo
e. no slanter

14. MAN SELLING HIS CAR: "True, there's a little wear and tear, but what are a few dents?" This statement contains what might best be called

a. a loaded question
b. an innuendo
c. a dysphemism
d. a euphemism

▲ **15.** MAN THINKING OF BUYING THE CAR IN EXERCISE 14, TO HIS WIFE: "Okay, okay, so it's got a few miles on it. Still, it may be the only Mustang in the whole country for that price." In this item, "few" and "still" could be said to belong to the same category of slanter. (T or F)

16. In Exercise 15, "it may be" is

a. a weaseler
b. a proof surrogate
c. a downplayer
d. not a slanter

17. Still in Exercise 15, "in the whole country" is an example of

a. innuendo
b. hyperbole
c. a euphemism
d. none of these

Exercise 4-2

▲ Determine which of the numbered, italicized words and phrases are used as rhetorical devices in the following passage. If the item fits one of the text's categories of rhetorical devices, identify it as such.

> The National Rifle Association's campaign *to arm every man, woman, and child in America*[1] received a setback when the President signed the Brady Bill. But the *gun-pushers*[2] know that the bill was only *a small skirmish in a big war*[3] over guns in America. They can give up some of their more *fanatic*[4] positions on such things as *assault weapons*[5] and *cop-killer bullets*[6] and still win on the one that counts: regulation of manufacture and sale of handguns.

Exercise 4-3

▲ Follow the directions for Exercise 4-2.

> The *big money guys*[1] who have *smuggled*[2] the Rancho Vecino development onto the November ballot *will stop at nothing to have this town run just exactly as they want.*[3] *It is possible*[4] that Rancho Vecino will cause traffic congestion on the east side of town, and *it's perfectly clear that*[5] the number of houses that will be built will overload the sewer system. *But*[6] a small number of individuals have taken up the fight. *Can the developers be stopped in their desire to wreck our town?*[7]

Exercise 4-4

Follow the directions for Exercise 4-2.

> The U.S. Congress has cut off funds for the superconducting supercollider that the *scientific establishment*[1] wanted to build in Texas. The *alleged*[2] virtues of the supercollider proved no match for the *huge*[3] *cost-overruns*[4] that had piled up *like a mountain alongside a sea of red ink.*[5] Despite original estimates of five to six billion dollars, the latest figure was over eleven billion and *growing faster than weeds.*[6]

Exercise 4-5

Read the passage below and answer the questions that follow it. Your instructor may have further directions.

> Another quality that makes [Texas Republican Tom] DeLay an un-Texas pol is that he's mean. By and large, Texas pols are an agreeable set of less-than-perfect humans and quite often well-intentioned. As Carl Parker of Port Arthur used to observe, if you took all the fools out of the [legislature], it would not be a representative body any longer. The old sense of collegiality was strong, and vindictive behavior—

punishing pols for partisan reasons—was simply not done. But those are Tom DeLay's specialties, his trademarks. The Hammer is not only genuinely feared in Washington, he is, I'm sorry to say, hated.

— *Excerpt from a column by Molly Ivins,* Ft. Worth Star-Telegram

1. What issue is the author addressing?
2. What position does the author take on that issue?
3. If the author supports this position with an argument, state that argument in your own words.
4. Does the author use rhetorical devices discussed in this chapter? If so, classify any that fall into the categories described in this chapter.

Exercise 4-6

Follow the directions for Exercise 4-5, using the same list of questions.

Schools are not a microcosm of society, any more than an eye is a microcosm of the body. The eye is a specialized organ which does something that no other part of the body does. That is its whole significance. You don't use your eyes to lift packages or steer automobiles. Specialized organs have important things to do in their own specialties. So schools, which need to stick to their special work as well, should not become social or political gadflies.

— *Thomas Sowell*

Exercise 4-7

Follow the directions for Exercise 4-5, using the same list of questions.

Here is what I believe: The country has just witnessed an interlude of religious hysteria, encouraged and exploited by political quackery. The political cynicism of Republicans shocked the nation. But even more alarming is the enthusiasm of self-described "pro-life" forces for using the power of the state to impose their obtuse moral distinctions on the rest of us. The Catholic Church and many Protestant evangelicals are acting as partisan political players in a very dangerous manner. Once they have mobilized zealots to their moral causes, they can expect others to fight back in the same blind, intolerant manner.

— *William Greider, "Pro-Death Politics," the* Nation, *April 2, 2005*

Exercise 4-8

Follow the directions for Exercise 4-5, using the same list of questions.

Asked whether he would be resigning, [U.N. Secretary General Kofi] Annan replied, "Hell, no. I've got lots of work to do, and I'm going to go ahead and do it." That's doubtful. His term is up at the end of 2006, and few—after the mess he's caused—take him seriously. He may have a lot of "work" he'd like to do, but he won't be permitted to do it. All around Annan is the wreckage of the U.N.'s spirit of high-level cronyism.

— *Editorial in the* National Review Online, *April 1, 2005*

Exercise 4-9

Follow the directions for Exercise 4-5, using the same list of questions.

"It is not the job of the state, and it is certainly not the job of the school, to tell parents when to put their children to bed," declared David Hart of the National Association of Head Teachers, responding to David Blunkett's idea that parents and teachers should draw up "contracts" (which you could be fined for breaching) about their children's behaviour, time-keeping, homework and bedtime. Teachers are apparently concerned that their five-to-eight-year-old charges are staying up too late and becoming listless truants the next day.

While I sympathise with Mr. Hart's concern about this neo-Stalinist nannying, I wonder whether it goes far enough. Is it not high time that such concepts as Bathtime, Storytime and Drinks of Water were subject to regulation as well? I for one would value some governmental guidance as to the number of humorous swimming toys (especially Hungry Hippo) allowable per gallon of water. Adopting silly voices while reading Spot's Birthday or Little Rabbit Foo-Foo aloud is something crying out for regulatory guidelines, while the right of children to demand and receive wholly unnecessary glasses of liquid after lights-out needs a Statutory Minimum Allowance.

— *John Walsh, the* Independent

Exercise 4-10

Identify any rhetorical devices you find in the following selections, and classify those that fit the categories described in the text. For each, explain its function in the passage.

▲ 1. I trust you have seen Janet's file and have noticed the "university" she graduated from.

2. The original goal of the Milosevic government in Belgrade was ethnic cleansing in Kosovo.

3. "National Health Care: The compassion of the IRS and the efficiency of the post office, all at Pentagon prices."

— *From a letter to the editor,* Sacramento Bee

▲ 4. Although it has always had a bad name in the United States, socialism is nothing more or less than democracy in the realm of economics.

5. We'll have to work harder to get Representative Burger reelected because of his little run-in with the law.

▲ 6. It's fair to say that, compared with most people his age, Mr. Beechler is pretty much bald.

7. During World War II, the U.S. government resettled many people of Japanese ancestry in internment camps.

▲ 8. "Overall, I think the gaming industry would be a good thing for our state."

— *From a letter to the editor,* Plains Weekly Record

9. Morgan has decided to run for state senator. I'm sorry to hear that he's decided to become a politician.

10. I'll tell you what capitalism is: Capitalism is Charlie Manson sitting in Folsom Prison for all those murders and still making a bunch of bucks off T-shirts.

▲ 11. Clearly, Antonin Scalia is the most corrupt Supreme Court Justice in the history of the country.

12. In a February 1 article, writer Susan Beahay says Bush's abortion decision will return abortions to secrecy, risking the mother's life having a back-alley abortion. That's really juicy. The ultra-left pro-abortion crowd sure can add a little levity into a deadly serious subject.

13. It may well be that many faculty members deserve some sort of pay increase. Nevertheless, it is clearly true that others are already amply compensated.

▲ 14. "The only people without [cable or satellite TV] are Luddites and people too old to appreciate it."

— *Todd Mitchell, industry analyst*

15. I love some of the bulleting and indenting features of Microsoft Word. I think it would have been a nice feature, however, if they made it easy to turn some of them off when you don't need them.

Exercise 4-11

Identify any rhetorical devices you find in the following passage, and classify any that fit into the categories described in this chapter.

> On March 11, the U.S. Senate passed the bankruptcy bill that will fill the coffers of the credit card companies while bleeding consumers dry.
>
> The bill passed by a whopping 74 to 25 margin, with eighteen Democratic Senators going over to the dark side.
>
> Here are the spineless 18: [There follows a list of senators.]
>
> "This is not where we as Democrats ought to be, for crying out loud," as Senator Tom Harkin noted. "We are making a terrible mistake by thinking that we can have it both ways. We have to remember where our base is."
>
> This bill is a fantasy come true for credit card companies, which have been pushing it for years. But it's not as though they're suffering. The made $30 billion in profits last year.
>
> The bill severely limits the ability of consumers to wipe away some of their debts and get a fresh start.
>
> Half the people who file for bankruptcy do so because of sky-high medical bills, and another 40 percent do so because of disability, job loss, family death, or divorce, according to the National Consumer Law

Center. If you make more than the median income in your state, no matter how high your bills are, you can't wipe the debts clean.

As a result, debtors will be at much greater risk of losing their cars or their homes.

And even if your debts are the consequence of identity theft, of someone stealing your credit card and running up charges, you still are on the hook for them, as the Senate amazingly voted down an amendment to shelter victims of identity theft.

— *Matthew Rothschild, "Democratic Senators Cave on Bankruptcy Bill,"* The Progressive, *March 12, 2005*

Exercise 4-12

Identify any rhetorical devices you find in the following passages, and explain their purposes. Note: Some items may contain *no* rhetorical devices.

▲ **1.** "If the United States is to meet the technological challenge posed by Japan, Inc., we must rethink the way we do everything from design to manufacture to education to employee relations."

— Harper's

2. According to UNICEF reports, several thousand Iraqi children died each month because of the U.N. sanctions.

3. Maybe Professor Daguerre's research hasn't appeared in the first-class journals as recently as that of some of the other professors in his department; that doesn't necessarily mean his work is going downhill. He's still a terrific teacher, if the students I've talked to are to be believed.

▲ **4.** "Let's put it this way: People who make contributions to my campaign fund get access. But there's nothing wrong with constituents having access to their representatives, is there?"

Loosely paraphrased from an interview with a California state senator

5. In the 2000 presidential debates, Al Gore consistently referred to his own tax proposal as a "tax plan" and to George W. Bush's tax proposal as a "tax scheme."

6. "This healthy food provides all the necessary ingredients to help keep your bird in top health."

— *Hartz Parrot Diet*

▲ **7.** [*Note:* Dr. Jack Kevorkian was instrumental in assisting a number of terminally ill people in committing suicide during the 1990s.] "We're opening the door to Pandora's Box if we claim that doctors can decide if it's proper for someone to die. We can't have Kevorkians running wild, dealing death to people."

— *Larry Bunting, assistant prosecutor, Oakland County, Michigan*

8. "LOS ANGELES—Marriott Corp. struck out with patriotic food workers at Dodger Stadium when the concession-holder ordered them to keep working instead of standing respectfully during the National Anthem. . . . Concession stand manager Nick Kavadas . . . immediately objected to a Marriott representative.

"Marriott subsequently issued a second memo on the policy. It read: 'Stop all activities while the National Anthem is being played.'

"Mel Clemens, Marriott's general manager at the stadium, said the second memo clarified the first memo."

— *Associated Press*

9. These so-called forfeiture laws are a serious abridgment of a person's constitutional rights. In some states, district attorneys' offices only have to *claim* that a person has committed a drug-related crime to seize the person's assets. So fat-cat DAs can get rich without ever getting around to proving that anybody is guilty of a crime.

▲ 10. "A few years ago, the deficit got so horrendous that even Congress was embarrassed. Faced with this problem, the lawmakers did what they do best. They passed another law."

— *Abe Mellinkoff, in the* San Francisco Chronicle

11. "[U]mpires are baseball's designated grown-ups and, like air-traffic controllers, are paid to handle pressure."

— *George Will*

12. "Last season should have made it clear to the moguls of baseball that something still isn't right with the game—something that transcends residual fan anger from the players' strike. Abundant evidence suggests that baseball still has a long way to go."

— *Stedman Graham,* Inside Sports

▲ 13. "As you know, resolutions [in the California State Assembly] are about as meaningful as getting a Publishers' Clearinghouse letter saying you're a winner."

— *Greg Lucas, in the* San Francisco Chronicle

14. The entire gain in the stock market in the first four months of the year was due to a mere fifty stocks.

▲ 15. Thinkers who entertain the possibility that there are lots of universes have invented a new term for the entire ensemble: "the multiverse." Why believe in the multiverse? The "pro" camp has essentially two kinds of arguments.

— *Jim Holt,* Slate *online magazine*

16. "[Supreme Court Justice Antonin] Scalia's ideology is a bald and naked concept called 'Majoritarianism.' Only the rights of the majority are protected."

— *Letter to the editor of the* San Luis Obispo Telegram-Tribune

17. "Mimi Rumpp stopped praying for a winning lottery ticket years ago. . . . But after a doctor told her sister Miki last year that she needed a kidney transplant, the family began praying for a donor. . . . Less than a year later, Miki has a new kidney, courtesy of a bank teller in Napa, Calif., to whom she had told her story. The teller was the donor; she was so moved by Miki's plight she had herself tested and discovered she was a perfect match. Coincidence? Luck? Divine intervention? Rumpp is sure: 'It was a miracle.'"

— Newsweek

▲ 18. "We are about to witness an orgy of self-congratulation as the self-appointed environmental experts come out of their yurts, teepees, and grant-maintained academic groves to lecture us over the impending doom of the planet and agree with each other about how it is evil humanity and greedy 'big business' that is responsible for it all."

— *Tim Worstall, in* New Times

19. "In the 1980s, Central America was awash in violence. Tens of thousands of people fled El Salvador and Guatemala as authoritarian governments seeking to stamp out leftist rebels turned to widespread arrests and death squads."

— USA Today

Exercise 4-13

Discuss the following stereotypes in class. Do they invoke the same kind of images for everyone? Which are negative and which are positive? How do you think they came to be stereotypes? Is there any "truth" behind them?

1. soccer mom
2. Religious Right
3. dumb blonde
4. tax-and-spend liberal
5. homosexual agenda
6. redneck
7. radical feminist
8. contented housewife
9. computer nerd
10. tomboy
11. interior decorator
12. Washington insider
13. Earth mother
14. frat rat
15. Deadhead
16. trailer trash

Exercise 4-14

Your instructor will give you three minutes to write down as many positive and negative stereotypes as you can. Are there more positive stereotypes on your list or more negative ones? Why do you suppose that is?

Exercise 4-15

Write two brief paragraphs describing the same person, event, or situation—that is, both paragraphs should have the same informative content. The first paragraph should be written in a *purely* informative way, using language that is as neutral as possible; the second paragraph should be slanted as much as possible either positively or negatively (your choice).

Exercise 4-16

Explain the difference between a weaseler and a downplayer. Find a clear example of each in a newspaper, magazine, or other source. Next find an example of a phrase that is sometimes used as a weaseler or downplayer but that is used appropriately or neutrally in the context of your example.

Exercise 4-17

Explain how rhetorical definitions, rhetorical comparisons, and rhetorical explanations differ. Find an example of each in a newspaper, magazine, or other source.

Exercise 4-18

Look through an issue of *Time, Newsweek,* or another newsmagazine, and find a photograph that portrays its subject in an especially good or bad light—that is, one that does a nonverbal job of creating slant regarding the subject.

Exercise 4-19

In groups, invent two newspaper or magazine headlines to go with the photograph of Senator Hillary Rodham Clinton on p. 215. Make one headline create a favorable impression in combination with the photo and make the other create an unfavorable impression.

Writing Exercises

1. Your instructor will select an essay from those in Appendix 1 and ask you to identify as many rhetorical devices as you can find. (Your instructor may narrow the scope of the assignment to just certain paragraphs.)
2. Over the past decade, reportedly more than 2,000 illegal immigrants have died trying to cross the border into the southwestern United States. Many deaths have resulted from dehydration in the desert in the desert heat and from freezing to death on cold winter nights. A San Diego–based non-profit humanitarian organization now leaves blankets, clothes, and water at stations throughout the desert and mountain regions for the immigrants. Should the organization do this? Its members say they are providing simple humanitarian aid, but critics accuse them of encouraging illegal activity. Take a stand on the issue and defend your position in writing. Then identify each rhetorical device you used.
3. Until recently, tiny Stratton, Ohio, had an ordinance requiring all door-to-door "canvassers" to obtain a permit from the mayor. Presumably the ordinance was intended to protect the many senior citizens of the town from harm by criminals who might try to gain entry by claiming to be conducting a survey. The ordinance was attacked by the Jehovah's Witnesses, who thought it violated their First Amendment right to free speech. The Supreme Court agreed and struck down the law in 2002. Should it have? Defend your position in a brief essay without using rhetoric. Alternatively, defend your position and use rhetorical devices, but identify each device you use.

Chapter 5

More Rhetorical Devices: Psychological and Related Fallacies

This ad employs scare tactics, discussed in this chapter.

Once upon a time, in an earlier edition of this book, we complained about how the level of political discussion had dropped. How little did we know! Since that time, we've watched the discussion of issues on radio, on television, and in issue-oriented books turn into shouting matches on television and radio as the presentation of evidence and argument give way everywhere to rhetoric, bombast, and plain old name-calling. Rush Limbaugh, Michael Savage, Sean Hannity, and others from the right wing of American politics have dominated the airwaves in recent years. Recently they've been joined by Al Franken, Mike Malloy, and others on *Air America,* a talk network from the other end of the political spectrum. "Issue oriented" programs on television, such as the *McLaughlin Group,* feature talking heads who debate points by out-shouting each other.

As it becomes more difficult to find a serious discussion of an important issue, it gets easier and easier to find examples of rhetorical devices designed to provoke emotional, knee-jerk reactions. Unfortunately (for us as individuals as well as for public policy), it can be altogether too easy to allow such responses to take the place of sound judgment and careful thinking. In this chapter, we'll target some specific devices designed to produce this effect—devices that go beyond the rhetorical coloration we talked about in the last chapter. The stratagems we'll discuss below sometimes masquerade as arguments, complete with premises and conclusions and language that would suggest argumentation. But while they may be made to *look* or *sound* like arguments, they don't really provide legitimate grounds for accepting a conclusion. In place of good reasons for a conclusion, most of the schemes we'll look at in this chapter offer us considerations that are emotionally or psychologically linked to the issue in question. The support they may appear to offer is really only pretended support; you might think of them as pieces of pretend reasoning, or *pseudoreasoning.*

The devices in this chapter thus all count as fallacies (a fallacy is a mistake in reasoning). The rhetorical devices we discussed in the last chapter—euphemisms, innuendo, and so forth—aren't fallacies. Of course, *we* commit a fallacy if we think a claim has been supported when the "support" is nothing more than rhetorically persuasive language.

People constantly accept fallacies as legitimate arguments; but the reverse mistake can also happen. We must be careful not to dismiss *legitimate* arguments as fallacies just because they *remind* us of a fallacy. Often beginning students in logic have this problem. They read about fallacies like the ones we cover here and then think they see them everywhere. These fallacies are common, but they are not everywhere; and you sometimes must consider a specimen carefully before accepting or rejecting it. The exercises at the end of the chapter will help you learn to do this, because they contain a few reasonable arguments mixed in with the fallacies.

THE "ARGUMENT" FROM OUTRAGE

We just tuned in to Rush Limbaugh for a few minutes, to see if he was outraged about something or other, and we were not disappointed. He was talking about some recent criticism of Tom DeLay, the majority leader in the House of Representatives. Rush's first words were,

> The left is just a drooling mob and it's ugly out there. The left wing and their attack on DeLay is not new. As a matter of fact, Tom DeLay was the first demon of choice of the left. But it went nowhere. No traction, no fund-raising, no focus group numbers, so the gangbangers on the left went after Cheney. Remember that?

Although we've heard him more worked up, his voice was still tense with disbelief and indignation that "the left" was causing problems for DeLay. The technique of expressing outrage—anybody who doesn't see *this* point must be a fool or a traitor!—is one we've identified with Limbaugh because he was one of the early masters of the method; we even referred to the use of outrage to persuade people as "the Limbaugh fallacy" in the previous edition. But the technique is not unique to Limbaugh, of course; it's typical of today's hardline talk show people. And apparently it works, if the people who call in to the programs are any indication, since they tend to be as outraged at the goings-on as the hosts of the programs. That's the idea, of course. If a person gets angry enough about something, if one is in the throes of righteous indignation, then it's all too easy to throw reason and good sense out the window and accept whatever alternative is being offered by the speaker just from indignation alone.

Now, does this mean that we never have a right to be angry about something? Of course not. Anger is not a fallacy, and there are times when it's entirely appropriate. However, when we are angry—and the angrier or more outraged we are the more true this becomes—it's easy to become illogical, and it can happen in two different ways. *First, we may think we have been given a reason for being angry when in fact we have not.* Were Tom DeLay's detractors "out to get him" because he had actually done something wrong, or were they simply trying to get rid of him because he was an effective leader in the Congress, as was claimed by his radio defenders? This would take some investigation to find out. (By investigation, we don't mean simply going down the dial to listen to another radio talk show host!) At any rate, it is a mistake to think that something is wrong just because it makes somebody angry, even if it's us whom it seems to anger. It's easy to mistake a feeling of outrage for evidence of something, but it isn't evidence of anything, really, except our anger.

■ Limbaugh seems to have no trouble finding things to get mad about. You'll find examples in the text, and if you're still not angry, you can try his Web site.

Second, we may let the anger we feel as the result of one thing influence our evaluations of an unrelated thing. If we're angry over what we take to be the motives of somebody's detractors, we must remember that their motives are a separate matter from that of whether their criticisms are accurate; they might still be right. Similarly, if a person does something that makes us mad, that doesn't provide us a reason for downgrading him on some other matter, nor would it be a reason for upgrading our opinion of someone else.

The **"argument" from outrage,*** then, consists in inflammatory words (or thoughts) followed by a "conclusion" of some sort. It substitutes anger for reason and judgment in considering an issue. It is a favorite strategy of demagogues. In fact, it is *the* favorite strategy of demagogues. Let's say the issue is whether gay marriages should be legal. Left-of-center demagogues may wax indignantly about "narrow-minded fundamentalist bigots dictating what people can do in their bedrooms"—talk calculated to get us steamed although it really has nothing to do with the issue. On the other side, conservative demagogues may allude to gays' demanding "special rights." Nobody wants someone else to get special rights, and when we hear about somebody "demanding" them, our blood pressure goes up. But wanting a right other people have is not wanting a special right; it's wanting an equal right.

A particularly dangerous type of "argument" from outrage is known as **scapegoating**—blaming a certain group of people—or even a single person (like George W. Bush or Bill Clinton) for all of life's troubles. George Wallace, the former governor of Alabama who ran for president in 1968 on a "states' rights platform" (which then was a code word for white supremacy) said he could get good old Southern boys to do anything by whooping them into a frenzy over Northern civil rights workers.

*In discussing this and several succeeding fallacies, we've used the word "argument" in quotation marks to indicate that we are not really talking about an argument at all. (Such marks are sometimes called "irony" quotation marks, and are not unrelated to the "downplaying" quotation marks described in Chapter 4.)

In the Media

Apple Polishing

The idea here, we suppose, is to make the viewer think that he or she, too, like Sanford Biggers, is a connoisseur of fine cognac. This is photographic "apple polishing."

> The idea behind [talk radio] is to keep the base riled up.
>
> – Republican political advisor Brent Lauder, explaining what talk radio is for ["the base" refers to the Republican rank and file]

"Arguments" based on outrage are so common that the fallacy ranks high on our list of the top ten fallacies of all time, which is contained in Appendix 2. It's unfortunate they are so common—history demonstrates constantly that anger is a poor lens through which to view the world. Policies adopted in anger are seldom wise, as any parent will tell you who has laid down the law in a fit of anger.

SCARE TACTICS

George Wallace didn't just try to anger the crowds when he told them what Northern civil rights workers were up to; he tried to *scare* them. When people become angry or afraid, they don't think clearly. They follow blindly. Demagogues like Wallace like to dangle scary scenarios in front of people.

Trying to scare people into doing something or accepting a position is using **scare tactics.** One way this might be done is the George Wallace method—dangling a frightening picture in front of someone. A simpler method might be just to threaten the person, a special case of scare tactics known as **"argument" by force.** Either way, if the idea is to get people to substitute fear for reason and judgment when taking a position on an issue, it is a fallacy. Likewise, it is a fallacy to succumb to such techniques when others use them on us.

On Language

Rhetoric and Social Security

As we go to press with this edition, Social Security reform is one of the big continuing news stories. Our friends on the left say the president and his advisors are using *scare tactics* to make everyone think that if Social Security isn't overhauled it will become bankrupt before long. Using a *rhetorical explanation,* they say the real reason the president wants to "reform" Social Security is to destroy it. As far as they are concerned, "reform" is just a *euphemism* for "destroy" or "abolish."

Meantime, our conservative friends say that liberals are the ones using scare tactics, trying to convince the public that the president wants to do away with Social Security.

Who is right? One objective place to look at the facts of Social Security solvency is at the Web site of the Congressional Budget Office, which offers a nonpartisan analysis of the situation. You'll find it at http://www.cbo.gov/SocialSecurity.cfm

Fear can befuddle us as easily as can anger, and the mistakes that happen are similar in both instances. Wallace's listeners may not have noticed (or not cared) that Wallace didn't actually give them *proof* that civil rights workers were doing whatever it was he portrayed them as doing; the portrayal was its own evidence, you might say. When we are befuddled with fear, we may not notice we lack evidence that the scary scenario is real. Imagine someone talking about global warming: The speaker may paint a picture so alarming we don't notice that he or she doesn't provide evidence that global warming is actually happening. Or take gay marriages again. Someone might warn us of presumably dire consequences if gay people are allowed to marry—we'll be opening "Pandora's box"; marriage will become meaningless; homosexuality will become rampant; society will collapse—but he or she may issue these warnings without providing details as to why (or how) the consequences might actually come about. The consequences are so frightening they apparently don't need proof.

Fear of one thing, X, may also affect evaluation of an unrelated thing, Y. You have your eye on a nice house and are considering buying it, and then the real estate agent frightens you by telling you the seller has received other offers and will sell soon. Some people, in this situation, might overestimate what they really can afford to pay.

To avoid translating fear of one thing into an evaluation of some unrelated thing, we need to be clear on what issues our fears are relevant to. Legitimate warnings do not involve irrelevancies and do not qualify as scare tactics. "You should be careful of that snake—it's deadly poisonous" might be a scary thing to say to someone, but we don't make a mistake in reasoning when we say it, and neither does the other person if he or she turns and runs into the house. Suppose, however, that the Michelin tire people show an ad featuring a sweet (and vulnerable) baby in a ring of automobile tires. Showing pictures of car tires around infants will produce disquieting associations in any observer, and it wouldn't be unreasonable to check our tires when we see this ad. But the issue raised by the Michelin people is whether to buy *Michelin* tires, and the fear of injuring or killing a child by driving on unsafe tires does not bear on the question of *which* tires to buy. The Michelin ad isn't a legitimate warning; it's scare tactics.

OTHER FALLACIES BASED ON EMOTIONS

Other emotions work much like anger and fear as sources of mistakes in reasoning. *Compassion,* for example, is a fine thing to have. There is absolutely nothing wrong with feeling sorry for someone. But when feeling sorry for someone drives us to a position on an unrelated matter, the result is the fallacy known as **"argument" from pity.** We have a job that needs doing; Helen can barely support her starving children and needs work desperately. But does Helen have the skills we need? We may not care if she does; and if we don't, nobody can fault us for hiring her out of compassion. But feeling sorry for Helen may lead us to misjudge her skills or overestimate her abilities, and that is a mistake in reasoning. Her skills are what they are regardless of her need. Or, suppose you need a better grade in this course to get into law school or avoid academic disqualification or whatever. If you think you *deserve* or have *earned* a better grade because you need a better grade, or you try to get your instructor to think you deserve a better grade by trying to make him or her feel sorry for you, that's the "argument" from pity. Or, if you think someone *else* deserves a better grade because of the hardships he or she (or his or her parents) suffered, that's also the "argument" from pity.

Envy and *jealousy* can also confuse our thinking. Compassion, a desirable emotion, may tempt us to emphasize a person's good points; envy and jealousy tempt us to exaggerate someone's bad points. When we find fault with a person because of envy, we are guilty of the fallacy known as **"argument" from envy.** "Well, he may have a lot of money but he certainly has bad manners" would be an example of this if it is envy that prompts us to criticize him.

Pride, on the other hand, can lead us to exaggerate *our own* accomplishments and abilities and lead to our making other irrelevant judgments as well.

Real Life

Knee Operation Judged Useless

Fake surgery worked just as well in cases of osteoarthritis.

> Here we are doing all this surgery on people and it's all a sham.
>
> — Dr. Baruch Brody, Baylor College of Medicine

Wishful thinking—allowing our desires and hopes to color our beliefs and influence our judgment—is common indeed. A powerful illustration of wishful thinking is the placebo effect, where subjects perceive improvement in a medical condition when they receive what they think is a medication but in fact is an inactive substance. Even surgical procedures, apparently, are subject to a placebo effect, judging from a study of a popular and expensive knee operation for arthritis. People who have had this procedure swear by it as significantly reducing pain. But researchers at the Houston Veterans Affairs Medical Center and Baylor College of Medicine discovered that subjects who underwent placebo (fake) surgery said exactly the same thing. Furthermore, when they tested knee functions two years after the surgery the researchers discovered that the operation doesn't improve knee functions at all.

Source: *Sacramento Bee,* July 11, 2002. From *New York Times* News Service.

It especially makes us vulnerable to **apple polishing.** Moore recently sat on a jury in a criminal case involving alleged prostitution and pandering at a strip club; the defendant's attorney told the members of the jury it would take *"an unusually discerning jury"* to see that the law, despite its wording, wasn't really intended to apply to someone like his client. Ultimately the jury members did find with the defense, but let us hope it wasn't because the attorney flattered their ability to discern things. Allowing praise of oneself to substitute for judgment about the truth of a claim, or trying to get others to do this, as the lawyer did, is the apple polishing fallacy.

Feelings of *guilt* work similarly. "How could you not invite Trixie to your wedding? She would never do that to you and you know she must be very hurt." The remark is intended to make someone feel sorry for Trixie, but even more fundamentally it is supposed to induce a sense of guilt. Eliciting feelings of guilt to get others to do or not do something, or to accept the view that they should or should not do it, is popularly known as putting a **guilt trip** on someone, which is to commit a fallacy. Parents sometimes use this tactic with children when they (the parents) won't (or can't) offer a clear explanation of why something should or shouldn't be done. Certainly, if the child knowingly does something wrong, he or she should feel guilty; but whatever has been done isn't wrong *because* he or she feels guilty.

Hopes, desires, and aversions can also lead us astray logically. The fallacy known as **wishful thinking** happens when we accept or urge acceptance (or rejection) of a claim simply because it would be pleasant (or unpleasant) if it were true. Some people, for example, may believe in God simply on the basis of wishful thinking or desire for an afterlife. A smoker may refuse to acknowledge the health hazards of smoking. We've had students who are in denial about the consequences of cutting classes. The wishful thinking fallacy also

Real Life

Positive Outlook Won't Delay Cancer Death, Study Says

NICE, France — New research has dealt a blow to the idea that a positive outlook might improve a patient's chances of surviving cancer, scientists said Saturday.

However, experts said it is still worthwhile for patients to improve their attitude, perhaps by joining a cancer support group, because often it does make them feel better.

The findings were presented Saturday at a meeting of the European Society of Medical Oncology in Nice, France. The researchers reviewed evidence to determine whether psychologist-run support groups kept patients alive.

"There were some studies out there showing that positive-thinking type of support will not only improve your quality of life—which undoubtedly it does, I'm not questioning that—but also will prolong the lives of cancer patients," said Dr. Edzard Ernst, a professor of complementary medicine at the University of Exeter in England who led the study.

"One study from 1989 gets cited over and over and over again, and we knew there were one or two negative studies on this, too, so we decided to see if it was true," he said.

The researchers analyzed 11 studies that included a total of 1,500 patients.

"The data provided no evidence at all to show that these types of approaches prolong life in cancer patients," Ernst said.

— *Associated Press*

More wishful thinking, apparently.

Source: *Sacramento Bee*, October 19, 2002.

underlies much of the empty rhetoric of "positive thinking"—rhetoric that claims "you are what you want to be" and other such slogans. As obvious (and as obviously fallacious) as it may appear when you read about it here, wishful thinking can be a powerful influence and can sometimes defeat all but our most committed efforts to do the rational thing.

Most people desire to be liked or accepted by some circle of other people and are averse to having the acceptance withdrawn. A *desire for acceptance* can motivate us to accept a claim not because of its merits, but because we will gain someone's approval (or will avoid having approval withdrawn). When we do this, or try to get someone else to do it, the fallacy is the **peer pressure "argument."** Now, obviously nobody ever said anything quite so blatant as "Ralph, this claim is true because we won't like you any more if you don't accept it." Peer pressure is often disguised or unstated, but anyone going through an American high school, where you can lose social standing merely by being seen with someone who isn't "in," knows it is a real force. Kids who feel ostracized sometimes take guns to school.

It doesn't have to be one's associates who exert peer pressure, either. In scientific experiments, people will actually revise what they say they saw if a group of strangers in the same room deny having seen the same thing.

One very common fallacy that is closely related to the peer pressure "argument" involves one's sense of *group identification,* which people experience when they are part of a group—a team, a club, a school, a gang, a state, a nation, the Elks, Wal-Mart, the U.S.A., Mauritius, you name it. Let's define the **group think fallacy** as happening when one substitutes pride of membership in a group for reason and deliberation in arriving at a position on an issue; and let's include the fallacy in our list of the top ten fallacies of all time, because it is exceedingly common. One obvious form of this fallacy involves national pride, or **nationalism**—a powerful and fierce emotion that can lead to blind endorsement of a country's policies and practices. ("My country right or wrong" explicitly discourages critical thinking and encourages blind patriotism.) Nationalism is also invoked to reject, condemn, or silence criticism of one's country as unpatriotic or treasonable (and may or may not involve an element of peer pressure). If a letter writer expresses a criticism of America on the opinion page of your local newspaper on Monday, you can bet that by the end of the week there will be a response dismissing the criticism with the "argument" that if so-and-so doesn't like it here, he or she ought to move to Russia (or Cuba or Afghanistan or Iraq).

This "Patriotism Bear" is all decked out with flags, medals, and patches. He sells for $119.99 from Dollsville on the Web. There are a lot of people out to cash in on the patriotism bandwagon.

Group think does not play cultural or political favorites, either. On the opposite side of the political spectrum are what some people call the "blame America first" folks. The group think ethic of this club includes, most importantly, automatically assuming that whatever is wrong in the world is the result of some U.S. policy. The club has no formal meetings or rules for membership, but flying an American flag would be grounds for derision and instant dismissal.

Group think "reasoning" is certainly not limited to political groups either. It occurs whenever one's affiliations are of utmost psychological importance.

Now, these various emotional fallacies, from the "argument" from outrage to the group think fallacy, all share certain properties. They often (though not always) contain assertions you might call "premises" and other assertions that you might call a "conclusion." But the "premises" don't actually *support* the "conclusion"; rather, they evoke emotions that make us want to accept the conclusion without support. So, although they can wear the clothing of *arguments,* they are really pieces of *persuasion* (Chapter 1). Whenever language is used to arouse emotions, it is wise to consider carefully whether any "conclusions" that come to mind have been supported by evidence.

RATIONALIZING

Let's say Mr. Smith decides to do something really nice for his wife on her birthday and buys her a new table saw. "This saw wasn't cheap," he tells her. "But you're going to be glad we have it, because it will keep me out in the garage and out of your way when you're working here in the house."

The fallacy in the reasoning in this made-up example is pretty obvious. Mr. Smith is confusing his wife's desires with his own.

When we do this, when we use a false pretext to satisfy our own desires or interests, we're guilty of **rationalizing,** a very common fallacy. It almost made our list of the top ten fallacies of all time (Appendix 2).

Now, there is nothing wrong with satisfying one's desires, at least if they don't harm someone or aren't illegal. But in this book we're talking logic, not morals. Rationalizing involves a confusion in thinking, and to the extent we wish to avoid being confused in our thinking, we should try to avoid rationalizing.

"But," you may be saying, "It is good to do nice things for other people. If you do something that helps them, or that they like, or that benefits the world, what difference does motivation make? If, for whatever reason, the table saw makes Mr. Smith's wife happy, that's what counts."

Now, there is something to be said for this argument, because it is good to make people happy. But whether Mr. Smith's wife is happy or not, there has been a confusion in his thinking, a fallacy. And it is a common fallacy indeed. Obviously most instances of rationalizing are not as blatant as Mr. Smith's, but people frequently deceive themselves as to their true motives.

Rationalizing need not be selfish, either. Let's say a former oilman is elected governor of a state that produces oil. He may act in what at some level he thinks are the best interests of his state—when in fact he is motivated by a desire to help the oil industry. (Incidentally, you can't just assume he would do this.) To the extent he is deceiving himself about his true motivation, he is rationalizing. But this isn't *selfish* rationalizing; his actions don't benefit him personally.

Rationalizing, then, involves an element of self-deception, but otherwise it isn't necessarily devious. However, some people encourage others to rationalize because they themselves stand to benefit in some way. "Hey, Smith," his buddy Jones says to him. "That's a fine idea! Really creative. Your wife will really like a saw. Maybe you could build a boat for her, and you and I could go fishing." Jones may or may not say this innocently: If he does, he too is guilty of rationalizing; if he doesn't, he's just cynical.

EVERYONE KNOWS . . .

In Chapter 4, we examined proof surrogates like "Everyone knows . . ." and "It's only common sense that. . . ." Phrases like this are used when a speaker or writer doesn't really have an argument.

Such phrases often appear in peer pressure "arguments" ("Pardner, in these parts everyone thinks. . . ."). They also are used in the group think fallacy ("As any red-blooded American patriot knows, . . .). There is, however, a third way these phrases can be used. An example would be when Robert Novak says on CNN's *Crossfire,* "Liberals are finally admitting what everyone knows, that airline safety demands compromise." Novak isn't applying or evoking peer pressure or group think; he is offering "proof" that airline safety demands compromise (and bad-mouthing liberals to boot). His proof is the fact that everyone knows it.

When we do this, when we urge someone to accept a claim (or fall prey to someone's doing it to us) simply on the grounds that all or most or some substantial number of people (other than authorities or experts, of course) believe it, we commit the fallacy known as the **"argument" from popularity.**

Real Life

The Great White Van

While searching for the serial sniper who terrorized the Washington, D.C., area in the fall of 2002, police encountered the suspects' blue Chevrolet Caprice several times in road checkpoints and once with the sniper asleep in the car on a side street in Baltimore. However, the vehicle did not arouse police suspicions, apparently because it did not fit the beliefs that were forming in the case. As one senior government official put it, everyone was focused on finding an angry white guy in a white van. A witness had reported seeing a white van fleeing a shooting, and then other witnesses at other shootings began to see a white van, too. (One report even turned out to have been fabricated.) One eyewitness did report seeing a fleeing Caprice, but the Caprice sighting just didn't catch on. By the end of the case, the white van theory had gained so much momentum that another person who saw a Caprice didn't file a report until after the suspects were apprehended. He said he assumed the sniper's vehicle was a white van. *Time* magazine even printed a picture of the white van the police were looking for.

In Chapter 3, we pointed out how eyewitness accounts can be untrustworthy. Here, we see the influence of popular belief.

That most people believe something is a fact is not evidence that it is a fact—most people believe in God, for example, but that isn't evidence that God exists. Likewise, if most people didn't believe in God, that wouldn't be evidence that God doesn't exist.

Most people seem to assume that bus driving and similar jobs are somehow less desirable than white-collar jobs. The widespread acceptance of this assumption creates its own momentum—that is, we tend to accept it because everybody else does, and we don't stop to think about whether it actually has anything to recommend it. For a lot of people, a job driving a bus might make for a much happier life than a job as a manager.

In *some* instances, we should point out, what people think actually *determines* what is true. The meanings of most words, for example, are determined by popular usage. In addition, it would not be fallacious to conclude that the word "ain't" is out of place in formal speech because most speakers of English believe that it is out of place in formal speech.

There are other cases where what people think is an *indication* of what is true, even if it cannot *determine* truth. If several Bostonians of your acquaintance think that it is illegal to drink beer in their public parks, then you have some reason for thinking that it's true. And if you are told by several Europeans that it is not gauche to eat with your fork in your left hand in Europe, then it is not fallacious to conclude that European manners allow eating with your fork in your left hand. The situation here is one of credibility, which we discussed in Chapter 3. Natives of Boston in the first case and Europeans in the second case can be expected to know more about the two claims in question, respectively, than others know. In a watered-down sense, they are "experts" on the subjects, at least in ways that many of us are not. In general, when the "everyone" who thinks that X is true includes experts about X, then what they think is indeed a good reason to accept X.

Thus it would be incorrect to automatically label as a fallacy any instance in which a person cites people's beliefs to establish a point. (No "argument" fitting a pattern in this chapter should *unthinkingly* be dismissed.) But it is important to view such references to people's beliefs as red alerts. These are cautionary signals that warn you to look closely for genuine reasons in support of the claim asserted.

Two variations of the "argument" from popularity deserve mention: **"Argument" from common practice** consists in trying to justify or defend an *action* or *practice* (as distinguished from an assertion or claim) on the grounds that it is common. "I shouldn't get a speeding ticket because everyone drives over the limit" would be an example. "Everyone cheats on their taxes, so I don't see why I shouldn't" would be another. Now there is something to watch out for here: When a person defends an action by saying that other people do the same thing, he or she might just be requesting fair play. He or she might just be saying, in effect, "OK, OK, I know it's wrong, but nobody else gets punished and it would be unfair to single me out." That person isn't trying to justify the action; he or she is asking for equal treatment.

The other variant of the argument from popularity is the **"argument" from tradition,** a name that is self-explanatory. People do things because that's the way things have always been done, and they believe things because that's what people have always believed. But, logically speaking, you don't prove a claim or prove a practice is legitimate on the basis of tradition; when you try to do so, you are guilty of "argument" from tradition. The fact that it's a tradition among most American children to believe in Santa Claus, for instance, doesn't prove Santa Claus exists; and the fact it's also a tradition for most American parents to deceive their kids about Santa Claus doesn't necessarily mean it is okay for them to do so. Where we teach, there has been a long tradition of fraternity hazing, and over the years several unfortunate hazing incidents have happened. We have yet to hear a defense of hazing that amounted to anything other than an "argument" from tradition, which is equivalent to saying we haven't heard a defense at all.

SUBJECTIVISM AGAIN

If somebody tells you sandpaper is slippery, you'll conclude one or more of the following:

1. This guy doesn't know what sandpaper is.
2. He doesn't know what "slippery" means.
3. He's using some kind of oddball metaphor.
4. He's on drugs.

In Chapter 1, we talked about subjectivism, the idea that each person's opinion is as good as the next person's, or the notion that thinking a claim is true makes it true. A big problem with subjectivism is that it fails to respect the rules of common language. You can assign a word any meaning you want, but it takes more than one person to make that meaning a part of language. Within language, some phrases, like "tastes great," or "that's cool!" can be used pretty much as you please. But other expressions are bound by fairly rigid rules; you can't just call any old thing sandpaper and expect people to understand you. Words like "slippery" are somewhere in the middle. "Slippery" has a subjective element that permits a broad range of application, but there are constraints. Sandpaper and campfires, for example, aren't slippery, and thinking that either of them is slippery doesn't make it so. Reasonable people might disagree as to whether your driveway is slippery after rain, but if your driveway is covered with ice, anyone who thought it wasn't slippery would be dreaming.

Plus, subjectivism is problematic because people just get their facts wrong. If you tell the doorman you are over 21 or under 40, he may believe you, but that won't make you over 21 or under 40 if you aren't.

Where subjectivism gets traction and enjoys a measure of popularity is when it comes to moral value judgments.* Some people find it wildly attractive to think that whether or not something is morally good or morally bad is purely a matter of subjective opinion. In our municipal park, there is a disk golf course, where you play golf with Frisbees. Recently, somebody took a chain saw to a tree in the golf course and used the tree as a dirt bike ramp. Perhaps the culprit thought the act was a good thing, or at any rate didn't think there was anything wrong with cutting down the tree; others disagreed. It is easy enough in a case like this to think, well, everyone is entitled to his or her own opinion. But if someone maintained there is nothing wrong with blinding toddlers or pets to see how they react, it would be clear this person doesn't understand right and wrong. We discussed subjectivism in Chapter 1: Thinking sandpaper is slippery just doesn't make it so; thinking the driveway is slippery might make it so in some instances; thinking someone is 21 never makes it so; and thinking something is morally acceptable, if it ever makes it so, doesn't always make it so.

Thus, it is probably best to think of subjectivism as a half-baked piece of philosophy, rather than as a "fallacy." Yes, some expressions, by common

*See Chapter 13 for a definition; or check the glossary.

agreement, can be used as you please. But not all expressions are like that, and not every claim you think is true is made true by the fact you think it is.

THE RELATIVIST FALLACY

Relativism is the idea that one culture's or society's opinion is as good as the next, and that a society/culture's thinking a claim is true makes it true in that society/culture. It's by no means clear what constitutes a "culture" or a "society," but adherents of relativism tend to think of this as a niggling theoretical detail, and we won't go into it. Certainly there is a point at which the beliefs, attitudes, and habits of two societies are so different that the two must be regarded as different cultures, but there are also borderline cases. Are blue states and red states different cultures? In some ways, yes, and in some ways, no. Is NASCAR racing a separate culture? We won't comment.

Very few people are relativists about every sort of claim. A water molecule consists of two atoms of hydrogen and one atom of oxygen, and if you assemble enough water molecules, you have a substance that does not flow uphill. If people on some island in the world speak English but don't believe water consists of hydrogen and oxygen, you'd figure they lack science. You'd forgive them, but they'd be mistaken nevertheless. You would not say, well, in America water consists of hydrogen and oxygen, but on your island maybe it doesn't. If they said, water flows uphill, you'd probably not know what to think; perhaps the island has unusual geophysical properties? But if you both look at the same creek, say, and you think the water is flowing downhill and they think it is flowing uphill, you'd conclude they had reversed the meanings of "uphill" and "downhill."

Which, of course, is possible. For instance, within certain hip English-speaking subcultures, it became common to use the word "bad" to denote a desirable quality, so "That's bad" meant what members of the British royal family and others still mean by "That's good." We the authors don't use "bad" this way. If one of us won the lottery, the other would not say, "Man, that's bad." But a community of speakers can develop its own system of shared meanings, obviously.

Likewise a community can have its own moral standards. It is here that relativism has its main appeal. Different societies not infrequently have different standards of acceptable behavior. For example, most societies do not approve of slavery or human sacrifice, but certainly there are societies that once did; maybe some still do. Clearly one part of American society views homosexual activity as seriously immoral; another part clearly doesn't. Members of the Taliban reportedly think it is good to keep women out of schools; red-state cultures and blue-state cultures are united in not sharing that view. Cross-cultural clashes of values are undeniable, and it can seem presumptuous to tell another society its standards are incorrect.

However, being presumptuous is not the same as being illogical. What is illogical is to think that a standard of your society applies universally, while simultaneously maintaining that it doesn't apply to societies that don't accept that standard. Unfortunately, relativists are sometimes guilty of just this confusion, and you occasionally hear statements like this:

> Well, I think bullfighting is wrong, but other cultures don't think so, and who am I to tell them what to believe? If they think there is

> nothing wrong with bullfighting, then I guess it isn't wrong for them to have bullfights.

We hope you can see that this paragraph is self-contradictory: The person is saying, in effect, that he or she thinks it is wrong to have bullfights, *and* that he or she thinks it isn't wrong for some people to have bullfights. You can think that whether bullfighting is wrong depends on what a culture thinks, *or* you can subscribe to what your culture thinks, but you can't do both.

This bit of inconsistency we shall call the **relativist fallacy**. To repeat the formula, the relativist fallacy consists in thinking a moral standard of your own group applies universally while simultaneously maintaining that it doesn't apply to groups that don't accept the standard. This is like saying that water is made out of oxygen and hydrogen but in Ethiopia it isn't made out of oxygen and hydrogen. If you think human sacrifice is wrong period, then you cannot also say it isn't wrong in some parts of the world.

Applying this to a more likely example, consider someone who says the following, or something that equates to it:

> Well, I think it is wrong to force women to wear veils, but other societies don't, and since they are entitled to their opinions as much as we are, it isn't wrong to force women in those societies to wear veils.

If "they are entitled to their opinion as much as we are" means "their opinion is just as correct as ours," then the passage commits the relativist fallacy.

TWO WRONGS MAKE A RIGHT

Let's say you get tired of the people upstairs stomping around late at night, and so, to retaliate, you rent a tow truck and deposit their car in the river. From an emotional standpoint, you're getting even. From a reasoning standpoint, you're committing the fallacy known as **"two wrongs make a right."** It's a fallacy because wrongful behavior on someone else's part doesn't convert wrongful behavior on your part into rightful behavior, any more than illegal behavior on someone else's part converts your illegal activity into legal activity. If an act is wrong, it is wrong. Wrong acts don't cross-pollinate such that one comes out shorn of wrongfulness.

However, there is a well-known and somewhat widely held theory known as *retributivism,* according to which it is acceptable to harm someone in return for a harm he or she has done to you. But we must distinguish legitimate punishment from illegitimate retaliation. A fallacy clearly occurs when we

"Yes, yes, I *know* that, Sidney—*every*body knows *that!* ... But look: Four wrongs *squared*, minus two wrongs to the fourth power, divided by this formula, *do* make a right."

consider a wrong to be justification for *any* retaliatory action, as would be the case if you destroyed your neighbors' car because they made too much noise at night. It is also a fallacy when the second wrong is directed at someone who didn't do the wrong in the first place—a brother or a child of the wrongdoer, for example. And it is a fallacy to defend doing harm to another on the grounds that that individual *would* or *might* do the same to us. This would happen, for example, if we didn't return excess change to a salesclerk on the grounds that "if the situation were reversed," the clerk wouldn't have given us back the money.

On the other hand, it isn't a fallacy to defend an action on the grounds it was necessary to prevent harm from befalling oneself; bopping a mugger to prevent him from hurting you would be an instance. To take another example, near the end of World War II, the United States dropped two atomic bombs on Japanese cities, killing tens of thousands of civilians. Politicians, historians, and others have argued that the bombing was justified because it helped end the war and thus prevented more casualties from the fighting, including the deaths of more Americans. People have long disagreed on whether the argument provides *sufficient* justification for the bombings, but there is no disagreement about its being a real argument and not empty rhetoric.

RED HERRING/SMOKESCREEN

When a person brings a topic into a conversation that distracts from the original point, especially if the new topic is introduced in order to distract, the person is said to have introduced a **red herring.** (It is so called because dragging a herring across a trail will cause a dog to leave the original trail and follow the path of the herring.) In the strip-joint jury trial we mentioned earlier, the defendant was charged with pandering; but the prosecuting attorney introduced evidence that the defendant had also sold liquor to minors. That was a red herring that had nothing to do with pandering.

The difference between red herrings and their close relatives, **smokescreens,** is subtle (and really not a matter of crucial importance). Generally speaking, red herrings distract by pulling one's attention away from one topic and toward another; smokescreens tend to pile issues on or to make them extremely complicated until the original is lost in the (verbal) "smoke." When Bill Clinton had missiles fired at terrorists in Sudan, he was accused of creating a red herring to deflect public scrutiny from the Monica Lewinsky business. When George W. Bush talked about Iraq having missiles capable of threatening the United States, about that country's potential of having a nuclear weapon "within six months," and about similar possible Iraqi threats, he was accused of putting up a smokescreen to hide his real reasons for wanting to attack Iraq, which were said to be oil interests and his own personal desire to complete his father's unfinished business.

We admit that this measure is popular. But we also urge you to note that there are so many bond issues on this ballot that the whole concept is getting ridiculous.

– A generic red herring (unclassifiable irrelevance) from a California ballot pamphlet

Let's look at another example, this one made up but fairly typical of what often happens. Let's say a reporter asks Michael Chertoff (secretary of the Department of Homeland Security) whether his office has made the country substantially safer from attacks by terrorists. "I'm pleased to say," Chertoff answers, "that the United States is the safest country in the world when it comes to terrorist attacks. Certainly nobody can give an absolute, one hundred percent guarantee of safety, but you are certainly safer here than in any other country of the world."

In the Media

A Red Herring in a Letter to *Time*

> *Time*'s coverage of the medical marijuana controversy was thoughtful and scrupulously researched. But what argues most persuasively for a ban on marijuana is the extraordinary threat the drug poses for adolescents. Marijuana impairs short-term memory, depletes energy and impedes acquisition of psychosocial skills. Perhaps the most chilling effect is that it retards maturation for young people. A significant number of kids who use lots of pot simply don't grow up. So it is hardly surprising that marijuana is the primary drug for more than half the youngsters in the long-term residential substance-abuse programs that Phoenix House operates throughout the country.
>
> — MITCHELL S. ROSENTHAL, M.D.
> President, Phoenix House
> New York City

The issue is legalization of marijuana for *adults;* the question of what it would do to children, who presumably would be prohibited from its use, is a red herring.

Source: *Time,* November 28, 2002

Chertoff has steered clear of the original question (whether his agency had made the country safer) and is leading the reporter on a tangent, toward the comparative safety of the United States (the United States may already have been the safest country before the creation of the agency). He has dragged a red herring across the trail, so to speak.

Imagine the conversation continues this way:

Reporter: "Mr. Chertoff, polls say about half of the public think your agency has failed to make them safer. How do you answer your critics?"

Michael Chertoff: "We are making progress toward reassuring people, but quite frankly our efforts have been hampered by the tendency of the press to concentrate on the negative side of the issue."

Once again Chertoff brings in a red herring to sidestep the issue raised by the reporter.

Whether a distraction or an obfuscation is a plain red herring or a smokescreen is often difficult to tell in real life, and it's better to spend your energy getting a discussion back on track rather than worrying which type you have before you.

Many of the other fallacies we have been discussing in this chapter (and will be discussing in the next chapter) qualify, in some version or other, as red herrings/smokescreens. For example, a defense attorney might talk about a defendant's miserable upbringing to steer a jury's attention away from the charges against the person; doing this would qualify as an argument from pity as well as a smokescreen/red herring. Likewise, a prosecuting attorney may try to get a jury so angry about a crime it doesn't notice the weakness of the evidence pointing to the defendant. This would be an argument from outrage—and a red herring.

Good point. Anyone know of a hospital or highway built by Rush Limbaugh or an automobile invented by him?

Could somebody please show me one hospital built by a dolphin? Could somebody show me one highway built by a dolphin? Could someone show me one automobile invented by a dolphin?

— RUSH LIMBAUGH, responding to the *New York Times*' claim that dolphins' "behavior and enormous brains suggest an intelligence approaching that of human beings."

To simplify things, your instructor may reserve the red herring/smokescreen categories for irrelevancies that don't qualify as one of the other fallacies mentioned in this or the next chapter. In other words, he or she may tell you that if something qualifies as, say, an argument from outrage, you should call it that rather than a red herring or smokescreen.

Recap

In an interview with CNN's Connie Chung (photo below), tennis champion Martina Navratilova asserted that when she left Communist Czechoslovakia for the United States she changed one system that suppresses free opinion for another. Connie Chung told Navratilova to go ahead and think that at home, but asserted that celebrities shouldn't "spill out" such thoughts in public, because "people will write it down and talk about what you said." (Chung thus ineptly confirmed the very point Navratilova was making.)

One can only speculate as to what exactly was going on in Connie Chung's head, if anything. Maybe she was worried that Navratilova's comment would make people think bad things about the United States. Maybe she thinks the tennis star's comment is unpatriotic. Maybe criticism of the United States just upsets her. Whatever her thoughts, the example nicely illustrates what we have been talking about in this chapter. Sometimes, instead of bringing forth considerations relevant to an issue, people give an unrelated "argument." Many of the fallacies we have examined are like Connie Chung's: The unrelated argument involves some kind of emotion, though it may be hard to pin down exactly what it is.

- "Argument" from outrage
- Scare tactics
- "Argument" by force
- "Argument" from pity
- "Argument" from envy
- Apple polishing
- Guilt trip
- Wishful thinking
- Peer pressure "argument"
- Group think fallacy
- Nationalism

Other fallacies discussed in this chapter don't invoke emotions directly, but are closely related to emotional appeals. These include

- Rationalization
- "Argument" from popularity
- "Argument" from common practice
- "Argument" from tradition
- Subjectivism
- Relativist fallacy
- Two wrongs make a right
- Red herring/smokescreen

In all these specimens, there is something one might call a "premise" and something one might call a "conclusion," but the "premise" either fails to support the conclusion or "supports" some tangential claim. In any case, a mistake in reasoning has been made, a fallacy has been committed.

Exercises

In the exercises that follow, we ask you to name fallacies, and your instructor may do the same on an exam.

Exercise 5-1

Working in groups, invent a simple, original, and clear illustration of each type of fallacy covered in this chapter. Then, in the class as a whole, select the illustrations that are clearest and most straightforward. Go over these illustrations before doing the remaining exercises in this chapter, and review them before you take a test on this material.

Exercise 5-2

Identify any instances of fallacies that occur in the following passages, either by naming them or, where you think they do not conform to any of the patterns we have described, by explaining in one or two sentences why the "argument" is irrelevant to the point at issue. (There are a few passages that contain no fallacies. Be sure you don't find one where none exist!)

▲ 1. The tax system in this country is unfair and ridiculous! Just ask anyone!

2. SHE: I think it was exceedingly boorish of you to finish off the last of their expensive truffles like that.
HE: Bosh. They certainly would have done the same to us, if given the chance.

3. Overheard:
"Hmmmm. Nice day. Think I'll go catch some rays."
"Says here in this magazine that doing that sort of thing is guaranteed to get you a case of skin cancer."

"Yeah, I've heard that, too. I think it's a bunch of baloney, personally. If that were true, you wouldn't be able to do anything—no tubing, skiing, nothing. You wouldn't even be able to just plain lay out in the sun. Ugh!"

▲ **4.** I've come before you to ask that you rehire Professor Johnson. I realize that Mr. Johnson does not have a Ph.D., and I am aware that he has yet to publish his first article. But Mr. Johnson is over forty now, and he has a wife and two high-school-aged children to support. It will be very difficult for him to find another teaching job at his age, I'm sure you will agree.

5. JUAN: But, Dad, I like Horace. Why shouldn't I room with him, anyway?
JUAN'S DAD: Because I'll cut off your allowance, that's why!

6. That snake has markings like a coral snake. Coral snakes are deadly poisonous, so you'd better leave it alone!

▲ **7.** DEMOCRAT: What do you think of the president's new plan for Social Security?
REPUBLICAN: I think it is pretty good, as a matter of fact.
DEMOCRAT: Oh? And why is that?
REPUBLICAN: Because you Democrats haven't even offered a plan, that's why!

8. The animal rights people shouldn't pick on rodeos. If they'd come out and see the clowns put smiles on kids' faces and see horses buck off the cowboys and hear the crowd go "ooh" and "ahh" at the bull riding, why then they'd change their minds.

9. HE: Tell you what. Let's get some ice cream for a change. Sunrise Creamery has the best—let's go there.
SHE: Not that old dump! What makes you think their ice cream is so good, anyway?
HE: Because it is. Besides, that old guy who owns it never gets any business any more. Every time I go by the place I see him in there all alone, just staring out the window, waiting for a customer. He can't help it that he's in such an awful location. I'm sure he couldn't afford to move.

▲ **10.** Student speaker: "Why, student fees have jumped by more than 300 percent in just two years! This is outrageous! The governor is working for a balanced budget, but it'll be on the backs of us students, the people who have the very least to spend! It seems pretty clear that these increased student fees are undermining higher education in this state. Anybody who isn't mad about this just doesn't understand the situation."

11. "Jim, I'm very disappointed you felt it necessary to talk to the media about the problems here in the department. When you join the FBI, you join a family, and you shouldn't want to embarrass your family."

▲ **12.** "I think it is wrong for anyone to mistreat animals, but in that society, they apparently don't think so, so I guess it is okay for them to do so."

▲ **13.** A fictitious Western governor: "Yes, I have indeed accepted $550,000 in campaign contributions from power companies. But as I stand here before you, I can guarantee you that not one dime of that money has affected any decision I've made. I make decisions based on data, not on donors."

14. "If you ask me, you are making a mistake to break up with Rasheed. Have you forgotten how he stood by you when you needed him last year? Is this how you repay him?"

15. "What? You aren't a Cornhuskers fan? Listen, around here *everybody* is for the Huskers! This is Nebraska!"

Exercise 5-3

Answer the following questions and explain your answers.

▲ 1. A brand of toothpaste is advertised as best-selling. How relevant is that to whether to buy the brand?

2. A brand of toothpaste is best-selling. How relevant is that to whether to buy that brand?

▲ 3. An automobile is a best-seller in its class. How relevant is that to whether to buy that kind of automobile?

4. A movie is a smash hit. Would that influence your opinion of it? Should it?

5. Your friends are all Republicans. Would that influence your decision on with which party to register? Should it?

6. Your friends are all Democrats. Would that influence what you say about Democrats to them? Should it?

▲ 7. Your friend's father wrote a novel. How relevant is that to whether you should say nice things about the book to your friend?

8. Your friend's mother is running for office. How relevant is that to whether you should vote for her?

9. Your own mother is running for office. How relevant is that to whether she will do a good job? To whether you should vote for her?

▲ 10. Movie critic Roger Ebert gives a movie a thumbs up and calls it one of the best of the year. How relevant is this to whether you should go see the movie?

Exercise 5-4

Which of the following do you believe? Which of the following do you *really* have evidence for? Which of the following do you believe on an "everyone knows" basis? Discuss your answers with other members of your class.

1. Small dogs tend to live longer than large dogs.
2. Coffee has a dehydrating effect.
3. Most people should drink at least eight glasses of water a day.
4. If you are thirsty, it means you are already dehydrated.
5. Rape is not about sex; it's about aggression.
6. Marijuana use leads to addiction to harder drugs.
7. The news media are biased.

8. You get just as much ultraviolet radiation on a cloudy day as on a sunny day.
9. If you don't let yourself get angry every now and then, your anger will build up to the exploding point.
10. Carrots make you see better.
11. Reading in poor light is bad for your eyes.
12. Sitting too close to the TV is bad for your eyes.
13. Warm milk makes you sleepy.
14. Covering your head is the most effective way of staying warm in cold weather.
15. Smoking a cigarette takes seven minutes off your life.

Exercise 5-5

For each of the passages that follow, determine whether fallacies are present and, if so, whether they fit the categories described in this chapter.

▲ 1. Boss to employee: "I'll be happy to tell you why this report needs to be finished by Friday. If it isn't ready by then, you'll be looking for another job. How's that for a reason?"

2. Mother: "I think he has earned an increase in his allowance. He doesn't have any spending money at all, and he's always having to make excuses about not being able to go out with the rest of his friends because of that."

3. Mother to father: "You know, I really believe that our third-grader's friend Joe comes from an impoverished family. He looks to me as though he doesn't get enough to eat. I think I'm going to start inviting him to have dinner at our house once or twice a week."

▲ 4. "Aw, c'mon, Jake, let's go hang out at Dave's. Don't worry about your parents; they'll get over it. You know, the one thing I really like about you is that you don't let your parents tell you what to do."

5. FIRST PERSON: You know, I might not agree with it, but I could understand it if a society decided to look down on a woman who had a child out of wedlock. But stoning to death? My God, that's barbaric and hideously immoral!
SECOND PERSON: But remember that you come from a background much different from that of the people in that part of Nigeria. It's less immoral in that situation. Besides, in Iran stoning to death has been a common punishment for adultery under the current regime.

6. FRED: I think we should just buy the new truck and call it a business expense so we can write it off on our taxes.
ETHEL: I don't know, Fred. That sounds like cheating to me. We wouldn't really use the truck very much in the business, you know.
FRED: Oh, don't worry about it. This kind of thing is done all the time.

▲ 7. I'm going to use the textbook that's on reserve in the library. I'll have to spend more time on the campus, but it's sure better than shelling out over a hundred bucks for one book.

8. Imagine yourself alone beside your broken-down car at the side of a country road in the middle of the night. Few pass by and no one stops to help. Don't get caught like that—don't get caught without your Polytech cellular phone!

9. One political newcomer to another: "I tell you, Sam, you'd better change those liberal views of yours. The general slant toward conservatism is obvious. You'll be left behind unless you change your mind about some things."

▲ 10. Reporter COKIE ROBERTS: Mr. Cheney, aside from the legal issues that stem from the various United Nations resolutions, isn't there an overriding moral dimension to the suffering of so many Kurdish people in Iraq?
DICK CHENEY: Well, we recognize that's a tragic situation, Cokie, but there are tragic situations occurring all over the world.
— *Adapted from an interview on National Public Radio's* Morning Edition

Exercise 5-6

For each of the passages that follow, determine whether fallacies are present and, if so, whether they fit the categories described in this chapter.

▲ 1. "Grocers are concerned about *sanitation problems* from beverage residue that Proposition 11 could create. Filthy returned cans and bottles—*over 11 billion a year*—don't belong in grocery stores, where our food is stored and sold. . . . Sanitation problems in other states with similar laws have caused increased use of *chemical sprays* in grocery stores to combat rodents and insects. Vote no on 11."
— *Argument against Proposition 11, California ballot pamphlet*

2. Schwarzenegger? You are going to vote for *Arnold Schwarzenegger*? And you expect me to *marry* you after you say that?

3. STUDENT: I think I deserve a better grade than this on the second question.
PROF: Could be. Why do you think so?
STUDENT: You think my answer's wrong.
PROF: Well, your answer *is* wrong.
STUDENT: Maybe you think so, but I don't. You can't mark me wrong just because my answer doesn't fit your opinion.

▲ 4. C'mon, George, the river's waiting and everyone's going to be there. You want me to tell 'em you're gonna worry on Saturday about a test you don't take 'til Tuesday? What're people going to think?

5. ATTENDANT: I'm sorry, sir, but we don't allow people to top off their gas tanks here in Kansas. There's a state law against it, you know.
RICHARD: What? You've got to be kidding! I've never heard of a place that stopped people from doing that!

6. One roommate to another: "I'm telling you, Ahmed, you shouldn't take Highway 50 this weekend. In this weather, it's going to be icy and dangerous. Somebody slides off that road and gets killed nearly every winter. And you don't even have any chains for your car!"

▲ 7. That, in sum, is my proposal, ladies and gentlemen. You know that I trust and value your judgment, and I am aware I could not find a more astute panel of experts to evaluate my suggestion. Thank you.

8. JARED: In Sweden, atheists and agnostics outnumber believers 2 to 1, and in Germany, less than half the population believes in God. Here in the United States, though, over 80 percent believe in God. I wonder what makes the States so different.
ALICE: You've answered your own question. If I didn't believe in God, I'd feel like I stuck out like a sore thumb.

9. Businessman to partner: "I'm glad Brownell has some competition these days. That means when we take estimates for the new job, we can simply ignore his, no matter what it is. That'll teach him a lesson for not throwing any business our way last year."

▲ **10.** One local to another: "I tell you, it's disgusting. These idiot college students come up here and live for four years—and ruin the town—and then vote on issues that affect us long after they've gone. This has got to stop! I say, let only those who have a real stake in the future of this town vote here! Transient kids shouldn't determine what's going to happen to local residents. Most of these kids come from Philadelphia . . . let them vote there."

Exercise 5-7

For each of the passages that follow, determine whether fallacies are present and, if so, whether they fit the categories described in this chapter.

▲ **1.** Chair, Department of Rhetoric (to department faculty): "If you think about it, I'm certain you'll agree with me that Mary Smith is the best candidate for department secretary. I urge you to join with me in recommending her to the administration. Concerning another matter, I'm now setting up next semester's schedule, and I hope that I'll be able to give you all the classes you have requested."

2. NELLIE: I really don't see anything special about Sunquist grapefruit. They taste the same as any other grapefruit to me.
NELLIE'S MOM: Hardly! Don't forget that your Uncle Henry owns Sunquist. If everyone buys his fruit, you may inherit a lot of money some day!

3. The ancient Mayans believed in human sacrifice and if that is what they believed, then that was right for them. Of course, I think human sacrifice is barbaric, but I'm not an ancient Mayan.

▲ **4.** *"Don't risk letting a fatal accident rob your family of the home they love—on the average more than 250 Americans die each day because of accidents.* What would happen to your family's home if you were one of them?

Your home is so much more than just a place to live. It's a community you've chosen carefully . . . a neighborhood . . . a school district . . . the way of life you and your family have come to know. And you'd want your family to continue sharing its familiar comforts, even if suddenly you were no longer there. . . . Now, as a Great Western mortgage customer, you can protect the home you love. . . . Just complete the Enrollment Form enclosed for you."

— *Insurance Company Brochure*

5. "You've made your mark and your scotch says it all."

— *Glen Haven Reserve*

6. Dear Senator Jenkins,
I am writing to urge your support for higher salaries for state correctional facility guards. I am a clerical worker at Kingsford Prison, and I know whereof I speak. Guards work long hours, often giving up weekends, at a dangerous job. They cannot afford expensive houses or even nice clothes. Things that other state employees take for granted, like orthodontia for their children and a second car, are not possibilities on their salaries, which, incidentally, have not been raised in five years. Their dedication deserves better.
Very truly yours, . . .

▲ 7. In *Shelley v. Kraemer,* 334 U.S.1 (1948), the "argument" was put before the Supreme Court that "state courts stand ready to enforce restrictive covenants excluding white persons from the ownership or occupancy of property covered by such agreements," and that therefore "enforcement of covenants excluding colored persons may not be deemed a denial of equal protection of the laws to the colored persons who are thereby affected." The court decided that "this contention does not bear scrutiny." In fact, the contention seems to be an example of what form of pseudoreasoning?

▲ 8. HER: Listen, honey, we've been dating for how long now? Years! I think it's time we thought seriously about getting married.
HIM: Right, ummm, you know what? I think it's time we went shopping for a new car! What do you say to that?

9. There are very good reasons for the death penalty. First, it serves as a deterrent to those who would commit capital offenses. Second, it is just and fair punishment for the crime committed. Third, reliable opinion polls show that over 70 percent of all Americans favor it. If so many people favor it, it has to be right.

▲ 10. NEWS ANCHOR: Do you think there is any substance to the ethics charges against Speaker Tom De Lay?
REPUBLICAN SPOKESPERSON: You know, Tim, the Democrats have been guilty of so many lapses over the years it is hard to keep track, Jim Wright, Dan Rostenkowski, Barney Frank, Adam Clayton Powell, Bill Clinton. . . .

11. Frankly, I think the Salvation Army, the Red Cross, and the Wildlife Fund will put my money to better use than my niece Alison and her husband would. They've wasted most of the money I've given them. So I think I'm going to leave a substantial portion of my estate to those organizations instead of leaving it all to my spendthrift relatives.

12. "The President's prosecution of the war on terror is being handled exactly right. He wasn't elected to do nothing!"

13. Student to teacher: "I've had to miss several classes and some quizzes because of some personal matters back home. I know you have a no-make-up policy, but there was really no way I could avoid having to be out of town; it really was not my fault."

▲ **14.** BUD: So here's the deal. I'll arrange to have your car "stolen," and we'll split the proceeds from selling it to a disposer. Then you file a claim with your insurance company and collect from it.
LOU: Gee, this sounds seriously illegal and dangerous.
BUD: Illegal, yeah, but do you think this is the first time an insurance company ever had this happen? Why, they actually expect it—they even budget money for exactly this sort of thing.

15. Kibitzer, discussing the job Lamar Alexander did as secretary of education: "It was absolutely clear to me that Alexander was not going to do any good for American education. He was way too involved in money-making schemes to give any attention to the job *we* were paying him for. Do you know that back before he was appointed, he and his wife invested five thousand dollars in some stock deal, and four years later that stock was worth over eight hundred thousand dollars? Tell me there's nothing fishy about a deal like that!"

16. My opponent, the evolutionist, offers you a different history and a different self-image from the one I suggest. While I believe that you and I are made in the image of God and are only one step out of the Garden of Eden, he believes that you are made in the image of a monkey and are only one step out of the zoo.

▲ **17.** Recently, two Colorado lawmakers got into a shouting match when one of them marched into a news conference the other was holding in opposition to same-sex marriage. Rep. Jim Welker had called the news conference to solicit support for a constitutional amendment to bar gays and lesbians from marrying. Rep. Angie Paccione objected, saying, "We have over 700,000 Coloradans without health care; how could we possibly say gay marriage is more important than health care?"

Welker then responded, "Gay marriage will open a Pandora's box. Where do you draw the line? A year and a half ago a lady in India married her dog!" Welker was referring to the marriage of a 9-year-old girl to a stray dog as part of a ritual to ward off an evil spell.

"Oh, for heaven's sake," Paccione said. "Come on, Jim."

"That is true. That's a fact," Welker said.

Paccione replied, "It 's not the same to have somebody marry a dog as it is to have two loving people get married. Come on."

18. "Boomers beware! The 76 million people born between 1946 and 1964 are beginning to think about retirement. They'd better listen carefully. Douglas Bernheim, an economics professor at Princeton, says current retirees were 'extraordinarily lucky' in that their home values climbed, high inflation took the sting out of their fixed-rate mortgages, and there were big increases in private and public pensions. 'The average baby boomer must triple his or her rate of savings to avoid a precipitous decline of living standards during retirement,' Bernheim said. . . .

"To be on the safe side, baby boomers should have an aggressive savings plan and not rely on government assurances of cushy retirement years. It is always best to err on the side of caution."

— Charleston *(W.Va.)* Daily Mail

Writing Exercises

1. Find an example of a fallacy in a newspaper editorial or opinion magazine (substitute an example from an advertisement or a letter to the editor only as a last resort and only if your instructor permits it). Identify the issue and what side of the issue the writer supports. Explain why the passage you've chosen does not really support that position—that is, why it involves a fallacy. If the writer's claims do support some other position (possibly on a different, related issue), describe what position they do support.
2. In 1998 the police in Harris County, Texas, responded to a false report about an armed man who was going crazy. They did not find such an individual; but when they entered the home of John Geddes Lawrence, they found him and another man, Tyron Garner, having sex. Both men were arrested and found guilty of violating a Texas law that criminalizes homosexual sex acts. The men challenged their conviction, and the case went to the United States Supreme Court in March 2003. A district attorney from the county argued, "Texas has the right to set moral standards of its people."

   Do you agree or disagree with the district attorney's statement? Defend your answer in a one-page essay written in class. Your instructor will have other members of the class read your essay to see if they can find your basic argument in the midst of any rhetoric you may have used. They also will note any fallacies that you may have employed.
3. Should there be an amendment to the U.S. Constitution prohibiting desecration of the U.S. flag? In a one-page essay, defend a "yes" or "no" answer to the question. Your instructor will have other members of the class read your essay, following the instructions in Exercise 2.

Chapter 6

More Fallacies

Photographs as well as words can introduce irrelevancies and fallacies into a discussion. For example, photos like this one of the Alaskan wilderness are sometimes shown to encourage opposition to oil and gas exploration and drilling in the Arctic National Wildlife Refuge. However, is the area shown actually where the exploration and drilling will take place? If not, then this is a photographic straw man, discussed later in the chapter.

What is the most common (and seductive) error in reasoning on the planet? You are about to find out. In this chapter we examine the infamous *argumentum ad hominem,* as well as other common fallacies.

To remind you of the overall picture, in Chapter 4 we explored ways the rhetorical content of words and phrases can be used to affect belief and attitude. In Chapter 5 we considered emotional appeals and related fallacies. The fallacies we turn to now, like the devices in the preceding chapters, can tempt us to believe something without giving us a legitimate reason for doing so.

THE AD HOMINEM FALLACY

The ad hominem fallacy (*argumentum ad hominem*) is the most common of all mistakes in reasoning. The fallacy rests on a confusion between the qualities of the person making a claim and the qualities of the claim itself. ("Claim" is to be understood broadly here, as including beliefs, opinions, positions, arguments, proposals and so forth.)

Parker is an ingenious fellow. It follows that Parker's opinion on some subject, whatever it is, is the opinion of an ingenious person. But it does not follow that Parker's *opinion itself* is ingenious. To think that it does follow would be to confuse the content of Parker's claim with Parker himself. Or let's suppose you are listening to somebody, your teacher perhaps, whom you regard as a bit strange or maybe even weird. Would it follow that the *car* your teacher drives is strange or weird? Obviously not. Likewise, it would not follow that some specific proposal that the teacher has put forth is strange or weird. A proposal made by an oddball is an oddball's proposal, but it does not follow that it is an oddball proposal. We must not confuse the qualities of the person making a claim with the qualities of the claim itself.

We commit the **ad hominem** fallacy when we think that considerations about a person "refute" his or her assertions. *Ad hominem* is Latin for "to the man," indicating it is not really the subject matter that's being addressed, but the person. The most common varieties of the ad hominem fallacy are as follows.

Personal Attack Ad Hominem

"Johnson has such-and-such a negative feature; therefore, his claim (belief, opinion, theory, proposal, etc.) stands refuted." This is the formula for the **personal attack ad hominem** fallacy. The name "personal attack" is self-explanatory, because attributing a negative feature to Johnson is attacking him personally.

Now there are many negative features that we might attribute to a person: Perhaps Johnson is said to be ignorant or stupid. Maybe he is charged with being self-serving or feathering his own nest. Perhaps he is accused of being a racist or a sexist or a fascist or a cheat or of being cruel or uncaring or soft on communism or prone to kick dogs or what-have-you. The point to remember is that shortcomings in *a person* are not equivalent to shortcomings in that person's ideas, proposals, theories, opinions, claims, or arguments.

Now it is true that there are exceptional circumstances we can imagine in which some feature of a person might logically imply that what that person says is false; but these circumstances tend to be far-fetched. "Johnson's claim is false because he has been paid to lie about the matter" might qualify as an example. "Johnson's claim is false because he has been given a drug that makes him say only false things" would qualify too. But such situations are rare. True, when we have doubts about the credibility of a source, we must be careful before we accept a claim from that source. But the doubts are rarely sufficient grounds for outright rejection of the claim. No matter what claim Johnson might make and no matter what his faults might be, we are rarely justified in rejecting the claim as false simply because he has those faults.

Man! As if sodomy in the people's Capitol isn't bad enough, they have to go and fund displays about it!

Leonard's remark is an example of an inconsistency ad hominem. (It also contains a wild syntactical ambiguity, as noted above.)

They believe the Boy Scouts' position on homosexuality was objectionable, but they gave no heed to people's objections about using state money to fund displays about sodomy in the people's Capitol.

– California Assemblyman Bill Leonard (R-San Bernardino), criticizing the legislature for funding a gay pride display in the state's Capitol

The Inconsistency Ad Hominem

"Moore's claim is inconsistent with something else Moore has said or done; therefore, his claim (belief, opinion, theory, proposal, etc.) stands refuted." This is the formula for the **inconsistency** ad hominem, and you encounter versions of this fallacy all the time. Suppose a political commentator exclaims (as we heard Rush Limbaugh say about George W. Bush), "The president says now that he believes in global warming, but ladies and gentlemen, when the president was campaigning he scoffed at the idea." Do we have a reason here for thinking something is wrong with the president's current view? Not at all. The fact that people change their minds has no bearing on the truth of what they say either before or after.

In Depth

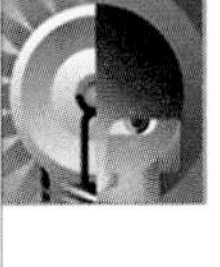

The Double Standard

Double standard: a rule or principle applied more strictly to some people than others (or oneself). *The Concise Oxford English Dictionary*

Let's look at an example of a claim of "double standard." In 2004, Laurence Tribe, a well-known and highly respected scholar at Harvard University, was found to have used language in a 1985 book that was taken verbatim from a book by another author, Henry J. Abraham. The campus newspaper, the *Harvard Crimson*, published an editorial noting that Professor Tribe was only "mildly chastised" by the university for the offense, and that no formal punishment was forthcoming. This, according to the paper, amounted to no more than "a slap on the wrist." On the other hand, students at Harvard who are found guilty of plagiarism are subject to suspension for one or more terms and even to expulsion. The editorial went on to say that "it is up to the university to levy a punishment that does not demonstrate such a lamentable disciplinary double standard." (*Harvard Crimson*, April 19th, 2005)

Claims about the application of a double standard are oftentimes entirely appropriate, but they can sometimes slide very quickly into an inconsistency ad hominem. Here's how: If the claim of a double standard is simply that two people or two groups or two situations that are similar in all relevant respects are being treated differently, then there is no fallacy; this is simply a call for fair play—one should treat like cases alike. But if one claims that because one person or group was held to one standard, the standard applied to some other person or group is automatically *wrong*, then we have a fallacy. It could be that the standard applied to the first person or group is now thought to be mistaken and that the standard now being applied is the correct one. As noted in the text, there is nothing wrong with a legitimate change of mind. Note, however, that *reasons* need to be given for the change of standard.

Would you say the editors of the *Harvard Crimson* have committed the fallacy, or is their criticism warranted? Can you explain and defend your answer?

Sometimes a person's claim seems inconsistent, not with previous statements but with that person's behavior. For example, Johnson might tell us to be more generous, when we know Johnson himself is as stingy as can be. Well, Johnson may well be a hypocrite, but we would be guilty of the inconsistency ad hominem fallacy if we regarded Johnson's stinginess or hypocrisy as grounds for rejecting what he says. This type of reasoning, where we reject what somebody says because what he or she says seems inconsistent with what he or she does, even has a Latin name: *tu quoque*, meaning "you too." This version of the inconsistency ad hominem often boils down to nothing more than saying "You too" or "You do it, too!" If a smoker urges another smoker to give up the habit, the second smoker commits the inconsistency ad hominem if she says, "Well, you do it too!"

Often an inconsistency ad hominem will accuse someone of having a double standard. Notice how this example is combined with ridicule.

I get calls from nutso environmentalists who are filled with compassion for every snail darter that is threatened by some dam somewhere. Yet, they have no interest in the 1.5 million fetuses that are aborted every year in the United States. I love to argue with them and challenge their double standard.

— Rush Limbaugh

Circumstantial Ad Hominem

"Parker's circumstances are such and such; therefore, his claim (belief, opinion, theory, proposal, etc.) stands refuted." This is the formula for the **circumstantial ad hominem.** An example would be "Well, you can forget about

what Father Hennesy says about the dangers of abortion because Father Hennesy's a priest, and priests are required to hold such views." The speaker in this example is citing Father Hennesy's circumstances (being a priest) to "refute" Father Hennesy's opinion. This example isn't a personal attack ad hominem because the speaker may think very highly of priests in general and of Father Hennesy in particular. Clearly, though, a person could intend to issue a personal attack by mentioning circumstances that (in the opinion of the speaker) constituted a defect on the part of the person attacked. For example, consider "You can forget about what Father Hennesy says about the dangers of abortion because he is a priest and priests all have sexual hang-ups." That would qualify as both a circumstantial ad hominem (he's a priest) and a personal attack ad hominem (priests have sexual hang-ups).

An inconsistency ad hominem

There were 750,000 people in New York's Central Park recently for Earth Day. They were throwing Frisbees, flying kites, and listening to Tom Cruise talk about how we have to recycle *everything* and stop corporations from polluting. Excuse me.

Didn't Tom Cruise make a stock-car movie in which he destroyed thirty-five cars, burned thousands of gallons of gasoline, and wasted dozens of tires? If I were given the opportunity, I'd say to Tom Cruise, "Tom, most people don't own thirty-five cars in their *life,* and you just trashed thirty-five cars for a movie. Now you're telling other people not to pollute the planet? Shut up, sir."

—Rush Limbaugh

Poisoning the Well

Poisoning the well can be thought of as an ad hominem in advance. If someone dumps poison down your well, you don't drink from it. Similarly, when A poisons your mind about B by relating unfavorable information about B, you may be inclined to reject what B says to you.

Well-poisoning is easier to arrange than you might think. You might suppose that to poison someone's thinking about Mrs. Jones, you would have to say or at least insinuate something deprecatory or derogatory about her. In fact, recent psycholinguistic research suggests you can poison someone's thinking about Mrs. Jones by doing just the opposite! If we don't know Mrs. Jones, even a sentence that expresses an outright denial of a connection between her and something unsavory is apt to make us form an unfavorable impression of her. Psychological studies indicate that people are more apt to form an unfavorable impression of Mrs. Jones from a sentence like "Mrs. Jones is not an ax murderer" than from a sentence like "Mrs. Jones has a sister."

Moral: Because it might be easy for others to arrange for us to have a negative impression of someone, we must be extra careful not to reject what a person says *just because* we have an unfavorable impression of the individual.

GENETIC FALLACY

The **genetic fallacy** occurs when we try to "refute" a claim (or urge others to do so) on the basis of its origin or history. For example, a person might "refute" the idea that God exists on the grounds that belief in God first rose in superstitious times or on the grounds we come to believe in God to comfort ourselves in the face of death. We have heard people declare the U.S. Constitution "invalid" because it was (allegedly) drafted to protect the interests of property owners. These are examples of the genetic fallacy.

If we "refute" a proposal (or urge someone else to reject it) on the grounds it was part of the Republican (or Democratic) party platform, we commit the genetic fallacy. If we "refute" a policy (or try to get others to reject it) on the grounds that a slave-holding state in the nineteenth century originated the policy, that also would qualify. If we "rebut" (or urge others to reject) a ballot initiative on the grounds that the insurance industry or the association of trial lawyers or the American Civil Liberties Union or "Big Tobacco" or "Big Oil" or multinational corporations or the National Education Association or the National Rifle Association or the National Organization for Women proposed it or back it, we commit the fallacy. Knowing that the NRA or the NEA or NOW proposed or backs or endorses a piece of legislation may give one reason (depending on one's politics) to be suspicious of it or to have a careful look at it; but a perceived lack of merit on the part of the organization that proposed or backs or endorses a proposal is not equivalent to a lack of merit in the proposal itself. Knowing the NRA is behind a particular ballot initiative is not the same as knowing about a specific defect in the initiative itself, even if you detest the NRA.

Obviously, the genetic fallacy is similar to the ad hominem arguments we have examined. The following examples might help you see a difference between the two:

Example of (Personal Attack) Ad Hominem
The Democrats never tire of criticizing the president's policy in Iraq, but all this criticism is completely unwarranted. These people just can't get over the fact that they've lost the last two presidential elections.

Example of Genetic Fallacy
All this criticism of the president's war plans is completely unwarranted. It all just comes from the Democrats.

Just remember what "ad hominem" means. It means "to the person." If we reject *Moore's* claim because *Moore* is, let us say, a member of the National Rifle Association, that's a (circumstantial) ad hominem. If we reject a *claim* because it originated with the National Rifle Association, that's the genetic fallacy.

Don't get into nuclear warfare with your classmates or with your instructor over whether a particular item is a genetic fallacy or this or that type of *argumentum ad hominem.* These mistakes all belong to the same family and resemble each other closely.

Gender-based inconsistency ad hominem

Whom are they kidding? Where are NOW's constitutional objections to the billions of dollars (including about $1 million to NOW itself) that women's groups receive under the Violence Against Women Act?

— Armin Brott, issuing an ad hominem response to opposition by the National Organization for Women to a proposal to provide poor fathers with parenting and marital-skills training and classes on money management

"POSITIVE AD HOMINEM FALLACIES"

An ad hominem fallacy, then, is committed if we rebut a person on the basis of considerations that, logically, apply to the person rather than to his or her claims. Strictly speaking, if we automatically transfer the positive or favorable attributes of a person to what he or she says, that's a mistake in reasoning, as well. The fact that you think Moore is clever does not logically entitle you to conclude that any specific opinion of Moore's is clever. The fact that in your view the NRA represents all that is good and proper does not enable you to infer that any specific proposal from the NRA is good and proper. Logicians did not always limit the ad hominem fallacy to cases of rebuttal, but that seems to be the usage now, and we shall follow that policy in this book. You should just remember that a parallel mistake in reasoning happens if you confuse the favorable qualities of a person with the qualities of his or her assertion.

STRAW MAN

A man made of straw is easier to knock over than a real one. And that's the reason this fallacy has its name. We get a **straw man fallacy** when a speaker or writer distorts, exaggerates, or otherwise misrepresents an opponent's

In the Media

Straw Man in the Elder Competition

In February of 2005 the conservative political group, USA NEXT, ran an ad attacking the American Association of Retired Persons (the AARP). The ad featured a photo of a soldier next to a photo of two men kissing at a wedding. An 'X' was imposed over the soldier and a check mark was imposed over the photo of the two men with a caption that read, "The REAL AARP Agenda." At first glance, this ad made it appear as if the AARP stood *against* American troops and *for* gay marriage, while in truth, the AARP has never taken a position on gays or same-sex marriage. It has, however, taken a stand against privatization of Social Security, which was proposed by President Bush early in 2005. USA Next offers itself as a political alternative to AARP and supports privatized Social Security by pouring millions of dollars into such policy battles. Charlie Jarvis, Chairman of USA Next, defended the ad by saying that an AARP affiliate in Ohio had come out against a same-sex marriage ban in that state. To claim that this is the same as saying the AARP endorses gay marriage while it opposes an American soldier is a perfect example of a straw man fallacy.

position. In such a case, the position attributed to the opponent isn't a real one; it's a position made of straw, and thus more easily criticized and rejected. Here's a simple example: Imagine that our editor's wife says to him, "Jon-David, it's time you got busy and cleaned out the garage." He protests, "What? Again? Do I have to clean out the garage every blasted day?" In saying this, he is attributing to his wife a much less defensible position than her real one, since nobody would agree that he should have to clean out the garage every day.

Here's a real-life example from a newspaper column by George Will:

> [Senator Lindsey] Graham believes that some borrowing is appropriate to make stakeholders of future generations, which will be the biggest beneficiaries of personal accounts. But substantially reducing the borrowing would deny Democrats the ability to disguise as fiscal responsibility their opposition to personal accounts, *which really is rooted in reluctance to enable people to become less dependent on government.*

It's the final portion, which we've put in italics, that's the straw man, and a wonderful example it is. Will describes the Democrats' position as being reluctant to enable people to become less dependent on government. We're pretty sure you could question every Democrat in Washington, D.C., and maybe every Democrat in the United States, and you could not find *even one* who is reluctant "to enable people to become less dependent on government." To be in favor of government programs to help people who need them is a far cry from being in favor of *keeping people on those programs as long as possible.*

A second point regarding this example, and one that is often a part of a straw man fallacy, is that the writer is presuming to read the minds of an entire group of people—how could he possibly know the "real" reason Democrats oppose personal accounts if they're claiming something entirely different? (This is sometimes called "reliance on an unknown fact.")

The straw man fallacy is so common that it ranks next to the top on our list of the top ten fallacies of all time (see Appendix 2). One person will say he wants to eliminate the words "under God" from the Pledge of Allegiance, and his opponent will act as if he wants to eliminate the entire pledge. A conservative will oppose tightening emission standards for sulfur dioxide, and a liberal will accuse him of wanting to relax the standards. A Democratic congresswoman will say she opposes cutting taxes, and her Republican opponent will accuse her of wanting to raise taxes.

The ad hominem fallacy attempts to "refute" a claim on the basis of considerations that logically apply to its source. The straw man fallacy attempts to "refute" a claim by altering it so that it seems patently false or even ridiculous.

I'm a very controversial figure to the animal rights movement. They no doubt view me with some measure of hostility because I am constantly challenging their fundamental premise that animals are superior to human beings.

– Rush Limbaugh, setting up another straw man for the kill

FALSE DILEMMA

Suppose our editor's wife in the example above says to him, "Look, Jon-David, either we clean out the garage or all this junk will run us out of house and home. Would you prefer that?" Now she is offering him a "choice": either clean out the garage or let the junk run them out of house and home. But the choice she offers is limited to just two alternatives, and there are alternatives that deserve consideration, such as doing it later or not acquiring additional junk.

The **false dilemma** fallacy occurs when you limit considerations to only two alternatives although other alternatives may be available. Like the straw man fallacy, it is encountered all the time. You say you don't want to drill for oil in the Alaskan National Wildlife Reserve? Would you prefer letting the Saudis dictate the price of oil?

Or take a look at this example:

CONGRESSMAN CLAGHORN: Guess we're going to have to cut back expenditures on social programs again this year.

YOU: Why's that?

CLAGHORN: Well, we either do that or live with this high deficit, and that's something we can't allow.

Here, Claghorn maintains that either we live with the high deficit or we cut social programs, and that therefore, because we can't live with the high deficit, we have to cut social programs. But this reasoning works only if cutting social programs is the *only* alternative to a high deficit. Of course, that is not the case (taxes might be raised or military spending cut, for example). Another example:

DANIEL: Theresa and I both endorse this idea of allowing prayer in public schools, don't we, Theresa?

THERESA: I never said any such thing!

DANIEL: Hey, I didn't know you were an atheist!

Here, Daniel's "argument" amounts to this: Either you endorse prayer in public schools, or you are an atheist; therefore, because you do not endorse school prayer, you must be an atheist. But a person does not have to be an atheist in

Real Life

Photo False Dilemma

Two photos like these appeared on a flyer urging a "no" vote on a proposed zoning law change in a western city. The message above the photos was, "Which is it going to be, Springfield?" Since the photos do not depict all reasonable alternatives, they present an excellent example of a false dilemma.

order to feel unfavorable toward prayer in public schools. The alternatives Daniel presents, in other words, could both be false. Theresa might not be an atheist and still not endorse school prayer.

The example Daniel provides us shows how this type of fallacy and the preceding one can work together: A straw man is often used as part of a false dilemma. A person who wants us to accept X may not only ignore other alternatives besides Y but also exaggerate or distort Y. In other words, this person leaves only *one* "reasonable" alternative because the only other one provided is really a straw man. You can also think of a false dilemma as a false dichotomy.

It might help in understanding false dilemmas to look quickly at a *real* dilemma. Consider: You know that the Smiths must heat their house in the winter. You also know that the only heating options available in their location are gas and electricity. Under these circumstances, if you find out that they do *not* have electric heat, it must indeed be true that they must use gas heat because that's the only alternative remaining. False dilemma occurs only when reasonable alternatives are ignored. In such cases, both X and Y may be false, and some other alternative may be true.

Therefore, before you accept X because some alternative, Y, is false, make certain that X and Y cannot *both* be false. Look especially for some third alternative, some way of rejecting Y without having to accept X. Example:

> MOORE: Look, Parker, you're going to have to make up your mind. Either you decide that you can afford this stereo, or you decide that you're going to do without music for a while.

Parker could reject both of Moore's alternatives (buying this stereo and going without music) because of some obvious third possibilities. One, Parker might find a less expensive stereo. Or, two, he might buy a part of this stereo now—just the CD player, amplifier, and speakers, say—and postpone until later purchase of the rest.

Before moving on, we should point out that there is more than one way to present a pair of alternatives. Aside from the obvious "either X or Y" version we've described so far, we can use the form "if not X, then Y." For instance, in the example at the beginning of the section, Congressman Claghorn can say, "Either we cut back on expenditures, or we'll have a big deficit," but he can accomplish the same thing by saying, "If we don't cut back on expenditures, then we'll have a big deficit." These two ways of stating the dilemma are equivalent to one another. Claghorn gets the same result: After denying that we can tolerate the high deficit, he concludes that we'll have to cut back expenditures. Again, it's the artificial narrowness of the alternatives—the falsity of the claim that says "if not one, then surely the other"—that makes this a fallacy.

Perfectionist Fallacy

A particular subspecies of false dilemma and common rhetorical ploy is something we call the **perfectionist fallacy.** It comes up when a plan or policy is under consideration, and it goes like this:

> If policy X will not meet our goals as well as we'd like them met (i.e., "perfectly"), then policy X should be rejected.

This principle downgrades policy X simply because it isn't perfection. It's a version of false dilemma because it says, in effect, "Either the policy is perfect, or else we must reject it."

An excellent example of the perfectionist fallacy comes from the National Football League's experience with the instant replay rule, which allows an off-field official to review videotape of a play to determine whether the on-field official's ruling was correct. To help the replay official, tape from several angles can be viewed, and the play run in slow motion.

One of the most often heard arguments against the use of videotape replays goes like this: "It's a mistake to use replays to make calls because no matter how many cameras you have following the action on the field, you're still going to miss some calls. There's no way to see everything that's going on."

According to this type of reasoning, we should not have police unless they can prevent *every* crime or apprehend *every* criminal. You can probably think of other examples that show perfectionist reasoning to be very unreliable indeed.

Line-Drawing Fallacy

Another version of the false dilemma is called the line-drawing fallacy. An example comes from the much-publicized Rodney King case mentioned in Chapter 4, in which four Los Angeles police officers were acquitted of charges of using excessive force when they beat King during his arrest. After the trial, one of the jurors indicated that an argument like the following finally convinced her and at least one other juror to vote "not guilty":

> Everybody agrees that the first time one of the officers struck King with a nightstick it did not constitute excessive force. Therefore, if we are to

> conclude that excessive force was indeed used, then sometime during the course of the beating (during which King was hit about fifty times) there must have been a moment—a particular blow—at which the force *became* excessive. Since there is no point at which we can determine that the use of force changed from warranted to excessive, we are forced to conclude that it did not become excessive at any time during the beating; and so the officers did not use excessive force.

False dilemma

[People] who are voyeurs, if they are not irredeemably sick, . . . feel ashamed at what they are witnessing.

— Irving Kristol, "Pornography, Obscenity, and the Case for Censorship"

These jurors accepted the **line-drawing fallacy,** the fallacy of insisting that a line must be drawn at some precise point when in fact it is not necessary that such a precise line be drawn.

To see how this works, consider another example: Clearly, it is impossible for a person who is not rich to become rich by our giving her one dollar. But, equally clearly, if we give our lucky person fifty million dollars, one at a time (very quickly, obviously—maybe we have a machine to deal them out), she will be rich. According to the line-drawing argument, however, *if we cannot point to the precise dollar that makes her rich, then she can never get rich, no matter how much money she is given!*

The problem, of course, is that the concepts referred to by "rich" and "excessive force" (and many others) are vague concepts. We can find cases where the concepts clearly apply and cases where they clearly do not apply. But it is not at all clear exactly where the borderlines are.

Many logicians interpret line drawing as a variety of slippery slope (discussed next). The King case might be seen this way: If the first blow struck against King did not amount to excessive violence, then there's nothing in the series of blows to change that fact. So there's no excessive violence at the end of the series, either.

Our own preference is to see the line-drawing fallacy as a version of false dilemma. It presents the following alternatives: Either there is a precise place where we draw the line, or else there is no line to be drawn (no difference) between one end of the scale and the other. Either there is a certain blow at which the force used against King became excessive, or else the force never became excessive.

Again, remember that our categories of fallacy sometimes overlap. When that happens, it doesn't matter as much which way we classify a case as that we see that an error is being made.

SLIPPERY SLOPE

We've all heard people make claims of this sort: "If we let X happen, the first thing you know Y will be happening." This is one form of the **slippery slope.** Such claims are fallacious when in fact there is no reason to think that X will lead to Y. Sometimes X and Y can be the same kind of thing or can bear some kind of similarity to one another, but that doesn't mean that one will inevitably lead to the other.

Opponents of handgun control sometimes use a slippery slope argument, saying that if laws to register handguns are passed, the next thing we know there will be laws to make owning any kind of gun illegal. This is fallacious if there is no reason to think that the first kind of law will make the second kind more likely. It's up to the person who offers the slippery slope claim to show *why* the first action will lead to the second.

Real Life

$8 Billion, Down the Tube!

> Eight billion dollars in utility ratepayers' money and 20 years of effort will be squandered if this resolution is defeated.
>
> – Senator FRANK MURKOWSKI, R-Alaska, using a slippery slope fallacy to argue for going forward with government plans to bury radioactive waste in Yucca Mountain, Nevada

The fact that we've spent money on it already doesn't make it a good idea.

It is also argued that one should not experiment with certain drugs because experimentation is apt to lead to serious addiction or dependence. In the case of drugs that are known to be addictive, there is no fallacy present—the likelihood of the progression is clear.

The other version of slippery slope occurs when someone claims we must continue a certain course of action simply because we have already begun that course. It was said during the Vietnam War that because the United States had already sent troops to Vietnam, it was necessary to send more troops to support the first ones. Unless there is some reason supplied to show that the first step *must* lead to the others, this is a fallacy. (Notice that it's easy to make a false dilemma out of this case as well; do you see how to do it?)

Sometimes we take the first step in a series, and then we realize that it was a mistake. To insist on taking the remainder when we could admit our mistake and retreat is to fall prey to the slippery slope fallacy. (If you're the sort who insists on following one bad move with another one, we'd like to tell you about our friendly Thursday night poker game.)

The slippery slope fallacy has considerable force because *psychologically* one item does often lead to another even though *logically* it does no such thing. When we think of X, say, we may be led immediately to think of Y. But this certainly does not mean that X itself is necessarily followed by Y. Once again, to think that Y has to follow X is to engage in slippery slope thinking; to do so when there is no particular reason to think Y must follow X is to commit a slippery slope fallacy.

MISPLACING THE BURDEN OF PROOF

Let's say Moore asks Parker, "Say, did you know that if you rub red wine on your head your gray hair will turn dark again?"

Parker, of course, will say, "Baloney."

Let's suppose Moore then says, "Baloney? Hey, how do you know it won't work?"

Moore's question is odd, because the **burden of proof** rests on him, not on Parker. Moore has misplaced the burden of proof on Parker, and this is a mistake, a fallacy.

Misplacing the burden of proof occurs when the burden of proof is placed on the wrong side of an issue. This is a common rhetorical technique, and sometimes you have to be on your toes to spot it. People are frequently tricked

In the Media

A Double Slippery Slope

"Next time it will be easier. It always is. The tolerance of early-term abortion made it possible to tolerate partial-birth abortion, and to give advanced thinkers a hearing when they advocate outright infanticide. Letting the courts decide such life-and-death issues made it possible for us to let them decide others, made it seem somehow wrong for anyone to stand in their way. Now they are helping to snuff out the minimally conscious. Who's next?"

– Editorial, *National Review Online,* March 31, 2005

There are actually two slippery slope arguments built into this passage. One says that one type of abortion (early-term) led to another (partial-birth); the second says that letting the courts decide some issues led to allowing them to decide more issues. Both cases are fallacious because in neither is there any evidence advanced for the slipperiness of the slope. Was it tolerance of early-term abortion that led to partial-birth abortion? In fact, the slope seems not to have been slippery, since a ban on partial-birth abortion became federal law in 2003. And many issues, including many life-and-death issues, are properly within the purview of the courts from the outset; there is no reason to think that some became matters for the judiciary simply because others were.

into thinking they have to prove their opponent's claim is wrong, when in fact the opponent should be proving that the claim is right. For example, back in 2003 you often heard people trying their darnedest to prove that we shouldn't go to war with Iraq, in a context in which the burden of proof rests on those who think we should go to war.

What reasonable grounds would make us place the burden of proof more on one side of an issue than the other? There are a variety of such grounds, but they fall mainly into three categories. We can express them as a set of rules of thumb:

1. *Initial plausibility.* In Chapter 3, we said that the more a claim coincides with our background information, the greater its initial plausibility. The general rule that most often governs the placement of the burden of proof is simply this: The less initial plausibility a claim has, the greater the burden of proof we place on someone who asserts that claim. This is just good sense, of course. We are quite naturally less skeptical about the claim that Charlie's now-famous eighty-seven-year-old grandmother drove a boat across Lake Michigan than we are about the claim that she swam across Lake Michigan. Unfortunately, this rule is a rule of thumb, not a rule that can be applied precisely. We are unable to assess the specific degree of a claim's plausibility and then determine with precision just exactly how much evidence its advocates need to produce to make us willing to accept the claim. But, as a rule of thumb, the initial plausibility rule can keep us from setting the requirements unreasonably high for some claims and allowing others to slide by unchallenged when they don't deserve to.

2. *Affirmative/negative.* Other things being equal, the burden of proof falls automatically on those supporting the affirmative side of an issue rather

Paleological misplacement of the burden of proof!

than on those supporting the negative side. In other words, we generally want to hear reasons why something *is* the case before we require reasons why it is *not* the case. Consider this conversation:

MOORE: The car won't start.

PARKER: Yeah, I know. It's a problem with the ignition.

MOORE: What makes you think that?

PARKER: Well, why not?

Parker's last remark seems strange because we generally require the affirmative side to assume the burden of proof; it is Parker's job to give reasons for thinking that the problem *is* in the ignition.

This rule applies to cases of existence versus nonexistence, too. Most often, the burden of proof should fall on those who claim something exists rather than on those who claim it doesn't. There are people who believe in ghosts, not because of any evidence that there *are* ghosts, but because nobody has shown there are no such things. (When someone claims that we should believe in such-and-such because nobody has proved that it *isn't* so, we have a subtype of burden of proof known as **appeal to ignorance.**) This is a burden-of-proof fallacy because it mistakenly places the requirement of proving their position on those who do not believe in ghosts. (Of course, the first rule applies here, too, because ghosts are not part of background knowledge for most of us.)

In general, the affirmative side gets the burden of proof because it tends to be much more difficult—or at least much more inconvenient—to prove the negative side of an issue. Imagine a student who walks up to the ticket window at a football game and asks for a discounted student ticket. "Can you prove you're a student?" he is asked. "No," the student replies, "can you prove

In Depth

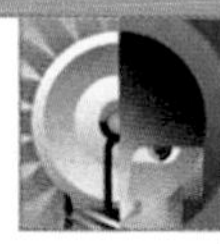

Innocent Until Proved Guilty

We must point out that sometimes there are specific reasons why the burden of proof is placed entirely on one side. The obvious case in point is in criminal court, where it is the prosecution's job to prove guilt. The defense is not required to prove innocence; it must only try to keep the prosecution from succeeding in its attempt to prove guilt. We are, as we say, "innocent until proved guilty." As a matter of fact, it's possible that more trials might come to a correct conclusion (i.e., the guilty get convicted and the innocent acquitted) if the burden of proof were equally shared between prosecution and defense. But we have wisely decided that if we are to make a mistake, we would rather it be one of letting a guilty person go free than one of convicting an innocent person. Rather than being a fallacy, then, this lopsided placement of the burden of proof is how we guarantee a fundamental right: the presumption of innocence.

I'm not?" Well, it may be possible to prove he's not a student, but it's no easy chore, and it would be unreasonable to require it.

Incidentally, some people say it's *impossible* to "prove a negative." But difficult is not the same as impossible. And some "negatives" are even easy to prove. For example, "There are no elephants in this classroom."

3. *Special circumstances.* Sometimes getting at the truth is not the only thing we want to accomplish, and on such occasions we may purposely place the burden of proof on a particular side. Courts of law provide us with the most obvious example. Specific agreements can also move the burden of proof from where it would ordinarily fall. A contract might specify, "It will be presumed that you receive the information by the tenth of each month unless you show otherwise." In such cases, the rule governing the special circumstances should be clear and acceptable to all parties involved.

One important variety of special circumstances occurs when the stakes are especially high. For example, if you're thinking of investing your life savings in a company, you'll want to put a heavy burden of proof on the person who advocates making the investment. However, if the investment is small, one you can afford to lose, you might be willing to lay out the money even though it has not been thoroughly proved that the investment is safe. In short, it is reasonable to place a higher burden of proof on someone who advocates a policy that could be dangerous or costly if he or she is mistaken.

In the Media

So Much for Presumed Innocence . . .

> I would rather have an innocent man executed than a guilty murderer go free.
>
> – caller on *Talk Back Live* (CNN)

This not uncommon thought is a bizarre false dilemma, since if the innocent man is executed, the guilty murderer *does* go free.

These three rules cover most of the ground in placing the burden of proof properly. Be careful about situations where people put the burden of proof on the side other than where our rules indicate it should fall. Take this example:

PARKER: I think we should invest more money in expanding the interstate highway system.

MOORE: I think that would be a big mistake.

PARKER: How could anybody object to more highways?

With his last remark, Parker has attempted to put the burden of proof on Moore. Such tactics can put one's opponent in a defensive position; Moore now has to show why we should *not* spend more on roads rather than Parker having to show why we *should* spend more. This is an inappropriate burden of proof.

You should always be suspicious when an inability to *disprove* a claim is said to show that one is mistaken in doubting the claim or in saying that it's false. It does no such thing, unless the burden was on that person to disprove the claim. Inability to disprove that there is extrasensory perception (ESP) is no reason to think that one is mistaken in doubting that ESP exists. But psychics' repeated failure to prove that ESP exists *does* weaken *their* case because the burden of proof is on them.

BEGGING THE QUESTION

Here's a version of a simple example of begging the question, one that's been around a long time (we'll return to it later):

> Two gold miners roll a boulder away from its resting place and find three huge gold nuggets underneath. One says to the other, "Great! That's one nugget for you and two for me," handing one nugget to his associate.
>
> "Wait a minute!" says the second miner. "Why do you get two and I get just one?"
>
> "Because I'm the leader of this operation," says the first.
>
> "What makes you the leader?" asks miner number two.
>
> "I've got twice the gold you do," answers miner number one.

This next example is as famous as the first one was silly: Some people say they can prove God exists. When asked how, they reply, "Well, the Scriptures say very clearly that God must exist." Then, when asked why we should believe the Scriptures, they answer, "The Scriptures are divinely inspired by God himself, so they must be true."

The problem with such reasoning is that the claim at issue—whether it's the case that God exists—turns out to be one of the very premises the argument is based on. If we can't trust the Scriptures, then the argument isn't any good, but the reason given for trusting the Scriptures requires the existence of God, the very thing we were arguing for in the first place! Examples like this are sometimes called circular reasoning or arguing in a circle because they start from much the same place as they end up.

If you examine this "reasoning" closely, it says that gay marriages shouldn't be legal because they aren't legal. This is not quite "X is true just because X is true," but it's close. The issue is whether the law should be changed. So giving the existence of the law as a "reason" for its *not* being changed can carry no weight, logically.

Gay marriages should not be legal because if there wasn't anything wrong with them they would already be legal, which they aren't.

– From a student essay

Rhetorical definitions can beg questions. Consider an example from an earlier chapter: If we define abortion as "the murder of innocent children," then it's obvious that abortion is morally wrong. But of course anyone who doubts that abortion is morally wrong is certainly not going to accept this definition. That person will most likely refuse to recognize an embryo or early-stage fetus as a "child" at all and will certainly not accept the word "murder" in the definition.

And this brings us to the real problem in cases of question begging: a misunderstanding of what premises (and definitions) it is reasonable for one's audience to accept. We are guilty of **begging the question** when we ask our audience to accept premises that are as controversial as the conclusion we're arguing for and are controversial on the same grounds. The sort of grounds on which people would disagree about the morality of abortion are much the same as those on which they would disagree about the definition of abortion above. The person making the argument has not "gone back far enough," as it were, to find common ground with the audience whom he or she wishes to convince.

Let's return to our feuding gold miners to illustrate what we're talking about. Clearly, the two disagree about who gets the gold, and, given what being the leader of the operation means, they're going to disagree just as much about that. But what if the first miner says, "Look, I picked this spot, didn't I? And we wouldn't have found anything if we'd worked where you wanted to work." If the second miner agrees, they'll have found a bit of common ground. Maybe—*maybe*—the first miner can then convince the second that this point, on which they agree, is worth considering when it comes to splitting the gold. At least there's a chance of moving the discussion forward when they proceed this way.

In fact, if you are ever to hope for any measure of success in trying to convince somebody of a claim, you should always try to argue for it based on whatever common ground you can find between the two of you. Indeed, the attempt to find common ground from which to start is what underlies the entire enterprise of rational debate.

Recap

The fallacies in this chapter, like those in Chapter 5, may resemble legitimate arguments, but none gives a reason for accepting (or rejecting) a claim. The discussions in this part of the book should help make you sensitive to the difference between relevant considerations and emotional appeals, factual irrelevancies, and other dubious argumentative tactics.

In this chapter we examined:

- Personal attack ad hominem—thinking a person's defects refute his or her beliefs
- Circumstantial ad hominem—thinking a person's circumstances refute his or her beliefs
- Inconsistency ad hominem—thinking a person's inconsistencies refute his or her beliefs
- Poisoning the well—encouraging others to dismiss what someone will say, by citing the speaker's defects, inconsistencies, circumstances, or other personal attributes
- Genetic fallacy—thinking that the origin or history of a belief refutes it
- Straw man—"rebutting" a claim by offering a distorted or exaggerated version of it
- False dilemma—an erroneous narrowing down of the range of alternatives; saying we have to accept X or Y (and omitting that we might do Z)
- Perfectionist fallacy—arguing that we either do something completely or not at all
- Line-drawing fallacy—requiring that a precise line be drawn someplace on a scale or continuum when no such precise line can be drawn; usually occurs when a vague concept is treated like a precise one
- Slippery slope—refusing to take the first step in a progression on unwarranted grounds that doing so will make taking the remaining steps inevitable or insisting erroneously on taking the remainder of the steps simply because the first one was taken
- Misplacing burden of proof—requiring the wrong side of an issue to make its case
- Begging the question—assuming as true the claim that is at issue and doing this as if you were giving an argument

Exercises

Exercise 6-1

Working in groups, invent a simple, original, and clear illustration of each fallacy covered in this chapter. Then in the class as a whole select the illustrations that are clearest and most straightforward. Go over these illustrations before doing the remaining exercises in this chapter, and review them before you take a test on this material.

Exercise 6-2

Identify any examples of fallacies in the following passages. Tell why you think they are present, and identify which category they belong in, if they fit any category we've described.

▲ 1. Of course Chinese green tea is good for your health. If it weren't, how could it be so beneficial to drink it?

2. Overheard: "No, I'm against this health plan business. None of the proposals are gonna fix everything, you can bet on that."

3. You have a choice: Either you let 'em out to murder and rape again and again, or you put up with a little prison overcrowding. I know what I'd choose.

▲ 4. "The legalization of drugs will not promote their use. The notion of a widespread hysteria sweeping across the nation as every man, woman, and child instantaneously becomes addicted to drugs upon their legalization is, in short, ridiculous."

— *From a student essay*

5. Way I figure is, giving up smoking isn't gonna make me live forever, so why bother?

6. "The trouble with [syndicated columnist Joseph] Sobran's gripe about Clinton increasing the power of the federal government is that Sobran is the one who wants the government to tell women they can't have abortions."

— *From a newspaper call-in column*

▲ 7. Aid to Russia? Gimme a break! Why should we care more about the Russians than about our own people?

8. Bush's tax cut stinks. He's just trying to please big business.

9. I believe Tim is telling the truth about his brother because he just would not lie about that sort of thing.

▲ 10. I think I was treated unfairly. I got a ticket out on McCrae Road. I was doing about sixty miles an hour, and the cop charged me with "traveling at an unsafe speed." I asked him just exactly what would have been a *safe* speed on that particular occasion—fifty? forty-five?—and he couldn't tell me. Neither could the judge. I tell you, if you don't know what speeds are unsafe, you shouldn't give tickets for "unsafe speeds."

Exercise 6-3

Classify each of the following cases of ad hominem as personal attack ad hominem, circumstantial ad hominem, inconsistency ad hominem, poisoning the well, or genetic fallacy. Identify the cases, if any, in which it might be difficult or futile to assign the item to any single one of these categories, as well as those cases, if any, where the item doesn't fit comfortably into any of these categories at all.

▲ 1. The proponents of this spend-now–pay-later boondoggle would like you to believe that this measure will cost you only one billion dollars. That's NOT TRUE. In the last general election some of these very same people argued against unneeded rail projects because they would cost taxpayers millions more in interest payments. Now they have changed their minds and are willing to encourage irresponsible borrowing. Connecticut is already awash in red ink. Vote NO.

2. Rush Limbaugh argues that the establishment clause of the First Amendment should not be stretched beyond its intended dimensions by precluding voluntary prayer in public schools. This is a peculiar argument, when you consider that Limbaugh is quite willing to stretch the Second Amendment to include the right to own assault rifles and Saturday night specials.

3. I think you can safely assume that Justice Scalia's opinions on the cases before the Supreme Court this term will be every bit as flaky as his past opinions.

▲ 4. Harvard now takes the position that its investment in urban redevelopment projects will be limited to projects that are environmentally friendly. Before you conclude that that is such a swell idea, stop and think. For a long time, Harvard was one of the biggest slumlords in the country.

5. REPUBLICAN: Finally! Finally the governor is getting around to reducing taxes—as he promised. What do you think of his plan?
DEMOCRAT: Not much. He's just doing it so the Democrats won't get all the credit.

6. Dear Editor—
I read with amusement the letter by Leslie Burr titled "It's time to get tough." Did anyone else notice a little problem in her views? It seems a little odd that somebody who claims that she "loathes violence" could also say that "criminals should pay with their life." I guess consistency isn't Ms. Burr's greatest concern.

▲ 7. YOU: Look at this. It says here that white males still earn a lot more than minorities and women for doing the same job.
YOUR FRIEND: Yeah, right. Written by some woman, no doubt.

8. "Steve Thompson of the California Medical Association said document-checking might even take place in emergency rooms. That's because, while undocumented immigrants would be given emergency care, not all cases that come into emergency rooms fall under the federal definition of an emergency.
"To all those arguments initiative proponents say hogwash. They say the education and health groups opposing the initiative are interested in protecting funding they receive for providing services to the undocumented."
— *Article in* Sacramento Bee

9. Horace, you're new to this town, and I want to warn you about the local newspaper. It's in cahoots with all them left-wing environmental nutcakes that are wrecking the economy around here. You can't believe a thing you read in it.

10. Are Moore and Parker guilty of the ad hominem fallacy or poisoning the well in their discussion of Rush Limbaugh on p. 146?

▲ 11. Creationism cannot possibly be true. People who believe in a literal interpretation of the Bible just never outgrew the need to believe in Santa Claus.

12. "Americans spend between $28 billion and $61 billion a year in medical costs for treatment of hypertension, heart disease, cancer and other illnesses attributed to consumption of meat, says a report out today from a pro-vegetarian doctor's group.
"Dr. Neal D. Barnard, lead author of the report in the *Journal of Preventive Medicine,* and colleagues looked at studies comparing the health of vegetarians and meat eaters, then figured the cost of treating illnesses suffered by meat eaters in excess of those suffered by vegetarians. Only

studies that controlled for the health effects of smoking, exercise and alcohol consumption were considered.

"The American Medical Association, in a statement from Dr. M. Roy Schwarz, charged that Barnard's group is an 'animal rights front organization' whose agenda 'definitely taints whatever unsubstantiated findings it may claim.'"

— USA Today

Exercise 6-4

Identify any fallacies in the following passages. Tell why you think they are present, and identify which category they belong in, if they fit any of those we've described. Instances of fallacies are all from the types found in Chapter 6.

▲ 1. Suspicious: "I would forget about whatever Moore and Parker have to say about pay for college teachers. After all, they're both professors themselves; what would you *expect* them to say?"

2. It's obvious to me that abortion is wrong—after all, everybody deserves a chance to be born.

3. Overheard: Well, I think that's too much to tip her. It's more than 15 percent. Next time it will be 20 percent, then 25 percent—where will it stop?

▲ 4. CARLOS: Four A.M.? Do we really have to start that early? Couldn't we leave a little later and get more sleep?
JEANNE: C'mon, don't hand me that! I know you! If you want to stay in bed until noon and then drag in there in the middle of the night, then go by yourself! If we want to get there at a reasonable hour, then we have to get going early and not spend the whole day sleeping.

5. I know a lot of people don't find anything wrong with voluntary euthanasia, where a patient is allowed to make a decision to die and that wish is carried out by a doctor or someone else. What will happen, though, is that if we allow voluntary euthanasia, before you know it we'll have the patient's relatives or the doctors making the decision that the patient should be "put out of his misery."

6. "Congress was elected to make laws, not Dr. David Kessler, commissioner of the Food and Drug Administration, who convinced Clinton to have the FDA regulate nicotine. What's next? Will Dr. Kessler have Clinton regulate coffee and Coca-Cola? Will Big Macs be outlawed and overeating prohibited?"

▲ 7. Whenever legislators have the power to raise taxes, they will always find problems that seem to require for their solution doing exactly that. This is an axiom, the proof of which is that the power to tax always generates the perception on the part of those who have that power that there exist various ills the remedy for which can only lie in increased governmental spending and hence higher taxes.

8. Don't tell me I should wear my seat belt, for heaven's sake. I've seen you ride a motorcycle without a helmet!

9. People who own pit bulls show a lack of respect for their friends, their neighbors, and anybody else who might come in contact with their dogs. They don't care if their dogs chew other people up.

▲ 10. When it comes to the issue of race relations, either you're part of the solution or you're part of the problem.

11. What! So now you're telling me we should get a new car? I don't buy that at all. Didn't you claim just last month that there was nothing wrong with the Plymouth?

12. Letter to the editor: "The Supreme Court decision outlawing a moment of silence for prayer in public schools is scandalous. Evidently the American Civil Liberties Union and the other radical groups will not be satisfied until every last man, woman and child in the country is an atheist. I'm fed up."

— Tri-County Observer

▲ 13. We should impeach the attorney general. Despite the fact that there have been many allegations of unethical conduct on his part, he has not done anything to demonstrate his innocence.

14. What do you mean, support Amnesty International? They only defend criminals.

15. Overheard: "Hunting immoral? Why should I believe that coming from you? You fish, don't you?"

16. "Will we have an expanding government, or will we balance the budget, cut government waste and eliminate unneeded programs?"

— *Newt Gingrich, in a Republican National Committee solicitation*

17. "Former House Speaker Newt Gingrich, who is amazingly still welcomed on television despite his fall from power in disgrace, groused that Mondale had served on a panel recently that recommended privatizing Social Security. But don't Republicans adore this notion, even though they now call it 'private retirement investments' in deference to the idea's unpopularity?"

— *Political columnist Marianne Means*

Exercise 6-5

Identify any fallacies in the following passages. Tell why you think they are present, and identify which category they belong in, if they fit in any of those we've described.

▲ 1. Despite all the studies and the public outcry, it's still true that nobody has ever actually *seen* cigarette smoking cause a cancer. All the anti-smoking people can do is talk about statistics; as long as there isn't real proof, I'm not believing it.

2. There is only one way to save this country from the domination by the illegal drug establishment to which Colombia has been subjected, and that's to increase tenfold the funds we spend on drug enforcement and interdiction.

3. I believe that the great flood described in the Bible really happened. The reason is simple: Noah would not have built the ark otherwise.

▲ 4. In 1996 a University of Chicago study gave evidence that letting people carry concealed guns appears to sharply reduce murders, rapes, and other violent crimes. Gun-control backer Josh Sugarman of the Violence Policy Center commented: "Anyone who argues that these laws reduce crime either doesn't understand the nature of crime or has a preset agenda."

5. Letter to the editor: "I strongly object to the proposed sale of alcoholic beverages at County Golf Course. The idea of allowing people to drink wherever and whenever they please is positively disgraceful and can only lead to more alcoholism and all the problems it produces—drunk driving, perverted parties, and who knows what else. I'm sure General Stuart, if he were alive today to see what has become of the land he deeded to the county, would disapprove strenuously."

— Tehama County Tribune

6. Letter to the editor: "I'm not against immigrants or immigration, but something has to be done soon. We've got more people already than we can provide necessary services for, and, at the current rate, we'll have people standing on top of one another by the end of the century. Either we control these immigration policies or there won't be room for any of us to sit down."

— Lake County Recorder

▲ 7. Letter to the editor: "So now we find our local crusader-for-all-that-is-right, and I am referring to Councilman Benjamin Bostell, taking up arms against the local adult bookstore. Is this the same Mr. Bostell who owns the biggest liquor store in Chilton County? Well, maybe booze isn't the same as pornography, but they're the same sort of thing. C'mon, Mr. Bostell, aren't you a little like the pot calling the kettle black?"

— Chilton County Register

8. Letter to the editor: "Once again the *Courier* displays its taste for slanted journalism. Why do your editors present only one point of view?

"I am referring specifically to the editorial of May 27, regarding the death penalty. So capital punishment makes you squirm a little. What else is new? Would you prefer to have murderers and assassins wandering around scot-free? How about quoting someone who has a different point of view from your own, for a change?"

— Athens Courier

9. "Clinton should have been thrown in jail for immoral behavior. Just look at all the women he has had affairs with since he left the presidency."

"Hey, wait a minute. How do you know he has had affairs since he was president?"

"Because if he didn't, then why would he be trying to cover up the fact that he did?"

▲ 10. It's practically a certainty that the government is violating the law in the arms deals with Saudi Arabians. When a reporter asked officials to describe how they were complying with the law, he was told that details about the arms sales were classified.

Exercise 6-6

Identify any examples of fallacies in the following passages. Tell why you think these are fallacies, and identify which category they belong in, if they fit any category we've described.

▲ 1. Letter to the editor: "I would like to express my feelings on the recent conflict between county supervisor Blanche Wilder and Murdock County Sheriff Al Peters over the county budget.

"I have listened to sheriffs' radio broadcasts. Many times there have been dangerous and life-threatening situations when the sheriff's deputies' quickest possible arrival time is 20 to 30 minutes. This is to me very frightening.

"Now supervisor Wilder wants to cut two officers from the Sheriff's Department. This proposal I find ridiculous. Does she really think that Sheriff Peters can run his department with no officers? How anyone can think that a county as large as Murdock can get by with no police is beyond me. I feel this proposal would be very detrimental to the safety and protection of this county's residents."

2. Letter to the editor: "Andrea Keene's selective morality is once again showing through in her July 15 letter. This time she expresses her abhorrence of abortion. But how we see only what we choose to see! I wonder if any of the anti-abortionists have considered the widespread use of fertility drugs as the moral equivalent of abortion, and, if they have, why they haven't come out against them, too. The use of these drugs frequently results in multiple births, which leads to the death of one of the infants, often after an agonizing struggle for survival. According to the rules of the pro-lifers, isn't this murder?"

— North-State Record

3. In one of her columns, Abigail Van Buren printed the letter of "I'd rather be a widow." The letter writer, a divorcée, complained about widows who said they had a hard time coping. Far better, she wrote, to be a widow than to be a divorcée, who are all "rejects" who have been "publicly dumped" and are avoided "like they have leprosy." Abby recognized the pseudoreasoning for what it was, though she did not call it by our name. What is our name for it?

▲ 4. Overheard: "Should school kids say the Pledge of Allegiance before class? Certainly. Why shouldn't they?"

5. Letter to the editor: "Once again the Park Commission is considering closing North Park Drive for the sake of a few joggers and bicyclists. These so-called fitness enthusiasts would evidently have us give up to them for their own private use every last square inch of Walnut Grove. Then anytime anyone wanted a picnic, he would have to park at the edge of the park and carry everything in—ice chests, chairs, maybe even grandma. I certainly hope the Commission keeps the entire park open for everyone to use."

6. "Some Christian—and other—groups are protesting against the placing, on federal property near the White House, of a set of plastic figurines representing a devout Jewish family in ancient Judaea. The protestors would of course deny that they are driven by any anti-Semitic motivation. Still, we wonder: Would they raise the same objections (of unconstitutionality, etc.) if the scene depicted a modern, secularized Gentile family?"

— National Review

▲ 7. "It's stupid to keep on talking about rich people not paying their fair share of taxes while the budget is so far out of balance. Why, if we raised the tax rates on the wealthy all the way back to where they were in 1980, it would not balance the federal budget."

— *Radio commentary by Howard Miller*

8. From a letter to the editor: "The counties of Michigan clearly need the ability to raise additional sources of revenue, not only to meet the demands of growth but also to maintain existing levels of service. For without these sources those demands will not be met, and it will be impossible to maintain services even at present levels."

9. In February 1992, a representative of the Catholic Church in Puerto Rico gave a radio interview (broadcast on National Public Radio) in which he said that the Church was against the use of condoms. Even though the rate of AIDS infection in Puerto Rico is much higher than on the U.S. mainland, the spokesman said that the Church could not support the use of condoms because they are not absolutely reliable in preventing the spread of the disease. "If you could prove that condoms were absolutely dependable in preventing a person from contracting AIDS, then the Church could support their use."

▲ 10. A 1991 book by a former member of the National Security Council indicated that supporters of Ronald Reagan may have made a deal with the Iranians who had been holding American hostages for months. The Iranians agreed not to release the hostages until after the 1980 election (in which Reagan defeated Jimmy Carter), and, it was alleged, the new administration promised to make weapons available to Iran. Here's one reaction to the announcement of the deal:

"I'm not surprised about Reagan's using trickery to get himself elected president. After all, he was nothing but an old actor, and he was used to using Hollywood trickery to fool people during his first career."

Exercise 6-7

Identify any examples of fallacies in the following passages. Tell why you think they are present, and identify which category they belong in, if they fit any category we've described.

▲ 1. The U.S. Congress considered a resolution criticizing the treatment of ethnic minorities in a Near Eastern country. When the minister of the interior was asked for his opinion of the resolution, he replied, "This is purely an internal affair in my country, and politicians in the U.S. should stay out of such affairs. If the truth be known, they should be more concerned with the plight of minority peoples in their own country. Thousands of black and Latino youngsters suffer from malnutrition in the United States. They can criticize us after they've got their own house in order."

2. It doesn't make any sense to speak of tracing an individual human life back past the moment of conception. After all, that's the beginning, and you can't go back past the beginning.

3. MOE: The death penalty is an excellent deterrent for murder.
JOE: What makes you think so?
MOE: Because there's no evidence that it's *not* a deterrent.
JOE: Well, states with capital punishment have higher murder rates than states that don't have it.
MOE: Yes, but that's only because there are so many legal technicalities standing in the way of executions that convicted people hardly ever get

executed. Remove those technicalities, and the rate would be lower in those states.

▲ 4. Overheard: "The new sculpture in front of the municipal building by John Murrah is atrocious and unseemly, which is clear to anyone who hasn't forgotten Murrah's mouth in Vietnam right there along with Hayden and Fonda calling for the defeat of America. I say: Drill holes in it so it'll sink and throw it in Walnut Pond."

5. Overheard: "Once we let these uptight guardians of morality have their way and start censoring *Playboy* and *Penthouse,* the next thing you know they'll be dictating everything we can read. We'll be in fine shape when they decide that *Webster's* should be pulled from the shelves."

6. It seems the biggest problem the nuclear industry has to deal with is not a poor safety record, but a lack of education of the public on nuclear power. Thousands of people die each year from pollution generated by coal-fired plants. Yet to date, there has been no death directly caused by radiation at a commercial nuclear power plant in the United States. We have a clear choice: an old, death-dealing source of energy or a safe, clean one. Proven through the test of time, nuclear power is clearly the safest form of energy and the least detrimental to the environment. Yet it is perceived as unsafe and an environmental hazard.

▲ 7. A high school teacher once told my class that if a police state ever arose in America, it would happen because we freely handed away our civil rights in exchange for what we perceived would be security from the government. We are looking at just that in connection with the current drug crisis.

For almost thirty years we've seen increasing tolerance, legally and socially, of drug use. Now we are faced with the very end of America as we know it, if not from the drug problem, then from the proposed solutions to it.

First, it was urine tests. Officials said that the innocent have nothing to fear. Using that logic, why not allow unannounced police searches of our homes for stolen goods? After all, the innocent would have nothing to fear.

Now we're looking at the seizure of boats and other property when even traces of drugs are found. You'd better hope some drug-using guest doesn't drop the wrong thing in your home, car, or boat.

The only alternative to declaring real war on the real enemies—the Asian and South American drug families—is to wait for that knock on the door in the middle of the night.

8. The mayor's argument is that because the developers' fee would reduce the number of building starts, ultimately the city would lose more money than it would gain through the fee. But I can't go along with that. Mayor Tower is a member of the Board of Realtors, and you know what *they* think of the fee.

9. Letter to the editor: "Next week the philosopher Tom Regan will be in town again, peddling his animal rights theory. In case you've forgotten, Regan was here about three years ago arguing against using animals in scientific experimentation. As far as I could see then and can see now, neither Regan nor anyone else has managed to come up with a good

reason why animals should not be experimented on. Emotional appeals and horror stories no doubt influence many, but they shouldn't. I've always wondered what Regan would say if his children needed medical treatment that was based on animal experiments."

▲ **10.** Not long before Ronald and Nancy Reagan moved out of the White House, former Chief of Staff Don Regan wrote a book in which he depicted a number of revealing inside stories about First Family goings-on. Among them was the disclosure that Nancy Reagan regularly sought the advice of a San Francisco astrologer. In response to the story, the White House spokesman at the time, Marlin Fitzwater, said, "Vindictiveness and revenge are not admirable qualities and are not worthy of comment."

Exercise 6-8

Elegant Country Estate

- Stunning Federal-style brick home with exquisite appointments throughout
- 20 picturesque acres with lake, pasture, and woodland
- 5 bedrooms, 4.5 baths
- 5800 sq. ft. living space, 2400 sq. ft. basement
- Formal living room; banquet dining with butler's pantry; luxurious foyer, gourmet kitchen, morning room
- 3 fireplaces, 12 chandeliers

Maude and Clyde are discussing whether to buy this nice little cottage. Identify as many fallacies and rhetorical devices as you can in their conversation. Many are from this chapter, but you may see something from Chapters 4 and 5 as well.

CLYDE: Maude, look at this place! This is the house for us! Let's make an offer right now. We can afford it!

MAUDE: Oh, Clyde, be serious. That house is way beyond our means.

CLYDE: Well, I think we can afford it.

MAUDE: Honey, if we can afford it, pigs can fly.

CLYDE: Look, do you want to live in a shack? Besides, I called the real estate agent. She says it's a real steal.

MAUDE: Well, what do you expect her to say? She's looking for a commission.

CLYDE: Sometimes I don't understand you. Last week you were pushing for a really upscale place.

MAUDE: Clyde, we can't make the payments on a place like that. We couldn't even afford to heat it! And what on earth are we going to do with a lake?

CLYDE: Honey, the payments would only be around $5000 a month. How much do you think we could spend?
MAUDE: I'd say $1800.
CLYDE: Okay, how about $2050?
MAUDE: Oh, for heaven's sake! Yes, we could do $2050!
CLYDE: Well, how about $3100?
MAUDE: Oh, Clyde, what is your point?
CLYDE: So $3100 is okay? How about $3200? Stop me when I get to exactly where we can't afford it.
MAUDE: Clyde, I can't say exactly where it gets to be too expensive, but $5000 a month is too much.
CLYDE: Well, I think we can afford it.
MAUDE: Why?
CLYDE: Because it's within our means!
MAUDE: Clyde, you're the one who's always saying we have to cut back on our spending!
CLYDE: Yes, but this'll be a great investment!
MAUDE: And what makes you say that?
CLYDE: Because we're bound to make money on it.
MAUDE: Clyde, honey, you are going around in circles.
CLYDE: Well, can you prove we can't afford it?
MAUDE: Once we start spending money like drunken sailors, where will it end? Next we'll have to get a riding mower, then a boat for that lake, a butler for the butler's pantry—where will it end?
CLYDE: Well, we don't have to make up our minds right now. I'll call the agent and tell her we're sleeping on it.
MAUDE: Asleep and dreaming.

Exercise 6-9

In groups, vote on which option best depicts the fallacy found in each passage; then compare results with other groups in the class. *Note:* The fallacies include those found in Chapter 5 and Chapter 6.

▲ **1.** The Health Editor for *USA Today* certainly seems to know what she is talking about when she recommends we take vitamins, but I happen to know she works for Tishcon, Inc., a large manufacturer of vitamin supplements.

a. smokescreen/red herring
b. subjectivism
c. argument from popularity
d. circumstantial ad hominem
e. no fallacy

2. The president is right. People who are against attacking Iraq are unwilling to face up to the threat of terrorism.

a. common practice
b. peer pressure
c. false dilemma
d. straw man
e. begging the question

3. Well, I for one think the position taken by our union is correct, and I'd like to remind you before you make up your mind on the matter that around here we employees have a big say in who gets rehired.

a. wishful thinking
b. circumstantial ad hominem
c. scare tactics
d. apple polishing
e. begging the question

▲ **4.** On the whole, I think global warming is a farce. After all, most people think winters are getting colder, if anything. How could that many people be wrong?

a. argument from outrage
b. argument from popularity
c. straw man
d. no fallacy

5. MARCO: I think global warming is a farce.
CLAUDIA: Oh, gad. How can you say such a thing, when there is so much evidence behind the theory?
MARCO: Because. Look. If it isn't a farce, then how come the world is colder now than it used to be?

a. begging the question
b. subjectivism
c. red herring
d. circumstantial ad hominem
e. no fallacy

6. Of course you should buy a life insurance policy! Why shouldn't you?

a. smokescreen/red herring
b. wishful thinking
c. scare tactics
d. peer pressure argument
e. misplacing burden of proof

▲ **7.** My opponent, Mr. London, has charged me with having cheated on my income tax. My response is, When are we going to get this campaign out of the gutter? Isn't it time we stood up and made it clear that vilification has no place in politics?

a. smokescreen/red herring
b. wishful thinking
c. argument from common practice
d. argument from popularity
e. circumstantial ad hominem

8. Either we impeach the man or we send a message to the kids of this country that it's all right to lie under oath. Seems like an easy choice to me.

a. smokescreen/red herring
b. straw man
c. false dilemma
d. inconsistency ad hominem
e. none of these

9. If cigarettes aren't bad for you, then how come it's so hard on your health to smoke?
   a. circumstantial ad hominem
   b. genetic fallacy
   c. slippery slope
   d. begging the question

▲ 10. Global warming? I don't care what the scientists say. Just 'cause it's true for them doesn't make it true for me.
   a. smokescreen/red herring
   b. subjectivism
   c. argument from tradition
   d. argument from common practice

Exercise 6-10

In groups, vote on which option best depicts the fallacy found in each passage, and compare results with other groups. (It is all right with us if you ask anyone who is not participating in the discussions in your group to leave.) *Note:* The fallacies include those found in Chapter 5 and Chapter 6.

▲ 1. So what if the senator accepted a little kickback money—most politicians are corrupt, after all.
   a. argument from envy
   b. argument from tradition
   c. common practice
   d. subjectivism
   e. no fallacy

2. Me? I'm going to vote with the company on this one. After all, I've been with them for fifteen years.
   a. genetic fallacy
   b. group think fallacy
   c. slippery slope
   d. no fallacy

3. Public opinion polls? They're rigged. Just ask anyone.
   a. argument from common practice
   b. guilt trip
   c. begging the question
   d. argument from popularity
   e. no fallacy

▲ 4. Hey! It can't be time for the bars to close. I'm having too much fun.
   a. false dilemma
   b. misplacing burden of proof
   c. wishful thinking
   d. argument from tradition
   e. no fallacy

5. A mural for the municipal building? Excuse me, but why should public money, *our* tax dollars, be used for a totally unnecessary thing like art? There are potholes that need fixing. Traffic signals that need to be put up.

There are a *million* things that are more important. It is an *outrage,* spending taxpayers' money on unnecessary frills like art. Give me a break!

a. inconsistency ad hominem
b. argument from outrage
c. slippery slope
d. perfectionist fallacy
e. no fallacy

6. Mathematics is more difficult than sociology, and I *really* need an easier term this fall. So I'm going to take a sociology class instead of a math class.

a. circumstantial ad hominem
b. argument from pity
c. false dilemma
d. begging the question
e. no fallacy

▲ **7.** Parker says Macs are better than PCs, but what would you expect him to say? He's owned Macs for years.

a. personal attack ad hominem
b. circumstantial ad hominem
c. inconsistency ad hominem
d. perfectionist fallacy
e. no fallacy

8. The congressman thought the president's behavior was an impeachable offense. But that's nonsense, coming from the congressman. He had an adulterous affair himself, after all.

a. inconsistency ad hominem
b. poisoning the well
c. circumstantial ad hominem
d. genetic fallacy
e. no fallacy

9. Your professor wants you to read Moore and Parker? Forget it. Their book is so far to the right it's falling off the shelf.

a. poisoning the well
b. inconsistency ad hominem
c. misplacing burden of proof
d. argument from tradition
e. no fallacy

▲ **10.** How do I know God exists? Hey, do you know he doesn't?

a. perfectionist fallacy
b. inconsistency ad hominem
c. misplacing burden of proof
d. slippery slope
e. begging the question

Exercise 6-11

In groups, vote on which option best depicts the fallacy found in each passage, and compare results with other groups. *Note:* The fallacies include those found in Chapter 5 and Chapter 6.

Real Life

Getting Really Worked Up over Ideas

Not long ago the editor of *Freethought Today* magazine won a court case upholding the constitutional separation of church and state. Following are a few samples of the mail she received as a result (there was much more), as they were printed in the magazine. We present them to remind you of how worked up people can get over ideas.

> Satan worshipping scum . . .
>
> If you don't like this country and what it was founded on & for *get the f–– out of it* and go straight to hell.
>
> F– you, you communist wh–.
>
> If you think that mathematical precision that governs the universe was established by random events then you truly are that class of IDIOT that cannot be aptly defined.

These remarks illustrate extreme versions of more than one rhetorical device mentioned in this part of the book. They serve as a reminder that some people become defensive and emotional when it comes to their religion. (As Richard Dawkins, professor of Public Understanding of Science at Oxford University, was prompted to remark, "A philosophical opinion about the nature of the universe, which is held by the great majority of America's top scientists and probably the elite intelligentsia generally, is so abhorrent to the American electorate that no candidate for popular election dare affirm it in public.")

– Adapted from *Free Inquiry*, Summer 2002

▲ **1.** Laws against teenagers drinking?—They are a total waste of time, frankly. No matter how many laws we pass, there are always going to be some teens who drink.

a. misplacing burden of proof
b. perfectionist fallacy
c. line-drawing fallacy
d. no fallacy

2. Even though Sidney was old enough to buy a drink at the bar, he had no identification with him and the bartender would not serve him.

a. perfectionist fallacy
b. inconsistency ad hominem
c. misplacing burden of proof
d. slippery slope
e. no fallacy

3. Just how much sex has to be in a movie before you call it pornographic? Seems to me the whole concept makes no sense.

a. perfectionist fallacy
b. line-drawing fallacy
c. straw man
d. slippery slope
e. no fallacy

▲ 4. Studies confirm what everyone already knows: Smaller classes make students better learners.

a. argument from common practice
b. begging the question
c. misplacing burden of proof
d. argument from popularity
e. no fallacy

5. The trouble with impeaching Bill Clinton is this: Going after every person who occupies the presidency will take up everyone's time and the government will never get anything else done.

a. inconsistency ad hominem
b. straw man
c. group think
d. argument from envy
e. red herring

6. The trouble with impeaching Bill Clinton is this. If we start going after Clinton, next we'll be going after senators, representatives, governors. Pretty soon no elected official will be safe from partisan attack.

a. inconsistency ad hominem
b. slippery slope
c. straw man
d. false dilemma
e. misplacing burden of proof

▲ 7. MR. IMHOFF: That does it. I'm cutting down on your peanut butter cookies. Those things blimp me up.
MRS. IMHOFF: Oh, Imhoff, get real. What about all the ice cream you eat?

a. circumstantial ad hominem
b. subjectivism
c. straw man
d. slippery slope
e. inconsistency ad hominem

8. KEN: I think I'll vote for Andrews. She's the best candidate.
ROBERT: Why do you say she's best?
KEN: Because she's my sister-in-law. Didn't you know that?

a. apple polishing
b. argument from pity
c. scare tactics
d. peer pressure argument
e. none of the above

9. MOE: You going to class tomorrow?
JOE: I s'pose. Why?
MOE: Say, don't you get tired of being a Goody Two-shoes? You must have the most perfect attendance record of anyone who ever went to this school—certainly better than the rest of us; right, guys?

a. poisoning the well
b. argument from pity
c. scare tactics

d. no fallacy
e. none of the above

▲ **10.** Morgan, you're down to earth and I trust your judgment. That's why I know I can count on you to back me up at the meeting this afternoon.

a. apple polishing
b. argument from pity
c. scare tactics
d. guilt trip
e. no fallacy

11. "Do you want to sign this petition to the governor?"

"What's it about?"

"We want him to veto that handgun registration bill that's come out of the legislature."

"Oh. No, I don't think I want to sign that."

"Oh, really? So are you telling me you want to get rid of the Second Amendment?"

a. false dilemma
b. personal attack ad hominem
c. genetic fallacy
d. misplacing burden of proof
e. no fallacy

12. Outlaw gambling? Man, that's a strange idea coming from you. Aren't you the one who plays the lottery all the time?

a. inconsistency ad hominem
b. circumstantial ad hominem
c. genetic fallacy
d. scare tactics
e. no fallacy

Exercise 6-12

Most of the following passages contain fallacies from Chapter 5 or Chapter 6. Identify them where they occur and try to place them in one of the categories we have described.

▲ **1.** "People in Hegins, Pennsylvania, hold an annual pigeon shoot in order to control the pigeon population and to raise money for the town. This year, the pigeon shoot was disrupted by animal rights activists who tried to release the pigeons from their cages. I can't help but think these animal rights activists are the same people who believe in controlling the human population through the use of abortion. Yet, they recoil at a similar means of controlling pigeons. What rank hypocrisy."

— *Rush Limbaugh*

2. Dear Mr. Swanson: I realize I'm not up for a salary increase yet, but I thought it might make my review a bit more timely if I pointed out to you that I have a copy of all the recent e-mail messages between you and Ms. Flood in the purchasing department.

3. I don't care if Nike has signed up Michael Jordan, Tiger Woods, and even Santa Claus to endorse their shoes. They're a crummy company that makes a crummy product. The proof is the fact that they pay poor women a dollar sixty for a long day's work in their Vietnamese shoe factories. That's not even enough to buy a day's worth of decent meals!

▲ 4. I don't care if Nike has signed up Michael Jordan, Tiger Woods, and even Santa Claus to endorse their shoes. They're a crummy company, and I wouldn't buy their shoes no matter what the circumstance. You don't need any reason beyond the fact that they pay poor women a dollar sixty for a long day's work in their Vietnamese shoe factories. That's not even enough to buy a day's worth of decent meals!

5. JULIA: Even this long after the 2000 presidential election, I still feel sort of unsettled about it. It still feels sort of illegitimate—do you know what I mean?
JEFF: Look, it's a done deal, and Bush is the president. Get over it!

6. POWELL FAN: Colin Powell says that diplomatic efforts to avoid war with Iraq were serious and genuine, and his word is good enough for me.
SKEPTIC: And what makes you so sure he's telling it like it is?
FAN: Because he's the one guy in the administration you can trust.

▲ 7. I know the repair guy in the service center screwed up my computer; he's the only one who's touched it since it was working fine last Monday.

8. If you give the cat your leftover asparagus, next thing you know you'll be feeding him your potatoes, maybe even your roast beef. Where will it all end? Pretty soon that wretched animal will be sitting up here on the table for dinner. He'll be eating us out of house and home.

9. Look, either we refrain from feeding the cat table scraps, or he'll be up here on the table with us. So don't go giving him your asparagus.

▲ 10. We have a simple choice. Saving Social Security is sure as hell a lot more important than giving people a tax cut. So write your representative now and let him or her know how you feel.

11. Let gays join the military? Give me a break. God created Adam and Eve, not Adam and Steve.

12. So my professor told me if he gave me an A for getting an 89.9 on the test, next he'd have to give people an A for getting an 89.8 on the test, and pretty soon he'd have to give everyone in the class an A. How could I argue with that?

▲ 13. Those blasted Democrats! They want to increase government spending on education again. This is the same outfit that gave us $10,000 toilets and government regulations up the wazoo.

14. All this yammering about Clinton having been a liar—spare me! Every president under the sun has lied—Reagan, Kennedy, Nixon, both Bushes, probably even Jimmy Carter.

15. Lauren did a better job than anyone else at the audition, so even if she has no experience, we've decided to give her the part in the play.

▲ 16. TERRY: I failed my test but I gave my prof this nifty argument. I said, "Look, suppose somebody did 0.0001 percent better than I, would that be a big enough difference to give him a higher grade?" And he had to say "no," so then I said, "And if someone did 0.0001 percent better than that second person, would that be a big enough difference?" And he had to say "no" to that, too, so I just kept it up, and he never could point to the place where the difference was big enough to give the other person a higher grade. He finally saw he couldn't justify giving anyone a better grade.

HARRY: Well? What happened?

TERRY: He had to fail the whole class.

17. There is an increasingly large likelihood of a war with Iraq this winter [of 2003]. It is not clear just what Saddam Hussein has in the way of nuclear, chemical, and biological weapons, but we believe he is not without some capability with weapons of those kinds. In fact, we are sure that, if it were within his capabilities at this moment, he would launch a preemptive strike against the United States. All the more reason that the United States strike first.

— *Loosely adapted from a conversation on NBC's* Meet the Press

18. Look, maybe you think it's okay to legalize tribal casinos, but I don't. Letting every last group of people in the country open a casino is a ridiculous idea, bound to cause trouble.

▲ **19.** What, you of all people complaining about violence on TV? You, with all the pro football you watch?

20. You have three Fs and a D on your exams, and your quizzes are on the borderline between passing and failing. I'm afraid you don't deserve to pass the course.

Exercise 6-13

Where we (Moore and Parker) teach, the city council recently debated relaxing the local noise ordinance. One student (who favored relaxation) appeared before the council and stated: "If 250 people are having fun, one person shouldn't be able to stop them."

We asked our students to state whether they agreed or disagreed with that student and to support their position with an argument. Here are some of the responses.

Divide into groups, and then identify any instances of fallacious reasoning you find in any answers, drawing from the materials in the last two chapters. Compare your results with those of other students, and see what your instructor thinks.

1. I support what the person is saying. If 250 people are having fun, one person shouldn't be able to stop them. Having parties and having a good time are a way of life for Chico State students. The areas around campus have always been this way.
2. A lot of people attend Chico State because of the social aspects. If rules are too tight, the school could lose its appeal. Without the students, local businesses would go under. Students keep the town floating. It's not just bars and liquor stores, but gas stations and grocery stores and apartment houses. This town would be like Orland.
3. If students aren't allowed to party, the college will go out of business.

4. We work hard all week long studying and going to classes. We deserve to let off steam after a hard week.
5. Noise is a fact of life around most college campuses. People should know what they are getting into before they move there. If they don't like it, they should just get earplugs or leave.
6. I agree with what the person is saying. If 250 people want to have fun, what gives one person the right to stop them?
7. I am sure many of the people who complain are the same people who used to be stumbling down Ivy Street twenty years ago doing the same thing that the current students are doing.
8. Two weeks ago I was at a party and it was only about 9:00 P.M. There were only a few people there and it was quiet. And then the police came and told us we had to break it up because a neighbor complained. Well, that neighbor is an elderly lady who would complain if you flushed the toilet. I think it's totally unreasonable.
9. Sometimes the noise level gets a little out of control, but there are other ways to go about addressing this problem. For example, if you are a neighbor and you are having a problem with the noise level, why don't you call the "party house" and let them know, instead of going way too far and calling the police?
10. I'm sure that these "narcs" have nothing else better to do than to harass the "party people."
11. You can't get rid of all the noise around a college campus no matter what you do.
12. The Chico noise ordinance was put there by the duly elected officials of the city and is the law. People do not have the right to break a law that was put in place under proper legal procedures.
13. The country runs according to majority rule. If the overwhelming majority want to party and make noise, under our form of government they should be given the freedom to do so.
14. Students make a contribution to the community, and in return they should be allowed to make noise if they want.
15. Your freedom ends at my property line.

Exercise 6-14

Listen to a talk-radio program (e.g., Al Franken, Rush Limbaugh, Michael Reagan, Michael Savage), and see how many minutes (or seconds) go by before you hear one of the following: ad hominem, straw man, ridicule, argument from outrage, or scare tactics. Report your findings to the class and describe the first item from the above list that you heard.

Exercise 6-15

Watch one of the news/public affairs programs on television (*NewsHour with Jim Lehrer, Nightline, Face the Nation,* and so on), and make a note of any examples of fallacies that occur. Explain in writing why you think the examples contain fallacious reasoning.

Alternatively, watch *Real Time* with Bill Maher. It usually doesn't take long to find a fallacy there.

Exercise 6-16

The following passages contain fallacies from both this and the preceding chapter. Identify the category in which each item belongs.

▲ **1.** "I can safely say that no law, no matter how stiff the consequence is, will completely stop illegal drug use. Outlawing drugs is a waste of time."

— From a student essay

2. "If we expand the commuter bus program, where is it going to end? Will we want to have a trolley system? Then a light rail system? Then expand Metrolink to our area? A city this size hardly needs and certainly cannot afford all these amenities."

— From a newspaper call-in column

3. YAEKO: The character Dana Scully on *The X-Files* really provides a good role model for young women. She's a medical doctor and an FBI agent, and she's intelligent, professional, and devoted to her work.
MICHAEL: Those shows about paranormal activities are so unrealistic. Alien abductions, government conspiracies—it's all ridiculous.

4. Overheard: "The reason I don't accept evolution is that ever since Darwin, scientists have been trying to prove that we evolved from some apelike primate ancestor. Well, they still haven't succeeded. Case closed."

▲ **5.** Ladies and gentlemen, as you know, I endorsed Council Member Morrissey's bid for reelection based on his outstanding record during his first term. Because you are the movers and shakers in this community, other people place the same high value on your opinions that I do. Jim and I would feel privileged to have your support.

6. It's totally ridiculous to suppose that creationism is true. If creationism were true, then half of what we know through science would be false, which is complete nonsense.

7. KIRSTI: I counted my CDs this weekend, and out of twenty-seven, ten of them were by U2. They are such a good band! I haven't heard anything by Bono for a long time. He has such a terrific voice!
BEN: Is he bisexual?

8. Was Gerhard a good committee chair? Well, I for one think you have to say he was excellent, especially when you consider all the abuse he put up with. Right from the start people went after him—they didn't even give him a chance to show what he could do. It was really vicious—people making fun of him right to his face. Yes, under the circumstances he has been quite effective.

▲ **9.** Medical research that involves animals is completely unnecessary and a waste of money. Just think of the poor creatures! We burn and blind and torture them, and then we kill them. They don't know what is going to happen to them, but they know something is going to happen. They are scared to death. It's really an outrage.

10. Dear Editor—

    If Christians do not participate in government, only sinners will.

    — *From a letter to the* Chico Enterprise Record

11. The HMO people claim that the proposal will raise the cost of doing business in the state to such a degree that insurers will be forced to leave the state and do business elsewhere. What nonsense. Just look at what we get from these HMOs. I know people who were denied decent treatment for cancer because their HMO wouldn't approve it. There are doctors who won't recommend a procedure for their patients because they are afraid the HMO will cancel their contract. And when an HMO does cancel some doctor's contract, the patients have to find a new doctor themselves—*if* they can. Everybody has a horror story. Enough is enough.

12. HOWARD: Dad, I really appreciate your letting me borrow the Chevy. But Melanie's parents just bought her a brand new Mercedes!
    DAD: Some people just refuse to buy American!

▲ 13. [Dole campaign chairman] SCOTT REID: There is a clear pattern of campaign finance abuse by the [Clinton] administration. Indonesian business interests have steered millions into the President's campaign using a gardener as a front, and [Democratic fund-raiser] John Huang, who apparently laundered money at a fund-raiser at a Buddhist temple in California, is suddenly nowhere to be found.
    [White House Senior Adviser] GEORGE STEPHANOPOULOS: I can't let these charges go unrefuted. Dole has received millions from foreign supporters like José Fanjul, and his vice chairman for finance, Simon Fireman, had to pay the largest fine in the history of the country for massive violations of campaign-finance laws.

    — *On NBC's* Meet the Press

14. The proposal to reduce spending for the arts just doesn't make any sense. We spend a paltry $620 million for the NEA [National Endowment for the Arts], while the deficit is closing in on $200 billion. Cutting support for the arts isn't going to eliminate the deficit; that's obvious.

15. Year-round schools? I'm opposed. Once we let them do that, the next thing you know they'll be cutting into our vacation time and asking us to teach in the evenings and on the weekends and who knows where it will end. We teachers have to stand up for our rights.

▲ 16. [NBC's *Meet the Press* host] TIM RUSSERT: Mr. Perot, Bob Dole says that every vote for Ross Perot is a vote for Bill Clinton. True?
    ROSS PEROT: Of course that's not true. They've been programmed from birth to say that if they are a Republican.

17. Even if we outlaw guns we're still going to have crime and murder. So I really don't see much point in it.

    — *From a student essay*

18. Do you think affirmative action programs are still necessary in the country?
    Answers:

    a. Yes, of course. I don't see how you, a woman, can ask that question. It's obvious we have a very long way to go still.
    b. No. Because of affirmative action, my brother lost his job to a minority who had a lot less experience than he did.

c. Yes. The people who want to end affirmative action are all white males who just want to go back to the good-old-boy system. It's always the same: Look out for number one.
d. No. The people who want it to continue know a good deal when they see one. You think I'd want to end it if I were a minority?

Exercise 6-17

Explain in a sentence or two how each of the following passages involves a type of fallacy mentioned in either this or the preceding chapter. *Many of these examples are difficult* and should serve to illustrate how fallacies sometimes conform only loosely to the standard patterns.

▲ **1.** I believe that the companies that produce passenger airliners should be more strictly supervised by the FAA. I mean, good grief, everybody knows that you can make more money by cutting corners here and there than by spending extra time and effort getting things just right, and you know there have got to be airlines that are doing exactly that.

2. From a letter to a college newspaper editor: "I really appreciated the fact that your editorial writer supports the hike in the student activity fee that has been proposed. Since the writer is a senior and won't even be here next year, he will escape having to pay the fee himself, so of course there's no downside to it as far as he's concerned. I'm against the fee, and I'll be one of those who pay it if it passes. Mine is an opinion that should count."

3. "'There's a certain sameness to the news on the Big Three [ABC, NBC, and CBS] and CNN,' says Moody, . . . who is in charge of Fox News's day-to-day editorial decisions. That's the message, Moody says, that 'America is bad, corporations are bad, animal species should be protected, and every cop is a racist killer. That's where "fair and balanced" [Fox's slogan] comes in. We don't think all corporations are bad, every forest should be saved, every government spending program is good. We're going to be more inquisitive.'"

— *From an interview with John Moody, vice president for news editorial at Fox News Network, in* Brill's Content *magazine*

▲ **4.** During the Reagan and G. H. W. Bush administrations, Democratic members of Congress pointed to the two presidents' economic policies as causing huge deficits that could ultimately ruin the country's economy. President Bush dismissed such charges as "the politics of doom and gloom." "These people will find a dark cloud everywhere," he has said. Was this response fallacious reasoning?

▲ **5.** "Louis Harris, one of the nation's most influential pollsters, readily admits he is in the polling business to 'have some impact with the movers and shakers of the world.' So poll questions are often worded to obtain answers that help legitimize the liberal Establishment's viewpoints."

— Conservative Digest

6. "At a White House meeting in February of 1983 with Washington, D.C., anchormen, Ronald Reagan was asked to comment on 'an apparent continuing perception among a number of black leaders that the White House continues to be, if not hostile, at least not welcome to black viewpoints.' President Reagan replied as follows: 'I'm aware of all that, and it's very disturbing to me, because anyone who knows my life story knows that long before there was a thing called the civil-rights movement, I was busy on that side. As a sports announcer, I didn't have any Willie Mayses or Reggie Jacksons to talk about when I was broadcasting major league baseball. The opening line of the Spalding Baseball Guide said, "Baseball is a game for Caucasian gentlemen." And as a sports announcer I was one of a very small fraternity that used that job to editorialize against that ridiculous blocking of so many fine athletes and so many fine Americans from participating in what was called the great American game.' Reagan then went on to mention that his father refused to allow him to see *Birth of a Nation* because it was based on the Ku Klux Klan and once slept in a car during a blizzard rather than stay at a hotel that barred Jews. Reagan's 'closest teammate and buddy' was a black, he said."

— *James Nathan Miller,* The Atlantic

7. From a letter to the editor of the *Atlantic Monthly:* "In all my reading and experience so far, I have found nothing presented by science and technology that precludes there being a spiritual element to the human being. . . . The bottom line is this: Maybe there are no angels, afterlife, UFOs, or even a God. Certainly their existence has not yet been scientifically proved. But just as certainly, their *nonexistence* remains unproved. Any reasonable person would therefore have to reserve judgment."

8. Stop blaming the developers for the fact that our town is growing! If you want someone to blame, blame the university. It brings the new people here, not the developers. Kids come here from God knows where, and lots of them like what they find and stick around. All the developers do is put roofs over those former students' heads.

▲ 9. Two favorite scientists of the Council for Tobacco Research were Carl Seltzer and Theodore Sterling. Seltzer, a biological anthropologist, believes smoking has no role in heart disease and has alleged in print that data in the huge 45-year, 10,000-person Framingham Heart Study—which found otherwise—have been distorted by anti-tobacco researchers. Framingham Director William Castelli scoffs at Seltzer's critique but says it "has had some impact in keeping the debate alive."

Sterling, a statistician, disputes the validity of population studies linking smoking to illness, arguing that their narrow focus on smoking obscures the more likely cause—occupational exposure to toxic fumes.

For both men, defying conventional wisdom has been rewarding. Seltzer says he has received "well over $1 million" from the Council for research. Sterling got $1.1 million for his Special Projects work in 1977–82, court records show.

— *From "How Tobacco Firms Keep Health Questions 'Open' Year After Year," Alix Freedman and Laurie Cohen. The article originally appeared in the* Wall Street Journal *and was reprinted in the* Sacramento Bee.

10. We have had economic sanctions in effect against China ever since the Tienanmen Square massacre. Clearly they haven't turned the Chinese leadership in Beijing into a bunch of good guys. All they've done, in fact, is cost American business a lot of money. We should get rid of the sanctions and find some other way to make them improve their human rights record.

Writing Exercises

1. Your instructor will assign one or more of the Essays for Analysis in Appendix 1 for you to scan for fallacies and rhetorical devices.
2. When Marshall Gardiner married J'Noel Gardiner, he was aware that his new wife had been born a male and had recently had a sex-change operation. When Marshall Gardiner died, his wife's right to inherit half of her husband's $2.5 million estate was challenged by Marshall Gardiner's son. The son claimed the marriage was invalid under Kansas law, which declares same-sex marriages invalid, but does not address marriages involving transsexuals. The case went to the state supreme court in 2002. How should the court have ruled, in your opinion? Defend your position, using whatever rhetorical devices from Chapters 4, 5, and 6 you want. When everyone is finished, read the essays in groups looking for fallacies and other rhetorical devices. Your instructor may have groups select one essay to read to the class.
3. Should Kansas (or any other state) make same-sex marriages illegal? Take a position and defend it following the instructions for Exercise 2.

Chapter 7

The Anatomy and Varieties of Arguments

When we evaluate a person's deeds, including those of a public official like Hillary Clinton here, we ordinarily use deductive arguments. When we surmise what an individual's future deeds will be, we ordinarily employ inductive arguments. Deduction and induction are explained in this chapter.

Recently, we read about a potential juror in a Los Angeles courtroom who yawned loudly during jury selection. Superior Court Judge Craig Veals, who was annoyed by this, asked the man if he had a problem. "I find this really boring," the man explained. The judge replied, "Well, I find you in contempt. That will cost you $1,000." He then asked the man if he was still bored.*

This chapter is about logic, which among other things is the study of the principles of reasoning; that is, those principles by which arguments must be evaluated. In the example above, Judge Veals was reasoning deductively. He was applying a general principle—a principle about the sorts of thing that count as being in contempt of court—to a specific case. The pattern of reasoning involved is known as a categorical syllogism, and it is a common form of reasoning about which we will say much in the next chapter. We'll return to Judge Veals in a moment.

*Based on an Associated Press report by Caroline Liss, April 22, 2005. The judge later reduced the fine to $100.

ARGUMENTS: GENERAL FEATURES AND REVIEW

We said a lot about arguments back in Chapter 1, and it wouldn't hurt to repeat the basics here, expanding where necessary. As we said, an argument consists of two parts: One part (the *premise* or *premises*) is supposedly a reason for believing the other part (the *conclusion*). Earlier we mentioned our friend Ken, who mows his lawn in his bare feet. Ken gave as his reason for this dangerous practice that most lawn-mowing accidents involve people wearing shoes, and he figured that meant his chances of getting hurt were less if he didn't wear shoes. Ken's argument was not a good one, but it was an argument. It had a premise *(Most lawn-mowing accidents involve people wearing shoes)* and a conclusion *(The chances of getting into a lawn-mowing accident therefore are less if you don't wear shoes).*

Another example of an argument: Recently, we read about a man, John McGivney, 64, who had much trouble starting his 1994 Chrysler LeBaron. As a result, he pulled out a .38-caliber semiautomatic and shot five rounds into the hood of the car, apparently to teach it a lesson. Sheriff's deputies in Broward County, Florida, tried to teach Mr. McGivney a different lesson and placed him in jail for discharging a firearm in public. McGivney, however, was unrepentant. The car, he asserted, had "outlived its usefulness" and the pleasure of putting it "out of its misery" was "worth every damn minute in that jail."* McGivney had thus presented an argument, that [premise] *the LeBaron had outlived its usefulness,* and therefore [conclusion] *it was justifiable for him to put it out of its misery.*

One more example of an argument, a little more complicated, might prove useful:

> It's morally wrong for a person to inflict awful pain on another sensitive creature, one that has done the first no harm. Therefore, the so-called scientists who perform their hideous and sadistic experiments on innocent animals are moral criminals just as were Hitler and his Nazi torturers.

The rhetoric used here is pretty obvious, and one might read the passage and, after the comparison with Hitler and Nazi torturers, simply pass the whole thing off. "No, those scientists are not like Hitler—this person is nuts." But doing this would be to ignore a real argument contained in the passage. Shorn of rhetoric, the argument is this:

1. Animals used in some experiments suffer serious pain as a result.
2. Those animals have caused no harm.
3. It is morally wrong to inflict pain upon a creature that has caused no harm.
4. Therefore, those who use animals in these experiments are committing morally wrong actions.

We've laid this argument out in more detail than is probably necessary—it could be done in two steps instead of four—because we want to use it as an

*Associated Press report by Caroline Liss, April 22, 2005.

In Depth

Conclusion Indicators

When the words in the following list are used in arguments, they usually indicate that a premise has just been offered and that a conclusion is about to be presented. (The three dots represent the claim that is the conclusion.)

Thus . . .	Consequently . . .
Therefore . . .	So . . .
Hence . . .	Accordingly . . .
This shows that . . .	This implies that . . .
This suggests that . . .	This proves that . . .

Example:

Stacy drives a Porsche. This suggests that either she is rich or her parents are.

The conclusion is

Either she is rich or her parents are.

The premise is

Stacy drives a Porsche.

illustration. The first three claims in the argument are the premises, and the fourth claim is the argument's conclusion.

Identifying our arguments—and those of others—is not always easy because they usually come expressed with rhetoric, go off on tangents, and bring in other extraneous material. The first part of this book provided practice in identifying arguments and spotting irrelevances and rhetorical flourishes; later in this chapter we'll explain a technique for diagramming written passages containing arguments, a technique that can be useful for identifying premises and conclusions. In the box above, and on p. 218, we repeat conclusion- and premise-indicating words and phrases, which can aid in spotting conclusions and premises.

Conclusions Used as Premises

Let's go back to Mr. McGivney, his Chrysler LeBaron, and his .38 caliber semiautomatic. When Mr. McGivney was asked for his reason (argument) for "putting his car out of its misery," he said, "It outlived its usefulness." We might imagine then asking him for his reasons for thinking his car had outlived its usefulness. He would then say (giving us a second argument), "Because it won't start anymore." In other words, what we have is a case in which the conclusion of one argument serves as a premise for a second argument, thus:

First argument
Premise: The LeBaron won't start.
Conclusion: Therefore, it has outlived its usefulness.

Second argument
Premise: The LeBaron has outlined its usefulness.
Conclusion: Therefore, it should be put out of its misery.

In Depth

Premise Indicators

When the words in the following list are used in arguments, they generally introduce premises. They often occur just *after* a conclusion has been given. A premise would replace the three dots in an actual argument.

Since . . .

Because . . .

For . . .

In view of . . .

This is implied by . . .

Example:

Either Stacy is rich or her parents are, since she drives a Porsche.

The premise is the claim that Stacy drives a Porsche; the conclusion is the claim that either Stacy is rich or her parents are.

As you can see, one and the same claim can be the conclusion of one argument and the premise in another argument. This, of course, happens each and every time we try to support or demonstrate the premises of an argument.

Obviously, every chain of reasoning must begin somewhere. If we ask Mr. McGivney what his reasons are for thinking his car won't start, he might well look at us oddly. However, if pressed, he might say that he had just *seen* that it wouldn't start. If we pressed harder and asked him to prove that he had just seen it not start, there is every chance Mr. McGivney would reach again for his .38.

What counts as a legitimate starting point for a chain of arguments, if anything, is a question in the branch of philosophy known as epistemology—the theory of knowledge. Though epistemology can be a lot of fun, we don't propose going into it here. The point we are making here, one that is fairly obvious, is that a premise can itself stand in need of support or demonstration; if support or demonstration is provided, that premise functions both as the conclusion of one argument and as a premise of another argument.

Unstated Premises and Conclusions

Arguments also contain unstated premises, a point to which we return in more detail momentarily. For example:

> [Premise] You can't check out books from the library without an ID card. [Conclusion] So Bill won't be able to check out any books.

The unstated premise must be "Bill has no ID card."

> Arguments can have unstated conclusions as well: [Premise] The political party that best reflects mainstream opinion will win the most seats in the next election, and [premise] the Republicans certainly best reflect mainstream opinion.

In Depth

Don't Confuse Arguments with Explanations!

Remember from Chapter 1, you use an *argument* to show that a claim is true. You use an **explanation** to show what caused something, or what it is, or how it works, or what purpose it serves.

> The reason I believe in God is because the universe couldn't just happen by chance.
>
> The reason I believe in God is because my parents were devout Christians who took great pains to instill this belief in me.

These two statements have similar wording, but the first one argues God exists, the second one explains the cause of my believing in God.

Arguments and explanations often use exactly the same words, and we have to be careful not to confuse them.

The unstated conclusion is: The Republicans will win the most seats in the next election.

DEDUCTIVE LOGIC

You may or may not remember from Chapter 1 that there are basically two kinds of argument, *deductive* arguments and *inductive* arguments. You also may or may not remember that a good deductive argument "demonstrates" or "proves" its conclusion (we use "demonstrate" and "prove" interchangeably). More precisely, a **good deductive argument** is one whose premises being true would mean the conclusion absolutely must be true (and cannot possibly be false—these being exactly the same thing). Judge Veals's reasoning, for example, involved an argument which roughly goes like this:

> Any juror who has disrupted the court in a way that disrespects the court should be found in contempt. This juror has disrupted the court in this way. Therefore, this juror should be found in contempt.

As you can see, the premises of this argument (the first two sentences) being true would mean that the conclusion could not possibly be false. The argument is therefore a good deductive argument. It *demonstrates* or *proves* the conclusion. Such arguments are said by logicians to be **valid.**

If you reflect on this definition of "valid argument," you will see that a good (valid) deductive argument can contain false premises. For example, "[Premise] George W. Bush is younger than his wife; therefore [Conclusion] his wife is older than he" is valid even though the premise is false. Even with the false premise, the argument is valid because *if* the premise were true, that would mean the conclusion must also be true. Another example:

> [Premise] Iraq is developing nuclear weapons that threaten our security.
>
> [Premise] We must take pre-emptive action against countries that do things that threaten our security.

■ **Tennis, anyone?** Like the buffalo mentioned later in this chapter, these buffalo also escaped, though these were inclined toward more athletic pursuits.

As an exercise, construct three deductive arguments and three inductive arguments, based on this photo.

> [Conclusion] Therefore, we must take pre-emptive action against Iraq.

This argument is valid, but the first premise, as it turned out, was false. To say that an argument is valid is only to say that its conclusion absolutely follows from its premises, which means that if the premises were true it would be impossible for the conclusion to be false. When logicians say that an argument is valid, they are not saying that the premises or conclusion is true.

The word logicians have for valid arguments whose premises *are* in fact true is "sound." A **sound** argument thus has these two characteristics: It is valid, and its premises are all true. "Hillary Clinton is a U.S. Senator from New York and is married to Bill Clinton; therefore, a U.S. Senator from New York is married to Bill Clinton" is an example of a sound argument, at least as we write these words.

A Mistaken Concept of Deduction

Some dictionaries (and some logic books) define a deductive argument as an argument that moves from a general premise to a specific conclusion about a particular thing. Judge Veals's argument as presented above certainly does this, but that's not what makes it deductive. What makes it deductive is that the premises are supposed to demonstrate or prove the conclusion. A valid argument can move just as easily from a premise about a specific to a conclusion also about a specific, or from a premise general in scope to a conclusion also general in scope. "Carol makes more money than Jennifer, and Jennifer makes more money than Christy; therefore Carol makes more money than Christy"

Real Life

Abe Lincoln Knew His Logic

Validity and Soundness in the Lincoln-Douglas Debates

Here's Abraham Lincoln speaking in the fifth Lincoln-Douglas debate:

> I state in syllogistic form the argument:
> Nothing in the Constitution . . . can destroy a right distinctly and expressly affirmed in the Constitution.
> The right of property in a slave is distinctly and expressly affirmed in the Constitution.
> Therefore, nothing in the Constitution can destroy the right of property in a slave.

Lincoln goes on to say:

> There is a fault [in the argument], but the fault is not in the reasoning; but the falsehood in fact is a fault of the premises. I believe that the right of property in a slave is *not* distinctly and expressly affirmed in the Constitution.

In other words, the argument is valid, Lincoln says, but unsound, and thus not a good argument.

Syllogisms, by the way, are covered in Chapter 8.

moves validly from a premise about a specific to a conclusion about a specific. "Penguins aren't fish; therefore no fish are penguins" moves validly from a general premise to a general conclusion.

INDUCTIVE LOGIC

A good inductive argument *supports* (rather than proves or demonstrates) its conclusion. More precisely: If the premise of a good inductive argument is true, the conclusion *probably* is true (and probably isn't false—these being the same). "I've never enjoyed long bike rides; so I won't enjoy riding in a century bicycle tour" is a good inductive argument: Never having enjoyed long bike rides makes it highly probable I won't enjoy sitting on a bicycle for 100 miles. "There is no record of any human surviving rabies; therefore, if you get rabies you will die" is another good inductive argument. Neither of these arguments is valid, given the way logicians use that word, because their premises don't make their conclusions absolutely, positively certain—it isn't absolutely impossible you might enjoy a 100-mile bike ride, and even stranger things have happened than a person surviving rabies. But they are good arguments nonetheless; they are good *inductive* arguments. The technical word for arguments like this—good inductive arguments—is **strong.** Both the above arguments, while not valid, are "strong."

One day recently one of our students was complaining about his vehicle, a used Dodge Dakota he bought. Among other problems, his truck constantly overheated and needed a new transmission with less than 50,000 miles on the vehicle. "Junk," he said about Dakotas in general. This too is an inductive argument. Paraphrasing loosely, here is the argument: [premise] This Dodge

On Language

Everyday English Definitions

In everyday English, "valid argument," "sound argument," and "strong argument" are used interchangeably and often just mean "good argument." Other terms people use to praise arguments include "cogent," "compelling," and "telling." Further, people often apply "valid," "sound," "cogent," and "compelling" to things other than arguments—claims, theories, and explanations, for example. So before you pounce on someone for using these words incorrectly, consider the context in which you hear them.

In everyday English, "weak argument" includes arguments that are invalid and unsound and has numerous synonyms, including "poor," "faulty," "fallacious," "specious," "unreasonable," "illogical," "stupid," and so forth.

Dakota is junk, therefore [conclusion] all Dodge Dakotas are junk. However, this inductive argument is not a strong one. The premise's truth adds *marginally* to the probability of the conclusion being true, but even conceding this may be too much. An isolated case like this certainly doesn't warrant such a sweeping generalization.

That's not to say, however, that you can never have a good inductive argument based on a single case. Some years ago, the children of one of the authors made a plate of cookies consisting of Play Doh, and offered their parent a cookie from the plate. Not realizing it wasn't a real cookie, this author bit into the thing, much to the delight of the kids. The inductive argument "This cookie doesn't taste right; therefore the next cookie on this plate won't taste right" was a strong inductive argument in that circumstance. "We fooled Daddy once; we can fool him again" was somewhat weaker.

Clearly, the strength of an argument is a matter of degrees; arguments can be evaluated as stronger or weaker depending on how likely the premises show the conclusion to be. Recently, we read about a buffalo that escaped from an auction in Rapid City, South Dakota; it eventually was located studying itself in a big mirror in a dressing room at the Rushmore Plaza Civic Center. Since the animal was happy and peaceful just staring at its image, the people running the auction figured what the heck and decided to keep the buffalo in the dressing room for the rest of the auction.* The argument "This buffalo liked looking at itself in a mirror; therefore the next buffalo will do so, too," isn't very strong; there may be something abnormal about this buffalo (or maybe the mirror). But now if experiments with numerous buffalo produced similar results, we'd have the premise for a much stronger argument.

Inductive reasoning includes, importantly, extrapolating from the properties of a sample of a class of things to the properties of all or most members of the class, drawing a conclusion about one thing by considering similar things, applying the lessons of past experience to future experience, and arriving at conclusions about the possible or likely causes of events. Inductive reasoning also underlies, or should underlie, many or most important decisions that one makes in life, including:

*Associated Press report, February 4, 2005.

An important life decision like buying a house requires careful inductive reasoning about future earning power, job security, the economy, interest rates, family and health needs, and lifestyle goals. Mistakes (or bad luck) hurt.

- Career choices
- Family planning
- Health decisions
- Retirement options
- Voting decisions

and many other things as well. Each of these things requires comparing the probabilities of the various outcomes of choices, actions, and events; each requires, therefore, constructing and evaluating inductive arguments.

UNSTATED PREMISES AGAIN

At this point, we need to return to unstated premises. As often as not in real life, a premise of an argument is left unstated. Suppose a husband and wife are dining out, and the wife says, "It's getting late; we should call for the check." For this little argument to be valid, this principle must be assumed: "If it is getting very late, then we should call for the check." The wife, no doubt, is assuming this principle (among many other things), and even if she is not assuming it, we must assume it, or something very much like it, if we are to credit her with a valid argument.

Most real-life arguments are like this, in that an unstated proposition must be assumed for the argument to be valid or strong. Many years ago, one of the authors and friends ordered a bottle of Chianti at The Tavern, in Yellow Springs, Ohio. After finishing the wine and taking the bottle home as a souvenir (in the old days young people did this sort of thing), somebody noticed there was a dead mouse in the bottle. "Whoa," everyone agreed. "We better send this out and get it analyzed." The argument, "That thing in the bottle is a dead mouse; therefore we should have it analyzed" assumes that drinking wine in which there is a dead mouse might be unhealthy and that the best way to ascertain the health risk as well as to know what to do is to have the situation evaluated by health officials. In short, to be valid the argument

In Depth

Unstated Arguments

There aren't any. An argument can contain unstated premises or an unstated conclusion, but the argument *itself* cannot be entirely unstated. A masked bandit who waves you against a wall with a gun is not presenting you with an argument, though his actions give you a good reason for moving; if you do not want to get shot, then you need to construct an argument in your own mind—and quickly, too—with the conclusion "I'd better move" and the premise "If I don't move, I may get my head blown off."

There is no such thing, then, as an unstated argument, though an argument can have unstated premises or an unstated conclusion. Further, it isn't possible for *all* the premises in an argument to be unstated.

assumes, "If there is a dead mouse in something you have drunk, you should have it analyzed by health officials.*

Most real-life arguments are like this: An unstated proposition must be assumed for the argument to be valid or strong. If someone says "I see your dog is a bloodhound; I suppose it has a keen sense of smell," he or she must assume that bloodhounds *all* have a keen sense of smell for the argument to be valid. And he or she must assume that *most* bloodhounds have a keen sense of smell for the argument to be strong.

Obviously, being able to spot what must be assumed for an argument to be valid or strong puts us in a better position to evaluate it. Take the argument:

He's related to Edward Kennedy, so he's rich.

This is the sort of remark that one is apt to toss off without much thought. But for the argument to be valid, one must assume that *everyone* related to Kennedy is rich, and that's not very plausible. For the argument to be strong, one must assume *most* people related to Kennedy are rich; this certainly is more plausible than the first assumption, but it still isn't very plausible. The most plausible relevant assumption is that *many* people related to Kennedy are rich, but with that assumption plugged into the argument, the argument is not particularly strong. In other words, if you look at the remark closely and consider what it assumes, you see that at best it is weak, unless you accept an implausible premise.

IDENTIFYING UNSTATED PREMISES

When someone produces an argument, it isn't productive to ask, What is this person assuming? No doubt the person is assuming many things, such as that you can hear (or read), that you understand English, that what he or she is saying is worth saying, that you aren't comatose or dead, and who knows what else. There are two better questions to ask, and the first is, "Is there a reason-

*The mouse turned out to be a bat, according to health officials, who also thought it would cause no harm. When the author went back to complain to the bartender (manager), he was told, "Next time, drink beer."

able assumption I could make that would make this argument valid?" And if what you must assume for the argument to be valid isn't plausible, then you ask the second question: "Is there a reasonable assumption I could make that would make this argument strong?"

As may be clear from the preceding section, an argument can be made valid by adding to it a general claim that appropriately connects the stated premises to the conclusion and says, in effect, that if the stated premises are true, then the conclusion is true. For example, take this argument:

> It's raining, so there is a south wind.

This argument is automatically valid if you add to it the general claim "Any time it is raining, there is a south wind." (Any variation of this claim will do equally well, such as "Whenever it is raining, there is a south wind," or "Only in the presence of a south wind is there rain.") But this claim isn't particularly plausible, at least where we live. And thus you should modify the claim by asking the second question, "What must I assume for this argument to be strong?" When you do this, you obtain a more plausible premise: "When it rains, there is usually a south wind." This is a reasonable claim (in our neck of the woods), and including it in the argument makes the argument a strong one.

Here's another example:

> You shouldn't let her pass. After all, this is the second time you caught her cheating.

A general claim that ties the stated premise to the conclusion and yields a valid argument would be "No person caught cheating two times should be permitted to pass." We'd accept this claim and, consequently, we'd also accept the conclusion of the argument, assuming that the stated premise (that this is the second time she was caught cheating) is true.

Here's one final example:

> Yes, Stacy and Harold are on the brink of divorce. They're remodeling their house.

When we try to make the argument valid by connecting the premise to the conclusion with a general claim, we get something like "A couple that remodels their house must be on the brink of divorce." But we can suppose that nobody would seriously subscribe to such a claim. So we attempt to make the argument strong, rather than valid, by modifying the claim to "Most couples remodeling their house are on the brink of divorce." However, this claim is also implausible. The only plausible thing to say is that *some* couples who remodel are on the brink of divorce. But this claim doesn't justify a conclusion that states unqualifiedly that Stacy and Harold are on the brink of divorce.

To summarize: Formulate a general claim that connects the stated premise with the conclusion in such a way as to make the argument valid, as explained above. If that premise isn't plausible, modify or qualify it as necessary to make the argument strong. If the argument just can't be made either valid or strong except by using an implausible premise, then you really shouldn't accept the argument—or use it yourself.

In your own essays, it is a good practice always to consider exactly what your readers must accept if they are to agree with your reasoning. You shouldn't

In Depth

Don't Forget Fallacies

In Chapters 5 and 6 we say that people will sometimes make statements in order to establish a claim when in reality their remarks have nothing to do with the claim. For example, "Margaret's qualifications are really quite good; after all, she'd be terribly hurt to think that you didn't think highly of them." Although Margaret's disappointment would no doubt be a reason for *something* (e.g., for keeping your views to yourself), it would not be a reason for altering your opinion of her qualifications. Her feelings are, in fact, thoroughly irrelevant to her qualifications. Extraneous material of all sorts can often be eliminated as argumentative material if you ask yourself simply, "Is this really relevant to the conclusion? Does this matter to what this person is trying to establish?" If you have worked through the exercises in Chapters 5 and 6, you have already had practice in spotting irrelevances. If you haven't done these exercises, it would be useful to go back and do them now.

require them to accept any claim that is implausible or unreasonable, whether or not you actually make the claim.

TECHNIQUES FOR UNDERSTANDING ARGUMENTS

Before we can evaluate an argument, we must understand it. Many arguments are difficult to understand because they are spoken and thus go by so quickly that we cannot be sure of the conclusion and the premises. Others are difficult to understand because they have a complicated structure. Still others are difficult to understand because they are embedded in nonargumentative material consisting of background information, prejudicial coloring, illustrations, parenthetical remarks, digressions, subsidiary points, and other window dressing. And some arguments are difficult to understand because they are confused or because the reasons they contain are so poor that we are not sure whether to regard them as reasons.

In understanding any argument, the first task is to find the conclusion—the main point or thesis of the passage. The next step is to locate the reasons that have been offered for the conclusion—that is, to find the premises. Next, we look for the reasons, if any, given for these premises. To proceed through these steps, you have to learn both to spot premises and conclusions when they occur in spoken and written passages and to understand the interrelationships among these claims—that is, the structure of the argument.

Clarifying an Argument's Structure

Let's begin with how to understand the relationships among the argumentative claims, because this problem is sometimes easiest to solve. If you are dealing with written material that you are free to mark up, one useful technique is to number the premises and conclusions and then use the numbers to lay bare the structure of the argument. Let's start with this argument as an example:

> I don't think we should get Carlos his own car. As a matter of fact, he is not responsible, because he doesn't care for his things. And anyway, we don't have enough money for a car, since even now we have trouble making ends meet. Last week you yourself complained about our financial situation, and you never complain without really good reason.

We want to display the structure of this argument clearly. First, circle all premise and conclusion indicators. Thus:

> I don't think we should get Carlos his own car. As a matter of fact, he is not responsible (because) he doesn't care for his things. And anyway, we don't have enough money for a car, (since) even now we have trouble making ends meet. Last week you yourself complained about our financial situation, and you never complain without really good reason.

Next, bracket each premise and conclusion, and number them consecutively as they appear in the argument. So what we now have is this:

> ① [I don't think we should get Carlos his own car.] As a matter of fact, ② [he is not responsible] because ③ [he doesn't care for his things.] And anyway, ④ [we don't have enough money for a car], since ⑤ [even now we have trouble making ends meet.] ⑥ [Last week you yourself complained about our financial situation], and ⑦ [you never complain without really good reason.]

And then we diagram the argument as follows: Using an arrow to mean "therefore" or "is intended as evidence [or as a reason or as a premise] for," the first three claims in the argument can be diagrammed as follows:

Now ⑥ and ⑦ together support ④; that is, they are part of the same argument for ④. To show that ⑥ and ⑦ go together, we simply draw a line under them, put a plus sign between them, and draw the arrow from the line to ④, like this:

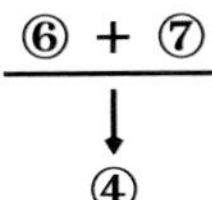

Because ⑤ and ⑥ + ⑦ are separate arguments for ④, we can represent the relationship between them and ④ as follows:

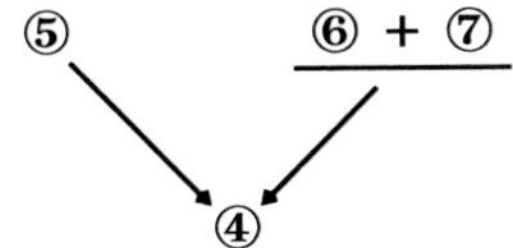

Finally, because ④ and ② are separate arguments for ①, the diagram of the entire argument is this:

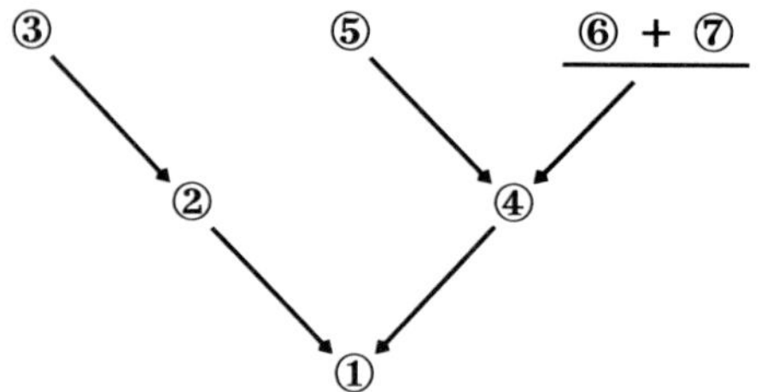

So, the conventions governing this approach to revealing argument structure are very simple: First, circle all premise- and conclusion-indicating words. Then, assuming you can identify the claims that function in the argument (a big assumption, as you will see before long), simply number them consecutively. Then display the structure of the argument using arrows for "therefore" and plus signs over a line to connect together two or more premises that depend on one another.

Some claims, incidentally, may constitute reasons for more than one conclusion. For example:

> ① [Carlos continues to be irresponsible.] ② [He certainly should not have his own car], and, as far as I am concerned, ③ [he can forget about that trip to Hawaii this winter, too.]

Structure:

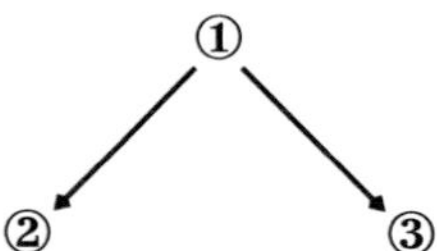

Frequently, too, we evaluate counterarguments to our positions. For example:

> ① We really should have more African Americans on the faculty. ② That is why the new diversity program ought to be approved. True, ③ it may involve an element of unfairness to whites, but ④ the benefits to society of having more black faculty outweigh the disadvantages.

Notice that claim ③ introduces a consideration that runs counter to the conclusion of the argument, which is stated in ②. We can indicate counterclaims by crossing the "therefore" arrow with lines, thus:

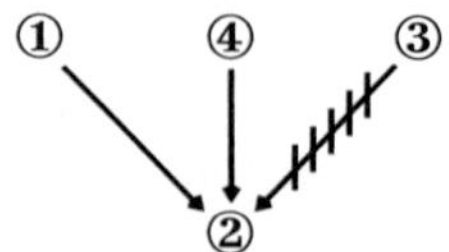

This diagram indicates that item ③ has been introduced by the writer as a consideration that runs counter to ②.

Of course, one might adopt other conventions for clarifying argument structure—for example, circling the main conclusion and drawing solid lines

On Language

Stupid Liberal!

The employer introduced himself to his new gardener.

"I am a professor of logic," the employer said.

"Oh. What's that?" the gardener asked.

"I shall give you a demonstration," announced the professor. "Do you own a wheelbarrow?"

"Yes," replied the gardener.

"Then I infer you are a hard worker," the professor continued. "And from that fact I infer you have a family. And from that I infer you are conscientious and responsible. And from that I infer you are a conservative. Am I right?"

"Wow!" exclaimed the gardener. "That's right! So that's logic?"

"That's logic," preened the professor.

Later the gardener met up with one of his buddies and told him he had a job with a professor of logic.

"Logic?" his friend asked, "What's that?"

"I'll show you," the gardener said. "Do you own a wheelbarrow?"

"No."

"Stupid liberal."

under supporting premises and wavy lines under the premises of subarguments. The technique we have described is simply one way of doing it; any of several others might work as well for you. However, *no* technique for revealing argument structure will work if you cannot spot the argumentative claims in the midst of a lot of background material.

Distinguishing Arguments from Window Dressing

It is not always easy to isolate the argument in a speech or a written piece. Often, speakers and writers think that because their main points are more or less clear to them, they will be equally apparent to their listeners or readers. But it doesn't always work that way.

If you are having trouble identifying a conclusion in what you hear or read, it *could* be that the passage is not an argument at all. Make sure that the passage in question is not a report, a description, an explanation, or something else altogether, rather than an argument. The key here is determining whether the speaker or writer is offering reasons intended to convince you of one or more of the claims made in the passage.

The problem could also be that the conclusion is left unstated. Sometimes it helps simply to put the argument aside and ask yourself, "What is this person trying to prove?" In any case, the first and essential step in understanding an argument is to spot the conclusion.

If you are having difficulty identifying the *premises,* consider the possibility that you have before you a case of rhetoric (see Chapter 4). (You can't find premises in a piece of rhetoric because there *are* no premises.) You have an advantage over many students in having learned about rhetorical devices in Chapters 4, 5, and 6. By this time you should be getting pretty good at recognizing them.

In the remainder of this book, we are concerned primarily with argument evaluation rather than argument clarification, so most of the arguments we present are straightforward and unconfusing; you probably won't need to use diagrams to clarify their structure. However, as you apply what you learn in this book to arguments you encounter in real life, you are apt to encounter arguments and argumentative essays whose organization is difficult to comprehend. When you do, you may find diagramming a useful technique. We also suggest that you attempt to diagram your own essays—if you find that you have difficulty, it is a good indication that you need to reorganize your essay and make the structure of your reasoning clearer.

EVALUATING ARGUMENTS

Thinking critically requires us to evaluate arguments, and evaluating arguments has two parts. First, there is the *logic* part: Does the argument either prove or demonstrate, or support its conclusion? Is this argument either deductively valid or inductively strong? You know now what these questions mean theoretically; in the next few chapters, we will see what they involve in fact.

The other part, of course, is the *truth* part. Are the premises actually true? As we explained in Chapter 3, it is best to be suspicious of a premise that conflicts with our background information or other credible claims, as well as a premise that comes from a source that lacks credibility. And, of course, as we developed at length in Chapters 4, 5, and 6, we want to avoid being tricked into accepting a claim by rhetoric or other psychological gimmickry. It also almost goes without saying that premises that are vague, ambiguous, or otherwise unclear require clarification before one accepts them—as we explained in Chapter 2. In general, determining the truth of premises requires knowledge, experience, a level head, and the inclination to look into things.

Recap

The main concepts and considerations of the chapter are as follows:

- An argument consists of a conclusion and one or more premises.
- Sometimes the conclusion of one argument is a premise in another argument.
- A good deductive argument is said to be valid. If an argument is valid, its premises being true make it impossible for the conclusion to be false.
- A valid argument with all true premises is said to be sound.
- A good inductive argument is said to be strong. If an argument is strong, its premises being true make it improbable for the conclusion to be false.
- Sometimes, premises and conclusions are unstated.

- When a premise is unstated, try to supply a reasonable assumption that would make the argument valid or strong.
- If you have trouble tracking the parts of an argument that appears in a written passage, try diagramming the passage.

Exercises

Exercise 7-1

Indicate which blanks would ordinarily contain premises and which would ordinarily contain conclusions.

▲ 1. ___a___, and ___b___. Therefore, ___c___.

▲ 2. ___a___. So, since ___b___, ___c___.

▲ 3. ___a___, because ___b___.

▲ 4. Since ___a___ and ___b___, ___c___.

▲ 5. ___a___. Consequently, ___b___, since ___c___ and ___d___.

Exercise 7-2

Identify the premises and conclusions in each of the following arguments.

▲ 1. Since all Communists are Marxists, all Marxists are Communists.

2. The Lakers almost didn't beat the Kings. They'll never get past Dallas.

3. If the butler had done it, he could not have locked the screen door. Therefore, since the door was locked, we know that the butler is in the clear.

▲ 4. That cat is used to dogs. Probably she won't be upset if you bring home a new dog for a pet.

5. Hey, he can't be older than his mother's daughter's brother. His mother's daughter has only one brother.

6. Moscone will never make it into the state police. They have a weight limit, and he's over it.

▲ 7. Presbyterians are not fundamentalists, but all born-again Christians are. So no born-again Christians are Presbyterians.

8. I guess he doesn't have a thing to do. Why else would he waste his time watching daytime TV?

9. "There are more injuries in professional football today than there were twenty years ago," he reasoned. "And if there are more injuries, then today's players suffer higher risks. And if they suffer higher risks, then they should be paid more. Consequently, I think today's players should be paid more," he concluded.

▲ 10. Let's see . . . If we've got juice at the distributor, the coil isn't defective, and if the coil isn't defective, then the problem is in the ignition switch. So the problem is in the ignition switch.

Exercise 7-3

Identify the premises and the conclusions in the following arguments.

▲ **1.** The darned engine pings every time we use the regular unleaded gasoline, but it doesn't do it with super. I'd bet that there is a difference in the octane ratings between the two in spite of what my mechanic says.

2. Kera, Sherry, and Bobby were all carded at JJ's, and they all look as though they're about thirty. Chances are I'll be carded too.

3. Seventy percent of freshmen at Wharfton College come from wealthy families; therefore, probably about the same percentage of all Wharfton College students come from wealthy families.

▲ **4.** When blue jays are breeding, they become very aggressive. Consequently, scrub jays, which are very similar to blue jays, can also be expected to be aggressive when they're breeding.

5. A cut in the capital gains tax will benefit wealthy people. Marietta says her family would be much better off if capital gains taxes were cut, so I'm sure her family is wealthy.

6. According to *Nature,* today's thoroughbred racehorses do not run any faster than their grandparents did. But human Olympic runners are at least 20 percent faster than their counterparts of fifty years ago. Most likely, racehorses have reached their physical limits but humans have not.

▲ **7.** It's easier to train dogs than cats. That means they're smarter than cats.

8. "Let me demonstrate the principle by means of logic," the teacher said, holding up a bucket. "If this bucket has a hole in it, then it will leak. But it doesn't leak. Therefore, obviously it doesn't have a hole in it."

9. I know there's a chance this guy might be different, but the last person we hired from Alamo Polytech was a rotten engineer, and we had to fire him. Thus I'm afraid that this new candidate is somebody I just won't take a chance on.

▲ **10.** If she were still interested in me, she would have called, but she didn't.

Exercise 7-4

Some of these passages contain separate arguments for the main conclusion. Others contain a single argument with more than one premise. Other passages contain both. Which passages contain separate arguments for the main conclusion?

▲ **1.** North Korea was always a much greater threat to its neighbors than Iraq. After all, North Korea has a million-man army lined up on the border ready to attack. Oh yes! They also have nuclear weapons and have said they'd use them.

2. Jim is going to ride with Mary to the party, and Sandra is going to ride with her, too. So Mary won't be driving all by herself to the party.

▲ **3.** Michael should go ahead and buy another car. The one he's driving is just about to fall apart, and he just got a new job and he can certainly afford another car now.

4. If Parker goes to Las Vegas, he'll wind up in a casino; and if he winds up in a casino, it's a sure thing he'll spend half the night at a craps table. So you can be sure: If Parker goes to Las Vegas, he'll spend half the night at a craps table.

5. It's going to be rainy tomorrow, and Moore doesn't like to play golf in the rain. It's going to be cold as well, and he *really* doesn't like to play when it's cold. So you can be sure Moore will be someplace other than the golf course tomorrow.

▲ 6. Hey, you're overwatering your lawn. See? There are mushrooms growing around the base of that tree—a sure sign of overwatering. Also, look at all the worms on the ground. They come up when the earth is oversaturated.

7. "Will you drive me to the airport?" she asked. "Why should I do that?" he wanted to know. "Because I'll pay you twice what it takes for gas. Besides, you said you were my friend, didn't you?"

8. If you drive too fast, you're more likely to get a ticket, and the more likely you are to get a ticket, the more likely you are to have your insurance premiums raised. So, if you drive too fast, you are more likely to have your insurance premiums raised.

▲ 9. If you drive too fast, you're more likely to get a ticket. You're also more likely to get into an accident. So you shouldn't drive too fast.

10. The war on terrorism had as its original goal the capture or elimination of Osama bin Laden. Since he's still at large, as of this point the war has not been very successful.

11. DANIEL: Where did that cat go, anyway?
THERESA: I think she ran away. Look, her food hasn't been touched in two days. Neither has her water.

▲ 12. There are several reasons why you should consider installing a solarium. First, you can still get a tax credit. Second, you can reduce your heating bill. Third, if you build it right, you can actually cool your house with it in the summer.

13. From a letter to the editor: "By trying to eliminate Charles Darwin from the curriculum, creationists are doing themselves a great disservice. When read carefully, Darwin's discoveries only support the thesis that species change, not that they evolve into new species. This is a thesis that most creationists can live with. When read carefully, Darwin actually supports the creationist point of view."

14. Editorial comment: "The Supreme Court's ruling that schools may have a moment of silence but not if it's designated for prayer is sound. Nothing stops someone from saying a silent prayer at school or anywhere else. Also, even though a moment of silence will encourage prayer, it will not favor any particular religion over any other. The ruling makes sense."

▲ 15. We must paint the house now! Here are three good reasons: (a) If we don't, then we'll have to paint it next summer; (b) if we have to paint it next summer, we'll have to cancel our trip; and (c) it's too late to cancel the trip.

Exercise 7-5

Some of these passages contain separate arguments for the main conclusion. Others contain a single argument with more than one premise. Other passages contain both. Which passages contain separate arguments for the main conclusion?

▲ 1. All mammals are warm-blooded creatures, and all whales are mammals. Therefore, all whales are warm-blooded creatures.

2. Jones won't plead guilty to a misdemeanor, and if he won't plead guilty, then he will be tried on a felony charge. Therefore, he will be tried on a felony charge.

3. John is taller than Bill, and Bill is taller than Margaret. Therefore, John is taller than Margaret.

▲ 4. Rats that have been raised in enriched environments, where there are a variety of toys and puzzles, have brains that weigh more than the brains of rats raised in more barren environments. Therefore, the brains of humans will weigh more if humans are placed in intellectually stimulating environments.

5. From a letter to the editor: "In James Kilpatrick's July 7 column it was stated that Scientology's 'tenets are at least as plausible as the tenets of Southern Baptists, Roman Catholics . . . and prayer book Episcopalians.' Mr. Kilpatrick seems to think that all religions are basically the same and fraudulent. This is false. If he would compare the beliefs of Christianity with the cults he would find them very different. Also, isn't there quite a big difference between Ron Hubbard, who called himself God, and Jesus Christ, who said 'Love your enemies, bless them that curse you, do good to them that hate you'?"

6. We've interviewed two hundred professional football players, and 60 percent of them favor expanding the season to twenty games. Therefore, 60 percent of all professional football players favor expanding the season to twenty games.

7. Exercise may help chronic male smokers kick the habit, says a study published today. The researchers, based at McDuff University, put thirty young male smokers on a three-month program of vigorous exercise. One year later, only 14 percent of them still smoked, according to the report. An equivalent number of young male smokers who did not go through the exercise program were also checked after a year and it was found that 60 percent still smoked. Smokers in the exercise program began running three miles a day and gradually worked up to eight miles daily. They also spent five and a half hours each day in modestly vigorous exercise such as soccer, basketball, biking, and swimming.

▲ 8. Letter to the editor: "I was enraged to learn that the mayor now supports the initiative for the Glen Royale subdivision. Only last year he himself proclaimed 'strong opposition' to any further development in the river basin. Besides, Glen Royale will only add to congestion, pollution, and longer lines at the grocery store, not that the grocers will mind."

9. Believe in God? Yes, of course I do. The universe couldn't have arisen by chance, could it? Besides, I read the other day that more and more physi-

cists believe in God, based on what they're finding out about the Big Bang and all that stuff.

▲ 10. From an office memo: "I've got a good person for your opening in Accounting. Jesse Brown is his name, and he's as sharp as they come. Jesse has a solid background in bookkeeping, and he's good with computers. He's also reliable, and he'll project the right image. Best of all, he's a terrific golfer. As you might gather, I know him personally. He'll be contacting you later this week."

Exercise 7-6

Which five of the following statements are probably intended to explain the cause of something, and which five are probably intended to argue that some claim is true?

▲ 1. The reason we've had so much hot weather recently is that the jet stream is unusually far north.

2. The reason Ms. Mossbarger looks so tired is that she hasn't been able to sleep for three nights.

3. The reason it's a bad idea to mow the lawn in your bare feet is that you could be seriously injured.

▲ 4. The reason Ken mows the lawn in his bare feet is that he doesn't realize how dangerous it is.

5. You can be sure that Ryan will marry Beth. After all, he told me he would.

6. If I were you, I'd change before going into town. Those clothes look like you slept in them.

▲ 7. Overeating can cause high blood pressure.

8. Eating so much salt can cause high blood pressure, so you'd better cut back a little.

▲ 9. It's a good bet the Saddam Hussein regime wanted to build nuclear weapons, because the U.N. inspectors found devices for the enrichment of plutonium.

10. The reason Saddam wanted to build nuclear weapons was to give him the power to control neighboring Middle Eastern countries.

Exercise 7-7

Fill in the blanks where called for, and answer true or false where appropriate.

1. Valid arguments are said to be strong or weak.

2. Valid arguments are always good arguments.

▲ 3. Sound arguments are _______ arguments whose premises are all _______.

4. The premises of a valid argument are never false.

5. If a valid argument has a false conclusion, then not all its premises can be true.

▲ **6.** If a strong argument has a false conclusion, then not all its premises can be true.

7. A sound argument cannot have a false conclusion.

8. A true conclusion cannot be derived validly from false premises.

▲ **9.** "Strong" and "weak" are absolute terms.

10. The following argument is valid: All swans are orange. You're a swan, so you're orange.

11. The following argument is *both* valid *and* sound: John McCain is one of New York's U.S. senators, and he is a Democrat. Therefore, he is a Democrat.

12. A strong argument with true premises has a conclusion that probably is true.

Exercise 7-8

Go back to Exercises 7-2 and 7-3, and determine which arguments are valid. In the answer section at the back of the book, we have answered items 1, 4, 7, and 10 in each set.

Exercise 7-9

▲ Given the premises, discuss whether the conclusion of each argument that follows is (a) true beyond a reasonable doubt, (b) probably true, or (c) possibly true or possibly false. You should expect disagreement on these items, but the closer your answers are to your instructor's, the better.

▲ **1.** The sign on the parking meter says "Out of Order," so the meter isn't working.

2. The annual rainfall in California's north valley averages twenty-three inches. So the rainfall next year will be twenty-three inches.

3. You expect to get forty miles to the gallon in *that?* Why, that old wreck has a monster V8; besides, it's fifty years old and needs an overhaul.

4. In three of the last four presidential races, the winner of the Iowa Republican primary has not captured the Republican nomination. Therefore, the winner of the next Iowa Republican primary will not capture the Republican nomination.

▲ **5.** The New York steak, the Maine lobster, and the beef stroganoff at that restaurant are all exceptionally good. All the entrees are excellent.

6. The number of cellular telephones has increased dramatically in each of the past few years. Therefore there will be even more of them in use this coming year.

7. Since the graduates of Harvard, Yale, Princeton, and other Ivy League schools generally score higher on the Graduate Record Examination than students from Central State, it follows that the Ivy League schools do more toward educating their students than Central State does.

8. Michael Jackson has had more plastic surgery than anybody else in California. You can bet he's had more than anybody in Connecticut!

▲ 9. Although Max bled profusely before he died, there was no blood on the ground where his body was found. Therefore, he was killed somewhere else and brought here after the murder.

10. When liquor was banned in 1920, hospitalizations for alcoholism and related diseases plummeted; in 1933, when Prohibition was repealed, alcohol-related illnesses rose sharply again. Legalization of cocaine, heroin, and marijuana would not curb abuse of those substances.

11. Relax. The kid's been delivering the paper for, how long? Three, four years maybe? And not once has she missed us. The paper will be here, just wait and see. She's just been delayed for some reason.

▲ 12. First, it seems clear that even if there are occasional small dips in the consumption of petroleum, the general trend shows no sign of a real permanent decrease. Second, petroleum reserves are not being discovered as fast as petroleum is currently being consumed. From these two facts we can conclude that reserves will eventually be consumed and that the world will have to do without oil.

Exercise 7-10

For each passage, supply a claim that turns it into a valid argument.

Example

The fan needs oil. It's squeaking.

Claim That Makes It Valid

Whenever the fan squeaks, it needs oil.

▲ 1. Jamal is well mannered, so he had a good upbringing.

2. Bettina is pretty sharp, so she'll get a good grade in this course.

3. It must have rained lately because there are puddles everywhere.

▲ 4. He'll drive recklessly only if he's upset, and he's not upset.

5. Let's see . . . they have tons of leftovers, so their party could not have been very successful.

6. I think we can safely conclude that the battery is still in good condition. The lights are bright.

▲ 7. Either the dog has fleas, or its skin is dry. It's scratching a lot.

8. Melton was a good senator. He'd make an excellent president.

9. Gelonek doesn't own a gun. He's sure to be for gun control.

▲ 10. The Carmel poet Robinson Jeffers is one of America's most outstanding poets. His work appears in many Sierra Club publications.

Exercise 7-11

▲ Go back to Exercise 7-10, and supply a claim that will produce a strong (but not valid) argument. In the answer section at the back of the book, we have answered items 1, 4, 7, and 10.

Example

The fan needs oil. It's squeaking.

Claim That Makes It Strong

When the fan squeaks, it usually needs oil.

Exercise 7-12

For each passage, supply a claim that turns it into a valid argument.

▲ 1. Prices in that new store around the corner are going to be high, you can bet. All they sell are genuine leather goods.

2. I had a C going into the final exam, but I don't see how I can make less than a B for the course because I managed an A on the final.

3. He's a good guitarist. He studied with Pepe Romero, you know.

▲ 4. That plant is an ornamental fruit tree. It won't ever bear edible fruit.

5. The Federal Reserve Board will make sure that inflation doesn't reach 8 percent again. Its chair is an experienced hand at monetary policy.

6. Murphy doesn't stand a chance of getting elected in this county. His liberal position on most matters is well known.

▲ 7. Jesse Ventura, the former Governor of Minnesota, was a professional wrestler. He couldn't have been a very effective governor.

8. Half the people in the front row believe in God; therefore, half the entire class believes in God.

9. Chaffee College students are all career-oriented. I say this because every Chaffee College student I ever met was career-oriented.

▲ 10. Population studies show that smoking causes lung cancer; therefore, if you smoke, you will get lung cancer.

Exercise 7-13

▲ Do Exercise 7-12 again, making the arguments strong but not valid. In the answer section at the back of the book, we have answered items 1, 4, 7, and 10.

Exercise 7-14

Diagram the following "arguments," using the method explained in the text.

▲ 1. ①, because ② and ③. [Assume that ② and ③ are part of the same argument for ①.]

2. ① and ②; therefore ③. [Assume that ① and ② are separate arguments for ③.]

3. Since ①, ②; and since ③, ④. And since ② and ④, ⑤. [Assume that ② and ④ are separate arguments for ⑤.]

▲ 4. ①; therefore ② and ③. But because ② and ③, ④. Consequently, ⑤. Therefore, ⑥. [Assume ② and ③ are separate arguments for ④.]

5. ①, ②, ③; therefore ④. ⑤, in view of ①. And ⑥, since ②. Therefore ⑦. [Assume ①, ②, and ③ are part of the same argument for ④.]

▲ Exercise 7-15

Go back to Exercises 7-2, 7-3, 7-4, and 7-5, and diagram the arguments using the method explained in the text. In the answer section at the back of the book, we have answered items 1, 4, 7, and 10 in Exercises 7-2 and 7-3; items 6, 9, 12, and 15 in Exercise 7-4; and items 1, 4, 8, and 10 in Exercise 7-5.

Exercise 7-16

Diagram the arguments contained in the following passages, using the method explained in the text.

▲ 1. Dear Jim,

Your distributor is the problem. Here's why. There's no current at the spark plugs. And if there's no current at the plugs, then either your alternator is shot or your distributor is defective. But if the problem were in the alternator, then your dash warning light would be on. So, since the light isn't on, the problem must be in the distributor. Hope this helps.

Yours,
Benita Autocraft

2. The federal deficit must be reduced. It has contributed to inflation, and it has hurt American exports.

3. It's high time professional boxing was outlawed. Boxing almost always leads to brain damage, and anything that does that ought to be done away with. Besides, it supports organized crime.

▲ 4. They really ought to build a new airport. It would attract more business to the area, not to mention the fact that the old airport is overcrowded and dangerous.

5. Vote for Jackson? No way. He's too radical, and he's too inexperienced, and his lack of experience would make him a dangerous council member.

Exercise 7-17

Diagram the arguments contained in the following passages, using the method explained in the text. (Your instructor may have different instructions for you to follow.)

▲ 1. Cottage cheese will help you to be slender, youthful, and more beautiful. Enjoy it often.

2. If you want to listen to loud music, do it when we are not at home. It bothers us, and we're your parents.

3. If you want to see the best version of *The Three Musketeers,* try the 1948 version. Lana Turner is luscious; Vincent Price is dastardly; Angela Lansbury is exquisitely regal; and nobody ever has or ever will portray D'Artagnan with the grace, athleticism, or skill of Gene Kelly. Rent it. It's a must.

▲ **4.** From a letter to the editor: "The idea of a free press in America today is a joke. A small group of people, the nation's advertisers, control the media more effectively than if they owned it outright. Through fear of an advertising boycott, they can dictate everything from programming to news report content. Politicians as well as editors shiver in their boots at the thought of such a boycott. This situation is intolerable and ought to be changed. I suggest we all listen to National Public Radio and public television."

5. Too many seniors, disabled veterans, and families with children are paying far too much of their incomes for housing. Proposition 168 will help clear the way for affordable housing construction for these groups. Proposition 168 reforms the outdated requirement for an election before affordable housing can even be approved. Requiring elections for every publicly assisted housing venture, even when there is no local opposition, is a waste of taxpayers' money. No other state constitution puts such a roadblock in front of efforts to house senior citizens and others in need. Please support Proposition 168.

6. More than forty years after President John F. Kennedy's assassination, it's no easier to accept the idea that a loser like Lee Harvey Oswald committed the crime of the century all by himself with a $12.78 mail-order rifle and a $7.17 scope. Yet even though two-thousand-plus books and films about the episode have been made, there is no credible evidence to contradict the Warren Commission finding that "the shots which killed President Kennedy and wounded Governor Connally were fired by Lee Harvey Oswald" and that "Oswald acted alone."

After all these years, it's time to accept the conclusion. The nation pays a heavy price for chronic doubts and mistrust. Confidence in the government has declined. Participation in the voting process has steadily slid downward. The national appetite for wild theories encourages peddlers to persist. Evil is never easy to accept. In the case of JFK, the sooner we let it go, the better.

▲ **7.** "Consumers ought to be concerned about the Federal Trade Commission's dropping a rule that supermarkets must actually have in stock the items they advertise for sale. While a staff analysis suggests costs of the rule outweigh the benefits to consumers, few shoppers want to return to the practices that lured them into stores only to find the advertised products they sought were not there.

"The staff study said the rule causes shoppers to pay $200 million to receive $125 million in benefits. The cost is a low estimate and the benefits a high estimate, according to the study.

"However, even those enormously big figures boil down to a few cents per shopper over a year's time. And the rule does say that when a grocer advertises a sale, the grocer must have sufficient supply of sale items on hand to meet reasonable buyer demand."

The Oregonian

8. "And we thought we'd heard it all. Now the National Rifle Association wants the U.S. Supreme Court to throw out the ban on private ownership of fully automatic machine guns.

"As the nation's cities reel under staggering murder totals, as kids use guns simply to get even after feuds, as children are gunned down by random bullets, the NRA thinks it is everybody's constitutional right to have their own personal machine gun.

"This is not exactly the weapon of choice for deer hunting or for a homeowner seeking protection. It is an ideal weapon for street gangs and drug thugs in their wars with each other and the police.

"To legalize fully automatic machine guns is to increase the mayhem that is turning this nation—particularly its large cities—into a continual war zone. Doesn't the NRA have something better to do?"

Capital Times, *Madison, Wisconsin*

9. From a letter to the editor: "Recently the California Highway Patrol stopped me at a drunk-drive checkpoint. Now, I don't like drunk drivers any more than anyone else. I certainly see why the police find the checkpoint system effective. But I think our right to move about freely is much more important. If the checkpoint system continues, then next there will be checkpoints for drugs, seat belts, infant car seats, drivers' licenses. We will regret it later if we allow the system to continue."

▲ 10. "Well located, sound real estate is the safest investment in the world. It is not going to disappear, as can the value of dollars put into savings accounts. Neither will real estate values be lost because of inflation. In fact, property values tend to increase at a pace at least equal to the rate of inflation. Most homes have appreciated at a rate greater than the inflation rate (due mainly to strong buyer demand and insufficient supply of newly constructed homes)."

Robert Bruss, The Smart Investor's Guide to Real Estate

11. "The constitutional guarantee of a speedy trial protects citizens from arbitrary government abuse, but it has at least one other benefit, too. It prevents crime.

"A recent Justice Department study found that more than a third of those with serious criminal records—meaning three or more felony convictions—are arrested for new offenses while free on bond awaiting federal court trial. You don't have to be a social scientist to suspect that the longer the delay, the greater the likelihood of further violations. In short, overburdened courts mean much more than justice delayed; they quite literally amount to the infliction of further injustice."

Scripps Howard Newspapers

12. "There is a prevailing school of thought and growing body of opinion that one day historians will point to a certain television show and declare: This is what life was like in small-town America in the mid-20th century.

"We like to think those future historians will be right about *The Andy Griffith Show.* It had everything, and in rerun life still does: humor, wisdom, wholesomeness and good old red-blooded American entertainment.

"That's why we are so puzzled that a group of true-blue fans of the show want to rename some suitable North Carolina town Mayberry. The group believes there ought to be a real-live city in North Carolina called Mayberry, even though everybody already knows that Mayberry was modeled on Mount Airy, sort of, since that is Sheriff Taylor's, uh, Andy Griffith's hometown.

"No, far better that the group let the whole thing drop. For one thing, we don't know of anyplace—hamlet, village, town, or city—that could properly live up to the name of Mayberry. Perhaps the best place for Mayberry to exist is right where it is—untouched, unspoiled and unsullied by the modern world. Ain't that right, Ernest T. Bass?"

Greensboro *(N.C.)* News & Record

▲ **13.** As we enter a new century, about 100 million Americans are producing data on the Internet as rapidly as they consume it. Each of these users is tracked by technologies ever more able to collate essential facts about them—age, address, credit rating, marital status, etc.—in electronic form for use in commerce. One Web site, for example, promises, for the meager sum of seven dollars, to scan "over two billion records to create a single comprehensive report on an individual." It is not unreasonable, then, to believe that the combination of capitalism and technology pose a looming threat to what remains of our privacy.

Loosely adapted from Harper's

14. Having your car washed at the carwash may be the best way to go, but there are some possible drawbacks. The International Carwashing Association (ICA) has fought back against charges that automatic carwashes, in recycling wash water, actually dump the salt and dirt from one car onto the next. And that brushes and drag cloths hurt the finish. Perhaps there is some truth to these charges.

The ICA sponsored tests that supposedly demonstrated that the average home car wash is harder on a car than an automatic wash. Maybe. But what's "the average" home car wash? And you can bet that the automatic carwashes in the test were in perfect working order.

There is no way you or I can tell for certain if the filtration system and washing equipment at the automatic carwash are properly maintained. And even if they are, what happens if you follow some mud-caked pickup through the wash? Road dirt might still be caught in the bristles of the brushes or strips of fabric that are dragged over your car.

Here's my recommendation: Wash your own car.

15. Letter to the editor: "The worst disease of the next decade will be AIDS, Acquired Immune Deficiency Syndrome.

"AIDS has made facing surgery scary. In the last ten years several hundred Americans got AIDS from getting contaminated blood in surgery, and it is predicted that within a few years more hundreds of people will receive AIDS blood each year.

"Shouldn't we be tested for AIDS before we give blood? As it is now, no one can feel safe receiving blood. Because of AIDS, people are giving blood to themselves so they will be safe if they have to have blood later. We need a very sensitive test to screen AIDS donors."

North State Record

▲ **16.** **Argument in Favor of Measure A**

"Measure A is consistent with the City's General Plan and City policies directing growth to the City's non-agricultural lands. A 'yes' vote on Measure A will affirm the wisdom of well-planned, orderly growth in the City of Chico by approving an amendment to the 1982 Rancho Arroyo Specific Plan. Measure A substantially reduces the amount of housing previously approved for Rancho Arroyo, increases the number of parks and amount of open space, and significantly enlarges and enhances Bidwell Park.

"A 'yes' vote will accomplish the following: • Require the development to dedicate 130.8 acres of land to Bidwell Park • Require the developer to dedicate seven park sites • Create 53 acres of landscaped corridors and greenways • Preserve existing arroyos and protect sensitive plant habitats and other environmental features • Create junior high school and church sites • Plan a series of villages within which, eventually, a total of 2,927 residential dwelling units will be developed • Plan area which will provide onsite job opportunities and retail services. . . ."

County of Butte Sample Ballot

17. Rebuttal to Argument in Favor of Measure A

"Villages? Can a project with 3,000 houses and 7,000 new residents really be regarded as a 'village'? The Sacramento developers pushing the Rancho Arroyo project certainly have a way with words. We urge citizens of Chico to ignore their flowery language and vote no on Measure A.

"These out-of-town developers will have you believe that their project protects agricultural land. Hogwash! Chico's Greenline protects valuable farmland. With the Greenline, there is enough land in the Chico area available for development to build 62,000 new homes. . . .

"They claim that their park dedications will reduce use of our overcrowded Bidwell Park. Don't you believe it! They want to attract 7,000 new residents to Chico by using Rancho Arroyo's proximity to Bidwell Park to outsell other local housing projects.

"The developers imply that the Rancho Arroyo project will provide a much needed school site. In fact, the developers intend to sell the site to the school district, which will pay for the site with taxpayers' money.

"Chico doesn't need the Rancho Arroyo project. Vote no on Measure A."

County of Butte Sample Ballot

18. Letter to the editor: "A relative of mine is a lawyer who recently represented a murderer who had already had a life sentence and broke out of prison and murdered someone else. I think this was a waste of the taxpayers' money to try this man again. It won't do any good. I think murderers should be executed.

"We are the most crime-ridden society in the world. Someone is murdered every 27 minutes in the U.S., and there is a rape every ten minutes and an armed robbery every 82 seconds. According to the FBI, there are 870,000 violent crimes a year, and you know the number is increasing.

"Also according to the FBI, only 10 percent of those arrested for the crimes committed are found guilty, and a large percentage are released on probation. These people are released so they can just go out and commit more crimes.

"Why are they released? In the end it is because there aren't enough prisons to house the guilty. The death sentence must be restored. This would create more room in prisons. It would also drastically reduce the number of murders. If a robber knew before he shot someone that if he was caught his own life would be taken, would he do it?

"These people deserve to die. They sacrificed their right to live when they murdered someone, maybe your mother. It's about time we stopped making it easy for criminals to kill people and get away with it."

Cascade News

▲ **19.** Letter to the editor: "In regard to your editorial, 'Crime bill wastes billions,' let me set you straight. Your paper opposes mandatory life sentences for criminals convicted of three violent crimes, and you whine about how criminals' rights might be violated. Yet you also want to infringe on a citizen's right to keep and bear arms. You say you oppose life sentences for three-time losers because judges couldn't show any leniency toward the criminals no matter how trivial the crime. What is your definition of trivial, busting an innocent child's skull with a hammer?"

North State Record

▲ **20.** Freedom means choice. This is a truth antiporn activists always forget when they argue for censorship. In their fervor to impose their morality, groups like Enough Is Enough cite extreme examples of pornography, such as child porn, suggesting that they are easily available in video stores.

This is not the way it is. Most of this material portrays, not actions such as this, but consensual sex between adults.

The logic used by Enough Is Enough is that if something can somehow hurt someone, it must be banned. They don't apply this logic to more harmful substances, such as alcohol or tobacco. Women and children are more adversely affected by drunken driving and secondhand smoke than by pornography. Few Americans would want to ban alcohol or tobacco even though they kill hundreds of thousands of people each year.

Writing Exercises

1. Write a one-page essay in which you determine whether, and why, it is better (you get to define "better") to look younger than your age, older than your age, or just your age. Then number the premises and conclusions in your essay and diagram it.

2. Should there be a death penalty for first-degree murder? On the top half of a sheet of paper, list considerations supporting the death penalty, and on the bottom half, list considerations opposing it. Take about ten minutes to compile your two lists. (A selection in Appendix 1 may give you some ideas. Your instructor may provide extra time for you to read this selection.)

After everyone is finished, your instructor will call on people to read their lists. He or she will then give everyone about twenty minutes to write a draft of an essay that addresses the issue, Should there be a death penalty for first-degree murder? Put your name on the back of your paper. After everyone is finished, your instructor will collect the papers and redistribute them to the class. In groups of four or five, read the papers that have been given to your group. Do not look at the names of the authors. Select the best essay in each group. Your instructor will ask each group to read the essay they have selected as best.

As an alternative, your instructor may have each group rank-order the papers. He or she will have neighboring groups decide which of their top-ranked papers is the best. The instructor will read the papers that have been top-ranked by two (or more) groups, for discussion.

3. Follow the instructions for Exercise 2, but this time address the question, Are free-needle programs a good idea? (Selections 14A and 14B in Appendix 1 may give you some ideas. Your instructor may provide extra time for you to read those selections.)
4. If you have not done so already, turn to Selection 7, 12, 19, or 20 in Appendix 1 and follow the first set of instructions.
5. Turn to Selection 8 or 13 in Appendix 1 and follow the instructions.
6. Turn to Selections 10A,B; 11A,B; 14A,B; 15A,B; 16A,B; 17A,B; or 18A,B in Appendix 1 and discuss which side has the stronger argument and why.

Chapter 8

Deductive Arguments I: Categorical Logic

For over a hundred years, the symbol of "the Science of Deduction."

> . . .The Science of Deduction and Analysis is one which can only be acquired by long and patient study, nor is life long enough to allow any mortal to attain the highest possible perfection in it.
>
> — *From an article by Sherlock Holmes, in* A Study in Scarlet *by Sir Arthur Conan Doyle*

Fortunately, the greatest detective was doing some serious exaggerating in this quotation. While it may be that few of us mortals will attain "the highest possible perfection" in "the Science of Deduction," most of us can learn quite a bit in a fairly short time if we put our minds to it. In fact, you already have an understanding of the basics from Chapter 7.* In this chapter and the next, you'll learn two kinds of techniques for making and evaluating deductive inferences—i.e., arguments.

If you flip through the pages of these two chapters, you'll see diagrams with circles and Xs, and in Chapter 9 page after page of weird symbols that remind some people of mathematics. These pages may look

*An understanding that's somewhat better than Sir Arthur's, as a matter of fact. Much of what he has Sherlock Holmes referring to as "deduction" turns out to be *inductive* arguments, not deductive ones. We mean no disrespect, of course; one of your authors is a dyed-in-the-wool Holmes fanatic.

intimidating. But there's nothing all that complicated about them if you approach them in the right way. Nearly anybody can catch on *if* they take one of Sherlock Holmes' points seriously: Most people need to apply themselves conscientiously in order to understand this material. The reason is that both here and in Chapter 9 most everything builds on what goes before; if you don't understand what happens at the beginning of the chapter, most of what happens later won't make much sense. So take our advice (and you'll probably hear this from your instructor, too): Keep up! Don't get behind. This stuff is not easy to learn the night before an exam. But if you apply yourself regularly, it really isn't all that hard. In fact, many of our students find this part of the book the most fun, because practicing the subject matter is like playing a game. So, be prepared to put in a little time on a regular basis, pay close attention to the text and your instructor's remarks, and just maybe you'll have a good time with this.

The first technique we'll discuss is **categorical logic.** Categorical logic is logic based on the relations of inclusion and exclusion among classes (or "categories") as stated in categorical claims. Its methods date back to the time of Aristotle, and it was the principle form that logic took among most knowledgeable people for over two thousand years. During that time, all kinds of bells and whistles were added to the basic theory, especially by monks and other scholars during the medieval period. So as not to weigh you down with unnecessary baggage, we'll just set forth the basics of the subject in what follows.

Like truth-functional logic, the subject of the next chapter, categorical logic is useful in clarifying and analyzing deductive arguments. But there is another reason for studying the subject: There is no better way to understand the underlying logical structure of our everyday language than to learn how to put it into the kinds of formal terms we'll introduce in these chapters.

To test your analytical ability, take a look at these claims. Just exactly what is the difference between them?

(1) Everybody who is ineligible for Physics 1A must take Physical Science 1.
(2) No students who are required to take Physical Science 1 are eligible for Physics 1A.

Here's another pair of claims:

(3) Harold won't attend the meeting unless Vanessa decides to go.
(4) If Vanessa decides to go, then Harold will attend the meeting.

You might be surprised at how many college students have a hard time trying to determine whether the claims in each pair mean the same thing or something different. In this chapter and the next, you'll learn a foolproof method for determining how to unravel the logical implications of such claims and for seeing how any two such claims relate to one another. (Incidentally, claims 1 and 2 do not mean the same thing at all, and neither do 3 and 4.) If you're signing a lease or entering into a contract of any kind, it pays to be able to figure out just what is being said in it and what is not; those who have trouble with claims like the ones above are at risk of being left in the dark.

Studying categorical and truth-functional logic can teach us to become more careful and precise in our own thinking. Getting comfortable with this type of thinking can be helpful in general, but for those who will someday be

■ Aristotle was interested in a lot of subjects besides logic—practically everything, in fact. Fortunately for his reputation, these remarks (which he *did* make!) are not typical of him.

applying to law school, medical school, or graduate school, it has the added advantage that many admission exams for such programs deal with the kinds of reasoning discussed in this chapter.

Let's start by looking at the four basic kinds of claims on which categorical logic is based.

CATEGORICAL CLAIMS

A **categorical claim** says something about classes (or "categories") of things. Our interest lies in categorical claims of certain standard forms. A **standard-form categorical claim** is a claim that results from putting names or descriptions of classes into the blanks of the following structures:

A: All _______ are _______.
(*Example:* All Presbyterians are Christians.)

E: No _______ are _______.
(*Example:* No Muslims are Christians.)

I: Some _______ are _______.
(*Example:* Some Christians are Arabs.)

O: Some _______ are not _______.
(*Example:* Some Muslims are not Sunnis.)

The phrases that go in the blanks are **terms;** the one that goes into the first blank is the **subject term** of the claim, and the one that goes into the second blank is the **predicate term.** Thus, "Christians" is the predicate term of the first example above and the subject term of the third example. In many of the examples and explanations that follow, we'll use the letters *S* and *P* (for "subject" and "predicate") to stand for terms in categorical claims. And we'll talk about the subject and predicate *classes,* which are just the classes that the terms refer to.

But first a caution: Only nouns and noun phrases will work as terms. An adjective alone, such as "red," won't do. "All fire engines are red" does *not* produce a standard-form categorical claim because "red" is not a noun or noun phrase. To see that it is not, try switching the places of the terms: "All red are fire engines." This doesn't make sense, right? But "red vehicles" (or even "red things") will do because "All red vehicles are fire engines" makes sense (even though it's false).

Looking back at the standard-form structures given above, notice that each one has a letter to its left. These are the traditional names of the four types of standard-form categorical claims. The claim "All Presbyterians are Christians" is an A-claim, and so are "All idolators are heathens," "All people born between 1946 and 1964 are baby boomers," and any other claim of the form "All S are P." The same is true for the other three letters and the other three kinds of claims.

Venn Diagrams

Each of the standard forms has its own graphic illustration in a **Venn diagram,** as shown in Figures 1 through 4. Named after British logician John Venn, these diagrams exactly represent the four standard-form categorical claim types. In the diagrams, the circles represent the classes named by the terms, shaded areas represent areas that are empty, and areas containing Xs represent areas that are not empty—that contain at least one item. An area that is blank is one that the claim says nothing about; it may be occupied, or it may be empty.*

Notice that in the diagram for the A-claim, the area that would contain any members of the S class that were not members of the P class is shaded—that is, it is empty. Thus, that diagram represents the claim "All S are P," since there is no S left that isn't P. Similarly, in the diagram for the E-claim, the area where S and P overlap is empty; any S that is also a P has been eliminated. Hence: "No S are P."

For our purposes in this chapter, the word "some" means "at least one." So, the third diagram represents the fact that at least one S is a P, and the X in the area where the two classes overlap shows that at least one thing inhabits this area. Finally, the last diagram shows an X in the area of the S circle that is outside the P circle, representing the existence of at least one S that is not a P.

We'll try to keep technical jargon to a minimum, but here's some terminology we'll need: The two claim types that *include* one class or part of one class within another, the A-claims and I-claims, are **affirmative claims;** the two that *exclude* one class or part of one class from another, the E-claims and O-claims, are **negative claims.**

Although there are only four standard-form claim types, it's remarkable how versatile they are. A large portion of what we want to say can be rewrit-

*There is one exception to this, but we needn't worry about it for a few pages yet.

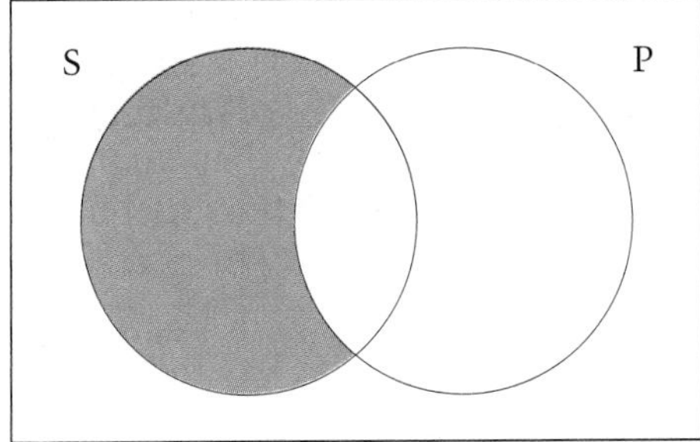

FIGURE 1 A-claim: All S are P.

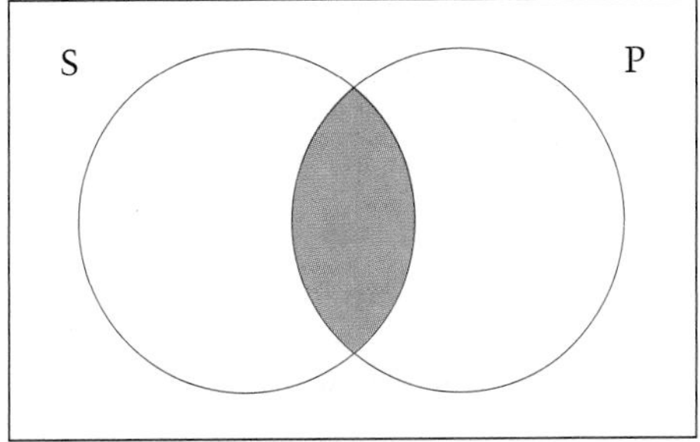

FIGURE 2 E-claim: No S are P.

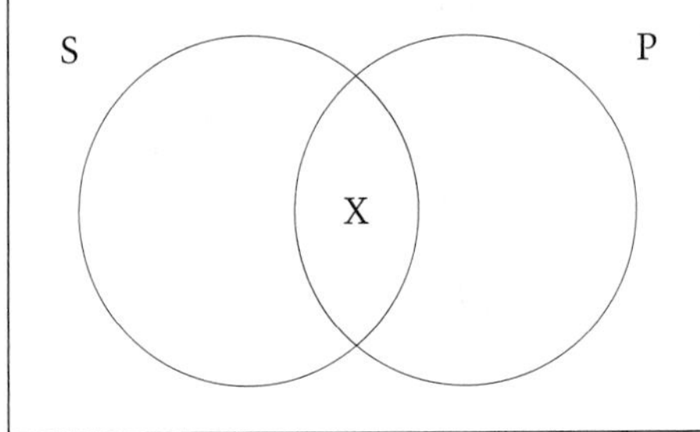

FIGURE 3 I-claim: Some S are P.

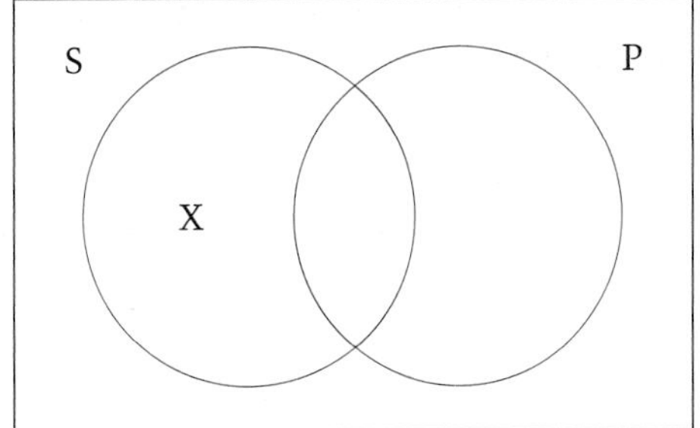

FIGURE 4 O-claim: Some S are not P.

ten, or "translated," into one or another of them. Because this task is sometimes easier said than done, we'd best spend a little while making sure we understand how to do it. And we warn you in advance: A lot of standard form translations are not very pretty—but it's accuracy we seek here, not style.

Translation into Standard Form

The main idea is to take an ordinary claim and turn it into a standard-form categorical claim that is exactly equivalent. We'll say that two claims are **equivalent claims** if, and only if, they would be true in all and exactly the same circumstances—that is, under no circumstances could one of them be true and the other false. (You can think of such claims as "saying the same thing," more or less.)

Lots of ordinary claims in English are easy to translate into standard form. A claim of the sort "Every X is a Y," for example, more or less automatically turns into the standard-form A-claim "All Xs are Ys." And it's easy to produce the proper term to turn "Minors are not eligible" into the E-claim "No minors are eligible people."

All standard-form claims are in the present tense, but even so we can use them to talk about the past. For example, we can translate "There were creatures weighing more than four tons that lived in North America" as "Some creatures that lived in North America are creatures that weighed more than four tons."

What about a claim like "Only sophomores are eligible candidates"? It's good to have a strategy for attacking such translation problems. First, identify the terms. In this case, the two classes in question are "sophomores" and "eligible candidates." Now, which do we have on our hands, an A-, E-, I-, or O-claim? Generally speaking, nothing but a careful reading can serve to answer this question. So, you'll need to think hard about just what relation between classes is being expressed and then decide how that relation is best turned into a standard form. Fortunately, we can provide some rules of thumb that help in certain frequently encountered problems, including one that applies to our current example. If you're like most people, you don't have too much trouble seeing that our claim is an A-claim, but *which* A-claim? There are two possibilities:

All sophomores are eligible candidates

and

All eligible candidates are sophomores.

If we make the wrong choice, we can change the meaning of the claim significantly. (Notice that "All sophomores are students" is very different from "All students are sophomores.") In the present case, notice that we are saying something about *every* eligible candidate—namely, that he or she must be a sophomore. (*Only* sophomores are eligible—i.e., no one else is eligible.) In an A-claim, the class so restricted is always the subject class. So, this claim should be translated into

All eligible candidates are sophomores.

In fact, *all claims of the sort "Only Xs are Ys" should be translated as "All Ys are Xs."*

But there are other claims in which the word "only" plays a crucial role and which have to be treated differently. Consider, for example, this claim: "The only people admitted are people over twenty-one." In this case, a restriction is being put on the class of people admitted; we're saying that *nobody else is admitted* except those over twenty-one. Therefore, "people admitted" is the subject class: "All people admitted are people over twenty-one." And, in fact, *all claims of the sort "The only Xs are Ys" should be translated as "All Xs are Ys."*

The two rules of thumb that govern most translations of claims that hinge on the word "only" are these:

The word "only," used by itself, introduces the *predicate* term of an A-claim.

The phrase "the only" introduces the *subject* term of an A-claim.

Note that, in accordance with these rules, we would translate both of these claims

Only matinees are half-price shows

and

Matinees are the only half-price shows

as

All half-price shows are matinees.

The kind of thing a claim directly concerns is not always obvious. For example, if you think for a moment about the claim "I always get nervous when I take logic exams," you'll see that it's a claim about *times*. It's about

On Language

The Most Versatile Word in English

Question:

There's only one word that can be placed successfully in any of the 10 numbered positions in this sentence to produce 10 sentences of different meaning (each sentence has 10 words): (1) *I* (2) *helped* (3) *my* (4) *dog* (5) *carry* (6) *my* (7) *husband's* (8) *slippers* (9) *yesterday* (10).

What is that word?

— GLORIA J., Salt Lake City, Utah

Answer:

The word is "only," which makes the following 10 sentences:

1. Only *I* helped my dog carry my husband's slippers yesterday. (Usually the cat helps too, but she was busy with a mouse.)
2. I only *helped* my dog carry my husband's slippers yesterday. (The dog wanted me to carry them all by myself, but I refused.)
3. I helped only *my* dog carry my husband's slippers yesterday. (I was too busy to help my neighbor's dog when he carried them.)
4. I helped my only *dog* carry my husband's slippers yesterday. (I considered getting another dog, but the cat disapproved.)
5. I helped my dog only *carry* my husband's slippers yesterday. (I didn't help the dog eat them; I usually let the cat do that.)
6. I helped my dog carry only *my* husband's slippers yesterday. (My dog and I didn't have time to help my neighbor's husband.)
7. I helped my dog carry my only *husband's* slippers yesterday. (I considered getting another husband, but one is enough.)
8. I helped my dog carry my husband's only *slippers* yesterday. (My husband had two pairs of slippers, but the cat ate one pair.)
9. I helped my dog carry my husband's slippers only *yesterday.* (And now the dog wants help again; I wish he'd ask the cat.)
10. I helped my dog carry my husband's slippers yesterday only. (And believe me, once was enough—the slippers tasted *terrible.*)

— MARILYN VOS SAVANT, author of the "Ask Marilyn" column

getting nervous and about logic exams indirectly, of course, but it pertains directly to times or occasions. The proper translation of the example is "All times I take logic exams are times I get nervous." Notice that the word "whenever" is often a clue that you're talking about times or occasions, as well as an indication that you're going to have an A-claim or an E-claim. "Wherever" works the same way for places: "He makes trouble wherever he goes" should be translated as "All places he goes are places he makes trouble."

There are two other sorts of claims that are a bit tricky to translate into standard form. The first is a claim about a single individual, such as "Aristotle is a logician." It's clear that this claim specifies a class, "logicians," and places Aristotle as a member of that class. The problem is that categorical claims are always about *two* classes, and Aristotle isn't a class. (We certainly couldn't talk about *some* of Aristotle being a logician.) What we want to do is treat such claims as if they were about classes with exactly one member—in the present case, Aristotle. One way to do this is to use the term "people who are identical with Aristotle," which of course has only Aristotle as a member. (Everybody is identical with himself or herself, and nobody else is.) The important thing to remember about such claims can be summarized in the following rule of thumb:

Claims about single individuals should be treated as A-claims or E-claims.

"Aristotle is a logician" can therefore be translated into "All people identical with Aristotle are logicians," an A-claim. Similarly, "Aristotle is not left-handed" becomes the E-claim "No people identical with Aristotle are left-handed people." (Your instructor may prefer to leave the claim in its original form and simply *treat* it as an A-claim or an E-claim. This avoids the awkward "people identical with Aristotle" wording and is certainly okay with us.)

It isn't just people that crop up in individual claims. Often this kind of treatment is called for when we're talking about objects, occasions, places, and other kinds of things. For example, the preferred translation of "St. Louis is on the Mississippi" is "All cities identical with St. Louis are cities on the Mississippi."

Other claims that cause translation difficulty contain what are called *mass nouns.* Consider this example: "Boiled okra is too ugly to eat." This claim is about a *kind of stuff.* The best way to deal with it is to treat it as a claim about *examples* of this kind of stuff. The present example translates into an A-claim about *all* examples of the stuff in question: "All examples of boiled okra are things that are too ugly to eat." An example such as "Most boiled okra is too ugly to eat" translates into the I-claim "Some examples of boiled okra are things that are too ugly to eat."

As we noted, it's not possible to give rules or hints about every kind of problem you might run into when translating claims into standard-form categorical versions. Only practice and discussion can bring you to the point where you can handle this part of the material with confidence. The best thing to do now is to turn to some exercises.

Exercise 8-1

Translate each of the following into a standard-form claim. Make sure that each answer follows the exact form of an A-, E-, I-, or O-claim and that each term you use is a noun or noun phrase that refers to a class of things. Remember that you're trying to produce a claim that's equivalent to the one given; it doesn't matter whether the given claim is actually true.

▲ **1.** Every salamander is a lizard.

2. Not every lizard is a salamander.

3. Only reptiles can be lizards.

▲ **4.** Snakes are the only members of the suborder Ophidia.

5. The only members of the suborder Ophidia are snakes.
6. None of the burrowing snakes is poisonous.
▲ 7. Anything that's an alligator is a reptile.
8. Anything that qualifies as a frog qualifies as an amphibian.
9. There are frogs wherever there are snakes.
▲ 10. Wherever there are snakes, there are frogs.
11. Whenever the frog population decreases, the snake population decreases.
12. Nobody arrived except the cheerleaders.
13. Except for vice presidents, nobody got raises.
14. Unless people arrived early, they couldn't get seats.
▲ 15. Most home movies are as boring as dirt.
▲ 16. Socrates is a Greek.
17. The bank robber is not Jane's fiancé.
18. If an automobile was built before 1950, it's an antique.
▲ 19. Salt is a meat preservative.
20. Most corn does not make good popcorn.

Exercise 8-2

Follow the instructions given in the preceding exercise.

▲ 1. Students who wrote poor exams didn't get admitted to the program.
2. None of my students is failing.
3. If you live in the dorms, you can't own a car.
▲ 4. There are a few right-handed first basemen.
5. People make faces every time Joan sings.
6. The only tests George fails are the ones he takes.
▲ 7. Nobody passed who didn't make at least 50 percent.
8. You can't be a member unless you're over fifty.
9. Nobody catches on without studying.
▲ 10. I've had days like this before.
11. Roofers aren't millionaires.
12. Not one part of Michael Jackson's face is original equipment.
▲ 13. A few holidays fall on Saturday.
14. Only outlaws own guns.
15. You have nothing to lose but your chains.
▲ 16. Unless you pass this test you won't pass the course.
17. If you cheat, your prof will make you sorry.
18. If you cheat, your friends couldn't care less.
▲ 19. Only when you've paid the fee will they let you enroll.
20. Nobody plays who isn't in full uniform.

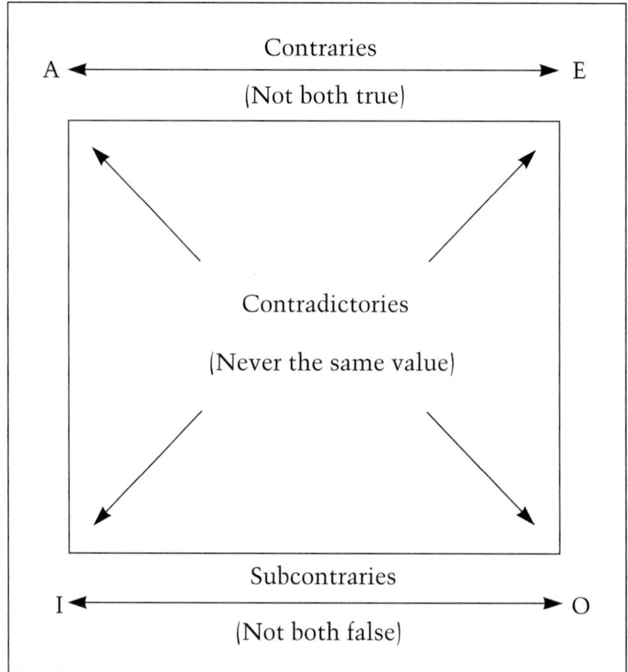

FIGURE 5 The square of opposition.

The Square of Opposition

Two categorical claims *correspond* to each other if they have the same subject term and the same predicate term. So, "All Methodists are Christians" corresponds to "Some Methodists are Christians": In both claims, "Methodists" is the subject term, and "Christians" is the predicate term. Notice, though, that "Some Christians are not Methodists" does *not* correspond to either of the other two; it has the same terms but in different places.

We can now exhibit the logical relationships between corresponding A-, E-, I-, and O-claims. The **square of opposition,** in Figure 5, does this very concisely. The A- and E-claims, across the top of the square from each other, are **contrary claims**—they can both be false, but they cannot both be true. The I- and O-claims, across the bottom of the square from each other, are **subcontrary claims**—they can both be true, but they cannot both be false. The A- and O-claims and the E- and I-claims, which are at opposite diagonal corners from each other, respectively, are **contradictory claims**—they never have the same truth values.

Notice that these logical relationships are reflected on the Venn diagrams for the claims (see Figures 1 through 4). The diagrams for corresponding A- and O-claims say exactly opposite things about the left-hand area of the diagram, namely, that the area *has* something in it and that it *doesn't;* those for corresponding E- and I-claims do the same about the center area. Clearly, exactly one claim of each pair is true no matter what—either the relevant area is empty, or it isn't.

The diagrams show clearly how both subcontraries can be true: There's no conflict in putting X's in both left and center areas. In fact, it's possible to diagram an A-claim and the corresponding E-claim on the same diagram; we just have to shade out the entire subject class circle. This amounts to saying that *both* an A-claim and its corresponding E-claim can be true *as long as there are no members of the subject class.* We get an analogous result for subcontraries: They can both be false as long as the subject class is empty.* We can easily avoid this result by making an assumption: *When making inferences from one contrary (or subcontrary) to another, we'll assume that the classes we're talking about are not entirely empty.* On this assumption, the A-claim or the corresponding E-claim (or both) must be false, and the I-claim or the corresponding O-claim (or both) must be true.

If we have the truth value of one categorical claim, we can often deduce the truth values of the other three corresponding claims by using the square of opposition. For instance, if it's true that "All serious remarks by Paris Hilton are hopeless clichés," then we can immediately infer that its contradictory claim, "Some serious remarks by Paris Hilton are not hopeless clichés," is false; the corresponding E-claim, "No serious remarks by Paris Hilton are hopeless clichés," is also false because it is the contrary claim of the original A-claim and cannot be true if the A-claim is true. The corresponding I-claim, "Some serious remarks by Paris Hilton are hopeless clichés," must be true because we just determined that *its* contradictory claim, the E-claim, is false.

However, we cannot *always* determine the truth values of the remaining three standard-form categorical claims. For example, if we know only that the A-claim is false, all we can infer is the truth value (true) of the corresponding O-claim. Nothing follows about either the E- or the I-claim. Because the A- and the E-claim can both be false, knowing that the A-claim is false does not tell us anything about the E-claim—it can still be either true or false. And if the E-claim remains undetermined, then so must its contradictory, the I-claim.

So here are the limits on what can be inferred from the square of opposition: Beginning with a *true* claim at the top of the square (either A or E), we can infer the truth values of all three of the remaining claims. The same is true if we begin with a *false* claim at the bottom of the square (either I or O): We can still deduce the truth values of the other three. But if we begin with a false claim at the top of the square or a true claim at the bottom, all we can determine is the truth value of the contradictory of the claim in hand.

*It is quite possible to interpret categorical claims this way. By allowing both the A- and the E-claims to be true and both the I- and the O-claims to be false, this interpretation reduces the square to contradiction alone. We're going to interpret the claims differently; however, at the level at which we're operating, it seems much more natural to see "All Cs are Ds" as conflicting with "No Cs are Ds."

Exercise 8-3

Translate the following into standard-form claims, and determine the three corresponding standard-form claims. Then, assuming the truth value in parentheses for the given claim, determine the truth values of as many of the other three as you can.

Example

Most snakes are harmless. (True)
Translation (I-claim): Some snakes are harmless creatures. (True)
Corresponding A-claim: All snakes are harmless creatures. (Undetermined)
Corresponding E-claim: No snakes are harmless creatures. (False)
Corresponding O-claim: Some snakes are not harmless creatures. (Undetermined)

▲ **1.** Not all anniversaries are happy occasions. (True)
2. There's no such thing as a completely harmless drug. (True)
3. There have been such things as just wars. (True)
▲ **4.** There are allergies that can kill you. (True)
5. Woodpeckers sing really well. (False)
6. Mockingbirds can't sing. (False)
7. Some herbs are medicinal. (False)
8. Logic exercises are easy. (False)

THREE CATEGORICAL OPERATIONS

The square of opposition allows us to make inferences from one claim to another, as you were doing in the last exercise. We can think of these inferences as simple valid arguments, because that's exactly what they are. We'll turn next to three operations that can be performed on standard-form categorical claims. They, too, will allow us to make simple valid arguments and, in combination with the square, some not-quite-so-simple valid arguments.

Conversion

You find the **converse** of a standard-form claim by switching the positions of the subject and predicate terms. The E- and I-claims, but not the A- and O-claims, contain just the same information as their converses; that is,

All E- and I-claims, but not A- and O-claims, are equivalent to their converses.

Each member of the following pairs is the converse of the other:

E: No Norwegians are Slavs.
No Slavs are Norwegians.

I: Some state capitals are large cities.
Some large cities are state capitals.

Notice that the claims that are equivalent to their converses are those with symmetrical Venn diagrams.

Obversion

To discuss the next two operations, we need a couple of auxiliary notions. First, there's the notion of a *universe of discourse.* With rare exceptions, we make claims within contexts that limit the scope of the terms we use. For example, if your instructor walks into class and says, "Everybody passed the last exam," the word "everybody" does not include everybody in the world. Your instructor is not claiming, for example, that your mother and the President of the United States passed the exam. There is an unstated but obvious restriction to a smaller universe of people—in this case, the people in your class who *took* the exam. Now, for every class within a universe of discourse, there is a *complementary class* that contains everything in the universe of discourse that is *not* in the first class. Terms that name complementary classes are complementary terms. So "students" and "nonstudents" are **complementary terms.** Indeed, putting the prefix "non" in front of a term is often the easiest way to produce its complement. Some terms require different treatment, though. The complement of "people who took the exam" is probably best stated as "people who did not take the exam" because the universe is pretty clearly restricted to people in such a case. (We wouldn't expect, for example, the complement of "people who took the exam" to include *everything* that didn't take the exam, including your Uncle Bob's hairpiece.)

Now, we can get on with it: To find the **obverse** of a claim, (a) change it from affirmative to negative, or vice versa (i.e., go horizontally across the square—an A-claim becomes an E-claim; an O-claim becomes an I-claim, and so on); then (b) replace the predicate term with its complementary term.

> **All categorical claims of all four types, A, E, I, and O, are equivalent to their obverses.**

The Mad Hatter is teaching Alice *not* to convert A-claims.

"You should say what you mean," the March Hare went on.

"I do," Alice hastily replied; "at least—at least I mean what I say—that's the same thing, you know."

"Not the same thing a bit!" said the Hatter. "Why, you might just as well say that 'I see what I eat' is the same thing as 'I eat what I see!'"

— Lewis Carroll, *Alice's Adventures in Wonderland*

Here are some examples; each claim is the obverse of the other member of the pair:

A: All Presbyterians are Christians.
No Presbyterians are non-Christians.

E: No fish are mammals.
All fish are nonmammals.

I: Some citizens are voters.
Some citizens are not nonvoters.

O: Some contestants are not winners.
Some contestants are nonwinners.

Contraposition

You find the **contrapositive** of a categorical claim by (a) switching the places of the subject and predicate terms, just as in conversion, and (b) replacing both terms with complementary terms. Each of the following is the contrapositive of the other member of the pair:

A: All Mongolians are Muslims.
All non-Muslims are non-Mongolians.

In Depth

Venn Diagrams for the Three Operations

Conversion: One way to see which operations work for which types of claim is to put them on Venn diagrams. Here's a regular diagram, which is all we need to explain *conversion:*

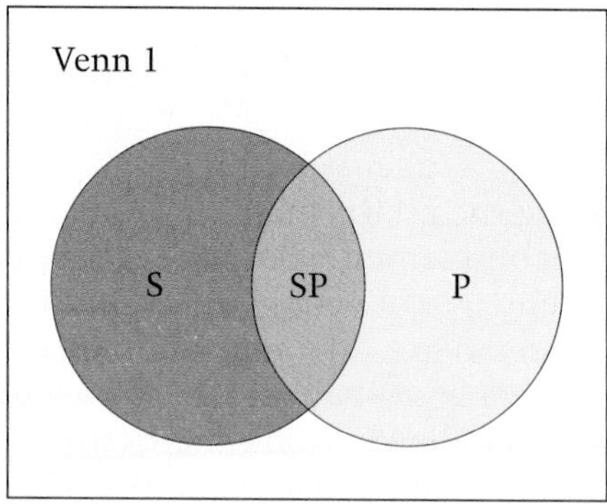

Imagine an I-claim, Some S are P, diagrammed on the above. It would have an X in the central area labeled SP, where S and P overlap. But its converse, Some P are S, would also have an X in that area, since that's where P and S overlap. So, the symmetry of the diagram shows that conversion works for I-claims. The same situation holds for E-claims, except we're shading the central area in both cases rather than placing Xs.

Now, let's imagine an A-claim, All S are P, the diagram for which requires us to shade all the subject term that's not included in the predicate term—i.e., the orange area above. But its converse, All P are S, would require that we shade out the yellow area of the diagram, since the subject term is now over there on the right. So the claims with asymmetrical diagrams cannot be validly converted.

We need a somewhat more complicated diagram to explain the other two operations. Let's use a rectangular box to represent the universe of discourse (see text for an explanation of the universe of discourse) within which our classes and their complements fall. In addition to the S and P labels, we'll add $\bar{S}$ anywhere we would *not* find S, and $\bar{P}$ anywhere we

O: Some citizens are not voters.
Some nonvoters are not noncitizens.

All A- and O-claims, but not E- and I-claims, are equivalent to their contrapositives.

The operations of conversion, obversion, and contraposition are important to much of what comes later, so make sure you can do them correctly and that you know which claims are equivalent to the results.

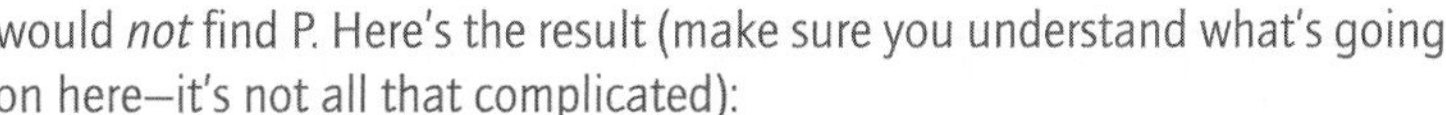

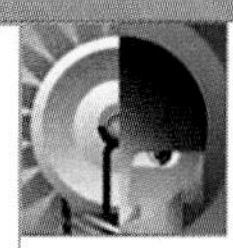

would *not* find P. Here's the result (make sure you understand what's going on here—it's not all that complicated):

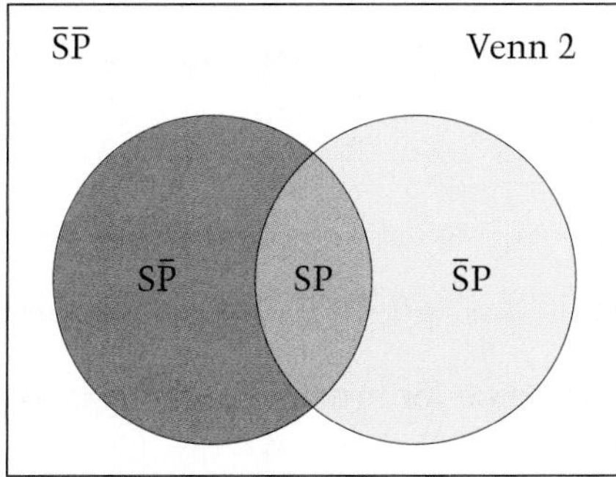

Obversion: Now let's look at *obversion.* Imagine an A-claim: All S are P, diagrammed on the above. We'd shade out the area labeled $S\bar{P}$ (the orange area), wouldn't we? (All the subject class that's not part of the predicate class.) Now consider its obverse, "No S are $\bar{P}$." Since it's an E-claim, we shade where the subject and predicate overlap (the peach area). And that turns out to be exactly the same area we shaded out for its obverse! So these two are equivalent: They produce the same diagram. If you check, you'll find you get the same result for each of the other three types of claim, since obversion is valid for all four types.

Contraposition: Finally, we'll see how *contraposition* works out on the diagram. The A-claim, All S are P, once again is made true by shading out the $S\bar{P}$ (orange) area of the diagram. But now consider this claim's contrapositive, All $\bar{P}$ are $\bar{S}$. Shading out all the subject class that's outside the predicate class produces the same diagram as the original, thus showing that they are equivalent. Try diagramming an O-claim and its contrapositive, and you'll find yourself putting an X in exactly the same area for each.

But if you diagram an I-claim, Some S are P, putting an X in the central SP area, and then diagram its contrapositive, Some $\bar{P}$ are $\bar{S}$, you'll find that the X would have to go entirely outside both circles, since that's the only place $\bar{P}$ and $\bar{S}$ overlap! Clearly, this says something different from the original I-claim. You'll find a similarly weird result if you consider an E-claim, since contraposition does *not* work for either I- or E-claims.

Exercise 8-4

Find the claim described, and determine whether it is equivalent to the claim you began with.

▲ **1.** Find the contrapositive of "No Sunnis are Christians."

2. Find the obverse of "Some Arabs are Christians."

3. Find the obverse of "All Sunnis are Muslims."

▲ 4. Find the converse of "Some Kurds are not Christians."
5. Find the converse of "No Hindus are Muslims."
6. Find the contrapositive of "Some Indians are not Hindus."
▲ 7. Find the converse of "All Shiites are Muslims."
8. Find the contrapositive of "All Catholics are Christians."
9. Find the converse of "All Protestants are Christians."
▲ 10. Find the obverse of "No Muslims are Christians."

Exercise 8-5

Follow the directions given in the preceding exercise.

▲ 1. Find the obverse of "Some students who scored well on the exam are students who wrote poor essays."
2. Find the obverse of "No students who wrote poor essays are students who were admitted to the program."
3. Find the contrapositive of "Some students who were admitted to the program are not students who scored well on the exam."
▲ 4. Find the contrapositive of "No students who did not score well on the exam are students who were admitted to the program."
5. Find the contrapositive of "All students who were admitted to the program are students who wrote good essays."
6. Find the obverse of "No students of mine are unregistered students."
▲ 7. Find the contrapositive of "All people who live in the dorms are people whose automobile ownership is restricted."
8. Find the contrapositive of "All commuters are people whose automobile ownership is unrestricted."
9. Find the contrapositive of "Some students with short-term memory problems are students who do poorly in history classes."
▲ 10. Find the obverse of "No first basemen are right-handed people."

Exercise 8-6

For each of the following, find the claim that is described.

Example

Find the contrary of the contrapositive of "All Greeks are Europeans." First, find the contrapositive of the original claim. It is "All non-Europeans are non-Greeks." Now, find the contrary of that. Going across the top of the square (from an A-claim to an E-claim), you get "No non-Europeans are non-Greeks."

1. Find the contradictory of the converse of "No clarinets are percussion instruments."
▲ 2. Find the contradictory of the obverse of "Some encyclopedias are definitive works."

In Depth

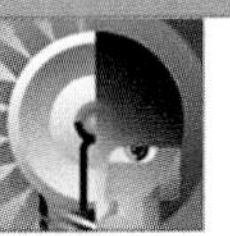

Two Common Mistakes

Some of the nuts and bolts on the imported Fords are metric; therefore, some are not.
Some of the nuts and bolts on the imported Fords are not metric; therefore, some are.

It's common for a person to make an inference from "Some As are Bs" to "Some As are not Bs," as the first sentence above specifies. But this is a mistake; it's an invalid inference. One might try to defend the mistake by saying, Look, if *all* As are Bs, why not just say so? By not saying so, you're implying that some As are *not* Bs, aren't you? Nope, in fact you're not. One reason we might say "Some As are Bs" is because we only *know* about some As; we may not know whether all of them are Bs.

The same kind of account, naturally, works for going the other way, as in the second sentence above.

3. Find the contrapositive of the subcontrary of "Some English people are Celts."
▲ 4. Find the contrary of the contradictory of "Some sailboats are not sloops."
5. Find the obverse of the converse of "No sharks are freshwater fish."

Exercise 8-7

For each of the numbered claims below, determine which of the lettered claims that follow are equivalent. You may use letters more than once if necessary. (Hint: This is a lot easier to do after all the claims are translated, a fact that indicates at least one advantage to putting claims into standard form.)

1. Some people who have not been tested can give blood.
▲ 2. People who have not been tested cannot give blood.
▲ 3. Nobody who has been tested can give blood.
4. Nobody can give blood except those who have been tested.
   a. Some people who have been tested cannot give blood.
   b. Not everybody who can give blood has been tested.
   c. Only people who have been tested can give blood.
   d. Some people who cannot give blood are people who have been tested.
   e. If a person has been tested, then he or she cannot give blood.

Exercise 8-8

Try to make the claims in the following pairs correspond to each other—that is, arrange them so that they have the same subject and the same predicate terms. Use only those operations that produce equivalent claims; for example, don't convert A- or O-claims in the process of trying to make the claims correspond. You can work on either member of the pair or both. (The main reason for practicing on these is to make the problems in the next two exercises easier to do.)

Example

a. Some students are not unemployed people.
b. All employed people are students.

These two claims can be made to correspond by obverting claim (a) and then converting the result (which is legitimate because the claim has been turned into an I-claim before conversion). We wind up with "Some employed people are students," which corresponds to (b).

▲ **1.** a. Some Slavs are non-Europeans.
b. No Slavs are Europeans.

2. a. All Europeans are Westerners.
b. Some non-Westerners are non-Europeans.

3. a. All Greeks are Europeans.
b. Some non-Europeans are Greeks.

▲ **4.** a. No members of the club are people who took the exam.
b. Some people who did not take the exam are members of the club.

5. a. All people who are not members of the club are people who took the exam.
b. Some people who did not take the exam are members of the club.

6. a. Some cheeses are not products high in cholesterol.
b. No cheeses are products that are not high in cholesterol.

▲ **7.** a. All people who arrived late are people who will be allowed to perform.
b. Some of the people who did not arrive late will not be allowed to perform.

8. a. No nonparticipants are people with name tags.
b. Some of the people with name tags are participants.

9. a. Some perennials are plants that grow from tubers.
b. Some plants that do not grow from tubers are perennials.

▲ **10.** a. Some decks that play digital tape are not devices equipped for radical oversampling.
b. All devices that are equipped for radical oversampling are decks that will not play digital tape.

Exercise 8-9

Which of the following arguments is valid? (Remember, an argument is valid when the truth of its premises guarantees the truth of its conclusion.)

▲ **1.** Whenever the battery is dead, the screen goes blank; that means, of course, that whenever the screen goes blank, the battery is dead.

2. For a while there, some students were desperate for good grades, which meant some weren't, right?

3. Some players in the last election weren't members of the Reform Party. Obviously, therefore, some members of the Reform Party weren't players in the last election.

▲ **4.** Since some of the students who failed the exam were students who didn't attend the review session, it must be that some students who weren't at the session failed the exam.

5. None of the people who arrived late were people who got good seats, so none of the good seats were occupied by latecomers.

6. Everybody who arrived on time was given a box lunch, so the people who did not get a box lunch were those who didn't get there on time.

▲ **7.** None of the people who gave blood are people who were tested, so everybody who gave blood must have been untested.

8. Some of the people who were not tested are people who were allowed to give blood, from which it follows that some of the people who were *not* allowed to give blood must have been people who were tested.

9. Everybody who was in uniform was able to play, so nobody who was out of uniform must have been able to play.

▲ **10.** Not everybody in uniform was allowed to play, so some people who were not allowed to play must not have been people in uniform.

Exercise 8-10

For each pair of claims, assume that the first has the truth value given in parentheses. Using the operations of conversion, obversion, and contraposition along with the square of opposition, decide whether the second claim is true, false, or remains undetermined.

Example

a. No aardvarks are nonmammals. (True)
b. Some aardvarks are not mammals.

Claim (a) can be obverted to "All aardvarks are mammals." Because all categorical claims are equivalent to their obverses, the truth of this claim follows from that of (a). Because this claim is the contradictory of claim (b), it follows that claim (b) must be false.

Note: If we had been unable to make the two claims correspond without performing an illegitimate operation (such as converting an A-claim), then the answer is automatically *undetermined.*

▲ **1.** a. No mosquitoes are poisonous creatures. (True)
b. Some poisonous creatures are mosquitoes.

2. a. Some students are not ineligible candidates. (True)
b. No eligible candidates are students.

▲ **3.** a. Some sound arguments are not invalid arguments. (True)
b. All valid arguments are unsound arguments.

4. a. Some residents are nonvoters. (False)
b. No voters are residents.

▲ **5.** a. Some automobile plants are not productive factories. (True)
b. All unproductive factories are automobile plants.

Many of the following will have to be rewritten as standard-form categorical claims before they can be answered.

6. a. Most opera singers take voice lessons their whole lives. (True)
   b. Some opera singers do not take voice lessons their whole lives.
7. a. The hero gets killed in some of Gary Brodnax's novels. (False)
   b. The hero does not get killed in some of Gary Brodnax's novels.
8. a. None of the boxes in the last shipment are unopened. (True)
   b. Some of the opened boxes are not boxes in the last shipment.
▲ 9. a. Not everybody who is enrolled in the class will get a grade. (True)
   b. Some people who will not get a grade are enrolled in the class.
10. a. Persimmons are always astringent when they have not been left to ripen. (True)
    b. Some persimmons that have been left to ripen are not astringent.

CATEGORICAL SYLLOGISMS

A **syllogism** is a two-premise deductive argument. A **categorical syllogism** (in standard form) is a syllogism whose every claim is a standard-form categorical claim and in which three terms each occur exactly twice in exactly two of the claims. Study the following example:

All Americans are consumers.
Some consumers are not Democrats.
Therefore, some Americans are not Democrats.

Notice how each of the three terms "Americans," "consumers," and "Democrats" occurs exactly twice in exactly two different claims. The *terms of a syllogism* are sometimes given the following labels:

***Major term:* the term that occurs as the predicate term of the syllogism's conclusion**

***Minor term:* the term that occurs as the subject term of the syllogism's conclusion**

***Middle term:* the term that occurs in both of the premises but not at all in the conclusion**

The most frequently used symbols for these three terms are *P* for major term, *S* for minor term, and *M* for middle term. We use these symbols throughout to simplify the discussion.

In a categorical syllogism, each of the premises states a relationship between the middle term and one of the other terms, as shown in Figure 6. If both premises do their jobs correctly—that is, if the proper connections between S and P are established via the middle term, M—then the relationship between S and P stated by the conclusion will have to follow—that is, the argument is valid.

In case you're not clear about the concept of validity, remember: An argument is valid if, and only if, it is not possible for its premises to be true while its conclusion is false. This is just another way of saying that *were* the premises of a valid argument true (whether or not they are in fact true), then the truth of the conclusion would be guaranteed. In a moment, we'll begin developing the first of two methods for assessing the validity of syllogisms.

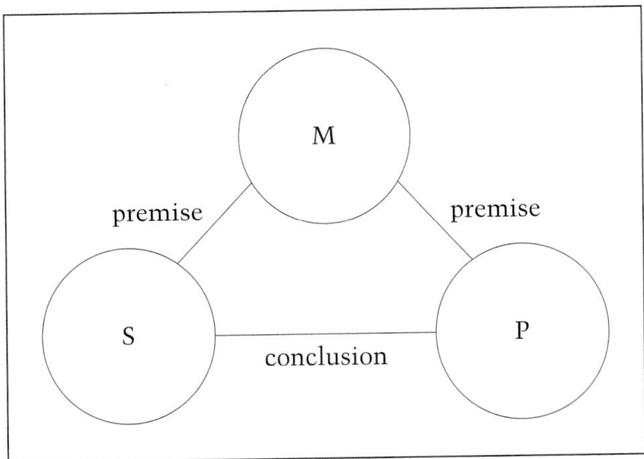

FIGURE 6 Relationship of terms in categorical syllogisms.

First, though, let's look at some candidates for syllogisms. In fact, only one of the following qualifies as a categorical syllogism. Can you identify which one? What is wrong with the other two?

1. All cats are mammals.
   Not all cats are domestic.
   Therefore, not all mammals are domestic.
2. All valid arguments are good arguments.
   Some valid arguments are boring arguments.
   Therefore, some good arguments are boring arguments.
3. Some people on the committee are not students.
   All people on the committee are local people.
   Therefore, some local people are nonstudents.

We hope it was fairly obvious that the second argument is the only proper syllogism. The first example has a couple of things wrong with it: Neither the second premise nor the conclusion is in standard form—no standard-form categorical claim begins with the word "not"—and the predicate term must be a noun or noun phrase. The second premise can be translated into "Some cats are not domestic creatures" and the conclusion into "Some mammals are not domestic creatures," and the result is a syllogism. The third argument is okay up to the conclusion, which contains a term that does not occur anywhere in the premises: "nonstudents." However, because "nonstudents" is the complement of "students," this argument can be turned into a proper syllogism by obverting the conclusion, producing "Some local people are not students."

Once you're able to recognize syllogisms, it's time to learn how to determine their validity. We'll turn now to our first method, the Venn diagram test.

The Venn Diagram Method of Testing for Validity

Diagramming a syllogism requires three overlapping circles, one representing each class named by a term in the argument. To be systematic, in our diagrams we put the minor term on the left, the major term on the right, and the middle term in the middle, but lowered a bit. We will diagram the following syllogism step by step:

No Republicans are collectivists.
All socialists are collectivists.
Therefore, no socialists are Republicans.

In this example, "socialists" is the minor term, "Republicans" is the major term, and "collectivists" is the middle term. See Figure 7 for the three circles required, labeled appropriately.

We fill in this diagram by diagramming the premises of the argument just as we diagrammed the A-, E-, I-, and O-claims earlier. The premises in the above example are diagrammed like this: First: No Republicans are collectivists (Figure 8). Notice that in this figure we have shaded the entire area where the Republican and collectivist circles overlap.

Second: All socialists are collectivists (Figure 9). Because diagramming the premises resulted in the shading of the entire area where the socialist and Republican circles overlap, and because that is exactly what we would do to diagram the syllogism's conclusion, we can conclude that the syllogism is valid. In general, a syllogism is valid if and only if diagramming the premises automatically produces a correct diagram of the conclusion.* (The one exception is discussed later.)

*It might be helpful for some students to produce two diagrams, one for the premises of the argument and one for the conclusion. The two can then be compared: Any area of the conclusion diagram that is shaded must also be shaded in the premises diagram, and any area of the conclusion diagram that has an X must also have one in the premises diagram. If both of these conditions are met, the argument is valid. (Thanks to Professor Ellery Eells of the University of Wisconsin, Madison, for the suggestion.)

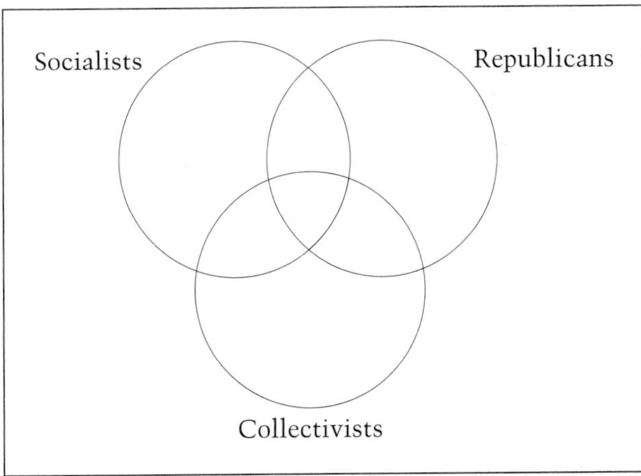

FIGURE 7 Before either premise has been diagrammed.

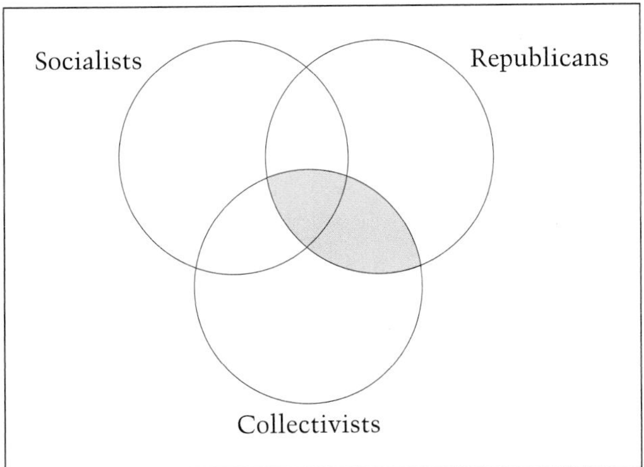

FIGURE 8 One premise diagrammed.

When one of the premises of a syllogism is an I- or O-premise, there can be a problem about where to put the required X. The following example presents such a problem (see Figure 10 for the diagram). Note in the diagram that we have numbered the different areas in order to refer to them easily.

Some S are not M.
All P are M.
Some S are not P.

(The horizontal line separates the premises from the conclusion.)

An X in either area 1 or area 2 of Figure 10 makes the claim "Some S are not M" true, because an inhabitant of either area is an S but not an M. How do we determine which area should get the X? In some cases, the decision can be made for us: *When one premise is an A- or E-premise and the other is an I- or O-premise, diagram the A- or E-premise first.* (Always shade before putting in Xs.) Refer to Figure 11 to see what happens with the current example when we follow this rule.

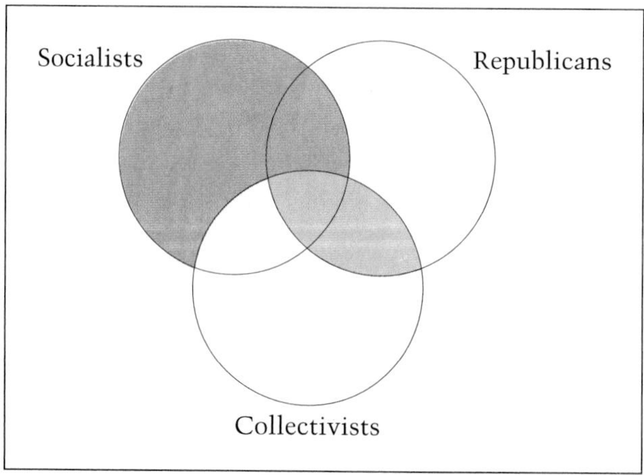

FIGURE 9 Both premises diagrammed.

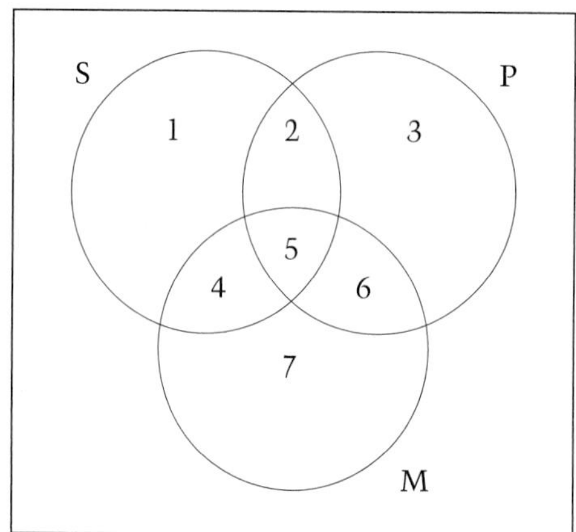

FIGURE 10

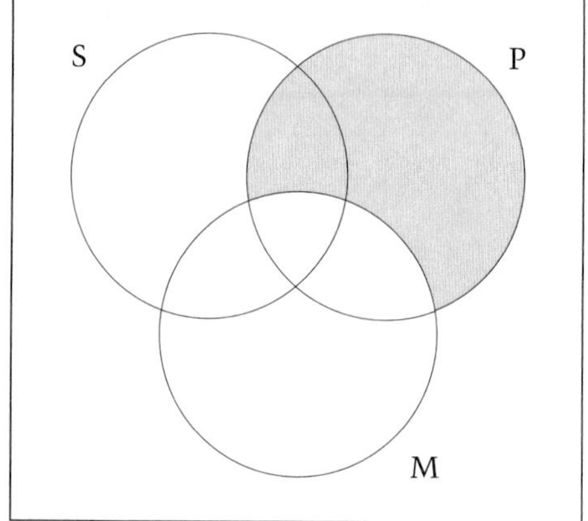

FIGURE 11

Once the A-claim has been diagrammed, there is no longer a choice about where to put the X—it has to go in area 1. Hence, the completed diagram for this argument looks like Figure 12. And from this diagram we can read the conclusion "Some S are not P," which tells us that the argument is valid.

In some syllogisms, the rule just explained does not help. For example,

All P are M.
Some S are M.
Some S are P.

A syllogism like this one still leaves us in doubt about where to put the X, even after we have diagrammed the A-premise (Figure 13): Should the X go in area 4 or 5? When such a question remains unresolved, here is the rule to follow: *An X that can go in either of two areas goes on the line separating the areas,* as in Figure 14.

In essence, an X on a line indicates that the X belongs in one or the other of the two areas, maybe both, but we don't know which. When the time comes

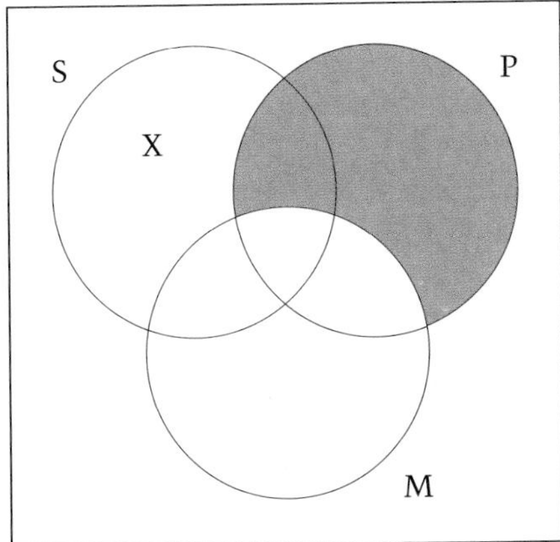

FIGURE 12

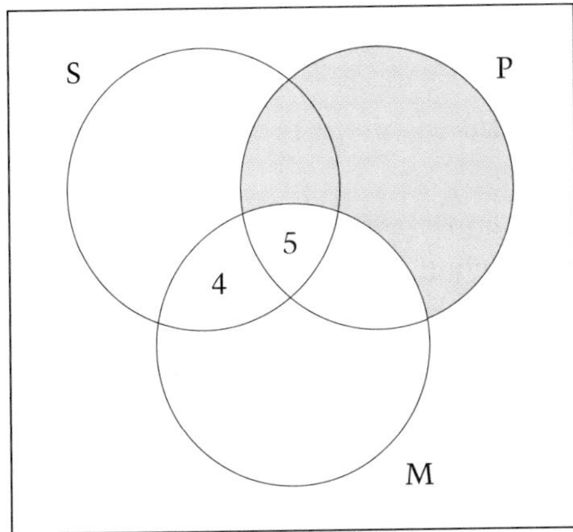

FIGURE 13

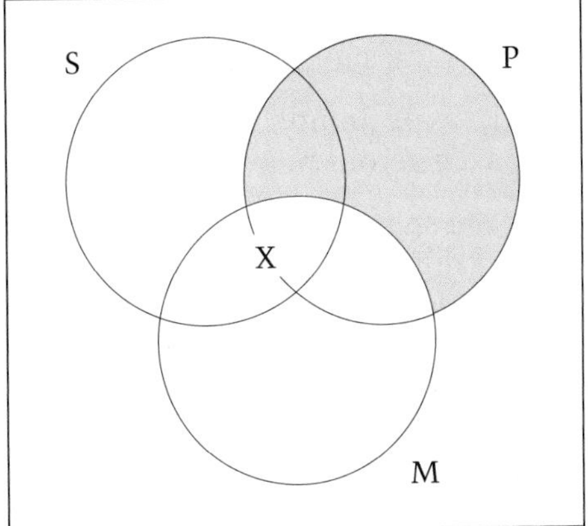

FIGURE 14

to see whether the diagram yields the conclusion, we look to see whether there is an X *entirely* within the appropriate area. In the current example, we would need an X entirely within the area where S and P overlap; because there is no such X, the argument is invalid. An X *partly* within the appropriate area fails to establish the conclusion.

Please notice this about Venn diagrams: When both premises of a syllogism are A- or E-claims and the conclusion is an I- or O-claim, diagramming the premises cannot possibly yield a diagram of the conclusion (because A- and E-claims produce only shading, and I- and O-claims require an X to be read from the diagram). In such a case, remember our assumption that every class we are dealing with has at least one member. This assumption justifies our looking at the diagram and determining whether any circle has all but one of its areas shaded out. *If any circle has only one area remaining unshaded, an X should be put in that area.* This is the case because any member of that class has to be in that remaining area. Sometimes placing the X in this way will enable us to read the conclusion, in which case the argument is valid (on the assumption that the relevant class is not empty); sometimes placing the X will not enable us to read the conclusion, in which case the argument is invalid, with or without any assumptions about the existence of a member within the class.

Categorical Syllogisms with Unstated Premises

Many "real-life" categorical syllogisms have unstated premises. For example, suppose somebody says:

> You shouldn't give chicken bones to dogs. They could choke on them.

The speaker's argument rests on the unstated premise that you shouldn't give dogs things they could choke on. In other words, the argument, when fully spelled out, is this:

> All chicken bones are things dogs could choke on.
> [No things dogs could choke on are things you should give dogs.]
> Therefore, no chicken bones are things you should give dogs.

The unstated premise appears in brackets.

To take another example:

> Driving around in an old car is dumb, since it might break down in a dangerous place.

Here the speaker's argument rests on the unstated premise that it's dumb to risk a dangerous breakdown. In other words, when fully spelled out, the argument is this:

> All examples of driving around in an old car are examples of risking dangerous breakdown.
> [All examples of risking dangerous breakdown are examples of being dumb.]
> Therefore, all examples of driving around in an old car are examples of being dumb.

When you hear (or give) an argument that looks like a categorical syllogism that has only one stated premise, usually a second premise has been assumed and not stated. Ordinarily this unstated premise remains unstated because the speaker thinks it is too obvious to bother stating. The unstated premises in the arguments above are good examples: "You shouldn't give dogs things they could choke on," and "It is dumb to risk a dangerous breakdown."

When you encounter (or give) what looks like a categorical syllogism that is missing a premise, ask: Is there a reasonable assumption I could make that would make this argument valid? We covered this question of unstated premises in more detail in Chapter 7, and you might want to look there for more information on the subject.

At the end of this chapter, we have included a few exercises that involve missing premises.

Real-Life Syllogisms

We'll end this section with a word of advice. Before you use a Venn diagram (or the rules method described below) to determine the validity of real-life arguments, it helps to use a letter to abbreviate each category mentioned in

■ Los Angeles ranks first in the country in the amount of time drivers spend stuck in gridlock. The mayor of L.A., Antonio Villaraigosa, believes making left turn lanes longer will speed up traffic flow. But the only way to speed up traffic flow is to reduce the number of cars on the highways, and making left turn lanes longer won't do that. Therefore, making left turn lanes longer will not speed up traffic flow. *This is a categorical syllogism, though not in standard form.*

the argument. This is mainly just a matter of convenience: It is easier to write down letters than to write down long phrases.

Take the first "real-life" categorical syllogisms given above:

> You shouldn't give chicken bones to dogs because they could choke on them.

The argument spelled out, once again, is this:

> All chicken bones are things dogs could choke on.
> [No things dogs could choke on are things you should give dogs.]
> Therefore, no chicken bones are things you should give dogs.

Abbreviating each of the three categories with a letter, we get

> C = chicken bones; D = things dogs could choke on; and S = things you should give dogs.

Then, the argument is

> All C are D
> [No D are S]
> Therefore, no C are S.

Likewise, the second argument was this:

> Driving around in an old car is dumb, since it might break down in a dangerous place.

When fully spelled out, the argument is

> All examples of driving around in an old car are examples of risking dangerous breakdown.
> [All examples of risking dangerous breakdown are examples of being dumb.]
> Therefore, all examples of driving around in an old car are examples of being dumb.

Abbreviating each of the three categories, we get

> D = examples of driving around in an old car; R = examples of risking dangerous breakdown; S = examples of being dumb.

Then, the argument is

All D are R
[All R are S]
Therefore, all D are S.

A final tip: Take the time to write down your abbreviation key clearly.

Exercise 8-11

Use the diagram method to determine which of the following syllogisms are valid and which are invalid.

▲ **1.** All paperbacks are books that use glue in their spines.
No books that use glue in their spines are books that are sewn in signatures.
No books that are sewn in signatures are paperbacks.

2. All sound arguments are valid arguments.
Some valid arguments are not interesting arguments.
Some sound arguments are not interesting arguments.

3. All topologists are mathematicians.
Some topologists are not statisticians.
Some mathematicians are not statisticians.

▲ **4.** Every time Louis is tired he's edgy. He's edgy today, so he must be tired today.

5. Every voter is a citizen, but some citizens are not residents. Therefore, some voters are not residents.

6. All the dominant seventh chords are in the mixolydian mode, and no mixolydian chords use the major scale. So no chords that use the major scale are dominant sevenths.

▲ **7.** All halyards are lines that attach to sails. Painters do not attach to sails, so they must not be halyards.

8. Only systems with removable disks can give you unlimited storage capacity of a practical sort. Standard hard drives never have removable disks, so they can't give you practical, unlimited storage capacity.

9. All citizens are residents. So, since no noncitizens are voters, all voters must be residents.

▲ **10.** No citizens are nonresidents, and all voters are citizens. So all residents must be nonvoters.

Exercise 8-12

Put the following arguments in standard form (you may have to use the obversion, conversion, or contraposition operations to accomplish this); then determine whether the arguments are valid by means of diagrams.

▲ **1.** No blank disks contain any data, although some blank disks are formatted. Therefore, some formatted disks do not contain any data.

Real Life

Brodie!

"Otterhounds are friendly, are fond of other dogs, bark a lot, and like to chase cats."
"That describes Brodie exactly! He must be an otterhound."

Not so fast, dog lover. The argument seems to be

All otterhounds are friendly, fond of other dogs, and like to chase cats. Brodie is friendly, fond of other dogs, and likes to chase cats.
Therefore, Brodie is an otterhound.

This argument has the form

All As are X
All Bs are X.
Therefore, all Bs are As.

If you use techniques described in this chapter, you will see that arguments with this form are invalid. If you just stumbled on this box or your instructor referred you to it, common sense should tell you the same. It's like arguing "All graduates of Harvard are warm-blooded, and Brodie is warm-blooded;" therefore, Brodie is a graduate of Harvard."

You'll find the dog in the cartoon on page 268 making the same mistake.

2. All ears of corn with white tassels are unripe, but some ears are ripe even though their kernels are not full-sized. Therefore, some ears with full-sized kernels are not ears with white tassels.
3. Prescription drugs should never be taken without a doctor's order. So no over-the-counter drugs are prescription drugs, because all over-the-counter drugs can be taken without a doctor's order.
4. All tobacco products are damaging to people's health, but some of them are addictive substances. Some addictive substances, therefore, are damaging to people's health.
5. A few CD players use 24× sampling, so some of them must cost at least fifty dollars, because you can't buy any machine with 24× sampling for less than fifty dollars.
6. Everything that Pete won at the carnival must be junk. I know that Pete won everything that Bob won, and all the stuff that Bob won is junk.
7. Only people who hold stock in the company may vote, so Mr. Hansen must not hold any stock in the company, because I know he was not allowed to vote.

In Depth

Additional Common Invalid Argument Forms

Other common invalid argument forms (see the box about Brodie) include these:

All As are X.
No As are Y.
Therefore, no Xs are Ys.

All Xs are Ys; therefore, all Ys are Xs.

Some Xs are not Ys. Therefore, some Ys are not Xs.

Some Xs are Ys. Therefore, some Xs are not Ys.

Some Xs are not Ys. Therefore, some Xs are Ys.

So you don't get lost in all the Xs and Ys, and to help you remember them, we recommend you make up examples of each of these forms and share them with a classmate.

8. No off-road vehicles are allowed in the unimproved portion of the park, but some off-road vehicles are not four-wheel-drive. So some four-wheel-drive vehicles are allowed in the unimproved part of the park.
9. Some of the people affected by the new drainage tax are residents of the county, and many residents of the county are already paying the sewer tax. So it must be that some people paying the sewer tax are affected by the new drainage tax, too.
10. ▲ No argument with false premises is sound, but some of them are valid. So some unsound arguments must be valid.

The Rules Method of Testing for Validity

The diagram method of testing syllogisms for validity is intuitive, but there is a faster method that makes use of three simple rules. These rules are based on two ideas, the first of which has been mentioned already: affirmative and negative categorical claims. (Remember, the A- and I-claims are affirmative; the E- and O-claims are negative.) The other idea is that of *distribution.* Terms that occur in categorical claims are either distributed or undistributed: Either the claim says something about every member of the class the term names, or it does not.* Three of the standard-form claims distribute one or more of their terms. In Figure 15, the circled letters stand for distributed terms, and the un-

*The above is a rough-and-ready definition of distribution. If you'd like a more technical version, here's one: A term is *distributed* in a claim if, and only if, on the assumption that the claim is true, the class named by the term can be replaced by *any* subset of that class without producing a false claim. Example: In the claim "All senators are politicians," the term "senators" is distributed because, assuming the claim is true, you can substitute *any* subset of senators (Democratic ones, Republican ones, tall ones, short ones . . .) and the result must also be true. "Politicians" is not distributed: The original claim could be true while "All senators are honest politicians" was false.

A-claim:	All Ⓢ are P.
E-claim:	No Ⓢ are Ⓟ.
I-claim:	Some S are P.
O-claim:	Some S are not Ⓟ.

FIGURE 15 Distributed terms.

circled ones stand for undistributed terms. As the figure shows, the A-claim distributes its subject term, the O-claim distributes its predicate term, the E-claim distributes both, and the I-claim distributes neither.

We can now state the three *rules of the syllogism.* A syllogism is valid if and only if all of these conditions are met:

1. **The number of negative claims in the premises must be the same as the number of negative claims in the conclusion.** (Because the conclusion is always one claim, this implies that no valid syllogism has two negative premises.)
2. **At least one premise must distribute the middle term.**
3. **Any term that is distributed in the conclusion of the syllogism must be distributed in its premises.**

These rules are easy to remember, and with a bit of practice, you can use them to determine quickly whether a syllogism is valid.

Which of the rules is broken in this example?

All pianists are keyboard players.
Some keyboard players are not percussionists.
Some pianists are not percussionists.

The term "keyboard players" is the middle term, and it is undistributed in both premises. The first premise, an A-claim, does not distribute its predicate term; the second premise, an O-claim, does not distribute its subject term. So this syllogism breaks rule 2.

Another example:

No dogs up for adoption at the animal shelter are pedigreed dogs.
Some pedigreed dogs are expensive dogs.
Some dogs up for adoption at the animal shelter are expensive dogs.

This syllogism breaks rule 1 because it has a negative premise but no negative conclusion.

A last example:

No mercantilists are large landowners.
All mercantilists are creditors.
No creditors are large landowners.

The minor term, "creditors," is distributed in the conclusion (because it's the subject term of an E-claim) but not in the premises (where it's the predicate term of an A-claim). So this syllogism breaks rule 3.

Real Life

Wolfowitz and the World Bank

When President Bush nominated Paul Wolfowitz to run the World Bank, he made the following remark: "I'd say he's a man with good experiences. He's helped manage a large organization. The World Bank's a large organization." His unstated conclusion, more or less, was: Wolfowitz would be good at helping manage the World Bank. Let's lay the argument out like this:

Wolfowitz has shown himself able to help manage a large organization.

The World Bank is a large organization.

Wolfowitz has shown himself able to manage the World Bank.

Can you put this argument into standard syllogistic form? Does it pass the test for validity?

Recap

The following list of topics covers the basics of categorical logic as discussed in this chapter:

- The four types of categorical claims include A, E, I, and O.
- There are Venn diagrams for the four types of claims.
- Ordinary English claims can be translated into standard-form categorical claims. Some rules of thumb for such translations are as follows:
  —"only" introduces predicate term of A-claim,
  —"the only" introduces subject term of A-claim,
  —"whenever" means times or occasions,
  —"wherever" means places or locations,
  —claims about individuals are treated as A- or E-claims.
- Square of opposition displays contradiction, contrariety, and subcontrariety among corresponding standard-form claims.
- Conversion, obversion, and contraposition are three operations that can be performed on standard-form claims; some are equivalent to the original and some are not.
- Categorical syllogisms are standardized deductive arguments; we can test them for validity by the Venn diagram method or by the rules method—the latter relies on the notions of distribution and the affirmative and negative qualities of the claims involved.

Additional Exercises

Exercise 8-13

In each of the following items, identify whether A, B, or C is the middle term.

▲ 1. All A are B.
All A are C.
———
All B are C.

2. All B are C.
No C are D.
———
No B are D.

3. Some C are not D.
All C are A.
———
Some D are not A.

▲ 4. Some A are not B.
Some B are C.
———
Some C are not A.

5. No C are A.
Some B are A.
———
Some C are not B.

Exercise 8-14

Which terms are distributed in each of the following?

▲ 1. All A are B.
   a. A only
   b. B only
   c. Both A and B
   d. Neither A nor B

2. No A are B.
   a. A only
   b. B only
   c. Both A and B
   d. Neither A nor B

3. Some A are B.
   a. A only
   b. B only
   c. Both A and B
   d. Neither A nor B

▲ 4. Some A are not B.
   a. A only
   b. B only
   c. Both A and B
   d. Neither A nor B

Exercise 8-15

How many negative claims appear in the premises of each of the following arguments? (In other words, how many of the premises are negative?) Your options are 0, 1, or 2.

▲ **1.** All A are B.
All A are C.
Therefore, all B are C.

2. All B are C.
No C are D.
Therefore, no B are D.

3. Some C are not D.
All C are A.
Therefore, some D are not A.

▲ **4.** Some A are not B.
Some B are C.
Therefore, some C are not A.

5. No A are B.
Some B are not C.
Some A are C.

Exercise 8-16

Which rules (if any) are broken in each of the following? Select from these options:

a. Breaks rule 1 only
b. Breaks rule 2 only
c. Breaks rule 3 only
d. Breaks more than one rule
e. Breaks no rule

▲ **1.** All A are B.
All A are C.
Therefore, all B are C.

2. All B are C.
No C are D.
Therefore, no B are D.

3. Some C are not D.
All C are A.
Therefore, some D are A.

▲ **4.** Some A are not B.
Some B are C.
Therefore, some C are not A.

5. Some A are C.
Some C are B.
Therefore, some A are B.

6. Some carbostats are framistans.
No framistans are arbuckles.
Some arbuckles are not carbostats.

▲ 7. All framistans are veeblefetzers.
Some veeblefetzers are carbostats.
Some framistans are carbostats.

8. No arbuckles are framistans.
All arbuckles are carbostats.
No framistans are carbostats.

9. All members of the class are registered students.
Some registered students are not people taking fifteen units.
Some members of the class are not people taking fifteen units.

▲ 10. All qualified mechanics are people familiar with hydraulics.
No unschooled people are people familiar with hydraulics.
No qualified mechanics are unschooled people.

Exercise 8-17

Which rules (if any) are broken in each of the following?

Note: If an argument breaks a rule, *which* rule is broken depends on how you translate the claims in the argument. For example, the claim "Dogs shouldn't be given chicken bones" could be translated as an *E-claim:* "No dogs are animals that should be given chicken bones." But it also could be translated as an *A-claim:* "All dogs are animals that shouldn't be given chicken bones." If the original claim appeared in an invalid argument, one rule would be broken if you translated it as the E-claim. A different rule would be broken if you translated it as the A-claim.

▲ 1. All tigers are ferocious creatures. Some ferocious creatures are zoo animals. Therefore, some zoo animals are tigers. (For this and the following items, it will help if you abbreviate each category with a letter. For example, let T = tigers, F = ferocious creatures, and Z = zoo animals.)

2. Some pedestrians are not jaywalkers. Therefore, some jaywalkers are not gardeners, since no gardeners are pedestrians.

3. Because all shrubs are ornamental plants, it follows that no ornamental plants are cacti, since no cacti qualify as shrubs.

▲ 4. Weightlifters aren't really athletes. Athletics requires the use of motor skills; and few, if any, weightlifters use motor skills.

5. The trick to finding syllogisms is to think categorically, as well as to focus on the key argument in a passage. For example, some passages contain a good bit of rhetoric, and some passages that do this make it hard to spot syllogisms, with the result that it is hard to spot syllogisms in some passages.

6. Every broadcast network has seen its share of the television audience decline during the past six years. But not every media outlet that has a decline in television audience share has lost money. So not every broadcast network has lost money.

▲ 7. Many students lift papers off the Internet, and this fact is discouraging to teachers. However, it must be noted that students who do this are only cheating themselves, and anyone who cheats himself or herself loses in the long run. Therefore, lifting papers off the Internet is a losing proposition in the long run.

8. When he was Speaker of the House, Mr. Newt Gingrich could be counted on to advance Republican causes. At the time, nobody who would do that could be accused of being soft on crime, which explains why at the time Gingrich could hardly be accused of being soft on crime.

9. It would be in everyone's interest to amend the Constitution to permit school prayer. And it is obviously in everyone's interest to promote religious freedom. It should be no surprise, then, that amending the Constitution to permit school prayer will promote religious freedom.

▲ 10. If you want to stay out all night dancing, it is fine with me. Just don't cry about it if you don't get good grades. Dancing isn't a total waste of time, but dancing the whole night certainly is. There are only so many hours in a day, and wasting time is bound to affect your grades negatively. So, fine, stay out dancing all night. It's your choice. But you have to expect your grades to suffer.

Exercise 8-18

▲ Refer back to Exercises 8-11 and 8-12 and check the arguments for validity using the rules. We recommend abbreviating each category with a letter.

Once again, remember: If an argument breaks a rule, *which* rule is broken depends on how you translate the claims in the argument. For example, the claim "Dogs shouldn't be given chicken bones" could be translated as an E-claim: "No dogs are animals that should be given chicken bones." But it also could be translated as an A-claim (the obverse of the other version): "All dogs are animals that shouldn't be given chicken bones." If the original claim appeared in an invalid argument, one rule would be broken if you translated it as an E-claim. A different rule would be broken if you translated it as an A-claim.

Answers to 2, 5, 7, and 8 are given in the answer section.

Exercise 8-19

For each of the following items: Abbreviate each category with a letter, then translate the argument into standard form using the abbreviations. Then test the argument for validity using either the diagram method or the rules method.

Note: For many of these items it can be difficult to translate the arguments into standard form.

▲ 1. Some athletes are not baseball players, and some baseball players are not basketball players. Therefore, some athletes are not basketball players.

2. Rats are disease-carrying pests, and as such should be eradicated, because such pests should all be eradicated.

▲ 3. This is not the best of all possible worlds, because the best of all possible worlds would not contain mosquitoes, and *this* world contains plenty of mosquitoes!

4. From time to time, the police have to break up parties here on campus, since some campus parties get out of control, and when a party gets out of control, well, you know what the police have to do.

5. I know that all fundamentalist Christians are evangelicals, and I'm pretty sure that all revivalists are also evangelicals. So, if I'm right, at least some fundamentalist Christians must be revivalists.

▲ 6. "Their new lawn furniture certainly looks cheap to me," she said. "It's made of plastic, and plastic furniture just looks cheap."

7. None of our intramural sports are sports played in the Olympics, and some of the intercollegiate sports are not Olympic sports either. So some of the intercollegiate sports are also intramural sports.

8. The moas were all Dinornithidae, and no moas exist anymore. So there aren't any more Dinornithidae.

▲ 9. Everybody on the district tax roll is a citizen, and all eligible voters are also citizens. So everybody on the district tax roll is an eligible voter.

10. Any piece of software that is in the public domain may be copied without permission or fee. But that cannot be done in the case of software under copyright. So software under copyright must not be in the public domain.

11. None of the countries that have been living under dictatorships for these past few decades are familiar with the social requirements of a strong democracy—things like widespread education and a willingness to abide by majority vote. Consequently, none of these countries will make a successful quick transition to democracy, since countries where the above-mentioned requirements are unfamiliar simply can't make such a transition.

▲ 12. Trust Senator Cobweb to vote with the governor on the new tax legislation. Cobweb is a liberal, and liberals just cannot pass up an opportunity to raise taxes.

13. Investor-held utilities should not be allowed to raise rates, since all public utilities should be allowed to raise rates, and public utilities are not investor-held.

14. Masterpieces are no longer recorded on cassettes. This is because masterpieces belong to the classical repertoire, and classical music is no longer recorded on cassettes.

15. It isn't important to learn chemistry, since it isn't very useful, and there isn't much point in learning something that isn't useful.

16. Stockholders' information about a company's worth must come from the managers of that company, but in a buy-out, the managers of the company are the very ones who are trying to buy the stock from the stockholders. So, ironically, in a buy-out situation, stockholders must get their information about how much a company is worth from the very people who are trying to buy their stock.

▲ 17. All of the networks devoted considerable attention to reporting poll results during the last election, but many of those poll results were not especially newsworthy. So the networks have to admit that some unnewsworthy items received quite a bit of their attention.

▲ 18. If a person doesn't understand that the earth goes around the sun once a year, then that person can't understand what causes winter and summer. Strange as it may seem, then, there are many American adults who don't know what causes winter and summer, because a survey a year or so ago showed that many such adults don't know that the earth goes around the sun.

19. Congress seems ready to impose trade sanctions on China, and perhaps it should. China's leaders cruelly cling to power. They flout American interests in their actions in Tibet, in their human-rights violations, in their weapons sales, and in their questionable trade practices. Any country with a record like this deserves sanctions.

▲ **20.** Since 1973, when the U.S. Supreme Court decided *Miller v. California,* no work can be banned as obscene unless it contains sexual depictions that are "patently offensive" to "contemporary community standards" and unless the work as a whole possesses no "serious literary, artistic, political or scientific value." As loose as this standard may seem when compared with earlier tests of obscenity, the pornographic novels of "Madame Toulouse" (a pseudonym, of course) can still be banned. They would offend the contemporary standards of *any* community, and to claim any literary, artistic, political, or scientific value for them would be a real joke.

21. All creationists are religious, and all fundamentalists are religious, so all creationists are fundamentalists.

22. Every sportscaster is an athlete, and no athlete is a college professor. Therefore, no sportscasters are college professors.

23. Anyone who voted for the Democrats favors expansion of medical services for the needy. So, the people who voted for the Democrats all favor higher taxes, since anyone who wants to expand medical services must favor higher taxes.

24. All cave dwellers lived before the invention of the radio, and no one alive today is a cave dweller. Thus, no person who lived before the invention of the radio is alive today.

25. Conservationists don't vote for Republicans, and all environmentalists are conservationists. Thus, environmentalists don't vote for Republicans.

26. Since all philosophers are skeptics, it follows that no theologian is a skeptic, since no philosophers are theologians.

27. Each philosopher is a skeptic, and no philosopher is a theologian. Therefore, no skeptic is a theologian.

28. Peddlers are salesmen, and confidence men are, too. So, peddlers are confidence men.

29. Should drug addicts be treated as criminals? Well, addicts are all excluded from the class of decent people, yet all criminals belong to that class. Accordingly, no addicts are criminals.

30. Critical thinkers recognize invalid syllogisms: therefore, critical thinkers are logicians, since logicians can spot invalid syllogisms, too.

31. The Mohawk Indians are Algonquin, and so are the Cheyenne. So, the Mohawks are really just Cheyenne.

32. Idiots would support the measure, but no one else would. Whatever else you may think of the school board, you can't say they are idiots. [Therefore . . .]

Exercise 8-20

This exercise is a little different, and you may need to work one or more such items in class in order to get the hang of them. Your job is to try to prove each of the following claims about syllogisms true or false. You may need to produce a general argument—that is, to show that *every* syllogism that does *this* must also do *that*—or you may need to produce a counterexample, that is, an example that proves the claim in question false. The definition of categorical syllogism and the rules of the syllogism are of crucial importance in working these examples.

▲ **1.** Every valid syllogism must have at least one A- or E-claim for a premise.

2. Every valid syllogism with an E-claim for a premise must have an E-claim for a conclusion.

3. Every valid syllogism with an E-claim for a conclusion must have an E-claim for a premise.

▲ **4.** It's possible for a syllogism to break two of the rules of the syllogism.

5. No syllogism can break all three of the rules of the syllogism.

Exercise 8-21

The following is an anonymous statement of opinion that appeared in a newspaper call-in column.

> This is in response to the person who called in that we should provide a shelter for the homeless, because I think that is wrong. These people make the downtown area unsafe because they have nothing to lose by robbing, mugging, etc. The young boy killed by the horseshoe pits was attacked by some of these bums, assuming that witnesses really saw people who were homeless, which no doubt they did, since the so-called homeless all wear that old worn-out hippie gear, just like the people they saw. They also lower property values. And don't tell me they are down and out because they can't find work. The work is there if they look for it. They choose for themselves how to live, since if they didn't choose, who did?

A lot of things might be said in criticism of this tirade, but what we want you to notice is the breakdown of logic. The piece contains, in fact, a gross logic error, which we ask you to make the focus of a critical essay. Your audience is the other members of your class; that is, you are writing for an audience of critical thinkers.

Exercise 8-22

> Pornography violates women's rights. It carries a demeaning message about a woman's worth and purpose and promotes genuine violence. This is indeed a violation of women's civil rights and justifies the Minneapolis City Council in attempting to ban pornography.

This letter to the editor is, in effect, two syllogisms. The conclusion of the first is that pornography violates women's rights. This conclusion also functions as a premise in the second syllogism, which has as its own conclusion the claim that the Minneapolis City Council is justified in attempting to ban pornography. Both syllogisms have unstated premises. Translate the entire argument into standard-form syllogisms, supplying missing premises, and determine whether the reasoning is valid.

Exercise 8-23

Each of the following arguments contains an unstated premise, which, together with the stated premise, makes the argument in question valid. Your job is to identify this unstated premise, abbreviate each category with a letter, and put the argument in standard form.

▲ **1.** Ladybugs eat aphids; therefore, they are good to have in your garden.

2. CEOs have lots of responsibility; therefore, they should be paid a lot.

3. Anyone who understands how a computer program works knows how important logic is. Therefore, anyone who understands how a computer program works understands how important unambiguous writing is.

▲ **4.** Self-tapping screws are a boon to the construction industry. They make it possible to screw things together without drilling pilot holes.

5. No baseball player smokes anymore. Baseball players all know that smoking hampers athletic performance.

6. You really ought to give up jogging. It is harmful to your health.

7. Camping isn't much fun. It requires sleeping on the hard ground and getting lots of bug bites.

8. Having too much coffee makes you sleep poorly. That's why you shouldn't do it.

9. Do you have writer's block? No problem. You can always hire a secretary.

10. "You think those marks were left by a—snake? That's totally crazy. Snakes don't leave footprints."

Writing Exercises

1. Should dogs be used in medical experiments, given that they seem to have the capacity to experience fear and feel pain? Write a short paper defending a negative answer to this question, taking about five minutes to do so. When you have finished, exchange your argument with a friend and rewrite each other's argument as a categorical syllogism or a combination of categorical syllogisms. Remember that people often leave premises unstated.
2. Follow the instructions for Exercise 1, but this time defend the position that it is not wrong to use dogs in medical experiments.
3. Turn to Selection 7 in Appendix 1 and follow the second set of instructions.
4. Turn to Selection 15A, 15B, 16A, or 16B and follow the second alternative assignment.

Chapter 9

Deductive Arguments II: Truth-Functional Logic

No logic, no computers. No logic, no critical thinking.

The earliest development of truth-functional logic took place among the Stoics, who flourished from about the third century B.C.E. until the second century C.E. But it was in the late nineteenth and twentieth centuries that the real power of **truth-functional logic** (known also as *propositional* or *sentential logic*) became apparent.

The "logic of sentences" is one of the bases on which modern symbolic logic rests, and as such it is important in such intellectual areas as set theory and the foundations of mathematics. It is also the model for electrical circuits of the sort that are the basis of digital computing. But truth-functional logic is also a useful tool in the analysis of arguments.

The study of truth-functional logic can benefit you in several ways. For one thing, you'll learn something about the structure of language that you wouldn't learn any other way. For another, you'll get a sense of what it's like to work with a very precise, nonmathematical system of symbols that is nevertheless very accessible to nearly any student willing to invest a modest amount of effort. The model of precision and clarity that such systems provide can serve you well when you communicate with others in ordinary language.

If you're not comfortable working with symbols, the upcoming sections on truth-functional arguments and deductions might look intimidating. But they are not as forbidding as they may appear. We presume that the whole matter of a symbolic system is unfamiliar to you, so we'll start from absolute scratch. Keep in mind, though, that everything builds on what goes before. It's important to master each concept as it's explained and not fall behind. Catching up can be very difficult. If you find yourself having difficulty with a section or a concept, put in some extra effort to master it before moving ahead. It will be worth it in the end.

TRUTH TABLES AND THE TRUTH-FUNCTIONAL SYMBOLS

Our "logical vocabulary" will consist of claim variables and truth-functional symbols. Before we consider the real heart of the subject, truth tables and the symbols that represent them, let's first clarify the use of letters of the alphabet to symbolize terms and claims.

Claim Variables

In Chapter 8, we used uppercase letters to stand for terms in categorical claims. Here we use uppercase letters to stand for claims. Our main interest is now in the way that words such as "not," "and," "or," and so on affect claims and link them together to produce compound claims out of simpler ones. So don't confuse the Ps and Qs, called **claim variables,** that appear in this chapter with the variables used for terms in Chapter 8.*

Truth Tables

Let's now consider truth tables and symbols. In truth-functional logic, any given claim, P, is either true or false. The following little table, called a **truth table,** displays both possible truth values for P:

P
T
F

Whichever truth value the claim P might have, its negation or contradictory, which we'll symbolize ~P, will have the other. Here, then, is the truth table for ***negation:***

P	~P
T	F
F	T

The left-hand column of this table sets out both possible truth values for P, and the right-hand column sets out the truth values for ~P based on P's values. This is a way of defining the negation sign, ~, in front of the P. The symbol means "change the truth value from T to F or from F to T, depending

*It is customary to use one kind of symbol, usually lowercase letters or Greek letters, as *claim variables* and plain or italicized uppercase letters for *specific claims.* Although this use has some technical advantages and makes possible a certain theoretical neatness, students often find it confusing. Therefore, we'll use uppercase letters for both variables and specific claims and simply make it clear which way we're using the letters.

■ The word "and," when used in questions, can produce some interesting and amusing results. In this case, Brutus means to ask "How many of them are boys and how many of them are girls?" But Jack thinks he asks "How many of them are girls and boys?" There's even a third version: "How many of them are *both* girls and boys?" Presumably none.

on P's values." Because it's handy to have a name for negations that you can say aloud, we read ~P as "not-P." So, if P were "Parker is at home," then ~P would be "It is not the case that Parker is at home," or, more simply, "Parker is not at home." In a moment we'll define other symbols by means of truth tables, so make sure you understand how this one works.

Because any given claim is either true or false, two claims, P and Q, must both be true, both be false, or have opposite truth values, for a total of four possible combinations. Here are the possibilities in truth-table form:

P	Q
T	T
T	F
F	T
F	F

A **conjunction** is a compound claim made from two simpler claims, called *conjuncts. A conjunction is true if and only if both of the simpler claims that make it up (its conjuncts) are true.* An example of a conjunction is the claim "Parker is at home and Moore is at work." We'll express the conjunction of P and Q by connecting them with an ampersand (&). The truth table for conjunctions looks like this:

P	Q	P & Q
T	T	T
T	F	F
F	T	F
F	F	F

P & Q is true in the first row only, where both P and Q are true. Notice that the "truth conditions" in this row match those required in the italicized statement above.

Here's another way to remember how conjunctions work: If either part of a conjunction is false, the conjunction itself is false. Notice finally that although the word "and" is the closest representative in English to our ampersand symbol, there are other words that are correctly symbolized by the ampersand: "but" and "while," for instance, as well as phrases such as "even though." So, if we let P stand for "Parsons is in class" and Q stand for "Quincy is absent," then we should represent "Parsons is in class even though Quincy is absent" by P & Q. The reason is that the compound claim is true only in one case: where both parts are true. And that's all it takes to require an ampersand to represent the connecting word or phrase.

A **disjunction** is another compound claim made up of two simpler claims, called *disjuncts. A disjunction is false if and only if both of its disjuncts are false.* Here's an example of a disjunction: "Either Parker is at home or Moore is at work." We'll use the symbol ∨ ("wedge") to represent disjunction when we symbolize claims—as indicated in the example, the closest word in English to this symbol is "or." The truth table for disjunctions is this:

P	Q	P ∨ Q
T	T	T
T	F	T
F	T	T
F	F	F

Notice here that a disjunction is false only in the last row, where both of its disjuncts are false. In all other cases a disjunction is true.

The third kind of compound claim made from two simpler claims is the **conditional claim.** In ordinary English, the most common way of stating conditionals is by means of the words "if . . . then . . . ," as in the example "If Parker is at home, then Moore is at work."

We'll use an arrow to symbolize conditionals: P→Q. The first claim in a conditional, the P in the symbolization, is the **antecedent,** and the second—Q in this case—is the **consequent.** *A conditional claim is false if and only if its antecedent is true and its consequent is false.* The truth table for conditionals looks like this:

P	Q	P → Q
T	T	T
T	F	F
F	T	T
F	F	T

Only in the second row, where the antecedent P is true and the consequent Q is false, does the conditional turn out to be false. In all other cases it is true.

Of the four types of truth-functional claims—negation, conjunction, disjunction, and conditional—the conditional typically gives students the most trouble. Let's have a closer look at it by considering an example that may shed light on how and why conditionals work. Let's say that Moore promises you that, if his paycheck arrives this morning, he'll buy you lunch. So now we can consider the conditional,

> If Moore's paycheck arrives this morning, then Moore will buy you lunch.

Negation (~)

Truth table:

P	~P
T	F
F	T

Closest English counterparts: "not," or "it is not the case that"

Conjunction (&)

Truth table:

P	Q	(P & Q)
T	T	T
T	F	F
F	T	F
F	F	F

Closest English counterparts: "and," "but," "while"

Disjunction (∨)

Truth table:

P	Q	(P ∨ Q)
T	T	T
T	F	T
F	T	T
F	F	F

Closest English counterparts: "or," "unless"

Conditional (→)

Truth table:

P	Q	(P →Q)
T	T	T
T	F	F
F	T	T
F	F	T

Closest English counterparts: "if . . . . then," "provided that"

FIGURE 1 The Four Basic Truth-Functional Symbols

We can symbolize this using P (for the claim about the paycheck) and L (for the claim about lunch): P → L. Now let's try to see why the truth table above fits this claim.

The easiest way to see this is by asking yourself what it would take for Moore to break his promise. A moment's thought should make this clear: Two things have to happen before we can say that Moore has fibbed to you. The first is that his paycheck must arrive this morning. (After all, he didn't say what he was going to do if his paycheck *didn't* arrive, did he?) Then, it being true that his paycheck arrives, he must then *not* buy you lunch. Together, these two items make it clear that Moore's original promise was false. Notice: Under no other circumstances would we say that Moore broke his promise. And *that* is why the truth table has a conditional false in one and only one case, namely, where the antecedent is true and the consequent is false. Basic information about all four symbols is summarized in Figure 1.

Our truth-functional symbols can work in combination. Consider, for example, the claim "If Paula doesn't go to work, then Quincy will have to work a double shift." We'll represent the two simple claims in the obvious way, as follows:

P = Paula goes to work.
Q = Quincy has to work a double shift.

And we can symbolize the entire claim like this:

~P → Q

Here is a truth table for this symbolization:

P	Q	~P	~P → Q
T	T	F	T
T	F	F	T
F	T	T	T
F	F	T	F

Notice that the symbolized claim ~P→Q is false in the *last* row of this table. That's because here and only here the antecedent, ~P, is true and its consequent, Q, is false. Notice that we work from the simplest parts to the most complex: The truth value of P in a given row determines the truth value of ~P, and that truth value in turn, along with the one for Q, determines the truth value of ~P→Q.

Consider another combination: "If Paula goes to work, then Quincy and Rogers will get a day off." This claim is symbolized this way:

P → (Q & R)

This symbolization requires parentheses in order to prevent confusion with (P→Q) & R, which symbolizes a different claim and has a different truth table. Our claim is a conditional with a conjunction for a consequent, whereas (P→Q) & R is a conjunction with a conditional as one of the conjuncts. The parentheses are what make this clear.

You need to know a few principles to produce the truth table for the symbolized claim P→(Q & R). First you have to know how to set up all the possible combinations of true and false for the three simple claims P, Q, and R. In claims with only one letter, there were two possibilities, T and F. In claims with two letters, there were four possibilities. *Every time we add another letter, the number of possible combinations of T and F doubles, and so, therefore, does the number of rows in our truth table.* The formula for determining the number of rows in a truth table for a compound claim is $r = 2^n$, where r is the number of rows in the table and n is the number of letters in the symbolization. Because the claim we are interested in has three letters, our truth table will have eight rows, one for each possible combination of T and F for P, Q, and R. Here's how we do it:

P	Q	R
T	T	T
T	T	F
T	F	T
T	F	F
F	T	T
F	T	F
F	F	T
F	F	F

The systematic way to construct such a table is to alternate Ts and Fs in the right-hand column, then alternate *pairs* of Ts and *pairs* of Fs in the next column to the left, then sets of *four* Ts and sets of *four* Fs in the next, and so forth. The leftmost column will always wind up being half Ts and half Fs.

The second thing we have to know is that the truth value of a compound claim in any particular case (i.e., any row of its truth table) depends entirely

In Depth

Test Yourself

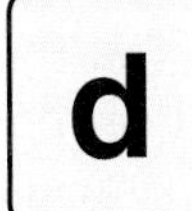

These cards are from a deck that has letters on one side and numbers on the other. They are supposed to obey the following rule: "If there is a vowel on one side, then the card has an even number on the other side."

Question: To see that the rule has been kept, how many cards must be turned over and checked?

P.S. Most university students flunk this simple test of critical thinking.

upon the truth values of its parts; and if these parts are themselves compound, their truth values depend upon those of their parts; and so on, until we get down to letters standing alone. The columns under the letters, which you have just learned to construct, will then tell us what we need to know. Let's build a truth table for P→(Q & R) and see how this works.

P	Q	R	Q & R	P→(Q & R)
T	T	T	T	T
T	T	F	F	F
T	F	T	F	F
T	F	F	F	F
F	T	T	T	T
F	T	F	F	T
F	F	T	F	T
F	F	F	F	T

The three columns at the left, under P, Q, and R, are our *reference columns,* set up just as we discussed above. They determine what goes on in the rest of the table. From the second and third columns, under the Q and the R, we can fill in the column under Q & R. Notice that this column contains a T only in the first and fifth rows, where both Q and R are true. Next, from the column under the P and the one under Q & R, we can fill in the last column, which is the one for the entire symbolized claim. It contains Fs in only rows two, three, and four, which are the only ones where its antecedent is true and its consequent is false.

What our table gives us is a *truth-functional analysis* of our original claim. Such an analysis displays the compound claim's truth value, based on the truth values of its simpler parts.

If you've followed everything so far without problems, that's great. If you've not yet understood the basic truth table idea, however, as well as the truth tables for the truth-functional symbols, then by all means stop now and go back over this material. You should also understand how to build a truth table for symbolizations consisting of three or more letters. What comes later builds on this foundation, and like any construction project, without a strong foundation the whole thing collapses.

A final note before we move on: Two claims are **truth-functionally equivalent** if they have exactly the same truth table—that is, if the Ts and Fs in the column under one claim are in the same arrangement as those in the column under the other. Generally speaking, when two claims are equivalent, one can be used in place of another—truth-functionally, they each imply the other.*

TRUTH-FUNCTIONAL LOGIC AND ELECTRICAL CIRCUITS

(This section can be skipped without loss of continuity)

We mentioned at the beginning of the chapter that truth-functional logic is the basis of digital computing. This is because, translated into hardware systems, "true" and "false" become "on" and "off." Although there's a lot more to it than this, we can illustrate in a crude way a little of how this works.

Let's construct a simple electrical circuit from an electrical source to a ground and put a light bulb in it somewhere, like this:

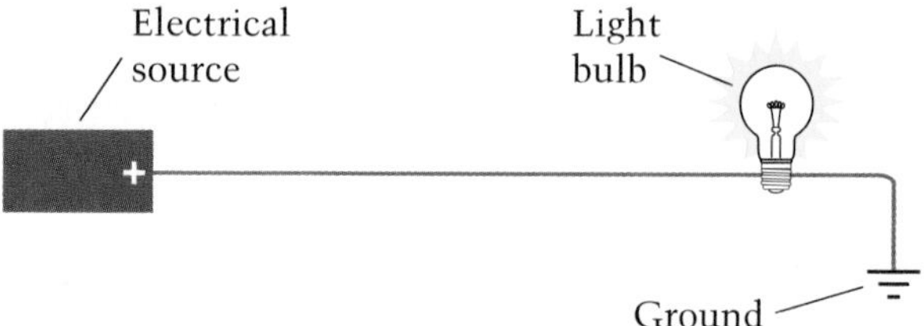

In this situation, the light burns all the time. Now, let's add a switch, and give it a name, "P," like so:

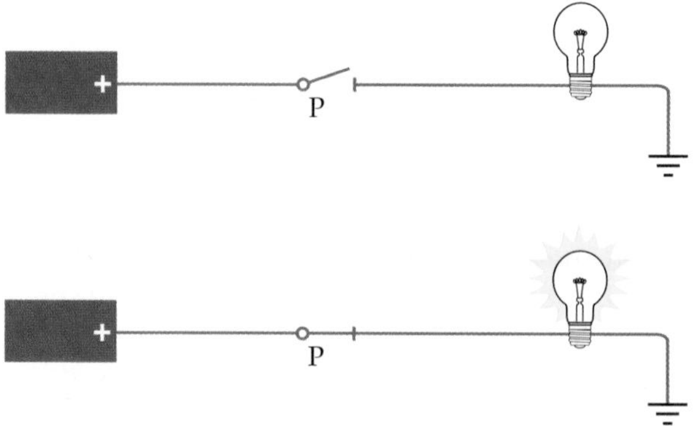

*The exceptions to this remark are due to *non*-truth-functional nuances that claims sometimes have. Most compound claims of the form P & Q, for example, are interchangeable with what are called their commutations, Q & P. That is, it doesn't matter which conjunct comes first. (Note that this is also true of disjunctions but *not* of conditionals.) But at times "and" has more than a truth-functional meaning, and in such cases which conjunct comes first can make a difference. In "Daniel got on the train and bought his ticket," the word "and" would ordinarily mean "and then." So "Daniel bought his ticket and got on the train" turns out to be a different claim from the previous one; it says that he did the two things in a different order from that stated in the first claim. This temporal-ordering sense of "and" is part of the word's occasional non-truth-functional meaning.

(Switch P represents a sentence that can be true or false, just as the switch can be open or closed.) When the switch is open (corresponding to false), as on the left, the light doesn't come on, but when it's closed (corresponding to true) as on the right, the light comes on. Now, let's add another switch in the same line, and call it "Q":

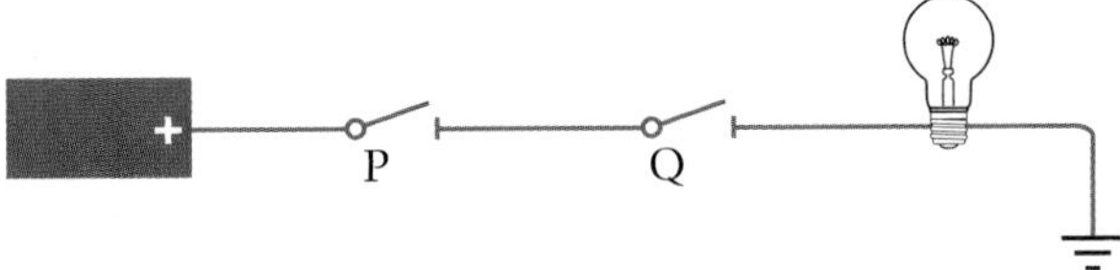

This simple circuit is analogous to a simple conjunction, "P & Q," because *both* switches must be closed for the bulb to come on, just as both conjuncts have to be true in order for the conjunction to be true. So, although there are four possible combinations for the switches (open + open, open + closed, closed + open, closed + closed) only one of them causes the bulb to burn, just as there is only one T in the truth-table for conjunction.

We can represent disjunction with a different circuit, one with the switches wired in parallel rather than in series:

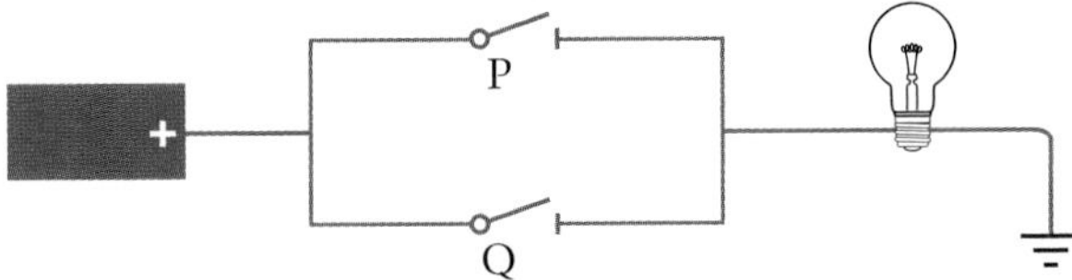

In this case, if *either* the P switch or the Q switch is on, the bulb will light up. So, it lights up in three of the four possible combinations of open/closed for the two switches, just as the disjunction, "P ∨ Q," is true in three of the rows in its truth-table.

We complicate our circuit-making chores somewhat when we bring in negation. If we have a switch labeled "~P," for example, we just treat it the same as if it were "P": It's either open or closed. But if our circuit contains a switch P and another switch, ~P, then we have to connect them (we'll do it with a dotted line) indicating that these switches are always opposite; when one closes, the other automatically opens. Now we get two interesting results: When two switches that are "negations" of each other are wired in series like this:

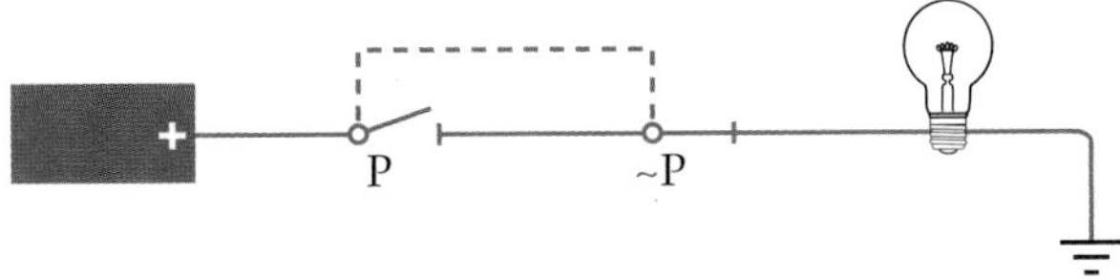

we have a dysfunctional circuit: The light can never come on! But we get the opposite result when we wire the two negation switches in parallel:

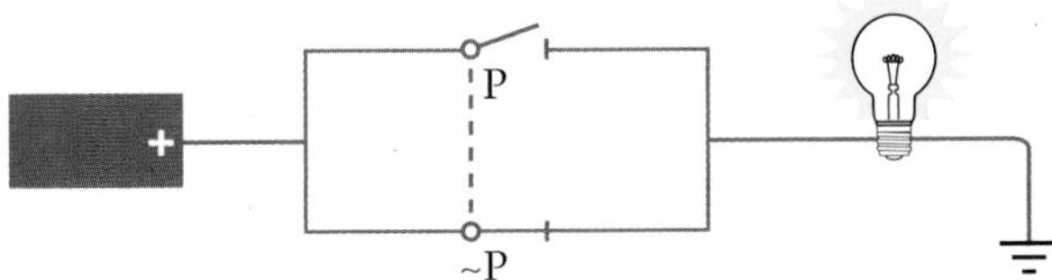

Here, the light can never go off! (This circuit is the exact equivalent of our original one, in which there were no switches at all.) In truth-functional logic, what is being represented here, of course, is that a contradiction is never true (bulb never comes on) and a tautology is never false (bulb never goes off). ("Tautology" is a traditional and somewhat fancy word for a sentence with nothing but "T"s in its truth-table.)

This gives you nothing more than a peek at the subject (among other things, truth-functional logic can help us design circuits that are the simplest possible for doing a certain job—i.e., for being on and off under exactly the right circumstances); unfortunately, we don't have room to go further into the subject here. An Introduction to Computer Science class would be the best next step.

Okay. It's time now to consider some tips for symbolizing truth-functional claims.

SYMBOLIZING COMPOUND CLAIMS

Most of the things we can do with symbolized claims are pretty straightforward; that is, if you learn the techniques, you can apply them in a relatively clear-cut way. What's less clear-cut is how to symbolize a claim in the first place. We'll cover a few tips for symbolization in this section and then give you a chance to practice with some exercises.

Remember, when you symbolize a claim, you're displaying its truth-functional structure. The idea is to produce a version that will be truth-functionally equivalent to the original informal claim—that is, one that will be true under all the same circumstances as the original and false under all the same circumstances. Let's go through some examples that illustrate some standard symbolization problems.

"If" and "Only If"

In symbolizing truth-functional claims, as in translating categorical claims in Chapter 8, nothing can take the place of a careful reading of what the claim in question says. It always comes down to a matter of exercising careful judgment. Nonetheless, there are some tips we can give you that should make the job a little easier.

Of all the basic truth-functional types of claim, the conditional is probably the most difficult for students to symbolize correctly. There are so many ways to make these claims in ordinary English that it's not easy to keep track. Fortunately, the phrases "if" and "only if" account for a large number of conditionals, so you'll have a head start if you understand their uses. Here are some rules of thumb to remember:

> The word "if," used alone, introduces the antecedent of a conditional.
>
> The phrase "only if" introduces the consequent of a conditional.

To put it another way: It's not the location of the part in a conditional that tells us whether it is the antecedent or the consequent; it's the logical words that identify it. Consider this example:

> Moore will get wet *if* Parker capsizes the boat.

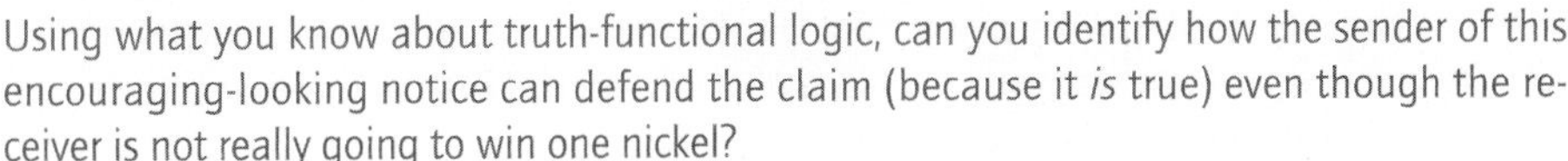

Real Life

Truth-Functional Trickery

Using what you know about truth-functional logic, can you identify how the sender of this encouraging-looking notice can defend the claim (because it *is* true) even though the receiver is not really going to win one nickel?

You Have Absolutely Won

$1,000,000.00

If you follow the instructions inside
and return the winning number!

Answer: Because there is not going to be any winning number inside (there are usually several *losing* numbers, in case that makes you feel better), the conjunction "You follow the instructions inside and [you] return the winning number" is going to be false, even if you do follow the instructions inside. Therefore, because this conjunction is the antecedent of the whole conditional claim, the conditional claim turns out to be true.

Of course, uncritical readers will take the antecedent to be saying something like "If you follow the instructions inside *by returning the winning number inside* (as if there were a winning number inside). These are the people who may wind up sending their own money to the mailer.

The "Parker" part of the claim is the antecedent, even though it comes *after* the "Moore" part. It's as though the claim had said,

> If Parker capsizes the boat, Moore will get wet.

We would symbolize this claim as P → M. Once again, it's the word "if" that tells us what the antecedent is.

> Parker will eat his hat *only if* Moore hits the target.

This claim is different. In this case, the "Parker" part is the antecedent because "only if" introduces the consequent of a conditional. This is truth-functionally the same as

> If Parker eats his hat (P), then Moore hit (or must have hit) the target (T).

Using the letters indicated in parentheses, we'd symbolize this as

> P → T

Don't worry about the grammatical tenses; we'll adjust those in whatever way necessary so that the claims make sense. We can use "if" in front of a conditional's antecedent, or we can use "only if" in front of its consequent; we produce exactly equivalent claims in the two cases. As in the case with "if," it doesn't matter where the "only if" part of the claim occurs. The part of this claim that's about Moore is the consequent, even though it occurs at the beginning of this version:

> Only if Moore hits the target will Parker eat his hat.

Real Life

Hell Hath Enlarged Herself

> The fearful, and unbelieving, and the abominable, and murderers, and whoremongers, and sorcerers, and idolators, and all liars, shall have their part in the lake which burneth with fire and brimstone.
>
> – Revelation 21:8

This came to us in a brochure from a religious sect offering salvation for the believer. Notice, though, that the passage from the Bible doesn't say that, if you believe, you won't go to hell. It says, if you don't believe, you will go to hell.

Exercise 9-1

Symbolize the following using the claim variables P and Q. (You can ignore differences in past, present, and future tense.)

▲ 1. If Quincy learns to symbolize, Paula will be amazed.
▲ 2. Paula will teach him if Quincy pays her a big fee.
▲ 3. Paula will teach him only if Quincy pays her a big fee.
▲ 4. Only if Paula helps him will Quincy pass the course.
▲ 5. Quincy will pass if and only if Paula helps him.

Claim 5 in the preceding exercise introduces a new wrinkle, the phrase "if and only if." Remembering our rules of thumb about how "if" and "only if" operate separately, it shouldn't surprise us that "if and only if" makes both antecedent and consequent out of the claim it introduces. We can make P both antecedent and consequent this way:

$$(P \rightarrow Q) \; \& \; (Q \rightarrow P)$$

There are other ways to produce conditionals, of course. In one of its senses, the word "provided" (and the phrase "provided that") works like the word "if" in introducing the antecedent of a conditional. "Moore will buy the car, provided the seller throws in a ton of spare parts" is equivalent to the same expression with the word "if" in place of "provided."

Necessary and Sufficient Conditions

Conditional claims are sometimes spelled out in terms of necessary and sufficient conditions. Consider this example:

> The presence of oxygen is a necessary condition for combustion.

This tells us that we can't have combustion without oxygen, or "If we have combustion (C), then we must have oxygen (O)." Notice that *the necessary condition becomes the consequent of a conditional:* C → O.

■ Comment: We often use "only if" when we mean to state both necessary and sufficient conditions, even though, literally speaking, it produces only the former. If Lew were a critical thinker, he'd check this deal more carefully before getting out the hose and bucket.

A sufficient condition *guarantees* whatever it is a sufficient condition for. Being born in the United States is a sufficient condition for U.S. citizenship—that's *all* one needs to be a U.S. citizen. *Sufficient conditions are expressed as the antecedents of conditional claims,* so we would say, "If John was born in the United States (B), then John is a U.S. citizen (C)": B → C.

You should also notice the connection between "if" and "only if" on the one hand and necessary and sufficient conditions on the other. The word "if," by itself, introduces a sufficient condition; the phrase "only if" introduces a necessary condition. So the claim "X is a necessary condition for Y" would be symbolized "Y → X."

From time to time, one thing will be both a necessary and a sufficient condition for something else. For example, if Jean's payment of her dues to the National Truth-Functional Logic Society (NTFLS) guaranteed her continued membership (making such payment a sufficient condition) and there was no way for her to continue membership *without* paying her dues (making payment a necessary condition as well), then we could express such a situation as "Jean will remain a member of the NTFLS (M) if and only if she pays her dues (D)": (M → D) & (D → M).

We often play fast and loose with how we state necessary and sufficient conditions. A parent tells his daughter, "You can watch television only if you clean your room." Now, the youngster would ordinarily take cleaning her room as both a necessary and a sufficient condition for being allowed to watch television, and probably that's what a parent would intend by those words. But notice that the parent actually stated only a necessary condition;

On Language

Another "If" and "Only if" Confusion

> Do you want to install and run News Menu 3.0 distributed by MSNBC Interactive News LLC? Caution: MSNBC Interactive News LLC asserts that this content is safe. You should install/view this content if you trust MSNBC Interactive News LLC to make that assertion.
>
> – Download caution on the MSNBC Web site

Presumably they mean not "if" but "only if." Do you see why? In any case, this caution contains one heck of a weaseler (Chapter 4).

technically, he would not be going back on what he said if room cleaning turned out not to be sufficient for television privileges. Of course he'd better be prepared for more than a logic lesson from his daughter in such a case, and most of us would be on her side in the dispute. But, literally, it's the necessary condition that the phrase "only if" introduces, not the sufficient condition.

"Unless"

Consider the claim "Paula will foreclose unless Quincy pays up." Asked to symbolize this, we might come up with ~Q→P because the original claim is equivalent to "If Quincy doesn't pay up, then Paula will foreclose." But there's an even simpler way to do it. Ask yourself, what is the truth table for ~Q → P? If you've gained familiarity with the basic truth tables by this time, you realize that it's the same as the table for P ∨ Q. And, as a matter of fact, you can treat the word "unless" exactly like the word "or" and symbolize it with a "∨."

"Either . . ."

Sometimes we need to know exactly where a disjunction begins; it's the job of the word "either" to show us. Compare the claims

Either P and Q or R

and

P and either Q or R.

These two claims say different things and have different truth tables, but the only difference between them is the location of the word "either"; without that word, the claim would be completely ambiguous. "Either" tells us that the disjunction begins with P in the first claim and Q in the second claim. So we would symbolize the first (P & Q) ∨ R and the second P & (Q ∨ R).

The word "if" does much the same job for conditionals as "either" does for disjunctions. Notice the difference between

P and if Q then R

and

If P and Q then R.

"If" tells us that the antecedent begins with Q in the first example and with P in the second. Hence, the second must have P & Q for the antecedent of its symbolization.

In general, the trick to symbolizing a claim correctly is to pay careful attention to exactly what the claim says—and this often means asking yourself just exactly what would make this claim false (or true). Then try to come up with a symbolization that says the same thing—that is false (or true) in exactly the same circumstances. There's no substitute for practice, so here's an exercise to work on.

Exercise 9-2

When we symbolize a claim, we're displaying its truth-functional structure. Show that you can figure out the structures of the following claims by symbolizing them. Use these letters for the first ten items:

P = Parsons signs the papers.
Q = Quincy goes (or will go) to jail.
R = Rachel files (or will file) an appeal.

Use the symbols ~, &, v, and →. We suggest that, at least at first, you make symbolization a two-stage process: First, replace simple parts of claims with letters; then, replace logical words with logical symbols, and add parentheses as required. We'll do an example in two stages to show you what we mean.

Example

If Parsons signs the papers, then Quincy will go to jail but Rachel will not file an appeal.

Stage 1: If P, then Q but ~R.
Stage 2: P→(Q & ~R)

▲ **1.** If Parsons signs the papers then Quincy will go to jail, and Rachel will file an appeal.

▲ **2.** If Parsons signs the papers, then Quincy will go to jail and Rachel will file an appeal.

3. If Parsons signs the papers and Quincy goes to jail then Rachel will file an appeal.

4. Parsons signs the papers and if Quincy goes to jail Rachel will file an appeal.

▲ **5.** If Parsons signs the papers then if Quincy goes to jail Rachel will file an appeal.

6. If Parsons signs the papers Quincy goes to jail, and if Rachel files an appeal Quincy goes to jail.

7. Quincy goes to jail if either Parsons signs papers or Rachel files an appeal.

8. Either Parsons signs the papers or, if Quincy goes to jail, then Rachel will file an appeal.

9. If either Parsons signs the papers or Quincy goes to jail then Rachel will file an appeal.

10. If Parsons signs the papers then either Quincy will go to jail or Rachel will file an appeal.

For the next ten items, use the following letters:

C = My car runs well.
S = I will sell my car.
F = I will have my car fixed.

▲ **11.** If my car doesn't run well, then I will sell it.

▲ **12.** It's not true that if my car runs well, then I will sell it.

13. I will sell my car only if it doesn't run well.

14. I won't sell my car unless it doesn't run well.

15. I will have my car fixed unless it runs well.

▲ **16.** I will sell my car, but only if it doesn't run well.

17. Provided my car runs well, I won't sell it.

18. My car's running well is a sufficient condition for my not having it fixed.

19. My car's not running well is a necessary condition for my having it fixed.

▲ **20.** I will neither have my car fixed nor sell it.

Exercise 9-3

▲ Construct truth tables for the symbolizations you produced for Exercise 9-2. Determine whether any of them are truth-functionally equivalent to any others. (Answers to items 1, 5, and 12 are provided in the answer section at the end of the book.)

TRUTH-FUNCTIONAL ARGUMENTS

Categorical syllogisms (discussed in Chapter 8) have a total of 256 forms. A truth-functional argument, by contrast, can take any of an infinite number of forms. Nevertheless, we have methods for testing for validity that are flexible enough to encompass every truth-functional argument. In the remainder of this chapter, we'll look at three of them: the truth-table method, the short truth-table method, and the method of deduction.

Before doing anything else, though, let's quickly review the concept of validity. An argument is *valid,* you'll recall, if and only if the truth of the premises guarantees the truth of the conclusion—that is, if the premises were true, the conclusion could not then be false. (In logic, remember, it doesn't matter whether the premises are *actually* true.)

The *truth-table test for validity* requires familiarity with the truth tables for the four truth-functional symbols, so go back and check yourself on those if you think you may not understand them clearly. Here's how the method works: We present all of the possible circumstances for an argument by building a truth table for it; then we simply look to see if there are any circumstances in which the premises are all true and the conclusion false. If there are such circumstances—one row of the truth table is all that's required—then the argument is invalid.

Let's look at a simple example. Let P and Q represent any two claims. Now look at the following symbolized argument:

P → Q
~P
Therefore, ~Q

We can construct a truth table for this argument by including a column for each premise and one for the conclusion:

P	Q	~P	P→Q	~Q
T	T	F	T	F
T	F	F	F	T
F	T	T	T	F
F	F	T	T	T

The first two columns are reference columns; they list truth values for the letters that appear in the argument. The third and fourth columns appear under the two premises of the argument, and the fifth column is for the conclusion. Note that in the third row of the table, both premises are true and the conclusion is false. This tells us that it is possible for the premises of this argument to be true while the conclusion is false; thus, the argument is invalid. Because it doesn't matter what claims P and Q might stand for, the same is true for *every* argument of this pattern. Here's an example of such an argument:

> If the Saints beat the Forty-Niners, then the Giants will make the playoffs. But the Saints won't beat the Forty-Niners. So the Giants won't make the playoffs.

Using S for "The Saints beat (or will beat) the Forty-Niners," and G for "The Giants make (or will make) the playoffs," we can symbolize the argument like this:

S → G
~S
———
~G

The first premise is a conditional, and the other premise is the negation of the antecedent of that conditional. The conclusion is the negation of the conditional's consequent. It has exactly the same structure as the argument for which we just did the truth table; accordingly, it too is invalid.

Let's do another simple one:

> We're going to have large masses of arctic air (A) flowing into the Midwest unless the jet stream (J) moves south. Unfortunately, there's no chance of the jet stream's moving south. So you can bet there'll be arctic air flowing into the Midwest.

Symbolization gives us

A ∨ J
~J
―――
A

Here's a truth table for the argument:

1	2	3	4
A	J	A ∨ J	~J
T	T	T	F
T	F	T	T
F	T	T	F
F	F	F	T

Note that the first premise is represented in column 3 of the table, the second premise in column 4, and the conclusion in one of the reference columns, column 1. Now, let's recall what we're up to. We want to know whether this argument is valid—that is to say, is it possible for the premises to be true and the conclusion false? If there is such a possibility, it will turn up in the truth table because, remember, the truth table represents every possible situation with respect to the claims A and J. We find that the premises are both true in only one row, the second, and when we check the conclusion, A, we find it is true in that row. Thus, there is *no* row in which the premises are true and the conclusion false. So the argument is valid.

Here's an example of a rather more complicated argument:

> If Scarlet is guilty of the crime, then Ms. White must have left the back door unlocked and the colonel must have retired before ten o'clock. However, either Ms. White did not leave the back door unlocked, or the colonel did not retire before ten. Therefore, Scarlet is not guilty of the crime.

Let's assign some letters to the simple claims so that we can show this argument's pattern.

S = Scarlet is guilty of the crime.
W = Ms. White left the back door unlocked.
C = The colonel retired before ten o'clock.

Now we symbolize the argument to display this pattern:

S → (W & C)
~W ∨ ~C
―――
~S

Let's think our way through this argument. As you read, refer back to the symbolized version above. Notice that the first premise is a conditional, with "Scarlet is guilty of the crime" as antecedent and a conjunction as consequent. In order for that conjunction to be true, both "Ms. White left the back door unlocked" and "The colonel retired before ten o'clock" have to be true, as you'll recall from the truth table for conjunctions. Now look at the second premise. It is a disjunction that tells us *either* Ms. White did not leave the back door unlocked *or* the colonel did not retire before ten. But if either or both of those disjuncts are true, at least one of the claims in our earlier con-

Real Life

Rule 1

> Hitler was clearly intent on taking over the world. Mr. Buchanan thinks we should have stood by silently watching, and so, no, I would not say he belongs in the Republican Party.

The remark by Senator John McCain of Arizona is actually Rule 1 (page 310) with an unstated premise, in effect:

> [If Mr. Buchanan thinks we should have stood by silently watching, then Mr. Buchanan does not belong in the Republican Party.]
>
> Mr. Buchanan thinks we should have stood by silently watching.
>
> Therefore, Mr. Buchanan does not belong in the Republican Party.

junction is false. So it cannot be that *both* parts of the conjunction are true. This means the conjunction symbolized by W & C must be false. And so the consequent of the first premise is false. How can the entire premise be true, in that case? The only way is for the antecedent to be false as well. And that means that the conclusion, "Scarlet is not guilty of the crime," must be true.

All of this reasoning (and considerably more that we don't require) is implicit in the following truth table for the argument:

1 S	2 W	3 C	4 ~W	5 ~C	6 W & C	7 S→(W & C)	8 ~W ∨ ~C	9 ~S
T	T	T	F	F	T	T	F	F
T	T	F	F	T	F	F	T	F
T	F	T	T	F	F	F	T	F
T	F	F	T	T	F	F	T	F
F	T	T	F	F	T	T	F	T
F	T	F	F	T	F	T	T	T
F	F	T	T	F	F	T	T	T
F	F	F	T	T	F	T	T	T

We've numbered the columns at the top to make reference somewhat easier. The first three are our reference columns, columns 7 and 8 are for the premises of the argument, and column 9 is for the argument's conclusion. The remainder—4, 5, and 6—are for parts of some of the other symbolized claims; they could be left out if we desired, but they make filling in columns 7 and 8 a bit easier.

Once the table is filled in, evaluating the argument is easy. Just look to see whether there is any row in which the premises are true and the conclusion is false. One such row is enough to demonstrate the invalidity of the argument.

In the present case, we find that both premises are true only in the last three rows of the table. And in those rows, the conclusion is also true. So there is no set of circumstances—no row of the table—in which both premises are true and the conclusion is false. Therefore, the argument is valid.

Although filling out a complete truth table always produces the correct answer regarding a truth-functional argument's validity, it can be quite a tedious chore—in fact, life is much too short to spend much of it filling in truth tables. Fortunately, there are shorter and more manageable ways of finding such an answer. The easiest systematic way to determine the validity or invalidity of truth-functional arguments is the *short truth-table method.* Here's the idea behind it: Because, if an argument is invalid, there has to be at least one row in the argument's truth table where the premises are true and the conclusion is false, we'll look directly for such a row. Consider this symbolized argument:

$$\begin{array}{l} P \rightarrow Q \\ \underline{\sim Q \rightarrow R} \\ \sim P \rightarrow R \end{array}$$

We begin by looking at the conclusion. Because it's a conditional, it can be made false only one way, by making its antecedent true and its consequent false. So we do that, by making P false and R false.

Can we now make both premises true? Yes, as it turns out, by making Q true. This case,

P	Q	R
F	T	F

makes both premises true and the conclusion false and thus proves the argument invalid. What we've done is produce the relevant row of the truth table without bothering to produce all the rest. Had the argument been valid, we would not have been able to produce such a row.

Here's how the method works with a valid argument. Consider this example:

$$\begin{array}{l} (P \vee Q) \rightarrow R \\ \underline{S \rightarrow Q} \\ S \rightarrow R \end{array}$$

The only way to make the conclusion false is to make S true and R false. So we do that:

P	Q	R	S
		F	T

Now, with S true, the second premise requires that we make Q true. So we do that next:

P	Q	R	S
	T	F	T

But now, there is no way at all to make the first premise true, because P ∨ Q is going to be true (because Q is true) and R is already false. Because there is no other way to make the conclusion false and the second premise true and because this way fails to make the first premise true, we can conclude that the argument is *valid.*

In some cases, there may be more than one way to make the conclusion false. Here's a symbolized example:

P & (Q ∨ R)
R → S
P → T
―――――
S & T

Because the conclusion is a conjunction, it is false if either or both of its conjuncts are false, which means we could begin by making S true and T false, S false and T true, or both S and T false. This is trouble we'd like to avoid if possible, so let's see if there's someplace else we can begin making our assignment. (Remember: The idea is to try to assign true and false to the letters so as to make the premises true and the conclusion false. If we can do it, the argument is invalid.)

In this example, to make the first premise true, we *must* assign true to the letter P. Why? Because the premise is a conjunction and both of its parts must be true for the whole thing to be true. That's what we're looking for: places where we are *forced* to make an assignment of true or false to one or more letters. Then we make those assignments and see where they lead us. In this case, once we've made P true, we see that, to make the third premise true, we are forced to make T true (because a true antecedent and a false consequent would make the premise false, and we're trying to make our premises true).

After making T true, we see that, to make the conclusion false, S must be false. So we make that assignment. At this point we're nearly done, needing only assignments for Q and R.

P	Q	R	S	T
T			F	T

Are there any other assignments that we're forced to make? Yes: We must make R false to make the second premise true. Once we've done that, we see that Q must be true to preserve the truth of the first premise. And that completes the assignment:

P	Q	R	S	T
T	T	F	F	T

This is one row in the truth table for this argument—the only row, as it turned out—in which all the premises are true and the conclusion is false; thus, it is the row that proves the argument invalid.

In Depth

Common Truth-Functional Argument Patterns

Some truth-functional patterns are so built into our thinking process that they almost operate at a subverbal level. But, rather than trust our subverbal skills, whatever those might be, let's identify three common patterns that are perfectly valid—their conclusions follow with certainty from their premises—and three invalid imposters—each of the imposters bears a resemblance to one of the good guys. We'll set them up in pairs:

Valid Argument Forms

In this case, the premises guarantee the conclusion.

1. Modus ponens (or affirming the antecedent)
   If P, then Q
   P
   ———
   Q
2. Modus tollens (or denying the consequent)
   If P, then Q
   Not-Q
   ———
   Not-P
3. Chain argument
   If P, then Q
   If Q, then R
   ———
   If P, then R

Invalid Argument Forms

Here, the premises can be true while the conclusion is false.

1-A. Affirming the consequent
   If P, then Q
   Q
   ———
   P

2-A. Denying the antecedent
   If P, then Q
   Not-P
   ———
   Not-Q

3-A. Undistributed middle (truth-functional version)
   If P, then Q
   If R, then Q
   ———
   If P, then R

In the preceding example, there was a premise that forced us to begin with a particular assignment to a letter. Sometimes neither the conclusion nor any of the premises forces an assignment on us. In that case we must use trial and error: Begin with one assignment that makes the conclusion false (or some premise true) and see if it will work. If not, try another assignment. If all fail, then the argument is valid.

Often, several rows of a truth table will make the premises true and the conclusion false; any one of them is all it takes to prove invalidity. Don't get the mistaken idea that, just because the premises are all true in one row and so is the conclusion, the conclusion follows from the premises—that is, that the argument must be valid. To be valid, the conclusion must be true in *every* row in which all the premises are true.

To review: Try to assign Ts and Fs to the letters in the symbolization so that all premises come out true and the conclusion comes out false. There may be more than one way to do it; any of them will do to prove the argument invalid. If it is impossible to make the premises and conclusion come out this way, the argument is valid.

Exercise 9-4

Construct full truth tables or use the short truth-table method to determine which of the following arguments are valid.

▲ 1. P ∨ ~Q
~Q
———
~P

2. P → Q
~Q
———
~P

3. ~ (P ∨ Q)
R → P
———
~R

▲ 4. P → (Q → R)
~ (P → Q)
———
R

5. P ∨ (Q → R)
Q & ~R
———
~P

6. (P → Q) ∨ (R → Q)
P & (~P → ~R)
———
Q

▲ 7. (P & R) → Q
~Q
———
~P

8. P & (~Q → ~P)
R → ~Q
———
~R

9. L ∨ ~J
R → J
———
L → ~R

10. ~F ∨ (G & H)
P → F
———
~H → ~P

Exercise 9-5

Use either the long or short truth-table method to determine which of the following arguments are valid.

▲ 1. K → (L & G)
M → (J & K)
B & M
———
B & G

▲ 2. L ∨ (W → S)
P ∨ ~S
~L → W
———
P

▲ **3.** M & P
R → ~P
F ∨ R
G → M
———
G & F

▲ **4.** (D & G) → H
M & (H → P)
M → G
———
D & P

▲ **5.** R → S
(S & B) → T
T → E
———
(R ∨ B) → E

DEDUCTIONS

The next method we'll look at is less useful for proving an argument *invalid* than the truth-table methods, but it has some advantages in proving that an argument is valid. The method is that of **deduction.**

When we use this method, we actually deduce (or "derive") the conclusion from the premises by means of a series of basic truth-functionally valid argument patterns. This is a lot like "thinking through" the argument, taking one step at a time to see how, once we've assumed the truth of the premises, we eventually arrive at the conclusion. We'll consider some extended examples showing how the method works as we explain the first few basic argument patterns. We'll refer to these patterns as truth-functional rules because they govern what steps we're allowed to take in getting from the premises to the conclusion. (Your instructor may ask that you simply learn some or all of the basic valid argument patterns. It's a good idea to be able to identify these patterns whether you go on to construct deductions from them or not.)

Group I Rules: Elementary Valid Argument Patterns

This first group of rules should be learned before you go on to the Group II rules. Study them until you can work Exercise 9-6 with confidence.

Rule 1: Modus ponens (MP), also known as *affirming the antecedent*

Any argument of the pattern

P → Q
P
———
Q

is valid. If you have a conditional among the premises and if the antecedent of that conditional occurs as another premise, then by **modus ponens** the consequent of the conditional follows from those two premises. The claims involved do not have to be simple letters standing alone—it would have made no difference if, in place of P, we had had something more complicated, such as (P ∨ R), as long as that compound claim appeared everywhere that P appears in the pattern above. For example:

1. $(P \vee R) \rightarrow Q$ Premise
2. $P \vee R$ Premise
3. Q From the premises, by modus ponens

The idea, once again, is that if you have *any conditional whatsoever* on a line of your deduction and if you have the antecedent of that conditional on some other line, you can write down the consequent of the conditional on your new line.

If the consequent of the conditional is the conclusion of the argument, then the deduction is finished—the conclusion has been established. If it is not the conclusion of the argument you're working on, the consequent of the conditional can be listed just as if it were another premise to use in deducing the conclusion you're after. An example:

1. $P \rightarrow R$
2. $R \rightarrow S$
3. P Therefore, S

We've numbered the three premises of the argument and set its conclusion off to the side. (Hereafter we'll use a slash and three dots [/∴] in place of "therefore" to indicate the conclusion.) Now, notice that line 1 is a conditional, and line 3 is its antecedent. Modus ponens allows us to write down the consequent of line 1 as a new line in our deduction:

4. R 1, 3, MP

At the right we've noted the abbreviation for the rule we used and the lines the rule required. These notes are called the *annotation* for the deduction. We can now make use of this new line in the deduction to get the conclusion we were originally after, namely, S.

5. S 2, 4, MP

Again, we used modus ponens, this time on lines 2 and 4. The same explanation as that for deriving line 4 from lines 1 and 3 applies here.

Notice that the modus ponens rule and all other Group I rules can be used only on whole lines. This means that you can't find the items you need for MP as *parts* of a line, as in the following:

$P \vee (Q \rightarrow R)$
Q
$P \vee R$ (erroneous!)

This is *not* a legitimate use of MP. We do have a conditional as *part* of the first line, and the second line is indeed the antecedent of that conditional. But the rule cannot be applied to parts of lines. The conditional required by rule MP must take up the entire line, as in the following:

$P \rightarrow (Q \vee R)$
P
$Q \vee R$

Rule 2: Modus tollens (MT), also known as *denying the consequent*

The **modus tollens** pattern is this:

$P \rightarrow Q$
$\sim Q$
$\sim P$

THE BORN LOSER reprinted by permission of Newspaper Enterprise Association, Inc.

If you have a conditional claim as one premise and if one of your other premises is the negation of the consequent of that conditional, you can write down the negation of the conditional's antecedent as a new line in your deduction. Here's a deduction that uses both of the first two rules:

1. (P & Q) → R	
2. S	
3. S → ~R	/∴~(P & Q)
4. ~R	2, 3, MP
5. ~(P & Q)	1, 4, MT

In this deduction we derived line 4 from lines 2 and 3 by modus ponens, and then 4 and 1 gave us line 5, which is what we were after, by modus tollens. The fact that the antecedent of line 1 is itself a compound claim, (P & Q), is not important; our line 5 is the antecedent of the conditional with a negation sign in front of it, and that's all that counts.

Rule 3: Chain argument (CA)

P → Q
Q → R
―――――
P → R

The **chain argument** rule allows you to derive a conditional from two you already have, provided the antecedent of one of your conditionals is the same as the consequent of the other.

Rule 4: Disjunctive argument (DA)

P ∨ Q	P ∨ Q
~P	~Q
Q	P

Real Life

If the Dollar Falls . . .

The valid argument patterns are in fact fairly common. Here's one in an article in *Time* as to why a weakening dollar is a threat to the stock market:

> Why should we care? . . . If the dollar continues to drop, investors may be tempted to move their cash to currencies on the upswing. That would drive the U.S. market lower. . . . Because foreigners hold almost 40% of U.S. Treasury securities, any pullout would risk a spike in interest rates that would ultimately slaughter the . . . market.

The chain argument here is reasonably obvious. In effect: If the dollar falls, then investors move their cash to currencies on the upswing. If investors move their cash to currencies on the upswing, then the U.S. market goes lower. If the U.S. market goes lower, then interest rates on U.S. Treasury securities rise. If interest rates on U.S. Treasury securities rise, then the . . . market dies. [Therefore, if the dollar falls, then the . . . market dies.]

From a disjunction and the negation of one disjunct, the other disjunct may be derived.

Rule 5: Simplification (SIM)

This one is obvious, but we need it for obvious reasons:

$$\frac{P \,\&\, Q}{P} \qquad \frac{P \,\&\, Q}{Q}$$

If the conjunction is true, then of course the conjuncts must all be true. You can pull out one conjunct from any conjunction and make it the new line in your deduction.

Rule 6: Conjunction (CONJ)

$$\frac{\begin{array}{l}P\\Q\end{array}}{P \,\&\, Q}$$

This rule allows you to put any two lines of a deduction together in the form of a conjunction.

Rule 7: Addition (ADD)

$$\frac{P}{P \vee Q} \qquad \frac{Q}{P \vee Q}$$

Clearly, no matter what claims P and Q might be, if P is true then *either* P or Q must be true. The truth of one disjunct is all it takes to make the whole disjunction true.

Rule 8: Constructive dilemma (CD)

$$\frac{\begin{array}{l}P \rightarrow Q\\R \rightarrow S\\P \vee R\end{array}}{Q \vee S}$$

The disjunction of the antecedents of any two conditionals allows the derivation of the disjunction of their consequents.

Rule 9: Destructive dilemma (CD)

P → Q
R → S
~Q ∨ ~S
~P ∨ ~R

The disjunction of the negations of the consequents of two conditionals allows the derivation of the disjunction of the negations of their antecedents. (Refer to the pattern above as you read this, and it will make a lot more sense.)

Exercise 9-6

For each of the following groups of symbolized claims, identify which of the Group I rules was used to derive the last line.

▲ **1.** P → (Q & R)
(Q & R) → (S ∨ T)
P → (S ∨ T)

▲ **2.** (P & S) ∨ (T → R)
~(P & S)
T → R

▲ **3.** P ∨ (Q & R)
(Q & R) →S
P → T
S ∨ T

▲ **4.** (P ∨ R) → Q
~Q
~(P ∨ R)

▲ **5.** (Q → T) → S
~S ∨ ~P
R → P
~(Q → T) ∨ ~R

Exercise 9-7

Construct deductions for each of the following using the Group I rules. Each can be done in just a step or two (except number 10, which takes more).

▲ **1.** 1. R → P
2. Q → R /∴Q → P

2. 1. P → S
2. P ∨ Q
3. Q → R /∴S ∨ R

3. 1. R & S
2. S → P /∴P

▲ **4.** 1. P → Q
2. ~P → S
3. ~Q /∴S

5. 1. (P ∨ Q) → R
2. Q /∴R

6. 1. ~P
2. ~(R & S) ∨ Q
3. ~P → ~Q /∴~(R & S)

▲ **7.** 1. ~S
2. (P & Q) → R
3. R → S /∴~(P & Q)

8. 1. P → ~(Q & T)
2. S → (Q & T)
3. P /∴~S

9. 1. (P ∨ T) → S
2. R → P
3. R ∨ Q
4. Q → T /∴S

▲ **10.** 1. (T ∨ M) → ~Q
2. (P → Q) & (R → S)
3. T /∴~P

Group II Rules: Truth-Functional Equivalences

A claim or part of a claim may be replaced by any claim or part of a claim to which it is equivalent by one of the following equivalence rules. Don't despair if this sounds complicated. The way such replacement works will become clear after a few examples.

There are a few differences between these rules about equivalences and the Group I rules. First, these rules allow us to go two ways instead of one—from either claim to its equivalent. Second, these rules allow us to replace part of a claim with an equivalent part, rather than having to deal with entire lines of a deduction all at once. In the examples that follow the first few rules, watch for both of these differences.

We'll use a double-headed arrow (↔) to indicate the equivalence of two claims.

Rule 10: Double negation (DN)

P ↔ ~~P

This rule allows you to add or remove two negation signs in front of any claim, whether simple or compound. For example, this rule allows the derivation of either of the following from the other

P → (Q ∨ R) P → ~~(Q ∨ R)

because the rule guarantees that (Q ∨ R) and its double negation, ~~(Q ∨ R), are equivalent. This in turn guarantees that P → (Q ∨ R) and P → ~~(Q ∨ R) are equivalent, and hence that each implies the other.

Here's an example of DN at work:

1. P ∨ ~(Q → R)
2. (Q → R) /∴P
3. ~~(Q → R) 2, DN
4. P 1, 3, DA

Rule 11: Commutation (COM)

(P & Q) ↔ (Q & P)
(P ∨ Q) ↔ (Q ∨ P)

This rule simply allows any conjunction or disjunction to be "turned around," so that the conjuncts or disjuncts occur in reverse order. Here's an example:

P → (Q ∨ R) P → (R ∨ Q)

Notice that commutation is used on *part* of the claim—just the consequent.

Rule 12: Implication (IMPL)

This rule allows us to change a conditional into a disjunction and vice versa.

(P → Q) ↔ (~P ∨ Q)

Notice that the antecedent always becomes the negated disjunct, or vice versa, depending on which way you're going. Another example:

(P ∨ Q) → R ↔ ~(P ∨ Q) ∨ R

Rule 13: Contraposition (CONTR)

This rule may remind you of the categorical operation of contraposition (see Chapter 8)—this rule is its truth-functional version.

(P → Q) ↔ (~Q → ~P)

This rule allows us to exchange the places of a conditional's antecedent and consequent, but only by putting on or taking off a negation sign in front of each. Here's another example:

(P & Q) → (P ∨ Q) ↔ ~(P ∨ Q) → ~(P & Q)

Sometimes you want to perform contraposition on a symbolization that doesn't fit either side of the equivalence because it has a negation sign in front of either the antecedent or the consequent but not both. You can do what you want in such cases, but it takes two steps, one applying double negation and one applying contraposition. Here's an example:

(P ∨ Q) → ~R
~~(P ∨ Q) → ~R Double negation
R → ~(P ∨ Q) Contraposition

Your instructor may allow you to combine these steps (and refer to both DN and CONTR in your annotation).

Rule 14: DeMorgan's Laws (DEM)

~(P & Q) ↔ (~P ∨ ~Q)
~(P ∨ Q) ↔ (~P & ~Q)

Notice that when the negation sign is "moved inside" the parentheses, the "&" changes into a "∨," or vice versa. It's important not to confuse the use of the negation sign in DeMorgan's Laws with that of the minus sign in algebra. Notice that when you take ~(P ∨ Q) and "move the negation sign in," you do *not* get (~P ∨ ~Q). The wedge must be changed to an ampersand or vice versa whenever DEM is used. You can think of ~(P ∨ Q) and (~P & ~Q) as saying "neither P nor Q," and you can think of ~(P & Q) and (~P ∨ ~Q) as saying "not both P and Q."

Rule 15: Exportation (EXP)

[P → (Q → R)] ↔ [(P & Q) → R]

Square brackets are used exactly as parentheses are. In English, the exportation rule says that "If P, then if Q, then R" is equivalent to "If both P and Q, then R." (The commas are optional in both claims.) If you look back to Exercise 9-2, items 3 and 5 (page 301), you'll notice that, according to the exportation rule, each of these can replace the other.

Rule 16: Association (ASSOC)

$[P \& (Q \& R)] \leftrightarrow [(P \& Q) \& R]$
$[P \vee (Q \vee R)] \leftrightarrow [(P \vee Q) \vee R]$

Association simply tells us that, when we have three items joined together with wedges or with ampersands, it doesn't matter which ones we group together. If we have a long disjunction with more than two disjuncts, it still requires only one of them to be true for the entire disjunction to be true; if it's a conjunction, then all the conjuncts have to be true, no matter how many of them there are, in order for the entire conjunction to be true. Your instructor may allow you to drop parentheses in such symbolizations, but if you're developing these rules as a formal system, he or she may not.

Rule 17: Distribution (DIST)

This rule allows us to "spread a conjunct across a disjunction" or to "spread a disjunct across a conjunction." In the first example below, look at the left-hand side of the equivalence. The P, which is conjoined with a disjunction, is picked up and dropped (distributed) across the disjunction by being conjoined with each part. (This is easier to understand if you see it done on a chalkboard than by trying to figure it out from the page in front of you.) The two versions of the rule, like those of DEM, allow us to do exactly with the wedge what we're allowed to do with the ampersand.

$[P \& (Q \vee R)] \leftrightarrow [(P \& Q) \vee (P \& R)]$
$[P \vee (Q \& R)] \leftrightarrow [(P \vee Q) \& (P \vee R)]$

Rule 18: Tautology (TAUT)

$(P \vee P) \leftrightarrow P$
$(P \& P) \leftrightarrow P$

This rule allows a few obvious steps; they are sometimes necessary to "clean up" a deduction.

The twelve-step and seven-step examples that follow show some deductions that use rules from both Group I and Group II. Look at them carefully, covering up the lines with a piece of paper and uncovering them one at a time as you progress. This gives you a chance to figure out what you might do before you see the answer. In any case, make sure you understand how each line was achieved before going on. If necessary, look up the rule used to make sure you understand it.

The first example is long, but fairly simple. Length is not always proportional to difficulty.

1. $P \rightarrow (Q \rightarrow R)$		
2. $(T \rightarrow P) \& (S \rightarrow Q)$		
3. $T \& S$		$/\therefore R$
4. $T \rightarrow P$	2, SIM	
5. $S \rightarrow Q$	2, SIM	
6. T	3, SIM	
7. S	3, SIM	
8. P	4, 6, MP	
9. Q	5, 7, MP	
10. $P \& Q$	8, 9, CONJ	
11. $(P \& Q) \rightarrow R$	1, EXP	
12. R	10, 11, MP	

Group I

1. Modus ponens (MP) $P \rightarrow Q$ $\underline{P}$ Q	2. Modus tollens (MT) $P \rightarrow Q$ $\underline{\sim Q}$ $\sim P$	3. Chain argument (CA) $P \rightarrow Q$ $\underline{Q \rightarrow R}$ $P \rightarrow R$
4. Disjunctive argument (DA) $P \vee Q \quad P \vee Q$ $\underline{\sim P} \quad \underline{\sim Q}$ $Q \quad\quad P$	5. Simplification (SIM) $\underline{P \,\&\, Q} \quad \underline{P \,\&\, Q}$ $P \quad\quad\quad Q$	6. Conjunction (CONJ) P $\underline{Q}$ $P \,\&\, Q$
7. Addition (ADD) $\underline{P} \quad\quad \underline{Q}$ $P \vee Q \quad P \vee Q$	8. Constructive dilemma (CD) $P \rightarrow Q$ $R \rightarrow S$ $\underline{P \vee R}$ $Q \vee S$	9. Destructive dilemma (DD) $P \rightarrow Q$ $R \rightarrow S$ $\underline{\sim Q \vee \sim S}$ $\sim P \vee \sim R$

Group II

10. Double negation (DN) $P \longleftrightarrow \sim\sim P$	11. Commutation (COM) $(P \,\&\, Q) \longleftrightarrow (Q \,\&\, P)$ $(P \vee Q) \longleftrightarrow (Q \vee P)$	12. Implication (IMPL) $(P \rightarrow Q) \longleftrightarrow (\sim P \vee Q)$
13. Contraposition (CONTR) $(P \rightarrow Q) \longleftrightarrow (\sim Q \rightarrow \sim P)$	14. DeMorgan's Laws (DEM) $\sim(P \vee Q) \longleftrightarrow (\sim P \,\&\, \sim Q)$ $\sim(P \,\&\, Q) \longleftrightarrow (\sim P \vee \sim Q)$	15. Exportation (EXPORT) $[P \rightarrow (Q \rightarrow R)] \longleftrightarrow [(P \,\&\, Q) \rightarrow R]$
16. Association (ASSOC) $[P \,\&\, (Q \,\&\, R)] \longleftrightarrow [(P \,\&\, Q) \,\&\, R]$ $[P \vee (Q \vee R)] \longleftrightarrow [(P \vee Q) \vee R]$	17. Distribution (DIST) $[P \,\&\, (Q \vee R)] \longleftrightarrow [(P \,\&\, Q) \vee (P \,\&\, R)]$ $[P \vee (Q \,\&\, R)] \longleftrightarrow [(P \vee Q) \,\&\, (P \vee R)]$	18. Tautology (TAUT) $(P \vee P) \longleftrightarrow P$ $(P \,\&\, P) \longleftrightarrow P$

FIGURE 2 Truth-Functional Rules for Deductions

It's often difficult to tell how to proceed when you first look at a deduction problem. One strategy is to work backward. Look at what you want to get, look at what you have, and see what you would need in order to get what you want. Then determine where you would get *that,* and so on. We'll explain in terms of the following problem.

1.	$P \rightarrow (Q \,\&\, R)$	
2.	$S \rightarrow \sim Q$	
3.	S	$/\therefore \sim P$
4.	$\sim Q$	2, 3, MP
5.	$\sim Q \vee \sim R$	4, ADD
6.	$\sim(Q \,\&\, R)$	5, DEM
7.	$\sim P$	1, 6, MT

We began by wanting ~P as our conclusion. If we're familiar with modus tollens, it's clear from line 1 that we can get ~P if we can get the negation of line 1's consequent, which would be ~(Q & R). That in turn is the same as ~Q ∨ ~R, which we can get if we can get either ~Q or ~R. So now we're looking for someplace in the first three premises where we can get ~Q. That's easy: from lines 2 and 3, by modus ponens. A little practice and you'll be surprised how easy these strategies are to use, at least *most* of the time!

Exercise 9-8

The annotations that explain how each line was derived have been left off the following deductions. For each line, supply the rule used and the numbers of any earlier lines the rule requires.

▲ **1.**
1. P → Q (Premise)
2. R → S (Premise)
3. Q → ~S (Premise) /∴P → ~R
4. P → ~S
5. ~S → ~R
6. P → ~R

2.
1. ~P (Premise)
2. (Q → R) & (R → Q) (Premise)
3. R ∨ P (Premise) /∴Q
4. R
5. R → Q
6. Q

3.
1. P → Q (Premise)
2. R → (~S ∨ T) (Premise)
3. ~P → R (Premise) /∴(~Q & S) → T
4. ~Q → ~P
5. ~Q → R
6. ~Q → (~S ∨ T)
7. ~Q → (S → T)
8. (~Q & S) → T

▲ **4.**
1. (P & Q) → T (Premise)
2. P (Premise)
3. ~Q → ~P (Premise) /∴T
4. P → Q
5. Q
6. P & Q
7. T

5.
1. ~(S ∨ R) (Premise)
2. P → S (Premise)
3. T → (P ∨ R) (Premise) /∴~T
4. ~S & ~R
5. ~S
6. ~P
7. ~R

8. ~P & ~R
9. ~(P ∨ R)
10. ~T

Exercise 9-9

Derive the indicated conclusions from the premises supplied.

▲ **1.** 1. P & Q
2. P→R /∴R

▲ **2.** 1. R → S
2. ~P ∨ R /∴P → S

3. 1. P ∨ Q
2. R & ~Q /∴P

▲ **4.** 1. ~P ∨ (~Q ∨ R)
2. P /∴Q → R

5. 1. T ∨ P
2. P → S /∴~T → S

6. 1. Q ∨ ~S
2. Q → P /∴S → P

7. 1. ~S ∨ ~R
2. P → (S & R) /∴~P

▲ **8.** 1. ~Q & (~S & ~T)
2. P → (Q ∨ S) /∴~P

9. 1. P ∨ (S & R)
2. T → (~P & ~R) /∴~T

10. 1. (S & P) → R
2. S /∴P → R

Exercise 9-10

Derive the indicated conclusions from the premises supplied.

▲ **1.** 1. P → R
2. R → Q /∴~P ∨ Q

2. 1. ~P ∨ S
2. ~T → ~S /∴P → T

3. 1. F → R
2. L → S
3. ~C
4. (R & S) → C /∴~F ∨ ~L

▲ **4.** 1. P ∨ (Q & R)
2. (P ∨ Q) → S /∴S

5. 1. (S & R) → P
2. (R → P) → W
3. S /∴W

6. 1. ~L → (~P → M)
2. ~(P ∨ L) /∴M

▲ **7.** 1. (M ∨ R) & P
2. ~S → ~P
3. S → ~M /∴R

8. 1. Q → L
2. P → M
3. R ∨ P
4. R → (Q & S) /∴~M → L

9. 1. Q → S
2. P → (S & L)
3. ~P → Q
4. S → R /∴R & S

▲ **10.** 1. P ∨ (R & Q)
2. R → ~P
3. Q → T /∴R → T

Conditional Proof

Conditional proof (CP) is both a rule and a strategy for constructing a deduction. It is based on the following idea: Let's say we want to produce a deduction for a conditional claim, P → Q. If we produce such a deduction, what have we proved? We've proved the equivalent of "If P were true, then Q would be true." One way to do this is simply to *assume* that P is true (that is, to add it as an additional premise) and then to prove that, on that assumption, Q has to be true. If we can do that—prove Q after assuming P—then we'll have proved that if P then Q, or P → Q. Let's look at an example of how to do this; then we'll explain it again.

Here is the way we'll use CP as a new rule: Simply write down the antecedent of whatever conditional we want to prove, drawing a circle around the number of that step in the deduction; in the annotation, write "CP Premise" for that step. Here's what it looks like:

1. P ∨ (Q → R) Premise
2. Q Premise /∴~P → R
(3.) ~P CP Premise

Then, after we've proved what we want—the consequent of the conditional—in the next step, we write the full conditional down. Then we draw a line in the margin to the left of the deduction from the premise with the circled number to the number of the line we deduced from it. (See below for an example.) In the annotation for the last line in the process, list *all the steps from the circled number to the one with the conditional's consequent,* and give CP as the rule. Drawing the line that connects our earlier CP premise with the step we derived from it indicates we've stopped making the assumption that the premise, which is now the antecedent of our conditional in our last step, is true. This is known as *discharging the premise.* Here's how the whole thing looks:

1. P ∨ (Q → R) Premise
2. Q Premise /∴~P → R
(3.) ~P CP Premise
4. Q → R 1, 3, DA
5. R 2, 4, MP
6. ~P → R 3–5, CP

Here's the promised second explanation. Look at the example. Think of the conclusion as saying that, given the two original premises, *if* we had ~P, we could get R. One way to find out if this is so is to *give ourselves* ~P and then see if we can get R. In step 3, we do exactly that: We give ourselves ~P. Now, by circling the number, we indicate that *this is a premise we've given ourselves* (our "CP premise") and therefore that it's one we'll have to get rid of before we're done. (We can't be allowed to invent, use, and keep just any old premises we like—we could prove *anything* if we could do that.) But once we've given ourselves ~P, getting R turns out to be easy! Steps 4 and 5 are pretty obvious, aren't they? (If not, you need more practice with the other rules.) In steps 3 through 5 what we've actually proved is that *if* we had ~P, then we could get R. So we're justified in writing down step 6 because that's exactly what step 6 says: If ~P, then R.

Once we've got our conditional, ~P→R, we're no longer dependent on the CP premise, so we draw our line in the left margin from the last step that depended on the CP premise back to the premise itself. We *discharge* the premise.

Here are some very important restrictions on the CP rule:

1. CP can be used only to produce a conditional claim: After we discharge a CP premise, the very next step must be a conditional with the preceding step as consequent and the CP premise as antecedent. [Remember that lots of claims are equivalent to conditional claims. For example, to get (~P ∨ Q), just prove (P → Q), and then use IMPL.]

2. If more than one use is made of CP at a time—that is, if more than one CP premise is brought in—they must be discharged in exactly the reverse order from that in which they were assumed. This means that the lines that run from different CP premises must not cross each other. See examples below.

3. Once a CP premise has been discharged, no steps derived from it—those steps encompassed by the line drawn in the left margin—may be used in the deduction. (They depend on the CP premise, you see, and it's been discharged.)

4. All CP premises must be discharged.

This sounds a lot more complicated than it actually is. Refer back to these restrictions on CP as you go through the examples, and they will make a good deal more sense.

Here's an example of CP in which two additional premises are assumed and discharged in reverse order.

1.	P → [Q ∨ (R & S)]	Premise	
2.	(~Q → S) → T	Premise	/∴P → T
③	P	CP Premise	
4.	Q ∨ (R & S)	1, 3, MP	
⑤	~Q	CP Premise	
6.	R & S	4, 5, DA	
7.	S	6, SIM	
8.	~Q → S	5–7, CP	
9.	T	2, 8, MP	
10.	P → T	3–9, CP	

Notice that the additional premise added at step 5 is discharged when step 8 is completed, and the premise at step 3 is discharged when step 10 is completed. Once again: Whenever you discharge a premise, you must make that premise the antecedent of the next step in your deduction. (You might try the preceding deduction without using CP; doing so will help you appreciate having the rule, however hard to learn it may seem at the moment. Using CP makes many deductions shorter, easier, or both.)

Here are three more examples of the correct use of CP:

1.	(R → ~P) → S	Premise	
2.	S → (T ∨ Q)	Premise	/∴~(R & P) → (T ∨ Q)
(3.)	~(R & P)	CP Premise	
4.	~R ∨ ~P	3, DEM	
5.	R → ~P	4, IMPL	
6.	S	1, 5, MP	
7.	(T ∨ Q)	2, 6, MP	
8.	~(R & P) → (T ∨ Q)	3–7, CP	

In this case, one use of CP follows another:

1.	(P ∨ Q) → R	Premise	
2.	(S ∨ T) → U	Premise	/∴(~R → ~P) & (~U → ~T)
(3.)	~R	CP Premise	
4.	~(P ∨ Q)	1, 3, MT	
5.	~P & ~Q	4, DEM	
6.	~P	5, SIM	
7.	~R → ~P	3–6, CP	
(8.)	~U	CP Premise	
9.	~(S ∨ T)	2, 8, MT	
10.	~S & ~T	9, DEM	
11.	~T	10, SIM	
12.	~U → ~T	8–11, CP	
13.	(~R → ~P) & (~U → ~T)	7, 12, CONJ	

In this case, one use of CP occurs "inside" another:

1.	R → (S & Q)	Premise	
2.	P → M	Premise	
3.	S → (Q→~M)	Premise	
4.	(J ∨ T) → B	Premise	/∴R → (J → (B & ~P))
(5.)	R	CP Premise	
(6.)	J	CP Premise	
7.	J ∨ T	6, ADD	
8.	B	4, 7, MP	
9.	(S & Q)	1, 5, MP	
10.	(S & Q) → ~M	3, EXP	
11.	~M	9, 10, MP	
12.	~P	2, 11, MT	
13.	B & ~P	8, 12, CONJ	
14.	J → (B & ~P)	6–13, CP	
15.	R → (J → (B & ~P))	5–14, CP	

Before ending this section on deductions, we should point out that our system of truth-functional logic has a couple of properties that are of great theoretical interest: It is both sound and complete. To say that a logic system is sound (in the sense most important to us here) is to say that *every deduction that can be constructed using the rules of the system constitutes a valid argument.* Another way to say this is that no deduction or string of deductions allows us to begin with true sentences and wind up with false ones.

To say that our system is complete is to say that *for every truth-functionally valid argument that there is (or even could be), there is a deduction in our system of rules that allows us to deduce the conclusion of that argument from its premises.* That is, if conclusion C really does follow validly from premises P and Q, then we know for certain that it is possible to construct a deduction beginning with just P and Q and ending with C.

We could have produced a system that is both sound and complete and that had many fewer rules than our system has. However, in such systems, deductions tend to be very difficult to construct. Although our system is burdened with a fairly large number of rules, once you learn them, producing proofs is not too difficult. So, in a way, every system of logic is a trade-off of a sort. You can make the system small and elegant but difficult to use, or you can make it larger and less elegant but more efficient in actual use. (The smaller systems are more efficient for some purposes, but those purposes are quite different from ours in this book.)

Recap

The following topics were covered in Chapter 9:

- Truth-functional symbols, their truth tables, and their English counterparts: negation, conjunction, disjunction, conditional (see chart, p. 291 for a summary.
- Symbolizations of truth functions can represent electrical circuits because "true" and "false" for sentences can be made to correspond to "on" and "off" for circuits.
- Sentences in normal English can be symbolized by claim letters and our four truth-functional symbols; care is required to make sure the result is equivalent.
- The truth-table method and the short truth-table method both allow us to determine whether an argument is truth-functionally valid.
- Certain elementary valid argument forms and equivalences are helpful in determining the validity of arguments (see chart, p. 318 for a summary).
- Deductions can be used to prove the validity of truth-functional arguments; they make use of the rules on the chart, p. 318, and the rule of conditional proof, p. 321.

Additional Exercises

Exercise 9-11

Display the truth-functional structure of the following claims by symbolizing them. Use the letters indicated.

D = We do something to reduce the deficit.
B = The balance of payments gets worse.
C = There is (or will be) a financial crisis.

▲ 1. The balance of payments will not get worse if we do something to reduce the deficit.

2. There will be no financial crisis unless the balance of payments gets worse.

3. Either the balance of payments will get worse or, if no action is taken on the deficit, there will be a financial crisis.

▲ 4. The balance of payments will get worse only if we don't do something to reduce the deficit.

5. Action cannot be taken on the deficit if there's a financial crisis.

6. I can tell you about whether we'll do something to reduce the deficit and whether our balance of payments will get worse: Neither one will happen.

▲ 7. In order for there to be a financial crisis, the balance of payments will have to get worse and there will have to be no action taken to reduce the deficit.

8. We can avoid a financial crisis only by taking action on the deficit and keeping the balance of payments from getting worse.

9. The *only* thing that can prevent a financial crisis is our doing something to reduce the deficit.

Exercise 9-12

For each of the numbered claims below, there is exactly one lettered claim that is equivalent. Identify the equivalent claim for each item. (Some lettered claims are equivalent to more than one numbered claim, so it will be necessary to use some letters more than once.)

▲ 1. Oil prices will drop if the OPEC countries increase their production.

2. Oil prices will drop only if the OPEC countries increase their production.

3. Neither will oil prices drop nor will the OPEC countries increase their production.

▲ 4. Oil prices cannot drop unless the OPEC countries increase their production.

5. The only thing that can prevent oil prices dropping is the OPEC countries' increasing their production.

6. A drop in oil prices is necessary for the OPEC countries to increase their production.

▲ 7. All it takes for the OPEC countries to increase their production is a drop in oil prices.

8. The OPEC countries will not increase their production while oil prices drop; each possibility excludes the other.

a. It's not the case that oil prices will drop, and it's not the case that the OPEC countries will increase their production.

b. If OPEC countries increase their production, then oil prices will drop.

c. Only if OPEC countries increase their production will oil prices drop.

d. Either the OPEC countries will not increase their production, or oil prices will not drop.

e. If the OPEC countries do not increase production, then oil prices will drop.

Exercise 9-13

Construct deductions for each of the following. (Try these first without using conditional proof.)

▲ **1.** 1. P
2. Q & R
3. (Q & P) → S   /∴S

2. 1. (P ∨ Q) & R
2. (R & P) → S
3. (Q & R) → S   /∴S

3. 1. P → (Q → ~R)
2. (~R → S) ∨ T
3. ~T & P   /∴Q → S

▲ **4.** 1. P ∨ Q
2. (Q ∨ U) → (P → T)
3. ~P
4. (~P ∨ R) → (Q → S)   /∴T ∨ S

5. 1. (P → Q) & R
2. ~S
3. S ∨ (Q → S)   /∴P → T

6. 1. P → (Q & R)
2. R → (Q → S)   /∴P → S

▲ **7.** 1. P → Q   /∴P → (Q ∨ R)

8. 1. ~P ∨ ~Q
2. (Q → S) → R   /∴P → R

9. 1. S
2. P → (Q & R)
3. Q → ~S   /∴~P

▲ **10.** 1. (S → Q) → ~R
2. (P→Q) → R   /∴~Q

Exercise 9-14

Use the rule of conditional proof to construct deductions for each of the following.

▲ **1.** 1. P → Q
2. P → R   /∴P → (Q & R)

2. 1. P → Q
2. R → Q   /∴(P ∨ R) → Q

3. 1. P → (Q → R)   /∴(P → Q) → (P → R)

▲ **4.** 1. P → (Q ∨ R)
2. T → (S & ~R) /∴(P & T) → Q

5. 1. ~P → (~Q → ~R)
2. ~(R & ~P) → ~S /∴S → Q

6. 1. P → (Q → R)
2. (T → S) & (R → T) /∴P → (Q → S)

▲ **7.** 1. P ∨ (Q & R)
2. T → ~(P ∨ U)
3. S → (Q → ~R) /∴~S ∨ ~T

8. 1. (P ∨ Q) → R
2. (P → S) → T /∴R ∨ T

9. 1. P → ~Q
2. ~R → (S & Q) /∴P → R

▲ **10.** 1. (P & Q) ∨ R
2. ~R ∨ Q /∴P → Q

Exercise 9-15

Display the truth-functional form of the following arguments by symbolizing them; then use the truth-table method, the short truth-table method, or the method of deduction to prove them valid or invalid. Use the letters provided. (We've used underscores in the example and in the first two problems to help you connect the letters with the proper claims.)

Example

If Maria does not go to the movies, then she will help Bob with his logic homework. Bob will fail the course unless Maria helps him with his logic homework. Therefore, if Maria goes to the movies, Bob will fail the course. (M, H, F)

Symbolization

1. ~M → H (Premise)
2. ~H → F (Premise) /∴M → F

Truth Table

M	H	F	~M	~H	~M→H	~H→F	M→F
T	T	T	F	F	T	T	T
T	T	F	F	F	T	T	F

We need to go only as far as the second row of the table, since both premises come out true and the conclusion comes out false in that row.

▲ **1.** If it's cold, Dale's motorcycle won't start. If Dale is not late for work, then his motorcycle must have started. Therefore, if it's cold, Dale is late for work. (C, S, L)

2. If profits depend on unsound environmental practices, then either the quality of the environment will deteriorate, or profits will drop. Jobs will be plentiful only if profits do not drop. So, either jobs will not be plentiful, or the quality of the environment will deteriorate. (U, Q, D, J)

3. The new road will not be built unless the planning commission approves the funds. But the planning commission's approval of the funds will come only if the environmental impact report is positive, and it can't be positive if the road will ruin Mill Creek. So, unless they find a way for the road not to ruin Mill Creek, it won't be built. (R, A, E, M)

▲ **4.** The message will not be understood unless the code is broken. The killer will not be caught if the message is not understood. Either the code will be broken, or Holmes's plan will fail. But Holmes's plan will not fail if he is given enough time. Therefore, if Holmes is given enough time, the killer will be caught. (M, C, K, H, T)

5. If the senator votes against this bill, then he is opposed to penalties against tax evaders. Also, if the senator is a tax evader himself, then he is opposed to penalties against tax evaders. Therefore, if the senator votes against this bill, he is a tax evader himself. (V, O, T)

6. If you had gone to class, taken good notes, and studied the text, you'd have done well on the exam. And, if you'd done well on the exam, you'd have passed the course. Since you did not pass the course and you did go to class, you must not have taken good notes and not studied the text.

▲ **7.** Either John will go to class, or he'll miss the review session. If John misses the review session, he'll foul up the exam. If he goes to class, however, he'll miss his ride home for the weekend. So John's either going to miss his ride home or foul up the exam.

8. If the government's position on fighting crime is correct, then if more people are locked up, then the crime rate should drop. But the crime rate has not dropped despite the fact that we've been locking up record numbers of people. It follows that the government's position on fighting crime is not correct.

9. The creation story in the Book of Genesis is compatible with the theory of evolution, but only if the creation story is not taken literally. If, as most scientists think, there is plenty of evidence for the theory of evolution, the Genesis story cannot be true if it is not compatible with evolution theory. Therefore, if the Genesis story is taken literally, it cannot be true.

▲ **10.** The creation story in the Book of Genesis is compatible with the theory of evolution, but only if the creation story is not taken literally. If there is plenty of evidence for the theory of evolution, which there is, the Genesis story cannot be true if it is not compatible with evolution theory. Therefore, if the Genesis story is taken literally, it cannot be true.

11. If there was no murder committed, then the victim must have been killed by the horse. But the victim could have been killed by the horse only if he, the victim, was trying to injure the horse before the race; and, in that case, there certainly was a crime committed. So, if there was no murder, there was still a crime committed.

12. Holmes cannot catch the train unless he gets to Charing Cross Station by noon; and if he misses the train, Watson will be in danger. Because

Moriarty has thugs watching the station, Holmes can get there by noon only if he goes in disguise. So, unless Holmes goes in disguise, Watson will be in danger.

▲ 13. It's not fair to smoke around nonsmokers if secondhand cigarette smoke really is harmful. If secondhand smoke were not harmful, the American Lung Association would not be telling us that it is. But they are telling us that it's harmful. That's enough to conclude that it's not fair to smoke around nonsmokers.

14. If Jane does any of the following, she's got an eating disorder: If she goes on eating binges for no apparent reason, if she looks forward to times when she can eat alone, or if she eats sensibly in front of others and makes up for it when she's alone. Jane does in fact go on eating binges for no apparent reason. So it's clear that she has an eating disorder.

15. The number of business majors increased markedly during the past decade; and if you see that happening, you know that younger people have developed a greater interest in money. Such an interest, unfortunately, means that greed has become a significant motivating force in our society; and if greed has become such a force, charity will have become insignificant. We can predict that charity will not be seen as a significant feature of this past decade.

Exercise 9-16

Use the box on page 308 to determine which of the following are valid arguments.

1. If Bobo is smart, then he can do tricks. However, Bobo is not smart. So he cannot do tricks.
2. If God is always on America's side, then America wouldn't have lost any wars. America has lost wars. Therefore, God is not always on America's side.
3. If your theory is correct, then light passing Jupiter will be bent. Light passing Jupiter is bent. Therefore, your theory is correct.
4. Moore eats carrots and broccoli for lunch, and if he does that, he probably is very hungry by dinner time. Conclusion: Moore is very hungry by dinner time.
5. If you value your feet, you won't mow the lawn in your bare feet. Therefore, since you do mow the lawn in your bare feet, we can conclude that you don't value your feet.
6. If Bobo is smart, then he can do tricks; and he can do tricks. Therefore, he is smart.
7. If Charles walked through the rose garden, then he would have mud on his shoes. We can deduce, therefore, that he did walk through the rose garden, because he has mud on his shoes.
8. If it rained earlier, then the sidewalks would still be wet. We can deduce, therefore, that it did rain earlier, because the sidewalks are still wet.
9. If you are pregnant, then you are a woman. We can deduce, therefore, that you are pregnant, because you are a woman.

10. If this stuff is on the final, I will get an A in the class because I really understand it! Further, the teacher told me that this stuff will be on the final, so I know it will be there. Therefore, I know I will get an A in the class.

11. If side A has an even number, then side B has an odd number, but side A does not have an even number. Therefore, side B does not have an odd number.

12. If side A has an even number, then side B has an odd number, and side B does have an odd number. Therefore, side A has an even number.

13. If the theory is correct, then we would have observed squigglyitis in the specimen. However, we know the theory is not correct. Therefore, we did not observe squigglyitis in the specimen.

14. If the theory is correct, then we would have observed dilation in the specimen. Therefore, since we did not observe dilation in the specimen, we know the theory is not correct.

15. If we observe dilation in the specimen, then we know the theory is correct. We observed dilation—so the theory is correct.

16. If the comet approached within 1 billion miles of the earth, there would have been numerous sightings of it. There weren't numerous sightings. So it did not approach within 1 billion miles.

17. If Baffin Island is larger than Sumatra, then two of the five largest islands in the world are in the Arctic Ocean. And Baffin Island, as it turns out, is about 2 percent larger than Sumatra. Therefore, the Arctic Ocean contains two of the world's largest islands.

18. If the danger of range fires is greater this year than last, then state and federal officials will hire a greater number of firefighters to cope with the danger. Since more firefighters are already being hired this year than were hired all last year, we can be sure that the danger of fires has increased this year.

19. If Jack Davis robbed the Central Pacific Express in 1870, then the authorities imprisoned the right person. But the authorities did not imprison the right person. Therefore, it must have not been Jack Davis who robbed the Central Pacific Express in 1870.

20. If the recent tax cuts had been self-financing, then there would have been no substantial increase in the federal deficit. But they turned out not to be self-financing. Therefore, there will be a substantial increase in the federal deficit.

21. The public did not react favorably to the majority of policies recommended by President Ronald Reagan during his second term. But if his electoral landslide in 1984 had been a mandate for more conservative policies, the public would have reacted favorably to most of those he recommended after the election. Therefore, the 1984 vote was not considered a mandate for more conservative policies.

22. Alexander will finish his book by tomorrow afternoon only if he is an accomplished speed reader. Fortunately for him, he is quite accomplished at speed reading. Therefore, he will get his book finished by tomorrow afternoon.

23. If higher education were living up to its responsibilities, the five best-selling magazines on American campuses would not be *Cosmopolitan, People, Playboy, Glamour,* and *Vogue.* But those are exactly the magazines that sell best in the nation's college bookstores. Higher education, we can conclude, is failing in at least some of its responsibilities.

24. Broc Glover was considered sure to win if he had no bad luck in the early part of the race. But we've learned that he has had the bad luck to be involved in a crash right after the start, so we're expecting another driver to be the winner.

25. If Boris is really a spy for the KGB, then he has been lying through his teeth about his business in this country. But we can expose his true occupation if he's been lying like that. So, I'm confident that if we can expose his true occupation, we can show that he's really a KGB spy.

26. The alternator is not working properly if the ammeter shows a negative reading. The current reading of the ammeter is negative. So, the alternator is not working properly.

27. Fewer than 2 percent of the employees of New York City's Transit Authority are accountable to management. If such a small number of employees are accountable to the management of the organization, no improvement in the system's efficiency can be expected in the near future. So, we cannot expect any such improvements any time soon.

28. If Charles did not pay his taxes, then he did not receive a refund. Thus, he did not pay his taxes, since he did not receive a refund.

29. If they wanted to go to the party, then they would have called by now. But they haven't, so they didn't.

30. "You'll get an A in the class," she predicted.
"What makes you say that?" he asked.
"Because," she said, "if you get an A, then you're smart, and you *are* smart."

31. If Florin arrived home by eight, she received the call from her attorney. But she did not get home by eight, so she must have missed her attorney's call.

32. The acid rain problem will be solved, but only if the administration stops talking and starts acting. So far, however, all we've had from the president is words. Words are cheap. Action is what counts. The problem will not be remedied, at least not while this administration is in office.

Writing Exercises

1. a. In a one-page essay, evaluate the soundness of the argument in the box on page 305. Alternatively, in a one-page essay evaluate the soundness of the argument in the box on p. 313. Write your name on the back of your paper.
b. When everyone is finished, your instructor will collect the papers and redistribute them to the class. In groups of four or five, read the papers

that have been given to your group and select the best one. The instructor will select one group's top-rated paper to read to the class for discussion.

2. Take about fifteen minutes to write an essay responding to the paper the instructor has read to the class in Exercise 1. When everyone is finished, the members of each group will read each other's responses and select the best one to share with the class.

Chapter 10

Inductive Arguments

Important public health decisions always depend on inductive reasoning—in this case projections about the spread of H5N1 avian influenza—and assumptions about causes and cures. This chapter discusses inductive reasoning; the next chapter discusses the reasoning we use to reach conclusions about cause and effect.

In July 2002, George Kapidian, of New Braunfels, Texas, lost his new home in a devastating flood. After four days of violent thunderstorms around San Antonio, the Guadalupe River rose twenty feet—flooding Mr. Kapidian's house and destroying everything in it. Seven people died in the raging floodwaters.

Seventy-two-year-old Mr. Kapidian should have known better. He was aware that the area was subject to flooding; in fact, his house was built on the foundation of a house washed away by a flood just three years earlier. But when he bought the house he reasoned, "What are the odds it would happen again?"

People often think this way, and the old saying "lightning never strikes twice in the same place" would seem to confirm their reasoning—if it were true. But it isn't true, and this kind of thinking can have unfortunate consequences. For example, it would lead one to swim where someone was recently mauled by a shark because, after all, "What are the chances it would happen again?" In truth, the odds are greater that it will happen again at this beach than at a beach where there has been no shark attack.

Do you believe this? Try the idea out on someone who works at a fire lookout on a mountaintop in thunderstorms.

Lightning never strikes the same place twice.

When we try to predict the future, we are reasoning inductively; we are producing inductive arguments. George Kapidian was trying to do this, though he was doing a poor job of it. That there had been flooding where he built his house made it more likely that it would flood there again, not less likely.

Inductive reasoning says, basically, these things have or had such-and-such a feature or property, therefore these other things probably will have that property as well. It in effect involves a prediction. It says previous thunderstorms caused the river to flood; therefore other thunderstorms will cause it to flood, too.

Because inductive reasoning involves a prediction, the premises of an inductive argument at best *support* a conclusion with a degree of *probability*; they do *not* demonstrate or prove it with certainty. No prediction is 100 percent certain; even if the Guadalupe River had flooded every July in recorded history, it still wouldn't be 100 percent certain that it would flood again this July.

If an inductive argument succeeds in showing that the conclusion probably is true, it is said to be *strong*. "Very few people live to be over 100; therefore you won't live to be over 100" is a strong argument. By contrast, if the argument provides little or no reason for thinking that the conclusion is true, the argument is *weak*. But "strong" and "weak" are matters of degree: Facts about life expectancy make it a better bet (stronger argument) that you will live to be 60 than that you will live to be 90.

Being able to reason well inductively is the key to success; in fact, it is the key to survival. That's because, to a certain extent, you must make predictions to survive. If you cannot predict what will happen if you drink arsenic or stick your finger into an electrical outlet, you will be in trouble. It is inductive reasoning that tells us not to repeat past mistakes—at least it does if we are reasoning well. It tells us not to pour gasoline on a fire and to wear gloves when we handle rose bushes or barbed wire. It tells us, or should tell us, not to build a house on the foundation of one that was swept away in a flood three years ago.

Unfortunately, people do not always reason well inductively. Each semester we encounter students who fail the first midterm but don't change their study habits. They then seem surprised when they fail the second midterm. Perhaps, like George Kapidian, they say to themselves "Hey, what are the odds this will happen again?"

We read recently about the Mid/East Acceptance Corporation, of Raleigh, N.C., a repossession company. When Jackie L. Eley missed two payments on her pickup, Mid/East swung into action and repossessed the vehicle, refusing to let her unload 130 watermelons she had in the bed. Later that day, they also refused to let her retrieve the melons from their storage yard. Unfortunately, this occurred in July, when the daytime temperature and humidity were both near 100, and within two days the melons rotted, creating a horrid mess and overpowering stench. At this point, Mid/East demanded that Eley remove the melons or pay someone to do so. She, understandably, refused; the case went to court and eventually Mid/East was ordered to pay Eley $1,365—three times the value of the melons—as well as legal fees. Well, this is what happens to unrefrigerated fruit in the July heat. If Mid/East had reasoned inductively, they would have known that they would have a problem on their hands when they refused to allow Ms. Eley to unload her melons.*

*Reported by Patricia Porter, Associated Press, July 8, 2005.

Now, before we discuss principles for evaluating the strength of inductive arguments, we should look at three more examples of this type of reasoning.

Three Examples of Inductive Arguments
Parker has had a Harley-Davidson motorcycle for years, and recently there was one for sale down the street that he was trying to talk Moore into buying. In truth, Moore has as much interest in motorcycles as he has in worm casts, which is to say, none whatsoever. In addition, he has noted that Parker's motorcycle leaks oil all over the place, making a mess. "I don't want oil all over my garage floor," he tells Parker. This is an inductive argument on Moore's part; he has made a prediction based on what he knows about Parker's motorcycle to what probably would be, or at least might be true of the motorcycle Parker wants him to buy. "Parker's Harley-Davidson has this property; therefore this other Harley-Davidson might well have this property"—that is the argument. This argument is what is called an *analogical argument.* We'll explain below.

Second example: One of us has a new neighbor, and the new neighbor has a dog. On the very first day after the neighbor moved in, his dog barked at the author when he took out his trash. The same thing happened on the second day, and again on the third day. The author thus expected the dog to bark at him when he took out the trash the next time. He had reasoned inductively from what happened before to what would (probably) happen in the future. The past trash-removing occasions had a certain property (dog barking); therefore the next trash-removing occasion would also have this property. This, too, is an analogical argument.

Last example: If you buy a batch of okay-looking peaches at A&P, but they turn out to be mushy, we assume you would not buy more peaches there for a while. You would, we assume, figure the rest of the current batch of peaches at the A&P, or at least many of them, probably are also mushy. Here, too, you are making a prediction; your thinking is that the peaches you bought have this undesirable property; therefore most or all of the current A&P peaches will have that property. This is an example of an *inductive generalization.*

If you have the feeling that these three arguments are very, very similar, you would be right. In the next section, we will look at analogical arguments, and in the section after that we will look at inductive generalizations.

ANALOGICAL ARGUMENTS

In the case of an **analogical argument**—or argument by analogy—we are generally drawing a conclusion about a single thing by comparing it to another, similar thing. In the motorcycle example above, Moore is comparing Parker's motorcycle to the one Parker wants him to buy. These items being compared are known as the **terms of the analogy.** (While there are often only two terms in an analogical argument, there can be more, as we'll see in a moment.) One of the terms, the one about which we draw the conclusion, is the **target.** In the above argument, the motorcycle Parker wants Moore to buy is the target. The issue in this case is whether the target motorcycle will leak oil. Leaking oil is said to be the "property in question" or "feature in question"—properties and

■ Inductive reasoning is at the heart of conclusions we reach about things around us. Take this truck. Reasoning from our past encounters with people who drive vehicles like this, we'd consider each of the following conclusions likely: The owner of this vehicle: 1) is a male, 2) doesn't worry about global warming, any other environmental problem, or his cholesterol level, 3) doesn't play chess.

features being the same thing. The **property (or feature) in question** is the property attributed to the target in the conclusion of the argument. Okay, do you have the terminology down? You will by the time we discuss a few more examples.

Look back to the barking dog case. The terms of the analogy are the four occasions of taking out the trash: Let's say Monday, Tuesday, Wednesday, and Thursday. Thursday's taking out of the trash is the target occasion, because it's the one about which you draw the conclusion: The dog will bark on this occasion as it has on the others; and it's the dog's barking at you that is the property in question.

With this bit of terminology digested, let's set out the general principle on which analogical arguments are based:

> The more similar the terms of the analogy, the higher the probability that the conclusion is true.

So, similarities between the target and the other term or terms of the analogy make the argument stronger; and, of course, dissimilarities between these items make the argument weaker.

With this principle in mind, let's look back at our other examples. In the motorcycle example, it should be clear that the more the target motorcycle resembles Parker's, the more likely it will be that it will leak oil just like Parker's. Lots of relevant similarities will make Moore's conclusion more likely to be true, and this will give him a good reason not to buy the cycle. (He may have lots of other reasons—not being as inclined as Parker to risk his life needlessly, for example—but that's another matter.) If the cycle is about the same age as Parker's, this is an important similarity; if they are in similar condition, this is another. You can probably think of others that are equally relevant.

When you take out the trash on Thursday, are the conditions the same as on the previous three days? Is it the same time of day, for example? If so, this similarity makes the argument stronger than it would be otherwise. Were the neighbors gone the first three days of the week but are home now? If so, this dissimilarity makes the argument weaker than it would be otherwise. Is there a chance that someone has shot the barking dog in the last twenty-four hours? If so, . . . well, you get the idea.

A peculiarity of arguments by analogy occurs when we consider a feature of the target that we don't know about. Strong arguments require strong similarities, we've said, but what if we don't know whether the target has such-and-such a feature? In that case, we get the strongest argument if the other terms of the analogy are varied—that is, if some have the feature and some do not. For example, if we don't know what time of day you're going to take the garbage out Thursday, then the conclusion that the dog will bark at you is more likely if he has barked at you at *various* times in previous days rather than always at the same time. Of course, if we do know you'll be taking the garbage out early in the morning, then the argument is strongest if your earlier episodes happened at a similar time.

Real Life

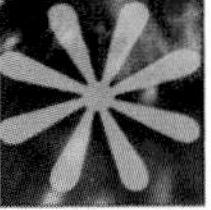

Bears!

The following was adapted from a financial advice newsletter: Most people who know about bears in the wild know that the best tactic to take when you and a bear come across each other is to hold stock still. Any motion is likely to cause the bear to become interested in you, something you definitely do not want. So, don't move until the danger is past.

What goes for bears also goes for bear markets: When threatened by falling prices, the best thing to do is nothing at all. Simply waiting the danger out is the safest policy. The time to review your portfolio is after the immediate danger is past, not while it is staring you in the face.

Comment: Although a lot of people might take this for an argument by analogy, it isn't. (Or, if someone insisted on taking it that way, it's a perfectly *terrible* argument.) That what this writer advises for bear markets happens to resemble the proper tactic for real bears is a matter of coincidence. The terms of this analogy allow for no conclusion at all!

Before going on to generalizations, one last point: Not all analogies are *arguments* by analogy. Indeed, it's probably true that the great majority of them are not. Some are explanatory analogies, designed to help explain something, and some are simply interesting comparisons, not designed to do much at all except point out a similarity. Many analogies also are rhetorical, intended primarily to express or evoke a positive or negative feeling about something. (We discussed rhetorical analogies in detail in Chapter 4.) If you remember that arguments are offered to support a conclusion, to give a reason or reasons for thinking that conclusion is true, it will help you sort analogical arguments out from other uses of analogy. Have a look at the "Bears!" box for a nice example.

INDUCTIVE GENERALIZATIONS

We noticed that analogical arguments usually have a single thing (or event or occasion) as a target. The next type of argument we'll look at, inductive generalizations (or simply "generalizations," for short), *always* has a class of things, events, or occasions as a target. And when we construct this type of argument, we always argue *from* a sample taken from the target class *to* the target class as a whole. One more time: In an **inductive generalization,** we base our reasoning on what we know about a **sample** taken from a class and we draw a conclusion about the entire **target class.** Our peaches example from a while back was a generalization. The target class was the entire batch of peaches at the A&P, and the sample was the peaches you bought from that batch. Based on your knowledge of the sample, you reached the conclusion that the whole batch was probably going to be mushy.

The connection between analogical arguments and inductive generalizations is a close one; indeed, they overlap, in a manner of speaking. We can see this if we change the conclusion of the peaches argument from one about the whole batch, "all the peaches in this batch are mushy," to a conclusion about a single peach, "the next peach I pick from that batch will be mushy." This turns it into an analogical argument. If we have a strong argument that the entire batch of peaches is mushy, then certainly we have at least as strong an argument that the next peach we select from that batch will be mushy.

We saw that it was similarities between the terms of an analogical argument that made it strong. Inductive generalizations draw their strength from similarities between the sample and the entire target class. But, since in generalizations the sample is *drawn from* the target, we use the term "representative" to describe these similarities. A sample is said to be **representative** when it is similar to the target class in all relevant respects. For example, if you had taken all the peaches you bought from the bottom of the bin, that's a significant difference between the sample and the target, since the target includes peaches on top and in the middle of the bin as well as those on the bottom. In such a case, we'd say your sample was not representative of the target in at least one relevant respect, and this would make the conclusion that *all* the peaches in the bin are mushy less likely; it would weaken your argument. Here's the general principle:

> **The more representative the sample of an inductive generalization is of the target, the stronger the argument (i.e., the more likely the conclusion is to be true.)**

When people generalize from a sample that is significantly different from the target in one or more relevant respects, they are said to be arguing from a **biased sample.** If some of the peaches in the sample had come from the bottom of the bin, some from the middle, and some from the top, this particular bias in the sample could have been avoided because a sample selected in this way would probably be more like the target class as a whole. The more representative sample that resulted would have produced a stronger argument.

It may seem to you that this business of a sample being representative is a lot like what we were talking about before when we said that analogical arguments are stronger when the target is more similar to the other term or terms of the analogy. If so, you're exactly right. Similarity of terms in an analogical argument amounts to the same thing as representativeness of the sample in a generalization.

It may occur to you that larger samples should produce stronger arguments than smaller ones, and you would be right, at least up to a point. But larger samples are mainly useful because they are more representative, or at least more likely to be representative, than small ones. A large sample, if it is biased, is of no more use, and in fact less use, than a small one that is not biased. But, given that equal efforts are made to keep bias out of a sampling method (and we'll see how this can be done in a minute), we can make the following rule:

> **Generally speaking, the larger the sample, the stronger the argument (i.e., the more likely that the conclusion is true.)**

If we can make one final reference to those (by now deteriorating) peaches, this rule tells us that, other things being equal, a larger sample of mushy ones will make it more likely that the whole batch is mushy than if we had a smaller sample.

This rule is most frequently applied to inductive generalizations, but it can also come into play in analogical arguments as well. If the wretched dog in our example has barked at you *ten* days in a row instead of *four,* it makes it more likely that he'll bark at you today when you take out the garbage (including those peaches). If Moore knows several people besides Parker who own Harleys that all leak oil, then it's more likely that if he buys the bike Parker is pushing him to buy he'll need a bag of kitty litter for his garage floor because it will leak like the rest of them.

So, let's sum up what we've got so far. Both analogical arguments and inductive generalizations are made stronger by similarities between the items we know about and the target; this is referred to as "representativeness" in the case of generalizations. Also, both types of argument are made stronger by having a larger number of items we know something about—that is, that we now have the property in question. This is expressed as having more terms in the analogy in the first case* and as having a bigger sample in the second.

Our two rules work together, but the first is more important. The crucial requirement for analogies is that the target be similar to the other terms; the crucial thing for generalizations is that the sample be representative of the target class. We simply cannot produce dependable arguments if we are arguing from something or some group of things that is different in some significant way from our target; even a generalization with a huge sample is unreliable if it fails to be representative. On the other hand, a sample consisting of just a single item can warrant a generalization to an entire class if that item is sufficiently similar to the other items in the class. If one copy of a book has a misprint on page 327, then it is extremely likely that every other copy of the book from that printing has a similar misprint. (If we know that all the items in a target class are exactly similar, then we get a different kind of situation. See the box titled "Typical Sample Cases: Deduction in Disguise.")

However, if the items in the class of things we are concerned about are not known to be homogeneous or are known to be nonhomogeneous, then we cannot get away with a small sample. For example, to draw conclusions about the political views of, say, Canadian truck drivers, we'd need a sample large enough to represent the diverse array of personalities, socioeconomic levels, educational background, life experiences, and so forth, that are found in such

*In analogical arguments, we could (and did, in previous editions) refer to the terms of the analogy that we compare to the target item as a "sample." (Parker's motorcycle is the sample; the one Moore is considering is the target.) This maintains the parallel with generalizations, but doing so leads to the question of what class it's a sample *from,* and that question can lead to unnecessary complications.

In Depth

Typical Sample Cases: Deduction in Disguise

Let's say you want to know whether gold is denser than lead. To find out, you take exactly one cubic centimeter of gold and the same volume of lead, and you place them on the two sides of a balance scale. The weighing shows that the cubic centimeter of gold is heavier than the lead (in fact, the weight of the lead is about 59 percent of that of the gold). You then conclude that, as a matter of fact, gold in general is more dense than lead—that is, that *every instance* of gold is more dense than *every instance* of lead.

Are you committing the fallacy of hasty generalization by basing your conclusion on only one case? No, of course not. The reason is that you can safely assume that every instance of gold is similar in density to every other instance of gold and that instances of lead are likewise similar with regard to properties like density, because gold and lead are elements.

Reasoning such as this is often made out to be a peculiar kind of inductive argument, one where a little sample goes a long way, as it were. In fact, though, arguments like this are really *deductive* arguments in disguise. The assumption that makes the argument inductively strong (namely, that in the matter of density, gold is all alike and so is lead) also makes the argument deductively valid! The argument turns out to be this:

General assumption: All gold is alike with regard to density, and so is all lead.

Result of weighing: This gold is denser than this lead.

Conclusion: Gold is denser than lead.

a large and nonhomogeneous population. How this is accomplished will be explained in a few moments.

FORMAL AND INFORMAL INDUCTIVE ARGUMENTS

Before we go on, we need to separate two levels of inductive argumentation. The first level, and the one that concerns most of us most of the time, is that of everyday, informal arguments. We encounter both generalizations and arguments by analogy at this level, and, if you pay close attention, you'll discover that you are making inferences like these practically all the time. They are integral to our rational process, with many such inferences occurring at a subargumentative level—that is, we don't reach the point of putting our thinking into words (which, you might recall, is a necessary condition of making an argument).

The second level is that of what we might call "scientific" or "formal" argumentation. At this level we find generalizations in the form of public opinion polls, ratings for television and radio stations, and research surveys of all sorts.

There are a couple of obvious differences between formal and informal arguments. First, most formal arguments turn out to be generalizations. You could certainly produce a formal, scientifically controlled argument by analogy, but you just won't happen upon one in your everyday life very often. Second, formal arguments require an attention to detail—including reliance on some moderately sophisticated mathematics—that is usually impossible to achieve and generally not necessary in their informal counterparts. But, as we're going to see, however different they may look, arguments at both levels depend entirely on exactly the same general principles. A long and complicated statistical study of the population decline of spotted owls and a quick inference about whether to return to a restaurant you tried last week are measured against the very same general criteria.

So here's our plan: We're going to make an excursus into formal arguments, explaining how several concepts operate at that level as we trace an example from beginning to end. It may get a little technical along the way, but it isn't really complicated. After the formal treatment, we'll show how the principles at that level have corresponding versions at the informal level and how we apply them to our everyday reasoning.

EXAMPLE OF A FORMAL GENERALIZATION: A POLITICAL POLL

Imagine that you graduate from college one of these days. (We're serious.) You take a position at a survey research firm that does political polling. Your first job is to manage a poll commissioned by a potential candidate for the presidency—say, Jeb Bush, who figures that it's his time to be president, his father and older brother having already had their turn. Bush wants to know whether the Republican voters of New Hampshire would vote for him rather than, say, John McCain in the presidential primary in that state. Your job is to produce a reasonably accurate assessment of public opinion on the issue at the lowest reasonable cost.

Of course, the most accurate way to settle the issue would be to ask all the Republican voters of New Hampshire. But that would be excessively expensive. So you will have to make do with asking a sample of those voters and extending the knowledge gained thereby to a conclusion about the whole class. How well that knowledge will extend to the whole class depends on how good a job you do. The two most important decisions you have to make are these: How will you select the sample so that it is representative of the entire target class of voters? How large will the sample need to be in order to adequately represent that class?

Clearly, it would be a mistake to let the Republicans on the faculty at the University of New Hampshire be the sample, even if doing so would produce a sample of the right size. It would be a mistake because those faculty at UNH are very likely *not* to represent the entire target class. Indeed, they are too different in too many relevant ways from many, many members of the target class. And this is a good place to elaborate a bit on what it means for a sample to be representative of a target. We'll say that *a sample is representative of a target class if, and only if, it possesses all the relevant features of the target class in proportions similar to those of the target class.* We should add that a feature is said to be relevant when it is likely that its presence or absence would affect the presence or absence of the property in question. The following should make this clear.

Let's ask ourselves whether there are features of the Republican UNH faculty that are not features of the entire target class. Sure there are: For example, there is a much higher percentage of advanced degrees among the former than among the latter. Now we ask ourselves, Is the possession of advanced degrees relevant to the property in question (which, you'll recall, is the likelihood of voting for Jeb Bush rather than John McCain)? It is very likely that the level of one's education affects the way a person votes, which means that this feature is relevant. Notice that this doesn't mean that *every* highly educated voter must vote differently from every less educated voter, only that the former *tend* to vote in certain ways somewhat more frequently than the latter.

Some people use statistics like a drunk uses a lamp post, more for support than illumination.

So, by possessing relevant properties that make them different from the target class, the UNH faculty members can't form the sample you want for your survey—they would give you a very biased sample indeed.

Notice also that we don't have to know with absolute certainty that higher levels of education have significant effects on the way a person votes; we only need a strong suspicion. The general rule is, if we're not sure whether a feature is relevant, the safe path is to presume that it *is* relevant. It's a matter of being safe rather than sorry.

You now have a problem: How are you going to find a group that will share relevant features with the entire target class? Setting out to construct such a group (which, as we'll see in the next chapter, actually has to be done sometimes) is a real chore. For starters, we don't usually know what all the relevant features are—Does the age of a Republican in New Hampshire help determine how he or she votes? Probably. Does being left-handed? Probably not. What about being a commuter versus working at home? Who knows? And, even if we knew what all the relevant features are, it would still be a big job getting our sample to exhibit them in just the proportions in which they occur in the target class.

Fortunately for you and the job at hand, there is a method that solves the problem we've been describing. You've probably already figured out what it is: a randomly selected sample. A **random selection process** gives every member of the target class an equal chance of becoming a member of the sample. If we randomly select our sample from the target population, we should, within certain limits, get a sample that possesses all the characteristics of the target class in proportions more or less similar to those found in the target class. We should point out that, as a practical matter, coming up with actual procedures for getting a random selection process can be a difficult problem; statisticians often have to settle for something that works only *pretty* well because it's affordable. Another word on that in a few moments.

RANDOM VARIATION: PROBLEMS AND SOLUTIONS

A lot of people misunderstand what random selection is all about in cases like the ones we're discussing. They often think that randomness is the goal of the process. And indeed it is *a* goal, but it is merely the means by which we try to achieve the *real* goal, which is representativeness. Fortunately, randomness does a pretty good job of helping us reach this goal; unfortunately, it doesn't do a perfect job. In fact, any given randomly selected sample from a target class might misrepresent that target to some extent or other. That is, there's nothing in a sample, even if it is perfectly random, that *guarantees* that it will be representative.

What does this mean for our need to come up with an answer to the question "How many New Hampshire Republican voters would prefer to vote for Bush over McCain?" It means we have to build some "wiggle room" into the answer. Fortunately, there are some perfectly reasonable ways to do that.

For one thing, nobody would expect you and your firm to be able to determine *exactly, to the precise number,* how many voters would prefer Bush. If you can get reasonably close, you'll have done a good job. So, you want to be able to tell the Bush people, "approximately such-and-such percent" prefer one candidate to the other, or "about so-and-so percent" prefer him. Giving yourself this wiggle room is known as providing an "error margin." An **error margin** is a range of percentage points within which an answer is claimed to fall (rather than a precise percentage point or even fraction of a percentage point). The idea is the same here as in the situation where a potential automobile buyer asks a salesman about a car's gas mileage: The salesman should only have to say *approximately* what mileage can be expected, not *exactly* how many miles per gallon one will get. Of course, if the error margin is too big, the survey is useless. If you have to tell the Bush campaign that somewhere between 10 and 90 percent of New Hampshire Republican voters prefer Bush, you haven't given them much for their money, have you? We'll return to this in a moment.

Statistics are like bikinis; what they show is important, but what they hide is vital.

– *Cornell Review*

The second way to make the argument provided by the survey a reasonable one is to allow that there is *some* chance that it might be wrong. Indeed, it would be a rare argument where a person is extending knowledge about a known thing to claims about an unknown thing and where the person would be willing to bet his or her life on the outcome. We don't usually bet the farm unless we *know* we're right. What you want to do here is identify a "confidence level" for your argument. A **confidence level** is a measure of the argument's strength; the higher the confidence level, the more likely the argument's conclusion is to be true. So, we can say that it is "very likely" that such and such a percentage of voters prefer Bush, or we can actually quantify mathematically what percentage of likelihood the conclusion has.

Given that the sample of a survey is randomly selected from the target class, the error margin of the generalization's conclusion and the argument's confidence level are determined entirely by the size of the sample. Here's the principle:

> **As the sample size of a generalization gets larger, either the error margin becomes more narrow, or the confidence level of the argument becomes greater, or a combination of both.**

Notice that this principle relates three variables—sample size, confidence level, and error margin—and shows how they are interdependent. It's very important that you understand how these three factors relate to one another.

Okay. We've determined that your sample of voters in the New Hampshire primary needs to be randomly selected—we're going to leave it to you to determine how to do that, but we'll warn you to be careful: You don't want to make the mistake the *Chicago Daily Tribune* made. (See the box on the following page.)

SAMPLE SIZE

By the end of the last section, we had come back around to the topic of **sample size,** and now it's time to deal with it. When it comes to surveys of the sort we're talking about, the question "How many individuals does the sample need to contain?" has a neat, short answer: somewhere between 1,000

Real Life

The Great Slip-Up of 1948

Because of a strike, the *Chicago Daily Tribune* had to go to press earlier than usual the night of the 1948 presidential election. So they relied on some early returns, some "expert" opinion, and public opinion polls to decide on the famous "Dewey Defeats Truman" headline. But the polls were not sufficiently accurate, as Truman edged Dewey in a narrow upset victory.

and 1,500. You may find it interesting that, no matter what the survey is about, it usually requires between 1,000 and 1,500 in the sample regardless of whether the target class is Republican primary voters in New Hampshire, voters of all parties in New England, citizens of the United States, or human beings on the entire planet. In short, as long as we're not talking about very small target classes (which we can safely ignore, since generalizations like these don't apply to them), the size of the target is not relevant to the size of the sample required. The reason for this will become clear in what follows.

We are not going to discuss the mathematics that lie behind the facts we're describing here, but they are among the most basic mathematics in this field—you can trust them. They guarantee the details that you'll find in Table 10-1, which you should look at now. Notice that the column on the left represents a series of increasing sample sizes. In the second column, we find the error margins that correspond to the various sample sizes expressed as "plus or minus *x* percentage points." This expression is the means by which statisticians express the amount of "wiggle room" an argument requires for its conclusion. The third column just shows the range of percentage points that the error margin produces.

The two most important things to notice about Table 10-1 are, first, that the error margin narrows very quickly as the size of the sample increases from

Table 10.1

Approximate Error Margins for Random Samples of Various Sizes

Confidence level of 95 percent in all cases.

Sample Size	Error Margin (%)	Corresponding Range (Percentage Points)
10	±30	60
25	±22	44
50	±14	28
100	±10	20
250	±6	12
500	±4	8
1,000	±3	6
1,500	±2	4

The error margin decreases rapidly as the sample size begins to increase, but this decrease slows markedly as the sample gets larger. It is usually pointless to increase the sample beyond 1,500 unless there are special requirements of precision or confidence level.

(We presume, both here and in the text, that the target class is large—that is, 10,000 or larger. When the target is small, there is a correction factor that can be applied to determine the appropriate error margin. But most reported polls have large enough targets that we need not concern ourselves with the calculation methods for correcting the error margin here.)

10 to 25 and then to 50, but as we go down the columns the narrowing of the error margin slows down. So, by the time we get to a sample size of 500, with an error margin of plus or minus 4 percent, we have to *double* the sample to 1,000 in order to decrease the error margin by one percentage point, to plus or minus 3 percent. It takes another 500 added to the sample to get it down one more percentage point. (These error margins are approximate; they've been rounded off for convenience's sake.) In order to get the error margin down to, say, 1 percent or less, we have to vastly increase the size of the sample, and for most practical purposes, the gain in a more precise conclusion (one with a narrow error margin) is outweighed by the difficulty and expense of having to add so many new members to the sample. And this explains the claim made above that we very seldom go beyond 1,000 to 1,500 members of a sample—because the trouble of increasing a sample beyond that is hardly worth the modest decrease produced in the error margin.

Now, throughout the preceding paragraphs, we've been making a presumption about confidence levels. We've been presuming that the people who hired you, the Bush campaign, would be satisfied with a 95 percent confidence level for the survey. We chose this figure because it is the standard of the polling industry—if a confidence level is not mentioned in a professionally done poll, the assumption is that it is 95 percent. This means simply that one can be 95 percent sure that the conclusion of the argument does indeed follow from the premises—in other words, that we can have considerable confidence in the conclusion.* If we have a smaller sample, we will, of course, have a lower confidence level or a larger error margin. On the other hand, if it is important to have a confidence level higher than 95 percent, then we need a larger sample, if the error margin is not to be affected.

In general, professional surveying and polling organizations have settled on the 95 percent figure for a standard level of confidence and an error margin of around 3 percentage points. And thus the figure of 1,000 or a little over is the standard sample size for most professionally done scientific polls.

This brings us to the second thing—or, actually, things—you should remember about Table 10.1. You should make a mental note of the three or four lines near the bottom of the table so that, if you run across a survey with a suspiciously small sample, you'll know what kind of error margins it would be reasonable—or unreasonable—to claim for it. We recently saw in a golf magazine that approximately 200 golfers had been surveyed about something or other and that less than half of them, 45 percent, in fact, had agreed with the poll question. Does this mean that less than half of all golfers can be expected to agree with the poll question? Not at all. If it has the usual confidence level, a sample of 200 must have an error margin of around plus or minus 8 percent, which means it may be that as many as 53 percent—a majority—actually agree with the poll question.

INFORMAL INDUCTIVE ARGUMENTS

Most of the inductive arguments we have to deal with in everyday life—both generalizations and arguments by analogy—are most definitely *not* of the formal, scientific variety we've been talking about in the last few pages. The most important difference between formal or scientific inductive arguments on one hand and informal, everyday arguments on the other is that the latter do not make use of randomly selected samples. In everyday inductive reasoning, we make use of whatever is at hand—the Harleys Moore is familiar with, the peaches you bought at the A&P this morning, and the like. For this reason, it should be obvious, we cannot make the kinds of calculations that make formal arguments precise.

Informal Error Margins: "Cautious" Conclusions

But many of the concepts and principles we've described in connection with formal arguments do have their place in their everyday counterparts—they just take a more easygoing form. We probably wouldn't say to a colleague, "Based on my experience in freshman courses, I'd conclude that the grade point for the freshman class is 2.1036." And we're not likely to say to a fishing partner, "Ed, I've looked at the Fish and Game Department statistics, and your chance of catching a fish in that lake that weighs more than three pounds is 12 percent, plus or minus 3 percent." Ed would probably throw us out of the boat. We'd actually say something like, "I'd conclude that the freshman grade point is somewhere around a two-point," or "You're not likely to catch a three-pounder in that lake." These are informal ways of providing error mar-

*If you held our feet to the fire about this, we'd have to say that the *real* meaning of a 95 percent confidence level is that an average of 95 out of every 100 random samples from this target class will have the property in question within the range of the error margin. But this translates into practical terms in the way we've put it in the text.

gins for our inferences. Increasing the informal "error margins" in everyday arguments makes the conclusion more cautious.

Informal Confidence Levels: Hedging Our Bets

In informal arguments we also set informal confidence levels (as distinct from informal error margins) by adjusting the cautiousness of the conclusion. For example, it's more cautious to conclude "there's a good chance" the Yankees will win the pennant than to conclude "You can be pretty sure" the Yankees will win the pennant. "There's a good chance" and "You can be pretty sure" are informal ways of expressing our "confidence level." Obviously, the informal "confidence level" and "error margin" for our conclusion should be appropriate for the premises of our argument. If the Yankees have won only 40 games, we must be more cautious in concluding they will win the pennant than if they won over a hundred.

Summing Up: Evaluating Inductive Generalizations and Analogical Arguments

When all is said and done, the issue of whether we have a strong inductive generalization (or analogical argument) or a weak one, or something in between, can be reduced to three key questions:

1. Are the sample and the target sufficiently alike? If it's a generalization we have before us, this can be stated in terms of representativeness: Does the sample adequately represent the target class? If we're looking at an argument by analogy, the question is simply, Do the other terms of the analogy adequately resemble the target item in relevant respects?

If the terms of the analogy (for analogical arguments) or sample and target class (for generalizations) are alike with regard to features that are relevant to the property in question, then the argument will be strong; it will be weaker to the extent they are unlike regarding these features. Notice that a significant difference with respect to only one relevant feature is all it takes to ruin an otherwise good inductive argument. If, in the barking dog example, we know that the owners of the dog were away from home during our earlier episodes but that now, as you take out the garbage, we know that they are at home, this makes it much more difficult to conclude that the dog will behave as he did before. This difference is enough to cast considerable doubt on our reasoning.

2. Is the sample of sufficient size? In a formal argument, we've seen that the size of the sample determines the calculated confidence level and error margin. In informal arguments, the general rule is, The bigger the sample, the better (given the same degree of caution in the conclusion). It is possible, as we've indicated, to get a pretty good argument from a small sample—as small as one single item, in fact. And analogical arguments often operate from just two terms, one of them the target. But this can occur only when we know that the sample item or items are very, very similar to the target item or to all the members of the target class. It's also helpful in such cases if we can stand a fairly large error margin. To illustrate this last point, consider this example: Let's say that Moore owns a five-year-old Toyota Camry, and he recommends a similar car to Parker when the latter decides he needs to buy one. Parker finds

On Language

Danger—Docs and Guns

The following was going around on the Internet not long ago. There have been a number of variations on this theme, but it's still good for a chuckle. Make sure you can identify the problem with the argument–it may take a moment's thought.

First, about physicians:

- There are approximately 700,000 physicians in the United States.
- Accidental deaths caused by physicians per year are about 120,000.
- The accidental death rate per physician is therefore 0.171.

Next, about guns:

- The number of gun owners in the United States is about 80,000,000.
- The number of accidental gun deaths per year is about 1,500.
- The number of accidental deaths per gun owner is therefore .000188.

Now, the math:

.171 divided by .000188 equals 909.

The conclusion: Statistically, doctors are approximately 900 times more dangerous than gun owners.

So remember: Guns don't kill people; doctors do.

one that is the same year and model as Moore's; it has approximately the same number of miles on it; it has been driven and maintained in similar fashion, and the various fittings—transmission, air conditioning, etc.—are also similar. Parker asks Moore what kind of gas mileage his car gets, and Moore says he averages 30 miles to the gallon. Now, on the assumption that Parker's driving habits are similar to Moore's,* it would be a pretty safe bet that Parker will get *fairly similar* mileage. If Parker were to conclude that he'll get, say, between 25 and 35 miles per gallon, we'd say he had a very strong argument. It's a high probability that his mileage will fall somewhere within this substantial range. Were he to conclude that he'll probably average between 28 and 32 mpg, he'd still have a pretty good case, but considerably less strong than when he adopted the wider error margin—the more cautious conclusion.

These considerations about Moore's gas mileage point to the third key question about inductive generalizations and analogical arguments:

*They aren't.

3. Is the level of confidence expressed in the conclusion appropriate for the premises? The confidence we express in our conclusion shouldn't exceed what the premises warrant. The more confidence we express in the conclusion, the harder it is to support it. If the Yankees have won 50 percent of their games so far, we cannot be as confident they will win their next game as we can if they won 66 percent. In short, we shouldn't go out on a limb with our conclusion, unless we have a nice, sturdy trunk (premise) to support us. To say that the premises of an inductive generalization or analogical argument don't warrant much confidence in the conclusion is just a way of saying that it is not a strong argument.

FALLACIES

Recently, a woman had a question for *Car Talk,* an automotive advice radio program that features automobile mechanics Tom and Ray Magliozzi.* Will it hurt my husband's car, she wondered, if he sits in it for an hour each day with the engine and AC running while eating lunch and listening to sports radio? The Magliozzis assured her it would not and encouraged her to leave the poor guy alone. After the call, one of them jokingly asserted that women apparently have a hard time relating to the emotional needs of men.

The Magliozzis, who are graduates of MIT, would be the first to acknowledge that generalizing like this to a sweeping conclusion about all women from an absurdly small sample (in this case a single incident) obviously involves poor reasoning. They, of course, were doing this with tongue in cheek. We all overgeneralize from time to time (as we are doing in this very sentence), and occasionally it can lead to problems. For example, people sometimes generalize about medical remedies and procedures on the basis of reports from friends about what seems to work for them, rather than on the basis of accumulated medical statistics. Selecting a medical procedure on this basis can lead to trouble, even serious trouble.

Look again at Table 10-1. As you can see, the problem logically with generalizing from a small sample is that at any reasonably interesting confidence level a small sample produces a large error margin and a very small sample produces a very large error margin. Thus it is that people refer to generalizing based on too small a sample as **hasty generalizing** or **overgeneralizing.** Recently, for example, two separate incidents in which pit bulls attacked humans were reported in the press; shortly after this, letters appeared in newspapers asserting that the attacks proved that pit bulls were all extremely dangerous. As a matter of fact, these two incidents don't prove this, or by themselves prove much of anything except that some pit bulls are extremely dangerous. The letter writers were overgeneralizing.**

**Car Talk* airs on National Public Radio. The Magliozzis also answer automotive questions in a syndicated newspaper column.

**The most reliable data source we can find on the subject of pit bulls is a report from the Centers for Disease Control, indicating that during the reporting period (1979–1996) pit bulls were responsible for about twice as many human fatalities (sixty) as the breed in second place (Rottweilers, which accounted for twenty-nine fatalities). We don't know how many dogs of each breed are out there; however, according to an Associated Press report (July 12, 2005), in San Francisco since 2003 pit bulls (and pit bull mixes) accounted for 27 percent of dog bites reported to the city's Animal Care and Control department, while pit bulls account for only 6 percent of licensed dogs in the city. "Anybody who has been in animal welfare understands there is a problem with pit bulls," said the deputy director of the Animal Care and Control.

One version of hasty generalizing deserves special mention. You often hear statisticians and scientists dismiss evidence as "merely anecdotal." An anecdote is a story, and the **fallacy of anecdotal evidence** is a version of hasty generalizing that consists in generalizing wildly about a target class on the basis of a story about a member of that class. For example, someone might tell us a story about how gentle and sweet her pit bull is, to demonstrate that the nasty reputation such dogs have is undeserved, that is, to indicate that pit bulls generally are not mean and aggressive. When we hear a personal story like this it can carry much weight psychologically, but in reality, the story is just a sample of one—and deriving a conclusion about pit bulls in general from it would be overgeneralizing. The fact that the Car Talk sample is couched in terms of an entertaining anecdote is logically beside the point.

While a generalization based on a very small sample has a very large error margin, it doesn't follow that generalizations based on large samples are automatically just fine. A generalization based on a large sample isn't worth much if it is biased, that is, unrepresentative of the target class. When people call in opinions to CNN on a question the network has posed, we may have a huge sample; but it would be a mistake to draw conclusions about public sentiment generally. The sample does not contain the views of people who do not have the time or inclination to call in their opinion or do not watch CNN, and so forth.

Thus, the two basic mistakes of generalizing are hasty (or over-) generalizing, which involves generalizing from too small a sample and includes the fallacy of anecdotal evidence, and **biased generalizing,** which involves generalizing from a nonrepresentative (i.e., biased) sample. Of course, most samples that are too small are also biased, especially if one finds more variety in the target class. However, customarily we apply the hasty generalization label to small samples, and we reserve the biased generalization label for arguments whose samples aren't especially small, but are indeed biased.

A related problem can crop up when we reason by analogy. This happens if the terms of the analogical argument are dissimilar. "I enjoyed Carl Hiaasen's last novel; I'll probably enjoy his next novel" is a reasonable inference. But "I enjoyed Carl Hiaasen's last novel; therefore I'll enjoy reading Moore and Parker's book on critical thinking" would be, logically speaking, ridiculous.

When the terms of an analogical argument are thought to be too dissimilar to warrant an inference from one term to the other, the argument is said to be a **weak** (or **poor**) **analogy.** The second Carl Hiaasen argument above would qualify as such, for instance. Or to take another example, people sometimes make assertions about federal spending based on comparisons between it and household spending. You hear people say, "It is unwise for a household to go into debt; therefore it is unwise for the federal government to go into debt." Unfortunately, the terms of this analogy (the federal government, an ordinary household) are hugely dissimilar: Among other things, the government can raise taxes and print money. Or to take another example, while it wouldn't be unreasonable to conclude that someone might well make a poor parent because he or she doesn't take very good care of a pet dog, it would be very weak reasoning to conclude that he or she would make a poor parent because he or she neglects houseplants.

"Similar" and "dissimilar," as well as "poor," "weak," "hasty," and "biased," are all relative terms and matters of degree. Taking care of a pet dog has more in common with taking care of a child than does taking care of a houseplant. Because of this relativity, there is no mathematical formula to tell us

Real Life

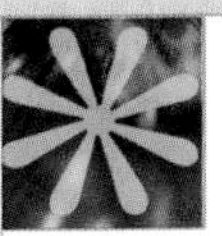

Who Do You Trust?

- When it comes to deciding which kind of car to buy, which do you trust more—the reports of a few friends or the results of a survey based on a large sample?
- When it comes to deciding whether an over-the-counter cold remedy (e.g., vitamin C) works, which do you trust more—a large clinical study or the reports of a few friends?

Many people trust the reports of friends over more reliable statistical information. We hope you aren't among 'em. (According to R. E. Nisbett and L. Ross, *Human Inference: Strategies and Shortcomings of Human Social Judgment* [Englewood Cliffs, N.J.: Prentice Hall, 1980], people tend to be insensitive to sample size when evaluating some product, being swayed more by the judgments of a few friends than by the results of a survey based on a large sample.)

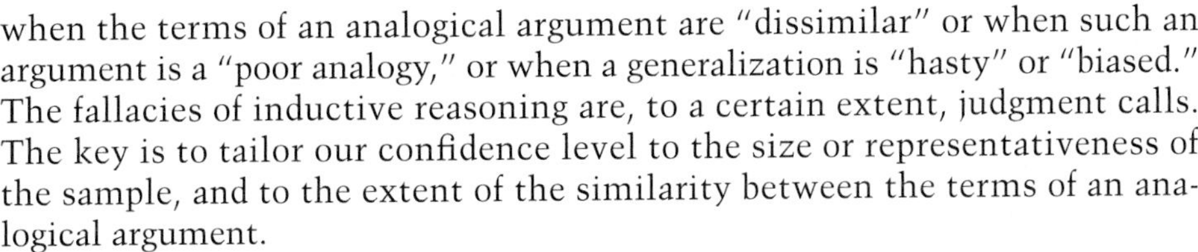

when the terms of an analogical argument are "dissimilar" or when such an argument is a "poor analogy," or when a generalization is "hasty" or "biased." The fallacies of inductive reasoning are, to a certain extent, judgment calls. The key is to tailor our confidence level to the size or representativeness of the sample, and to the extent of the similarity between the terms of an analogical argument.

POLLS: PROBLEMS AND PITFALLS

One of the most frequently encountered uses of inductive arguments is in polls, especially public opinion polls (and most especially in election years). We explained many of the concepts that are important in conducting and reporting polls a bit earlier in the chapter, but it's time now to look at a couple of the problems that crop up in this important use of inductive argumentation.

We should emphasize first that a properly conducted and accurately reported poll can be a very reliable source of information. But we hasten to add that a lot of polls that you hear or read about are *not* properly done and often the people who report on the results cannot tell the difference between a good poll and a bad one. We can't go into every possible way a poll can fail, but in what follows we'll take notice of two of the most common ones.

Self-Selected Samples

Recall that a generalization from a sample is only as good as the representativeness of the sample. Therefore, keep this in mind: *No poll should be trusted if the members of the sample are there by their own choice.* When a television station asks its viewers to call in to express an opinion on some subject, the results tell us very, very little about what the entire population thinks about that subject. There are all kinds of differences possible—indeed, likely—between the people who call in and the population in general. The same goes for polls conducted by mail-in responses. One of the most massive polls ever processed—and one of the most heavily flawed, we should add—was done in 1993. The political organization of H. Ross Perot, a very wealthy businessman

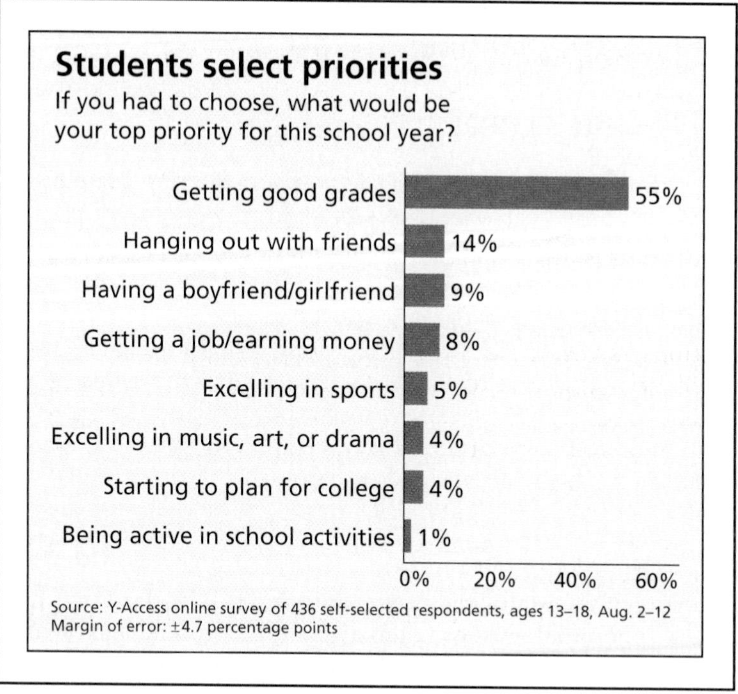

■ Comment: A good example of a worthless poll . . .

who ran for president as a member of the Reform Party, paid for a poll that was conducted by means of the magazine *TV Guide.* People were asked to answer questions posed in the magazine, then tear out or reproduce the pages and send them in for processing. There were other things wrong with this poll, and we'll get to some of them in a minute, but you've already heard all you need to know to discount any results that it produced. In such polls, the sample consists only of people who have strong enough feelings on the issues to respond and who have the time to go to the trouble of doing it. Such a situation almost guarantees that the sample will have views that are significantly different from those of the target population as a whole—it will be fatally biased.

Another example, just for fun: A few years ago the late Abigail Van Buren ("Dear Abby") asked her female readers to write in answering the question "Which do you like more, tender cuddling or 'the act' (sex)?" More of her responders preferred cuddling, it turned out, and when she published this fact it provoked another columnist, Mike Royko, to ask his male readers which *they* liked better, tender cuddling or bowling. Royko's responders preferred bowling. Although both surveys were good fun, neither of them could be taken to reflect accurately the views of either columnist's readership, let alone society in general.

It should go without saying that person-on-the-street interviews (which have become extremely popular in our neck of the woods) should be utterly discounted as indications of popular opinion. They include small samples, almost always biased because, among other reasons, the interviews are usually conducted at a single location and include only people willing to stick their faces in front of a camera. You should read these interviews as fun, not as a reflection of the views of the general public.

Slanted Questions

A major source of unreliability in polling practices is the wording of the questions that are asked. It is possible to ask nearly any question of importance in many different ways. Consider this pair of questions:

- Do you think the school board should agree to teachers' demands for higher pay?
- Do you think it is reasonable for local public school teachers to seek pay raises?

These questions ask essentially the same thing, but you would be smart to expect more negative answers to the first version than to the second. The context in which a question is asked can be important too. Imagine a question asking about approval of pay raises for public school teachers, but imagine it coming after one or the other of the following questions:

- Are you aware that teachers in this district have not had a salary increase for the past six years?
- Are you aware that the school district is facing a budget shortfall for the coming fiscal year?

We'd expect the approval of raises would fare better when asked after the first of these questions than after the second.

We might add that the inclusion of slanted questions is not always accidental. Oftentimes a group or an organization will want to produce results that are slanted in their direction, and so they will include questions that are designed to do exactly that. This is an exercise in deception, of course, but unfortunately it is more widespread than we'd wish.

Have a look at the box ("Ask Us No [Loaded] Questions . . .") and you'll see how one large, very expensive poll can contain most of the errors we've been discussing.

Is this evidence of discrimination against blondes and redheads, as the writer of the letter thought?

Nope; there are more brunettes to begin with. We'd be suspicious if *fewer* brunettes had high-paying corporate jobs.

Studies indicate that more brunettes than blondes or redheads have high-paying corporate jobs.

– From a letter in the *San Francisco Chronicle*

PLAYING BY THE NUMBERS

What if your instructor were to flip a coin ten times, and it came up heads seven times out of that ten? Would this make you think your teacher is a wizard or a sleight-of-hand artist? Of course not. There's nothing unusual in the coin coming up heads seven times out of ten, despite the fact that we all know the chance of heads in a fair coin flip is 50-50 (or 1 in 2, or, as the statisticians put it, 0.5). But what if your instructor were to get heads 70 percent of the time after flipping the coin a *hundred* times? This would be much more unexpected, and if he or she were to flip the coin a *thousand* times and get 70 percent heads—well, the whole class should leave right now for Las Vegas, where your instructor will make you all rich.

Why is 70 percent heads so unsurprising in the first case and so nearly miraculous in the last? The answer lies in what we call the **law of large numbers,** which says,

> **The larger the number of chance-determined repetitious events considered, the closer the alternatives will approach predictable ratios.**

On Language

Ask Us No [Loaded] Questions; We'll Tell You No Lies

In the spring of 1993, H. Ross Perot did a nationwide survey that received a lot of publicity. But a survey is only as good as the questions it asks, and loaded questions can produce a biased result. *Time* and CNN hired the Yankelovich Partners survey research firm to ask a split random sample of Americans two versions of the questions; the first was Perot's original version, the second was a rewritten version produced by the Yankelovich firm. Here is what happened for three of the topics covered.

Question 1

PEROT VERSION: "Do you believe that for every dollar of tax increase there should be two dollars in spending cuts with the savings earmarked for deficit and debt reduction?"

YANKELOVICH VERSION: "Would you favor or oppose a proposal to cut spending by two dollars for every dollar in new taxes, with the savings earmarked for deficit reduction, even if that meant cuts in domestic programs like Medicare and education?"

RESULTS: Perot version: 67 percent yes; 18 percent no
Yankelovich version: 33 percent in favor; 61 percent opposed

Question 2

PEROT VERSION: "Should the President have the Line Item Veto to eliminate waste?"

YANKELOVICH VERSION: "Should the President have the Line Item Veto, or not?"

RESULTS: Perot version: 71 percent in favor; 16 percent opposed
Yankelovich version: 57 percent in favor; 21 percent opposed

Question 3

PEROT VERSION: "Should laws be passed to eliminate all possibilities of special interests giving huge sums of money to candidates?"

YANKELOVICH VERSION: "Should laws be passed to prohibit interest groups from contributing to campaigns, or do groups have a right to contribute to the candidate they support?"

RESULTS: Perot version: 80 percent yes; 17 percent no
Yankelovich version: 40 percent for prohibition; 55 percent for right to contribute

This is not as complicated as it sounds; metaphorically, it just says that large numbers "behave" better than small numbers. Here's the idea: Because a single fair coin flip (i.e., no weighted coin, no prestidigitation) has a 50 percent chance of coming up heads, we say that the **predictable ratio** of heads to tails is 50 percent. The law of large numbers says that the more flips you include, the closer to 50 percent the heads-to-tails ratio will get.

The reason smaller numbers don't fit the percentages as well as bigger ones is that any given flip or short series of flips can produce nearly any kind of result. There's nothing unusual about several heads in a row or several tails—in fact, if you flip a thousand times, you'll probably get several "streaks" of heads and tails (and a sore thumb, too). Such streaks will balance

Real Life

Welcome to Saint Simpson's

There are many ways that statistical reports can be misleading. The following illustrates one of the stranger ways, known to statisticians as "Simpson's Paradox":

Let's say you need a fairly complicated but still routine operation, and you have to pick one of the two local hospitals, Mercy or Saint Simpson's, for the surgery. You decide to pick the safer of the two, based on their records for patient survival during surgery. You get the numbers: Mercy has 2,100 surgery patients in a year, of whom 63 die—a 3 percent death rate. Saint Simpson's has 800 surgery patients, of whom 16 die—a 2 percent death rate. You decide it's safer to have your operation done at Saint Simpson's.

The fact is, you could actually be *more* likely to die at Saint Simpson's than at Mercy Hospital, despite the former hospital's lower death rate for surgery patients. But you would have no way of knowing this without learning some more information. In particular, you need to know how the total figures break down into smaller, highly significant categories.

Consider the categories of high-risk patients (older patients, victims of trauma) and low-risk patients (e.g., those who arrive in good condition for elective surgery). Saint Simpson's may have the better looking overall record, not because it performs better, but because *Saint Simpson's gets a higher proportion of low-risk patients than does Mercy.* Let's say Mercy had a death rate of 3.8 percent among 1,500 high-risk patients, whereas Saint Simpson's, with 200 high-risk patients, had a death rate of 4 percent. Mercy and Saint Simpson's each had 600 low-risk patients, with a 1 percent death rate at Mercy and a 1.3 percent rate at Saint Simpson's.

So, as it turns out, it's a safer bet going to Mercy Hospital whether you're high risk or low, even though Saint Simpson's has the lower overall death rate.

The moral of the story is to be cautious about accepting the interpretation that is attached to a set of figures, especially if they lump together several categories of the thing being studied.

– Adapted from a story in the *Washington Post,* which quoted extensively from DAVID S. MOORE, professor of statistics at Purdue University

each other out in a series of a thousand flips, but even a short streak can skew a small series of flips. The idea is that when we deal with small numbers, every number counts for a very large number of percentage points. Just two extra cases of heads can produce a 70:30 ratio in ten flips, a ratio that would be astounding in a large number of flips.

The law of large numbers operates in many circumstances. It is the reason we need a minimum sample size even when our method of choosing a sample is entirely random. To infer a generalization with any confidence, we need a sample of a certain size before we can trust the numbers to "behave" as they should. Smaller samples increase the likelihood of random sampling error.

The law of large numbers also keeps knowledgeable gamblers and gambling establishments in business. They know that if they make a bet that gives them even a modest advantage in terms of a predictable ratio, then all they have to do is make the bet often enough (or, more frequently, have some chump make the opposing bet against them often enough) and they will come out winners.

Let's consider an example. A person who plays roulette in an American casino gives away an advantage to the house of a little over 5 percent. The odds of winning are 1 in 38 (because there are slots for thirty-six numbers plus a zero and a double-zero), but when the player wins, the house pays off only at the rate of 1 in 36 (as if there were no zeros). Now, this advantage to the house doesn't mean you might not walk up to a table and bet on your birthday and win four times in a row. But the law of large numbers says that if you pull up a chair and play long enough, eventually the house will win it all back—and the rent money, too.

Almost no one in Las Vegas believes the gambler's fallacy is in fact a fallacy.

– From an anonymous reviewer of this book

A final note while we're speaking about gambling. There is a famous error known as the **gambler's fallacy,** and it is as seductive as it is simple. Let's say that you're flipping a coin, and it comes up heads four times in a row. You succumb to the gambler's fallacy if you think that the odds of its coming up heads the next time are anything except 50 percent. It's true that the odds of a coin coming up heads five times in a row are small—only a little over 3 in 100—but once it has come up heads four times in a row, the odds are still 50-50 that it will come up heads the next time. Past performance may give you a clue about a horse race, but not about a coin flip (or any other event with a predictable ratio).

Recap

This list summarizes the topics covered in this chapter:

- Inductive arguments include analogical arguments (or arguments by analogy), inductive generalizations, and a third variety that will be discussed in the next chapter.
- An analogical argument compares the terms of an analogy and, based on similarities, arrives at a conclusion about the target term.
- An inductive generalization reaches a conclusion about a target class based on a sample drawn from the target.
- The conclusions of both arguments attribute a property or feature (the "property" or "feature in question") to the target term or members of the target class.
- Analogical arguments' strength lies in how similar the terms of the analogy are; the strength of inductive generalizations depends on how representative its sample is.
- Arguments are generally stronger when the sample or number of terms compared is greater.
- Arguments are generally stronger when the conclusions are given with the proper level of cautiousness.
- Fallacies of inductive generalizing includes hasty generalizing or overgeneralizing (generalizing from too small a sample), and biased generalizing (generalizing from a sample that isn't especially small but is not representative).
- The fallacy of anecdotal evidence is a special case of hasty generalizing, in which the sample is presented in the form of a story or anecdote.

In Depth

Which Is More Likely?

Which is more likely to have a week in which over 60 percent of new babies are boys—a large hospital or small hospital? If you thought it was a large hospital, you need to reread the section on the law of large numbers. (The example is from R. E. Nisbett and L. Ross, *Human Inference: Strategies and Shortcomings of Human Social Judgment.* Englewood Cliffs, N.J.:Prentice Hall, 1980.)

- When the terms of an analogical argument are too dissimilar to sustain the conclusion, the argument is said to commit the fallacy of weak (or poor) analogy.
- The law of large numbers governs statistically predictable outcomes of events—the longer you play against the house, the more odds will favor it in precisely predictable ways. (Stay away from bets in the center of a craps table.)

Exercises

Exercise 10-1

In groups (or individually, if the instructor prefers), decide whether each of the following comments is (a) an analogical argument or (b) an analogy that isn't in an argument. If the passage contains an argument, identify the terms of the analogy and specify which is the target.

▲ 1. These shrubs look rather similar to privet. I bet they keep their leaves in the winter, just like privet.

2. Working in this office is just about exactly as much fun as driving in Florida without air conditioning.

3. The last version of Word was filled with bugs; that's why I know the new version will be the same way.

▲ 4. If you ask me, Dr. Walker has as much personality as a piece of paving concrete.

5. I hate math, and soon as I saw all those formulas and junk, I knew I'd hate this symbolic logic stuff too.

6. Your new boyfriend has been married five times?! Say—do you seriously think it'll work out better the next time?

▲ 7. Too much sun will make your face all wrinkly; I suppose it would have that effect on your hands, too.

8. A Democrat who got caught taking trips financed by a lobbyist and who put family members on the payroll and paid them hundreds of thousands of dollars would be run out of Washington on a rail these days. That's why they should force Tom DeLay into resigning.

9. Look, advertising our magazine on AM radio is like Paris Hilton doing ads for the *Encyclopaedia Britannica.*

▲ 10. Here, you can use your screwdriver just like a chisel, if you want. Just give it a good whack with this hammer.

11. In elections during economic hard times, the party out of the White House has always made major gains in the Congress. That's why we can expect the president's party to suffer losses in the next election.

12. "Those thinkers in whom all stars move in cyclic orbits are not the most profound. Whoever looks into himself as into vast space and carries galaxies in himself, also knows how irregular all galaxies are; they lead into the chaos and labyrinth of existence."

— *Friedrich Nietzsche*

▲ 13. "Religion . . . is the *opium* of the people. To abolish religion as the *illusory* happiness of the people is to demand their *real* happiness."

— *Karl Marx*

14. "Publishing is to thinking as the maternity ward is to the first kiss."

— *Friedrich Von Schlegel*

15. She's not particularly good at tennis, so I doubt she'd be good at racquetball.

▲ 16. "A book is like a mirror. If an ape looks in, a saint won't look out."

— *Ludwig Wittgenstein*

17. As odd as it sounds, historically the stock market goes up when there is bad news on unemployment, and the latest statistics show the unemployment rate is skyrocketing. This could be a good time to buy stocks.

18. I never met anyone from North Carolina who didn't have an accent thicker than molasses.

▲ 19. Yamaha makes great motorcycles, so I'll bet their pianos are pretty good, too.

20. The last time we played Brazil in soccer we got run through the washer and hung out to dry.

Exercise 10-2

In groups (or individually if the instructor prefers), decide whether each of the following is (a) an analogical argument or (b) an inductive generalization.

▲ 1. Paulette, Georgette, Babette, and Brigitte are all Miami University English majors, and they are all atheists. Therefore, probably all the English majors at Miami University are atheists.

2. Paulette, Georgette, Babette, and Brigitte are all Miami University English majors, and they are all atheists. Therefore Janette, who is a Miami University English major, probably is also an atheist.

3. Gustavo likes all the business courses he has taken at Harvard to date. Therefore, he'll probably like all the business courses he takes at Harvard.

▲ 4. Gustavo likes all the business courses he has taken at Harvard to date. Therefore, he'll probably like the next business course he takes at Harvard.

5. Gustavo likes all the business courses he has taken at Harvard to date. Therefore, his brother, Sergio, who also attends Harvard, will probably like all the business courses he takes there, too.

6. Forty percent of Moore's 8:00 A.M. class are atheists. Therefore, 40 percent of all Moore's students are atheists.

▲ 7. Forty percent of Parker's 8:00 A.M. class are atheists. Therefore, probably 40 percent of Parker's 9:00 A.M. class are atheists.

8. Forty percent of Moore's 8:00 A.M. class are atheists. Therefore, probably 40 percent of all the students at Moore's university are atheists.

9. Bill Clinton lied to the American public about his relationship with Monica Lewinsky; therefore, he probably lied to the American public about Iraq, too.

▲ 10. Bill Clinton lied to the American public about his relationship with Monica Lewinsky; therefore, he probably lied to the American public about most things.

Exercise 10-3

In groups (or individually, if the instructor prefers), decide whether each of the following is (a) an analogical argument or (b) an inductive generalization.

▲ 1. With seven out of the last nine El Niños, we saw below-average rainfall across the northern United States and southern Canada. Therefore, chances are we'll see the same with the next El Niño.

2. I've been to at least twenty Disney movies in my lifetime, and not one of them has been especially violent. I guess the Disney people just don't make violent movies.

3. Most of my professors wear glasses; it's a good bet most professors everywhere do the same.

▲ 4. Seems like the Christmas decorations go up a little earlier each year. I bet next year they're up by Halloween.

5. The conservatives I've met dislike Olympia Snowe. Based on that, I'd say most conservatives feel the same way.

6. FIRST PROF: I can tell after just one test exactly what a student's final grade will be.
SECOND PROF: How many tests do you give, just a couple?
FIRST PROF: As a matter of fact, I give a test every week of the semester.

▲ 7. MRS. BRUDER: Bruder! Bruder! Guess what! The music department is selling two of their grand pianos!
MR. BRUDER: Well, let's check it out, but remember the last pianos they sold were way overpriced. Probably it'll be the same this time.

8. A 35 percent approval rating? Those polls are rigged by the liberal media. Most of the people I know say the man ought to be given a third term.

9. The New England Patriots have won six of their last seven home games. They're playing at home on Sunday. Don't bet against them.

▲ 10. You're going out with a Georgette? Well, don't expect much because I've known three Georgettes and all of them have been stuck up, spoiled yuckheads. I'll bet this one will be a yuckhead, too.

Exercise 10-4

Go through the preceding exercise and for each item identify (1) the sample, or the terms of the analogy, (2) the target or target class, and (3) the property (feature) in question.

Exercise 10-5

In groups (or individually, if the instructor prefers), determine in which of the following inductive generalizations or analogical arguments the sample, the terms of the analogy, the target or target class, or property in question is excessively vague or ambiguous.

▲ 1. The tests in this class are going to be hard, judging from the first midterm.

2. Judging from my experience, technical people are exceedingly difficult to communicate with sometimes.

3. The transmissions in 2003 Chrysler minivans tend to fail prematurely, if my Voyager is any indication.

▲ 4. Women can tolerate more stress than can men. My husband even freaks when the newspaper is a little late.

5. Movies are much too graphic these days. Just go to one—you'll see what I mean.

6. Violent scenes in the current batch of movies carry a message that degrades women. Just go see any of the movies playing downtown right now.

▲ 7. You'll need to get better clothing than that if you're going to Iowa. In my experience, the weather there sucks much of the year.

8. Entertainment is much too expensive these days, judging from the cost of movies.

9. Art majors sure are weird! I roomed with one, once. Man.

▲ 10. Artsy people bug me. They're all like, aaargh, you know what I mean?

11. The French just don't like Americans. Why, in Paris, they won't give you the time of day.

12. All the research suggests introverts are likely to be well-versed in computer skills.

▲ 13. Suspicious people tend to be quite unhappy, judging from what I've seen.

Exercise 10-6

For analogical arguments among the following, decide how similar the terms of the analogy are; for generalizations, decide how well the sample represents the target class. In groups (or individually), choose from the following options:

a. Very well
b. Pretty well
c. Not very well
d. Very poorly

▲ 1. The coffee in that pot is lousy—I just had a cup.

2. The coffee at that restaurant is lousy—I just had a cup.

3. The food in that restaurant is lousy—I just ate there.

▲ 4. This student doesn't write very well, judging from how poorly she wrote on the first paper.

5. Terrence didn't treat her very well on their first date; I can't imagine he will treat her better next time.

6. I expect I'll have trouble sleeping after this huge feast. Whenever I go to bed on a full stomach, I never sleep very well.

▲ 7. Lupe's sister and mother both have high blood pressure; chances are Lupe does too.

8. Every movie Courtney Cox Arquette has been in has been great! I bet her next movie will be great, too!

▲ 9. Women don't play trombones; leastwise, I never heard of one who did.

10. I'm sure Blue Cross will cover that procedure because I have Blue Cross and they covered it for me.

11. Cocker spaniels are nice dogs, but they eat like pigs. When I was a kid, we had this little cocker that ate more than a big collie we had.

▲ 12. Cadillacs are nice cars, but they are gas hogs. When I was a kid, we owned this Cadillac that got around ten miles per gallon.

13. Cockatoos are great birds, but they squawk. A lot. Had one when I was a kid, and even the neighbors complained, it was so raucous.

14. The parties at the university always turn into drunken brawls. Why, just last week the police had to go out and break up a huge party at Fifth and Ivy.

Exercise 10-7

Analyze the following argument. What kind of argument is it? Is it really as good as Dan Walters believes it is?

> The proponents of [school] vouchers say, in essence, that if competition produces excellence in other fields—consumer products, athletics and higher education, to name but three—it would be healthy for the schools as well. Their logic is difficult to refute.
>
> — *Dan Walters, political columnist*

Exercise 10-8

Arrange the alternative conclusions of the following arguments in order of decreasing confidence level and then compare your rankings with those of three or four classmates. Some options are pretty close to being tied. Don't get in feuds with classmates or the teacher over close calls.

▲ 1. Not once this century has this city gone Republican in a presidential election. Therefore . . .

a. I wouldn't count on it happening this time.
b. it won't happen this time.
c. in all likelihood it won't happen this time.
d. there's no chance whatsoever it will happen this time.

e. it would be surprising if it happened this time.
f. I'll be a donkey's uncle if it happens this time.

2. Byron doesn't know how to play poker, so . . .

a. he sure as heck doesn't know how to play blackjack.
b. it's doubtful he knows how to play blackjack.
c. there's a possibility he doesn't know how to play blackjack.
d. don't bet on him knowing how to play blackjack.
e. you're nuts if you think he knows how to play blackjack.

3. Every time I've used the Beltway, the traffic has been heavy, so I figure that . . .

a. the traffic is almost always heavy on the Beltway.
b. frequently the traffic on the Beltway is heavy.
c. as a rule, the traffic on the Beltway is heavy.
d. the traffic on the Beltway can be heavy at times.
e. the traffic on the Beltway is invariably heavy.
f. typically, the traffic on the Beltway is heavy.
g. the traffic on the Beltway is likely to be heavy most of the time.

Exercise 10-9

In which of the following arguments is the implied confidence level too high or low, given the premises? After you have decided, compare your results with those of three or four classmates.

▲ **1.** We spent a day on the Farallon Islands last June, and was it ever foggy and cold! So dress warmly when you go there this June. Based on our experience, it is 100 percent certain to be foggy and cold.

2. We've visited the Farallon Islands on five different days, two during the summer and one each during fall, winter, and spring. It's been foggy and cold every time we've been there. So dress warmly when you go there. Based on our experience, there is an excellent chance it will be foggy and cold whenever you go.

3. We've visited the Farallon Islands on five different days, all in June. It's been foggy and cold every time we've been there. So dress warmly when you go there in June. Based on our experience, it could well be foggy and cold.

▲ **4.** We've visited the Farallon Islands on five different days, all in June. It's been foggy and cold every time we've been there. So dress warmly when you go there in June. Based on our experience, there is a small chance it will be foggy and cold.

5. We've visited the Farallon Islands on five different days, all in January. It's been foggy and cold every time we've been there. So dress warmly when you go there in June. Based on our experience, it almost certainly will be foggy and cold.

Exercise 10-10

For the past four years, Clifford has gone on a hundred-mile bicycle ride on the Fourth of July. He has always become too exhausted to finish the entire hundred miles. He decides to try the ride once again, but thinks, "Well, I probably won't finish it this year, either, but no point in not trying."

▲ 1. Is the confidence level expressed in the conclusion appropriate?

2. Suppose the past rides were done in a variety of different weather conditions. With this change, would the argument be stronger than the original, weaker, or about the same?

3. Suppose that Clifford is going to ride the same bike this year that he's ridden in all the previous rides. Does this make the argument stronger than the original version, weaker, or neither?

▲ 4. Suppose the past rides were all done on the same bike, but that bike is not the bike Clifford will ride this year. Does this make the argument stronger than the original version, weaker, or neither?

5. Suppose Clifford hasn't yet decided what kind of bike to ride in this year's ride. Now, is the argument made stronger or weaker or neither if the past rides were done on a variety of different kinds of bike (e.g., road bikes, mountain bikes, racing bikes, etc.)?

6. Suppose the past rides were all done on flat ground and this year's ride will also be on flat ground. Does this make the argument stronger than the original version, weaker, or neither?

7. Suppose the past rides were all done on flat ground and this year's ride will be done in hilly territory. Does this make the argument stronger than the original version, weaker, or neither?

▲ 8. Suppose Clifford doesn't know what kind of territory this year's ride will cover. Is his argument made stronger or weaker or neither if the past rides were done on a variety of kinds of territory?

9. Suppose the past rides were all done in hilly territory and this year's ride will be done on flat ground. Does this make the argument stronger than the original version, weaker, or neither?

▲ 10. In answering the preceding item, did you take into consideration information you have about bike riding in different kinds of terrain or did you consider only the criteria for evaluating inductive arguments in general?

Exercise 10-11

During three earlier years Kirk has tried to grow artichokes in his backyard garden, and each time his crop has been ruined by mildew. Billie prods him to try one more time, and he agrees to do so, though he secretly thinks: "This is probably a waste of time. Mildew is likely to ruin this crop, too." Decide in each of the following cases whether the supposition would make the argument stronger, weaker, or neither, given the confidence level expressed in Kirk's conclusion.

▲ 1. Suppose this year Kirk plants the artichokes in a new location.

2. Suppose on the past three occasions Kirk planted his artichokes at different times of the growing season.

3. Suppose this year Billie plants marigolds near the artichokes.

▲ 4. Suppose the past three years were unusually cool.

5. Suppose only two of the three earlier crops were ruined by mildew.
6. Suppose one of the earlier crops grew during a dry year, one during a wet year, and one during an average year.
▲ 7. Suppose this year, unlike the preceding three, there is a solar eclipse.
8. Suppose this year Kirk fertilizes with lawn clippings for the first time.
9. Suppose this year Billie and Kirk acquire a large dog.
▲ 10. Suppose this year Kirk installs a drip irrigation system.

Exercise 10-12

Every student I've met from Ohio State believes in God. My conclusion is that most of the students from Ohio State believe in God. Decide whether the following suppositions would make the argument stronger, weaker, or neither.

▲ 1. Suppose (as is the case) that Ohio State has no admission requirements pertaining to religious beliefs. Suppose further the students in the sample were all interviewed as they left a local church after Sunday services.
2. Suppose all those interviewed were first-year students.
3. Suppose all students interviewed were on the Ohio State football team.
▲ 4. Suppose the speaker selected all the students interviewed by picking every tenth name on an alphabetical list of students' names.
5. Suppose the students interviewed all responded to a questionnaire published in the campus newspaper titled "Survey of Student Religious Beliefs."
6. Suppose the students interviewed were selected at random from the record office's list of registered automobile owners.

Exercise 10-13

Read the passage below, and answer the questions that follow.

> In the Georgia State University History Department, students are invited to submit written evaluations of their instructors to the department's personnel committee, which uses those evaluations to help determine whether history instructors should be recommended for retention and promotion. In his three history classes, Professor Ludlum has a total of one hundred students. Six students turned in written evaluations of Professor Ludlum; four of these evaluations were negative, and two were positive. Professor Hitchcock, who sits on the History Department Personnel Committee, argued against recommending Ludlum for promotion. "If a majority of the students who bothered to evaluate Ludlum find him lacking," he stated, "then it's clear to me that a majority of all his students find him lacking."

▲ 1. What is the sample in Professor Hitchcock's reasoning?
2. What is the target or target class?
3. What is the property in question?

▲ 4. Is this an analogical argument or a generalization?

5. Are there possibly important differences between the sample and the target (or target class) that should reduce our confidence in Professor Hitchcock's conclusion?

▲ 6. Is the sample random?

7. How about the size of Professor Hitchcock's sample? Is it large enough to help ensure that the sample and target or target classes won't be too dissimilar?

▲ 8. Based on the analysis of Professor Hitchcock's reasoning that you have just completed in the foregoing questions, how strong is his reasoning?

Exercise 10-14

George's class is doing a survey of student opinion on social life and drinking. One of the questions is "Do you believe that students who are members of fraternities and sororities drink more alcohol than students who are not members of such organizations?" Let's say that George would wager a large sum on a bet only if he had a 95 percent chance of winning. Answer the following questions for him. (Use Table 10-1 on page 345 to help you with this exercise.)

▲ 1. Exactly 60 percent of a random sample of 250 students at George's college believe that students in fraternities and sororities drink more than others. Should George bet that exactly 60 percent of the student population hold the same belief?

2. Should he bet that *at least* 60 percent hold that belief?

3. Should he bet that *no more than* 66 percent hold the belief?

▲ 4. According to the text, the largest number that he can safely bet hold the belief mentioned is ______ percent.

5. Let's change the story a bit. Let's make the sample size 100 and once again say exactly 60 percent of it hold the belief in question. Should George bet that at least 55 percent of the total student population hold the belief?

6. Should he bet that at least 50 percent of the total hold it?

▲ 7. It is safe for George to bet that no more than ______ percent of the total population share the belief in question. What's the smallest number that can be placed in the blank?

Exercise 10-15

Critically analyze these arguments by analogy. Do this by specifying what things are compared in the analogy and then identifying important relevant dissimilarities between these things. If any of the arguments seem pretty strong—that is, if the dissimilarities are not relevant or particularly important—say so.

Example

Earth and Venus are twin planets; both have atmospheres that protect them from the harsh environment of outer space, both are about the same size and exert similar gravitational force, both have seasons, both have days and nights, and there are other similarities. Earth has life; therefore, Venus may well have life, too.

Analysis

1. The terms of the analogy are Earth and Venus.
2. Important relevant dissimilarities are that Venus's atmosphere is composed of 96 percent carbon dioxide, whereas Earth's contains about 0.03 percent. Also, the surface temperature of Venus is higher than the boiling point of lead.

▲ **1.** Tiger Woods began playing golf at the age of two, and look what he's accomplished. I'm going to start golf lessons for my two-year-old, too, by golly.

2. A household that doesn't balance its budget is just asking for trouble. It's the same with the federal government. Balance the federal budget, or watch out.

3. Saccharin has been determined to cause cancer in rats; in similar doses, it's likely to do so in humans as well.

▲ **4.** Senator Clinton has been an excellent senator for New York; therefore, she would make an excellent president.

5. Ross Perot really knows how to run a business; therefore, he'd have made an excellent president.

6. There's no way I can actually feel other people's pain or experience their fear or anxiety. Nevertheless, I can be quite sure other people experience these things because they behave as I do when I experience them. Therefore, I can be equally sure animals experience these things when they behave in a similar fashion.

▲ **7.** Jeb Bush has an 80 percent approval rating in Georgia. It's safe to assume he is equally popular in Massachusetts.

8. Suppose you had never seen a clock before and one day you found one lying on the ground somewhere. You'd be certain it had been made by an intelligent being who was up to the task of creating such a thing. Now think of the Earth. It displays a far more complex design than a clock. It is safe to conclude that it, too, just like a clock, is the product of an intelligent creator, and one up to such a momentous task as creating a world. This is a very good reason to think that God exists.

9. Trying to appease Adolf Hitler was totally counterproductive; trying to appease Kim Jong Il will likely have similar results.

▲ **10.** The Barneses are traveling to Europe for a year and decide to find a student to house-sit for them. They settle on Warren because he is neat and tidy in his appearance. "If he takes such good care of his personal appearance," Mrs. Barnes thinks, "he's likely to take good care of our house, too."

11. Abortion consists in killing a living person. If abortion is wrong, therefore so is capital punishment.

12. Hey! This ant poison looks like Windex! I bet we can clean our windows with it.

13. (Refers to preceding item) I don't know about that, but maybe the Windex will work as well on ants as the poison.
14. Says here, "Lysol kills germs." Well, that's what body odor is all about, germs! I bet Lysol will make a great deodorant!
15. Saddam was just like Hitler. That's why we had to take him out.*

Exercise 10-16

Identify any fallacies that are present in the following passages:

▲ 1. From a letter to the editor: "I read with great interest the May 23 article on the study of atheists in federal prisons, according to which most of these atheists identify themselves as socialists, communists, or anarchists. That most atheists, along with all their other shortcomings, turn out to be political wackos surprises yours truly not one bit."

2. I ordered a packet of seeds from Hansen Seed Company last year, and only half of them germinated. I'll bet you get only half the plants you're expecting from the order you just sent them.

3. My cousin has a Dodge truck that he drives around on the ranch and back and forth to town as well. It now has 120,000 miles on it without any major overhaul. I've started to believe the commercials: Dodge does build tough trucks!

▲ 4. Drug abuse among professional athletes is a serious and widespread problem. Three players from a single team admitted last week that they had used cocaine.

5. Most Americans favor a national lottery to reduce the federal debt. In a poll taken in Las Vegas, more than 80 percent said they favored such a lottery.

6. I think collies are one of the easiest breeds of dog to train. I had one when I was young, and she was really easy to teach. Of course, if you need more evidence, there's Lassie.

7. From a letter to the editor: "Last week, members of the Animal Liberation Front stole several hours of videotapes of experiments done to animals at the University of Pennsylvania's Head Injury Clinical Research Center. According to reliable reports, one of the tapes shows baboons having their brains damaged by a piston device that smashed into their skulls with incredible force. The anesthetic given the baboons was allegedly insufficient to prevent serious pain. Given that this is what animal research is all about, Secretary of Health and Human Services Margaret Heckler acted quite properly in halting federal funding for the project. Federal funding for animal research ought to be halted, it seems to me, in the light of these atrocities."

▲ 8. Overheard: "You're not going to take a course from Harris, are you? I know at least three people who say he's terrible. All three flunked his course, as a matter of fact."

---

*Example from James Anderson.

9. A majority of Ohio citizens consider the problem of air pollution critical. According to a survey taken in Cleveland, more than half the respondents identified air pollution as the most pressing of seven environmental issues and as having either "great" or "very great" importance.

▲ 10. Comment: What are we getting for the billions we spend on these new weapons? Absolutely nothing. Just look at the Apache helicopter. I read where they can't fly one of them for more than ten hours without grounding it for major repairs.

11. The IRS isn't interested in going after the big corporations, just middle-class taxpayers like you and me. I was audited last year, and I know several people who have been audited. You ever hear of ExxonMobil getting nailed?

12. I am totally outraged by the ethics of our elected representatives. Just look around: Bill Clinton accepted illegal campaign donations; Tom DeLay is being investigated for misuse of funds. I tell you, they are all just a bunch of crooks.

▲ 13. When he was president, Ronald Reagan occasionally would wave a copy of the "Help Wanted" section of some newspaper to demonstrate that U.S. unemployment wasn't really so bad. What was the fallacy in this "argument"?

Exercise 10-17

1. In the text, it is said that a person playing roulette has a disadvantage of about 5 percent compared with the house. Explain what this means.
2. Choose two or three other gambling bets for which you can calculate or look up the odds against the bettor. (Stick with games of pure chance; those that can involve a bit of skill, such as twenty-one—also known as blackjack—are much more difficult to deal with.) Determine which bet gives the house the smallest advantage.
3. Choose a state lottery and determine the odds against winning for a given ticket. Can you determine what kind of advantage the "house" has in such a gamble?

Exercise 10-18

1. Explain in your own words what the law of large numbers says.
2. "Over the long term, human births will approximate 50 percent males and 50 percent females." Is this a reasonable application of the law of large numbers? What facts can you think of that are relevant to determining whether this is a reasonable application of the law?
3. A person is betting on flips of a coin. He always bets on heads. After he loses three in a row, you hear him say, "Okay, I'm due for one now!" as he raises his bet. Write a brief note in which you give him some friendly advice.

Writing Exercises

1. Which of the following general claims do you accept? Select one that you accept and write a one-page essay presenting evidence (giving arguments) for the claim. When you are finished, write down on a separate piece of paper a number between 1 and 10 that indicates how strong you think your overall "proof" of the general claim is, with 10 = very strong and 1 = very weak. Take about two minutes to complete your essay. Write your name on the back of your paper.

   General claims:

   You get what you pay for.
   Nice guys finish last.
   Everything else being equal, men prefer blondes.
   Women are more gentle and nurturing than men.
   Politicians are untrustworthy.
   Government intrudes into our private lives/business affairs too much.
   Too many welfare recipients don't deserve assistance.
   College teachers are liberals.
   Jocks are dumb.
   The superwealthy pay less in taxes than they should.

2. When everyone is finished, the instructor will collect the papers and redistribute them to the class. In groups of four or five, read the papers and assign a number from 1 to 10 to each one (10 = very strong; 1 = very weak). When all groups are finished, return the papers to their authors. When you get your paper back, compare the number you assigned to your work with the number the group assigned to it. The instructor may ask volunteers to defend their own judgment of their work against the judgment of the group. Do you think there is as much evidence for the claim you selected as you did when you argued for it initially?

Chapter 11

Causal Arguments

This boulder landing on this highway is a specific event caused by a combination of various other specific factors. Cause-and-effect statements about specific events are different from general cause-and-effect statements. This chapter discusses both.

A few months ago Uncle Pete came down with pneumonia. His condition was life-threatening. Aunt Clara prayed for Pete—and, we are happy to report, Uncle Pete recovered. Did Aunt Clara's prayers help? Aunt Clara is certain they did. ("Can you prove they didn't?" she asks.) Pete's doctor is keeping his thoughts to himself.

We don't know whether Aunt Clara's prayers helped Uncle Pete—and, in fact, neither does Aunt Clara. We know only that Aunt Clara prayed and then Uncle Pete recovered. Knowing that, however, is not the same as knowing that the prayers had anything at all to do with the recovery.

Thinking that X being followed by Y means that X caused Y is a common mistake in reasoning. It's known as the **post hoc fallacy** and is one of the most common mistakes people make.

"Post hoc fallacy" is short for the Latin phrase *post hoc, ergo propter hoc,* which translates as "After that, therefore because of that," or to put it a bit more loosely, "This thing happened right after that other thing, so this thing was caused by that other thing." Whenever we reason this way, we make that mistake. Uncle Pete's cure happened when, or just after, Aunt Clara prayed; therefore the praying caused the cure—this is post hoc reasoning.

That this kind of reasoning is a mistake should be obvious. Moore's birthday happened just before Parker's, but Moore's birthday didn't cause Parker's.

On the other hand, suppose Howard topples over with a heart attack immediately after sprinting up two flights of stairs. Doesn't the fact that the heart attack came on the heels of the sprint suggest the one thing caused the other? The answer is no. After all, the heart attack also came on the heels of Howard's sweating heavily, and it would be peculiar to suppose on these grounds that his sweating caused his heart attack. Something else obviously needs to be considered before we can say that the sprinting caused the heart attack. What other things? To answer this, we need to look at the principles involved when we reason our way to a statement about cause and effect.

INFORMAL CAUSAL REASONING

A **causal claim** (or **cause-and-effect claim**) states or suggests the presence (or absence) of causation. An example is worth several words, so here are examples of causal claims:

- Aunt Clara's prayers helped Uncle Pete recover from pneumonia.
- At high concentrations, some enzymes damage healthy tissue.
- Pressing the two surfaces together produced a permanent bond.
- Dnase significantly improves lung function.
- Vitamin C does not cure colds.
- Fertilizing with Scott's didn't do anything for my lawn.
- Sprinting caused Howard to have a heart attack.

A statement to the effect that X causes or caused Y can, of course, be offered as a hypothesis rather than as a claim: A **hypothesis** is a supposition offered as a starting point for further investigation. When you hypothesize, you aren't actually claiming something, you are conjecturing (which is a rather fancy way to say you're making a guess). However, the reasoning that supports a claim and the reasoning that tests a hypothesis is the same, so, for practical purposes we can treat causal claims and **causal hypotheses** as the same kind of thing.

TWO BASIC PATTERNS OF CAUSAL REASONING

When we assert (or hypothesize) that one thing causes or caused another, our reasoning often will rely on either (or some combination) of two distinct patterns of inference: relevant-difference reasoning and common-thread reasoning.

Relevant-Difference Reasoning

Last summer, one of us was driving north on Interstate 680 near Walnut Creek, California, when he noticed the temperature needle on his Dodge pickup suddenly moving into the danger zone. He needed to pull over immediately, but I-680 at that point had ten lanes of vehicles traveling bumper-to-bumper at approximately the speed of light, and the large trailer he was towing

■ Jeff Fulcher, a former student of ours, read this book and now flies airplanes in Alaska. See what an exciting career can come from reading this book? (This is an example of post hoc, ergo propter hoc.)

made lane changes dicey. It didn't help that the three dogs thought this was the perfect time to bark raucously for a potty stop.

Fortunately, an off-ramp was handy. The author coasted to a safe spot off the highway, got the dogs out, and pondered what to do.

What had caused the vehicle to overheat? It had never done that before. What was different about this occasion? If something happens in one situation that doesn't happen in similar situations, you try to find something that is different, and you suspect it as the cause.

Relevant difference reasoning is frequently employed when we try to figure out the cause of something. If you wake up one morning with a splitting headache and you remember doing something different the night before, such as reading in poor light, you will suspect that this variation caused the headache. Is a colleague suddenly chummy and warm—the very same person who ordinarily doesn't give you the time of day? You ask yourself, what's different now—did he win the lottery? (Or did you?) Why isn't the post office open? Oh, that's what's different—it's Martin Luther King, Jr.'s birthday.

Unfortunately, as to the overheated Dodge, the author couldn't think of any difference between this occasion and earlier ones, or any difference that might be relevant. He hadn't been driving faster than usual; he often towed a trailer; he wasn't fighting a head wind. He hadn't gone up any unusual grade. The engine hoses looked the same and felt the same. There was no difference; nothing was out of the ordinary, except for the dogs' peculiar timing. That was unusual but not relevant.

Could the problem be in the temperature gauge rather than the engine? A quick check of the fluids and the feel of the oil dipstick and hoses—very hot, but not obviously hotter than normal—suggested (inductive reasoning) the engine was not in fact verging on meltdown. If the engine wasn't super hot, then (deductive reasoning) the problem was in the temperature gauge or connecting apparatus. Still, the author let the engine cool, and then drove side roads long enough to see the needle behaving normally; he continued driving several more hours and reached home without incident.

This, then, is relevant-difference reasoning. Something happens that hasn't happened in similar situations. If there is a relevant difference between this

Real Life

Converting Correlation to Causation

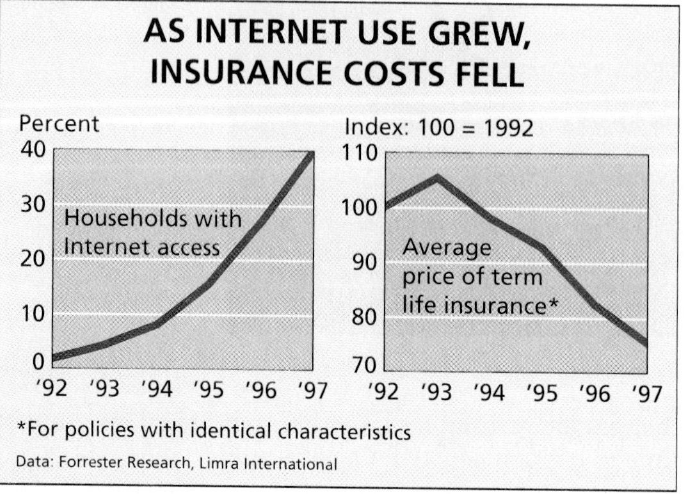

From a study by two economists (Jeffrey R. Brown and Austan Goolsbee), reported by Gene Koretz in *Business Week*, January 8, 2001.

The graphs show that as the number of houses with Internet access increased, the price of term life insurance decreased. So far, this is just (inverse) correlation; no inference to cause and effect is warranted. However, in the same time frame, the price of whole-life insurance did not decrease. Why? The economists found a relevant difference: online quotes for whole life insurance were not available during the period. This additional information makes it reasonable to hypothesize cause and effect: The cause of the decline in term-life prices was due to increased availability of price quotes. Assuming that increased availability of price quotes could only be due to increased Internet access, it is reasonable to conclude, as the economists did, that the Internet apparently drove term insurance prices down.

situation and the others, you suspect the difference played a role in causing the effect. Although the author followed this line of reasoning in our example, the relevant difference that caused the temperature gauge malfunction at that point still remained a mystery to him.

Common-Thread Reasoning

Now, a different pattern of reasoning is illustrated by considering what happens when you have *multiple* occurrences of some effect. For example, what happens when a group of people all come down with the same mysterious health symptoms such as those that accompany SARS? The first thing health officials do is look for a **common thread** among the victims. Did they all breathe the same air? Were they all present in the same location? Is there some person they all contacted? Common threads are immediately suspicious as possible causes of the illness.

On Language

The Great 9/11 Mystery

How could all these facts be mere coincidence?

- The day was 9/11 (9 plus 1 plus 1 equals 11).
- American Airlines Flight 11 was the first to hit the World Trade Center.
- 92 people were on board (nine placed alongside 1 plus 1 equals 92).
- September 11 is the 254th day of the year (2 plus 5 plus 4 equals 11).
- "New York City" has 11 letters in it.
- "The Pentagon" has 11 letters in it.
- "Saudi Arabia" (where most of the 9/11 terrorists were from) has 11 letters in it.
- "Afghanistan" has 11 letters in it.
- And get this: Within eleven months of September 11, 2001, eleven men, all connected to bioterror and germ warfare, died in strange and violent circumstances: One suffocated; another was stabbed, another hit by a car; another shot dead by a fake pizza delivery boy; one was killed in an airplane crash; one died from a stroke while being mugged; and the rest met similar ends.

Could this possibly be coincidence? What are the odds against all these things happening and being connected by the number 11?

Well, if you think these events must somehow be causally interconnected, you'd have a lot of company. But it wouldn't include mathematicians—or us. Why not? In a world where so many things happen, strange and seemingly improbable coincidences are bound to happen every second of every day.

In the movie *Signs,* Mel Gibson is worried about the dark secrets of the universe.

Not convinced? Ask each of your classmates to think of as many events or things connected with the 9/11 attack that involve the number 11. Give each person a week to work on this. We'll bet the collected list of "suspicious" coincidences is very long. There are even Web sites devoted to 9/11 coincidences.

As for the men connected with bioterrorism and germ warfare, you might be interested to know that the American Society for Microbiology alone has 41,000 members, and the total number of people "connected" in some way or other with bioterrorism and germ warfare would be indefinitely larger than that. We'd bet our royalties that in the eleven months following September 11, a lot more than just eleven people connected with bioterrorism and germ warfare died mysteriously and/or violently.

Lisa Belkin of the *New York Times Magazine* wrote an article on this subject (August 18, 2002), from which we learned about the coincidences mentioned above.

Incidentally, "Moore/Parker" has eleven letters.

If some years the azaleas bloom prolifically and other years they don't, you look for a common thread among the years they bloom well (or among the years they don't). For example, if, whenever they bloomed well you always pruned in the fall rather than the winter, you'd suspect time of pruning might have something to do with quality of bloom.

One summer, every Saturday evening mosquitoes swarmed in the backyard of one of the authors, making it unpleasant to be out there. Other evenings they were not particularly noticeable. What was it about Saturday evenings? What did they have in common, the author wondered. It finally dawned on him that he mowed the grass on late Saturday afternoons, and that practice therefore seemed a reasonable cause of his insect problem.

Likewise, returning to the Dodge pickup story, when that author returned to Chico, everything was fine with the car for a few weeks. But then one day the temperature needle again floated into the red zone. This time the needle returned to its normal position while he continued to drive. Similar episodes, in which the needle briefly went to danger and then returned to normal, occurred several times over the next several weeks—and the author looked for a common thread among the episodes. He eventually found a loose electrical connection at the temperature gauge sensor; maybe the connection was jiggling open from time to time? After he secured the connection, the needle stopped misbehaving, and the author concluded—using relevant-difference reasoning—that his hypothesis was correct.

To summarize these two types of reasoning:

Relevent-Difference Reasoning
Something happens in one situation that hasn't happened in similar situations. Any relevant difference between this situation and the others may well have caused the effect in question.

Common-Thread Reasoning
Some effect is present in multiple situations. Any common thread uniting those situations may have caused the effect in question.

Common-thread reasoning is best suited as a method for forming hypotheses that can be tested in some other way, usually involving relevant-difference reasoning. Relevant-difference reasoning, on the other hand, can be reasonably conclusive—at least in experimental conditions. If a piece of litmus paper turns red when you dip it in a liquid, it is safe to think the liquid caused the alteration. That's because the litmus paper prior to dipping and the litmus paper during dipping were exactly the same, except for the liquid. This may sound like post hoc reasoning, but it isn't: The reason for saying the liquid caused the litmus paper to turn red isn't just that it turned red after touching the liquid. The reason is that touching the liquid was the only relevant difference that could explain the paper's turning red.

Even apart from carefully controlled experimental conditions, relevant-difference reasoning yields conclusions that are certain by everyday standards of rigor. If the car won't start immediately after you installed a new electrical device, and you are sure the before-installation and after-installation conditions are the same except for the device and the failure to start, you are right to think the device or its installation is the problem.

– **On the other hand, maybe parents with higher IQs are more aware of the health advantages of breastfeeding and as a result are more likely to breastfeed their children.**

According to a report in the *Journal of the American Medical Association*, infants who are breastfed have higher IQs later in life.

Real Life

See What Happens If You Watch the Tube?

Recent research indicates that people who watch several hours of TV each day, as compared with those who don't watch very much, express more racially prejudiced attitudes, perceive women as having more limited abilities and interests than men, overestimate the prevalence of violence in society, and underestimate the number of old people. Does this suggest to you that these attitudes and misconceptions are the *result* of watching a lot of TV, that TV *causes* people to have these attitudes and misconceptions? If so, that's fine. But remembering not to overlook possible underlying common causes should lead you to contemplate another idea. It's possible that what accounts for these attitudes and misconceptions isn't too much TV, but rather *ignorance,* and that ignorance is also what makes some people happy spending hours in front of the tube. An underlying common cause?

COMMON MISTAKES IN INFORMAL CAUSAL REASONING

When we use relevant-difference or common-thread reasoning, we can make mistakes. Those that follow are pretty common. The strength of the reasoning depends on the extent to which we can eliminate these mistakes. Post hoc reasoning essentially involves a failure to eliminate the following mistakes.

- *We can overlook alternative common threads or differences.* Let's say the azaleas don't bloom well this spring. Well, we failed to fertilize the azaleas last winter; but let's not overlook other relevant differences—for example, the fact that we also failed to prune them last winter.
- *We can focus on irrelevant differences or common threads.* What if, this year, we read two new books on ornamental horticulture? This is a difference between this year and previous years all right, but it isn't a *relevant* difference if we don't actually *do* anything different to the azaleas. Just *reading* about them plays no role in whether or not they bloom. *What do we mean when we say a difference or thread is relevant?* We mean it is not unreasonable to suppose the difference might have caused the feature in question. Obviously, the more you know about a subject, the better able you are to say whether a given difference is relevant. If you knew nothing about anything, then you would have no idea what is relevant and what isn't.

In the Media

"Teen Smoking Surge Reported After Joe Camel's 1988 Debut"

So said the Associated Press headline that accompanied this graphic. The article, however, stated that the Centers for Disease Control *attributed* the surge in part to kid-friendly cartoon advertising like the Joe Camel ads. It also noted that then-president Clinton had blamed the increase on the Joe Camel ad campaign.

It is true that the CDC studies showed that the rate for beginning smokers had been *declining* steadily for over a decade before it started increasing again in 1988. It is also true that *something* caused the rate to start increasing again, beginning in 1988. And finally, it is true that R. J. Reynolds introduced *Joe Camel* in its advertising for Camel cigarettes in 1988.

But *this* information, while suspicious, does not show that the increase was *caused,* even in part, *by* the ad campaign. For example, reportedly there was a notable increase in the appearance of cigarette smoking in movies beginning about then, too. As it stands, this too is post hoc, ergo propter hoc.

Rise in youth smoking

The incidence of youths becoming regular smokers jumped 50 percent between 1988 and 1996. A look at the rate of youths who started smoking daily, age 12–17:

Per 1,000 nonsmoking youths*

*Considered nonsmokers at start of year

Source: Centers for Disease Control and Prevention

- *We can overlook the possibility that causation is the reverse of what has been asserted.* Did his fall cause the rope to break? Or did the rope's breaking cause his fall? Does your back ache because of your poor posture? Or is your poor posture the result of your aching back?
- *We can overlook the possibility that the stated cause and the stated effect are both effects of some third, underlying cause.* We know people, and you may do so as well, who think that cold weather causes the leaves to turn yellow in the fall. In fact, the cold weather and the yellowing leaves are both caused by the waning sunlight.
- *We can fail to consider the possibility of coincidence.* For example, if the cancer rate in one neighborhood is higher than in others, you'd look both for common threads among the cancer victims and relevant differences between this neighborhood and others. But it could be coincidence. Cancer cases won't be distributed evenly throughout a region; some neighborhoods will have a higher-than-average cancer rate and others a rate that is lower than average, just due to chance.

If we fail to take these possibilities into consideration, we are apt to think A caused B just because of its spatial-temporal proximity to B, which is the post-hoc fallacy.

GENERAL CAUSAL CLAIMS

Recently, we met an older man who began discussing his health, as older people sometimes do. "You look pretty good for your age," we said, lying.

"Used to have arthritis," he continued. "Bad. I took vitamin E and that really helped."

Well, maybe. But from the mere fact that your arthritis improved after taking vitamin E you cannot conclude that the improvement *resulted* from taking vitamin E. That would be post hoc, ergo propter hoc. Unless the man had good reason to think the vitamin E was the only relevant difference between the two conditions, the most he should say is "I took vitamin E and *it got better,*" not "I took vitamin E and it *helped.*"

It is an interesting fact about human psychology that if we were to read about a "clinical trial" that consisted of a single arthritic person taking vitamin E, we would laugh out loud. However, if a *friend* tells us vitamin E helped her arthritis, we might very well take it ourselves, if we suffered from that malady, or recommend vitamin E to someone else who is arthritic. But logically there is no difference between a "clinical trial" consisting of a single subject and a report from a friend.

What's wrong with a report from friend, or a "clinical trial" with one subject? The problem is that, generally, you can't control for all the variables, and as a result you can't calculate the probability that the outcome was not just chance. If you drink herbal tea and your cold goes away, that result might be the effect of some entirely unrelated cause, which is to say that its going away when you drank herbal tea is sheer coincidence. Since you haven't eliminated other possible causes (relevant differences), you cannot calculate the probability that this was just a chance occurrence.

The way scientists resolve the problem is to concern themselves with *general* causal claims, such as "Vitamin E improves arthritis." "Taking vitamin E improved *my* arthritis" is a claim about a specific cause-and-effect event, and as such it can be difficult to establish. Likewise, "My uncle got lung cancer because he smoked" is a statement about a specific cause-effect event, whereas "Smoking causes lung cancer" is a general claim. It's with general hypotheses that science is mainly concerned.

A general causal claim has to be understood somewhat differently from a claim about a specific cause-effect event.* General causal claims can be given a statistical interpretation that makes them subject to scientific confirmation. A general claim, such as "drinking causes cancer of the mouth," should not be interpreted as meaning that drinking will cause mouth cancer for any given individual, or even that drinking will cause mouth cancer for the majority of individuals. The claim is that drinking is a *causal factor* for mouth cancer—that is, there would be more cases of mouth cancer if everyone drank than if no one did. And so it is with other claims about causation in populations: To say that X causes Y in population P is to say that there would be more cases of Y in population P if every member of P were exposed to X than if no member of P were exposed to X.

*For the following analysis, we follow Ronald N. Giere, Understanding Scientific Reasoning, 3rd ed (Fort Worth: Holt, Rinehart, and Winston, 1991).

Real Life

Television's Effect on Kids

Let's say increased TV watching *correlates* with increased incidence of violent behavior. Maybe watching TV *leads* to the violent behavior—but, equally as likely, maybe both are a result of an underlying cause (whatever causes kids to act violently also causes them to like to watch violent behavior). Or maybe kids who act violently become more interested in looking at violence (in the same way that signing up for a sport may heighten one's interest in watching the sport on TV).

Correlations, like the one reported in this graphic, do not establish causation. Thinking they do is a type of post hoc reasoning.

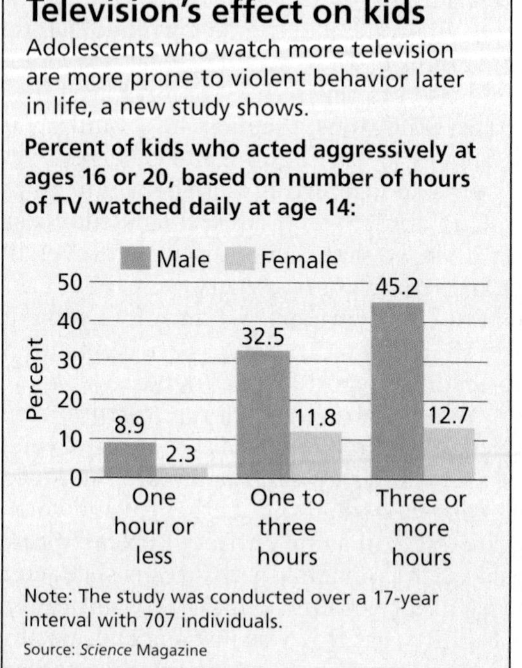

The evidence on which such claims may be soundly based comes principally from three kinds of investigations or "arguments" All are applications of relevant-difference reasoning, which we explained in the previous section.

The basic idea behind these investigations is this. Someone once told us port wine applied to bald men's heads promotes hair growth. How would you find out? You would round up a group of bald men and divide them into two subgroups. On the heads of the men in one subgroup. you'd apply port wine. If the men in both subgroups are the same in all respects except for the port wine applied to the heads of the men in the one subgroup (a big "if"), then if the men in that subgroup sprout hair, you conclude that the port wine caused the hair growth, because it, the port wine, is the only relevant difference between the two groups.

With that as background, let's look at these types of investigations just a bit more closely.

Controlled Cause-to-Effect Experiments

In **controlled cause-to-effect experiments,** a random sample of a target population is itself randomly divided into two groups: (1) an experimental group, all of whose members are exposed to a suspected causal factor, C (e.g., exposure of the skin to nicotine), and (2) a control group, whose members are all treated exactly as the members of the experimental group, except that they are not exposed to C. Both groups are then compared with respect to frequency of some effect, E (e.g., skin cancer). If the difference, *d*, in the frequency of E in the two groups is sufficiently large, then C may justifiably be said to cause E in the population.

This probably sounds complicated, but the principles involved are matters of common sense. You have two groups that are essentially alike, except that the members of one group are exposed to the suspected causal agent. If the effect is then found to be sufficiently more frequent in that group, you conclude that the suspected causal agent does indeed cause the effect in question.

Familiarizing yourself with these concepts and abbreviations will help you understand cause-to-effect experiments:

> **experimental group**—the sample of the target population whose members are all exposed to the suspected causal agent
>
> **control group**—the sample of the target population whose members are treated exactly as the members of the experimental group are except that they are not exposed to the suspected causal agent
>
> C—the suspected causal agent
> E—the effect whose cause is being investigated
> *d*—the difference in the frequency of this effect in the experimental group and in the control group

Let us suppose that the frequency of the effect in the experimental group is found to be greater than in the control group. *How much greater* must the frequency of the effect in the experimental group be for us to say that the suspected causal agent actually is a causal factor? That is, how great must *d* be for us to believe that C is really a causal factor for E? After all, even if nicotine does *not* cause skin cancer, the frequency of skin cancer found in the experimental group *might* exceed the frequency found in the control group because of some chance occurrence.

Suppose that there are one hundred individuals in our experimental group and the same number in our control group, and suppose that *d* was greater than 13 percentage points—that is, suppose the frequency of skin cancer in the experimental group exceeded the frequency in the control group by more than 13 percentage points. Could that result be due merely to chance? Yes, but there is a 95 percent probability that it was *not* due to chance. If the frequency of skin cancer in the experimental group were to exceed the frequency in the control group by more than 13 percentage points (given one hundred members in each group), then this finding would be *statistically significant at the .05 level*, which simply means that we could say with a 95 percent degree of confidence that the elevated cancer rate wasn't just coincidence. If we were content to speak with less confidence, or if our samples were larger, then the difference in the frequency of skin cancer between the experimental group and control group would not have to be as great to qualify as statistically significant.

Thus, saying that the difference in frequency of the effect between the experimental and control groups is **statistically significant** at some level (e.g., .05) simply means that it would be unreasonable to attribute this difference in frequency to chance. Just how unreasonable it would be depends on what level is cited. If no level is cited—as in reports of controlled experiments that stipulate only that the findings are "significant"—it is customary to assume

Real Life

Hey, Couch Potato—Read This!

You sometimes hear people say they avoid exercise because they know of someone who had a heart attack while working out. We trust you now recognize such reasoning as post hoc: To show that Uncle Ned's heart attack was caused by lifting weights, or whatever, you have to do more than show that the one thing happened and then the other thing happened.

There is a further problem here. To wonder whether strenuous exercise causes heart attacks is to wonder whether such exercise is a **causal factor** for heart attacks. And you can't really answer such questions by appealing to specific incidents, as we explain in the text. To think that you can show that something is (or isn't) a causal factor in a population by referring to isolated, specific events is to appeal illegitimately to anecdotal evidence, as we discuss at the end of this chapter.

(For the record: According to research published in the *New England Journal of Medicine* at the end of 1993, males who undertake heavy physical exertion increase their risk of a heart attack by around 100 times *if* they are habitually sedentary–out of shape. For those who do exercise regularly, strenuous exertion doesn't increase their risk of heart attack.)

Percentage increases from a small baseline can be misleading.

If you look at the new cases of death from AIDS, the fastest growing category could be ladies over the age of 70. If last year one woman over 70 died from AIDS and this year two do, you get a 100 percent increase in AIDS deaths for that category.

— John Allen Paulos

that the results were significant at the .05 level, which simply means that the result could have arisen by chance in about five cases out of one hundred. Recall from Chapter 10 that we referred to a 95 percent confidence level, which is another way of saying we have the kind of probability found in a .05 significance level.

Media reports of controlled experiments usually state or clearly imply whether the difference in frequency of the effect found in the experimental and control groups is significant. However, if, as occasionally happens, there is a question about whether the results are statistically significant (i.e., are unlikely to have arisen by chance), it is important not to assume uncritically or automatically either of the following:

1. *That the sample is large enough to guarantee significance.* A large sample is no guarantee that the difference (d) in the frequency of the effect in the experimental group and in the control group is statistically significant. (However, the larger the sample, the smaller d—expressed as a difference in percentage points—needs to be to count as significant.) People are sometimes overly impressed by the mere size of a study.

2. *That the difference in frequency is great enough to guarantee significance.* The fact that there seems to be a pronounced difference in the frequency of the effect in the experimental group and in the control group is no guarantee that the difference is statistically significant. If the sample size is small enough, it may not be. If there are fifty rats in an experimental group and fifty more in a control group, then even if the frequency of skin cancer found in the experimental group exceeds the frequency of skin cancer found in the control group by as much as 18 percentage points, this finding would not be statistically significant (at the .05 level). If each group contained a thousand rats, a difference in frequency of 3 points would not qualify as significant. (And remember that a 3-point difference can be referred to as a

Table 11.1

Approximate Statistically Significant *d*'s at .05 Level

Number in Experimental Group *(with Similarly Sized Control Group)*	Approximate Figure That *d* Must Exceed to Be Statistically Significant *(in Percentage Points)*
10	40
25	27
50	19
100	13
250	8
500	6
1,000	4
1,500	3

"whopping" 50 percent difference if it is the difference between 6 points and 3 points.) Unless you have some knowledge of statistics, it is probably best not to assume that findings are statistically significant unless it is clearly stated or implied that they are.

Nevertheless, it may be helpful to you to have some rough idea of when a difference in frequency of effect in the experimental and control groups may be said to be statistically significant at the .05 level. Table 11-1 provides some examples.

Suppose there are ten individuals each in the randomly selected experimental and control groups. To be statistically significant at the .05 level, the difference between experimental and control group in frequency of the effect must exceed 40 percentage points. If there are twenty-five people in each group, then *d* must exceed 27 points to be statistically significant, and so forth.

Even if it is clear in a controlled experiment that *d* is significant, there are a few more considerations to keep in mind when reviewing reports of experimental findings. First, the results of controlled experiments are often extended analogically from the target population (e.g., rats) to another population (e.g., humans). Such analogical extensions should be evaluated in accordance with the criteria for analogical arguments discussed in the previous chapter. In particular, before accepting such extensions of the findings, you should consider carefully whether there are important relevant differences between the target population in the experiment and the population to which the results of the experiment are analogically extended.

Second, it is important in controlled experiments that the sample from which the experimental and control groups are formed be representative of the target population, and thus it is essential that the sample be taken at random. Further, because the experimental and control groups should be as similar as possible, it is important that the assignment of subjects to these groups also be a random process. In reputable scientific experiments it is safe to assume that randomization has been so employed, but one must be suspicious of informal "experiments" in which no mention of randomization is made.

In Depth

Cigarettes, Cancer, and the Genetic-Factors Argument

For years the tobacco industry challenged the data showing that smoking causes lung cancer. The industry argued that certain unknown genetic factors (1) predispose some people to get cancer and also (2) predispose those same people to smoke.

The tobacco people are just doing what critical thinkers should do, looking for a common underlying cause for two phenomena that seem on the face of things to be related directly by cause and effect. However, they have never found any such common cause, and the claim that there *might be* one is not equivalent to the claim that there *is* one. Further, even if the industry theory is correct, that wouldn't diminish the other risks involved in smoking.

We should point out, however, that scientists have recently discovered that a chemical found in cigarette smoke damages a gene, known as p53, that acts to suppress the runaway growth of cells that lead to tumors. Researchers regard the discovery as finding the exact mechanism of causation of cancer by cigarette smoke; the discovery seems to put the whole issue of whether cigarettes cause cancer beyond much doubt.

And while we're talking about reputable sources, remember that any outfit can call itself the "Cambridge Institute for Psychological Studies" and publish its reports in its own "journal." Organizations with prestigious-sounding place names (Princeton, Berkeley, Palo Alto, Bethesda, and so on), proper names (Fulbright, Columbia, and so on), or concepts (institute, academy, research, advanced studies) *could* consist of little more than a couple of university dropouts with a dubious theory and an axe to grind.

Nonexperimental Cause-to-Effect Studies

A **nonexperimental cause-to-effect study** (or argument) is another type of study designed to test whether something is a causal factor for a given effect. In this type of study, members of a target population (say, humans) who have not yet shown evidence of the suspected effect E (e.g., cancer of the colon) are divided into two groups that are alike in all respects except one. The difference is that members of one group, the experimental group, have all been exposed to the suspected cause C (fatty diets, for example), whereas the members of the other group, the control group, have not. Such studies differ from controlled experiments in that the members of the experimental group are not exposed to the suspected causal agent *by the investigators*—clearly, one limit of experimental studies is that investigators can't purposely expose human subjects to potentially dangerous agents. Eventually, just as in the controlled experiment, experimental and control groups are both compared with respect to the frequency of E. If the frequency in the experimental group exceeds the frequency in the control group by a statistically significant margin, we may conclude that C is the cause of E in the target population.

In reports of nonexperimental cause-to-effect studies, as in reports of controlled experiments, if it is not stated or clearly implied that the findings are significant, do not assume that they are merely because either (1) the samples are large or (2) the difference in the frequency of the effect in absolute terms or percentages is striking.

Likewise, (3) if a causal relationship found to hold in the target population on the basis of such a study is extended analogically to other populations, you should evaluate this analogical extension very carefully, especially with respect to any relevant differences between the target population and the analogical population.

And, finally, (4) note the following important difference between controlled experiments and nonexperimental cause-to-effect studies: In a *controlled* experiment, the subjects are assigned to experimental and control groups by a random process, after which the experimental subjects are exposed to C. This randomization ensures that experimental and control groups will be alike except for the suspected causal agent that the experimental group is then exposed to. But in the *nonexperimental* study, the experimental group (which is still so called even though no experiment is performed) is composed of randomly selected individuals who have already been exposed to the suspected causal agent or who say they were. And the individuals who have already been exposed to C (or who say they were) may differ from the rest of the target population in some respect in addition to having been exposed to C. For example, there is a positive correlation between having a fatty diet and drinking alcoholic beverages. Thus, an experimental group composed by random means from those in the general population who have fatty diets would include more than its fair share of drinkers. Consequently, the high rate of colon cancer observed in this experimental group might be due in part to the effects of drinking.

It is important, then, that the process by which the individuals in the general population "self-select" themselves (regarding their exposure to C) not be biased in any way related to the effect. In good studies, any factors that might bias the experimental group are controlled by one means or another. Often, for example, the control group is not randomly selected, but rather is selected to match the experimental group for any other relevant factors. Thus, in a study that seeks to relate fatty diets to cancer of the colon, an experimenter will make certain that the same percentage of drinkers is found in the control group as in the experimental group.

Nonexperimental studies of the variety explained here and in the next section are *inherently* weaker than controlled experiments as arguments for

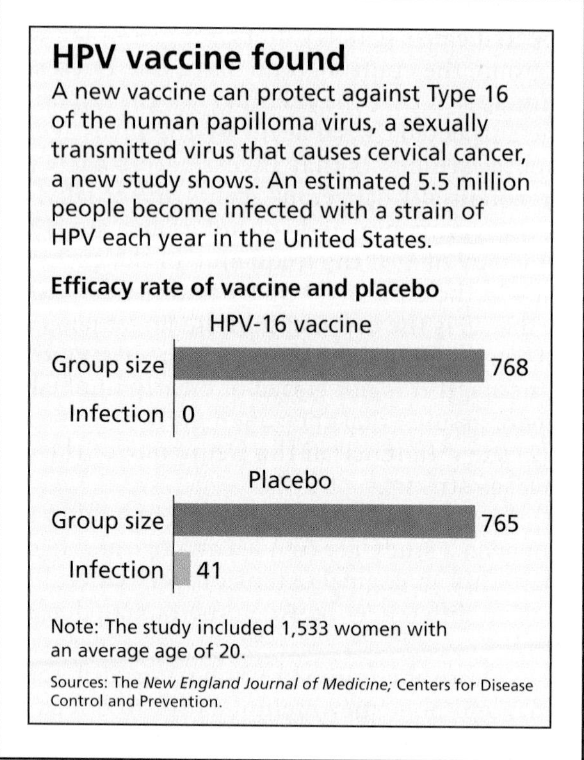

■ Graphics like this, while leaving out important details, help readers understand cause-and-effect investigations.

causal claims. Because we do not have complete knowledge of what factors are causally related to what other factors, it is impossible to say for certain that all possibly relevant variables in such studies have been controlled. It is good policy to imagine what characteristics those who have been exposed to the suspected causal agent might have and contemplate whether any of these factors may be related to the effect. If you can think of any relevant variables that have not been controlled, you should have doubts about any causal claim that is made on the basis of such studies.

Nonexperimental Effect-to-Cause Studies

A **nonexperimental effect-to-cause study** is a third type of study designed to test whether something is a causal factor for a given effect. In this type of study, the "experimental group," whose members already display the *effect* being investigated, E (e.g., cancer of the mouth), is compared with a control group none of whose members have E, and the frequency of the suspected cause, C (e.g., using chewing tobacco), is measured. If the frequency of C in the experimental group significantly exceeds its frequency in the control group, then C may be said to cause E in the target population.

Cautionary remarks from the discussion of nonexperimental cause-to-effect studies apply equally to nonexperimental effect-to-cause studies. That is, if it isn't clear that the findings are significant, don't assume that they are

Real Life

A Fool and His or Her Money Are Soon Parted

In the old days, traveling salesmen would sell "snake oil"—a worthless elixir claimed to cure numerous maladies. Sales were largely generated by testimonials from people who had used the product and found it had "cured" some ailment.

There was no need to make up the testimonials. Almost necessarily, *some malady or other* will disappear after *someone or other* takes a potion, just as sheer coincidence. And if an ailment disappears after you take the medicine—purely as a coincidence—you might well be inclined to attribute the cure to the medicine (post hoc, ergo propter hoc). Others, in turn, would be persuaded by your testimonial and give the product a try.

The modern-day equivalent of the elixir is found on the shelves of any health-food store, where people lay down good money for this or that "supplement," often for no better reason than that a friend tried it and found that it "worked."

merely because (1) the samples seem large or (2) the difference in the frequency expressed in absolute terms seems striking; and (3) evaluate carefully analogical extensions of the results to other populations.

Notice further that (4) the subjects in the experimental group may differ in some important way (in addition to showing the effect) from the rest of the target population. Thus, for instance, former smokers are more likely than others to use chewing tobacco and are also more likely to get mouth cancer. If you sample randomly from a group of victims of mouth cancer, therefore, you are likely to produce more ex-smokers in your sample than occur in the general population. The result is that you are likely to discover more chewing-tobacco users in the sample, even if chewing tobacco plays no role whatsoever in causing cancer of the mouth. Any factor that might bias the experimental group in such studies should be controlled. If, in evaluating such a study, you can think of any factor that has not been controlled, you can regard the study as having failed to demonstrate causation.

Notice, finally, that (5) effect-to-cause studies show only the probable frequency of the cause, not the effect, and thus provide no grounds for estimating the percentage of the target population that would be affected if everyone in it were exposed to the cause.

APPEAL TO ANECDOTAL EVIDENCE

In Chapter 10, we discussed the mistake of trying to reach a conclusion by citing one or two examples—i.e., by appealing to anecdotes. There is another type of appeal to anecdotal evidence that relates to causal arguments, as distinct from generalizations: trying to either prove or disprove that X is a causal factor for Y by citing an example or two of an X that did (or didn't) cause a Y. Thinking that red wine prevents colds because we know someone who drinks red wine and never catches cold would be an instance of this type of weak reasoning. It would be similarly weak to argue that red wine doesn't prevent colds because we've never observed that effect in us. Those who submit that smoking

On Language

The Wrong Initials Can Shorten Your Life

Researchers at the University of California, San Diego, looking at twenty-seven years of California death certificates, found that men with "indisputably positive" initials like JOY and WOW and ACE and GOD and WIN and VIP lived 4.48 years longer than a control group of men with neutral initials and ambiguous initials, like DAM and WET and RAY and SUN, that had both positive and negative interpretation. Further, men with "plainly negative" initials like ASS or DUD died on average 2.8 years earlier than did the men in the control group.

As an exercise, propose an explanation for these findings that isn't defective in terms of the criteria discussed in this chapter. Explain how you would test the explanation.

doesn't cause cancer because they know a smoker who lived to ninety-eight and died of old age are guilty of the causal type of anecdotal argument.

To establish that X is a causal factor for Y, we have to show that there would be more cases of Y if everyone did X than if no one did, and you can't really show this—or demonstrate that X isn't a causal factor for Y—by citing an example or two. Isolated incidents can reasonably serve to raise suspicions about causal factors, but that is all.

One of the most common mistakes made in everyday reasoning is to appeal to anecdotal evidence in one or the other of the ways discussed here and in Chapter 10. And now that you know what is involved in saying that something is a causal factor, you know why you can't establish this sort of causal claim by appealing to an anecdote.

DOUBTFUL CAUSAL CLAIMS/HYPOTHESES

You have trouble sleeping at night and go to the doctor to find out what's wrong. He runs several tests and then informs you that, at long last, he has the explanation.

"The cause of your not sleeping," he announces, "is insomnia."

Here you wouldn't need to know what your doctor's reasoning was. His explanation is *inherently* defective. Some causal claims and hypotheses are like that. They suffer from inherent difficulties, problems that lie within the claim itself.

Here are some common defects of this nature.

1. Circularity: A causal claim might be circular. This happens when the "cause" merely restates the effect. When your doctor says you can't sleep because of insomnia, his claim is circular. Insomnia just *is* not sleeping. "She has trouble writing because she has writer's block" would be another example of circular causal explanation. Having trouble writing and having writer's block amount to the same thing. A circular causal claim cannot teach you anything new about causes and effects (although it might teach you a new *name* for an effect).

2. Nontestability: "AIDS is God's punishment for evil." The problem with this assertion lies in the fact you cannot test whether it is true. There is no way

■ If somebody told you that cows stand up and talk to each other, you'd say he or she was nuts, right? After all, nobody has ever seen cows doing that. But suppose the person were to respond by telling you that cows stand up only when nobody can see them? Or suppose a psychic were to explain that his or her psychic abilities disappear when threatened or contaminated by the skepticism of an investigating scientist.

What's wrong with those explanations? Read the rest of the chapter to find out.

to detect when the hand of God is present and when it isn't. "You can't sleep because you are possessed" would be another example of a nontestable claim.

Do bear in mind that being *difficult* to test is *not* necessarily a defect in a causal hypothesis. Scientific hypotheses can be enormously difficult to test. The problem is with claims for which a test is *unimaginable,* like the examples above.

3. Excessive vagueness: "The reason Nasim has trouble in his relationships? Bad karma." The trouble with this claim is that "bad karma" is too vague: What does "bad karma" include, and what does it exclude? A similar problem of vagueness would arise if someone tried to attribute Nasim's difficulty to his having "impure thoughts." ("Trouble in his relationships" is pretty vague as well, but if we know Nasim and the speaker we might have an idea what the phrase refers to.) These two claims about Nasim are also untestable; indeed, in general, if a claim is too vague, we won't know exactly how to go about testing it. But not all untestable claims are too vague: "An invisible gremlin inside your car's engine explains why it misses occasionally" is untestable, but not especially vague.

4. Unnecessary assumptions: The assertion above about an invisible gremlin causing the engine to miss involves unnecessary assumptions, because there are *other* explanations for the car's missing that do *not* assume gremlins. Similarly, you sometimes hear déjà vu explained as being caused by memories from previous lives. But that claim, as well as being untestable, requires assuming past lives, which isn't necessary since déjà vu experiences can be induced by electric stimulation of areas within the brain.

5. A causal claim or hypothesis might **conflict with well-established theory.** For example, we once heard someone assert that a person's height is due to something the person did in a past life. This notion conflicts with genetic theory. Now, that an assertion conflicts with a well-established theory is not necessarily a *fatal* flaw, because theoretical advances often involve rejecting ideas that once counted as well-established. The theory of continental drift, for example, conflicted with other geological principles. Likewise, the theories of Einstein and other twentieth-century physicists conflicted with Newtonian physics. But evidence was required to establish the new ideas. If a proffered explanation conflicts with well-established theory, we have good reasons to look for an alternative account and to demand powerful evidence of its truth. Also, the fact that there are many examples in which well-established theory is later rejected is itself no evidence at all of the truth of any specific causal claim.

CAUSAL EXPLANATIONS AND ARGUMENTS

Recently we complained to a friend about the paint on a Chevy truck one of us owns.

"What's wrong with it?" he asked.

"It's peeling all over the place," we said.

"Why's it doing that?" he asked.

"That's what we would like to know," we said.

Our friend wasn't confused about this conversation. He understood clearly what it was we wanted to know: We wanted an *explanation* of why the paint on the truck was peeling. We wanted to know what caused it to peel.

Although our friend wasn't confused, causal explanations—explanations of the causes of something—are often confused with arguments, mainly because they involve some of the same words and phrases. But arguing and explaining are different enterprises. They respond to different questions. If someone questions *whether* the paint is peeling, he needs an argument that it either is or isn't. The question of what caused it to peel, on the other hand, assumes that it is peeling and just asks why. (See Chapter 1 for more on this subject.)

People shouldn't confuse causal explanations with arguments because causal explanations assert or imply cause and effect. A few examples make this clear. The items on the left all assert cause and effect. Those on the right do not—they are arguments.

Causal Claim/Explanation	**Argument**
The reason Republicans are fiscally conservative is that big business gives a lot of money to fiscal conservatives.	The reason you should vote for Republicans is that they are fiscally conservative.
Scott didn't live up to expectations; that's why they fired him.	I heard that Scott didn't live up to expectations; that's why I am pretty sure they will fire him.
The water in the eastern Pacific was 5 degrees above normal in 2004, making 2004 a wetter year across the southern tier of states.	The water in the eastern Pacific was 5 degrees above normal in 2004, making it safe to assume 2004 was a wetter year across the southern tier of states.

So, the moral is obvious. Don't be fooled by superficial similarities. Causal explanations can look superficially like arguments, but they assert cause and effect. Arguments try to prove that something is the case.

The only complication is that, unfortunately, *sometimes causal explanations are used as premises in arguments.* For example, you might explain *what caused* the carburetor on a lawn mower to be gummed up to argue *that* the carburetor is gummed up. A Ford ad might explain *what causes* Ford trucks to be best-sellers in order to argue *that* they are great trucks. Your doctor might explain what caused you to get scarlet fever in order to argue that what you have is indeed scarlet fever.

Consider the following additional example:

> You won't be able to see the comet from here tonight. The reason is that we're too close to the lights of the city to see anything that faint in the sky.

The speaker explains what it is that *will cause* you to not be able to see the comet from here; but it is very likely that he or she wants to provide you with evidence that you won't be able to see the comet from here. In that case, he or she is using this causal explanation to *argue* that you won't be able to see the comet from here tonight.

The lesson is simple: Causal explanations can function as premises of arguments. If someone tells you not to wear a dress because it makes you look tacky, the premise of the argument is that the dress makes you look tacky—a causal claim.

Explanations and Excuses

You are late to class—a tire went flat over night. You don't want the professor to mark you down, so you explain why you are late. This is a causal explanation (the flat tire caused me to be late) used as the premise of the argument that you should be excused for being late. When we try to justify or defend or excuse something we (or someone else) did, we sometimes explain its causes. David was caught stealing a loaf of bread; he then explained to the authorities that he needed the bread to feed his children. David was attempting to argue

Real Life

Study Backs an Old Idea about Crime

Target petty offenses to prevent serious ones, the theory goes.

Maybe you know about the Broken Windows theory of law enforcement. According to that theory, graffiti, petty vandalism, and other misdemeanor crimes in a neighborhood lead to more serious crime problems; and curtailing blight in a neighborhood prevents it from descending into a world of burglary, drugs, car theft, and violent crimes. Mayor Rudolph Giuliani vigorously subscribed to this theory during his term in office, during which New York City became a cleaner, safer place.

However, the theory had apparently not had much statistical support until an analysis of crime rates for all California counties from 1989 to 2000, by the California Institute for County Government, disclosed that the rate of arrests for serious property crimes indeed fell (overall by 3.6 percent) as the ratio for misdemeanor arrests increased. In some counties, where efforts were made to streamline prosecution for petty crimes, the decline in serious crimes was quite dramatic.

This makes sense, because some people who commit petty crimes also commit more serious crimes, and locking them up automatically reduces the number of serious crimes. But the findings (or at least the newspaper reports of them) leave room for skepticism as to the Broken Windows idea. One, the reduction in the rate of serious crimes might be the cause rather than the effect of an increase in petty crime arrest. The study was limited to property crimes like burglary and auto theft, which may well have declined anyway in this period of relative prosperity, thus increasing enforcement opportunities for misdemeanors. Two, apparently the crime rates were the averages for the counties, which gives rural counties disproportionate weight in the final results. In rural counties, even a small increase or decrease in absolute numbers can produce dramatic percentage shifts.

The most you can say is that the findings at least don't contradict the Broken Windows theory.

Source: *Sacramento Bee.*

that his behavior should be excused, and his explanation of what caused him to steal the bread was the premise of his argument.

Not every attempt to explain behavior is an attempt to excuse or defend the behavior. After the September 11 suicide attacks on the World Trade Center, speakers on some university campuses offered explanations of the causes of the attacks. In some cases they were accused of trying to excuse the attacks, and perhaps some of them were trying to do that. But others weren't trying to excuse the attacks; they were simply trying to explain their causes. The distinction was lost on some people; attempts to explain the causes of the attacks were frequently condemned as traitorous. (In fact, one of our own colleagues who tried to express his views about the geopolitical causes of the attacks made the national news and was promptly invited by Rush Limbaugh to move to Afghanistan.)

If you assume without thinking about it that anyone who tries to explain the causes of bad behavior is trying to excuse it, you commit a fallacy. (Remember that a fallacy is a mistake in reasoning.) This fallacy, which we shall call **confusing explanations and excuses,** is common. For example, someone may try to explain why many Germans adopted the vicious anti-Semitic views of the Nazi party during the 1930s. The speaker may point out that the German economy was in a mess, that the country still suffered from terms imposed on it at the end of World War I, and, furthermore, that people often look for scapegoats on whom they can blame their troubles. These remarks may help us understand why the German people were easily led into anti-Semitism, but an uncritical listener may believe that the speaker is trying to muster sympathy for those people and their actions. As a matter of fact, just such an explanation was given by Phillipp Jenniger in the German parliament on the fiftieth anniversary of the *Kristallnacht,* a night when Nazis attacked Jewish neighborhoods and shops. Many of Jenniger's fellow Germans misunderstood his account, thinking it was designed to make excuses for the Nazis' actions. But it does not follow that a person proposing explanations has any sympathy at all for the views or actions being explained.

To sum things up, sometimes we explain the causes of something that sounds bad in order to excuse it; but sometimes such explanations are simply used to explain. Causal explanations can be entirely neutral with regard to approval or disapproval of an action. If we fail to see the difference between explaining behavior and excusing it, we may stifle attempts to explain it. The speaker may worry that we will think he or she is defending the bad behavior. This would be unfortunate because, lacking an explanation for such behavior, we may be hampered in our attempts to discourage it.

Recap

The following topics were covered in this chapter:

- When we reason about cause and effect in informal, real-life situations, we often (but not always) want to know what caused some effect that interests us.
- It is never legitimate to conclude that one thing caused another just because the two things occurred around the same time—this is the *post hoc* fallacy.
- Instead, we must use either relevant-difference reasoning or common-thread reasoning.
- However, we must be careful not to focus on irrelevant differences or common threads, and we must not overlook alternative relevant common threads and differences.
- In addition, we should consider whether the causation is the reverse of what we suspect or that the effect and suspected cause are both the effects of some third, underlying cause.
- Further, we must consider whether the effect and suspected cause are connected merely through coincidence.
- We establish that something is a causal factor in a population on the basis of cause-to-effect experimentation or on the basis of cause-to-effect or effect-to-cause studies.

- We cannot establish a general causal claim on the basis of an example or two that looks like cause and effect.
- Causal claims can suffer from inherent defects, most notably circularity, nontestability, excessive vagueness, dependence on unnecessary assumptions, or conflict with well-established theory.
- Despite superficial similarities in phrasing, causal claims and arguments respond to different questions.
- A complication is that causal claims can be used as premises of arguments.
- Sometimes arguments that use causal claims in this way attempt to excuse something, but it is a mistake to think they all do.

Exercises

Exercise 11-1

Which of the following are causal claims (hypotheses)?

▲ **1.** Webber's being healthy is probably what made Philadelphia more competitive this year.

2. Dress more warmly! It's windy out there.

3. Gilbert's disposition has deteriorated since he and his wife separated; it isn't just a coincidence.

▲ **4.** Senator Lott praised Strom Thurmond and that forced some conservatives to call for Lott's resignation.

5. Getting that new trumpet player certainly improved the brass sections.

6. When men wear a swimsuit, they have difficulty doing math problems.

▲ **7.** Despite all the injuries, the Dolphins managed to keep winning. It must have something to do with their positive attitude.

8. Too little sleep will slow down your reaction time.

9. Women are worse drivers than men.

▲ **10.** He's a creep! That's why Chaz removes the toilet paper from his bathroom before his mother-in-law visits.

11. Randomized clinical trials produce unbiased data on the benefits of drugs.

12. The batteries in this dang flashlight are completely dead!

▲ **13.** The reason that flashlight won't work is that the batteries are completely dead.

14. Believe me, the batteries in that flashlight are dead. Try it. You'll see.

15. Aunt Clara thinks her prayers cured Uncle Pete. [Caution!]

▲ **16.** The risk of having a heart attack is 33 percent higher in the winter than in the summer in Philadelphia.

Exercise 11-2

What is the cause and what is the effect in each of the following?

1. The cat won't eat, so Mrs. Quibblebuck searches her mind for a reason. "Now, could it be," she muses, "that I haven't heard mice scratching around in the attic lately?" "That's the explanation," she concludes.

2. Each time one of the burglaries occurred, observers noticed a red Mustang in the vicinity. The police, of course, suspect the occupants as being responsible.
3. Violette is a strong Cowboys fan. Because of her work schedule, however, she has been able to watch their games only twice this season, and they lost both times. She resolves not to watch any more. "It's bad luck," she decides.
4. ▲ Giving the little guy more water could have prevented him from getting dehydrated, said Ms. Delacruz.
5. OAXACA, Mexico (AP)—Considered by many to be Mexico's culinary capital, this city took on McDonald's and won, keeping the hamburger giant out of its colonial plaza by passing around tamales in protest.
6. Eating fish or seafood at least once a week lowers the risk of developing dementia, researchers have found.
7. ▲ It has long puzzled researchers why people cannot detect their own bad breath. One theory is that people get used to the odor.
8. Researchers based at McDuff University put thirty young male smokers on a three-month program of vigorous exercise. One year later, only 14 percent of them still smoked. An equivalent number of young male smokers who did not go through the exercise program were also checked after a year, and it was found that 60 percent still smoked. The experiment is regarded as supporting the theory that exercise helps chronic male smokers kick the habit.
9. The stronger the muscles, the greater the load they take off the joint, thus limiting damage to the cartilage, which explains why leg exercise helps prevent osteoarthritis.
10. ▲ Many judges in Oregon will not process shoplifting, trespassing, and small-claims charges. This saves the state a lot of money in court expenses.

Exercise 11-3

Identify each reasoning pattern as (a) relevant-difference reasoning or (b) common-thread reasoning.

1. ▲ Pat never had trouble playing that passage before. I wonder what the problem is. It must have something to do with the piano she just bought.
2. Sometimes the fishing is pretty good around here; sometimes it isn't. When I try to pin down why, it seems like the only variable is the wind. Strange as it sounds, the fish just don't bite when it's windy.
3. The price of gas has gone up more than 40 cents a gallon in the past three or four weeks. It all started when they had that fire down there in that refinery in Texas. Must have really depleted supplies somehow.
4. ▲ You know, it has occurred to me, whenever we have great roses like this, it's always after a long period of cloudy weather. I'll bet they don't like direct sun.

Real Life

Birthday Coincidences

Jeff's birthday is January 24, and guess what? So is his girlfriend's. Wow! Jeff and Samantha regard this as a sign. "It was meant to be," they say, referring to their relationship.

Is the fact their birthdays fall on the very same day really a sign of something "deeper"?

Probably not. The odds that their birthdays both fall on January 24 is (if we forget about leap years) $1/365^2$. But no matter what two days their birthdays happen to fall on, the chances of their falling on just those days is also $1/365^2$. For example, suppose Jeff's birthday is January 16 and Samantha's is, say, March 30. The odds of this happening is also $1/365^2$. Would Jeff and Samantha regard it as special if he was born on January 16 and Samantha was born on March 30? Probably not.

In fact, no matter what combination of events happens, the odds of exactly that combination of events happening is likely to be very small. So, when we think about it that way, most everything is a coincidence—which amounts to saying that nothing more coincidental than most other things.

Let's do a little experiment. Ask the person who sits next to you what his or her birthday is. If you and this person have the same birthday will you be more surprised than you would be by any other specific combination of birth dates? You shouldn't be.

5. All of a sudden he's all "Let's go to Beano's for a change." Right. Am I supposed to think it's just coincidence his old girlfriend started working there?
6. You really want to know what gets me and makes me be so angry? It's you! You and your stupid habit of never lifting up the toilet seat.
7. ▲ Why in heck am I so tired today? Must be all the studying I did last night. Thinking takes a lot of energy.
8. The computer isn't working again. Every time it happens the dang kids have been playing with it. Why can't they just use the computers they have down at school?
9. What makes your dog run away from time to time? I bet it has to do with that garbage you feed him. You want him to stay home? Feed him a better brand of dog food.
10. ▲ I'll tell you what caused all these cases of kids taking guns to school and shooting people. Every single one of those kids liked to play violent videogames, that's what caused it.
11. Gag! What did you do to this coffee, anyway—put Ajax in it?
12. Can you beat that? I set this battery on the garage floor last night and this morning it was dead. I guess the old saying about cement draining a battery is still true.
13. ▲ Clinton was impeached. Then his standing went up in the opinion polls. Just goes to show: No publicity is bad publicity.
14. Why did the dog yelp? Are you serious? You'd yelp if someone stomped on your foot, too.

15. Dennis certainly seems more at peace with himself these days. I guess starting up psychotherapy was good for him.

▲ 16. Every time we have people over, the next morning the bird is all squawky and grumpy. The only thing I can figure is it must not get enough sleep when people are over in the evening.

17. The lawn mower started up just fine last week, and now it won't start at all. Could the fact I let it stand out in the rain have something to do with it?

18. Every time Moore plays soccer, his foot starts to hurt. It also hurts right after he goes jogging. But when he bicycles, or uses an elliptical trainer, he doesn't have a problem. He decides to avoid exercise that involves pounding his feet on the ground.

▲ 19. You know, all of a sudden she's been, like, cool toward me? A bit, you know, icy? I don't think she liked it when I told her I was going to start playing poker with you guys again.

20. Your Chevy Suburban is hard to start. My Chevy Suburban starts right up. You always use Chevron gas; I use Texaco. You'd better switch to Texaco.

Exercise 11-4

Identify the numbered items as A, B, or C, where

A = possible coincidence

B = possible reversed causation

C = possibly a case in which the stated cause and stated effect both result from some third thing, an underlying cause

▲ 1. Whenever I mow the lawn I end up sneezing a lot more than usual. Must be gas fumes from the mower.

2. Maybe the reason he's sick is all the aspirin he's taking.

3. The only thing that could possibly account for Clark and his two brothers all having winning lottery tickets is that all three had been blessed by the Reverend Dim Dome just the day before. I'm signing up for the Reverend's brotherhood.

▲ 4. What else could cause the leaves to turn yellow in the fall? It's got to be the cold weather!

5. Perhaps Jason is nearsighted because he reads so many books.

6. First, Rodrigo gets a large inheritance. Then Charles meets the girl of his dreams. And Amanda gets the job she was hoping for. What did they all have in common? They all thought positively. It can work for you, too.

▲ 7. It's common knowledge that osteoarthritis of the knee causes weakness in the quadriceps.

8. Ever since the country lost its moral direction, the crime rate has gone through the ceiling. What more proof do you need that the cause of skyrocketing crime is the breakdown in traditional family values?

9. Wow! Is Johnson hot or what? After that rocky start, he has struck out the last nine batters to face him. That's what happens when ol' Randy gets his confidence up.

▲ **10.** Research demonstrates that people who eat fish are smarter. I'm going to increase my intake.

11. What a night! All those dogs barking made the coyotes yap, and nobody could get any sleep.

12. Isn't it amazing how when the leaves drop off in the winter, it makes the branches brittle?

▲ **13.** What explains all the violence in society today? TV. Just look at all the violence they show these days.

14. On Monday, Mr. O'Toole came down with a cold. That afternoon, Mrs. O'Toole caught it. Later that evening, their daughter caught it, too.

15. Retail sales are down this year. That's because unemployment is so high.

▲ **16.** Yes, they're saying electric blankets aren't really a health threat, but I know better. A friend had cancer and know what? He slept with an electric blanket.

17. At finals time, the bearded man on the front campus offers prayers in return for food. Donald is thinking, "Sure. Why not?—can't hurt anything." He approaches the bearded man with a tidbit. Later: The bearded man prays. Donald passes his finals. To skeptical friends: "Hey, you never know. I'll take all the help I can get."

18. It is an unusually warm evening, and the birds are singing with exceptional vigor. "Hot weather does make a bird sing," Uncle Irv observes.

▲ **19.** Why did Uncle Ted live such a long time? A good attitude, that's why.

20. Studies demonstrate that people who are insecure about their relationships with their partners have a notable lack of ability to empathize with others. That's why we recommend that partners receive empathy training before they get married.

21. Lack of self-confidence can be difficult to explain, but common sense suggests that stuttering is among the causes, judging from how often the two things go together.

▲ **22.** When I went to Munich last summer I went to this movie, and who was there? This guy I went to school with and hadn't seen in 15 years! No way that could be coincidence!

23. It's odd. I've seen a huge number of snails this year, and the roses have mildew. Don't know which caused which, but one of them obviously caused the other.

24. Her boyfriend is in a bad mood, you say? I'll bet it's because she's trying just a bit too hard to please him. Probably gets on his nerves.

▲ **25.** Many people note that top executives wear expensive clothes and drive nice cars. They do the same, thinking these things must be a key to success.

26. ". . . and let's not underestimate the importance of that home field advantage, guys."

"Right, Dan. Six of the last seven teams that had the home field advantage went on to win the Super Bowl."

27. On your trip across the country, you note that the traffic is awful at the first intersection you come to in Jersey. "They certainly didn't do anyone a favor by putting a traffic light at this place," you reflect. "Look at all the congestion it caused."

Exercise 11-5

Identify each of the following as (a) a claim about a specific case of cause and effect, (b) a general causal claim, or (c) neither of these.

▲ 1. The hibiscus died while we were away. There must have been a frost.
2. Carlos isn't as fast as he used to be; that's what old age will do.
3. Kent's college education helped him get a high-paying job.
▲ 4. The most frequently stolen utility vehicle is a 2000 Jeep Wrangler.
5. Vitamin C prevents colds.
6. The man who put this town on the map was Dr. Jaime Diaz.
▲ 7. The high reading on the thermometer resulted from two causes: This thermometer was located lower to the ground than at other stations, and its shelter was too small, so the ventilation was inadequate.
8. Oily smoke in the exhaust was caused by worn rings.
9. The initial tests indicate that caffeine has toxic effects in humans.
▲ 10. Neonatal sepsis is usually fatal among newborns.
11. WIN 51,711 halted development of paralysis in mice that had recently been infected with polio-2.
12. A stuck hatch cover on *Spacelab* blocked a French ultraviolet camera from conducting a sky survey of celestial objects.
13. An experimental drug has shown broad antiviral effects on a large number of the picornaviruses against which it has been tested.
▲ 14. Investigation revealed the problem was a short-circuited power supply.
15. Arteriovenous malformations—distortions of the capillaries connecting an arteriole and a small vein in the brain—can bleed, causing severe headaches, seizures, and even death.
16. Because of all the guns that its citizens own, the United States has never been invaded.
▲ 17. According to two reports in the *New England Journal of Medicine,* oil from fish can prevent heart disease.
18. The most important cause in the growing problem of illiteracy is television.
19. "Raymond the Wolf passed away in his sleep one night from natural causes; his heart stopped beating when the three men who slipped into his bedroom stuck knives in it."

— *Jimmy Breslin,* The Gang That Couldn't Shoot Straight

▲ 20. The dramatic increases in atmospheric CO_2, produced by the burning of fossil fuels, are warming the planet and will eventually alter the climate.

Exercise 11-6

Go to Church and Live Longer

According to Bill Scanlon, a reporter for the Scripps Howard News Service, researchers from the University of Colorado, the University of Texas, and Florida State University determined that twenty-year-olds who attend church

Real Life

Auberry Drive Cancer Toll at 7

A new state review will try to see if more than coincidence is at work.

Another two related cancers on Auberry Drive have surfaced, bringing to seven the number of similarly stricken children and adults within one square mile just north of Elk Grove.

The news reinforces some residents' suspicions that they are witnessing a disease cluster perpetuated by some unknown toxic exposure.

"It's no surprise to me," said Dee Lewis, a nearby resident who has been investigating possible environmental links for the past three years.

At *The Bee's* request, state officials on Wednesday agreed to re-evaluate the area's cancer incidence to determine whether the concentration is more than a coincidence.

Rosemary Cress, an epidemiologist with the state-run California Cancer Registry, has concluded from earlier statistical analyses that the area's incidence of childhood leukemia is not outside the range of chance. She does not expect further analyses to change the conclusion.

By Chris Bowman

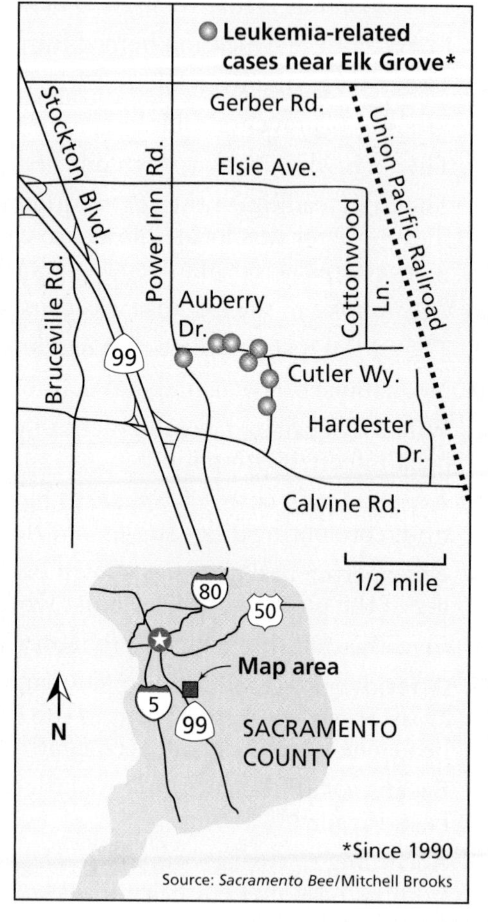

The incidence of cancer will be higher on some streets in a community than on others simply due to chance. But as a matter of psychology, it may be difficult to accept that fact if you live on one of the streets that has a high incidence of cancer.

at least once a week for a lifetime live on the average seven years longer than twenty-year-olds who never attend. The data came from a 1987 National Health Interview Survey that asked 28,000 people their income, age, church-attendance patterns, and other questions. The research focused on 2,000 of those surveyed who subsequently died between 1987 and 1995.

Propose two different causal hypotheses to explain these findings.

Hypothesis One:

What data would you need to have greater confidence in this hypothesis?

Hypothesis Two:

What data would you need to have greater confidence in this hypothesis?

Other Hypotheses:

What data would you need to have greater confidence in these hypotheses?

Exercise 11-7

> There is no single event, activity, decision, law, judgment, in this period of time that I call the "three strikes" era—other than "three strikes"—that could explain the tremendous acceleration in the drop in crime.
>
> — *Dan Lungren, former California Attorney General, who helped draft California's Three Strikes law*

Under this law, conviction for a third felony carried with it a mandatory sentence of twenty-five years to life. Although the crime rate in California had been falling before the law took effect in 1994, it reportedly fell even faster after the law was enacted, and California's crime rate dropped to levels not seen since the 1960s.

Provide two reasonable alternative hypotheses to explain the acceleration of the drop in the crime rate in California. What data would you need to be convinced that Lungren's hypothesis is the best?

Exercise 11-8

Suppose a university teacher wants to know whether or not requiring attendance improves student learning. How could she find out? In groups (or individually if the instructor prefers), describe an experiment that an instructor might actually use. Groups may then compare proposals to see who has the best idea.

Exercise 11-9

For each of the following investigations:

a. Identify the causal hypothesis at issue.
b. Identify what kind of investigation it is.
c. Describe the control and experimental groups.
d. State the difference in effect (or cause) between control and experimental groups.
e. Identify any problems in either the investigation or in the report of it, including but not necessarily limited to uncontrolled variables.
f. State the conclusion you think is warranted by the report.

▲ 1. Scientists have learned that people who drink wine weekly or monthly are less likely to develop dementia, including Alzheimer's disease. (Daily wine drinking, however, seems to produce no protective effect.) The lead researcher was Dr. Thomas Truelsen, of the Institute of Preventive Medicine at Kommunehospitalet in Copenhagen. The researchers identified the drinking patterns of 1,709 people in Copenhagen in the 1970s and then assessed them for dementia in the 1990s, when they were aged 65 or older. When they were assessed two decades later, 83 of the participants developed dementia. People who drank beer regularly were at an increased risk of developing dementia.

— *Adapted from* BBC News *(online), November 12, 2002*

2. Learning music can help children do better at math. Gordon Shaw of the University of California, Irvine, and Frances Rauscher at the University of Wisconsin compared three groups of second-graders: 26 received piano instruction plus practice with a math videogame, 29 received extra English lessons plus the game, and 28 got no special lessons. After four months the piano kids scored 15 to 41 percent higher on a test of ratios and fractions than the other participants.

— *Adapted from Sharon Begley,* Newsweek, *July 24, 2000*

3. The Carolina Abecedarian Project [A-B-C-D, get it?] selected participants from families thought to be at risk for producing mildly retarded children. These families were all on welfare, and most were headed by a single mother, who had scored well below average on a standardized IQ test (obtaining IQs of 70 to 85). The project began when the participating children were 6 to 12 weeks old, and continued for the next 5 years. Half of the participants were randomly assigned to take part in a special day-care program designed to promote intellectual development. The program ran from 7:15 to 5:15 for 5 days a week for 50 weeks each year until the child entered school. The other children received the same dietary supplements, social services, and pediatric care, but did not attend day-care. Over the next 21 years, the two groups were given IQ tests and tests of academic achievement. The day-care program participants began to outperform their counterparts on IQ tests starting at 18 months and maintained this IQ advantage through age 21. They also outperformed the others in all areas of academic achievement from the third year of school onward.

— *Adapted from* Developmental Psychology, *6th ed., David R. Schaffer*

▲ 4. Research at the University of Pennsylvania and the Children's Hospital of Philadelphia indicates that children who sleep in a dimly lighted room until age two may be up to five times more likely to develop myopia (nearsightedness) when they grow up.

The researchers asked the parents of children who had been patients at the researchers' eye clinic to recall the lighting conditions in the children's bedroom from birth to age two.

Of a total of 172 children who slept in darkness, 10 percent were nearsighted. Of a total of 232 who slept with a night light, 34 percent were nearsighted. Of a total of 75 who slept with a lamp on, 55 percent were nearsighted.

The lead ophthalmologist, Dr. Graham E. Quinn, said that, "just as the body needs to rest, this suggests that the eyes need a period of darkness."

— *Adapted from an AP report by Joseph B. Verrengia*

5. You want to find out if the coffee grounds that remain suspended as sediment in French press, espresso, and Turkish and Greek coffee can cause headaches.

You divide fifty volunteers into two groups and feed both groups a pudding at the same time every day. However, one group mixes eight grams of finely pulverized used coffee grounds into the pudding before eating it (that's equivalent to the sediment in about one and a half liters of Turkish coffee). Within three weeks, you find that 50 percent of the group that has eaten grounds have had headaches; only 27 percent of the other group have experienced a headache. You conclude that coffee grounds may indeed cause headaches and try to get a grant for further studies. (This is a fictitious experiment.)

6. Do you enjoy spicy Indian and Asian curries? That bright yellow-orange color is due to curcumin, an ingredient in the spice turmeric. An experiment conducted by Bandaru S. Reddy of the American Health Foundation in Valhalla, New York, and reported in *Cancer Research,* suggests that curcumin might suppress the development of colon cancer

Places where turmeric is widely used have a low incidence of colon cancer, so the research team decided to investigate. They administered a powerful colon carcinogen to sixty-six rats, and then added curcumin at the rate of 2,000 parts per million to the diet of thirty of them. At the end of a year, 81 percent of the rats eating regular rat food had developed cancerous tumors, compared with only 47 percent of those that dined on the curcumin-enhanced diet. In addition, 38 percent of the tumors in rats eating regular food were invasive, and that was almost twice the rate in rodents eating curcumin-treated chow.

— *Adapted from* Science News

▲ **7.** Does jogging keep you healthy? Two independent researchers interested in whether exercise prevents colds interviewed twenty volunteers about the frequency with which they caught colds. The volunteers, none of whom exercised regularly, were then divided into two groups of ten, and one group participated in a six-month regimen of jogging three miles every other day. At the end of the six months the frequency of colds among the joggers was compared both with that of the nonjoggers (group A) and with that of the joggers prior to the experiment (group B). It was found that, compared with the nonjoggers, the joggers had 25 percent fewer colds. The record of colds among the joggers also declined in comparison with their own record prior to the exercise program.

8. "In the fifty-seven-month study, whose participants were all male physicians, 104 of those who took aspirin had heart attacks, as compared with 189 heart attacks in those who took only a sugar pill. This means ordinary aspirin reduced the heart attack risk for healthy men by 47 percent. At least seven long-term studies of more than 11,000 heart attack victims have shown that one-half or one aspirin per day can reduce the risk of a second attack by up to 20 percent."

— *Adapted from the* Los Angeles Times

9. "Although cigarette ads sometimes suggest that smoking is 'macho,' new studies indicate that smoking can increase the risk of impotence. In a study of 116 men with impotence caused by vascular problems, done at the University of Pretoria, South Africa, 108 were smokers. Two independent studies, one done by the Centre d'Etudes et de Recherches di l'Impuissance in Paris, and reported in the British medical journal *Lancet,* and the other done by Queen's University and Kingston General Hospital in Ontario, found that almost two-thirds of impotent men smoked.

"To test whether smoking has an immediate effect on sexual response, a group of researchers from Southern Illinois and Florida State universities fitted 42 male smokers with a device that measures the speed of arousal.

The men were divided into three groups, one group given high-nicotine cigarettes, one group cigarettes low in nicotine, and one group mints. After smoking one cigarette or eating a mint, each man was placed in a private room and shown a two-minute erotic film while his sexual response was monitored. Then he waited ten minutes, smoked two more cigarettes or ate another mint, and watched a different erotic film, again being monitored.

"The results: Men who smoked high-nicotine cigarettes had slower arousal than those who smoked low-nicotine cigarettes or ate mints."

— *Adapted from* Reader's Digest

10. "A study published in the July 27 *Journal of the American Medical Association* indicates that taking androgen (a male sex hormone) in high doses for four weeks can have important effects on the high density lipoproteins (HDLs) in the blood, which are believed to protect against the clogging of vessels that supply the heart. Ben F. Hurley, an exercise physiologist from the University of Maryland in College Park who conducted the study at Washington University, monitored the levels of HDL in the blood of sixteen healthy, well-conditioned men in their early thirties who were taking androgens as part of their training program with heavy weights. Prior to use of the hormone, all had normal levels of HDLs. After four weeks of self-prescribed and self-administered use of these steroids the levels dropped by about 60 percent.

"Hurley is cautious in interpreting the data. 'You can't say that low HDL levels mean that a specified person is going to have a heart attack at an earlier age. All you can say is that it increases their risk for heart disease.'"

— *D. Franklin,* Science News

11. "New studies reported in the *Journal of the American Medical Association* indicate that vasectomy is safe. A group headed by Frank Massey of UCLA paired 10,500 vasectomized men with a like number of men who had not had the operation. The average follow-up time was 7.9 years, and 2,300 pairs were followed for more than a decade. The researchers reported that, aside from inflammation in the testes, the incidence of diseases for vasectomized men was similar to that in their paired controls.

"A second study done under federal sponsorship at the Battelle Human Affairs Research Centers in Seattle compared heart disease in 1,400 vasectomized men and 3,600 men who had not had the operation. Over an average follow-up time of fifteen years, the incidence of heart diseases was the same among men in both groups."

— *Edward Edelson,* New York Daily News; *reprinted in* Reader's Digest

12. "A new study shows that the incidence of cancer tumors in rats exposed to high doses of X-rays dropped dramatically when the food intake of the rats was cut by more than half. Dr. Ludwik Gross of the Veterans Administration Medical Center noted that this study is the first to demonstrate that radiation-induced tumors can be prevented by restricting diet.

"The experimenters exposed a strain of laboratory rats to a dose of X-rays that produced tumors in 100 percent of the rats allowed to eat their fill—about five or six pellets of rat food a day.

"When the same dose of X-rays was given to rats limited to two pellets of food a day, only nine of 29 females and one of 15 males developed tumors, the researchers reported.

"The weight of the rats on the reduced diet fell by about one-half, but they remained healthy and outlived their counterparts who died of cancer, Gross said. He noted that the restricted diet also reduced the occurrence of benign tumors. There is no evidence that restriction of food intake will slow the growth of tumors that have already formed in animals, he said."

— *Paul Raeburn,* Sacramento Bee

13. "Encephalitis, or sleeping sickness, has declined greatly in California during the past thirty years because more people are staying inside during prime mosquito-biting hours—7 P.M. to 10 P.M., researchers said. Paul M. Gahlinger of San Jose State University and William C. Reeves of the School of Public Health at UC Berkeley conducted the study. 'People who watch television on warm summer evenings with their air conditioners on are less likely to be exposed during the peak biting period of mosquitoes that carry encephalitis,' Reeves said.

"The researchers found that those counties in California's Central Valley with the highest television ownership had the lowest encephalitis rates for census years. Of 379 Kern County residents interviewed by telephone, 79 percent said they used their air conditioners every evening and 63 percent said they watched television four or more evenings a week during the summer.

"The percentage of residents who spend more time indoors now because of air conditioning than in 1950 more than doubled, from 26 percent to 54 percent, the researchers said."

— *Associated Press,* Enterprise-Record *(Chico, California)*

▲ **14.** "A study released last week indicated that Type A individuals, who are characteristically impatient, competitive, insecure and short-tempered, can halve their chances of having a heart attack by changing their behavior with the help of psychological counseling.

"In 1978, scientists at Mt. Zion Hospital and Medical Center in San Francisco and Stanford University School of Education began their study of 862 predominantly male heart attack victims. Of this number, 592 received group counseling to ease their Type A behavior and improve their self-esteem. After three years, only 7 percent had another heart attack, compared with 13 percent of a matched group of 270 subjects who received only cardiological advice. Among 328 men who continued with the counseling for the full three years, 79 percent reduced their Type A behavior. About half of the comparison group was similarly able to slow down and cope better with stress.

"This is the first evidence 'that a modification program aimed at Type A behavior actually helps to reduce coronary disease,' says Redford Williams of Duke University, an investigator of Type A behavior."

— Science News

Exercise 11-10

Here's a news report on the costs of drug abuse that appeared during the administration of George H. W. Bush. See if you can find any flaws in the reasoning by which the figures were reached.

J. Michael Walsh, an officer of the National Institute on Drug Abuse, has testified that the "cost of drug abuse to U.S. industry" was nearly $50 billion a year, according to "conservative estimates." President Bush has rounded this figure upward to "anywhere from $60 billion to $100 billion." This figure would seem to be a difficult one to determine. Here's how Walsh arrived at it. After a survey of 3,700 households, a NIDA contractor analyzed the data and found that the household income of adults who had *ever* smoked marijuana daily for a month (or at least twenty out of thirty days) was 28 percent less than the income of those who hadn't. The analysts called this difference "reduced productivity due to daily marijuana use." They calculated the total "loss," when extrapolated to the general population, at $26 billion. Adding the estimated costs of drug-related crimes, accidents, and medical care produced a grand total of $47 billion for "costs to society of drug abuse."

Exercise 11-11

Use letter grades (A, B, C, etc., with plusses and minuses if you wish) to evaluate each of the following explanations as to its degree of testability, its freedom from vagueness, and its noncircularity. ("A, A, A," for example, would indicate an explanation that was clearly testable, contained little or no vagueness, and was not at all circular.)

▲ **1.** What causes your engine to miss whenever you accelerate? Perhaps a spark plug is firing sporadically.

2. Antonio certainly had a run of hard luck—but then I warned him not to throw out that chain letter he got.

3. Divine intervention can cure cancer.

4. Having someone pray for you can cure cancer.

5. Having your mother pray for you brings good luck.

▲ **6.** Good luck is the result of being very fortunate.

7. Why did Claudia catch a cold? She's just prone to that sort of thing, obviously.

8. Federer won the match simply because he wanted it more than Roddick.

9. Tuck can play high notes so well because he has an excellent command of the upper register.

▲ **10.** Parker's trip to Spain last year is the reason his Spanish is not quite as bad as it used to be.

Exercise 11-12

Use the criteria discussed in the text to evaluate the following causal explanations. The criteria, once again, are

Testability
Noncircularity
Freedom from excessive vagueness
Freedom from conflict with well-established theory

▲ 1. The reason he has blue eyes is that he acquired them in a previous incarnation.

2. The Pacers did much better in the second half of the game. That's because they gained momentum.

3. "Men are biologically weaker than women and that's why they don't live as long, a leading expert declares."

— Weekly World News

▲ 4. PARKER: Gad, there are a lot of lawyers in this country today.
MOORE: That's because there are so many lawsuits that there's a huge demand for lawyers.

5. Why did he come down with the flu? He's just prone to that sort of thing, I guess.

6. If God had meant for people to fly, he'd have given them wings.

▲ 7. Alcoholics find it so difficult to give up drinking because they have become physiologically and psychologically addicted to it.

8. Alcoholics find it so difficult to give up drinking because they have no willpower.

9. The reason the latest episode of *The Rings* was a box-office hit is that Roger Ebert, one of the most influential movie critics, gave it a good review.

▲ 10. According to some psychologists, we catch colds because we want to. Most of the time we are not aware of this desire, which may, therefore, be said to be subconscious. Viruses are present when we have a cold, but unless we desire to catch cold, the viruses do not affect us.

11. Why does she sleep so late? I guess she's just one of those people who have a hard time waking up in the morning.

12. I wonder what made me choose Budweiser. Maybe I've been subjected to subliminal advertising.

▲ 13. The area along this part of the coast is especially subject to mudslides because of the type of soil that's found on the slopes and because there is not enough mature vegetation to provide stability with root systems.

14. How did he win the lottery twice? I'd have to say he's psychic.

15. "Parapsychologist Susan Blackmore failed to find evidence of ESP in numerous experiments over more than a decade. *Fate* magazine's consulting editor D. Scott Rogo explained her negative results as follows: 'In the course of my conversations with Blackmore I have come to suspect that she resists—at a deeply unconscious level—the idea that psychic phenomena exist. . . . *If* Blackmore is ever fortunate enough to witness a poltergeist or see some other striking display of psychic phenomena, I am willing to bet that her experimental results will be more positive.'"

— The Skeptical Inquirer

16. According to a report by Scotty Paul, writing in *Weekly World News,* thousands of tourists who defied an ancient curse and took home souvenir chunks of lava rock from Hawaii's Volcanoes National Park have felt the bitter wrath of a vengeful volcano goddess. The curse explains why a Michigan man tumbled to his death down a stairway and why a Canadian tourist died in a head-on auto accident, as well as why a Massachusetts widow lost her life savings in the stock market. The three

Real Life

When Is Affirmative Action Not Affirmative Action?

A letter-writer to the "Ask Marilyn" column in *Parade* magazine mentions a case worth your attention:

The writer, Christopher McLaughlin, of Orange Park, Florida, reported a company that opened a factory generating 70 white-collar jobs and 385 blue-collar jobs.

For the 70 white-collar positions, 200 males and 200 females applied; 15 percent of the males were hired, and 20 percent of the females were hired.

For the 385 blue-collar jobs, 400 males applied and 100 females applied; 75 percent of the males were hired, and 85 percent of the females were hired.

In short, the percentage of female applicants hired was greater than the percentage of male applicants hired in both categories. A victory for women, yes?

Nope—at least not according to the Equal Employment Opportunity Commission. The EEOC calculated that a female applying for a job at the factory had a 59 percent chance of being denied employment, whereas a male applicant had only a 45 percent chance of not being hired. So the company actually discriminated against women, the EEOC said.

Here's why: When you consider *total* applications, out of 600 male applicants, 330 were hired, and out of 300 female applicants, 125 were hired. That means that 55 percent of the male applicants—but only 41 percent of the female applicants—were hired.

(This case should remind you of the Saint Simpson's example in Chapter 10—see the box on page 355.)

suffered their misfortunes after taking lava rocks from the volcano and defying the curse of Madame Pele, the volcano goddess.

▲ **17.** Why is there so much violence these days? Rap music, that's why. That and the fact that there's so much violence on TV and in the movies.

18. The reason I got into so much trouble as a kid is that my father became a heavy drinker.

19. In their book *The Gulf Breeze Sightings: The Most Astounding Multiple Sightings of UFOs in U.S. History,* authors Ed and Frances Walters provide photographs of UFOs. According to the *Pensacola News Journal,* the man who now lives in the house the Walters family occupied at the time they photographed the UFOs discovered a flying saucer hidden under some insulation in the attic of the garage. With this model, news photographers were able to create photos of "UFOs" that looked like the Walterses' photos. Walters denies the model was his, but the paper in which it was wrapped contains part of a house plan Walters drew up (Walters is a building contractor). Walters says that model was planted by someone who wished to discredit him.

A Gulf Breeze youngster named Tom Smith also has come forth, admitting that he and Walters's son helped produce the fake saucer photos. He has five UFO photos of his own to substantiate his claim. Walters says Smith's photos are genuine. Which of the two explanations given for the original UFO photos is more plausible, and why? (This report is from *The Skeptical Inquirer.*)

▲ **20.** According to mathematician and science writer Martin Gardner, in Shivpuri, a village near Poona, India, there is a large stone ball weighing about 140 pounds in front of a mausoleum containing the remains of Kamarali Darvesh, a Muslim saint. It is possible for five men to stand around the ball and touch it with a forefinger at spots on or below the ball's equator. After they recite in unison "Kamarali Darvesh," an attendant gives a signal, and the ball slowly rises. The explanation of this phenomenon, according to devout Muslims, is that it is a miracle of Allah's.

Exercise 11-13

In twenty-five words or less, argue *that* a lot of kids cheat in high school. Then, again in twenty-five words or less, explain *why* a lot of kids cheat in high school. You may be asked by your instructor to read your response. The idea here is to make sure you understand the difference between an argument and an explanation.

Exercise 11-14

In this exercise, five items are best seen as arguments and five are best seen as explanations. Sort the items into the proper categories.

1. I got sick because I didn't get enough rest over the weekend.

2. You shouldn't buy that computer because it doesn't have very much memory.

3. The president should resign because foreign leaders are going to lose faith in his leadership skills.

4. Pine trees are called "evergreens" because they don't lose their leaves in the fall.

5. You are making a mistake to wear that outfit because it makes you look too old.

6. Stephanie won't wear outfits like that because she thinks they are tacky.

7. Used couches are so plentiful here because the students give them away at the end of each school year.

8. If I were you, I wouldn't open up a furniture store in this town, because students give good furniture away at the end of each school year.

9. Freestone peaches are better than clingstone, because they are easier to eat and have a crisper texture.

10. The sky appears blue because of the way light reflects off the atmosphere.

Exercise 11-15

In this exercise there are ten items. Some are arguments and some are explanations. One or two might even be explanations used to justify or excuse behavior. Determine which items fall into which categories.

▲ 1. Collins is absent again today because she's ill.

2. I told you Collins was ill. Just look at her color.

3. Did Bobbie have a good time last night? Are you kidding? She had a *great* time! She stayed up all night, she had such a good time.

▲ 4. The reason Collins was ill is that she ate and drank more than she should have.

5. For a while there, Jazzercise was really popular. But you don't hear much about it anymore. That's probably because rock makes you feel more like moving than jazz. Jazz just makes you feel like moving into another room.

6. How come light beer has fewer calories than real beer? It has less alcohol, that's why.

▲ 7. The senator's popularity goes up and down, up and down. That's because sometimes he says things that make sense, and other times he says things that are totally outrageous.

8. VIKKI: Say, remember the California Raisins? Whatever happened to them, anyway?
NIKKI: They faded. I guess people got tired of them or something.

9. Programs of preferential treatment may seem unfair to white males, but a certain amount of unfairness to individuals can be tolerated for the sake of the common good. Therefore, such programs are ethically justified.

▲ 10. I'm telling him, "Let's book!" and he's like, "Relax, dude," and since it's his wheel, what can I do? That's why we're late, man.

Exercise 11-16

Which of the following are arguments and which are explanations? Do any of the arguments involve explanations used as premises to justify or excuse behavior?

1. What a winter! And to think it's all just because there's a bunch of cold water off the California coast.

2. Hmmmm. I'm pretty sure you have the flu. You can tell because if you had a cold you wouldn't have aches and a fever. Aches and fever are a sure sign you have the flu.

3. You know, it occurs to me the reason the band sounded so bad is the new director. They haven't had time to get used to him or something.

▲ 4. For a while there it seemed like every male under thirty was shaving his head. It was probably the Michael Jordan influence.

▲ 5. Believe it or not, couples who regard each other as relatively equal are more likely to suffer from high blood pressure than are couples who perceive one or the other as dominant. This is an excellent reason for marrying someone you think is beneath (or above) you.

6. Believe it or not, couples who regard each other as relatively equal are more likely to suffer from high blood pressure than are couples who perceive one or the other as dominant. The reason seems to be that couples who see their partners as relatively equal tend to argue more often and more vigorously, pushing up blood pressure.

Exercise 11-17

Which of the following contain an explanation used as a premise in an argument intended to justify or excuse something?

▲ 1. You don't believe me when I say sometimes you can see Pluto with the naked eye? Just think of how the solar system works. The planets all orbit around the sun, and at a certain point, Pluto's orbit gets very close to Earth's orbit.

▲ 2. Yes, yes, I know Susan never goes out, but you can hardly blame her. She thinks it is important to study, and she may be right.

▲ 3. Harold didn't return the book when it was due, but he couldn't help it. Somebody broke into his car and stole his backpack, and the book was in it.

4. Maria really does have perfect pitch. See, her parents were both musicians, and perfect pitch is hereditary. She inherited it from them.

5. It takes time and effort to write decent essays. If you doubt it, just let me tell you what all is involved. You have to pick a topic. You have to think about the audience. You have to organize things and compose an outline. And you have to write about 50 million drafts.

6. Believe it or not, in Germany, it is illegal to name a child "Osama bin Laden." Maybe you think no government has the right to tell someone they can't name their kid what they want; but the way the Germans look at it, the government should protect children, and children with names like "Osama bin Laden" could be picked on at school.

7. "I'm really sorry our dogs made so much noise last night. They thought someone was trying to break into the house, and it took a long time for us to quiet them down."

8. Well, ordinarily I wouldn't be happy if I saw someone cutting down trees in his yard, but those trees are diseased and constantly losing branches. He's doing the right thing to take them out.

9. Sanctions against South Africa are usually cited as bringing down apartheid, but the real explanation was the diplomatic isolation and the threat from guerrillas in neighboring countries.

10. Why in heck would anyone plant zucchini when they could be growing something good like tomatoes or eggplant? The only reason I can see is she must be nuts.

Exercise 11-18

Do any of the following items that are arguments use an explanation as a premise?

1. If you ask a person to pick a number between 12 and 5, he'll probably say 7. That's because his brain automatically subtracts 5 from 12.
2. Ask a person to name a vegetable, and the first thing to come to mind is a carrot. Don't believe me? Ask someone.
3. To be acid-free, take Pepcid AC.

4. Why, just look at all the dog hair on this keyboard. Where do you let your dog sleep, anyway? No wonder your computer isn't working right.
5. On September 19, Mike Tyson will make the holy trek to Las Vegas, to ask the Nevada Athletic Commission to reinstate his boxing license, and chances are they will. Why would they do that for a man who bit another boxer, attacked a sixty-two-year-old man, and kicked another older man in the groin? The answer can be stated in a sentence: Vegas likes big money.
6. Feet hurt? Really hurt? Chances are you have weak or fallen arches.
7. "Let me explain to you why you know the public opinion polls are all rigged. Everybody I know loves Bush, and if you listen to talk radio you can tell that most people agree with us."

   —*Adapted from a newspaper call-in column*
8. Linda takes care of two youngsters, puts in a forty-hour week at her job, is troop leader for the local chapter of the Girl Scouts, serves half a day each week as a teacher's aide, and is almost finished with a book on time management. So it shouldn't surprise you that she hasn't been able to come out to the coast for a visit lately.
9. I believe God exists because my parents brought me up that way.
10. I believe God exists because there obviously had to be a first cause for everything, and that first cause was God.

Exercise 11-19

Do any of these items contain an argument that uses an explanation as a premise?

▲ 1. I can't understand how the garage got this cluttered. Must be we just never throw anything away.

2. When the sun reaches its equinox, it is directly over the equator, a fact that explains why the days are exactly the same length every place on the globe at that time.

3. Awww, don't get on her, Mom. The reason she didn't rake the leaves is that her stomach began hurting. She *had* to go lie down.

▲ 4. Watch out! Parker's giving a test today. I saw him carrying a big manila folder into the classroom.

5. Moore gave a test on Friday because he wanted to surprise everyone.

6. They get so many fires in southern California in the fall because that's when you get the Santa Ana winds, which blow in from the desert and make everything hot and extremely dry.

7. Give 'em a break. That kind of work makes noise, and they gotta start work early to get done on time.

▲ 8. HOSTESS: You know, I really think you should shave. The company's coming in less than an hour and you look like a hairy pig.
HOST: Hey, I told you! I can't shave because my razor is broken. What am I supposed to do, shave with my pocket knife?

9. So you actually believe he knows the names of the people in the audience because God tells him? Here's how he really does it. He's got a wireless radio receiver in his ear, okay? And the people fill out prayer cards before the show. Then his wife collects them and radios the details to him during the show.

▲ 10. Let me explain to you why that was a great movie. The acting was good, the story was interesting, the photography was a knockout, and the ending was a killer.

11. Harold must be rich. Just look at the car he's driving.

▲ 12. The water contamination around here is getting worse and worse. It's because we've allowed people to install septic systems whenever and wherever they want.

13. "I could never endure to shake hands with Mr. Slope. A cold, clammy perspiration always exudes from him, the small drops are ever to be seen standing on his brow, and his friendly grasp is unpleasant."

— *Anthony Trollope,* Parchester Towers

14. I know you think I wasted my vote by voting for Ralph Nader, but that isn't so. I didn't approve of either of the main candidates, and if I'd voted for one of them and he had won, then my vote would have counted as an endorsement of him and his views. I don't want to add my endorsement to what I think are bad policies.

▲ 15. It could be that you're unable to sleep because of all that coffee you drink in the evening.

16. The coffee I drink in the evening can't be why I'm not sleeping, because I drink only decaffeinated coffee.

17. Of *course* the real estate industry depends on tax benefits. Just look at how hard the real estate lobby fought to preserve those benefits.

▲ 18. Although the computer case is double-insulated, the pins in the cable connections are not insulated at all. In fact, they are connected directly to the logic board inside the machine. So, if you are carrying a charge of static electricity and you touch those connector pins, you can fry the logic circuits of your computer.

19. The orange is sour because it didn't have a chance to ripen properly.

20. "In 1970 Chrysler abandoned reverse-thread lug bolts on the left-hand side of its cars and trucks. One of those engineers must have realized, after about fifty years of close observation, that sure enough, none of the wheels were falling off the competition's cars, which had your ordinary, right-hand wheel fastenings."

— *John Jerome,* Truck

▲ 21. "Economically, women are substantially worse off than men. They do not receive any pay for the work that is done in the home. As members of the labor force their wages are significantly lower than those paid to men, even when they are engaged in similar work and have similar educational backgrounds."

— *Richard Wasserstrom, "On Racism and Sexism," in* Today's Moral Problems

22. Some people think that Iowa has too much influence in determining who becomes a leading presidential candidate, but I don't agree. Having early

caucuses in a relatively small state makes it possible for a person to begin a run at the presidency without spending millions and millions of dollars. And it may as well be Iowa as any other state.

23. She appears hard-hearted, but in reality she is not. She maintains strict discipline because she believes that if her children learn self-discipline, in the long run they will lead happier, more productive lives.

▲ 24. Letter to the editor: "Many people are under the impression that the Humane Society is an animal rights organization. Let me correct this misconception. Our purpose is that of an animal welfare organization. Animal rights groups have some excellent ideas but they are too broad of scope for us. We focus our attention on the care and welfare of the animals in our community. It is our primary purpose to provide humane care for homeless and owner-surrendered animals. However, we are against mistreatment of animals and we assist the State Humane Officer who investigates cases of animal abuse."

▲ 25. "American Airlines, United Airlines and TWA confirmed [before September 11, 2001] to the *Los Angeles Times* that some of their crews bypass passenger metal detectors. They said their current security procedures are effective and argued that switching to metal detectors would be costly and inefficient. Furthermore, they said, their security policies have been approved by the Federal Aviation Administration."

— Los Angeles Times

Exercise 11-20

Which of these items involves an explanation as a premise of an argument? Remember, trying to justify behavior is giving an argument.

▲ 1. The reason the door keeps banging is that the windows are open on the south side of the house and there is a strong south breeze.

2. Moore always starts his class exactly on the hour, because he has a lot to cover, and he can't afford to waste time.

3. Moore always starts his class exactly on the hour. Don't believe me? Just ask anyone.

▲ 4. The Rotary Club provides free dinners on Thanksgiving, the reason being that they want to help the poor.

5. So you think the lawn mower won't start because it's too old? Here's what's really going on. We let gas sit in the carburetor all winter and it gums up the works—that's why it won't start. It has nothing to do with its being too old.

6. "If slavery had been put to a vote, slavery never would have been overturned. We don't accept that you can put civil rights to a vote in a sexist and racist society."

— *Heather Bergman, member of the Coalition to Defend Affirmative Action by Any Means Necessary*

▲ 7. Rejecting a last-minute bid by Democrats to give President Clinton's lawyers a few days for review, House Republican leaders on Thursday arranged to make public today 445 pages of Independent Counsel

Kenneth Starr's report on possible impeachable offenses by the president. It may seem as if the Republicans are seeking to embarrass the president as much as they can, but in fact they called for the release because they feel the public deserves to know as soon as possible why Starr believes he has credible evidence that Clinton committed several crimes.

8. The share of public-school budgets devoted to regular education plummeted from 80 percent in 1967 to less than 59 percent in 1996. The rest goes to students with special needs. This at least partially accounts for declines in test scores among America's average students.

9. Just as Mary Shelley's Frankenstein monster fascinated us, computer viruses have come to do the same because they are much like a man-made life-form. Because of this fascination, you'll see more and more viruses turn up in hoaxes, urban legends, television shows, and movies.
— *Adapted from* Scientific American

▲ 10. It is becoming more and more clear that child molestation is passed down from one generation to another. What isn't clear is whether the tendency is actually an inherited trait or whether a young child's being molested by a parent psychologically conditions the child to be a molester when he becomes an adult. Either way, it looks as though a child with a molester for a parent is not the same as the rest of us; he has something to overcome that we don't, and it may be impossible for us to understand what a difficult problem he may have in avoiding the forbidden behavior.

Exercise 11-21

According to statistics from the Department of Transportation (reported by John Lang of the Scripps Howard News Service), in 1996 men accounted for a little more than 50 percent of licensed drivers and women for a little more than 49 percent. But according to these 1996 statistics, 41,010 male drivers were involved in fatal crashes, as opposed to only 14,145 female drivers. (This works out to about 74 percent male.) Of the drivers killed in those crashes, it was 17,822 male and 6,632 female. (This works out to about 73 percent male.)

Also, according to DOT statistics, in 1996, 86 percent of the people killed while pedaling a bicycle were men.

Which of the following conclusions can you derive from this information? (Assume all the conclusions pertain to 1996.)

1. Men were more likely than women to be involved in a fatal automobile crash.
2. If an automobile crash involved a fatality, it was more likely to have been a man than a woman.
3. Your brother was more likely to have been involved in a fatal automobile crash than your sister.
4. If your sibling was involved in a fatal automobile crash, it's more likely a brother than a sister.
5. Male drivers were more likely than females drivers to be killed in an automobile crash.
6. Men were less skilled than women at avoiding fatal automobile crashes.

7. Men were less able than women to avoid fatal automobile crashes.
8. Men were more likely than women to be killed while pedaling a bicycle.
9. If someone you know was killed while pedaling a bicycle, chances are the victim was a male.
10. If someone you know was killed in a traffic accident, it is more likely it was a bicycle accident than an auto accident.

Exercise 11-22

Men are involved in far more fatal automobile crashes than are women. List as many plausible explanations for this as you can.

Exercise 11-23

Let's say you randomly divide 700 men in the early stages of prostate cancer into two groups. The men in one group have their prostate removed surgically; those in the other group are simply watched to let the disease take its course. Researchers did this to 700 Scandinavian men and reported the results in the *New England Journal of Medicine* in fall 2002. As it turns out, 16 of those who underwent surgery died from prostate cancer, as compared with 31 of those who did not undergo surgery. On the face of it, these figures suggest your chances of not dying from prostate cancer are better if you have surgery. But put on your thinking caps and answer the following questions.

1. Suppose that despite these findings, there was no statistically significant difference in how long the men in each group lived. What would that suggest?
2. The follow-up comparison lasted six years. Suppose that after ten years the death rates from prostate cancer were the same for the two groups. What would that suggest?
3. Suppose Scandinavian men are not screened for prostate cancer as aggressively as American men and tend to be older when they get their first diagnosis.
4. Suppose Scandinavian men are screened more aggressively for prostate cancer than are American men and tend to be younger when they get their first diagnosis.

Here, as elsewhere, you need to know the whole picture to make a judgment. How old were the men to begin with? If they were relatively young men, how long did the study last? Was there a difference in how long the men in the two groups lived? (Note that prostate removal has risks and sometimes produces important negative side effects.)

Writing Exercises

1. How might one determine experimentally whether or not gender-based or ethnicity-based discrimination occurs in hiring? (Differences in unemployment rates can be powerful evidence, but it is not experimental.) See if you can design an experiment, and describe it in a brief essay.

Real Life

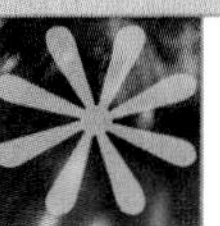

Are Women Less Competitive?

Studies uncover a striking pattern

Although women have made huge strides in catching up with men in the workplace, a gender gap persists both in wages and levels of advancement. Commonly cited explanations for this gap range from charges of sex discrimination to claims that women are more sensitive than men to work-family conflicts and thus less inclined to make sacrifices for their careers.

Now, however, two new studies by economists Uri Gneezy of the University of Chicago and Aldo Rustichini of the University of Minnesota suggest that another factor may be at work: a deeply ingrained difference in the way men and women react to competition that manifests itself even at an early age.

The first study focused on short races run by some 140 9- and 10-year-old boys and girls in a physical education class. At that age, there was no significant difference between the average speeds of boys and girls when each child ran the course alone. But when pairs of children with similar initial speeds ran the race again, things changed. Boys' speeds increased appreciably when running against either a boy or a girl, but more so when paired with a girl. Girls showed no increase when running against a boy and even ran a bit more slowly when paired with a girl.

The second study, by Gneezy, Rustichini, and Muriel Niederle of Stanford University, involved several hundred students at an elite Israeli technical university. Groups of six students were paid to solve simple maze problems on a computer. In some groups, subjects were paid 50¢ for each problem they solved during the experiment. In others, only the person solving the most problems got rewarded—but at the rate of $3 for each maze solved.

Regardless of the sexual makeup of the groups, men and women, on average, did equally well when students were paid for their own performance. But when only the top student was paid, average male performance rose sharply—by about 50%—while female performance remained the same.

The authors conclude that females tend to be far less responsive to competition than males—a tendency with important implications for women and business. It may hurt women in highly competitive labor markets, for example, and hamper efficient job placement—especially for positions in which competitiveness is not a useful trait.

That's something companies with highly competitive atmospheres may need to consider, says Rustichini. If they don't, the results could be "both a subtle bias against women and, in many cases, foregone worker productivity."

By Gene Koretz

Source: Business Week, December 9, 2002.

Let's Race: Boys' speeds went up.

2. Are women less competitive than men? In a brief essay, (a) explain what you think the investigations in the box show, if anything; or (b) set forth alternative explanations for the results; or (c) describe what implications you think these investigations have.
3. Which of the following causal hypotheses do you accept? Select one that you accept and write a one-page essay presenting evidence (giving arguments) for the claim. When you are finished, write down on a separate piece of paper a number between 1 and 10 that indicates how strong you think your overall "proof" of the claim is, with 10 = very strong and 1 = very weak. Take about ten minutes to complete your essay. Write your name on the back of your paper.

   Causal hypotheses:

   Pot leads to heroin/crack addiction.
   The death penalty is a deterrent to murder.
   The death penalty is not a deterrent to murder.
   Chocolate causes acne.
   Welfare makes people lazy.
   Spare the rod and spoil the child.
   People think better after a few beers.
   Pornography contributes to violence against women.
   If you want to get someone to like you, play hard to get.
   Vitamin C prevents colds.
   Rap music (TV, the movies) contributes to the crime problem.

   When everyone is finished, the instructor will collect the papers and redistribute them to the class. In groups of four or five, read the papers and assign a number from 1 to 10 to each one (10 = very strong; 1 = very weak). When all groups are finished, return the papers to their authors. When you get your paper back, compare the number you assigned to your work with the number the group assigned to it. The instructor may ask volunteers to defend their own judgment of their work against the judgment of the group. Do you think there is as much evidence for the claim you selected as you did when you argued for it initially?

Chapter 12

Moral, Legal, and Aesthetic Reasoning

with Nina Rosenstand and Anita Silvers

Art pieces, such as this painting by Otto Dix, can have monetary value and aesthetic value, but no moral value.

In early winter 2003, our friend Elliott Howard was offered a position as the manager of a country club near Winston-Salem, North Carolina.* For Elliott, this was the chance of a lifetime. Unfortunately, there was a problem. Elliott's father, who lived near Elliott in California, was old and had non-Hodgkins lymphoma. It was vital that Elliott live close by to care for him.

This presented a dilemma. On the one hand, Elliott's father depended on Elliott. On the other, Elliott knew he would not get another chance like this. He was getting on in years himself, and the job offer had come to him only through an unusual chain of events, one that would not likely ever be repeated.

Elliott attempted to find a way to accept the position and still provide for his father. Unfortunately, this turned out not to be possible. In the end, Elliott was faced with this hard choice: He could take the job, or he could take care of his father, but he could not do both.

Finally, reluctantly, Elliott turned down the job offer.

From time to time we all face tough moral decisions like this. Sometimes we must weigh our own interests against our responsibilities

*We have altered the circumstances slightly and changed our friend's name to protect his identity.

to people we love. Sometimes we face moral dilemmas of a different sort. When he was governor of Texas, George W. Bush had to decide whether to bestow clemency on Karla Faye Tucker, a woman whose life had undergone a transformation in prison and whose execution many people believed to be unwarranted. A mother may have to determine whether her daughter's birthday takes precedence over a professional responsibility. It can be excruciating to decide whether a dear pet's time has finally come.

When we think abstractly, we might have the idea that morality is a mere matter of personal opinion and that moral issues offer little room for reasoning. But when we are confronted with a real moral dilemma, we see instantly that this view is not correct. We reason about moral issues. We consider options, weigh consequences, think about what is right and wrong and why. Some considerations are more important than others, and some arguments are better than others. If Elliott decided what to do by flipping a coin, we would think there was something wrong with him.

In the first part of this chapter, we want to look at the basic concepts and principles that are always involved in moral reasoning.

MORAL EVALUATIONS

Recently, our colleague Becky White debated what to do about a student who had copied parts of someone else's term paper and was silly enough to think Professor White wouldn't notice.

There are many things one could say about the student; what Professor White said is, "He deserves an F." And that's what she gave him—for the entire course.

Our colleague's statement is what philosophers call a value judgment, a claim that expresses a value.* The value she expressed was a *moral* value, a value having to do with morals; she believed that submitting someone else's ideas as if they are your own is morally wrong.

Moral reasoning is distinguished from other kinds of reasoning in that the conclusions it tries to establish are moral value judgments. Because moral reasoning is all about moral value judgments, you need to be able to identify one when you see or hear it. A difficulty is that not every value judgment expresses a moral value. As we write this, the supposedly last-ever installment of the *Star Wars* movies has been released, and many think it is pretty good. Others think it is pretty good that it is the last installment. Both judgments are value judgments, though neither is a moral value judgment. Similarly, we know people who like Pepsi more than Coke, or vice versa; they are making a taste value judgment.

Recently, we read about Keith Lewis, a 49ers football player, who honored his mother by having her name tattooed into his arm in Japanese characters. Presumably, underlying his decision to do this was a value judgment, though one difficult to classify. "I should do this to honor my mother" would qualify as a moral value judgment; but doing something because you think it will look cool would involve a taste value judgment. *Possibly* Mr. Lewis decided to honor his mother and then looked around for the best way to do this,

*Philosophers often refer to value judgments as "normative" or "prescriptive" claims, and your instructor may do so as well.

finally settling on a tattoo. *Possibly,* for example, his mother once said, "Keith, if you want to do something really nice for me, why don't you tattoo my name into your arm in Japanese?" More likely, Mr. Lewis wanted a tattoo and then decided to honor his mother by having it spell out her name.*

To help solidify your grasp of the important concept of a moral value judgment, the claims in the left column are all moral value judgments; those in the right are value judgments, but not of the moral variety. Exercises on moral reasoning are at the end of the section titled "Moral Deliberation" in this chapter.

Moral Value Judgments	**Nonmoral Value Judgments**
1. It was wrong for Senator Kennedy to have withheld information.	1. Senator Kennedy dresses well.
2. Karl Rove ought to spend more time with his family.	2. The latest *Star Wars* movie has some of the best special effects of any movie ever made.
3. Abortion is immoral.	3. As an actress, Paris Hilton is a nice clothes rack.
4. Children should be taught to respect their elders.	4. Karl Rove is an excellent cellist.
5. I don't deserve to be flunked for an honest mistake.	5. Keith Lewis must be a total flake.

Typically, moral value judgments employ such words as "good," "bad," "right," "wrong," "ought," "should," "proper," and "justified," "fair," and so forth, and their opposites. But you need to bear in mind that, although these words often signal a moral evaluation, they do not always do so. Telling someone she should keep her promise is to make a moral value judgment; telling her she should keep her knees bent when skiing is assigning a positive value to keeping bent knees, but not a moral value.

It's also worth noticing that implicit value judgments can be made inside claims that are not themselves value judgments. For example, "Karl Rove, a good man, engineered President Bush's re-election" is not a value judgment, but the part about Karl Rove being a good man is.

Moral vs. Nonmoral; Moral vs. Immoral

A source of confusion in discussions that involve moral reasoning is the word "moral." The word has two separate and distinct meanings. First, "moral" may be used as the opposite to "nonmoral." This is the sense in which we have been using the term. The claim "Karl Rove weighs more than 200 pounds" is a nonmoral claim, meaning it has nothing to do with morality. "Karl Rove is an evil man," by contrast, has a lot to do with morality: It is a moral value judgment, a claim that expresses a moral value.

The second meaning of "moral" is the opposite not of "nonmoral" but of "immoral." Kicking a cat for the heck of it would be immoral; taking care of it would be moral. In this sense of the word, "moral" is used to mean "good," "right," "proper," and so forth.

*Unfortunately, the Japanese characters Mr. Lewis had tattooed into his arm turned out to be gibberish.

To avoid confusion, when we use the word "moral" in this chapter, we *always* mean moral as opposed to nonmoral; i.e., as having to do with morality. Thus, as we use the word, "It was wrong to kick the cat" and "It wasn't wrong to kick the cat" are both moral judgments.

Deriving Moral Value Judgments

From the standpoint of logic, there is something puzzling about deriving a value judgment from a premise that is not a value judgment. For example, consider the argument:

> 1a. Elliott's father depends on Elliott. Therefore, Elliott should take care of him.

We hear such arguments in everyday life, and tend to think nothing of them; they certainly do not seem illogical. If facts and statistics are not grounds for making moral decisions, what is? Nevertheless, logically, arguments like this—the basic kind of argument of moral reasoning—are puzzling, because the premise ("Elliott's father depends on Elliott") is not a value judgment; whereas the conclusion ("Elliott should take care of him") is. How, logically, can we get from the "is" premise to the "should" conclusion? How does the "should" get in there?

The answer is that the conclusion of this argument follows logically from the stated premise, only if a *general* moral principle is assumed. In this case, a principle that would work is: Adult children should take care of parents who are dependent on them. Here is the argument with its conclusion:

> 1b. Premise: Elliott's father depends on Elliott. [Unstated general moral principle: Adult children should take care of their parents who are dependent on them.] Conclusion: Therefore, Elliott should take care of his father.

The result is a valid deductive argument. Likewise, any chain of moral reasoning that starts from a claim about facts and ends up with a moral value judgment assumes a general principle that ties the fact-stating "is" premise to the value-stating "should" conclusion.

So far, this is just a point about the logic of moral reasoning. But there is a practical point to be made here as well. It helps clarify matters to consider our general moral principles when we advance moral arguments. If we agree with the premise that Elliott's father depends on Elliott, but disagree with the conclusion that Elliott should take care of his father, then our quarrel must be with the unstated general principle that adult children should take care of their parents who are dependent on them. For example, should an adult take care of parents even if it means sacrificing the welfare of his or her spouse? Considering the assumed general moral principle that ties the fact-stating premise with the value-judging conclusion can go a long way toward clarifying the issues involved in a moral decision.

For another example, you sometimes hear it said:

> Homosexuality is unnatural. Therefore, it ought not be practiced.

A general moral principle assumed here might be: Whatever is unnatural ought not be done. Bringing that principle to light sets the stage for fruitful discussion. What counts as unnatural? Is it unnatural to fly? To wear clothing? To live to 100? To have sex beyond the reproductive years? And is it true that unnatural things never should be done? In the natural world severely disabled offspring are left to fend for themselves; are we wrong to care for our own severely disabled children? Scratching oneself in public certainly qualifies as natural, but in our culture not doing so is considered the proper thing to do.

Earlier we mentioned our colleague Becky White, who failed a student for copying parts of another student's paper. As it so happens, Professor White also considered whether to penalize the student who allowed his paper to be read by the classmate. Was it wrong for Charles (whose name we have changed) to show his work to a classmate who then copied parts of it? Thinking that it was wrong would require a general principle, and one that would work would be: It is wrong to show your work to classmates before they have turned in their own work. This principle would yield a deductively valid argument, and there is something to be said for the principle. For example, showing your exam answers to the classmate sitting next to you is grounds for dismissal in many universities. At the same time, showing a term paper to a classmate to get constructive feedback is a good thing. Careful consideration of the principle above might lead to the conclusion that, in fact, Charles has done nothing wrong.

Later in this chapter, we examine the most general and fundamental moral principles assumed in most moral reasoning.

Consistency and Fairness

A common mistake made in moral reasoning is inconsistency—treating cases that are similar as if they weren't that way. For example, suppose Moore announces on the first day of class that the final in the class will be optional. "Except," he says, pointing at some person at random, "for the young woman there in the third row. For you," he says, "the final is mandatory."

The problem is that Moore is treating a student who is similar to the rest of the class as if she were different. And the student will want to know, of course, why she has been singled out: "What's so different about me?" she will wonder (as she drops the course).

A similar sort of problem occurs if Moore gives two students the same grade despite the fact that one student did far better in the course than the other. Treating dissimilar cases as if they were similar isn't inconsistent; it just involves a failure to make relevant discriminations.

As you have probably foreseen by now, when we treat people inconsistently, the result is often *unfair.* It is unfair to the woman in the third row to require her alone to take the final; alternatively, it would be unfair to the rest of the class to make the final mandatory for them and to make it optional for the woman in the third row. From the perspective of critical thinking, what is so troubling about unfairness is that it is illogical. It is like saying "All Xs are Y" and then adding, "Some Xs are not Y."

This doesn't mean, of course, that if you have been treating people unfairly, you should *continue* to treat them unfairly on the grounds that it would be inconsistent for you to change your policy. There is nothing illogical in saying, in effect, "I treated the Xs I encountered to date wrongly, but now I will not treat the Xs I encounter wrongly." People sometimes adhere to a bad policy simply on the grounds that it would be inconsistent of them to change, but there is no basis in logic for this idea.

Not all cases of inconsistency result in unfairness. For example, let's imagine that Harlan approved of the war in Iraq and opposed the war in Vietnam but is unable to point out any relevant differences between the two cases. This isn't a matter of unfairness, exactly; it's just inconsistency on Harlan's part.

When are two or more cases sufficiently similar to warrant our calling somebody inconsistent who treats them as if they were different? The answer is that there is no hard-and-fast rule. The point to keep in mind, however, is that the burden of proof is on the person who appears inconsistent to show that he or she is not treating similar cases dissimilarly. If, when challenged, Harlan cannot *tell* us what's different about Vietnam and Iraq that justifies his difference in attitude between the two, then we are justified in regarding him as inconsistent.

Imagine that Carol is a salesperson who treats black customers and white customers differently: She is, let us imagine, much more polite to customers of her own racial group (we needn't worry about which group that is). Can Carol explain to us what is so different about black and white customers that would justify her treating them differently? If not, we are justified in regarding her practices as inconsistent.

Suppose, however, that Carol thinks that skin color itself is a difference between blacks and whites relevant to how people should be treated, and she charges us with failing to make relevant discriminations. Here it would be easy for us to point out to Carol that skin color is an immutable characteristic of birth like height or eye color; does Carol adjust her civility to people depending on those characteristics?

It isn't difficult to perceive the inconsistency on the part of a salesperson who is more polite to customers of one group; but other cases are far tougher, and many are such that reasonable people will disagree about their proper assessment. Is a person inconsistent who approves of abortion but not capital punishment? Is a person inconsistent who, on the one hand, believes that the states should be free to reduce spending on welfare but, on the other, does not think that the states should be able to eliminate ceilings on punitive damages in tort cases? No harm is done in asking "What's the difference?" and because much headway can be made in a discussion by doing so, it seems wise to ask.

In Chapter 6, we talked about the inconsistency ad hominem, a fallacy we commit when we think we rebut the content of what someone says by pointing out inconsistency on his or her part. Now, let's say Ramesh tells us it is wrong to hunt, and then we find out Ramesh likes to fish. And let's say that, when we press Ramesh, he cannot think of any relevant moral difference between the two activities. Then he is being inconsistent. But that does not mean that it is right to hunt; nor does it mean that it is wrong to fish. An inconsistency ad hominem occurs if we say something like "Ramesh, you are mistaken when you say it is wrong to hunt, because you yourself fish." It is not an inconsistency ad hominem to say "Ramesh, you are being inconsistent. You must change your position either on hunting or on fishing."

Similarly, let's suppose Professor Moore gives Howard an A and gives James a C, but cannot think of any differences between their performance in his course. It would be the inconsistency ad hominem if we said "Moore, James does not deserve a C, because you gave Howard an A." Likewise, it would be the inconsistency ad hominem if we said "Moore, Howard does not deserve an A, because you gave James a C." But it is *not* illogical to say "Moore, you are being inconsistent. You have misgraded one of these students."

MAJOR PERSPECTIVES IN MORAL REASONING

Moral reasoning usually takes place within one or more frameworks or perspectives. Here we present some of the perspectives that have been especially influential in Western moral thought.

Relativism

As we mentioned early on in this book, a popular view of ethics, especially perhaps among undergraduates taking a first course in philosophy, is **moral relativism,** the idea that what is right and wrong depends on and is determined by one's group or culture.

A mistake sometimes made in moral reasoning is to confuse the following two claims:

1. What is *believed* to be right and wrong may differ from group to group, society to society, or culture to culture.
2. What *is* right and wrong may differ from group to group, society to society, or culture to culture.

The second claim, but not the first, is moral relativism. Please read the two claims carefully. They are so similar it takes a moment to see they are actually quite different. But they are different. The first claim is incontestable; the second claim is controversial and problematic. It may well have been the majority belief in ancient Greece that there was nothing wrong with slavery. But that does not mean that at that time there was nothing wrong with slavery.

Another popular moral perspective is **moral subjectivism,** the idea that what is right and wrong is merely a matter of subjective opinion, that thinking that something is right or wrong makes it right or wrong for that individual. We considered subjectivism in Chapter 1 and saw there the mistake in thinking that all value judgments are subjective.

Utilitarianism

The perspective we call **utilitarianism** rests on the idea that if an individual can feel pleasure and pain, then he or she deserves moral consideration. (This broad criterion has led many utilitarians to include animals in their considerations.) The theory is based on one principle, the **principle of utility:** Maximize happiness and minimize unhappiness. This means that the utilitarian is concerned with the *consequences* of actions and decisions. If an act will produce more happiness than will the alternatives, the act is the right one to do; if it will produce less happiness, it would be morally wrong to do it in place of one of its alternatives.

Many of us use a pro-and-con list of consequences as a guideline when considering what course of action to take. Let's assume you have to decide whether to go home for Thanksgiving or to spend the long weekend writing a term paper that is due. Your family is expecting you, and they will be disappointed if you don't come home. However, their disappointment will be lessened by their knowing that your studies are important to you. On the other hand, if you stay to finish the paper, you will miss seeing your friends at home. But if you go home, you will not finish the paper on time, and your final grade may be adversely affected. As a utilitarian, you try to weigh the consequences of the alternatives on everyone's happiness. You also have to factor in how *certain* the outcomes of each alternative are with respect to happiness, assigning relatively more weight to relatively more certain positive outcomes. Because you can generally be more certain of the effect of an act on your own happiness and on the happiness of others you know well, it is often morally proper to favor that act that best promotes your own or their happiness. Of course, you must not use this as an excuse to be entirely self-serving: Your own happiness isn't more important morally than another's. The best course of action morally is not always the one that best promotes your own happiness.

In sum, utilitarians weigh the consequences of the alternatives, pro and con, and then choose the alternative that maximizes happiness. One of the original and most profound intellects behind utilitarianism, Jeremy Bentham (1748–1832), even went so far as to devise a *hedonistic calculus*—a method of assigning actual numerical values to pleasures and pains based on their intensity, certainty, duration, and so forth. Other utilitarians think that some pleasures are of a higher quality (e.g., reading Shakespeare is of a higher quality than watching SpongeBob). Although there are other important issues in utilitarianism, the basic idea involves weighing the consequences of possible actions in terms of happiness. Utilitarianism has considerable popular appeal, and real-life moral reasoning is often utilitarian to a considerable extent.

Nevertheless, some aspects of the theory are problematic. Typically, when we deliberate whether or not to do something, we don't always take into consideration just the effect of the action on happiness. For example, other people have *rights* that we sometimes take into account. We would not make someone in our family a slave even if the happiness produced for the family by doing so outweighed the unhappiness it created for the slave. We also consider our *duties* and *obligations.* We think it is our duty to return a loan to someone even if we are still short on cash and the other person doesn't need the money and doesn't even remember having loaned it to us. If we make a date and then want to break it because we've met the love of our life, we think twice about standing up our original date, even if we believe that our overall happiness will far outweigh the temporary unhappiness of our date. To many, the moral obligation of a promise cannot be ignored for the sake of the overall happiness that might result from breaking it.

In estimating the moral worth of what people do, utilitarianism also seems to discount people's *intentions.* Suppose a mugger attacks somebody just as a huge flower pot falls from a balcony above. The mugger happens to push the individual the instant before the flower pot lands on the exact spot where the victim had been standing. The mugger has saved the victim's life, as it turns out. But would we say that the mugger did a morally good deed just because his action had a happy result? According to utilitarianism we would, assuming the net result of the action was more happiness than would otherwise have been the case. So utilitarianism doesn't seem to be the complete story in moral reasoning.

Duty Theory/Deontologism

Immanuel Kant (1724–1804), who witnessed the beginning phases of the utilitarian philosophy, found that philosophy deficient because of its neglect,

In Depth

Acts and Rules

Thinking of cheating on a test? Maybe the sum total of happiness in the world would be increased by this single *act* of cheating. But it isn't inconceivable that if the *principle* involved were adopted widely, the sum total of happiness would be decreased.

This raises the question: When calculating happiness outcomes, should we contemplate happiness outcomes of the particular *act* in question? Or should we contemplate happiness outcomes of adoption of the *principle* involved in the act?

Accordingly, some philosophers make a distinction between "act utilitarianism," which evaluates the moral worth of an act on the happiness it would produce, and "rule utilitarianism," which evaluates the moral worth of an act on the happiness that would be produced by adoption of the principle it exemplifies. (A possible middle ground might be to attempt to factor in, as a part of the happiness outcomes of a particular act, the likelihood that doing it will contribute to a general adoption of the principle involved. This is often what we do when we ask, "But what if everyone did this?")

among other things, of moral duty. Kant's theory is a version of what is called **duty theory,** or **deontologism.**

Kant acknowledged that our lives are full of imperatives based on our own situations and our objectives. If we want to advance at work, then it is imperative that we keep our promises; if we are concerned about our friends' happiness, then it is imperative that we not talk about them behind their backs. But this type of **hypothetical imperative,** which tells us we ought to do (or ought not to do) something in order to achieve such and such a result, is not a *moral* imperative, Kant argued. Keeping a promise so we'll get a solid reputation is neither morally praiseworthy nor morally blameworthy, he said. For our act to be *morally* praiseworthy, it must be done, not for the sake of some objective, but simply because *it is right.* Our action of keeping our promise is morally praiseworthy, he said, only if we do it simply because it is right to keep our promises. A moral imperative is unconditional or **categorical;** it prescribes an action, not for the sake of some result, but simply because that action is our moral duty.

It follows from this philosophy that when it comes to evaluating an action morally, what counts is not the result or consequences of the action, as utilitarianism maintains, but the intention from which it is done. And the morally best intention, indeed in Kant's opinion the *only* truly morally praiseworthy intention, is that according to which you do something just because it is your moral duty.

But what makes something our moral duty? Some deontologists ground duty in human nature; others ground it in reason; in Western culture, of course, many believe moral duty is set by God. How can we tell what our duty is? Some believe our duty is to be found by consulting conscience; others believe that it is just self-evident or is clear to moral intuition. Those who maintain that human moral duties are established by God usually derive their specific understanding of these duties through interpretations of religious

Real Life

Inmate Who Got New Heart While Still in Prison Dies

A California prison inmate believed to be the first in the nation to receive a heart transplant while incarcerated has died, officials said Tuesday.

Department of Corrections spokesman Russ Heimerich said the inmate, whose identity has been withheld, died late Monday at Stanford University Medical Center.

Heimerich said the exact cause of death was still undetermined, "but it looks like his body was rejecting the heart" he received in an expensive and controversial taxpayer-financed operation in January.

Officials estimated the surgery and subsequent care—including the $12,500 a day it cost to keep him in the Stanford facility after he was admitted Nov. 23—have cost more than $1.25 million. Heimerich said that figure does not include transportation, medication or providing round-the-clock security while the inmate was in the hospital.

"It could easily reach $2 million when it's all added in," Heimerich said.

The prisoner was a 32-year-old two-time felon serving a 14-year sentence for robbing a Los Angeles convenience store in 1996. He was eligible for parole in October 2008.

He became the center of a national controversy after The Bee disclosed the surgery, which also took place at Stanford.

The operation raised questions about whether there should be limits on the kinds of medical care to which prison inmates are entitled.

At the time of the transplant, prison officials said they were required under numerous court orders, including a 1976 U.S. Supreme Court decision, to provide necessary health care to all inmates.

The decision to provide the inmate, who had longtime heart problems caused by a viral infection, with a new heart was made by a medical panel at Stanford. The surgery was performed on a day when at least 500 other Californians were waiting for similar operations.

But medical professionals and organ transplant centers said they can make decisions about who gets organs and who doesn't based only on medical protocols and not social factors.

While the first of its kind, the transplant is not likely to be the last. As California's prison population ages, authorities are concerned the cost of inmate health care will soar far above last fiscal year's $663 million.

Compounding the problem, Heimerich said, is that many inmate patients don't follow doctor's orders. He said the heart recipient apparently did not follow all of the medical recommendations, although it wasn't clear his failure to do so played a role in his death.

"We can treat them," Heimerich said, "but we can't baby-sit them."

By Steve Wiegand
BEE STAFF WRITER

Comment: Such cases involve legal reasoning (see next section of this chapter) as well as moral reasoning. The position taken here by medical professionals is duty theory; they are explicitly ruling out utilitarian considerations in deciding to whom to give transplants.

Source: The *Sacramento Bee*, December 17, 2002.

texts such as the Bible, though there is disagreement over what the correct interpretation is and even over who should do the interpreting.

Kant answered the question, How can we tell what our moral duty is? as follows: Suppose you are considering some course of action—say, whether to borrow some money you need very badly. But suppose that you know you can't pay back the loan. Is it morally permissible for you to borrow money under such circumstances? Kant said to do this: First, find the *maxim* (principle of action) involved in what you want to do. In the case in question, the maxim is "Every time I'm in need of money, I'll go to my friends and promise I'll pay it back, even if I know I can't." Next, ask yourself, "Could I want this maxim to be a *universal* law or rule, one that everyone should follow?" This process of *universalization* is the feature that lets you judge whether something would work as a moral law, according to Kant. Could you make it a universal law that it is okay for everybody to lie about paying back loans? Hardly: If everyone adopted this principle, then there would be no such thing as loan making. In short, the universalization of your principle undermines the very principle that is universalized. If everyone adopted the principle, then nobody could possibly follow it. The universalization of your principle is illogical, so it is your duty to pay back loans.

As you can see, the results of acting according to Kant's theory can be radically different from the results of acting according to utilitarianism. Utilitarianism would condone borrowing money with no intention of repaying it, assuming that doing so would produce more happiness than would be produced by not doing so. But Kant's theory would not condone it.

Kant also noted that if you were to borrow a friend's money with no intention of repaying it, you would be treating your friend merely as a means to an end. If you examine cases like this, in which you use other people as mere tools for your own objectives, then, Kant said, you will find in each case a transgression of moral duty, a principle of action that cannot be universalized. Thus, he warned us, it is our moral duty never to treat someone else *merely* as a tool, as means to an end. Of course Kant did not mean that Moore cannot ask Parker for help on some project; doing so would not be a case of Moore's using Parker *merely* as a tool.

Kant's theory of the moral necessity of never treating other people as mere tools can be modified to support the ideas that people have rights and that treatment of others must always involve fair play. Regardless of whether you subscribe to Kant's version of duty theory, the chances are that your own moral deliberations are more than just strictly utilitarian and may well involve considerations of what you take to be other moral requirements, including your duties and the rights of others.

Divine Command Theory

Those who believe moral duty is set by an authority of some sort subscribe to "command" duty theory. (Some authorities view Kant's duty theory as a version of command duty theory, with the authority for Kant being *reason*.) In our culture, probably the most popular version of command duty theory is that according to which our moral duty is set by God; it thus is known as **divine command theory.** As noted above, those who hold this view generally derive their understanding of God's commandments by interpretation of religious texts like the Bible. How, for example, is "Thou shalt not kill" to be understood? Should it be understood as prohibiting capital punishment, or killing in self-defense, or killing in wartime? Does it cover abortion? There is obviously room for disagreement here; likewise, there is room for disagreement over who is to do the interpreting, whether it is to be oneself, or one's minister, or the head of one's church, or whoever.

I'm not guilty of murder. I'm guilty of obeying the laws of the Creator.

— Benjamin Matthew Williams, who committed suicide while awaiting sentencing for having murdered a gay couple

A philosophical difficulty in divine command theory lies in the question, Is God *justified* in decreeing an act to be right, or is his decree simply arbitrary? On the one hand, we don't want to say that God hands down rules arbitrarily; yet the first alternative seems to imply that there is some standard of rightness and wrongness *above* or *apart* from God, in terms of which God finds the justification for his edicts.

Virtue Ethics

Utilitarianism and duty theory, as well as most other classical approaches to moral theory, focus on the question of what to do. For that reason they are commonly referred to as ethics of conduct. However, another approach was predominant in classical Greek thinking and has regained popularity in recent years. That approach, known as **virtue ethics,** focuses not on *what to do,* but on *how to be*; in other words, the moral issue is not one of single actions or types of actions but of developing a *good character.*

The ancient Greeks believed it was supremely important for a person to achieve psychological and physical balance; and to do that, the person needed to develop a consistently good character. A person out of balance will not be able to assess a situation properly and will tend to overreact or not react strongly enough; moreover, such a person will not know his or her proper limits. People who recognize their own qualifications and limitations and who are capable of reacting to the right degree, at the right time, toward the right person, and for the right reason are virtuous persons. They understand the value of the idea of moderation: not too much and not too little, but in each case a response that is just right.

Aristotle (384–322 B.C.E.) regarded virtue as a trait, like wisdom, justice, or courage, that we acquire when we use our capacity to reason to moderate our impulses and appetites. The largest part of Aristotle's major ethical writing, the *Nicomachean Ethics,* is devoted to analysis of specific moral virtues as means between extremes (for example, courage is the mean between fearing everything and fearing nothing). He also emphasized that virtue is a matter of habit; it is a trait, a way of living.

Virtue ethics is not an abstruse ethical theory. Many of us (fortunately) wish to be (or become) persons of good character. And as a practical matter, when we are deliberating a course of action, our approach often is to consider what someone whose character we admire would do in the circumstances.

Still, it is possible that virtue theory alone cannot answer all moral questions. Each of us may face moral dilemmas of such a nature that it simply isn't clear what course of action is required by someone of good character.

MORAL DELIBERATION

Before you began this chapter, you may have assumed that moral discussion is merely an exchange of personal opinion or feeling, one that reserves no place for reason or critical thinking. But moral discussion usually assumes some

In Depth

Why Moral Problems Seem Unresolvable

Differences of opinion over ethical issues sometimes seem irreconcilable. Yet this fact often strikes thoughtful people as amazing, because ethical opponents often share a great deal of common ground. For example, pro-life and pro-choice adherents agree on the sanctity of human life. So why in the world can't they resolve their differences? Likewise, those who favor affirmative action and those who agree that racism and sexism still exist and are wrong and need to be eradicated—why on earth can't they resolve their differences?

The answer, in some cases, comes down to a difference in moral perspective. Take affirmative action. Those who favor affirmative action often operate within a utilitarian perspective: They assume that whether a policy should be adopted depends on whether adopting the policy will produce more happiness than will not adopting it. From this perspective, if policies of affirmative action produce more happiness over the long run, then they should be adopted—end of discussion. But those who oppose affirmative action (on grounds other than blatant racism) do so because they believe deontologism trumps utilitarianism. From the deontologist perspective, even if affirmative action policies would produce more happiness in the long run, if they involve even temporarily using some people as a means to that objective, then they are wrong—end of discussion.

In other disputes the root difference lies elsewhere. Pro-life and pro-choice adherents often both are deontologists and agree, for example, that in the absence of a powerful justification, it is wrong to take a human life. They may disagree, however, either as to what counts as a human life or as to what counts as a powerful justification. This difference, then, comes down to a difference in basic definitions—which fact, incidentally, illustrates how silly it can be to dismiss a discussion as "mere semantics."

sort of perspective like those we have mentioned here. Actually, in real life, moral reasoning is often a mixture of perspectives, a blend of utilitarian considerations weighted somewhat toward one's own happiness, modified by ideas about duties, rights, and obligations, and mixed often with a thought, perhaps guilty, about what the ideally virtuous person (a parent, a teacher) would do in similar circumstances. It also sometimes involves mistakes—factual and nonfactual claims may be confused, inconsistencies may occur, inductive arguments may be weak or deductive arguments may be invalid, fallacious reasoning may be present, and so forth.

We can make headway in our own thinking about moral issues by trying to get clear on what perspective, if any, we are assuming. For example, suppose we are thinking about the death penalty. Our first thought might be that society is much better off if murderers are executed. Are we then assuming a utilitarian perspective? Asking ourselves this question might lead us to consider whether there are *limits* on what we would do for the common good—for example, would we be willing to risk sacrificing an innocent person? It might also lead us to consider how we might *establish* whether society is better off if murderers are executed—if we are utilitarians, then ultimately we will have to establish this if our reasoning is to be compelling.

Or suppose we have seen a friend cheating on an exam. Should we report it to the teacher? Whatever our inclination, it may be wise to consider our perspective. Are we viewing things from a utilitarian perspective? That is, are we assuming that it would promote the most happiness overall to report our friend? Or do we simply believe that it is our duty to report him or her, come what may? Would a virtuous person report the person? Each of these questions will tend to focus our attention on a particular set of considerations—those that are the most relevant to our way of thinking.

It may occur to you to wonder at this point if there is any reason for choosing among perspectives. The answer to this question is yes: Adherents of these positions, philosophers such as those we mentioned, offer grounding or support for their perspectives in theories about human nature, the natural universe, the nature of morality, and other things. In other words, they have *arguments* to support their views. If you are interested, we recommend a course in ethics.

Exercise 12-1

Which of the following claims are value judgments?

▲ 1. Lizards make fine pets.

2. You can get a clothes rack at True Value for less than $15.00.

3. The last haircut I got at Supercuts was just totally awful.

▲ 4. It was a great year for regional politics.

5. Key officials of the Department of Defense are producing their own unverified intelligence reports about an arms buildup.

6. Texas leads the nation in accidental deaths caused by police chases.

▲ 7. Napoleon Bonaparte was the greatest military leader of modern times.

8. Racial segregation is immoral anytime anywhere.

9. President Bush is deploying a "missile defense" that hasn't been adequately tested.

▲ 10. Air consists mainly of nitrogen and oxygen.

Exercise 12-2

Which of the following claims are value judgments?

▲ 1. T-shirts made by Fruit of the Loom are soft and luxurious.

2. Rumsfeld is not nearly as detailed in reports to the press as is Rice.

3. The Pentagon was not nearly as supportive of a war as it should have been.

▲ 4. Tens of billions of dollars have been wasted on worthless public transportation schemes.

5. Atlanta is sultry in the summer.

6. Religious school teachers are stricter than their nonreligious counterparts.

▲ 7. Six Flags has the scariest rides in the state.

8. The politician with the best sense of humor? That would have to have been Al Sharpton.

9. Eugene is not nearly as happy as his wife, Polly.
10. Polly is more selfish than she should be.

Exercise 12-3

Which of the following are moral value judgments?

▲ 1. Marina's car puts out horrible smoke; for the sake of us all, she should get it tuned up.
2. After the surgery, Nicky's eyesight improved considerably.
3. Ms. Beeson ought not to have embezzled money from the bank.
▲ 4. Violence is always wrong.
5. Matthew ought to wear that sweater more often; it looks great on him.
6. Sandy, you are one of the laziest people I know!
▲ 7. My computer software is really good; it even corrects my grammar.
8. Lisa has been very good tonight, according to the babysitter.
9. Judge Ramesh is quite well-informed.
▲ 10. Judge Ramesh's decision gave each party exactly what it deserved.
11. The editor couldn't use my illustrations; she said they were not particularly interesting.
12. Wow. That was a tasty meal!
13. The last set of essays was much better than the first set.
14. Do unto others as you would have them do unto you.
15. People who live in glass houses shouldn't throw stones.
16. You really shouldn't make so much noise when the people upstairs are trying to sleep.
17. It is unfair the way Professor Smith asks questions no normal person can answer.
18. "Allegro" means fast, but not that fast!
19. Being in touch with God gives your life meaning and value.
20. Thou shalt not kill.

Exercise 12-4

In each of the following passages, a general moral principle must be added as an extra premise to make the argument valid. Supply such a principle.

Example

Mrs. Montez's new refrigerator was delivered yesterday, and it stopped working altogether. She has followed the directions carefully but still can't make it work. The people she bought it from should either come out and make it work or replace it with another one.

Principle

People should make certain that the things they sell are in proper working order.

1. After borrowing Morey's car, Leo had an accident and crumpled a fender. So, Leo ought to pay whatever expenses were involved in getting Morey's car fixed.
▲ 2. When Sarah bought the lawn mower from Jean, she promised to pay another fifty dollars on the first of the month. Since it is now the first, Sarah should pay Jean the money.
3. Kevin worked on his sister's car all weekend. The least she could do is let him borrow the car for his job interview next Thursday.
4. Harold is obligated to supply ten cords of firewood to the lodge by the beginning of October, since he signed a contract guaranteeing delivery of the wood by that date.
▲ 5. Since it was revealed yesterday on the 11:00 news that Mayor Ahearn has been taking bribes, he should step down any day now.
6. As a political candidate, Havenhurst promised to put an end to crime in the inner city. Now that she is in office, we'd like to see results.
▲ 7. Since he has committed his third felony, he should automatically go to prison for twenty-five years.
▲ 8. Laura's priest has advised Laura and her husband not to sign up for the in vitro fertilization program at the hospital because such treatments are unnatural.
9. Ali has been working overtime a lot lately, so he should receive a bonus.
10. It is true there are more voters in the northern part of the state. But that shouldn't allow the north to dictate to the south.

Exercise 12-5

Answer the question or respond to the statement that concludes each item.

1. Tory thinks women should have the same rights as men. However, he also thinks that although a man should have the right to marry a woman, a woman should not have the right to marry a woman. Is Tory being consistent in his views?
2. At Shelley's university, the minimum GPA requirement for admission is relaxed for 6 percent of incoming students. Half of those admitted under this program are women and minorities, and the other half are athletes, children of alumni, and talented art and music students. Shelley is opposed to special admissions programs for women and minority students; she is not opposed to special admission programs for art and music students, athletes, or children of alumni. Is she consistent?
▲ 3. Marin does not approve of abortion because the Bible says explicitly, "Thou shalt not kill." "'Thou shalt not kill' means thou shalt not kill," he says. Marin does, however, approve of capital punishment. Is Marin consistent?
4. Koko believes that adults should have the unrestricted right to read whatever material they want to read, but she does not believe that her seventeen-year-old daughter Gina should have the unrestricted right to read whatever she wants to read. Is Koko consistent?
5. Jack maintains that the purpose of marriage is procreation. On these grounds he opposes same-sex marriages. "Gays can't create children," he

explains. However, he does not oppose marriages between heterosexual partners who cannot have children due to age or medical reasons. "It's not the same," he says. Is Jack being consistent?

6. Alisha thinks the idea of outlawing cigarettes is ridiculous. "Give me a break," she says. "If you want to screw up your health with cigarettes, that's your own business." However, Alisha does not approve the legalization of marijuana. "Hel-loh-o," she says. "Marijuana is a *drug,* and the last thing we need is more druggies." Is Alisha being consistent?

7. California's Proposition 209 amends the California state constitution to prohibit "discrimination or preferential treatment" in state hiring based on race, gender, or ethnicity. Opponents say that Proposition 209 singles out women and members of racial and ethnic minorities for unequal treatment. Their argument is that Proposition 209 makes it impossible for members of these groups to obtain redress for past discrimination through preferential treatment, whereas members of other groups who may have suffered past discrimination (gays, for example, or members of religious groups) are not similarly restricted from seeking redress. Evaluate this argument.

▲ 8. Harold prides himself on being a liberal. He is delighted when a federal court issues a preliminary ruling that California's Proposition 209 (see previous item) is unconstitutional. "It makes no difference that a majority of California voters approved the measure," Harold argues. "If it is unconstitutional, then it is unconstitutional." However, California voters also recently passed an initiative that permits physicians to prescribe marijuana, and Harold is livid when the U.S. Attorney General says that the federal government will ignore the California statute and will use federal law to prosecute any physician who prescribes marijuana. Is Harold consistent?

9. Graybosch is of the opinion that we should not perform medical experiments on people against their will, but he has no problem with medical experiments being done on dogs. His wife disagrees. She sees no relevant difference between the two cases.

   "What, no difference between people and dogs?" Graybosch asks.

   "There are differences, but no differences that are relevant to the issue," Graybosch's wife responds. "Dogs feel pain and experience fear just as much as people."

   Is Graybosch's wife correct?

10. Mr. Bork is startled when a friend tells him he should contribute to the welfare of others' children as much as to his own.

    "Why on earth should I do that?" Mr. Bork asks his friend.

    "Because," his friend responds, "there is no relevant difference between the two cases. The fact that your children are yours does not mean that there is something different about them that gives them a greater entitlement to happiness than anyone else's children."

    How should Mr. Bork respond?

11. The university wants to raise the requirements for tenure. Professor Peterson, who doesn't have tenure, says that doing so is unfair to her. She argues that those who received tenure before she did weren't required to meet such exacting standards; therefore, neither should she. Is she correct?

12. Reverend Heintz has no objection to same-sex marriages, but is opposed to polygamous marriages. Is there a relevant difference between the two cases, or is Reverend Heintz being inconsistent?

Exercise 12-6

1. Roy needs to sell his car, but he doesn't have money to spend on repairs. He plans to sell the vehicle to a private party without mentioning that the rear brakes are worn. Evaluate Roy's plan of action from a Kantian perspective—that is, can the maxim of Roy's plan be universalized?
2. Defend affirmative action from a utilitarian perspective.
3. Criticize affirmative action from a Kantian perspective. (Hint: Consider Kant's theory that people must never be treated as means only.)
4. Criticize or defend medical experimentation on animals from a utilitarian perspective.
5. Criticize or defend medical experimentation on animals from a divine command perspective.
6. A company has the policy of not promoting women to be vice presidents. What might be said about this policy from the perspective of virtue ethics?
7. What might be said about the policy mentioned in item 6 from the perspective of utilitarianism?
8. Evaluate embryonic stem cell research from a utilitarian perspective.
9. In your opinion, would the virtuous person, the person of the best moral character, condemn, approve, or be indifferent to bisexuality?
10. "We can't condemn the founding fathers for owning slaves; people didn't think there was anything wrong with it at the time." Comment on this remark from the standpoint of duty theory.
11. "Let's have some fun and see how your parrot looks without feathers." (The example is from philosopher Joseph Grcic.) Which of the following perspectives seems best equipped to condemn this suggestion?
    a. utilitarianism
    b. Kantian duty theory
    c. divine command theory
    d. virtue ethics
    e. relativism
12. "Might makes right." Could a utilitarian accept this? Could a virtue ethicist? Could Kant? Could a relativist? Could someone who subscribes to divine command theory?

Exercise 12-7

> This is Darwin's natural selection at its very best. The highest bidder gets youth and beauty.

These are the words of fashion photographer Ron Harris, who auctioned the ova of fashion models via the Internet. The model got the full bid price, and the Web site took a commission of an additional 20 percent. The bid price included no medical costs, though it listed specialists who were willing to perform the procedure. Harris, who created the video "The 20 Minute Workout," said the egg auction gave people the chance of reproducing beautiful children who would have an advantage in society. Critics, however, were numerous. "It screams of unethical behavior," one said. "It is acceptable for an infertile couple to choose an egg donor and compensate her for her time, inconvenience and discomfort," he said. "But this is something else entirely. Among other things, what happens to the child if he or she turns out to be unattractive?"

Discuss the (moral) pros and cons of this issue for five or ten minutes in groups. Then take a written stand on the question "Should human eggs be auctioned to the highest bidder?" When you are finished, discuss which moral perspective seems to be the one in which you are operating.

Exercise 12-8

> Jesus wants to be our best friend. . . . If we let him direct our lives, he will give us the desires of our heart . . . we must yield to God and let him direct our future plans.

Where we live, a student was denied permission to deliver a valedictorian speech at his public high school graduation that contained this statement.

The principal held that religious points of view cannot be presented at an event sponsored by a publicly funded agency. If the student had given his speech, the principal said, it would be as if the school had condoned the strong religious message the words contained.

The student, on the other hand, said he should be free to express his opinions and beliefs in a graduation speech. He said:

> I would not object if a Buddhist student gave a graduation speech and thanked Buddha, or a graduation speaker thanked Satan and urged people to follow Satan's example. Our country was founded on godly principles. God is on all of our money. It's pretty absurd that you can't even mention God at a graduation.

Should the student have been denied permission to include the statement we've quoted in his graduation speech? Think about the issue for a few minutes and then discuss it in groups of four or five for another five or ten minutes. After that, take a position on the issue and, on a piece of paper, defend the position with the best argument you can think of. Groups should then decide which moral perspective or combination of moral perspectives your defense seems to adopt.

LEGAL REASONING

When we think about arguments and disputes, the first image to come to most minds is probably that of an attorney arguing a case in a court of law. Although it's true that lawyers require a solid understanding of factual matters related to their cases and of psychological considerations as well, especially where juries are involved, it is still safe to say that a lawyer's stock-in-trade is argument. Lawyers are successful—in large part—to the extent that they can produce evidence in support of the conclusion that most benefits their client—in other words, their success depends on how well they can put premises and conclusions together into convincing arguments.

Legal Reasoning and Moral Reasoning Compared

There are some obvious similarities between moral and legal claims. For example, they are both often prescriptive—they tell us what we should do. Both play a role in guiding our conduct, but legal prescriptions carry the weight of society behind them in a way that moral prescriptions do not: We can be punished if we fail to follow the former. In terms of specific actions, it's obvious that the class of illegal activities and the class of immoral activities greatly overlap. Indeed, a society whose moral and legal codes were greatly at odds would be very difficult to understand.

In our own society, we use the term "morals offenses" for a certain class of crimes (usually related to sexual practices), but in reality, most of the crimes we list in our penal codes are also offenses against morality: murder, robbery, theft, rape, and so on. There are exceptions both ways. Lying is almost always considered immoral, but it is illegal only in certain circumstances—under oath or in a contract, for example. On the other hand, there are many laws that have little or nothing to do with morality: laws that govern whether two people are married, laws that determine how far back from the street you must build your house, laws that require us to drive on the right side of the road, and so on. (It may be morally wrong to endanger others by driving on the wrong side of the road, but it is of no moral consequence whether the *correct* side is the right or the left. Hence, the actual content of the law is morally neutral.)

Two Types of Legal Studies: Justifying Laws and Interpreting Laws

Two principal kinds of questions are asked in legal studies. (Such studies, incidentally, are known variously as "jurisprudence" and "philosophy of law.") The first kind of question asks what the law *should be* and what procedures for making law should be adopted; the second kind asks what the law *is* and how it should be applied. Typically, philosophers are more interested in the former type of question and practicing attorneys in the latter.

By and large, reasoning about the first kind of question differs very little from moral reasoning as described in the first part of this chapter. The difference is simply that the focus is on justifying *laws* rather than on justifying moral statements or principles. We are often most interested in the justification of laws when those laws forbid us from doing something we might otherwise want to do or when they require us to do something we might otherwise want not to do. Justifications are simply arguments that try to establish the goodness, value, or acceptability of something. Here, they are used to try to answer the question, What should the law be?

Consider whether a law that forbids doing X should be enacted by your state legislature.* Typically, there are four main grounds on which a supporter of a law can base his or her justification. The first is simply that doing X is

---

*The example here is of a criminal law—part of a penal code designed to require and forbid certain behaviors and to punish offenders. The situation is a little different in civil law, a main goal of which is to shift the burden of a wrongful harm (a "tort") from the person on whom it falls to another, more suitable person—usually the one who caused the harm.

immoral. The claim that the law should make illegal anything that is immoral is the basis of the position known as **legal moralism.** One might use such a basis for justifying laws forbidding murder, assault, or unorthodox sexual practices. For a legal moralist, the kinds of arguments designed to show that an action is immoral are directly relevant to the question of whether the action should be illegal.

The next ground on which a law can be justified is probably the one that most people think of first. It is very closely associated with John Stuart Mill (1806–1873) and is known as the **harm principle:** The only legitimate basis for forbidding X is that doing X causes harm to others. Notice that the harm principle states not just that harm to others is a good ground for forbidding an activity, but that it is the *only* ground. (In terms of the way we formulated such claims in Chapter 9, on truth-functional logic, the principle would be stated, "It is legitimate to forbid doing X *if and only if* doing X causes harm to others.") A person who defends this principle and who wants to enact a law forbidding X will present evidence that doing X does indeed cause harm to others. Her arguments could resemble any of the types covered in earlier chapters.

A third ground on which our hypothetical law might be based is legal paternalism. **Legal paternalism** is the view that laws can be justified if they prevent a person from doing harm to him- or herself; that is, they forbid or make it impossible to do X, *for a person's own good.* Examples include laws that require that seat belts be worn while riding in automobiles and that helmets be worn while riding on motorcycles.

The last of the usual bases for justifying criminal laws is that some behavior is generally found offensive. The **offense principle** says that a law forbidding X can be justifiable if X causes great offense to others. Laws forbidding burning of the flag are often justified on this ground.

The second question mentioned earlier—What *is* the law and how should it be applied?—may be more straightforward than the first question, but it can still be very complicated. We needn't go into great detail here about why this is the case, but an example will provide an indication. Back in Chapter 2 we discussed vague concepts, and we found that it is impossible to rid our talk entirely of vagueness. Here's an example from the law. Let's suppose that a city ordinance forbids vehicles on the paths in the city park. Clearly, a person violates the law if he or she drives a truck or a car down the paths. But what about a motorbike? A bicycle? A go-cart? A child's pedal car? Just what counts as a vehicle and what does not? This is the kind of issue that must often be decided in court because—not surprisingly—the governing body writing the law could not foresee all the possible items that might, in somebody's mind, count as a vehicle.

The process of narrowing down when a law applies and when it does not, then, is another kind of reasoning problem that occurs in connection with the law.

The Role of Precedent in Legal Reasoning

Generally speaking, legal reasoning is like other reasoning insofar as it makes use of the same kinds of arguments: They are deductive or inductive; if the former, they can be valid or invalid; if the latter, they can range from strong to weak. The difference between legal and other types of reasoning is mainly in the subject matter to which the argumentative techniques are applied, a taste of which we have sampled in the preceding paragraphs.

There is one kind of argument that occupies a special place in reasoning about legal matters, however: the **appeal to precedent.** This is the practice in the law of using a case that has already been decided as an authoritative guide in deciding a new case that is similar. The appeal to precedent is a variety of argument by analogy in which the current case is said to be sufficiently like the previous case to warrant deciding it in the same way. The general principle of treating like cases alike, discussed in the previous section on moral reasoning, applies here for exactly the same reasons. It would be illogical—and most would say, in some cases at least, unfair or immoral—to treat similar cases in different ways. The Latin name for the principle of appeal to precedent is ***stare decisis*** ("don't change settled decisions," more or less). Using terminology that was applied in the Chapter 10 discussion of analogical argument, we'd say that the earlier, settled case and the current case are the terms of the analogy, with the latter the target case. The property in question is the way in which the first case was decided. If the target case is sufficiently like the sample case, then, according to the principle of *stare decisis,* it should be decided the same way. Arguments in such situations, naturally, tend to focus on whether the current case really is like the precedent in enough relevant respects. Aside from the fact that such disputes sometimes have more significant consequences for the parties involved, they are not importantly different from those over analogies in other subject matters.

Exercise 12-9

For each of the following kinds of laws, pick at least one of the four grounds for justification discussed in the text—legal moralism, the harm principle, legal paternalism, and the offense principle—and construct an argument designed to justify the law. You may not agree either with the law or with the argument; the exercise is to see if you can connect the law to the (allegedly) justifying principle. For many laws, there is more than one kind of justification possible, so there can be more than one good answer for many of these.

▲ **1.** Laws against shoplifting

▲ **2.** Laws against forgery

3. Laws against suicide

▲ **4.** Laws against spitting on the sidewalk

5. Laws against driving under the influence of drugs or alcohol

▲ **6.** Laws against adultery

7. Laws against marriage between two people of the same sex

8. Laws that require people to have licenses before they practice medicine

9. Laws that require drivers of cars to have driver's licenses

▲ **10.** Laws against desecrating a corpse

11. Laws against trespassing

12. Laws against torturing your pet (even though it may be legal to kill your pet, if it is done humanely)

Exercise 12-10

This exercise is for class discussion or a short writing assignment. In the text, "Vehicles are prohibited on the paths in the park" was used as an example of a law that might require clarification. Decide whether the law should be interpreted to forbid motorcycles, bicycles, children's pedal cars, and battery-powered remote-control cars. On what grounds are you deciding each of these cases?

Exercise 12-11

The U.S. Supreme Court came to a decision not long ago about the proper application of the word "use." Briefly, the case in point was about a man named John Angus Smith, who traded a handgun for cocaine. The law under which Smith was charged provided for a much more severe penalty—known as an enhanced penalty—if a gun was used in a drug-related crime than if no gun was involved. (In this case, the enhanced penalty was a mandatory thirty-year sentence; the "unenhanced" penalty was five years.) Justice Antonin Scalia argued that Smith's penalty should not be enhanced because he did not use the gun in the way the writers of the law had in mind; he did not use it *as a gun.* Justice Sandra Day O'Connor argued that the law only requires the *use* of a gun, not any particular *kind* of use. If you were a judge, would you vote with Scalia or with O'Connor? Construct an argument in support of your position. (The decision of the court is given in the answer section at the back of the book.)

AESTHETIC REASONING

Like moral and legal thinking, aesthetic thinking relies on a conceptual framework that integrates fact and value. Judgments about beauty and art—even judgments about whether something is a work of art or just an everyday object—appeal to principles that identify sources of aesthetic or artistic value. So when you make such a judgment, you are invoking aesthetic concepts, even if you have not made them explicit to yourself or to others.

Eight Aesthetic Principles

Here are some of the aesthetic principles that most commonly support or influence artistic creation and critical judgment about art. The first three identify value in art with an object's ability to fulfill certain cultural or social functions.

1. *Objects are aesthetically valuable if they are meaningful or teach us truths.* For example, Aristotle says that tragic plays teach us general truths about the human condition in a dramatic way that cannot be matched by real-life experience. Many people believe art shows us truths that are usually hidden from us by the practical concerns of daily life.

2. *Objects are aesthetically valuable if they have the capacity to convey values or beliefs that are central to the cultures or traditions in which they originate or that are important to the artists who made them.* For example, John Milton's poem *Paradise Lost* expresses the seventeenth-century Puritan view of the relationship between human beings and God.

Christo, *The Gates.*

3. *Objects are aesthetically valuable if they have the capacity to help bring about social or political change.* For instance, Abraham Lincoln commented that Harriet Beecher Stowe's *Uncle Tom's Cabin* contributed to the antislavery movement.

Another group of principles identifies aesthetic value with objects' capacities to produce certain subjective—that is, psychological—states in persons who experience or appreciate them. Here are some of the most common or influential principles of the second group:

4. *Objects are aesthetically valuable if they have the capacity to produce pleasure in those who experience or appreciate them.* For instance, the nineteenth-century German philosopher Friedrich Nietzsche identifies one kind of aesthetic value with the capacity to create a feeling of ecstatic bonding in audiences.

5. *Objects are aesthetically valuable if they have the capacity to produce certain emotions we value, at least when the emotion is brought about by art rather than life.* In the *Poetics,* Aristotle observes that we welcome the feelings of fear created in us by frightening dramas, whereas in everyday life fear is an experience we would rather avoid. The psychoanalyst Sigmund

■ **Rachel Steiner, *Mrs. Hubbub.*** Ms. Steiner is the high school daughter of a colleague. Apart from technical considerations, does the age of an artist bear any relation to the merit of the art work?

Freud offers another version of this principle: While we enjoy art, we permit ourselves to have feelings so subversive that we have to repress them to function in everyday life.

6. *Objects are aesthetically valuable if they have the capacity to produce special nonemotional experiences, such as a feeling of autonomy or the willing suspension of disbelief.* This principle is the proposal of the nineteenth-century English poet Samuel Taylor Coleridge. One of art's values, he believes, is its ability to stimulate our power to exercise our imaginations and consequently to free ourselves from thinking that is too narrowly practical.

Notice that principles 4 through 6 resemble the first three in that they identify aesthetic value with the capacity to fulfill a function. According to these last three, the specified function is to create some kind of subjective or inner state in audiences; according to the first three, however, art's function is to achieve such objective outcomes as conveying information or knowledge or preserving or changing culture or society. But there are yet other influential aesthetic principles that do not characterize art in terms of capacities for performing functions. According to one commonly held principle, art objects attain aesthetic value by virtue of their possessing a certain special aesthetic property or certain special formal configurations:

7. *Objects are aesthetically valuable if they possess a special aesthetic property or exhibit a special aesthetic form.* Sometimes this aesthetic property is called "beauty," and sometimes it is given another name. For instance, the early-twentieth-century art critic Clive Bell insists that good art is valuable for its own sake, not because it fulfills any function. To know whether a work is good aesthetically, he urges, one need only look at it or listen to it to see or hear whether it has "significant form." "Significant form" is valuable for itself, not for any function it performs.

Finally, one familiar principle insists that no reasons can be given to support judgments about art. Properly speaking, those who adhere to this principle think that to approve or disapprove of art is to express an unreasoned preference rather than to render judgment. This principle may be stated as follows:

8. *No reasoned argument can conclude that objects are aesthetically valuable or valueless.* This principle is expressed in the Latin saying *"De gustibus non est disputandum,"* or "Tastes can't be disputed."

The principles summarized here by no means exhaust the important views about aesthetic value, nor are they complete expositions of the views they represent. Historically, views about the nature of art have proven relatively fluid, for they must be responsive to the dynamics of technological and cultural change. Moreover, even though the number of familiar conceptions of aesthetic value is limited, there are many alternative ways of stating these that combine the thoughts behind them in somewhat different ways.

Consequently, to attempt to label each principle with a name invites confusion. For example, let's consider whether any of the principles might be designated *formalism,* which is an important school or style of art. Although the seventh principle explicitly ascribes aesthetic value to a work's form as opposed to its function, the formal properties of artworks also figure as valuable, although only as means to more valuable ends, in certain formulations of the first six principles. For instance, some scholars, critics, and artists think certain formal patterns in works of art can evoke corresponding emotions, social patterns, or pleasures in audiences—for example, slow music full of minor chords is commonly said to make people feel sad.

You should understand that all of the principles presented here merely serve as a basic framework within which you can explore critical thinking about art. If you are interested in the arts, you will very likely want to develop a more complex and sophisticated conceptual framework to enrich your thinking about this subject.

The story is told of the American tourist in Paris who told Pablo Picasso that he didn't like modern paintings because they weren't realistic. Picasso made no immediate reply. A few minutes later the tourist showed him a snapshot of his house.

"My goodness," said Picasso, "is it really *as small as that?*"

— Jacob Braude

Using Aesthetic Principles to Judge Aesthetic Value

The first thing to notice about the aesthetic principles we've just discussed is that some are compatible with each other. Thus, a reasonable thinker can appeal to more than one in reaching a verdict about the aesthetic value of an object. For instance, a consistent thinker can use both the first and the fifth principle in evaluating a tragic drama. Aristotle does just this in his *Poetics.* He tells us that tragedies are good art when they both convey general truths about the human condition and help their audiences purge themselves of the pity and fear they feel when they face the truth about human limitations. A play that presents a general truth without eliciting the proper catharsis (release of emotion) in the audience, or a play that provokes tragic emotions unaccompanied by recognition of a general truth, is not as valuable as a play that does both.

However, some of these principles cannot be used together consistently to judge aesthetic value. These bear the same relationship to each other as do contrary claims (recall the square of opposition in Chapter 8). They cannot both be true, although both might be false. For instance, the principle that art is valuable in itself, by virtue of its form or formal configuration (not because it serves some function), and the principle that art is valuable because it serves a social or political function cannot be used consistently together. You might have noticed also that the eighth principle contradicts the others; that is, the first seven principles all specify kinds of reasons for guiding and supporting our appreciation of art, but the last principle denies that there can be any such good reasons.

Finally, it is important to understand that the same principle can generate both positive and negative evaluations, depending on whether the work in question meets or fails to meet the standard expressed in the principle. For example, the fourth principle, which we might call aesthetic hedonism, generates positive evaluations of works that produce pleasure but negative evaluations of works that leave their audiences in pain or displeased.

Exercise 12-12

Suppose that the two statements in each of the following pairs both appear in a review of the same work of art. Identify which of the eight aesthetic principles each statement in the pair appeals to. Then state whether the principles are compatible (that is, they do not contradict each other) and thus form the basis for a consistent critical review or whether they contradict each other and cannot both be used in a consistent review.

▲ **1.** a. Last weekend's performance of the Wagnerian operatic cycle was superb; the music surged through the audience, forging a joyous communal bond.
   b. Smith's forceful singing and acting in the role of Siegfried left no doubt why Wagner's vision of heroic morality was attractive to his Teutonic contemporaries.

2. a. Leni Riefenstahl's film *Triumph of the Will* proved to be effective art because it convinced its audiences that the Nazi party would improve the German way of life.
   b. Despite its overtly racist message, *Triumph of the Will* is great art, for films should be judged on the basis of their visual coherence and not in terms of their moral impact.

3. a. All lovers of art should condemn Jackson Pollock's meaningless abstract expressionist splatter paintings.
   b. These paintings create neither sadness nor joy; those who view them feel nothing, neither love nor hate nor any of the other passions that great art evokes.

▲ **4.** a. Laurence Olivier's film production of *Hamlet* has merit because he allows us to experience the impact of the incestuous love that a son can feel for his mother.
   b. Nevertheless, Olivier's *Hamlet* is flawed because it introduces a dimension inconceivable to an Elizabethan playwright.

5. a. There is no point arguing about or giving reasons for verdicts about art, because each person's tastes or responses are so personal.
   b. Those who condemn sexually explicit performance art do not recognize that art is valuable to the extent it permits us to feel liberated and free of convention.

Evaluating Aesthetic Criticism: Relevance and Truth

Is any evaluation of a work of art as good as any other in creating a critical treatment of that work? The answer is no, for two reasons: (1) the principles of art one adopts function as a conceptual framework that distinguishes relevant from irrelevant reasons; (2) even a relevant reason is useless if it is not true of the work to which it is applied.

Let's consider the first reason. What would convince you of the value of a work if you accepted principles 4 through 6—all of which maintain that aesthetic value resides in the subjective responses art evokes in its audiences? In this case, you are likely to be drawn to see Picasso's *Guernica* if you are told that it has the power to make its viewers experience the horrors of war; but you would not be attracted by learning, instead, that *Guernica* explores the relationship of two- and three-dimensional spatial concepts. Suppose you reject principles 1 through 3, which conceive of aesthetic value in terms of the work's capacity to perform an objective, cognitive, moral, social, or political function. The fact that Picasso was a Communist will strike you as irrelevant to appreciating *Guernica* unless you accept one or more of the first three principles.

> The aim of art is to represent not the outward appearance of things, but their inward significance.
>
> — Aristotle

To illustrate the second reason, look at the nearby reproduction of *Guernica.* Suppose a critic writes, "By giving his figures fishlike appearances and showing them serenely floating through a watery environment, Picasso makes us feel that humans will survive under any conditions." But no figures in *Guernica* look anything like fish; moreover, they are surrounded by fire, not water, and they are twisted with anguish rather than serene. So, this critic's reasons are no good. Because they are not true of the work, they cannot guide us in perceiving features that enhance our appreciation. A similar problem occurs if reasons are implausible. For instance, an interpretation of *Guernica* as

■ Pablo Picasso, *Guernica*

a depiction of the Last Supper is implausible, because we cannot recognize the usual signs of this theme, the twelve disciples and Christ at a table (or at least at a meal), in the far fewer figures of the painting.

Exercise 12-13

State whether each of the reasons below is relevant according to any one of the aesthetic principles. If the reason is relevant, identify the principle that makes it so. If no principle makes the reason relevant, state that it is irrelevant.

▲ 1. Raphael's carefully balanced pyramidal compositions give his paintings of the Madonna such beautiful form that they have aesthetic value for Christian and atheist alike.

2. By grouping his figures so that they compose a triangle or pyramid, Raphael directs the viewer's eye upward to heaven and thereby teaches us about the close connection between motherhood and God.

3. The melody from the chorus "For unto Us a Child Is Born" in Handel's *Messiah* was originally composed by Handel for an erotic love song. Consequently, it evokes erotic responses which distract and detract from the devotional feeling audiences are supposed to experience when they hear *Messiah* performed.

▲ 4. Vincent van Gogh tells us that he uses clashing reds and greens in *The Night Café* to help us see his vision of "the terrible passions of humanity"; it is the intensity with which he conveys his views of the ugliness of human life that makes his work so illuminating.

5. The critics who ignored van Gogh's painting during his lifetime were seriously mistaken; by damaging his self-esteem, they drove him to suicide.

6. Moreover, these critics misjudged the aesthetic value of his art, as evidenced by the fact that his paintings now sell for as much as $80 million.

▲ 7. By showing a naked woman picnicking with fully clothed men in *Déjeuner sur l'herbe,* Édouard Manet treats women as objects and impedes their efforts to throw off patriarchal domination.

Exercise 12-14

Asuka, a three-year-old chimpanzee in Japan, has been sad and lonely, so the zoo director gave her paper, paints, and brushes to keep her busy. Look at this photograph of Asuka and her painting on page 448. Does the painting have aesthetic value? Use each of the eight aesthetic principles to formulate one reason for or against the aesthetic value of Asuka's work. You should end up with eight reasons, one appealing to each principle.

Why Reason Aesthetically?

The various aesthetic principles we've introduced are among those most commonly found, either explicitly or implicitly, in discussions about art. Moreover, they have influenced both the creation of art and the selection of art for

Asuka the chimpanzee

both private and public enjoyment. But where do these principles come from? There is much debate about this; to understand it, we can draw on notions about definition (introduced in Chapter 2) as well as the discussion of generalizations (Chapter 10).

Some people think that aesthetic principles are simply elaborate definitions of our concepts of art or aesthetic value. Let's explain this point. We use definitions to identify things; for example, by definition we look for three sides and three angles to identify a geometric figure as a triangle. Similarly, we can say that aesthetic principles are definitions; that is, these principles provide an aesthetic vocabulary to direct us in recognizing an object's aesthetic value.

If aesthetic principles are true by definition, then learning to judge art is learning the language of art. But because artists strive for originality, we are constantly faced with talking about innovative objects to which the critic's familiar vocabulary does not quite do justice. This aspect of art challenges even the most sophisticated critic to continually extend the aesthetic vocabulary.

Others think that aesthetic principles are generalizations that summarize what is true of objects treated as valuable art. Here, the argument is by analogy from a sample class to a target population. Thus, someone might hold that all or most of the tragic plays we know that are aesthetically valuable have had something important to say about the human condition; for this reason, we can expect this to be true of any member of the class of tragic plays we have not yet evaluated. Or, also by inductive analogy, musical compositions that are valued so highly that they continue to be performed throughout the centuries all make us feel some specific emotion, such as joy or sadness; so we can predict that a newly composed piece will be similarly highly valued if it also evokes a strong, clear emotion. Of course, such arguments are weakened to the extent that the target object differs from the objects in the sample class. Because there is a drive for originality in art, newly created works may diverge so sharply from previous samples that arguments by analogy sometimes prove too weak.

It is sometimes suggested that these two accounts of the source of aesthetic principles really reinforce each other: Our definitions reflect to some extent our past experience of the properties or capacities typical of valuable art, and our past experience is constrained to some extent by our definitions. But if art changes, of what use are principles, whether analytic or inductive, in guiding us to make aesthetic judgments and—even more difficult—in fostering agreement about these judgments?

At the very least, these principles have an emotive force that guides us in perceiving art. You will remember that emotive force (discussed briefly in Chapter 2) is a dimension of language that permits the words we use to do something more than convey information. In discussion about art, the words that constitute reasons can have an emotive force directing our attention to particular aspects of a work. If the critic can describe these aspects accurately and persuasively, it is thought, the audience will focus on these aspects and experience a favorable (or unfavorable) response similar to the critic's. If a critic's reasons are too vague or are not true of the work to which they are applied, they are unlikely to bring the audience into agreement with the critic.

The principles of art, then, serve as guides for identifying appropriate categories of favorable or unfavorable response, but the reasons falling into these categories are what bring about agreement. They are useful both in developing our own appreciation of a work of art and in persuading others. The reasons must be accurately and informatively descriptive of the objects to which they are applied. The reasons enable us (1) to select a particular way of viewing, listening, reading, or otherwise perceiving the object and (2) to recommend, guide, or prescribe that the object be viewed, heard, or read in this way.

So, aesthetic reasons contain descriptions that prompt ways of perceiving aspects of an object. These prescribed ways of seeing evoke favorable (or unfavorable) responses or experiences. For instance, suppose a critic states that van Gogh's brush strokes in *Starry Night* are dynamic and his colors intense. This positive critical reason prescribes that people focus on these features when they look at the painting. The expectation is that persons whose vision is swept into the movement of van Gogh's painted sky and pierced by the presence of his painted stars will, by virtue of focusing on these formal properties, enjoy a positive response to the painting.

To learn to give reasons and form assessments about art, practice applying these principles as you look, listen, or read. Consider what aspects of a painting, musical performance, poem, or other work each principle directs you to contemplate. It is also important to expand your aesthetic vocabulary so that you have words to describe what you see, hear, or otherwise sense in a work. As you do so, you will be developing your own aesthetic expertise. And, because your reasons will be structured by aesthetic principles others also accept, you will find that rational reflection on art tends to expand both the scope and volume of your agreement with others about aesthetic judgments.

Recap

The key points in this chapter are as follows:

- Value judgments are claims that express values.
- Moral value judgments express moral values.
- Certain words, especially "ought," "should," "right," "wrong," and their opposites are used in moral value judgments, though they can also be used in a nonmoral sense.
- Reasoning about morality is distinguished from other types of reasoning in that the conclusions it tries to establish are moral value judgments.
- Conclusions containing a value judgment cannot be reached solely from premises that do not contain a value judgment ("you cannot get an 'ought' from an 'is'"). A general moral principle must be supplied to tie together the fact-stating premise and the value-judgment conclusion.
- In a case in which we disagree with a value-judgment conclusion but not with the fact-stating premise, we can point to this general moral principle as the source of disagreement.
- People are sometimes inconsistent in their moral views: They treat similar cases as if they were different even when they cannot tell us what is importantly different about them.
- When two or more cases that are being treated differently seem similar, the burden of proof is on the person who is treating them differently to explain what is different about them.
- Moral reasoning is usually conducted within a perspective or framework. Influential Western perspectives include relativism, subjectivism, utilitarianism, Kantian duty theory, divine command theory, and virtue ethics.
- Often different perspectives converge to produce similar solutions to a moral issue.
- Keeping in mind our own perspective can help focus our own moral deliberations on relevant considerations.
- Legal reasoning, like moral reasoning, is often prescriptive.
- Legal studies are devoted to problems like that of justifying laws that prescribe conduct.
- Legal moralism, the harm principle, legal paternalism, and the offense principle are grounds for justifying laws that prescribe conduct.
- Determining just when and where a law applies often requires making vague claims specific.
- Precedent is a kind of analogical argument by means of which current cases are settled in accordance with guidelines set by cases decided previously.
- Whether a precedent governs in a given case is decided on grounds similar to those of any other analogical argument.
- To reason aesthetically is to make judgments within a conceptual framework that integrates facts and values.
- Aesthetic value is often identified as the capacity to fulfill a function, such as to create pleasure or promote social change.

- Alternatively, aesthetic value is defined in terms of a special aesthetic property or form found in works of art.
- Still another view treats aesthetic judgments as expressions of tastes.
- Reasoned argument about aesthetic value helps us to see, hear, or otherwise perceive art in changed or expanded ways and to enhance our appreciation of art.
- A critic who gives reasons in support of an aesthetic verdict forges agreement by getting others to share perceptions of the work. The greater the extent to which we share such aesthetic perceptions, the more we can reach agreement about aesthetic value.

Additional Exercises

Exercise 12-15

State whether the following reasons are (a) helpful in focusing perception to elicit a favorable response, (b) helpful in focusing perception to elicit an unfavorable response, (c) too vague to focus perception, (d) false or implausible and therefore unable to focus perception, or (e) irrelevant to focusing perception. The information you need is contained in the reasons, so try to visualize or imagine what the work is like from what is said. All of these are paraphrases of testimony given at a hearing in 1985 about a proposal to remove *Tilted Arc*, an immense abstract sculpture, from a plaza in front of a federal office building.

▲ 1. Richard Serra's *Tilted Arc* is a curved slab of welded steel 12 feet high, 120 feet long, weighing over 73 tons, covered completely with a natural oxide coating. The sculpture arcs through the plaza. By coming to terms with its harshly intrusive disruption of space, we can learn much about how the nature of the spaces we inhabit affects our social relations.

2. Richard Serra is one of our leading artists, and his work commands very high prices. The government has a responsibility to the financial community. It is bad business to destroy this work because you would be destroying property.

3. *Tilted Arc*'s very tilt and rust remind us that the gleaming and heartless steel and glass structures of the state apparatus can one day pass away. It therefore creates an unconscious sense of freedom and hope.

▲ 4. *Tilted Arc* looks like a discarded piece of crooked or bent metal; there's no more meaning in having it in the middle of the plaza than in putting an old bicycle that got run over by a car there.

5. *Tilted Arc* launches through space in a thrilling and powerful acutely arched curve.

6. *Tilted Arc* is big and rusty.

▲ 7. Because of its size, thrusting shape, and implacably uniform rusting surface, *Tilted Arc* makes us feel hopeless, trapped, and sad. This sculpture would be interesting if we could visit it when we had time to explore these feelings, but it is too depressing to face every day on our way to work.

Richard Serra's *Tilted Arc*

8. Serra's erotically realistic, precise rendering of the female figure in *Tilted Arc* exhibits how appealingly he can portray the soft circularity of a woman's breast.
9. *Tilted Arc* is sort of red; it probably isn't blue.

Exercise 12-16

The artist Artemisia Gentileschi was very successful in her own time. Success came despite the trauma of her early life, when she figured as the victim in a notorious rape trial. But after she died, her work fell into obscurity; it was neither shown in major museums nor written about in art-history books. Recently, feminist scholars have revived interest in her work by connecting the style and/or theme of such paintings as her *Judith* with her rape and with feelings or issues of importance to women. But other scholars have pointed out that both her subject matter and her treatment of it are conventionally found as well in the work of male painters of the Caravaggist school, with which she is identified. Based on this information, and using one or more of the aesthetic principles described in this chapter, write an essay arguing either that the painting *Judith* has aesthetic value worthy of our attention or that it should continue to be ignored.

Writing Exercises

1. In the movie *Priest,* the father of a young girl admits to the local priest—in the confessional—that he has molested his daughter. However, the man lacks remorse and gives every indication that he will continue to abuse

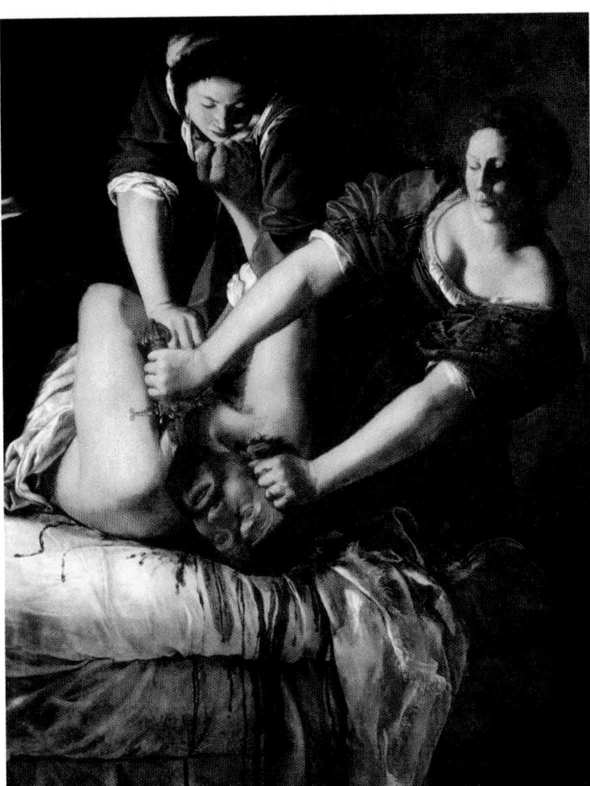

Artemisia Gentileschi's *Judith*

the girl. For the priest to inform the girl's mother or the authorities would be for him to violate the sanctity of the confessional, but to not inform anyone would subject the girl to further abuse. What should the priest do? Take about fifteen minutes to do the following:

a. List the probable consequences of the courses of action available to the priest.
b. List any duties or rights or other considerations that bear on the issue.

When fifteen minutes are up, share your ideas with the class.

Now take about twenty minutes to write an essay in which you do the following:

a. State the issue.
b. Take a stand on the issue.
c. Defend your stand.
d. Rebut counterarguments to your position.

When you are finished, write down on a separate piece of paper a number between 1 and 10 that indicates how strong you think your argument is (10 = very strong; 1 = very weak). Write your name on the back of your paper.

When everyone is finished, the instructor will collect the papers and redistribute them to the class. In groups of four or five, read the papers and assign a number from 1 to 10 to each one (10 = very strong; 1 = very weak). When all groups are finished, return the papers to their authors.

When you get your paper back, compare the number you assigned to your work with the number the group assigned it. The instructor may ask volunteers to defend their own judgment of their work against the judgment of the group. Do you think there is as much evidence for your position as you did at the beginning of the period?

2. Follow the same procedure as above to address one of the following issues:

a. A friend cheats in the classes he has with you. You know he'd just laugh if you voiced any concern. Should you mention it to your instructor?

b. You see a friend stealing something valuable. Even though you tell your friend that you don't approve, she keeps the item. What should you do?

c. Your best friend's fiancé has just propositioned you for sex. Should you tell your friend?

d. Your parents think you should major in marketing or some other practical field. You want to major in literature. Your parents pay the bills. What should you do?

Appendix 1

Essays for Analysis (and a Few Other Items)

Selection 1

Three Strikes and the Whole Enchilada

In this first selection, we've taken a real-life case of some importance and identified how various sections of the book bear on the issue and various aspects of the controversy that surround it. As we said at the beginning, this material is not designed to operate just in the classroom.

As you no doubt know, several states have "three strikes" laws, which call for life terms for a criminal convicted of any felony—if the criminal already has two prior felony convictions that resulted from serious or violent crime.

Have such laws helped to reduce crime in the states that have them? This is an objective question, a question of causation (Chapter 11). How might the issue be resolved?

In California, Frank Zimring, a University of California, Berkeley, law professor, analyzed the records of 3,500 criminal defendants in Los Angeles, San Diego, and San Francisco before and after California's law was enacted. Zimring found no evidence the law was a deterrent to crime. For our purposes we do not need to go into the details of the study.

People Against Crime, an organization that favors tougher penalties for criminals, denounced the study as "so much more left-wing propaganda coming out of a notoriously liberal university."

This charge is an ad hominem fallacy (Chapter 6). But is it nevertheless a reasonable challenge to Zimring's credibility that warrants not outright rejection of the study but suspension of judgment about its findings (Chapter 3)? The answer is no. Stripped of its rhetoric (Chapter 4), the charge is only that the author of the study is a professor at Berkeley; and that charge gives no reason to suspect bias on his part.

Other criticisms of the study were reported in the news. A spokesperson for the California secretary of state said, "When you see the crime rate going down 38 percent since three strikes you can't say it doesn't work."

This remark is an example of the fallacy "post hoc, ergo propter hoc," discussed in Chapter 11. In fact, that's being charitable. According to Zimring's research, the crime rate had been declining at the same rate before the law was passed.

The same spokesperson also criticized the Zimring study for ignoring the number of parolees leaving the state (to avoid getting a third strike, presumably). This is a red herring (Chapter 5). If the decline in the crime rate was unaffected after the law passed, as the Zimring study reportedly learned, then the law had no effect regardless of what parolees did or did not do.

The spokesperson also said, "Clearly when people are committing 20 to 25 crimes a year, the year they are taken off the street, that's 20 to 25 crimes that aren't going to happen." This too is a red herring (Chapter 5): If the decline in the crime rate remained the same before and after the "three strikes" law, then that's the end of the story. The criticism assumes criminals will continue to commit crimes at the same rate if there is no mandatory life sentence for a third felony. It therefore also begs the question (Chapter 6)—it assumes the law works in order to prove the law works. You will also have noticed the proof surrogate "clearly" (Chapter 4) in the criticism.

One might, of course, maintain that without the law the crime rate would have *stopped* declining, which would mean that the law had an effect after all. But the burden of proof (Chapter 6) is not on Zimring to *disprove* the possibility that the crime rate would have stopped declining if the law had not been passed.

A critic might also say that Zimring's study was conducted too soon after the law for the effects of the law to show up. This is another red herring (Chapter 5). It is not a weakness in the study that it failed to find an effect that might show up at a *later* time.

Selection 2

Controlling Irrational Fears After 9/11*

We present this selection as an example of a fairly well-reasoned argumentative essay. There is more here than arguments—there's some window dressing and you'll probably find some slanters here and there as well. You should go through the selection and identify the issues, the positions taken on those issues, and the arguments offered in support of those arguments. Are any arguments from opposing points of view considered? What is your final assessment of the essay?

The terrorist attacks of September 11, 2001, produced a response among American officials, the media, and the public that is probably matched only by the attack on Pearl Harbor in 1941. Since it is the very nature of terrorism not only to cause immediate damage but also to strike fear in the hearts of the population under attack, one might say that the terrorists were extraordinarily successful, not just as a result of their own efforts but also in consequence of the American reaction. In this essay, I shall argue that this reaction was irrational to a great extent and that to that extent Americans unwittingly cooperated with the terrorists in achieving a major goal: spreading fear and thus disrupting lives. In other words, we could have reacted more rationally and as a result produced less disruption in the lives of our citizens.

There are several reasons why one might say that a huge reaction to the 9/11 attacks was justified. The first is simply the large number of lives that were lost. In the absence of a shooting war, that 2,800 Americans should die from the same cause strikes us as extraordinary indeed. But does the sheer size of the loss of life warrant the reaction we saw? Clearly sheer numbers do not always impress us. It is unlikely, for example, that many Americans

*Note: This essay borrows very heavily from "A Skeptical Look at September 11th," an article in the *Skeptical Inquirer* of September/October 2002 by Clark R. Chapman and Alan W. Harris. Rather than clutter the essay with numerous references, we simply refer the reader to the original, longer piece.

remember that, earlier in 2001, an earthquake in Gujarat, India, killed approximately 20,000 people. One might explain the difference in reaction by saying that we naturally respond more strongly to the deaths of Americans closer to home than to those of others halfway around the world. But then consider the fact that, every *month* during 2001 more Americans were killed in automobile crashes than were killed on 9/11 (and it has continued every month since as well). Since the victims of car accidents come from every geographical area and every social stratum, one can say that those deaths are even "closer to home" than the deaths that occurred in New York, Washington, and Pennsylvania. It may be harder to identify with an earthquake victim in Asia than with a 9/11 victim, but this cannot be said for the victims of fatal automobile accidents.

One might say that it was the *malice* of the perpetrators that makes the 9/11 deaths so noteworthy, but surely there is plenty of malice present in the 15,000 homicides that occur every year in the United States. And while we have passed strict laws favoring prosecution of murderers, we do not see the huge and expensive shift in priorities that has followed the 9/11 attacks.

It seems clear, at least, that sheer numbers cannot explain the response to 9/11. If more reasons were needed, we might consider that the *actual total* of the number of 9/11 deaths seemed of little consequence in post-attack reports. Immediately after the attacks, the estimated death toll was about 6,500. Several weeks later it was clear that fewer than half that many had actually died, but was there a great sigh of relief when it was learned that over 3,000 people who were believed to have died were still alive? Not at all. In fact, well after it was confirmed that no more than 3,000 people had died, Secretary of Defense Donald Rumsfeld still talked about "over 5,000" deaths on 9/11. So the actual number seems to be of less consequence than one might have believed.

We should remember that fear and outrage at the attacks are only the beginning of the country's response to 9/11. We now have a new cabinet-level Department of Homeland Security; billions have been spent on beefing up security and in tracking terrorists and potential terrorists; billions more have been spent supporting airlines whose revenues took a nosedive after the attacks; the Congress was pulled away from other important business; the National Guard was called out to patrol the nation's airports; air travelers have been subjected to time-consuming and expensive security measures; you can probably think of a half-dozen other items to add to this list.

It is probable that a great lot of this trouble and expense is unwarranted. We think that random searches of luggage of elderly ladies getting on airplanes in Laramie, Wyoming, for example, is more effective as a way of annoying elderly ladies than of stopping terrorism.

We might have accomplished something if we had been able to treat the terrorist attacks of 9/11 in a way similar to how we treat the carnage on the nation's highways—by implementing practices and requirements that are directly related to results (as in the case of speed limits, safety belts, and the like, which took decades to accomplish in the cause of auto safety)— rather than by throwing the nation into a near panic and using the resulting fears to justify expensive but not necessarily effective or even relevant measures.

But we focused on 9/11 because of its terrorist nature and because of the spectacular film that was shown over and over on television, imprinting forever the horrific images of the airliner's collision with the World Trade Center and the subsequent collapse of the two towers. The media's instant obsession with the case is understandable, even if it is out of proportion to the actual damage, as awful as it was, when we compare the actual loss to the loss from automobile accidents.

Finally, our point is that marginal or even completely ineffective expenditures and disruptive practices have taken our time, attention, and national treasure away from other matters with more promise of making the country a better place. We seem to have all begun to think of ourselves as terrorist targets, but, in fact, reason tells us we are in much greater danger from our friends and neighbors behind the wheels of their cars.

The remainder of the essays in this section are here for analysis and evaluation. Your instructor will probably have specific directions if he or she assigns them, but at a minimum, they offer an opportunity to identify issues, separate arguments from other elements, identify premises and conclusions, evaluate the likely truth of the premises and the strength of the arguments, look for unstated assumptions or omitted premises, and lots of other stuff besides. We offer sample directions for many of the pieces.

Selection 3

Excerpts from Federal Court Ruling on the Pledge of Allegiance

The following are excerpts from the ruling by a three-judge federal appeals court panel in San Francisco that reciting the Pledge of Allegiance in public schools is unconstitutional because it includes the phrase "one nation under God." The vote was 2 to 1. Judge Alfred T. Goodwin wrote the majority opinion, in which Judge Stephen Reinhardt joined. Judge Ferdinand F. Fernandez wrote a dissent.

From the Opinion by Judge Goodwin

1 In the context of the pledge, the statement that the United States is a nation "under God" is an endorsement of religion. It is a profession of a religious belief, namely, a belief in monotheism. The recitation that ours is a nation "under God" is not a mere acknowledgment that many Americans believe in a deity. Nor is it merely descriptive of the undeniable historical significance of religion in the founding of the republic. Rather, the phrase "one nation under God" in the context of the pledge is normative. To recite the pledge is not to describe the United States; instead, it is to swear allegiance to the values for which the flag stands: unity, indivisibility, liberty, justice, and—since 1954—monotheism. The text of the official pledge, codified in federal law, impermissibly takes a position with respect to the purely religious question of the existence and identity of god. A profession that we are a nation "under God" is identical, for Establishment Clause purposes, to a profession that we are a nation "under Jesus," a nation "under Vishnu," a nation "under Zeus," or a nation "under no god," because none of these professions can be neutral with respect to religion. "The government must pursue a course of complete neutrality toward religion." Furthermore, the school district's practice of

teacher-led recitation of the pledge aims to inculcate in students a respect for the ideals set forth in the pledge, and thus amounts to state endorsements of these ideals. Although students cannot be forced to participate in recitation of the pledge, the school district is nonetheless conveying a message of state endorsement of a religious belief when it requires public school teachers to recite, and lead the recitation, of the current form of the pledge. . . .

The pledge, as currently codified, is an impermissible government endorsement of religion because it sends a message to unbelievers "that they are outsiders, not full members of the political community, and an accompanying message to adherents that they are insiders, favored members of the political community." 2

From the Dissent by Judge Fernandez

We are asked to hold that inclusion of the phrase "under God" in this nation's Pledge of Allegiance violates the religion clauses of the Constitution of the United States. We should do no such thing. We should, instead, recognize that those clauses were not designed to drive religious expression out of public thought; they were written to avoid discrimination. We can run through the litany of tests and concepts which have floated to the surface from time to time. Were we to do so, the one that appeals most to me, the one I think to be correct, is the concept that what the religion clauses of the First Amendment require is neutrality; that those clauses are, in effect, an early kind of equal protection provision and assure that government will neither discriminate for nor discriminate against religion or religions. But, legal world abstractions and ruminations aside, when all is said and done, the danger that "under God" in our Pledge of Allegiance will tend to bring about a theocracy or suppress somebody's belief is so miniscule as to be de minimis. The danger that phrase presents to our First Amendment freedoms is picayune at most. 3

Selection 4

Gays' Impact on Marriage Underestimated

Jeff Jacoby

It was a year ago last month that the Vermont law authorizing same-sex civil unions—a marriage by another name—took effect, and the *New York Times* marked the anniversary with a story July 25. "Quiet Anniversary for Civil Unions," the double headline announced. "Ceremonies for Gay Couples Have Blended Into Vermont Life." It was an upbeat report, and its message was clear: Civil unions are working just fine. 1

The story noted in passing that most Vermonters oppose the law. Presumably, they have reasons for not wanting legal recognition conferred on homosexual couples, but the *Times* had not room to mention them. It did have room, though, to dismiss those reasons—whatever they might be—as meritless: "The sky has not fallen," Gov. Howard Dean said, "and the institution of marriage has not collapsed. None of the dire predictions have come true. . . . There was a big rhubarb, a lot of fear-mongering, and now people realize there was nothing to be afraid of." 2

3 In the *Wall Street Journal* two days later, much the same point was made by Jonathan Rauch, the esteemed Washington journalist and vice president of the Independent Gay Forum. Opponents of same-sex marriage, he wrote, worry "that unyoking marriage from its traditional male-female definition will destroy or severely weaken it. But this is an empirical proposition, and there is reason to doubt it. Opponents of same-sex marriage have done a poor job of explaining why the health of heterosexual marriage depends on the exclusion of a small number of homosexuals."

4 The assertion that same-sex marriage will not damage traditional family life is rarely challenged, as Rep. Barney Frank, D-Mass., said during the 1996 congressional debate over the Defense of Marriage Act.

5 "I have asked and I have asked and I have asked, and I guess I will die . . . unanswered," Frank taunted. "How does the fact that I love another man and live in a committed relationship with him threaten your marriage? Are your relations with your spouses of such fragility that the fact that I have a committed, loving relationship with another man jeopardizes them?"

6 When another congressman replied that legitimizing gay unions "threatens the institution of marriage," Frank said, "That argument ought to be made by someone in an institution because it has no logical basis whatsoever."

7 But Frank's sarcasm, Rauch's doubts and Dean's reassurances notwithstanding, the threat posed by the same-sex unions to traditional marriage and family life is all too real. Marriage is harmed by anything that diminishes its privileged status. It is weakened by anything that erodes the social sanctions that Judeo-Christian culture developed over the centuries for channeling men's naturally unruly sexuality into a monogamous, lasting, and domestic relationship with one woman. For proof, just look around.

8 Over the past 40 years, marriage has suffered one blow after another. The sexual revolution and the pill made it much easier for men to enjoy women sexually without having to marry them. Legalized abortion reduced pressure on men to marry women they impregnated and reduced the need for women to wait for lasting love. The widespread acceptance of unmarried cohabitation—which used to be disdained as "shacking up"—diminished marriage further. Why get married if intimate companionship can be had without public vows and ceremony?

9 The rise of the welfare state with its subsidies for single mothers subverted marriage by sending the unmistakable message that husbands were no longer essential for family life. And the rapid spread of no-fault divorce detached marriage from any assumption of permanence. Where couples were once expected to stay married "for as long as you both shall live"—and therefore to put effort into making their marriage work—the expectation today is that they will remain together only "for as long as you both shall love."

10 If we now redefine marriage so it includes the union of two men or two women, we will be taking this bad situation and making it even worse.

11 No doubt the acceptance of same-sex marriage would remove whatever stigma homosexuality still bears, a goal many people would welcome. But it would do so at a severe cost to the most basic institution of our society. For all the assaults marriage has taken, its fundamental purpose endures: to uphold and encourage the union of a man and a woman, the framework that is the healthiest and safest for the rearing of children. If marriage stops meaning even that, it will stop meaning anything at all.

Selection 5

Bush's Environmental Record

Bob Herbert

Bob Herbert is a *New York Times* columnist.

Do you remember the character "Pig-Pen" in the "Peanuts" cartoons? He was always covered with dirt and grime. He was cute, but he was a walking sludge heap, filthy and proud of it. He once told Charlie Brown, "I have affixed to me the dirt and dust of countless ages. Who am I to disturb history?" 1

For me, Pig-Pen's attitude embodies President Bush's approach to the environment. 2

We've been trashing, soiling, even destroying the wonders of nature for countless ages. Why stop now? Who is Bush to step in and curb this venerable orgy of pollution, this grand tradition of fouling our own nest? 3

Oh, the skies may once have been clear and the waters sparkling and clean. But you can't have that and progress too. Can you? 4

Last week we learned that the Bush administration plans to cut funding for the cleanup of 33 toxic waste sites in 18 states. As the *New York Times'* Katharine Seelye reported, this means "that work is likely to grind to a halt on some of the most seriously polluted sites in the country." 5

The cuts were ordered because the Superfund toxic waste cleanup is running out of money. Rather than showing the leadership necessary to replenish the fund, the president plans to reduce its payouts by cleaning up fewer sites. 6

Pig-Pen would have been proud. 7

This is not a minor matter. The sites targeted by the Superfund program are horribly polluted, in many cases with cancer-causing substances. Millions of Americans live within a few miles of these sites. 8

The Superfund decision is the kind of environmental move we've come to expect from the Bush administration. Mother Nature has been known to tremble at the sound of the president's approaching footsteps. He's an environmental disaster zone. 9

In February, a top enforcement official at the Environmental Protection Agency, Eric Schaeffer, quit because of Bush administration policies that he said undermined the agency's efforts to crack down on industrial polluters. 10

Schaeffer said he felt he was "fighting a White House that seems determined to weaken the rules we are trying to enforce." 11

That, of course, is exactly what this White House is doing. 12

Within weeks of Schaeffer's resignation came official word that the administration was relaxing the air quality regulations that applied to older coal-fired power plants, a step backward that delighted the administration's industrial pals. 13

During this same period the president broke his campaign promise to regulate the industrial emissions of carbon dioxide, a move that, among other things, would have helped in the fight to slow the increase in global warming. Bush has also turned his back on the Kyoto Protocol, which would require industrial nations to reduce their emissions of carbon dioxide and other greenhouse gases. 14

The president was even disdainful of his own administration's report on global warming, which acknowledged that the U.S. would experience far-reaching and, in some cases, devastating environmental consequences as a result of the climate change. 15

16 The president's views on global warming seem aligned with those of the muddle-headed conservative groups in Texas that have been forcing rewrites in textbooks to fit their political and spiritual agendas. In one environmental science textbook, the following was added: "In the past, Earth has been much warmer than it is now, and fossils of sea creatures show us that the sea level was much higher than it is today. So does it really matter if the world gets warmer?"

17 Sen. Joseph Lieberman, not exactly a left-winger on the environment or anything else, gave a speech in California in February in which he assailed the president's lack of leadership on global warming and other environmental issues. He characterized the president's energy policy as "mired in crude oil" and said Bush had been "AWOL in the war against environmental pollution."

18 Several states, fed up with Bush's capitulation to industry on these matters, have moved on their own to protect the environment and develop more progressive energy policies.

19 Simply stated, the president has behaved irresponsibly toward the environment and shows no sign of changing his ways.

20 You could laugh at Pig-Pen. He was just a comic strip character. But Bush is no joke. His trashing of the environment is a deadly serious matter.

Selection 6

Death Penalty Has No Place in U.S.

Cynthia Tucker

1 Many Americans will applaud the decision of a Jasper, Texas, jury to condemn John William King to die. They will argue that the death penalty is exactly what King deserves for chaining James Byrd Jr. to the back of a pickup truck and dragging him until his body was torn apart—his head and right arm here, his torso there.

2 If there is to be capital punishment in this country, isn't this just the sort of case that demands it? King is the epitome of cold-blooded evil, a man who bragged about his noxious racism and attempted to win converts to his views. He believed he would be a hero after Byrd's death. He has proved himself capable of the sort of stomach-churning cruelty that most of us would like to believe is outside the realm of human behavior.

3 Besides, there is the matter of balancing the books. King is a white man who (with the help of accomplices, apparently) killed a black man. For centuries, the criminal justice system saw black lives as so slight, so insignificant, that those who took a black life rarely got the death penalty. Isn't it a matter of fairness, of equity, of progress, that King should be put to death?

4 No. Even though King is evil. Even though he is utterly without remorse. Even though he is clearly guilty. (After the prosecution mounted a case for five days, King's lawyers mounted a defense of only one hour. The jury of 11 whites and one black then deliberated only two and half hours to determine King's guilt.)

5 This is no brief for King, who would probably chain me to the back of a pickup truck as quickly as he did Byrd. This is a plea for America, which is strong enough, just enough and merciful enough to have put aside, by now, the thirst for vengeance.

The question is not, Does John William King deserve the death penalty? 6
The question is, Does America deserve the death penalty?

Capital punishment serves no good purpose. It does not deter crime. If it 7
did, this country would be blessedly crime-free. It does not apply equally to all. King notwithstanding, the denizens of death row are disproportionately blacks and Latinos who have killed whites. It remains true that the lives of blacks and Latinos count for less, that their killers are less likely to be sentenced to die.

Death row also counts among its inmates a high quotient of those who 8
are poor, dumb and marginalized. Those criminals blessed with education,
status and connections can usually escape capital punishment: 9

Last Tuesday, William Lumpkin, an attorney in Augusta, Ga., was found guilty of capital murder in the death of real estate agent Stan White, who owned the title to Lumpkin's home and was about to evict him. Lumpkin beat White to death with a sandbag and dumped the body in the Savannah River. But Lumpkin descends from Georgia gentry; one ancestor was a state Supreme Court justice. He was sentenced to life in prison.

Worse than those inequities, capital punishment is sometimes visited 10
upon the innocent. Lawrence C. Marshall, a law professor at Northwestern University, is director of the National Conference on Wrongful Convictions and the Death Penalty. Since 1972, he says, 78 innocent people have been released from death row.

It does not strain the imagination to think that maybe, just maybe, the 11
system did not catch all of its errors and some of those who were wrongly convicted have already been sent to their deaths. How many? There is no way to know, but even one is too many. The execution of even one innocent man puts us law-abiding citizens uncomfortably close to the level of a John William King.

Selection 7

Identify the main issue in this essay and the author's position on this issue. Then state in your own words three arguments given by the author in support of his position.

As an additional exercise, show how at least two of these arguments can be treated as categorical syllogisms (Chapter 8), as truth-functional arguments (Chapter 9), or as common deductive argument patterns.

Hetero by Choice?

A radio commentary by Richard Parker

For a while there, everybody who could get near a microphone was claiming 1
that only he or she and his or her group, party, faction, religion, or militia stood for real American family values.

Now, it was seldom made clear just what those values were supposed to 2
be. I have a notion that if [my son] Alex and I were to go out and knock over a few gas stations and convenience stores, the mere fact that we did it together would make it count as somebody's family values.

For some, the phrase "family values" never amounted to more than a eu- 3
phemism for gay-bashing. I remember a [few] years ago, during the loudest

squawking about values, when a reporter asked Dan Quayle whether he believed that a gay person's homosexuality was a matter of his or her psychological makeup or whether it was a matter of choice. He answered that he believed it was mainly a matter of choice. Two weeks later, Barbara Bush was quoted as saying that sexual orientation is mainly a matter of choice. Since then, it's turned up frequently.

4 It seems to me that people who make such a remark are either being remarkably cynical (if they don't really believe it themselves) or remarkably fatuous (if they do believe it).

5 If it were *true* that a person's sexual preference were a matter of choice, then it must have happened that each of us, somewhere back along the way, *decided* what our sexual preference would be. Now, if we'd made such decisions, you'd think that somebody would remember doing it, but nobody does.

6 In my case, I just woke up one morning when I was a kid and discovered that girls were important to me in a way that boys were not. I certainly didn't sit down and *decide* that it was girls who were going to make me anxious, excited, terror-struck, panicky, and inclined to act like an idiot.

7 Now, if the people who claim to hold the "choice" view were right, it must mean that gay people have always chosen—they've *decided*—to have the sexual orientation they have. Can you imagine a person, back in the '50s, say, who would *choose* to have to put up with all the stuff gay people had to put up with back then? It's bad enough now, but only the mad or the criminally uninformed would have *chosen* such a life back then.

8 (Actually, it seems clear to me that the whole idea of a preference rules out the notion of choice. I choose to eat chocolate rather than vanilla, but I don't choose to *prefer* chocolate to vanilla. One simply discovers what one prefers.)

9 If it's clear that people don't consciously choose their sexual preferences, why would anybody make such claims? I can think of a cynical reason: It only makes sense to condemn someone for something they choose, not for things they can't do anything about.

10 Is it just a coincidence that people who claim we choose our sexual preferences are often the same people who demonize homosexuals? No, of course not. In fact, their cart comes before their horse: They are damned sure going to condemn gay people, and so, since you can only condemn someone for voluntary actions, it *must* be that one's sexuality is a voluntary choice. Bingo! Consistent logic. Mean, vicious, and mistaken. But consistent.

Selection 8

In a brief essay, argue for whether Bonnie and Clyde should receive the same or different punishment.

Bonnie and Clyde

1 Bonnie and Clyde are both driving on roads near a mountain community in northern California. Both are driving recklessly—much faster than the posted speed limit. Each of them has a passenger in the car.

2 At a sharp and very dangerous curve, Bonnie loses control of her car and crashes into some nearby trees; only moments later, on another dangerous

section of road, Clyde's car goes into a skid, leaving the road and rolling over several times down an embankment.

3 As a result of their accidents, Bonnie and Clyde are bruised and shaken, but not seriously hurt. However, both of their passengers are hurt badly and require medical attention. Passersby call an ambulance from the next town, and soon it arrives, taking the injured passengers to the only medical facility in the area.

4 A neurosurgeon who is on duty examines both passengers when they arrive at the medical center. She determines that both have suffered serious head injuries and require immediate cranial surgery if they are to survive. However, she is the only person available who is competent to perform the surgery, and she cannot operate on both patients at once. Not knowing what to do, she tries to find someone to call for advice. But she can reach nobody. So she flips a coin.

5 As a result of the coin flip, the surgeon operates on Bonnie's passenger and leaves Clyde's passenger in the care of two medical technicians. The latter do the best they can, but Clyde's passenger dies. Because of the attention of the physician, Bonnie's passenger survives and, in time, makes a complete recovery.

Selection 9

Determine the author's main point. Identify any rhetorical devices present; identify and evaluate any arguments present.

Disinformation on Judges

Thomas Sowell

1 Judges who decide cases on the basis of the plain meaning of the words in the laws—like Justices Brown and Owen—may be what most of the public want but such judges are anathema to liberals.

2 The courts are the last hope for enacting the liberal agenda because liberals cannot get enough votes to control Congress or most state legislatures. Unelected judges can cut the voters out of the loop and decree liberal dogma as the law of the land.

3 Liberals don't want that stopped.

4 The damage that is done by judicial activism extends beyond the particular policies that happen to catch the fancy of judges. Judicial ad-libbing creates a large area of uncertainty, making the law a trap for honest people and a bonanza for the unscrupulous.

5 A disinformation campaign has already been launched to depict judges who believe in following the written law as being "activist" conservatives, just like liberal activists.

6 Those who play this game of verbal equivalence can seldom, if ever, come up with concrete examples where conservative judges made rulings that went directly counter to what the written law says or who made rulings for which there is no written law.

7 Meanwhile, nothing is easier to come up with than such examples among liberal judicial activists who have made decisions based on "evolving

standards," "world opinion" or other such lofty hokum worthy of the Wizard of Oz.

8 "Pay no attention to that man behind the curtain," the Wizard said—and "Don't attack our judges" the liberals say.

9 Even some conservative Republicans have fallen for this line. President Bush's former Solicitor General Theodore Olson recently condemned "personal attacks" on judges by their critics, and somehow lumped those critics with criminals or crackpots who have committed violence against judges or their family members.

10 Criticizing someone's official conduct is not a "personal attack." Nor does criticism equate with violence. An independent judiciary does not mean judges independent of the law. Nor is the rule of judges the same as the rule of law. Too often it is the rule of lawlessness from the bench.

Selections 10A and 10B

Evaluate the arguments on both sides. Who has the stronger arguments, and why? Make certain your response does not rest too heavily on rhetorical devices. As an alternative assignment, determine which author relies more heavily on rhetorical devices to persuade the audience.

Equal Treatment Is Real Issue—Not Marriage

USA Today

Our view: The fact is that marriage is already a messy entanglement of church and state.

1 With shouting about "gay marriage" headed for a new decibel level . . . chances for an amicable resolution seem bleak.

2 Traditionalists see the issue in private, religious terms, and with legislators in many states mobilizing around their cause, they're in no mood to compromise. They say marriage, by common definition, involves a man and a woman. And for most people, it's just that. In polls, two-thirds of the public supports the status quo.

3 But looking through the lenses of history and law, as judges must, marriage is far from a private religious matter. So much so that short of a constitutional amendment, compromise is inevitable.

4 Not only does the state issue marriage licenses and authorize its officers to perform a civil version of the rite, it gives married couples privileged treatment under law.

5 For example, when one spouse dies the house and other property held jointly transfer easily for the other's continued use and enjoyment. The survivor gets a share of continuing Social Security and other benefits. Joint health and property insurance continues automatically.

6 If there's no will, the law protects the bereaved's right to inherit. There's no question of who gets to make funeral arrangements and provide for the corpse.

7 It's the normal order of things, even for households that may have existed for only the briefest time, or for couples who may be long estranged though not divorced.

But some couples next door—even devoted couples of 20 or 30 years' standing—don't have those rights and can't get them because of their sex. 8

Support for marriage is justified as important to community stability, and it undoubtedly is. But when it translates into economic and legal discrimination against couples who may be similarly committed to each other, that should be disturbing. 9

The U.S. Constitution says every person is entitled to equal protection under law. Some state constitutions go farther, specifically prohibiting sexual discrimination. . . . 10

Ironically, people who oppose gay marriages on religious grounds would have their way but for the fact that marriage has evolved as a messy entanglement of church and state. To millions, marriage is a sacrament, and the notion that the state would license or regulate a sacrament ought to be an outrage. Imagine the uproar if a state legislature tried to license baptisms or communions, and wrote into law who could be baptized or who could receive bread and wine. Or worse yet gave tax breaks to those who followed those practices. 11

Short of getting out of the marriage business altogether, which isn't likely to happen, the state must figure a way to avoid discrimination. The hundreds of employers now extending workplace benefits to unmarried but committed couples and the handful of municipalities offering informal "domestic partner" status may be pointing in the right direction. 12

The need is not necessarily to redefine marriage but to assure equal treatment under the law. 13

Gay Marriage "Unnatural"

The Rev. Louis P. Sheldon

The Rev. Louis P. Sheldon is chairman of the Traditional Values Coalition, a California-based organization of some 32,000 churches.

Opposing view: Opinion polls show that nearly 80% of Americans don't accept "homosexual marriage."

In everything which has been written and said about . . . homosexual marriage . . . , the most fundamental but important point has been overlooked. Marriage is both culturally and physiologically compatible but so-called homosexual marriage is neither culturally nor physiologically possible. 1

Homosexuality is not generational. The family tree that starts with a homosexual union never grows beyond a sapling. Without the cooperation of a third party, the homosexual marriage is a dead-end street. In cyber language, the marriage is not programmed properly and there are hardware problems as well. 2

. . . Across America, "rights" are being created and bestowed routinely by judges indifferent to the wishes and values of their communities. This new wave of judicial tyranny confers special rights upon whichever group can cry the shrillest claim of victimhood. 3

At the core of the effort of homosexuals to legitimize their behavior is the debate over whether or not homosexuality is some genetic or inherited trait or whether it is a chosen behavior. The activists argue that they are a minority and homosexuality is an immutable characteristic. 4

But no school of medicine, medical journal or professional organization such as the American Psychological Association or the American Psychiatric 5

Association has ever recognized the claim that homosexuality is genetic, hormonal or biological.

6 While homosexuals are few in number, activists claim they represent about 10% of the population. More reliable estimates suggest about 10% of Americans are homosexual. They also are the wealthiest, most educated and most traveled demographic group measured today. Per capita income for the average homosexual is nearly twice that for the average American. They are the most advantaged group in America.

7 Homosexuality is a behavior-based life-style. No other group of Americans have ever claimed special rights and privileges based solely on their choice of sexual behavior, and the 1986 Supreme Court decision of Bowers vs. Hardwick said sodomy is not a constitutionally protected right.

8 When the state enacts a new policy, it must be reflected in its public school curriculum. Textbook committees and boards of education will ensure that all of that flows into the classroom. American families do not want the "normalcy" of homosexual marriage taught to their children.

9 Churches may not be forced to perform homosexual weddings but individual churches that resist may be subjected to civil suit for sexual discrimination. Resistance may be used as a basis for denying them access to federal, state or local government programs. In the Archdiocese of New York, Catholic churches were singled out by the city and denied reimbursement given to every other church for providing emergency shelter to the city's homeless. The reason cited was Catholic opposition to homosexual "rights" ordinances.

10 Whatever the pronouncements of the . . . nation's highest court, Americans know that "homosexual marriage" is an oxymoron. Calling a homosexual relationship a marriage won't make it so. There is no use of rhetoric that can sanitize it beyond what it is: unnatural and against our country's most basic standards. Every reputable public opinion poll demonstrates that nearly 8 of every 10 Americans don't accept the pretense of "homosexual marriage."

Selection 11

Determine the author's main point. Identify and evaluate any arguments; identify any rhetorical devices present.

Paying the Price for Bush's Retro Energy Policy

Arianna Huffington

1 . . . But when it comes to dealing with the many energy-related crises we're facing, can the Bushies really go on pretending that their policies are any more forward-looking than a rerun of "That '70s Show"?

2 Exhibit A is the president's bizarre and long-standing obsession with drilling for oil in the Arctic National Wildlife Refuge, which just got Senate approval last week. I mean, how retro can you get? Instead of pushing to increase fuel efficiency standards that could save millions of barrels of oil each day and calling for a national commitment to investing in renewable energy sources, he's after one more fix of dinosaur byproducts from one of the world's last pristine places.

3 Which might be understandable if making an Exxon Mobil theme park out of the refuge would actually reduce our dependence on foreign oil. But it

won't. At best, there's only enough oil there to satisfy U.S. demand for about six months. And it won't be available for least a decade—which is the only forward-looking aspect to Bush's ANWR dream.

The consequences of Bush's head-in-the-tundra policies are already all 4
around us—starting with the record prices Americans are paying to gas up their cars. The national average just raced past $2.10 a gallon—up 21 percent
from last year. The U.S. remains the world's largest oil consumer, but with 3
growing countries like China and India demanding more and more oil, and the world's refineries already close to maxed out, things are only going to get worse. How long will it be before filling stations are asking: "Cash, Credit or Home Equity Loan?"

Selection 12

Same directions as previous selection.

Liberals Love America Like O.J. Loved Nicole

Ann Coulter

Let's review. 1

The *New York Times* calls the U.S. "stingy" and runs letters to the editor redoubling the insult, saying: "The word 'stingy' doesn't even come close to accurately describing the administration's pathetic initial offer of aid. . . . I am embarrassed for our country." 2

Al Franken flies into a rage upon discovering that O'Reilly imagines the U.S. is the most generous nation in the world. 3

The *Washington Post* criticizes Bush for not rushing back to Washington in response to the tsunami—amid unfavorable comparisons to German Chancellor Gerhard Schroeder, who immediately cut short his vacation and returned to Berlin. (Nothing snaps a German to attention like news of mass death!). 4

The prestigious Princeton "ethicist" Peter Singer, who endorses sex with animals and killing children with birth defects, says "when it comes to foreign aid, America is the most stingy nation on Earth." 5

And has some enterprising reporter asked Sen. Patty Murray what she thinks about the U.S.'s efforts on the tsunami? How about compared to famed philanthropist Osama bin Laden? 6

In December 2002, Murray was extolling Osama bin Laden's good works in the Middle East, informing a classroom of students: "He's been out in these countries for decades building roads, building schools, building infrastructure, building day-care facilities, building health-care facilities, and the people are extremely grateful. It made their lives better." What does Murray say about bin Laden's charity toward the (mostly Muslim) tsunami victims? 7

Speaking of world leaders admired by liberals, why isn't Fidel Castro giving the tsunami victims some of that terrific care liberals tell us he has been providing the people of Cuba? 8

Stipulating that liberals love America—which apparently depends on what the meaning of "love" is—do they love America as much as they love bin Laden and Castro? 9

Selection 13

Determine whether this essay contains an argument and, if it does, what it is.

Alternative assignment: Identify rhetorical devices, including slanters and fallacious reasoning.

Is God Part of Integrity?

Editorial from *Enterprise Record,* Chico, California

1 What Oroville High School was trying to do last Friday night, said Superintendent Barry Kayrell, was "maintain the integrity of the ceremony."

2 The ceremony was graduation for approximately 200 graduates.

3 The way to maintain "integrity," as it turned out, was to ban the words "God" and "Jesus Christ."

4 The result was a perfect example of out-of-control interpretation of the separation of church and state.

5 The high school's action in the name of "integrity" needlessly disrupted the entire proceeding as almost the entire graduating class streamed out of their seats in support of Chris Niemeyer, an exemplary student who had been selected co-valedictorian but was barred from speaking because he wanted to acknowledge his belief in God and Jesus Christ.

6 The speech, said Kayrell, "was more of a testimonial."

7 It was preaching, added OHS principal Larry Payne.

8 "I truly believe in the separation (of church and state)," explained Kayrell.

9 It was a complicated story that led to last Friday night.

10 Niemeyer and fellow senior Ferin Cole had prepared their speeches ahead of time and presented them to school officials. Cole, who plans to attend Moody Bible College, had been asked to deliver the invocation.

11 Both mentioned God and Jesus Christ. Both were told that was unacceptable.

12 Both filed a last-minute action in federal court, challenging the school's censorship. At a hearing Friday, just hours before graduation, a judge refused to overrule the school on such short notice. The suit, however, continues, and the judge acknowledged it will involve sorting out complex constitutional questions.

13 Defeated in court, Niemeyer and Cole met with school officials to see what could be salvaged.

14 Both agreed to remove references to the deity, but Cole wanted to mention why, in an invocation—by definition a prayer—he was not allowed to refer to God. That was nixed, and Cole simply bowed out.

15 Niemeyer was supposed to deliver his revised draft to Payne by 5 P.M.

16 He missed the deadline, but brought the draft with him to the ceremony.

17 When it was his turn to speak, Niemeyer came forward, but Payne instead skipped over the program listing for the valedictory address and announced a song. The two debated the question on stage as the audience and graduates-to-be looked on.

18 Finally turned away, Niemeyer left the stage, tears of frustration on his cheeks, and his classmates ran to his side in a dramatic show of support.

19 You might say they were inspired by integrity.

The object of the First Amendment to the U.S. Constitution is to bar government-enforced religion. It was not designed to obliterate belief in God. 20

To stretch that command to denying a student the right to acknowledge what has spurred him on to the honor he has won is a bitter perversion. 21

That would apply whether the student was Islamic, Buddhist or any belief—atheist included. There is room, it would seem, for diversity in valedictory speeches, too. 22

Not at Oroville High School. There God and integrity don't mix. 23

It's spectacles like that played out last Friday night that have prompted Congress to consider a constitutional amendment aimed at curbing such misguided excess. 24

Earlier in the week it drew a majority vote in House, but fell short of the two-thirds margin needed. 25

Maybe such actions as witnessed locally can push it over the top. 26

Selection 14

Determine the author's main point. Identify and evaluate any arguments present; identify any rhetorical devices present.

Calling the Kettle Gay

Ann Coulter

It's been a tough year for Democrats. They lost the presidential election, their favorite news outlets have been abjectly humiliated, they had to sit through a smashingly successful election in Iraq, and most painfully, they had to endure unwarranted attacks on a cartoon sponge. So I understand liberals are upset. *Let go, let God* . . . Oops—I'm talking to liberals! *Let go, let Spongebob* . . . 1

Democrats tried working out their frustrations on blacks for a while, but someone—I can't remember who, but it probably wasn't Sen. Robert Byrd—must have finally told them it really wasn't helping to keep disparaging every single black person in a position of authority in this Republican administration. 2

So now liberals are lashing out at the gays. Two weeks ago, *The New York Times* turned over half of its op-ed page to outing gays with some connection to Republicans. There is no principled or intellectual basis for these outings. Conservatives don't want gays to die; we just don't want to transform the Pentagon into the Office of Gay Studies. 3

By contrast, liberals say: "We love gay people! Gay people are awesome! Being gay is awesome! Gay marriage is awesome! Gay cartoon characters are awesome! And if you don't agree with us, we'll punish you by telling everyone that you're gay!" 4

In addition to an attack on a Web site reporter for supposedly operating a gay escort service and thereby cutting into the business of the *Village Voice*, another *Times* op-ed article the same day gratuitously outed the children of prominent conservatives. 5

These are not public figures. No one knows who they are apart from their famous parents. I didn't even know most of these conservatives had children until the *Times* outed them. Liberals can't even cite their usual "hypocrisy" fig leaf to justify the public outing of conservatives' family members. No 6 outsider can know what goes on inside a family, but according to the public version of one family matter being leered over by liberals, a prominent conservative threw his daughter out of the house when he found out she was gay.

7 Stipulating for purposes of argument that that's the whole story—which is absurd—isn't that the opposite of hypocrisy? Wouldn't that be an example of someone sacrificing other values on the mantle of consistency?

8 Outing relatives of conservatives is nothing but ruthless intimidation: *Stop opposing our agenda—or your kids will get it.* This is a behavioral trope of all totalitarians: Force children to testify against their parents to gain control by fear.

Selections 15A and 15B

Evaluate the arguments on both sides. Who has the stronger arguments, and why?

Alternative assignment: Identify rhetorical devices and determine which author relies more heavily on them.

Second alternative assignment: In the first essay, find as many arguments as you can that can be treated as categorical syllogisms. Set up a key, letting a letter stand for a relevant category. Be sure you identify the category in plain English. Then circle all and only the distributed terms. Then state whether each syllogism is valid, identifying rules broken by any syllogisms that are not.

Make Fast Food Smoke-Free

USA Today

Our view: The only thing smoking in fast-food restaurants should be the speed of the service.

1 Starting in June, if you go to Arby's, you may get more than a break from burgers. You could get a break from tobacco smoke, too.

2 The roast-beef-sandwich chain on Tuesday moved to the head of a stampede by fast-food restaurants to limit smoking.

3 Last year, McDonald's began experimenting with 40 smokeless restaurants. Wendy's and other fast-food chains also have restaurants that bar smoking.

4 But Arby's is the first major chain to heed a call from an 18-member state attorneys general task force for a comprehensive smoking ban in fast-food restaurants. It will bar smoking in all its 257 corporate-owned restaurants and urge its 500 franchisees to do the same in their 2,000 restaurants.

5 Other restaurants, and not just the fast-food places, should fall in line.

6 The reason is simple: Smoke in restaurants is twice as bad as in a smoker's home or most other workplaces, a recent report to the *Journal of the American Medical Association* found.

7 Fast-food restaurants have an even greater need to clear the air. A quarter of their customers and 40% of their workers are under 18.

8 Secondhand smoke is a class A carcinogen. It is blamed for killing an estimated 44,000 people a year. And its toxins especially threaten youngsters' health.

9 The Environmental Protection Agency estimates that secondhand smoke causes up to 1 million asthma attacks and 300,000 respiratory infections that lead to 15,000 hospitalizations among children each year.

All restaurants should protect their workers and customers. If they won't, then local and state governments should do so by banning smoking in them, as Los Angeles has. 10

A person's right to a quick cigarette ends when it threatens the health of innocent bystanders, and even more so when many of them are youngsters. 11

They deserve a real break—a meal in a smoke-free environment that doesn't threaten their health. 12

Don't Overreact to Smoke

Brennan M. Dawson

Opposing view: With non-smoking sections available, and visits brief, what's the problem?

If the attorneys general from a handful of states—those charged with upholding the law—were to hold a forum in Washington, you might expect them to be tackling what polls say is the No. 1 public issue: crime. 1

Not these folks. They're worried someone might be smoking in the smoking section of a fast-food restaurant. And, there might be children in the non-smoking section. Thus, they say, fast-food chains should ban all smoking. 2

Some would argue that this raises serious questions about priorities. But it may be worth debating, since this is supposed to be about protecting children. Everyone is (and should be) concerned with children's health and well-being. 3

But what are we protecting them from—the potential that a whiff of smoke may drift from the smoking section to the non-smoking section during the average 20-minute visit for a quick burger? 4

Anyone knowledgeable would tell you that none of the available studies can reasonably be interpreted to suggest that incidental exposure of a child to smoking in public places such as restaurants is a problem. After all, with the almost universal availability of non-smoking sections, parents have the option of keeping their kids out of the smoking section. 5

A recent study published in the *American Journal of Public Health* reported that the separate smoking sections in restaurants do a good job of minimizing exposure to tobacco smoke. According to the figures cited, customers would have to spend about 800 consecutive hours in the restaurants to be exposed to the nicotine equivalent of one cigarette. 6

That would represent about 2,400 fast-food meals. Under those conditions, most parents would worry about something other than smoking. 7

Selections 16A and 16B

Evaluate the arguments on both sides. Who has the stronger arguments, and why?

Alternative assignment: Identify rhetorical devices and determine which author relies more heavily on them.

Second alternative assignment: In each of the two essays, find as many arguments as you can that can be treated as categorical syllogisms. Set up a key, letting a letter stand for a relevant category. Be sure you identify the category in plain English. Then circle all and only the distributed terms. Then state whether each syllogism is valid, identifying rules broken by any syllogisms that are not.

Buying Notes Makes Sense at Lost-in-Crowd Campuses

USA Today

Our view: Monster universities and phantom professors have only themselves to blame for note-selling.

1 Higher education got a message last week from a jury in Gainesville, Fla.: Its customers, the students across the nation, deserve better service.

2 The jury found entrepreneurs are free to sell notes from college professors' lectures. And Ken Brickman is an example of good, old free enterprise, even if his services encourage students to skip class.

3 Brickman is a businessman who pays students to take notes in classes at the University of Florida. From a storefront a block off campus, he resells the notes to other students with a markup.

4 Professors and deans bemoan Brickman's lack of morals. They even use the word "cheating." They'd be more credible if their complaints—and the university's legal resources—were directed equally at Brickman's competitor in the note-selling business a few blocks away.

5 The difference: The competition pays professors for their notes; Brickman pays students. Morals are absent, it seems, only when professors aren't getting their cut.

6 The deeper issue is why Brickman has found a lucrative market. It's easy to say that uninspired students would rather read someone else's notes than spend time in class, but that's not the point.

7 Why are students uninspired? Why are they required to learn in auditorium-size classes where personal attention is non-existent, taking attendance impossible, and students can "cut" an entire semester with no one noticing?

8 Why are students increasingly subjected to teaching assistants—graduate students who know little more than they—who control classes while professors are off writing articles for esoteric journals that not even their peers will read?

9 Why are there not more professors—every former student can remember one—who transmit knowledge of and enthusiasm for a subject with a fluency and flair that make students eager to show up? No one would prefer to stay away and buy that professor's notes.

10 The debate over professorial priorities—students vs. research—is old. But so long as students come in second, they'll have good reasons to go to Ken Brickman for their notes.

Buying or Selling Notes Is Wrong*

Opposing view: Note-buyers may think they're winners, but they lose out on what learning is all about.

1 It's tough being a college student. Tuition costs and fees are skyrocketing. Classes are too large. Many professors rarely even see their students, let alone

*The author of the companion piece to the *USA Today* editorial on this subject would not give us permission to reproduce her essay in a critical thinking text, so we wrote this item ourselves.

know their names or recognize their faces. The pressure for grades is intense. Competition for a job after graduation is keen.

But that's no excuse for buying the notes to a teacher's course. What goes around comes around. Students who buy someone else's notes are only cheating themselves—by not engaging in the learning process to the fullest extent. They aren't learning how to take notes. Or how to listen. Or how to put what someone is saying into their own words. 1

What happens if the notes are inaccurate? Will a commercial note-taker guarantee the notes? Would you want to take a test using someone else's notes? 2

Besides, what the professor says is her own property. It is the result of hard work on her part. A professor's lectures are often her principal means of livelihood. Nobody but the professor herself has the right to sell her property. Buying the notes to her lectures without her permission is just like selling a book that she wrote and keeping the money for yourself. 3

And buying the notes from someone who is selling them without the teacher's permission is the same as receiving stolen goods. 4

And that's assuming that there will be anyone out there to buy the notes in the first place. After all, most students will want to take notes for themselves, because they know that is their only guarantee of accuracy. People who think they can get rich selling the notes to someone's lectures should take a course in critical thinking. 5

The pressure for good grades doesn't justify buying or selling the notes to a professor's lectures without her permission. If you can't go to class, you shouldn't even be in college in the first place. Why come to school if you don't want to learn? 6

Selections 17A and 17B

Evaluate the arguments on both sides. Who has the stronger arguments, and why?

Alternative assignment: Identify rhetorical devices and determine which author relies more heavily on them.

Next, Comprehensive Reform of Gun Laws

USA Today

Our view: Waiting periods and weapon bans are welcome controls, but they're just the start of what's needed.

The gun lobby got sucker-punched by the U.S. Senate last weekend. It couldn't happen to a more deserving bunch. 1

For seven years, gun advocates have thwarted the supersensible Brady bill, which calls for a national waiting period on handgun purchases. Through a mix of political intimidation, political contributions and perverse constitutional reasoning, gun lobbyists were able to convince Congress to ignore the nine out of 10 Americans who support that idea. 2

But suddenly, after two days of filibuster, the Senate abruptly adopted the Brady bill. The House has already acted, so all that remains is to do some slight tinkering in a House-Senate conference, and then it's off to the White House for President Clinton's signature. 3

4 That's not the end of welcome gun control news, though. As part of the anti-crime bill adopted last week, the Senate agreed to ban the manufacture and sale of 19 types of assault-style semiautomatic weapons. Although these weapons constitute fewer than 1% of all guns in private hands, they figure in nearly 10% of all crime. The bill also bans some types of ammunition and restricts gun sales to, and ownership by, juveniles.

5 These ideas are worthy, but they can't do the whole job. Waiting periods and background checks keep criminals from buying guns from legal dealers. Banning certain types of anti-personnel weapons and ammunition will keep those guns and bullets from growing more common and commonly lethal.

6 Yet the wash of guns and gun violence demands much, much more. The judicial ability to process firearm-related crimes with certainty and speed is part of the solution. But even more so is the adoption of laws that permit gun licensing, gun registration and firearm training and education.

7 After years of denying the popular mood, Congress appears ready to honor it. That merits applause. But its new laws are just a start. Without truly comprehensive controls, the nationwide slick of gun carnage is bound to continue its bloody, inexorable creep.

Gun Laws Are No Answer

Alan M. Gottlieb

Opposing view: Disarming the law-abiding populace won't stop crime. Restore gun owners' rights.

8 Every time another gun control law is passed, violent crime goes up, not down, and the gun-ban crowd starts to yelp for more anti-gun laws.

9 So it's no surprise that the gun-banners are already snapping at the heels of our Bill of Rights.

10 They turn a blind eye to the fact that California, with a 15-day waiting period, experienced a 19% increase in violent crime and a 20% increase in homicide between 1987 and 1991. And that a 1989 ban on "assault weapons" in that state has also resulted in increased violent crime.

11 In Illinois, after a 30-day waiting period was installed, that state experienced a 31% increase in violent crime and a 36% increase in the homicide rate.

12 And, a handgun ban in Washington, D.C., has made it the murder capital of the world!

13 The results are in. Gun control makes the streets safe for violent criminals. It disarms their victims—you and me. The people's right to protect themselves should be restored, not restricted.

14 Case in point: Bonnie Elmasri of Wisconsin, who was being stalked by her estranged husband despite a court restraining order, was killed along with her two children while she waited for the handgun she purchased under that state's gun-waiting-period law.

15 Bonnie and her children are dead because of gun control laws, as are thousands of other victims each year.

16 Anybody who believes that disarming the law-abiding populace will help reduce crime has rocks in the head.

17 The next time a violent criminal attacks you, you can roll up your copy of USA TODAY and defend yourself with it. It may be all you'll have left for self-protection.

Selection 18

The following letter was sent to one of our students from the National Rifle Association. Notice the tendency—more and more common recently—to use repetition in place of argument. Are there any arguments present in the letter? Are there rhetorical devices?

Dear Friend,

It is critical that you accept the enclosed Black-and-Gold National Rifle 1
Association membership card today.

Joining the National Rifle Association (NRA) is the single most impor- 2
tant thing you can do to protect your Second Amendment rights and promote safe, responsible firearms ownership.

There has never been amore important time for America's gun owners to 3
unite and stand up for our freedom.

Anti-gun members of Congress, including Senators Hillary Clinton and 4
Charles Schumer, Representative Patrick Kennedy and others, are aggressively pushing for more harsh anti-gun legislation.

Their agenda includes *gun-owner licensing* and *fingerprinting, gun regis-* 5
tration, and *rationing, gun show bans* and *much more.*

Only a united effort by freedom-loving Americans can stop this assault 6
on our rights from doing irreversible damage to our freedoms.

That's why the National Rifle Association needs patriotic Americans 7
like you to join our organization and help defend our cherished freedoms.

Since our formation over 132 years ago, the NRA has led the effort to de- 8
fend the rights of law-abiding gun owners.

The NRA reaches out to America's 80 million gun owners to bring them 9
together through sponsorship of gun safety programs, hunter education courses, self-defense training, legislative advocacy and family events like our "Friends of NRA" gatherings.

Remember, *the NRA is a non-partisan grassroots membership organiza-* 10
tion, an association of millions of patriotic Americans who care about freedom and who enjoy and treasure our nation's heritage of firearms ownership and use.

We represent your "special-interest"—*YOUR FREEDOM!* 11

The NRA's efforts are based on the needs and concerns of our members, 12
men and women like you from all around the country.

That's why we are asking you to join and help serve as *"the eyes and* 13
ears" of the NRA to make sure grassroots gun owners in your area have their concerns addressed and your interests protected.

Our goal is to build a fire-wall around the Second Amendment by re- 14
cruiting at least ten thousand NRA members in each Congressional district.

I know this may sound ambitious, but most Congressional elections are decided by less than 10,000 votes.

Each NRA member we sign up means more leverage to convince the politi- 15
cians to keep their hands off the Second Amendment, or hunting lands and our other firearm freedoms—because politicians know NRA members vote!

. . .

As a member of the NRA, you can have a far-reaching impact on the fu- 16
ture of our Second Amendment right to keep and bear arms.

. . .

17 As a *BONUS GIFT* for joining today you'll receive a NRA Black-and Gold Shooter's Cap. This cap, like your membership card, is recognized around the world as a symbol of the organization dedicated to defending the United States Constitution, especially our Second Amendment right to keep and bear arms.

18 Of course the most important benefit of joining the NRA is knowing you are leading the fight to protect our right to keep and bear arms.

19 That's why I want you to carry your NRA Black-and-Gold membership card with pride as a reminder of all your membership does to protect your Second Amendment rights.

20 *We will never take your membership for granted and we will always remain committed to protecting your interests—your freedom—*

21 Remember, accepting your Black-and-Gold NRA membership card is the *most important step you can take to help preserve America's cherished heritage* of hunting, sport shooting, gun collecting and firearms ownership.

. . .

22 Our rights face many great challenges in Congress and throughout the country, but by working together, we can protect our freedom for today and for future Americans to enjoy.

23 Thank you in advance for accepting NRA Membership.

Sincerely,

Wayne LaPierre
Executive Vice President

P.S. *The NRA needs the active support of patriotic Americans like you to help promote safe, responsible hunting and gun ownership.* By accepting your NRA membership today you can help us *fight back against anti-gun media bias* and educate the public about the Second Amendment's critical role in our nation. Your membership in the NRA is critical to protecting our Second Amendment rights for future generations. Please use the enclosed reply form and postage-paid envelope to send your NRA Membership dues today. Thank you.

[All emphases present in the original. —Ed.]

Selections 19A and 19B

Evaluate the arguments on both sides. Who has the stronger arguments, and why?

Alternative assignment: Identify rhetorical devices and determine which author relies more heavily on them.

How Can School Prayer Possibly Hurt? Here's How

USA Today

Our view: Mississippi case shows how people's rights can be trampled by so-called "voluntary prayer."

1 What harm is there in voluntary prayer in school?

2 That's the question . . . House Speaker Newt Gingrich and others pose in their crusade to restore prayer to the classroom. They argue that a constitu-

tional amendment to "protect" so-called voluntary school prayer could improve morals and at worst do no harm.

Well, a mother's lawsuit filed Monday against Pontotoc County, Miss., schools says otherwise. It shows government-sponsored voluntary prayer in school threatens religious liberty. 3

All the mother, Lisa Herdahl, wants is that her six children get their religious instruction at home and at their Pentecostal church, not at school. 4

But their school hasn't made that easy. Prayers by students go out over the public address system every day. And a Bible study class is taught at every grade. 5

School officials argue that since no one is ordered to recite a prayer or attend the class, everything is voluntary.

But to Herdahl's 7-year-old son, it doesn't seem that way. She says he was nicknamed "football head" by other students after a teacher told him to wear headphones so he wouldn't have to listen to the "voluntary" prayers. 6

And she says her 11-year-old son was branded a "devil worshiper" after a teacher told students he could leave a Bible class because he didn't believe in God. 7

Indeed, Herdahl's children have suffered exactly the kind of coercion to conform that the Supreme Court found intolerable when it banned state-written prayers in 1962 and outlawed Alabama's moment of silence for meditation or voluntary prayer in 1985. 8

As the court noted in those cases, when government—including schools—strays from neutrality in religious matters, it pits one religion against another. And youngsters especially can feel pressured to submit to a majority's views. 9

That's why a constitutional amendment to protect "voluntary prayer" in school is so dangerous. 10

Students don't need an amendment to pray in school now. They have that right. And they can share their religious beliefs. They've formed more than 12,000 Bible clubs nationwide that meet in schools now, only not during class time. 11

For the Herdahls, who refused to conform to others' beliefs, state-sponsored voluntary prayer and religious studies have made school a nightmare. 12

For the nation, a constitutional amendment endorsing such ugly activities could make religious freedom a joke.

We Need More Prayer

Armstrong Williams

Armstrong Williams is a Washington, D.C.–based business executive, talk-show host, and author of The Conscience of a Black Conservative.

Opposing view: The tyranny of the minority was never envisioned by the nation's Founding Fathers.

The furor aroused by . . . Newt Gingrich's remarks about renewing school prayer illustrates how deep cultural divisions in American society really are. 1

A few moments of prayer in schools seems a small thing—harmless enough, almost to the point of insignificance. Yet it has provoked an impassioned firestorm of debate about the dangers of imposing viewpoints and the potential for emotionally distressing non-religious children. 2

3 The Constitution's framers were wary of a "tyranny of the majority," and so they imposed restraints on the legislature. They never foresaw, nor would they have believed, the tyranny of the minority made possible through an activist judiciary changing legal precedents by reinterpreting the Constitution.

4 The American ideal of tolerance has been betrayed by its use in directly attacking the deeply held convictions of millions of Americans.

5 The fact that this country was once unashamedly Christian did not mean that it was necessarily intolerant of other views—at least not nearly so intolerant of them as our rigid secular orthodoxy is toward all religious expression. Through the agency of the courts, a few disgruntled malcontents have managed to impose their secular/humanist minority views on the majority.

6 But it has not always been so.

7 The confidence with which some maintain that school prayer is manifestly unconstitutional belies an ignorance of our nation's history. America was founded by religious men and women who brought their religious beliefs and expressions with them into public life.

8 It was in 1962 that an activist Supreme Court ruled that denominationally neutral school prayer was judged to violate the establishment clause of the First Amendment. Since then, the "wall of separation" between church and state has rapidly become a prison wall for religious practice.

9 The drive to protect the delicate sensibilities of American children from the ravages of prayer is particularly ironic when our public schools have become condom clearinghouses that teach explicit sex.

10 The real heart of the school prayer issue is the role of religion in our public life.

Selection 20

Summarize the author's argument or arguments, if any.

Alternative assignment: Identify rhetorical devices, if any.

Do Women Really Need Affirmative Action?

Joanne Jacobs

Joanne Jacobs is a columnist for the *San Jose Mercury News.*

1 I was an affirmative action hire, back in 1978. As a result, I became the first woman on my newspaper's editorial board. Was I qualified? I certainly didn't have much experience. My boss took a chance on me. I like to think it paid off for him, as well as for me.

2 At any rate, I made the editorial board safe for women, who now make up half the editorial pages staff.

3 Defenders of affirmative action have a new strategy: Consider the ladies. Recently, a liberal coalition kicked off a campaign to cast affirmative action as a gender issue rather than a racial issue. Affirmative action is essential for women's advancement, argued feminist leaders. "Women will not quietly accept a rollback of our rights that have been part of the American scene for over a generation," said Katherine Spillar of the Feminist Majority.

4 It's a smart, though doomed, strategy.

The smart part is that women (if not feminists) are a majority of the population. If women were persuaded that affirmative action guarantees not only our benefits but also our "rights," public thinking would shift dramatically. 5

Poll data suggest that the majority of Americans accept preferences for women in jobs and college admissions; most are deeply hostile to preferences for minority group members. 6

The doomed part is that most white women don't think they'd lose their rights or their jobs if affirmative action ceased to exist; some are concerned about the job prospects of their white male husbands. 7

Affirmative action used to mean reaching out to people excluded from opportunities by overt discrimination or old-boy networks, giving everyone a chance to compete fairly. Now it means judging members of previously excluded groups by different, generally lower, standards than others. 8

Are women less able to compete [today] because of past discrimination? Certainly not women under the age of 45. 9

In the past, affirmative action helped women—especially educated, middle-class women—enter occupations previously reserved for men. Some argue that affirmative action primarily benefited white women who were most prepared to take advantage of opportunities, and most likely to have connections to powerful men. 10

Certainly, it appears that affirmative action has done most for those who needed it least. It has opened doors; it has not built ladders. 11

While women haven't achieved parity in income or in top executive ranks or in all careers, affirmative action can provide little help in achieving those goals in the future. 12

In education, affirmative action already is passé. Women don't need to be judged by different standards to get into college, and they're not. Females earn higher high school grades than males, and are more likely to attend college. 13

Women are underrepresented in the mathematical sciences and in engineering studies. An affirmative action program that admitted calculus-deficient women to physics class would do them no favor. The solution is not changing the standards; it's persuading more girls to take more math in high school. 14

Women do worry about workplace equity, but here too affirmative action isn't likely to play much of a role. The much-discussed "glass ceiling" for women in business is related to two factors: family and calculus. 15

Women are more likely than men to put family needs ahead of career advancement. These choices have consequences. Women who work more at home don't get to be CEO. 16

Selection 21

Want Better Schools? Support Teachers

Dean Simpson Jr.

Dean Simpson Jr. is a journalist and English teacher at Mount Whitney High School in Visalia.

In the education business we have a saying—you get what you get. That means we teachers deal with everyone who comes through the schoolhouse 1 door and do our best to send them out at the end of their term as educated, productive citizens. We don't always succeed, but overall I think we do a pretty good job, particularly considering the circumstances.

2 So it really aggravated me when my local newspaper, the *Visalia Times-Delta,* ran an editorial the essence of which was that teachers need to quit complaining about things we can't control, "a diverse population, poorly prepared students, television, parents who don't want to be involved and per-pupil spending," and focus on what we can control, "more rigorous course offerings, return to heavy concentration of reading and writing, longer school sessions and updated curriculum." Unfortunately, such admonitions seem to be on the lips of every legislator and a good many citizens in California today.

3 The implication is that teachers are a bunch of crybabies for complaining about conditions. Has it ever occurred to anyone that education is the only industry that cannot control the raw materials with which it works? No other industry is accused of whining if it advocates and lobbies for better conditions within its business.

4 If US Steel receives a shipment of substandard pig iron from a supplier, no one accuses it of whining when it sends it back. If Ford Motor Co. is sent a batch of defective tires, it's not expected to refabricate them. It sends them back. In education—we get what we get.

5 Imagine the newspaper has 10 openings to fill and must hire the first 10 people who walk through the door. A blind man running the press? Non-English speakers writing and editing copy? Editors who have no concept of personnel management? Advertising sales people with no communication skills? And you'd better be able to show an increase in profit and decline in the number of errors in the copy. After all, standards must be raised and met. Oh, and there's no money for additional training.

6 Now let's take a look at some of the things teachers are told we need to do to improve education, which will apparently overcome all the problems in the schools today. The first need supposedly is for more rigorous course offerings.

7 From kindergarten up, the curriculum is more rigorous than it has ever been. When I attended kindergarten in 1951, children learned "socialization," finger-painting and maybe their ABCs. Now they learn to read and write and do addition and subtraction up to 10s and sometimes beyond. Kindergartners also learn geometric shapes and handle thought problems using, among other things, simple graphs.

8 All the math I needed for admission to college in 1964 was geometry. Now students must have Algebra II and trigonometry to have much of a chance of college acceptance.

9 Advanced Placement classes—high school classes where students may earn college credit after completing the course and passing a rigorous test—didn't exist when I graduated. Today, virtually every high school in California offers these.

10 As far as the need for a heavy concentration on reading and writing, my students not only read a lot, I also expect them to interpret what they read. No fill-in-the-bubbles tests. They dig into what they've read, understand it, apply it to their lives and write about what they learn from the literature and its application in the world. None of these skills, unfortunately, show up on standardized tests.

Freshman enter my journalism class as experienced writers having written much more, and with greater depth of thought, than was expected of my generation until we entered college. 11

The next element that supposedly would make "for better trained, better educated students" is "longer school sessions." I'm not sure whether that refers to a longer school day or longer school year, but it doesn't really matter. If it's a longer school day, we must do away with all school sports, as they do in other countries. Those who wish can play club sports—for a fee. Other electives and extracurricular activities? Gone. We can't cherry pick here. We either do it as it's done in Europe and Japan, or we don't. 12

Is a longer school year the goal? Why? I know the Japanese have a longer school year, and they score better on standardized tests, too. But if those schools are so far superior to ours, why are their students, and students from nearly every country in the world, clamoring to get into our universities? And why are our high school graduates able to compete successfully with those foreign students at our universities? 13

A graduate from Redwood, one of our Central Valley high schools, received a Nobel Prize last year. If foreign schools are so great, why is the United States, with its allegedly awful schools, so far ahead in technology, industrial production and every other category worth mentioning? 14

As far as updating curriculum, can anyone update his home or business without money? Textbooks cost money. Lab materials, technology, and continuing education and training for teachers cost money. Show me the money or shut up and get out of the way. 15

What we need in education is support. If we set standards—and we've actually been fighting for high standards for a long time—parents and community members must help us enforce them, not just by paying lip service, but by feeling real pain when necessary. Standards are inherently hard to reach and not everyone will reach them, at least not easily. We in education have been doing our part for years. Remember CLAS and CAP tests? Educators didn't dump them in the trash can. Politicians and the public did. 16

Instead of accusing us of being whiners, see us as advocates for improvement of all conditions that contribute to educational success for all children. Help us by addressing the social problems we can't control and we'll continue to improve the conditions we can. 17

Images

Photographs are not essays, but they nevertheless serve to convey ideas and associations in their own ways. Each of the following advertisements makes strong use of photographs, and each is suitable for in-class discussion. You might consider such questions as, What is the target audience of each ad? How does the ad appeal to that audience?

■ Do you know what product is advertised here, or do you think the ad is intentionally ambiguous in that regard? What do you think is the age range and gender of the target audience? How do you think the ad is supposed to motivate the targeted audience to buy the product? Critically evaluate a classmate's answers to these questions.

■ This ad promotes Skechers footwear for women, yet arguably it might appeal as much to men as to women, within the targeted age bracket. Why would the advertiser do this? Is there a sexual message contained in this ad, and if so, what is it? Critically evaluate your instructor's answers to these questions.

■ You have to look carefully to see what product is being advertised here. Why has the advertiser downplayed the product so markedly? Explain how the facial expression of Serena Williams and the statements below her face might be thought by the advertiser to promote the product. Defend your assertions with arguments.

■ Is this ad designed to appeal more to men or women or both equally? How do you suppose the ad is supposed to translate into increased sales for KMART? In your opinion, is the ad a successful one? Explain.

Appendix 2

The Top Ten Fallacies of All Time

First, we should say that we are not exactly reporting on a scientific study of reasoning errors. Far from it. We're simply listing for you what we think, based on our experience, are the top ten fallacies that crop up in spoken and written discourse. While we're disclaiming, we should point out that some of the items on our list are not really *errors* of reasoning, but *failures to reason at all.* We've included a remark or two for each, but we remind you that all of them are discussed at greater length in the text.

Ad Hominem/Genetic Fallacy

If it operated no place but in politics, ad hominem would still be among the most ubiquitous examples of flawed thinking. While the fact that a claim came from a prominent Democrat or Republican might be reason to suspect that it is political spin, we constantly see people refuse even to consider—and sometimes even to hear—claims from a political perspective not their own.

But what goes in politics also goes in other arenas. Adversaries in practically every field of endeavor put less, or no, stock in their opponents' claims. We've seen this happen in disputes between physical scientists and behavioral scientists, between factions of a single academic department and between members of the same family. If they're the enemy, they cannot be right.

Wishful Thinking

It may surprise some that this category makes the list, but in observing people's behavior, we've come to think that they frequently put a lot more trust in what they *want* to be true than in what they have sufficient evidence for. Advertising, our beliefs about famous people, and many other aspects of life play upon this tendency. How frequently do we see people buy products that claim they'll make them younger-looking or more attractive only to see no results? And then those same people will buy the next product that comes along, possibly with the same ingredients but with a bigger advertising budget or better-looking models. We can't explain this in any other way except the triumph of wishful thinking.

Neither of your authors is sure about capital punishment. But we'd seriously consider an exception for people who invent scams based on wishful thinking and milk elderly people out of money they've spent their lives saving up.

"Argument" from Popularity

Operating in conjunction with wishful thinking, appeal to the authority of one's peers and predecessors accounts for a great proportion of the belief in the supernatural aspects of the world's religions down through history. This alone is sufficient to place it prominently on the list.

If a person thought that none of her peers believed in miracles, and she had never witnessed anything firsthand herself that she considered miraculous, what are the chances that she would believe in miracles in general? We believe it is very slight. But most people (well over half of Americans) do believe in miracles, and we're pretty sure such a belief rests at least in substantial part on the fact that most of one's peers share the belief.

Hasty Generalizing

The human mind is quick to notice connections between and among things, events, people, and such. Often, its ability to latch on to similarities is a matter of survival. ("A snake like that bit Oog the other day, and he died. I'm leaving this one alone.") But connections that we make "naturally" need to be sifted through our reasoning faculty. ("When I dreamed that it would rain on Easter, it did. Last night I dreamed the stock market would go up . . . I think I'll add to the portfolio.") We must learn to distinguish psychological connections from logical ones and real causes from coincidence.

Some related fallacies fall under this headline: One is the mistake of making generalizations from evidence that is merely anecdotal. We are very quick to conclude that our own experience or that of our friends is sufficient to arrive at a conclusion about the entire world. But the fact that your friend had no trouble quitting smoking is no reason to think that others won't.

A second variation is drawing conclusions (or generalizing) based on a bad analogy. The fact that two (or more) things are alike in *some* way is not all by itself a reason to think they're alike in some other way. Analogous items have to be very carefully scrutinized for relevant similarities and dissimilarities before we can draw conclusions about one from the other.

A final variety of the fallacy of hasty generalizing, and a sad one, is the way the public (following the media) jump to conclusions about a person's guilt when in fact the person has merely been mentioned as a possible suspect. Examples range from the famous Sam Shepard case (on which the TV series and movie titled *The Fugitive* were based) to the case of Richard Jewell, who was actually a hero in the bomb incident at the 1996 Atlanta Olympics—he spotted the fateful knapsack and warned people away from what turned out to be a pipe bomb, but later his name was leaked as a suspect. Although he was soon cleared by the authorities, the stigma of suspicion stuck to him and he was hounded for months at ball games and other events. His hopes for a career in law enforcement went down the drain. This, and similar stories, are the result of a public that makes up its mind on the basis of mere slivers of information.

"Argument" from Outrage

This category makes the list because of the increase in polarizing political discourse. The mere mention of Bill Clinton (on one hand) or George Bush (on the other) has the power to raise the blood pressure of large numbers of citizens. Animosity and bile have taken over from the presentation and evaluation of evidence, with the result that national political discussion has been on a downward trend for over a generation. We attribute at least part of the decline to the electronic media. Radio and television, although they had the potential to raise the level of public discourse, have had the opposite effect. ("Television is a medium," said Ernie Kovacs, "because it is neither rare nor well done.") Many television shows where politics are "discussed" have turned into shouting matches in which several morons compete for the loudest volume and sharpest insults. They may look vaguely like debates, but they are nothing of the sort. "Talk radio" is even worse, with meaningless statistics, false allegations, the spread of rumor, and general name-calling taking the place of argument and evidence. Most of these shows are designed solely to raise the heart rate of people who already believe the nonsense the host is talking about (no matter which side of the political spectrum he or she claims to represent).

It's worth pointing out that this "argument" almost always involves straw men (see the following entry) and very often involves scapegoating as well. The easiest way to deal with an issue is to identify an enemy, distort his real position, and blame everything on him amidst a flurry of name-calling.

Straw Man

One principal weapon of the indignation-mongers just described is the distortion and exaggeration of the views of others. This tactic is widespread in the talk media and in mainstream politics as well. In fact, the latter seem to be taking their cue from the former in recent years. (In the early 1990's, Newt Gingrich, former Republican Speaker of the U.S. House of Representatives, mailed a pamphlet to fellow Republicans, entitled *Language, a Key Mechanism of Control.* When discussing political opponents and their policies, he said, you should use such terms as "incompetent," "self-serving," "traitor," "anti-family," "ideological," and "radical." When discussing Republicans and their policies you should use such terms as "vision," "courage," "lead," "empower," "strength," and "pro-family.") Some, it seems, don't trust the American people to make political choices based on straightforward information. And, judging from the number of Americans who make no effort to obtain such information, there may be some basis for such an attitude.

Post Hoc

We usually explain post hoc reasoning in terms of simple-minded examples of cause and effect. But the real bamboozling takes place at more complicated levels. For example, while Jimmy Carter was president, interest rates went through the roof; while George Bush (the first such) was president, the economy went into a recession. Both presidents were blamed for these occurrences, but were the policies of either the cause of these effects? Probably not. At least most people did not stop to ask whether it was anything the president did or refused to do that might have caused them. It is our tendency to seize on easy, simple answers that helps give this fallacy, and most of the others, such a high profile.

Red Herring/Smokescreen

One might think of this as the "attention span" fallacy, since it seems to work best on listeners and readers who are unable to stay focused on an issue when they are tempted by distractions. These days, when politicians and other public figures dodge hard questions, they are generally allowed to get away with it. How long has it been since you've heard a reporter say, "But sir, you didn't answer the question!" Probably even longer than it's been since you heard a politician give a direct answer to a hard question. We've all heard it said that the media and the people they interview are interdependent—that is, they each depend on the other and have fundamentally the same interests (at the highest government and corporate levels), and that accounts for the easy treatment officials often get from interviewers. But we think it's also true that reporters themselves are prone to fall for the fallacy in question here. They are too likely to move on to the next question on their list when the public would be better served by a pointed follow-up question on an issue that has just been ducked. We think this is a serious failure and damaging to the public good.

Group Think Fallacy

This fallacy has undergone a major revival since the terrorist attacks of September 11, 2001. An understandable emotional shock followed those attacks, but even before the shock began to wear off, the motto for the country became "United We Stand." There's nothing unreasonable about a united stand, of course, but this motto soon began to stand for an intolerance of any position that ran counter to the official view of the United States government (as voiced by the White House). The prevailing view in many quarters, including many places in the government itself, was that all "good" Americans agreed with this official position. Considerable force was brought to bear in enforcing this group thinking, including describing critics as "giving aid and comfort" and so forth.

Of course, it isn't just national policy that can cause this phenomenon to occur. At what may be the other end of the spectrum, notice how the referees in a basketball game call way too many fouls on your team and not nearly enough on the other team. Our loyalty to our group can affect our judgments in ways that range from the amusing to the dangerous.

Scare Tactics

Reasoning that uses scare tactics is like rain in Seattle: It happens all the time. The scare tactics fallacy ranks up there with the "argument" from outrage as a staple of talk radio hosts and other demagogues, which means it is easy to find examples. What's wrong with raising fuel-efficiency standards? Well, how would you like to drive around in an elfmobile?—Because that's what you're going to be driving if the car companies are forced to make cars more efficient. What's wrong with the proposed big tax cut? Nothing—if you'd just as soon eliminate Social Security and Medicare.

The fallacy of scare tactics is an appeal to fear, and fear can often provide a perfectly reasonable motivation: Evidence that some frightening thing will result from X is certainly a good reason for avoiding X. But mere *mention* of the frightening thing is not, nor is a vivid portrayal or depiction of the ominous event. You don't prove we should overthrow a dictator merely by describing what would happen if he set off a nuclear bomb in New York City—or by showing gruesome photos of what he did to someone else. When the danger depicted is not shown to be relevant, the thinking is fallacious.

The use of scare tactics is not uncommon in advertising, either. But getting consumers to worry about having dandruff or halitosis or odors in their carpets is no argument for purchasing some particular brand of shampoo or mouthwash or carpet cleaner. People are often motivated to buy a house or car because they fear someone else will make an offer ahead of them and they'll lose the opportunity. This is unreasonable when it results in a purchase they would not otherwise have made. We wonder how many people live in houses they decided they liked just because they were afraid they'd lose them if they didn't make their offer *right now.*

Appendix 3

The Scrapbook of Unusual Issues

This section includes a number of items from here and there, mainly from newspapers, that struck us as amusing, out-of-the-ordinary, or just plain weird. All of them involve issues that can make for interesting discussions or subjects for writing assignments. (There's no reason critical thinking subjects have to be dull.) Like the essays in Appendix 1, these present opportunities to exercise your critical thinking skills.

Strange Stuff: News Out of the Ordinary

Golf-ball retriever's jail term tees off public

London — For 10 years John Collinson made a modest living diving for lost golf balls and selling them for 20 cents each. But after police caught him on a midnight expedition, a court frowned on his unusual job and jailed him for six months for theft.

The sentence provoked a public outcry, made the 36-year-old father of two a cause célèbre and prompted lawmakers, celebrities and the British media to campaign for this release.

Police arrested Collinson in August at Whetstone Golf Course in Leicester, central England. He and a colleague had fished 1,158 balls from Lily Pond, the bane of hundreds of golfers playing the difficult par 3 fifth hole.

Collinson, who made roughly $21,500 a year collecting balls at courses throughout the country, claimed in his defense they didn't belong to anyone. He told a jury at Leicester Crown Court last week he even filled out tax returns on his earnings. But the judge jailed him, saying, "It is obvious you show no remorse and no intention of quitting."

Gavin Dunnett, managing director of UK Lakeballs—a firm that buys balls from hundreds of divers and sells more than a million worldwide every year via the Internet—said Thursday that recovered balls are not stolen, but are abandoned property. He said more than 2,000 people had signed his online petition to "Free the Whetstone One."

Doodle crosses the line

MOUNT LEBANON, Pa. — A school suspended an 11-year-old girl for drawing two teachers with arrows through their heads, saying the stick figures were more death threat than doodle.

Becca Johnson, an honor-roll sixth grader at Mellon Middle School, drew the picture on the back of a vocabulary test on which she had gotten a D.

"That's my way of saying I'm angry," Becca said, adding she meant no harm to the teachers.

The stick figures, on a crudely drawn gallows with arrows in their heads, had the names of Becca's teacher and a substitute teacher written underneath. Another teacher spotted the doodle in the girl's binder Tuesday and reported it, prompting the three-day suspension.

Becca's parents, Philip and Barbara Johnson, denied the school's contention the drawings were "terrorist threats."

"She had done poorly on a test that was handed back to her. We've always told her that you can't take your feelings out on your teacher, so write about it or draw it, as a catharsis," Barbara Johnson said.

Brief lapse in judgment?

Poway — A high school vice principal was placed on leave Wednesday after she allegedly lifted girls' skirts—in front of male students and adults—to make sure they weren't wearing thong underwear at a dance.

"Everyone saw everything," said Kim Teal, whose 15-year-old daughter attended the dance but was not checked. "It was a big peep show."

Rita Wilson was placed on administrative leave Wednesday while the school district investigates the allegations concerning the dance last Friday for students at Rancho Bernardo High School.

Girls said they were told to line up outside the gym before entering the dance so Wilson could check their underwear. Those wearing thongs were turned away.

Cities Give Psychics License to Entertain, Not Exorcise

Believers in the occult and thrill-seekers are the bread and butter of psychic parlors.

For a few dollars, psychics foretell a client's future by gazing into a crystal ball or reading a palm.

Such transactions are legal entertainment, said Detective Jan Cater of the Sacramento County Sheriff's Department.

What is illegal, she said, is when clients are led to believe that they are cursed and must pay large sums of money to purge the evil.

"So-called psychics terrify people into believing that awful things will happen to them . . . . unless they pay to have the curses removed, Cater said.

Sacramento and other cities require that psychics and others in the "seer" trades undergo background checks before receiving a license issued by the police department.

But other communities, including unincorporated sections of Sacramento County, have no requirements—a situation that, according to Cater, can lead to big-time swindles.

"Psychic fraud isn't a major problem in the unincorporated areas (of the county), but it has the potential to be," Cater said.

In the city of Sacramento, the safeguards in place for several years are working, officials said. . . .

In San Francisco and other cities without license laws, psychic swindles are on the rise, authorities said.

One of Cater's biggest cases involved Ingrid, a Sonoma County woman who said she paid more than $265,000 over five years to "psychics" Louie Stevens and Nancy Uwnawich. The couple convinced Ingrid, 66, that she had a curse that had to be removed by them—or she would suffer, Ingrid said.

After wiping out her savings, Ingrid told the pair she had no more cash—except for $2,000 in her son's college trust fund.

"What's more important—your health or your son?" Uwnawich shouted, according to Ingrid.

Ingrid said she gave them the $2,000. . . .

An arrest warrant has been issued for Uwnawich, who remains at large.

— *By Edgar Sanchez*
BEE STAFF WRITER

Monogamy? Don't Cheat Yourself

DEAR ANN: Why do you come down so hard on married men who cheat? I don't understand why you believe monogamy is the only "right" way when it comes to marriage. If monogamy works so well, how come so many men cheat and so many women want divorces?

Many other cultures openly accept polygamy. Even the Bible says a man can have more than one wife. And in many countries, adultery is accepted and shrugged off as nothing to get excited about. The wife gets the financial support and social position, and the mistress gets the sex. This sounds like a fair exchange to me.

The truth is, there is not a woman on the planet who can fully satisfy the needs of a powerful male. When women quit asking men to make them the center of their universe and learn to accept a strong man's desire for more than one female companion, families will live together longer, more happily and with less rancor.

— *Truth Hurts In Texas*

DEAR AUSTIN: Men in biblical times had multiple wives in order to ensure an abundance of offspring because so many women died in childbirth. It was not a license to cheat.

I am sure your approach appeals to a lot of men, but I doubt that the women in your life would go for it. And without their cooperation, you're not going to get very far. Of course, if you would like to live in one of those foreign countries that condones adultery, be my guest. Most women would be delighted to see you go. A few might even be willing to buy you a ticket.

— *Ann Landers (By permission of Esther P. Lederer and Creators Syndicate, Inc.)*

Writer to "Dear Abby" Faces Child-Porn Counts

MILWAUKEE — A man who wrote to "Dear Abby" for advice on how to handle his fantasies about having sex with young girls was charged Wednesday with possessing child pornography after the columnist turned him in, authorities say.

Paul Weiser, 28, was charged with three counts of possession of child pornography. He was ordered released on $10,000 bail on condition he avoid computers and contact with anyone under 18.

Police said 40 pornographic photographs of children were found in his computer after his arrest Monday.

"He acknowledges he needs help and denies ever acting upon any desires," said prosecutor Paul Tiffin.

"Dear Abby" columnist Jeanne Phillips, daughter of column founder Pauline Phillips, called police after receiving the letter.

Jeanne Phillips, who shares her mother's pen name, Abigail Van Buren, told the Milwaukee Journal Sentinel she agonized over whether to report Weiser, since the column's credibility is based on anonymity given those seeking advice.

"I lost sleep. Didn't sleep for days, because I really believe this man wrote to me genuinely seeking help," she said. "I was torn, because my readers do turn to me for help, yet there was the priority of the safety of those young girls."

She was said to be traveling on Wednesday and did not return a call seeking comment.

Weiser could get up to five years in prison and a $10,000 fine on each count, if convicted.

He did not speak during Wednesday's court hearing except to answer "yes" when asked if he understood the proceedings.

A preliminary hearing was set for March 25.

— *Associated Press*

Strange Stuff: News Out of the Ordinary

"Whites" Send a Message

GREELEY, Colo. — Unable to persuade a local school to change a mascot name that offends them, some students at the University of Northern Colorado have named their intramural basketball team "The Fighting Whites."

The students are upset with Eaton High School for using an American Indian caricature on the team logo. The team is called the Reds.

The university team said it chose a white man as its mascot to try to raise awareness of stereotypes that some cultures endure.

"The message is 'Let's do something that will let people see the other side of what it's like to be a mascot,'" said Solomon Little Owl, a team member and director of Native American Student Services at the university.

The team, made up of American Indians, Latinos and Anglos, wears jerseys that say, "Every thang's going to be all white."

"It's not meant to be vicious. It is meant to be humorous," said Ray White, a Mohawk American Indian on the team.

No "ATHEISTS" Allowed

ST. PETERSBURG, Fla — Steven Miles has tooled around Gainesville, Fla., for 16 years with a license plate that says "ATHEIST."

To Miles, it is a form of self-expression, one he is happy to spend a few extra dollars every year to keep.

But to the state of Florida now, the tag is "obscene or objectionable," according to a letter Miles received last month from the Department of Highway Safety and Motor Vehicles.

"The plate must be canceled," the department ordered.

Miles said he is incensed and that giving up his tag is out of the question.

The vice president of Atheists of Florida said he intends to fight and is in touch with the American Civil Liberties Union.

Dummy is no woman

RENTON, Wash. — A woman with a full-size mannequin buckled into the front seat of her minivan tried to sneak into the car pool lane on Interstate 405 and became involved in a chain of crashes that backed up traffic for hours Tuesday morning, according to the Washington State Patrol.

Susan Aeschliman-Hill, 59, of Kent, Wash., acknowledged using the dummy—complete with a woman's sweater, makeup and wig—to drive illegally in the car pool lane. "When traffic gets real bad, I sometimes use (the mannequin)," she said.

State Patrol Trooper Monica Hunter said the woman likely will be cited for driving in the high-occupancy vehicle lane and making an unsafe lane change.

"Her passenger wasn't breathing, and that's one of our requirements," Hunter said.

— By Rick Nelson, compiled from the Associated Press

Christian School Expels Nude Dancer's Daughter

A Sacramento private school has expelled a kindergarten student three weeks before the end of the school year, saying her mother's work as a nude dancer clashes with its Christian philosophy.

Christina Silvas, 24, of Rancho Cordova said one reason she took the job as a dancer at Gold Club Centerfolds off Highway 50 was so she could afford the $400 monthly tuition at Capital Christian School.

"If you choose to do the wrong thing willfully, then God's word instructs me as to what my responsibility is," said Rick Cole, head pastor of Capital Christian Center. "I need to be faithful to my calling."

Silvas, who previously worked at the church as a Sunday school teacher, has a different view.

"I thought the church was supposed to accept everybody," she said. "That's my understanding of what God is about. My daughter is the one who goes to school there, not me, and they're turning her away."

Silvas, who is single, said school administrators telephoned her last week and told her that in response to persistent rumors, a parent went to the strip club's Web site, downloaded pictures of Silvas and brought them to school staff. Silvas told them she does dance at the all-nude bar, which doesn't serve alcohol, and subsequently met with Cole.

As head pastor of Capital Christian, which at 4,000 members is one of the largest Assemblies of God churches in the country, Cole had final say on the matter.

Silvas said Cole told her not only will her 5-year-old daughter be expelled, but as long as she keeps her job at the club, neither she nor her daughter can attend church there.

Silvas said her daughter enjoys the school's daily worship sessions and was looking forward to the end-of-the-year pool party and graduation ceremony. She hasn't told the girl why she won't be able to go to school next week.

"I'm still trying to figure out what I'm going to tell her," she said.

Silvas said that when she enrolled her daughter, she signed a statement that stipulated she would abide by the school's Christian commitment/philosophy and that "weekly church attendance is necessary for continued enrollment at CCS."

The statement also reads, in part, "CCS is interested in maintaining a partnership with our parents regarding the standards and criteria of a Christian learning structure that involves the entire family."

By working as an exotic dancer and refusing to change her vocation, Silvas violated the school's philosophy, Cole said.

"She was not in compliance with what she agreed to," he said. "There's a commitment form that parents sign. They agree to our Christian commitment and standard of living."

Seeking a resolution, Silvas and Cole met privately Tuesday. "I talked to her for over an hour, letting her know how much God cares about her and loves her and that he has a much better plan for her than what she is doing with her life right now," Cole said.

He promised that if Silvas quit her job, he and the church would forgive her, help her and even waive tuition for the month of June.

"My understanding was she would come back to me after thinking about it and let me know her decision," Cole said. "It's very stunning to me to see it on the news. We've been thrust into this media craze, but not by our desire."

Silvas said the decision is not simple and couldn't be made that quickly.

"I have other expenses besides my daughter's tuition," she said. "I am also concerned with providing a comfortable life for my daughter."

Silvas said she feels she is being demonized.

"I'm trying to let them know we're not evil because of our work, and we do have an awareness of God. My job is legal, it's not illegal."

Though Silvas is considering legal action, experts in education law say that may not be a good option.

"In a private school, it's hard to make a breach of contract action because they have the right to kick a kid out at any time for any reason," said Michael Sorgen, an education lawyer in San Francisco.

Even though the school has the legal right to expel the child, that doesn't make it right, Sorgen said.

— *By Erika Chavez*
BEE STAFF WRITER

Ill Boy's New Hurdle: School Drug Rules

Life just got more complicated for an 8-year-old boy and his mother who's had great success battling his mental disorders with a doctor-approved marijuana therapy.

The youngster's medical condition has improved so dramatically that he can now attend public school, but school officials won't permit a school nurse to administer his cannabis capsules and won't let him take the pills himself on campus, the child's mother said Monday.

"Other kids get their medication," she complained. But the drug her son needs daily at 1 p.m. must be delivered by her personally, off the school grounds, she said.

"It makes him feel he's not normal, that he's being treated differently. He wonders why he's being targeted. He just wants to be normal," she said.

She hopes to persuade school officials to change their minds and allow the capsules to be given on campus.

The woman, whose name is being withheld by *The Bee* to protect the boy's identity, has been treating her son with medical cannabis for the past year, at home and at the private school he had been attending.

But in April, they moved from Rocklin to El Dorado County. She presented her son's new school with the required permission slip for students who need medication at school, a form she and the boy's doctor signed.

The day before the boy was to report to his new school, however, a message left on the family answering machine informed the mother that her son's recommended medication could not be administered on campus.

So, she says, she's been forced to drive a round trip of 26 miles each noontime to remove him from the school grounds, give him his capsules, and return him to class.

Vicki L. Barber, superintendent of the El Dorado County Office of Education, said she could not comment on any specific case. But she said state law permits schools to dispense drugs only when they are formally "prescribed" by a physician. The boy's doctor made a "recommendation," and there is a difference,

Barber added, between a "prescription" and a doctor's "recommendation."

Proposition 215, the Compassionate Use Act of 1996, permits the use of medical marijuana and the possession of the drug by the patient or a primary caregiver.

A school district cannot be legally defined as a "primary caregiver," Barber said.

Because the district has a zero-tolerance policy, students are not permitted to have in their possession or to self-administer drugs of any kind, she said.

The boy's mother said the school district is relying on a technicality to dodge responsibility.

"There is no 'prescription' for 'oral cannabis,'" the capsule she prepares in a five-hour cooking and drying process at home, she said.

But it is a part of her son's "individual education plan" or IEP, the state's "prescription" for helping children with special needs, the mother said.

School district officials would not comment on the boy's specific IEP.

— *By Wayne Wilson*
BEE STAFF WRITER

A letter to the editor of the local paper by one of your authors.

5 Million Teen-agers Perfect

You recently ran an Associated Press story that first appeared in the New York Times about a Port Orchard, Wash., Eagle Scout who was given a week to abandon his atheism or be kicked out of Boy Scouts of America. Boy Scout law requires scouts to be trustworthy, loyal, helpful, friendly, courteous, kind, obedient, cheerful, thrifty, brave, clean and reverent. An atheist, of course, finds it difficult to be reverent in the intended sense of the term.

Unfortunately, you ended the article with a paraphrase from Gregg Shields, a Boy Scout spokesman: "Mr. Shields said for the Boy Scouts to insist on anything less would be unfair to the 5 million members."

But there were two more sentences in the New York Times article and you missed the best point of the piece by leaving them out. Shields said: "It would be a disservice to all the other members to allow someone to selectively obey or ignore our rules."

The Times piece then added, "As for the other 11 points of the Scout Law, Mr. Shields could not say whether anyone had been ejected for being untrustworthy, disloyal, unhelpful, unfriendly, discourteous, unkind, disobedient, cheerless, unthrifty, cowardly or sloppy."

I for one believe it is a credit to scouting that none of those 5 million teen-age boys has ever been found guilty of any of those other 11 defects.

— *Richard Parker, Chico*

Strange Stuff: News Out of the Ordinary

As if the goings-on of government weren't scary enough, the state of North Carolina is calling in a Ghostbusters-like group to do a paranormal screening of the old state Capitol.

Although there have been no sightings of a huge marshmallow man, staffers at the Capitol say they have heard floorboards creak with invisible footsteps, keys jangle, and doors squeak open and shut.

"To be honest with you, I've always made it a rule to be out of the building at quitting time," said Raymond Beck, the Capitol historian. "I've had enough of those strange vibes here that I don't like sticking around after it gets dark."

Researchers from the Ghost Research Foundation will give the 162-year-old Raleigh landmark where the governor has his offices a "spectral inspection," using infrared cameras, electromagnetic field detectors and audio recorders.

The Capitol has gone through a number of night watchmen who begged off the duty after one night of creepy noises, Beck said.

But Owen J. Jackson, 84, managed the job for 12 years before retiring in 1990. He apparently never was slimed, and strains of gospel hymns, the thump-thump-thumps that followed him down stairs and the angry slams of doors never bothered him, Jackson said.

"You get used to something like that," Jackson said. "I think there's a couple (of) million dollars buried somewhere there, and they're just trying to tell us where it was."

It's hormonal

A Harvard research team has found that married men, whether fathers or not, have significantly less testosterone than single men, regardless of age or overall health status.

Anthropology graduate student Peter Gray and his colleagues also found that men who spent lots of time with their wives had even lower testosterone levels than other married men. The team tested 58 men in the Boston area, according to an article in a recent Harvard University Gazette.

Gray suggests that married men don't produce as much testosterone after they shift from dating to parenting roles.

"Married men, particularly fathers, are less likely to engage in dominance interaction and aggression," he said. "That means less risk taking, less conflicts or other behaviors that could lead, for example, to death by homicide.

And couldn't it be Mother Nature's way of keeping men from straying? After all, other studies have found that men with high levels of testosterone were more likely to commit adultery than those with less of the stuff.

"That's an interesting question," Gray said. "That's a topic that will be harder to get at."

Is skydiving dog cruelty?

Animal lovers are howling over a skydiving dog.

The parachuting dachshund, known as Brutus the Skydiving Dog, is set to perform at this weekend's Air and Space show at Vandenberg Air Force Base.

"What we feel is this is cruelty to animals," said Shirley Cram, shelter director and treasurer for the Volunteers for Inter-valley Animals. "It's exploiting the dog. It certainly isn't fun for that dog to jump out of the plane."

Brutus' skydiving partner disagrees.

"He gets all excited when I'm getting my gear ready," said Ron Sirull of Delray Beach, Fla., contending Brutus enjoys his aerial activities. He added, "He's totally up for it."

Sirull said his dog's veterinarian and the Arizona Humane Society have signed off the activity being safe for man's best friend.

Brutus is tucked into a special pouch affixed to his owner's chest for the jump and dons custom-made goggles for what Sirull calls his "fleafall." While Sirull has 1,000 jumps, Brutus has logged 100.

"That's equal to 700 jumps in dog years," his owner joked.

— *Compiled by Caroline Liss from the Associated Press and Washington Post. In SAC BEE, 1 Nov. 2002.*

10 Commandments Monument Must Go

MONTGOMERY, Ala. — A Ten Commandments monument in the rotunda of Alabama's judicial building violates the Constitution's ban on government promotion of religion, a federal judge ruled Monday.

U.S. District Judge Myron Thompson gave Alabama Chief Justice Roy Moore, who had the 5,300-pound granite monument installed in the state building, 30 days to remove it.

Thompson said previous court rulings have allowed displays on government property if they have a secular purpose and do not foster "excessive government entanglement with religion." He said the Ten Commandments monument fails this test.

"His fundamental, if not sole, purpose in displaying the monument was non-secular; and the monument's primary effect advances religion," Thompson said.

Moore testified during the trial that the commandments are the moral foundation of American law. He said the monument acknowledges God, but does not force anyone to follow the justice's conservative Christian religious beliefs.

A lawsuit seeking removal of the monument argued that it promoted the judge's faith in violation of the Constitution.

Moore installed the monument after the building closed on the night of July 31, 2001, without telling any other justices.

"This monument was snuck in during the middle of the night, and they can sneak it out just as easily. It's a gross violation of the rights of the citizens of Alabama," said Morris Dees, lead counsel and co-founder of the Southern Poverty Law Center. He urged Moore to remove the monument immediately.

The monument, which features the King James Bible version of the Ten Commandments sitting on top of a granite block, is one of the first things visitors see upon entering the building.

"Its sloping top and the religious air of the tablets unequivocally call to mind an open Bible resting on a podium," Thompson said.

In his ruling, Thompson said he found the monument to be more than just a display of the Ten Commandments.

"The court is impressed that the monument and its immediate surroundings are, in essence, a consecrated place, a religious sanctuary, within the walls of the courthouse," Thompson wrote.

An appeal is expected. Neither Moore nor his lead attorney, Stephen Melchior, had any immediate comment. An assistant to Melchior said they were reserving comment until they had read the opinion.

Moore fought to display a wooden plaque of the commandments on his courtroom wall in Etowah County before he won election as chief justice in November 2000.

"The basic issue is whether we will still be able to acknowledge God under the First Amendment, or whether we will not be able to acknowledge God," Moore testified.

The Rev. Barry Lynn, executive director of Americans United for Separation of Church and State, call the ruling a setback for "Moore's religious crusade."

"It's high time Moore learned that the source of U.S. law is the Constitution and not the Bible," Lynn said.

One of Moore's supporters, Alabama Christian Coalition President John Giles, said he believes there may be a backlash against the ruling in Alabama.

"I am afraid the judge's order putting a 30-day limit on removal of the monument will lead to an uprising of citizens protesting removal of that monument," Giles said.

— *Associated Press*

Teen Claims Bias After School Bars Her Bid to Be Prom King

SACRAMENTO — An 18-year-old Encina High School senior is not being allowed to run for prom king because . . . she is a female.

Kristine Lester said Thursday that school officials told her that her name would not be on the ballot because only males can run for king and only females can run for queen.

"I just wanted to do something different," said Lester, who is openly gay and plans to wear a tuxedo at Saturday's prom. "I'm not the feminine type to run for queen."

Lester said she believes the school is discriminating against her because of her sexual orientation.

Officials with the San Juan Unified School District back Encina Principal Myrtle Berry's decision and denied that there was any discrimination involved.

"We don't discriminate," said district spokeswoman Deidra Powell.

— *Sandy Louey*

Point, Click . . . Fire!

According to a Knight-Ridder newspaper article, a gent from Texas has now made it possible to hunt pigs and kill them from anywhere you can carry your laptop. John Lockwood, who is a San Antonio body shop estimator, has set up a computer-directed firing range operated from a trailer installation on a 220-acre ranch 15 miles east of Boerne, Texas. Patrons can use their computers to sight, aim, and fire either a .22 caliber rifle (for target practice) or a .30-06 caliber hunting rifle for the pigs that range on the ranch.

More than 350 people have signed up as members of Live-Shot.com. They come from as far away as Hong Kong, France, and Peru. But they'd better give it their best shot soon, as Representative Todd Smith, a Republican member of the state legislature, has introduced a bill that would prohibit remote control hunting in Texas.

Boerne, United States: The Latest Internet Craze . . . Hunting Wild Animals Online: John Lockwood, owner of the real-time, online hunting and shooting Web site Live-Shot.com, demonstrates how one can use the internet to shoot targets on a ranch outside Boerne, Texas, 26 February, 2005. Now anyone with a computer and a modem can log on and fire real weapons, but the idea of Internet hunting has generated plenty of criticism. A Republican representative in the Texas Legislature, Todd Smith, himself an occasional hunter, has offered a bill to ban the practice. "I don't think we should be able to kill God's creatures with the click of a mouse," Smith said. "I think hunters are offended by the concept, much less non-hunters."

Marine General: "It's Fun to Shoot Some People"

WASHINGTON – A decorated Marine Corps general said, "It's fun to shoot some people" and poked fun at the manhood of some Afghans as he described the wars U.S. troops are fighting in Iraq and Afghanistan.

His boss, the commandant of the Marine Corps, said Thursday that the comments reflected "the unfortunate and harsh realities of war" but that the general has been asked to watch his words in public.

Lt. Gen James Mattis, a career infantry officer who is now in charge of developing better ways to train and equip Marines, made the comments Tuesday while speaking to a forum in San Diego.

According to an audio recording, he said: "Actually, it's a lot of fun to fight. You know, it's a hell of a hoot. . . . It's fun to shoot some people. I'll be right upfront with you—I like brawling."

He added: "You go into Afghanistan, you got guys who slap women around for five years because they didn't wear a veil. You know, guys like that ain't got no manhood left anyway. So it's a hell of a lot of fun to shoot them."

His comments were met with laughter and applause from the audience. Mattis was speaking during a panel discussion hosted by the Armed Forces Communications and Electronics Association, a spokeswoman for the general said.

Thursday, Gen. Mike Hagee, Commandant of the Marine Corps, issued a statement saying: "Lt. Gen. Mattis often speaks with a great deal of candor. I have counseled him concerning his remarks, and he agrees he should have chosen his words more carefully."

Hagee also said, "While I understand that some people may take issue with the comments made by him, I also know he intended to reflect the unfortunate and harsh realities of war."

Among Marines, Mattis is regarded as a fighting general and an expert in the art of warfare. Among his decorations are the Bronze Star with a combat distinguishing device and a combat action ribbon, awarded for close-quarters fighting.

He is the commanding general of the Marine Corps Combat Development Command in Quantico, Va., and deputy commandant for combat development.

The Council on American Islamic Relations, a Muslim civil liberties group, called on the Pentagon to discipline Mattis for the remarks.

"We do not need generals who treat the grim business of war as a sporting event," said the council's executive director, Nihad Awad. "These disturbing remarks are indicative of an apparent indifference to the value of human life."

—By John J. Lumpkin
ASSOCIATED PRESS

Women's Affair Not Adultery, Court Rules

CONCORD, N.H. — If a married woman has sex with another woman, is that adultery? The New Hampshire Supreme Court, ruling in a divorce case, says no.

The court was asked to review a case in which a husband accused his wife of adultery after she had a sexual relationship with another woman. Robin Mayer of Brownsville, Vt., was named in the divorce proceedings of David and Sian Blanchflower of Hanover.

A Family Court judge decided Mayer and Sian Blanchflower's relationship did constitute adultery, but Mayer appealed to the Supreme Court, arguing that gay sex is not adultery under New Hampshire divorce law.

Three of the five justices agreed. Two others—generally considered the court's more conservative members—did not.

Part of the problem is that New Hampshire's divorce laws do not define adultery. So the court looked up "adultery" in Webster's dictionary and found that it mentions intercourse. And it found an 1878 case that referred to adultery as "intercourse from which spurious issue may arise."

Other states have defined adultery in broader terms—beyond intercourse—to include gay sex.

Marcus Hurn, a professor at Franklin Pierce Law Center, suggested that the New Hampshire court's majority opinion is unintentionally trivializing same-sex relations and violating modern notions of the sanctity of marriage.

A sexual relationship, whether heterosexual or homosexual, is "exactly an equivalent betrayal and that, I think, is the ordinary meaning most people would give," he said.

— Associated Press

Stop Barring Men, Feminist Professor Told

Boston College gives her an ultimatum to allow males in class— or quit teaching

BOSTON — A radical feminist professor at Boston College has been given an ultimatum from the school: admit men to her classes or stop teaching.

Theologian Mary Daly lets only women take her courses.

Daly, whose seven major books, including "Outercourse," have made her a pioneer in feminist circles, has said she won't back down. Opening her classes to men would compromise her belief that women tend to defer to a man whenever one is in the room, she said.

Daly took a leave of absence from the Jesuit college this semester rather than bow to demands that she admit senior Duane Naquin into her class in feminist ethics.

Naquin, who claimed discrimination, has the backing of the Center for Individual Rights, a conservative law firm in Washington whose lawsuit ended affirmative action at the University of Texas. The firm sent a letter to BC in the fall threatening legal action if Daly did not relent.

Daly has argued Naquin did not have the prerequisite of another feminist studies course.

College officials said a second male student also complained of discrimination.

Daly has rejected a retirement offer from the college, the Boston Globe reported.

Daly, who is 70, taught only men when she first arrived at the Newton campus in 1966. The college of arts and science did not begin admitting women until 1970. In the early '70s, she said, she observed problems in her coed classes.

"Even if there were only one or two men with 20 women, the young women would be constantly on an overt or a subliminal level giving their attention to the men because they've been socialized to nurse men," she said.

Boston College officials said Daly's ground rules violate federal civil rights laws and school policy.

If a male professor tried to bar women from his classes, college spokesman Jack Dunn said, "we'd be run out of town."

Daly, who abandoned her Roman Catholic faith in the early 1970s, describes herself as a radical feminist, which she interprets as "going to the roots" of societal problems.

Her books include "The Church and the Second Sex," "Gyn/Ecology: The Metaethics of Radical Feminism" and "Outercourse," a theological autobiography.

She said she views the controversy as an attack on academic freedom and an assault on feminism by "an extreme right-wing organization" trying to "assert white male supremacy."

Daly's students are rallying around her, and 14 of them wrote a letter to college administrators.

"I think there comes a point where women need to claim their own space," said Kate Heekin, a Greenwich, Conn., senior. "If that needs to be a classroom, so be it."

— *By Robin Estrin*
ASSOCIATED PRESS

In Short . . .

She is Barbie's oldest friend, happily married and visibly pregnant with her second child—and some parents think she's a little too real for children. The pregnant version of Midge, which pops out a curled-up baby when her belly is opened, has been pulled from Wal-Mart shelves across the nation following complaints from customers, a company spokeswoman said.

— *Associated Press; from* The Sacramento Bee,
December 26, 2002

Glossary

ad hominem Attempting to rebut a source's argument or claim or position, etc., on the basis of considerations that logically apply to the source rather than to the argument or claim or position.

affirmative claim A claim that includes one class or part of one class within another: A- and I-claims.

affirming the antecedent *See* modus ponens.

affirming the consequent An argument consisting of a conditional claim as one premise, a claim that affirms the consequent of the conditional as a second premise, and a claim that affirms the antecedent of the conditional as the conclusion.

ambiguous claim A claim that could be interpreted in more than one way and whose meaning is not made clear by the context.

analogical argument An argument in which something that is said to hold true for one thing is claimed also to hold true of a similar thing.

analogy A comparison of two or more objects, events, or other phenomena.

analytic claim A claim that is true or false by virtue of the meanings of the words that compose it. *Contrast with* synthetic claim.

analytical definition A definition that specifies (1) the type of thing the defined term applies to and (2) the difference between that thing and other things of the same type.

antecedent *See* conditional claim.

appeal to anecdotal evidence, fallacy of A form of hasty generalization presented in the form of an anecdote or story. Also the fallacy of trying to prove (or disprove) a general causal claim citing an example or two.

appeal to ignorance The view that an absence of evidence *against* a claim counts as evidence *for* that claim.

appeal to indignation *See* outrage, "argument" from.

appeal to pity *See* pity, "argument" from.

appeal to precedent The claim (in law) that a current case is sufficiently similar to a previous case that it should be settled in the same way.

apple polishing A pattern of fallacious reasoning in which flattery is disguised as a reason for accepting a claim.

argument An attempt to support or prove a claim or an assertion by providing a reason or reasons for accepting it. The claim that is supported is called the conclusion of the argument, and the claim or claims providing the support are called the premises.

argument from analogy *See* analogical argument.

argument pattern The structure of an argument. This structure is independent of the argument's content. Several arguments can have the same pattern (e.g., modus ponens) yet be about quite different subjects. Variables are used to stand for classes or claims in the display of an argument's pattern.

background information The body of justified beliefs that consists of facts we learn from our own direct observations and facts we learn from others.

bandwagon *See* popularity, "argument" from.

begging the question *See* question-begging argument.

biased generalizing from, fallacy of Generalizing from a biased sample.

biased sample A sample that is not representative.

burden of proof, misplacing A form of fallacious reasoning in which the burden of proving a point is placed on the wrong side. One version occurs when a lack of evidence on one side is taken as evidence for the other side, in cases where the burden of proving the point rests on the latter side.

categorical claim Any standard-form categorical claim or any claim that means the same as some standard-form categorical claim. *See* standard-form categorical claim.

categorical imperative Kant's term for an absolute moral rule that holds unconditionally or "categorically."

categorical logic A system of logic based on the relations of inclusion and exclusion among classes ("categories"). This branch of logic specifies the logical relationships among claims that can be expressed in the forms "All Xs are Ys," "No Xs are Ys," "Some Xs are Ys," and "Some Xs are not Ys." Developed by Aristotle in the fourth century B.C.E., categorical logic is also known as Aristotelian or traditional logic.

categorical syllogism A two-premise deductive argument in which every claim is categorical and each of three terms appears in two of the claims—for example, all soldiers are martinets and no martinets are diplomats, so no soldiers are diplomats.

causal claim A statement that says or implies that one thing caused or causes another.

causal factor A causal factor for some specific effect is something that contributes to the effect. More precisely, in a given population, a thing is a causal factor for some specified effect if there would be more occurrences of the effect if every member of the population were exposed to the thing than if none were exposed to the thing. To say that C is a causal factor for E in population P, then, is to say that there would be more cases of E in population P if every member of P were exposed to C than if no member of P were exposed to C.

causal hypothesis A statement put forth to explain the cause or effect of something, when the cause or effect has not been conclusively established.

cause-and-effect claim *See* causal claim.

chain argument An argument consisting of three conditional claims, in which the antecedents of one premise and the conclusion are the same, the consequents of the other premise and the conclusion are the same, and the consequent of the first premise and the antecedent of the second premise are the same.

circularity The property of a "causal" claim where the "cause" merely restates the effect.

circumstantial ad hominem Attempting to discredit a person's claim by referring to the person's circumstances.

claim variable A letter that stands for a claim.

common practice, "argument" from Attempts to justify or defend an action or a practice on the grounds that it is common—that "everybody," or at least lots of people, do the same thing.

common thread When an effect is present on multiple occasions, look for some other shared feature (common thread) as a possible cause.

complementary term A term is complementary to another term if and only if it refers to everything that the first term does not refer to.

composition, fallacy of To think that what holds true of a group of things taken individually necessarily holds true of the same things taken collectively.

conclusion In an argument, the claim that is argued for.

conclusion indicator A word or phrase (e.g., "therefore") that ordinarily indicates the presence of the conclusion of an argument.

conditional claim A claim that state-of-affairs A cannot hold without state-of-affairs B holding as well—e.g., "If A then B." The A-part of the claim is called the *antecedent;* the B-part is called the *consequent.*

conditional proof A deduction for a conditional claim "If P then Q" that proceeds by assuming that P is true and then proving that, on that assumption, Q must also be true.

confidence level *See* statistical significance.

conflicting claims Two claims that cannot both be correct.

confusing explanations and excuses, fallacy of Mistaking an explanation of something for an attempt to excuse it.

conjunction A compound claim made from two simpler claims. A conjunction is true if and only if both of the simpler claims that compose it are true.

consequent *See* conditional claim.

contradictory claims Two claims that are exact opposites—that is, they could not both be true at the same time and could not both be false at the same time.

contrapositive The claim that results from switching the places of the subject and predicate terms in a claim and replacing both terms with complementary terms.

contrary claims Two claims that could not both be true at the same time but could both be false at the same time.

control group *See* controlled cause-to-effect experiment.

controlled cause-to-effect experiment An experiment designed to test whether something is a causal factor for a given effect. Basically, in such an experiment two groups are essentially alike, except that the members of one group, the *experimental group,* are exposed to the suspected causal factor, and the members of the other group, the *control group,* are not. If the effect is then found to occur with significantly more frequency in the experimental group, the suspected causal agent is considered a causal factor for the effect.

converse The converse of a categorical claim is the claim that results from switching the places of the subject and predicate terms.

deduction (proof) A numbered sequence of truth-functional symbolizations, each member of which validly follows from earlier members by one of the truth-functional rules.

deductive argument *See* good deductive argument.

definition by example Defining a term by pointing to, naming, or describing one or more examples of something to which the term applies.

definition by synonym Defining a term by giving a word or phrase that means the same thing.

denying the antecedent An argument consisting of a conditional claim as one premise, a claim that denies the antecedent of the conditional as a second premise, and a claim that denies the consequent of the conditional as the conclusion.

denying the consequent *See* modus tollens.

deontologism *See* duty theory.

dependent premises Premises that depend on one another as support for their conclusion.

If the assumption that a premise is false cancels the support another provides for a conclusion, the premises are dependent.

descriptive claim A claim that states facts or alleged facts. Descriptive claims tell how things are, or how they were, or how they might be. *Contrast with* prescriptive claims.

disjunction A compound claim made up of two simpler claims. A disjunction is false only if both of the simpler claims that make it up are false.

divine command theory The view that our moral duty (what's right and wrong) is dictated by God.

division, fallacy of To think that what holds true of a group of things taken collectively necessarily holds true of the same things taken individually.

downplayer An expression used to play down or diminish the importance of a claim.

duty theory The view that a person should perform an action because it is his or her moral duty to perform it, not because of any consequences that might follow from it.

dysphemism A word or phrase used to produce a negative effect on a reader's or listener's attitude about something or to tone down the positive associations the thing may have.

emotive force The feelings, attitudes, or emotions a word or an expression expresses or elicits.

envy, "argument" from Trying to induce acceptance of a claim by arousing feelings of envy.

equivalent claims Two claims are equivalent if and only if they would be true in all and exactly the same circumstances.

error margin Expression of the limit of random variation among random samples of a population.

euphemism An agreeable or inoffensive expression that is substituted for an expression that may offend the hearer or suggest something unpleasant.

experimental group *See* controlled cause-to-effect experiment.

expert A person who, through training, education, or experience, has special knowledge or ability in a subject.

explanation A claim or set of claims intended to make another claim, object, event, or state of affairs intelligible.

explanatory comparison A comparison that is used to explain.

explanatory definition A definition used to explain, illustrate, or disclose important aspects of a difficult concept.

extension The set of things to which a term applies.

factual claim A claim about a factual issue.

factual issue/question An issue that there are generally accepted methods for settling.

fallacy An argument in which the reasons advanced for a claim fail to warrant acceptance of that claim.

false dilemma This pattern of fallacious reasoning: "X is true because either X is true or Y is true, and Y isn't," said when X and Y could both be false.

feature in question In an inductive generalization, the property you are generalizing about. In an analogical argument, the property you are attributing to one thing because of its similarity to another thing

force, "argument" by Using a threat rather than legitimate argument to "support" a "conclusion."

functional explanation An explanation of an object or occurrence in terms of its function or purpose.

gambler's fallacy Believing that recent past events in a series can influence the outcome of the next event in the series is fallacious when the events have a predictable ratio of results, as flipping a coin.

genetic fallacy Rejecting a claim on the basis of its origin or history.

good deductive argument An argument whose premises being true would mean the conclusion absolutely must be true.

good inductive argument An argument whose premises being true would mean the conclusion probably is true.

grouping ambiguity A kind of semantic ambiguity in which it is unclear whether a claim refers to a group of things taken individually or collectively.

group think fallacy Fallacy that occurs when someone lets identification with a group cloud reason and deliberation when arriving at a position on an issue.

guilt trip Trying to get someone to accept a claim by making him or her feel guilty for not accepting it.

harm principle The claim that the only way to justify a restriction on a person's freedom is to show that the restriction prevents harm to other people.

hasty generalizing, fallacy of Generalizing from too small a sample.

horse laugh A pattern of fallacious reasoning in which ridicule is disguised as a reason for rejecting a claim.

hyperbole Extravagant overstatement.

hypothesis A supposition offered as a starting point for further investigation.

hypothetical imperative Kant's term for a command that is binding only if one is interested in a certain result.

inconsistency (ad hominem) A pattern of fallacious reasoning of the sort, "I reject your claim because you act inconsistently with it yourself," or "You can't make that claim now because you have in the past rejected it."

indirect proof Proof of a claim by demonstrating that its negation is false, absurd, or self-contradictory.

inductive analogical argument *See* analogical argument.

inductive argument *See* good inductive argument.

inductive generalization *See* generalization.

innuendo An insinuation of something deprecatory.

intension The set of characteristics a thing must have for a term correctly to apply to it.

invalid argument An argument that isn't valid.

issue A point that is or might be disputed, debated, or wondered about. Essentially, a question.

law of large numbers A rule stating that the larger the number of chance-determined, repetitious events considered, the closer the alternatives will approach predictable ratios. Example: The more times you flip a coin, the closer the results will approach 50 percent heads and 50 percent tails.

legal moralism The theory that, if an activity is immoral, it should also be illegal.

legal paternalism The theory that a restriction on a person's freedom can sometimes be justified by showing that it is for that person's own benefit.

leveling The process of omitting or de-emphasizing features in a description of a person, thing, or event, when the person doing the describing does not think those features are important. The result can be a distorted description.

line-drawing fallacy The fallacy of insisting that a line must be drawn at some precise point when in fact it is not necessary that such a line be drawn.

loaded question A question that rests on one or more unwarranted or unjustified assumptions.

logic The branch of philosophy concerned with whether the reasons presented for a claim, if those reasons were true, would justify accepting the claim.

mean A type of average. The arithmetic mean of a group of numbers is the number that results when their sum is divided by the number of members in the group.

median A type of average. In a group of numbers, as many numbers of the group are larger than the median as are smaller.

mode A type of average. In a group of numbers, the mode is the number occurring most frequently.

modus ponens An argument consisting of a conditional claim as one premise, a claim that affirms the antecedent of the conditional as a second premise, and a claim that affirms the consequent of the conditional as the conclusion.

modus tollens An argument consisting of a conditional claim as one premise, a claim that denies the consequent of the conditional as a second premise, and a claim that denies the antecedent of the conditional as the conclusion.

moral relativism The view that what is morally right and wrong depends on and is determined by one's group or culture.

nationalism A powerful and often fierce emotional attachment to one's country that can lead a person to blind endorsement of any policy or practice of that country. ("My country, right or wrong!") It is a subdivision of the group think fallacy.

naturalistic fallacy The assumption that one can conclude directly from a fact (what "is") what a rule or a policy should be (an "ought") without a value-premise.

negation The contradictory of a particular claim.

negative claim A claim that excludes one class or part of one class from another: E- and O-claims.

nonexperimental cause-to-effect study A study designed to test whether something is a causal factor for a given effect. Such studies are similar to controlled cause-to-effect experiments, except that the members of the experimental group are not exposed to the suspected causal agent by the investigators; instead, exposure has resulted from the actions or circumstances of the individuals themselves.

nonexperimental effect-to-cause study A study designed to test whether something is a causal factor for a given effect. Such studies are similar to nonexperimental cause-to-effect studies, except that the members of the experimental group display *the effect,* as compared with a control group whose members do not display the effect. Finding that the suspected cause is significantly more frequent in the experimental group is reason for saying that the suspected causal agent is a causal factor in the population involved.

non sequitur The fallacy of irrelevant conclusion; an inference that does not follow from the premises.

objective claim A claim that is not subjective. An objective claim does not owe its truth or falsity to someone's thinking it is true or false.

obverse The obverse of a categorical claim is that claim that is directly across from it in the square of opposition, with the predicate term changed to its complementary term.

offense principle The claim that an action or activity can justifiably be made illegal if it is sufficiently offensive.

opinion A claim that somebody believes to be true.

outrage, "argument" from An attempt to persuade others by provoking anger in them, usually by inflammatory words, followed by a "conclusion" of some sort.

peer pressure "argument" A fallacious pattern of reasoning in which you are in effect threatened with rejection by your friends, relatives, etc., if you don't accept a certain claim.

perfectionist fallacy Concluding that a policy or proposal is bad simply because it does not accomplish its goal to perfection.

personal attack ad hominem A pattern of fallacious reasoning in which we refuse to accept another's argument because there is something about the person we don't like or of which we disapprove. A form of ad hominem.

pity, "argument" from Supporting a claim by arousing pity rather than offering legitimate argument.

poisoning the well Attempting to discredit in advance what a person might claim by relating unfavorable information about the person.

popularity, "argument" from Accepting or urging others to accept a claim simply because all or most or some substantial number of people believe it—to do this is to commit a fallacy.

***post hoc, ergo propter hoc,* fallacy of** Reasoning that X caused Y simply because Y occurred after X, or around the same time.

precising definition A definition that limits the applicability of a term whose usual meaning is too vague for the use in question.

predicate term The noun or noun phrase that refers to the second class mentioned in a standard-form categorical claim.

predictable ratio The ratio that results of a series of events can be expected to have given the antecedent conditions of the series. Examples: The predictable ratio of a fair coin flip is 50 percent heads and 50 percent tails; the predictable ratio of sevens coming up when a pair of dice is rolled is 1 in 6, or just under 17 percent.

premise The claim or claims in an argument that provide the reasons for believing the conclusion.

premise indicator A word or phrase (e.g., "because") that ordinarily indicates the presence of the premise of an argument.

prescriptive claim A claim that states how things ought to be. Prescriptive claims impute values to actions, things, or situations. *Contrast with* descriptive claims.

principle of utility The basic principle of utilitarianism, to create as much overall happiness and/or to limit unhappiness for as many as possible.

proof surrogate An expression used to suggest that there is evidence or authority for a claim without actually saying that there is.

property in question *See* feature in question.

pseudoreason A consideration offered in support of a position that is not relevant to the truth or falsity of the issue in question.

question-begging argument An argument whose conclusion restates a point made in the premises or clearly assumed by the premises. Although such an argument is technically valid, anyone who doubts the conclusion of a question-begging argument would have to doubt the premises, too.

random sample *See* random selection process.

random selection process Method of drawing a sample from a target population so that each member of the target population has an equal chance of being selected.

rationalizing Using a false pretext in order to satisfy our desires or interests.

red herring *See* smokescreen.

reductio ad absurdum An attempt to show that a claim is false by demonstrating that it has false or absurd logical consequences; literally, "reducing to an absurdity."

relativism The idea that the beliefs of one society or culture are as true as those of the next, or the idea that what is true is determined by what a society/culture believes.

relativist fallacy Claiming a moral standard holds universally while simultaneously maintaining it doesn't hold within societies that don't accept it.

relevant/relevance A consideration is relevant to an issue if it is not unreasonable to suppose that its truth has some bearing on the truth or falsity of the issue. *See also* relevant difference

relevant difference If an effect occurs in one situation and doesn't occur in similar situations, look for something else that is different as a possible cause.

representative sample A sample that possesses all relevant features of a target population and possesses them in proportions that are similar to those of the target population.

rhetoric In our usage, "rhetoric" is language used primarily to persuade or influence beliefs or attitudes rather than to prove logically.

rhetorical analogy An analogy used to express or influence attitudes or affect behavior; such analogies often invoke images with positive or negative emotional associations.

rhetorical definition A definition used to convey or evoke an attitude about the defined term and its denotation.

rhetorical devices Rhetorical devices are used to influence beliefs or attitudes through the associations, connotations, and implications of words, sentences, or more extended passages. Rhetorical devices include slanters and fallacies. While rhetorical devices may be used to enhance the persuasive force of arguments, they do not add to the logical force of arguments.

rhetorical explanation An explanation intended to influence attitudes or affect behavior; such explanations often make use of images with positive or negative emotional associations.

rhetorical force *See* emotive force.

sample That part of a class referred to in the premises of a generalizing argument.

sample size One of the variables that can affect the size of the error margin or the confidence level of certain inductive arguments.

scapegoating Placing the blame for some bad effect on a person or group of people who are not really responsible for it, but who provide an easy target for animosity.

scare tactics Trying to scare someone into accepting or rejecting a claim. A common form includes merely describing a frightening scenario rather than offering evidence that some activity will cause it.

self-contradictory claim A claim that is analytically false.

semantically ambiguous claim An ambiguous claim whose ambiguity is due to the ambiguity of a word or phrase in the claim.

sharpening The process of exaggerating those points that a speaker thinks are important when he or she is describing some person, thing, or event. The result can be a distorted description.

slanter A linguistic device used to affect opinions, attitudes, or behavior without argumentation. Slanters rely heavily on the suggestive power of words and phrases to convey and evoke favorable and unfavorable images.

slippery slope A form of fallacious reasoning in which it is assumed that some event must inevitably follow from some other, but in which no argument is made for the inevitability.

smokescreen An irrelevant topic or consideration introduced into a discussion to divert attention from the original issue.

social utility A focus on what is good for society (usually in terms of overall happiness) when deciding on a course of action. *See also* principle of utility.

sound argument A valid argument whose premises are true.

spin A type of rhetorical device, often in the form of a red herring or complicated euphemism to disguise a politician's statement or action that might otherwise be perceived in an unfavorable light.

square of opposition A table of the logical relationships between two categorical claims that have the same subject and predicate terms.

standard-form categorical claim Any claim that results from putting words or phrases that name classes in the blanks of one of the following structures: "All ____ are _____"; "No _____ are _____"; "Some _____ are _____"; and "Some _____ are not _____."

stare decisis "Letting the decision stand." Going by precedent.

"statistically significant" This expression means from a statistical point of view probably not due to chance.

stereotype An oversimplified generalization about the members of a class.

stipulative definition A definition used to introduce an unfamiliar term or to assign a new meaning to a familiar term.

straw man A type of fallacious reasoning in which someone ignores an opponent's actual position and presents in its place a distorted, exaggerated, or misrepresented version of that position.

strong argument *See* good inductive argument.

subcontrary claims Two claims that can both be true at the same time but cannot both be false at the same time.

subject term The noun or noun phrase that refers to the first class mentioned in a standard-form categorical claim.

subjective claim A claim not subject to meaningful dispute if the speaker thinks it is true.

subjective expression An expression you can use pretty much as you please and still be using it correctly.

subjectivism The idea that one opinion is as good as the next, or that what is true is what you think is true.

subjectivist fallacy This pattern of fallacious reasoning: "Well, X may be true for you, but it isn't true for me," said with the intent of dismissing or rejecting X.

syllogism A deductive argument with two premises.

syntactically ambiguous claim An ambiguous claim whose ambiguity is due to the structure of the claim.

synthetic claim A claim whose truth value cannot be determined simply by understanding the claim—an observation of some sort is also required. *Contrast with* analytic claim.

target In the conclusion of an inductive generalization, the members of an entire class of things is said to have a property or feature. This class is the "target" or "target class." In the conclusion of an analogical argument, one or more individual things is said to have a property or feature. The thing or things is the "target" or "target item."

target class The population, or class, referred to in the conclusion of a generalizing argument.

target item *See* target.

term A word or an expression that refers to or denotes something.

terms of the comparison The entities referred to on both sides on an analogy.

tradition, "argument" from "Arguing" that a claim is true on the grounds that it is traditional to believe it is true.

truth-functional equivalence Two claims are truth-functionally equivalent if and only if they have exactly the same truth table.

truth-functional logic A system of logic that specifies the logical relationships among truth-functional claims—claims whose truth values depend solely upon the truth values of their simplest component parts. In particular, truth-functional logic deals with the logical functions of the terms "not," "and," "or," "if . . . then," and so on.

truth table A table that lists all possible combinations of truth values for the claim variables in a symbolized claim or argument and then specifies the truth value of the claim or claims for each of those possible combinations.

two wrongs make a right This pattern of fallacious reasoning: "It's acceptable for A to do X to B because B would do X to A," said where A's doing X to B is not necessary to prevent B's doing X to A.

utilitarianism The moral position unified around the basic idea that we should promote happiness as much as possible and weigh actions or derivative principles in terms of their utility in achieving this goal.

vague claim A claim that lacks sufficient precision to convey the information appropriate to its use.

valid argument *See* good deductive argument.

Venn diagram A graphic means of representing a categorical claim or categorical syllogism by assigning classes to overlapping circles. Invented by English mathematician John Venn (1834–1923).

virtue ethics The moral position unified around the basic idea that each of us should try to perfect a virtuous character that we exhibit in all actions.

weaseler An expression used to protect a claim from criticism by weakening it.

wishful thinking Accepting a claim because you want it to be true, or rejecting it because you don't want it to be true.

Answers, Suggestions, and Tips for Triangle Exercises

Chapter 1: Critical Thinking Basics

Exercise 1-1

1. An argument offers a reason or reasons for believing a claim is true. More technically, an argument consists of a conclusion and the premise or premises (the reason or reasons) said to support it.
4. False
7. All arguments have a conclusion, though the conclusion may not be explicitly stated.
10. It can be implied.
13. No
16. False
19. True
20. True

Exercise 1-3

1. Argument
4. No argument
7. No argument; Professor X is simply expressing an opinion. Saying that "there is good reason for increasing the class size" doesn't actually introduce a reason.
8. Argument. Conclusion: The dentist's billing practices are justified.
11. *Consumer Reports* seems to be suggesting that the watch may not really be water resistant, and giving a reason to support this suggestion. We'd call this an argument.

Exercise 1-4

1. No argument
4. Argument. Conclusion: Computers will never be able to converse intelligently through speech.
7. Argument. Conclusion: Fears that chemicals in teething rings and soft plastic toys may cause cancer may be justified.
10. No argument
13. No argument (Warren says that there are reasons for her conclusion, but she doesn't tell us what they are.)
16. No argument
19. No argument

Exercise 1-5

1. a. The other three claims in the paragraph are offered as *reasons* for the claim that Hank ought not to take the math course.

3. d. Answers a and b are given as reasons for believing claim d; they are premises of an argument and claim d is the conclusion. (Claim c misstates the issue.)

4. c. The remainder of the passage provides examples of what is claimed in c. The claims in which these examples appear function as premises for c.

13. b. There is a lot of information in this passage, but answer (b) is certainly the *main* issue of the selection. The easiest way to see this is to notice that almost all of the claims made in the passage support this one. We'd put answer (c) in second place.

14. c. Answers (a) and (b) don't capture the futility of the prison policy expressed in the passage; answer (d) goes beyond what is expressed in the passage.

15. b

16. b

20. c

Exercise 1-6

1. Whether police brutality happens very often
4. Whether there exists a world that is essentially independent of our minds
7. Whether a person who buys a computer should take some lessons
10. Whether Native Americans, as true conservationists, have something to teach readers about our relationship to the earth. There are other points made in the passage, but they are subsidiary to this one.

Exercise 1-7

1. There are two issues: whether they're going on Standard Time the next weekend and whether they'll need to set the clocks forward or back. Both speakers address both issues.
4. The issue is whether complaints about American intervention abroad are good or bad. Both speakers address this issue.

Exercise 1-8

1. Suburbanite misses Urbanite's point. Urbanite addresses the effects of the requirement; Suburbanite addresses the issue of whether he and his neighbors can afford to comply with it.
3. On the surface, it may seem that both Hands address the issue of whether a person such as One Hand can feel safe in her own home. But it's clear that One Hand's real issue is whether the large number of handguns makes one unsafe in

one's own home. Other Hand ignores this issue completely.

5. The issue for both parties is whether Fed-Up will be happier if he retires to Arkansas.

Exercise 1-9

The distinction used is between claims that address subjective issues and those that do not.

1. Not subjective
4. Subjective
7. Not subjective
10. Not subjective

Exercise 1-10

1. Not subjective
4. Not subjectived
7. Not subjective. Although this is not possible to resolve as a practical matter, we can at least imagine circumstances under which we could test for life on any given planet.
10. Subjective
13. This is clearly a question about a moral value judgment. This one is very controversial, of course, and if there were an agreed-upon method of settling the issue, it would have long since ceased to be so controversial. But controversy as such does not mean that the question raises a purely subjective issue; on the contrary, the controversy in this case suggests that at least some of the moral issues raised are not subjective. They are certainly not seen as subjective by those who take sides in the controversy.

Exercise 1-11

The subjective claims are all but 2, 4, 6, 8.

Exercise 1-12

1. The house, a two-story colonial-style building, burned to the ground.
4. The Coors Brewing Company began offering gay partners the same benefits as spouses in 1995.
7. McCovey was able to finish the assignment on time.
10. The Reverend Jesse Jackson's visit to Pakistan has been delayed due to lack of support from the Bush administration.
13. For two years the rapidly expanding global computer matrix had concerned Gates.

Exercise 1-13

1. No subjective elements present
4. No subjective elements present
7. The second sentence is arguably subjective, since the phrase "on the face of it" is something about which disagreements might be difficult to settle. On the other hand, the phrase "might be" is such a strong weaseler (see Chapter 4), one might say that this sentence commits to very little at all.
10. One might change the second sentence to read, "Those who felt character was important went on to elect one who some think has the feeblest intellect of any president in history."

Exercise 1-14

1. b
4. b
7. b
10. a

Exercise 1-15

1. Argument
4. Argument
7. Explanation
10. Explanation

Chapter 2: Clear Thinking, Critical Thinking, and Clear Writing

Exercise 2-1

In order of decreasing vagueness:

1. (d), (e), (b), (c), (f), and (a). Compare (e) and (b). If Eli and Sarah made plans for the future, then they certainly discussed it. But just discussing it is more vague—they could do that with or without making plans.
4. (c), (d), (e), (a), (b)

Exercise 2-2

1. a
4. b
7. **a.** But it's close.
10. b
15. a

Exercise 2-3

1. Too vague. Sure, you can't say exactly how much longer you want it cooked, but you can provide guidelines; for example, "Cook it until it isn't pink."
4. Not too vague.
7. Not too vague.

10. If this is the first time you are making frosting or if you are an inexperienced cook, this phrase is too vague.

Exercise 2-5

"Feeding" simply means "fertilizing" and is not too vague. "Frequently" is too vague. "No more than half" is not too vague. "Label-recommended amounts" is not too vague. "New year's growth begins" and "each bloom period ends" are pretty vague for a novice gardener, but because pinpoint timing apparently isn't crucial, the vagueness here is acceptable. "Similar" is too vague for a novice gardener. "Immediately after bloom" suggests that precise timing is important here, and we find the phrase too vague, at least for novices. "When the nights begin cooling off" is too vague even if precision in timing isn't terribly important.

Exercise 2-6

1. Twenty percent more than what? (You might wonder what "real dairy butter" is, but it's probably safe to assume that it's just plain old butter.)
4. This is not too bad, but the word "desert" covers a lot of territory—not all deserts are like the Sahara.
7. The comparison is okay, but don't jump to the conclusion that today's seniors are better students. Maybe the teachers are easier graders.
10. In the absence of absolute figures, this claim does not provide any information about how good attendance was (or about how brilliant the season was).

Exercise 2-7

1. Superior? In what way? More realistic character portrayal? Better expression of emotion? Probably the claim means only "I like Paltrow more than I like Blanchett."
4. Fine, but don't infer that they both grade the same. Maybe Smith gives 10 percent A's and 10 percent F's, 20 percent B's and 20 percent D's, and 40 percent C's, whereas Jones gives everyone a C. Who do you think is the more discriminating grader, given this breakdown?
7. Well, first of all, what is "long-distance"? Second, and more important, how is endurance measured? People do debate such issues, but the best way to begin a debate on this point would be by spelling out what you mean by "requires more endurance."
10. This is like a comparison of apples and oranges. How can the popularity of a movie be compared with the popularity of a song?

Exercise 2-8

1. The price-earnings ratio is a traditional (and reasonable) measure of a stock, and the figure is precise enough. Whether this is good enough reason to worry about the stock market is another matter; such a conclusion may not be supported by the price-earnings figure.
4. "Attend church regularly" is a bit vague; a person who goes to church each and every Christmas and Easter is a regular, although infrequent, attender. We don't find "majority" too vague in this usage.
7. "Contained more insights" is much too vague. The student needs to know more specifically what was the matter with his or her paper, or at least what was better about the roommate's paper.
10. These two sorts of things are much too different to be compared in this way. If you're starving, the chicken looks better; if you need to get from here to there, it's the Volkswagen. (This is the kind of question Moore likes to ask people. Nobody can figure out why.)

Exercise 2-10

1. The Raider tackle blocked the Giants linebacker.
4. How Therapy Can Help Victims of Torture
7. Susan's nose resembles Hillary Clinton's.
10. 6 Coyotes That Maul Girl Are Killed by Police
13. Second sentence: More than one disease can be carried and passed along to humans by a single tick.
16. We give to life good things.
19. Dunkelbrau—for those who crave the best-tasting real German beer
22. Jordan could write additional profound essays.
25. When she lay down to nap, she was disturbed by a noisy cow.
28. When Queen Elizabeth appeared before her troops, they all shouted "harrah."
31. AT&T, for as long as your business lasts.
32. This class might have had a member of the opposite sex for a teacher.
33. Married 10 times before, woman gets 9 years in prison for killing her husband.

Exercise 2-11

1. As a group
4. As a group
7. It's more likely that the claim refers to the Giants as a group, but it's possible that it refers to the play of individuals.
10. As individuals
12. Probably as individuals
15. Ambiguous. If the claim means that people are living longer than they used to, the reference is to people as individuals. If the claim means that the human race is getting older, then the reference is to people as a group. If the claim expresses the truism that to live is to age, then the reference is to people as individuals.

Exercise 2-12

1. "Piano" is defined analytically.
4. "Red planet" is defined by synonym. (This one is tricky because it looks like a definition by example. But there is only one red planet, so the phrase refers to exactly the same object as the word "Mars.")
8. "Chiaroscuro" is defined by synonym.
11. "Significant other" is defined by example—several of them.

Exercise 2-14

7, 6, 4, 1, 3, 2, 5

Exercise 2-15

1. Students should choose their majors with considerable care.
4. If a nurse can find nothing wrong with you in a preliminary examination, a physician will be recommended to you. However, in this city physicians wish to protect themselves by having you sign a waiver.
7. Soldiers should be prepared to sacrifice their lives for their comrades.
10. Petitioners over sixty should have completed form E-7.
13. Language is nature's greatest gift to humanity.
16. The proof must be acceptable to the rational individual.
17. The country's founders believed in the equality of all.
20. Athletes who want to play for the National Football League should have a good work ethic.
24. Most U.S. senators are men.
27. Mr. Macleod doesn't know it, but Ms. Macleod is a feminist.
30. To be a good politician, you have to be a good salesperson.

Exercise 2-16

In case you couldn't figure it out, the friend is a woman.

Chapter 3: Credibility

Exercise 3-5

Something like number 9 is probably true, given the huge, almost unimaginable difference in wealth between the richest and the poorest people on the planet, but we have no idea what the actual numbers are. We've seen number 12 going around the Web, but we don't know whether there's anything to it and we're not interested in conducting the appropriate experiments. We think the rest of these don't have much of a chance (although there are conspiracy theorists who seem to believe number 10.)

Exercise 3-8

1. In terms of expertise, we'd list (d), (c), and (b) first. Given what we've got to go on, we wouldn't assign expert status to either (a) or (e). We'd list all entries as likely to be fairly unbiased except for (a), which we would expect to be very biased.
3. Expertise: (b) first, then (a), then (c) and (d) about equal, and (e) last. We'd figure that (b) is most likely to be unbiased, with (c), (d), and (e) close behind; Choker would be a distant last on this scale. Her bad showing on the bias scale more than makes up for her high showing on the expertise scale.

Exercise 3-9

1. The most credible choices are either the FDA or *Consumer Reports*, both of which investigate health claims of the sort in question with reasonable objectivity. The company that makes the product is the least credible source because it is the most likely to be biased. The owner of the health food store may be very knowledgeable regarding nutrition but is not a credible source regarding drugs. Your local pharmacist can reasonably be regarded as credible, but he or she may not have access to as much information as the FDA or *CR*.
2. It would probably be a mistake to consider any of the individuals on this list more expert than the others, although different kinds and different levels of bias are fairly predictable on the parts of the victim's father, the NRA representative, and possibly the police chief. The senator might be expected to have access to more data that are relevant to the issue, but that would not in itself make his or her credibility much greater than that of the others. The problem here is that we are dealing with a value judgment that depends very heavily upon an individual's point of view rather than his or her expertise. What is important to this question is less the credibility of the person who gives us an answer than the strength of the supporting argument, if any, that he or she provides.
3. Although problem 2 hinges on a value judgment, this one calls for an interpretation of the original intent of a constitutional amendment. Here our choices would be either the Supreme

Court justice or the constitutional historian, with a slight preference for the latter because Supreme Court justices are concerned more with constitutional issues as they have been interpreted by other courts than with original intent. The NRA representative is paid to speak for a certain point of view and would be the least credible in our view. The senator and the U.S. President would fall somewhere in between: Both might reasonably be expected to be knowledgeable about constitutional issues, but much less so than our first two choices.

Exercise 3-10

1. Professor Jensen would possess the greatest degree of credibility and authority on (d), (f), and (h), and, compared with someone who had not lived in both places, on (i).

Exercise 3-12

1. We'd accept this as probably true—but probably only *approximately* true. It's difficult to be precise about such matters; Campbell will most likely lay off *about* 650 workers, including *about* 175 at its headquarters.
8. We'd accept this as likely.
12. No doubt cats that live indoors do tend to live longer than cats that are subject to the perils of outdoor life. If statistics on how much longer indoor cats live on the average were available, we'd expect the manufacturer to know them. But we suspect that such statistics would be difficult to establish (and probably not worth the effort), and we therefore have little confidence in the statistic cited here.
20. It's quite possible, though the Defamer blog bills itself as "the Hollywood gossip sheet" (which suggests it trades in rumor and innuendo) and does not say whether the request, if it was really made, was granted. The Defamer may be fun, scurrilous reading, and may even get the information correct sometimes, but it's not a reliable source.

Chapter 4: Persuasion Through Rhetoric: Common Devices and Techniques

Exercise 4-1

2. a
4. b
7. a
10. d
12. c
13. a
15 T

Exercise 4-2

(1) hyperbole (in Chapter 6 we'll call this "straw man"), (2) dysphemism, (3) not a rhetorical device, (4) dysphemism, (5) not a rhetorical device, (6) dysphemism

Exercise 4-3

(1) dysphemism, (2) dysphemism, (3) hyperbole, (4) weaseler, (5) proof surrogate, (6) not a downplayer in this context, (7) loaded question

Exercise 4-10

1. The quotation marks downplay the quality of the school.
4. Persuasive definition
6. No rhetorical device present
8. "Gaming" is a euphemism for "gambling."
11. "Clearly" is a proof surrogate; the final phrase is hyperbole.
14. "Luddites" (those opposed to technological progress) is a rhetorical analogy; the entire passage is designed to suggest that cable and satellite TV are near universal in acceptance and use and to characterize in a negative light those (few?) who haven't become subscribers.

Exercise 4-12

1. "Japan, Inc." is a dysphemism.
4. "Getting access" is a euphemism, and, in this context, so is "constituents." We'll bet it isn't just *any* old constituent who gets the same kind of "access" as big campaign contributors.
7. The last sentence is hyperbolic.
10. (We really like this one.) "Even," in the first sentence, is innuendo, insinuating that members of Congress are more difficult to embarrass than others. The remainder is another case of innuendo with a dash of downplaying. Although it's a first-class example, it's different from the usual ones. Mellinkoff makes you think that Congress *merely* passes a law in response to the situation. But stop and think for a moment: Aside from the odd congressional hearing or impeachment trial, *all that Congress can do is pass laws!* So Mellinkoff's charge really should not be seen as belittling Congress at all.
13. "As you know" is a variety of proof surrogate. The remainder is a rhetorical analogy, in this case a comparison.

15. Proof surrogate. A claim that there are "two kinds of arguments" in favor of a multiverse does not actually provide those reasons.
18. Lots of them here! To begin, "orgy" is a dysphemism; "self-appointed" is a downplayer. The references to yurts and teepees is ridicule, and "grant-maintained" is a downplayer. The rest of it employs a heavy dose of sarcasm.

Chapter 5: More Rhetorical Devices: Psychological and Related Fallacies

Exercise 5-2

1. "Argument" from popularity
4. "Argument" from pity
7. Smokescreen/red herring; rather than provide support for the claim that the president's plan for Social Security is "pretty good," Republican changes the subject and accuses the Democrats of not even offering a plan.
10. "Argument" from outrage. There is also an example of straw man in the last sentence—we'll meet straw man in Chapter 6.
12. Subjectivism
13. Rationalism (almost certainly)

Exercise 5-3

1. Not very.
3. Very relevant. A popular automobile may have continued support from its maker, and this can be advantageous to the owner of such a car.
7. It is a relevant consideration if you want to be polite or if you want to criticize the novel when you speak to your friend. But note that it would not be relevant if the issue had been whether the novel was well-written.
10. Relevant, especially if you have reason to think that Ebert likes or dislikes the same kinds of movies you do, or if you have opposite views (then you can avoid movies he recommends).

Exercise 5-5

1. Scare tactics
4. Apple polishing, with a touch of peer pressure
7. No fallacy
10. Smokescreen/red herring

Exercise 5-6

1. No fallacy
4. Peer pressure
7. Apple polishing
10. "Argument" from outrage

Exercise 5-7

1. Scare tactics
4. Scare tactics. Just how fallacious this passage is depends largely on one's assessment of how likely one is to be among the 250 who die from accidents on a given day. In any case, it is not an argument for buying *this company's* accident insurance.
7. Two wrongs make a right
8. Smokescreen/red herring
10. Smokescreen/red herring
14. "Argument" from common practice
17. The most obvious fallacy present here is the scare tactics we see from Rep. Welker. He is also guilty of a slippery slope fallacy, discussed in the next chapter. Under one interpretation of the situation, one might also find Rep. Paccione guilty of a red herring, since the original point of the news conference was whether there should be a constitutional amendment barring gays and lesbians from marrying and Rep. Paccione introduces a separate issue having to do with health care. But her claim—that as long as the health care issue remains unsolved it is not good policy to argue about other matters such as same-sex marriage—is relevant. Whether it's true is another matter; argument would be necessary to establish that.

Chapter 6: Ad Hominem and More Fallacies

Exercise 6-2

1. Begging the question
4. Straw man
7. Straw man
10. Line-drawing fallacy (false dilemma)

Exercise 6-3

1. Inconsistency ad hominem
4. Inconsistency ad hominem
7. Circumstantial ad hominem
11. Personal attack ad hominem

Exercise 6-4

1. Circumstantial ad hominem
4. Straw man (Jeanne responds as if Carlos wanted to sleep until noon). Can also be analyzed as false dilemma ("Either we get up right now, at 4:00 A.M., or we sleep until noon.")
7. This begs the question. The conclusion merely restates the premise.
10. False dilemma
13. Misplaced burden of proof

Exercise 6-5

1. This is an example of burden of proof. Yes, it is indeed slightly different from the varieties explained in the text, and here's what's going on. The speaker is requiring proof of a sort that *cannot be obtained*—actually *seeing* smoke cause a cancer. So he or she is guilty of one type of "inappropriate burden of proof."
4. This is false dilemma because Sugarman's alternatives are certainly not the only ones. Notice that he is giving *no argument* against the Chicago study; he is simply using the false dilemma to deny the study's conclusion.
7. Inconsistency ad hominem
10. This is a case of misplaced burden of proof. The speaker maintains that the government is violating the law. The burden of proof therefore falls on the speaker to justify his or her opinion. Instead of doing that, he or she acts as if the fact that officials haven't disproved the claim is proof that the claim is true.

Exercise 6-6

1. Assuming that the sheriff's department has more than two officers, the speaker is misrepresenting her opponent's position. Straw man.
4. Misplaced burden of proof
7. Perfectionist fallacy (false dilemma)
10. This is an ad hominem. It rides the border between personal attack and the circumstantial variety.

Exercise 6-7

1. Ad hominem: inconsistency. You hear this kind of thing a lot.
4. Ad hominem: personal attack
7. Slippery slope
10. Ad hominem: personal attack

Exercise 6-9

1. d
4. b
7. a
10. b

Exercise 6-10

1. c
4. c
7. b
10. c

Exercise 6-11

1. b
4. b
7. e
10. a

Exercise 6-12

1. Straw man, smokescreen/red herring
4. No fallacy. Notice that the passage is designed to attack the company, not the company's product. The wages it pays are relevant to the point at issue.
7. No fallacy
10. False dilemma
13. Genetic fallacy
16. Line-drawing fallacy (false dilemma)
19. Inconsistency ad hominem

Exercise 6-16

1. Perfectionist fallacy (false dilemma)
5. Apple polishing
9. "Argument" from pity and "argument" from outrage
13. Two wrongs; a case can easily be made for common practice as well.
16. Straw man, technically, but this is also ridicule.

Exercise 6-17

1. This is an example of misplaced burden of proof. The fact that the airplane builders *might* be cutting corners is not evidence that they are *in fact* cutting corners. The speaker's contention that the manufacturers may be tempted to cut corners may be good grounds for scrutinizing their operations, but it's not good grounds for the conclusion that they really are cutting corners.
4. Yes—this is clearly fallacious. Bush's sweeping generalization would be irrelevant to the Democrats' claim even if it were true. That it isn't true makes the response a straw man. One can also see this as a smokescreen.
5. The quoted remark from Harris is not relevant to the conclusion drawn in this passage. This passage doesn't fit neatly into any of our categories, although ad hominem would not be a bad choice. Notice a possible ambiguity that may come into play: "Having an impact" might mean simply that Harris wants his work to be noticed by "movers and shakers"—or it could mean that he wishes to sway people toward a certain political view. It's likely that he intended his remark the first way, but it's being taken in the second way in this passage.

9. This is a borderline circumstantial ad hominem. It certainly does not follow that Seltzer and Sterling are making false claims from the fact that they are being paid by an interested party. But remember the cautions from Chapter 3: Expertise can be bought, and we should be very cautious about accepting claims made by experts who are paid by someone who has a vested interest in the outcome of a controversy.

Chapter 7: The Anatomy and Varieties of Arguments

Exercise 7-1

1. a. Premise; b. Premise; c. Conclusion
2. a. Premise; b. Premise; c. Conclusion
3. a. Conclusion; b. Premise
4. a. Premise; b. Premise; c. Conclusion
5. a. Premise; b. Conclusion; c. Premise; d. Premise

Exercise 7-2

1. Premise: All Communists are Marxists.
Conclusion: All Marxists are Communists.
4. Premise: That cat is used to dogs.
Conclusion: Probably she won't be upset if you bring home a new dog for a pet.
7. Premise: Presbyterians are not fundamentalists.
Premise: All born-again Christians are fundamentalists.
Conclusion: No born-again Christians are Presbyterians.
10. Premise: If we've got juice at the distributor, the coil isn't defective.
Premise: If the coil isn't defective, then the problem is in the ignition switch.
[Unstated premise: We've got juice at the distributor.]
Conclusion: The problem is in the ignition switch.

Exercise 7-3

1. Conclusion: There is a difference in the octane ratings between the two grades of gasoline.
4. Conclusion: Scrub jays can be expected to be aggressive when they're breeding.
7. Conclusion: Dogs are smarter than cats.
10. Unstated conclusion: She is not still interested in me.

Exercise 7-4

1. Separate arguments
3. Separate arguments
6. Separate arguments
9. Separate arguments
12. Separate arguments
15. Single argument with more than one premise

Exercise 7-5

1. Single argument with more than one premise
4. Single argument with more than one premise; one premise is unstated: What's true for rats is probably true for humans.
8. Separate arguments
10. Separate arguments

Exercise 7-6

1. To explain
4. To explain
7. To explain
9. To argue

Exercise 7-7

3. Valid; true
6. False
9. False

Exercise 7-8

(Refer to Exercise 7-2)

1. Invalid
4. Invalid
7. Valid
10. Valid

(Refer to Exercise 7-3)

1. Invalid
4. Invalid
7. The unstated premise, "Being more easily trained is a *sure* sign of greater intelligence" would make the argument valid. An unstated premise such as "Being more easily trained is a *good* sign of greater intelligence" would make the argument fairly strong but invalid.
10. Valid

Exercise 7-9

1. Probably true; had "out of order" been written in pencil on the meter, we'd have a different opinion, since most of the meters in our town have those words scrawled on them.
5. Probably true; a restaurant that does a good job on these three different kinds of entrees will probably do a good job on the rest.
9. Probably true; it's possible that the killer cleaned up very thoroughly, but it's more likely that the body was brought from somewhere else.
12. True beyond a reasonable doubt; it may be that consumption will drop in the future or that dis-

covery of new reserves will increase, but as long as consumption at some level continues, *eventually* all the oil will be used up.

Exercise 7-10

1. Assumed premise: All well-mannered people had a good upbringing.
4. Assumed conclusion: He will not drive recklessly.
7. Assumed premise: All dogs that scratch a lot have fleas or dry skin.
10. Assumed premise: Every poet whose work appears in many Sierra Club publications is one of America's outstanding poets.

Exercise 7-11

1. Assumed premise: Most people who are well-mannered had a good upbringing.
4. Assumed conclusion: He will drive safely.
7. Assumed premise: Most dogs that scratch a lot have fleas or dry skin. (Or: When this dog scratches a lot, he usually has either fleas or dry skin.)
10. Assumed premise: Most poets whose work appears in many Sierra Club publications are among American's outstanding poets.

Exercise 7-12

1. Assumed premise: All stores that sell only genuine leather goods have high prices.
4. Assumed premise: No ornamental fruit trees bear edible fruit.
7. Assumed premise: No former professional wrestler could be a very effective governor.
10. Assumed premise: If population studies show that smoking causes lung cancer, then all smokers will get lung cancer.

Exercise 7-13

1. Assumed premise: Most stores that sell only genuine leather goods have high prices.
4. Assumed premise: Few ornamental fruit trees bear edible fruit.
7. Assumed premise: Few people who were professional wrestlers could be very effective governors.
10. Assumed premise: If population studies show that smoking causes lung cancer, then most smokers will get lung cancer.

Exercise 7-14

1.

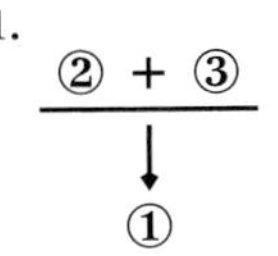

4.

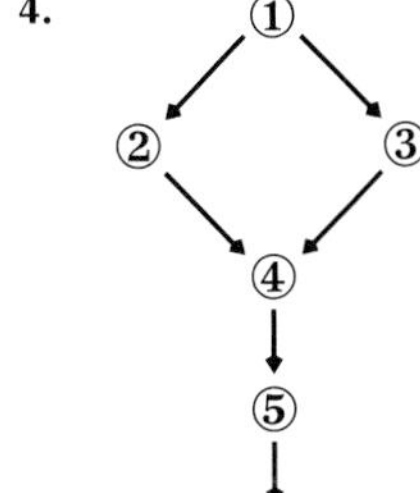

Exercise 7-15

(See Exercise 7-2)

1. ① All Communists are Marxists.
② All Marxists are Communists.

4. ① That cat is used to dogs.
② She won't be upset if you bring home a new dog for a pet.

7. ① Presbyterians are not fundamentalists.
② All born-again Christians are fundamentalists.
③ No born-again Christians are Presbyterians.

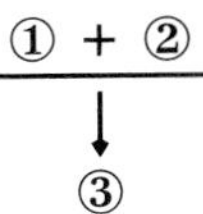

10. ① If we've got juice at the distributor, the coil isn't defective.
② If the coil isn't defective, then the problem is in the ignition switch.
③ The problem is in the ignition switch.

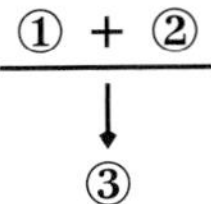

(See Exercise 7-3)

1. ① The engine pings every time we use the regular unleaded gasoline.
② The engine doesn't ping when we use super.
③ There is a difference in octane ratings between the two.

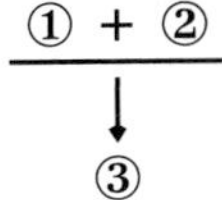

4. ① When blue jays are breeding, they become very aggressive.
② Scrub jays are very similar to blue jays.
③ Scrub jays can be expected to be aggressive when breeding.

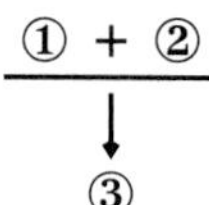

7. ① It's easier to train dogs than cats.
② Dogs are smarter than cats.

① → ②

10. ① If she were still interested in me, she would have called.
② She didn't call.
③ [Unstated] She's not still interested in me.

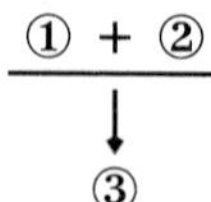

(See Exercise 7-4)

6. ① You're overwatering your lawn.
② There are mushrooms growing around the base of the tree.
③ Mushrooms are a sure sign of overwatering.
④ There are worms on the ground.
⑤ Worms come up when the earth is oversaturated.

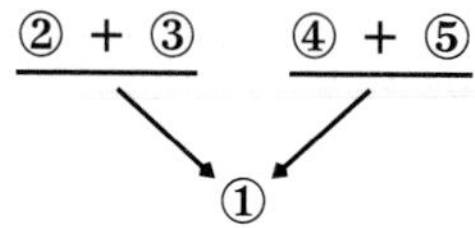

9. ① If you drive too fast, you're more likely to get a ticket.
② (If you drive too fast,) you're also more likely to get into an accident.
③ You shouldn't drive too fast.

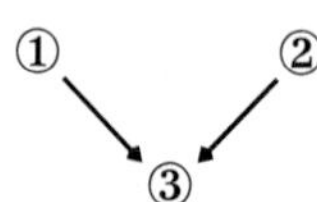

12. ① You should consider installing a solarium.
② Installing a solarium can get you a tax credit.
③ Installing a solarium can reduce your heating bill.
④ Installing a solarium correctly can help you cool your house in the summer.

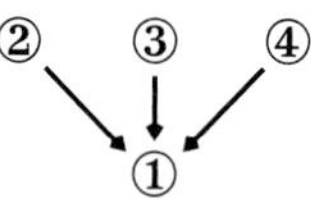

15. ① We must paint the house now.
② If we don't, we'll have to paint it next summer.
③ If we have to paint it next summer, we'll have to cancel our trip.
④ It's too late to cancel our trip.

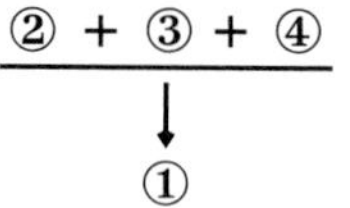

(See Exercise 7-5)

1. ① All mammals are warm-blooded creatures.
② All whales are mammals.
③ All whales are warm-blooded creatures.

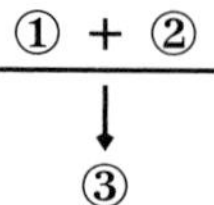

4. ① Rats that have been raised . . . have brains that weigh more. . . .
② The brains of humans will weigh more if humans are placed in intellectually stimulating environments.

8. ① The mayor now supports the initiative for the Glen Royale subdivision.
② Last year the mayor proclaimed strong opposition to further development in the river basin.
③ Glen Royale will add to congestion.
④ Glen Royale will add to pollution.
⑤ Glen Royale will make the lines longer at the grocery.
⑥ [Unstated] The mayor should not support the Glen Royale subdivision.

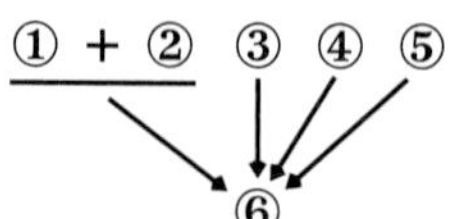

10. ① Jesse Brown is a good person for your opening in Accounting.

(2) He's as sharp as they come.
(3) He has a solid background in bookkeeping.
(4) He's good with computers.
(5) He's reliable.
(6) He'll project the right image.
(7) He's a terrific golfer.
(8) I know him personally.

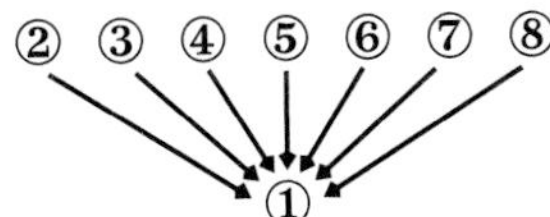

Exercise 7-16

1. (1) Your distributor is the problem.
(2) There's no current at the spark plugs.
(3) If there's no current at the plugs, then either your alternator is shot or your distributor is defective.
(4) [Unstated] Either your alternator is shot or your distributor is defective.
(5) If the problem were in the alternator, then your dash warning light would be on.
(6) The light isn't on.

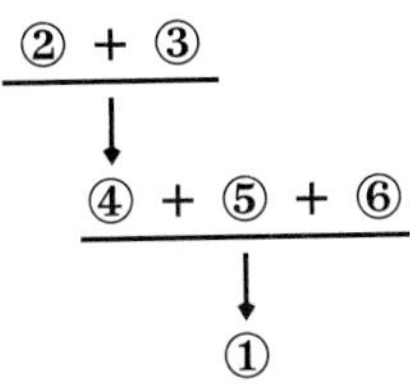

4. (1) They really ought to build a new airport.
(2) It [a new airport] would attract more business to the area.
(3) The old airport is overcrowded and dangerous.

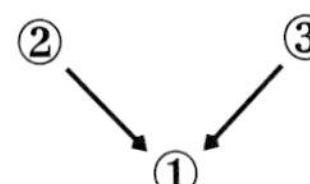

Note: Claim number 3 could be divided into two separate claims, one about overcrowding and one about danger. This would be important if the overcrowding were clearly offered as a reason for the danger.

Exercise 7-17

1. (1) Cottage cheese will help you to be slender.
(2) Cottage cheese will help you to be youthful.
(3) Cottage cheese will help you to be more beautiful.
(4) Enjoy cottage cheese often.

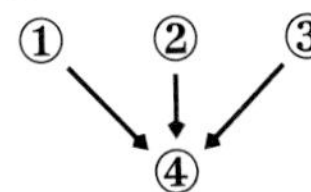

4. (1) The idea of a free press in America is a joke.
(2) The nation's advertisers control the media.
(3) Advertisers, through fear of boycott, can dictate programming.
(4) Politicians and editors shiver at the thought of a boycott.
(5) The situation is intolerable.
(6) I suggest we all listen to NPR and public television.

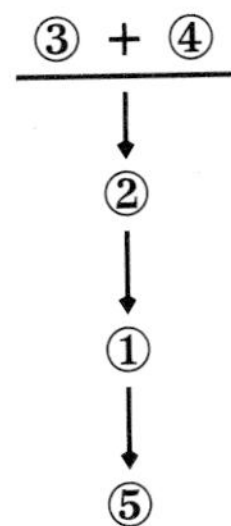

Note: The writer may see claim (1) as the final conclusion and claim (5) as his comment upon it. Claim (6) is probably a comment on the results of the argument, although it too could be listed as a further conclusion.

7. (1) Consumers ought to be concerned about the FTC's dropping the rule requiring markets to stock advertised items.
(2) Shoppers don't like being lured to stores and not finding advertised products.
(3) The rule costs at least $200 million and produces no more than $125 million in benefits.
(4) The figures boil down to a few cents per shopper over time.
(5) The rule requires advertised sale items to be on hand in reasonable numbers.

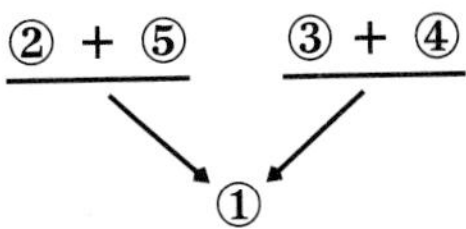

10. (1) Well-located, sound real estate is the safest investment in the world.
(2) Real estate is not going to disappear as can dollars in savings accounts.
(3) Real estate values are not lost because of inflation.
(4) Property values tend to increase at a pace at least equal to the rate of inflation.
(5) Most homes have appreciated at a rate greater than the inflation rate. . . .

13. ① About 100 million Americans are producing data on the Internet. . . . .
② Each user is tracked so private information is available in electronic form.
③ One Web site . . . promises, for seven dollars, to scan . . . etc.
④ The combination of capitalism and technology poses a threat to our privacy.

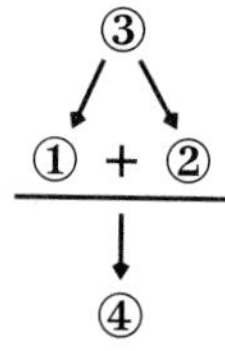

16. ① Measure A is consistent with the City's General Plan and city policies. . . .
② A "yes" vote will affirm the wisdom of well-planned, orderly growth. . . .
③ Measure A substantially reduces the amount of housing previously approved for Rancho Arroyo.
④ Measure A increases the number of parks and amount of open space.
⑤ Measure A significantly enlarges and enhances Bidwell Park.
⑥ Approval of Measure A will require dedication of 130.8 acres to Bidwell Park.
⑦ Approval of Measure A will require the developer to dedicate seven park sites.
⑧ Approval of Measure A will create 53 acres of landscaped corridors and greenways.
⑨ Approval of Measure A will preserve existing arroyos and protect sensitive plant habitats. . . .
⑩ Approval of Measure A will create junior high school and church sites.
⑪ Approval of Measure A will plan villages with 2,927 dwellings.
⑫ Approval of Measure A will provide onsite job opportunities and retail services.
⑬ [Unstated conclusion:] You should vote for Measure A.

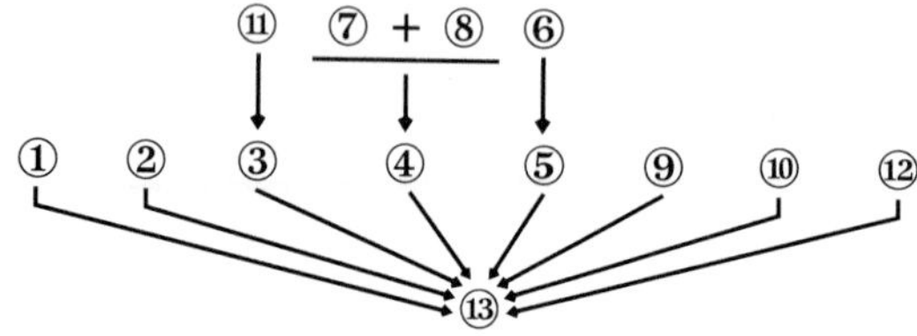

19. 1 In regard to your editorial, "Crime bill wastes billions," let me set you straight. [Your position is mistaken.]
② Your paper opposes mandatory life sentences for criminals convicted of three violent crimes, and you whine about how criminals' rights might be violated.
③ Yet you also want to infringe on a citizen's rights to keep and bear arms.
④ You say you oppose life sentences for three-time losers because judges couldn't show any leniency toward the criminals no matter how trivial the crime.
⑤ What is your definition of trivial, busting an innocent child's skull with a hammer?

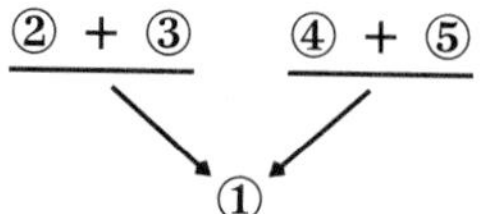

20. ① Freedom means choice.
② This is a truth antiporn activists always forget when they argue for censorship.
③ In their fervor to impose their morality, groups like Enough Is Enough cite extreme examples of pornography, such as child porn, suggesting that they are available in video stores.
④ This is not the way it is.
⑤ Most of this material portrays, not actions such as this, but consensual sex between adults.
⑥ The logic used by Enough Is Enough is that if something can somehow hurt someone, it must be banned.
⑦ They don't apply this logic to more harmful substances, such as alcohol or tobacco.
⑧ Women and children are more adversely affected by drunken driving and secondhand smoke than by pornography.
⑨ Few Americans would want to ban alcohol or tobacco even though they kill hundreds of thousands of people each year.
⑩ [Unstated conclusion] Enough Is Enough is inconsistent.
⑪ [Unstated conclusion] Enough Is Enough's antiporn position is incorrect.

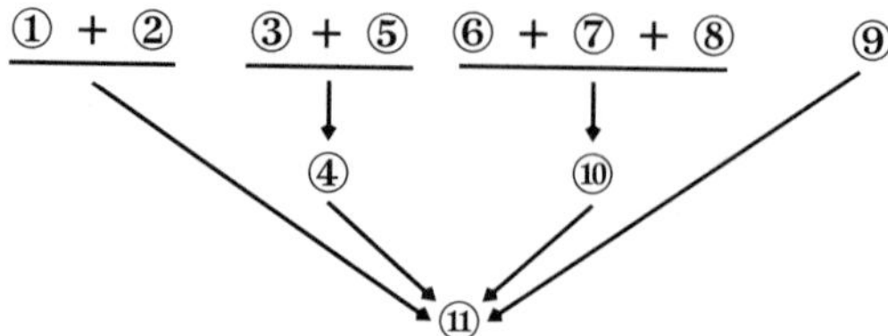

Chapter 8: Deductive Arguments I: Categorical Logic

Exercise 8-1

1. All salamanders are lizards.
4. All members of the suborder Ophidia are snakes.
7. All alligators are reptiles.
10. All places there are snakes are places there are frogs.
13. All people who got raises are vice presidents
15. Some home movies are things that are as boring as dirt.
16. All people identical with Socrates are Greeks.
19. All examples of salt are things that preserve meat.

Exercise 8-2

1. No students who wrote poor exams are students who were admitted to the program.
4. Some first-basemen are right-handed people.
7. All passers are people who made at least 50 percent.
10. Some prior days are days like this day.
13. Some holidays are holidays that fall on Saturday.
16. All people who pass the course are people who pass this test. Or: No people who fail this test are people who pass the course.
19. All times they will let you enroll are times you've paid the fee.

Exercise 8-3

1. Translation: Some anniversaries are not happy occasions. (True)
   Corresponding A-claim: All anniversaries are happy occasions. (False)
   Corresponding E-claim: No anniversaries are happy occasions. (Undetermined)
   Corresponding I-claim: Some anniversaries are happy occasions. (Undetermined)
4. Translation: Some allergies are things that can kill you. (True)
   Corresponding A-claim: All allergies are things that can kill you. (Undetermined)
   Corresponding E-claim: No allergies are things that can kill you. (False)
   Corresponding O-claim: Some allergies are not things that can kill you. (Undetermined)

Exercise 8-4

1. No non-Christians are non-Sunnis. (Not equivalent)
4. Some Christians are not Kurds. (Not equivalent)
7. All Muslims are Shiites. (Not equivalent)
10. All Muslims are non-Christians. (Equivalent)

Exercise 8-5

1. Some students who scored well on the exam are not students who didn't write poor essays. (Equivalent)
4. No students who were not admitted to the program are students who scored well on the exam. (Not equivalent)
7. All people whose automobile ownership is not restricted are people who don't live in the dorms. (Equivalent)
10. All first basemen are people who aren't right-handed. (Equivalent)

Exercise 8-6

2. All encyclopedias are nondefinitive works.
4. No sailboats are sloops.

Exercise 8-7

Translations of the lettered claims:

a. Some people who have been tested are not people who can give blood.

b. Some people who can give blood are not people who have been tested.

c. All people who can give blood are people who have been tested.

d. Logically equivalent to: "Some people who have been tested are people who cannot give blood" [converse]. Logically equivalent to: "Some people who have been tested are not people who can give blood" [obverse of the converse].

e. Logically equivalent to: "All people who have been tested are people who cannot give blood." Logically equivalent to: "No people who have been tested are people who can give blood" [obverse].

2. Logically equivalent to: "All people who have not been tested are people who cannot give blood." Logically equivalent to: "All people who can give blood are people who have been tested" [contraposition], which is equivalent to c.
3. Logically equivalent to: "No people who have been tested are people who can give blood," which is equivalent to e.

Exercise 8-8

1. Obvert (a) to get "some Slavs are not Europeans."
4. Obvert the conversion of (b) to get "Some members of the club are not people who took the exam."
7. Contrapose (a) to get "All people who will not be allowed to perform are people who did not arrive late." Translate (b) into "Some people who did not arrive late are people who will not be allowed to perform" and convert: "Some

people who will not be allowed to perform are people who did not arrive late."

10. Convert the obverse of (b) to get "No decks that will play digital tape are devices that are equipped for radical oversampling."

Exercise 8-9

1. Invalid (this would require the conversion of an A-claim).
4. Valid (the converse of an I-claim is logically equivalent to the original claim).
7. Valid (the premise is the obverse of the conclusion).
10. The premise translates to "Some people in uniform are people not allowed to play." Thus (translating the conclusion) "Some people not allowed to play are people not in uniform" does not follow and the argument is invalid. But the subcontrary of the conclusion ("Some people not allowed to play are people in uniform"), does follow since this claim, and the premise, are the converse of each other and therefore logically equivalent.

Exercise 8-10

1. The converse of (a) is the contradictory of (b), so (b) is false.
3. The contrapositive of (a) is a true O-claim that corresponds to (b); and that means that (b), its contradictory, is false.
5. Contrapose (a) to get "Some unproductive factories are not plants not for automobiles." Then obvert (b) to get "No unproductive factories are plants not for automobiles." Because (a) is true, (b) is undetermined.
9. The translation of (a) is "Some people enrolled in the class are not people who will get a grade." The obverse of the converse of (b) is "Some people enrolled in the class are not people who will get a grade." Wow! They're identical! So (b), too, is true.

Exercise 8-11

1. Valid:
All P are G.
No G are S.
No S are P.

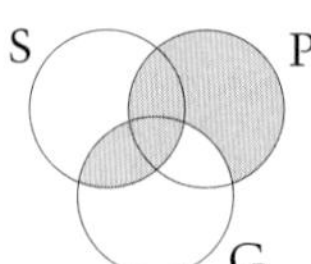

4. Invalid:
All T are E.
All T-T are E. (T = times Louis is tired, etc.)
All T-T are T. (T-T = times identical with today)

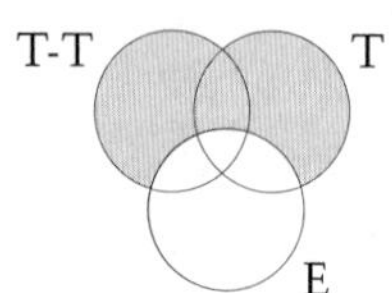

7. Valid:
All H are S.
No P are S.
No P are H.

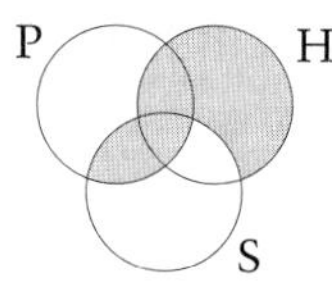

10. Invalid:
All C are R.
All V are C.
No R are V.

(Note: There is more than one way to turn this into standard form. Instead of turning nonresidents into residents, you can do the opposite.)

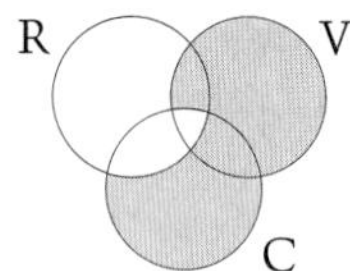

Exercise 8-12

1. No blank disks are disks that contain data.
Some blank disks are formatted disks.
Some formatted disks are not disks that contain data.
Valid:

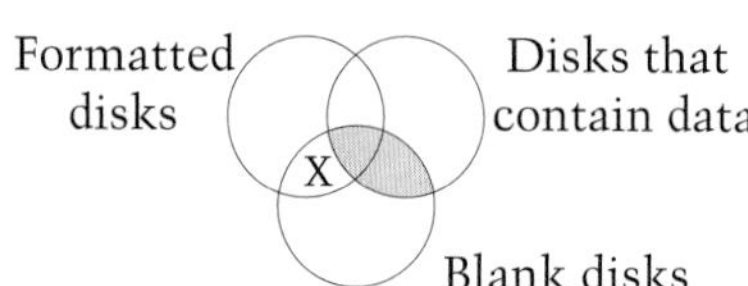

4. All tobacco products are substances damaging to people's health.
Some tobacco products are addictive substances.
Some addictive substances are substances damaging to people's health.
Valid:

Addictive substances
Substances damaging to people's health
X
Tobacco products

7. All people who may vote are stockholders in the company.
No people identical with Mr. Hansen are people who may vote.
No people identical with Mr. Hansen are stockholders in the company.
Invalid:

Mr. Hansen
Stockholders in the company
People who may vote

Note: Remember that claims with individuals as subject terms are treated as A- or E-claims.

10. After converting, then obverting the conclusion:
    No arguments with false premises are sound arguments.
    Some arguments with false premises are valid arguments.

    Some valid arguments are not sound arguments.
    Valid:

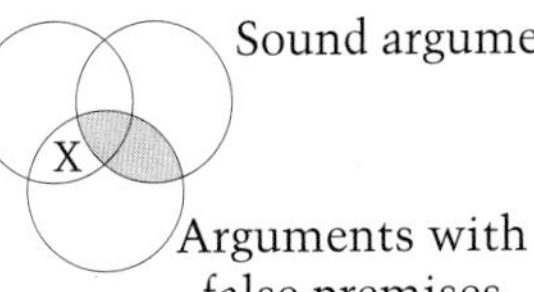

Exercise 8-13

1. A
4. B

Exercise 8-14

1. a
4. b

Exercise 8-15

1. 0
4. 1

Exercise 8-16

1. c
4. c
7. b
10. e

Exercise 8-17

1. All T are F.
   Some F are Z.

   Some Z are T.
   Invalid; breaks rule 2
4. There are two versions of this item, depending on whether you take the first premise to say *no* weightlifters use motor skills or only some don't. We'll do it both ways:

   All A are M.
   No W are M.

   No W are A.
   Valid

   All A are M.
   Some W are not M.

   No W are A.
   Invalid; breaks rule 3
7. Using I = people who lift papers from the Internet
   C = people who are cheating themselves
   L = people who lose in the long run

   All I are C.
   All C are L.

   All I are C.
   Valid
10. D = people who dance the whole night
    W = people who waste time
    G = people whose grades will suffer

    All D are W.
    All W are G.

    All D are G.
    Valid

Exercise 8-18

(Refer to Exercise 8-11 for these first four items.)

2. (Given in standard form in the text)
   Invalid: breaks rule 2
5. All voters are citizens.
   Some citizens are not residents.

   Some voters are not residents.
   Invalid: breaks rule 2
7. All halyards are lines that attach to sails.
   No painters are lines that attach to sails.

   No painters are halyards.
   Valid
8. All systems that can give unlimited storage . . . are systems with removable disks.
   No standard hard disks are systems with removable disks.

   No standard hard disks are systems that can give unlimited storage. . . .
   Valid

(Refer to Exercise 8-12 for the next four items.)

2. After obverting both premises, we get:
   No ears with white tassels are ripe ears.
   Some ripe ears are not ears with full-sized kernels.

   Some ears with full-sized kernels are not ears with white tassels.
   Invalid: breaks rule 1
5. After obverting the second premise:
   Some CD players are machines with 24x sampling.
   All machines with 24x sampling are machines that cost at least $100.

   Some CD players are machines that cost at least $100.
   Valid
7. All people who may vote are people with stock.
   No [people identical with Mr. Hansen] are people who may vote.

   No [people identical with Mr. Hansen] are people with stock.
   Invalid: breaks rule 3 (major term)
8. No off-road vehicles are vehicles allowed in the unimproved portion of the park.
   Some off-road vehicles are not four-wheel-drive vehicles.

   Some four-wheel-drive vehicles are allowed in the unimproved portion of the park.
   Invalid: breaks rule 1

Exercise 8-19

1. A = athletes; B = baseball players; C = basketball players
   Some A are not B.
   Some B are not C.
   Some A are not C.
   Invalid: breaks rule 1
3. T = worlds identical to this one; B = the best of all possible worlds; M = mosquito-containing worlds
   No B are M.
   All T are M.
   No T are B.
   Valid
6. P = plastic furniture; C = cheap furniture; L = their new lawn furniture
   All L are P.
   All P are C.
   All L are C.
   Valid
9. D = people on the district tax roll; C = citizens; E = eligible voters
   All D are C.
   All E are C.
   All D are E.
   Invalid: breaks rule 2
12. C = people identical to Cobweb; L = liberals; T = officials who like to raise taxes
    All C are L.
    All L are T.
    All C are T.
    Valid
17. P = poll results; U = unnewsworthy items; I = items receiving considerable attention from the networks
    All P are I.
    Some P are U.
    Some I are U.
    Valid
18. E = people who understand that the Earth goes around the Sun; W = people who understand what causes winter and summer; A = American adults
    All W are E.
    Some A are not E.
    Some A are not W.
    Valid
20. N = the pornographic novels of "Madame Toulouse"; W = works with sexual depictions patently offensive to community standards and with no serious literary, artistic, political, or scientific value; O = works that can be banned as obscene since 1973
    All O are W.
    All N are W.
    All N are O.
    Invalid: breaks rule 2

Exercise 8-20

1. True. A syllogism with neither an A- nor an E-premise would have (I) two I-premises, which would violate rule 2; or (II) two O-premises, which would violate rule 1; or (III) an I-premise and an O-premise. Alternative (III) would require a negative conclusion by rule 1, and a negative conclusion would require premises that distribute at least two terms, the middle term and (by rule 3) at least one other. Because an I-premise and an O-premise collectively distribute only one term, alternative (III) won't work either.
4. True. An AIE syllogism whose middle term is the subject of the A-premise breaks exactly two rules. If the middle term is the predicate of the A-premise, this syllogism breaks three rules.

Exercise 8-23

1. L = ladybugs; A = aphid-eaters; G = good things to have in your garden
   All L are A.
   [All A are G.]
   All L are G.
   Valid
4. S = self-tapping screws; B = boons to the construction industry; P = things that make it possible to screw things together without drilling pilot holes
   All S are P.
   [All P are B.]
   All S are B.
   Valid

Chapter 9: Deductive Arguments II: Truth-Functional Logic

Exercise 9-1

1. $Q \rightarrow P$
2. $Q \rightarrow P$
3. $P \rightarrow Q$
4. $Q \rightarrow P$
5. $(P \rightarrow Q) \& (Q \rightarrow P)$

Exercise 9-2

1. $(P \rightarrow Q) \& R$
2. $P \rightarrow (Q \& R)$
   Notice that the only difference between (1) and (2) is the location of the comma. But the symbolizations have two different truth tables, so moving the comma actually changes the mean-

ing of the claim. And we'll bet you thought that commas were there only to tell you when to breathe when you read aloud.

5. P → (Q → R). Compare (5) with (3).

11. ~C → S

12. ~(C → S)

16. S → ~C. Ordinarily, the word *but* indicates a conjunction, but in this case it is present only for emphasis—*only if* is the crucial truth-functional phrase.

20. ~(F ∨ S) or (~F & ~S). Notice that when you "move the negation sign in," you have to change the wedge to an ampersand (or vice versa). Don't treat the negation sign as you would treat a minus sign in algebra class, or you'll wind up in trouble.

Exercise 9-3

1.

P	Q	R	(P → Q)	(P → Q) & R
T	T	T	T	T
T	T	F	T	F
T	F	T	F	F
T	F	F	F	F
F	T	T	T	T
F	T	F	T	F
F	F	T	T	T
F	F	F	T	F

5.

P	Q	R	Q → R	P → (Q → R)
T	T	T	T	T
T	T	F	F	F
T	F	T	T	T
T	F	F	T	T
F	T	T	T	T
F	T	F	F	T
F	F	T	T	T
F	F	F	T	T

12.

C	S	C → S	~(C → S)
T	T	T	F
T	F	F	T
F	T	T	F
F	F	T	F

Exercise 9-4

1. Invalid:

		(Premise)	(Premise)	(Conclusion)
P	Q	~Q	P ∨ ~Q	~P
T	T	F	T	F
T	F	T	T	F
F	T	F	F	T
F	F	T	T	T

(Row 2)

4. Invalid:

			(Conclusion)	(Premise)		(Premise)
P	Q	R	(P → Q)	~(P → Q)	(Q → R)	P→(Q→R)
T	T	T	T	F	T	T
T	T	F	T	F	F	F
T	F	T	F	T	T	T
T	F	F	F	T	T	T
F	T	T	T	F	T	T
F	T	F	T	F	F	T
F	F	T	T	F	T	T
F	F	F	T	F	T	T

(Row 4)

7. Invalid:

			(Premise)		(Premise)	(Conclusion)
P	Q	R	~Q	P & R	(P & R) → Q	~P
T	T	T	F	T	T	F
T	T	F	F	F	T	F
T	F	T	T	T	F	F
T	F	F	T	F	T	F
F	T	T	F	F	T	T
F	T	F	F	F	T	T
F	F	T	T	F	T	T
F	F	F	T	F	T	T

(Row 4)

Exercise 9-5

We've used the short truth-table method to demonstrate invalidity.

1. Valid. There is no row in the argument's table that makes the premises all T and the conclusion F.

2. Invalid. There are two rows that make the premises T and the conclusion F. (Such rows are sometimes called "counterexamples" to the argument.) Here they are:

L	W	S	P
T	F	F	F
T	T	F	F

(Remember: You need to come up with only *one* of these rows to prove the argument invalid.)

3. Invalid. There are two rows that make the premises T and the conclusion F:

M	P	R	F	G
T	T	F	F	T
T	T	F	T	F

4. Invalid. There are three rows that make the premises true and the conclusion F:

D	G	H	P	M
F	T	T	T	T
F	T	F	T	T
F	T	F	F	T

5. Invalid. There are two rows that make the premises T and the conclusion F:

R	S	B	T	E
T	T	F	F	F
F	F	T	F	F

Exercise 9-6

1. Chain argument
2. Disjunctive argument
3. Constructive dilemma
4. Modus tollens
5. Destructive dilemma

Exercise 9-7

1. 1. $R \rightarrow P$ (Premise)
2. $Q \rightarrow R$ (Premise) $/\therefore Q \rightarrow P$
3. $Q \rightarrow P$ 1, 2, CA

4. 1. $P \rightarrow Q$ (Premise)
2. $\sim P \rightarrow S$ (Premise)
3. $\sim Q$ (premise) $/\therefore S$
4. $\sim P$ 1, 3, MT
5. S 2, 4, MP

7. 1. $\sim S$ (Premise)
2. $(P \& Q) \rightarrow R$ (Premise)
3. $R \rightarrow S$ (Premise) $/\therefore \sim(P \& Q)$
4. $\sim R$ 1, 3, MT
5. $\sim(P \& Q)$ 4, 2, MT

10. 1. $(T \vee M) \rightarrow \sim Q$ (Premise)
2. $(P \rightarrow Q) \& (R \rightarrow S)$ (Premise)
3. T (Premise) $/\therefore \sim P$
4. $T \vee M$ 3, ADD
5. $\sim Q$ 1, 4, MP
6. $P \rightarrow Q$ 2, SIM
7. $\sim P$ 5, 6, MT

Exercise 9-8

1. 4. 1,3, CA
5. 2, CONTR
6. 4,5, CA

4. 4. 3, CONTR
5. 2,4, MP
6. 2,5, CONJ
7. 1,6, MP

Exercise 9-9

There is usually more than one way to do these.

1. 1. $P \& Q$ (Premise)
2. $P \rightarrow R$ (Premise) $/\therefore R$
3. P 1, SIM
4. R 2, 3, MP

2. 1. $R \rightarrow S$ (Premise)
2. $\sim P \vee R$ (Premise) $/\therefore P \rightarrow S$
3. $P \rightarrow R$ 2, IMPL
4. $P \rightarrow S$ 1, 3, CA

4. 1. $\sim P \vee (\sim Q \vee R)$ (Premise)
2. P (Premise) $/\therefore Q \rightarrow R$
3. $P \rightarrow (\sim Q \vee R)$ 1, IMPL
4. $\sim Q \vee R$ 2, 3, MP
5. $Q \rightarrow R$ 4, IMPL

8. 1. $\sim Q \& (\sim S \& \sim T)$ (Premise)
2. $P \rightarrow (Q \vee S)$ (Premise) $/\therefore \sim P$
3. $(\sim Q \& \sim S) \& \sim T$ 1, ASSOC
4. $\sim Q \& \sim S$ 3, SIM
5. $\sim(Q \vee S)$ 4, DEM
6. $\sim P$ 2,5, MT

Exercise 9-10

1. 1. $P \rightarrow R$ (Premise)
2. $R \rightarrow Q$ (Premise) $/\therefore \sim P \vee Q$
3. $P \rightarrow Q$ 1, 2, CA
4. $\sim P \vee Q$ 3, IMPL

4. 1. $P \vee (Q \& R)$ (Premise)
2. $(P \vee Q) \rightarrow S$ (Premise) $/\therefore S$
3. $(P \vee Q) \& (P \vee R)$ 1, DIST
4. $P \vee Q$ 3, SIM
5. S 2,4, MP

7. 1. $(M \vee R) \& P$ (Premise)
2. $\sim S \rightarrow \sim P$ (Premise)
3. $S \rightarrow \sim M$ (Premise) $/\therefore R$
4. $P \rightarrow S$ 2, CONTR
5. P 1, SIM
6. S 4,5, MP
7. $\sim M$ 3,6, MP
8. $M \vee R$ 1, SIM
9. R 7,8, DA

10. 1. $P \vee (R \& Q)$ (Premise)
2. $R \rightarrow \sim P$ (Premise)
3. $Q \rightarrow T$ (Premise) $/\therefore R \rightarrow T$
4. $(P \vee R) \& (P \vee Q)$ 1, DIST
5. $P \vee Q$ 4, SIM
6. $\sim P \rightarrow Q$ 5, DN/IMPL
7. $R \rightarrow Q$ 2,6, CA
8. $R \rightarrow T$ 3,7, CA

Exercise 9-11

1. $D \rightarrow \sim B$
4. $B \rightarrow \sim D$
7. $C \rightarrow (B \& \sim D)$

Exercise 9-12

1. Equivalent to (b)
4. Equivalent to (c)
7. Equivalent to (c)

Exercise 9-13

1.

1.	P	(Premise)
2.	Q & R	(Premise)
3.	(Q & P) → S	(Premise) /∴ S
4.	Q	2, SIM
5.	Q & P	1,4, CONJ
6.	S	3,5, MP

4.

1.	P ∨ Q	(Premise)
2.	(Q ∨ U) → (P → T)	(Premise)
3.	~P	(Premise)
4.	(~P ∨ R) → (Q → S)	(Premise) /∴ T ∨ S
5.	Q	1,3, DA
6.	Q ∨ U	5, ADD
7.	P → T	2,6, MP
8.	~P ∨ R	3, ADD
9.	Q → S	4,8, MP
10.	T ∨ S	1,7,9, CD

7.

1.	P → Q	(Premise) /∴ P → (Q ∨ R)
2.	~P ∨ Q	1, IMPL
3.	(~P ∨ Q) ∨ R	2, ADD
4.	~P ∨ (Q ∨ R)	3, ASSOC
5.	P → (Q ∨ R)	4, IMPL

10.

1.	(S → Q) → ~R	(Premise)
2.	(P → Q) → R	(Premise) /∴ ~ Q
3.	~R → ~(P → Q)	2, CONTR
4.	(S → Q) → ~(P → Q)	1,3, CA
5.	~(S → Q) ∨ ~(P → Q)	4, IMPL
6.	~(~S ∨ Q) ∨ ~(~P ∨ Q)	5, IMPL (twice)
7.	(S & ~Q) ∨ (P & ~Q)	6, DEM/DN (twice)
8.	((S & ~Q) ∨ P) & ((S & ~Q) ∨ ~Q)	7, DIST
9.	(S & ~Q) ∨ ~Q	8, SIM
10.	~Q ∨ (S & ~Q)	9, COM
11.	(~Q ∨ S) & (~Q ∨ ~Q)	10, DIST
12.	~Q ∨ ~Q	11, SIM
13.	~Q	12, TAUT

Exercise 9-14

1.

1.	P → Q	(Premise)
2.	P → R	(Premise) /∴ P → (Q & R)
(3)	P	CP Premise
4.	Q	1,3, MP
5.	R	2,3, MP
6.	Q & R	4,5, CONJ
7.	P → (Q & R)	3–6, CP

4.

1.	P → (Q ∨ R)	(Premise)
2.	T → (S & ~R)	(Premise) /∴ (P & T) → Q
(3)	P & T	CP Premise
4.	P	3, SIM
5.	T	3, SIM
6.	Q ∨ R	1,4, MP
7.	S & ~R	2,5, MP
8.	~R	7, SIM
9.	Q	6,8, DA
10.	(P & T) → Q	3–9, CP

7.

1.	P ∨ (Q & R)	(Premise)
2.	T → ~(P ∨ U)	(Premise)
3.	S → (Q → ~R)	(Premise) /∴ ~S ∨ ~T
(4)	S	CP Premise
5.	Q → ~R	3,4, MP
6.	~Q ∨ ~R	5, IMPL
7.	~(Q & R)	6, DEM
8.	P	1,7, DA
9.	P ∨ U	8, ADD
10.	~~(P ∨ U)	9, DN
11.	~T	2,10, MT
12.	S → ~T	4–11, CP
13.	~S ∨ ~T	12, IMPL

10.

1.	(P & Q) ∨ R	(Premise)
2.	~R ∨ Q	(Premise) /∴ P → Q
(3)	P	CP Premise
(4)	~Q	CP Premise
5.	~R	2,4, DA
6.	P & Q	1,5, DA
7.	Q	6, SIM
8.	~Q → Q	4–7, CP
9.	Q ∨ Q	8, IMPL
10.	Q	9, TAUT
11.	P → Q	3–10, CP

Exercise 9-15

1. C → ~S
~L → S
———
C → L
Valid

4. ~M ∨ C
~M → ~K
C ∨ H
T → ~ H
———
T → K
Invalid

7. C ∨ S
S → E
C → R
———
R ∨ E
Valid

10. C → ~L
(E → (~C → ~T)) & E
———
L → ~T
Valid

13. S → ~F
~S → ~T
T
———
~F
Valid

Chapter 10: Inductive Arguments

Exercise 10-1

1. a. The two terms are "these shrubs" and "privet." The target is "these shrubs" and the issue is whether they will keep their leaves in the winter.
4. b
7. a. The two terms are "your face" and "your hands." The target is "your hands"; the issue is whether too much sun will make one's hands wrinkly.
10. b
13. b
16. b
19. a. The two terms are "Yamaha motorcycles" and "Yamaha pianos." The target is "Yamaha pianos" and the issue is whether Yamaha makes good pianos.

Exercise 10-2

1. b
4. a
7. a
10. b

Exercise 10-3

1. a
4. a
7. a
10. a

Exercise 10-5

1. "Tests in this class" is perfectly clear, "hard" (the property in question) is a little bit vague.
4. "Tolerant of stress" (the property in question) is vague.
7. Weather in Iowa is pretty vague, and so is "weather that sucks."
10. Everything in this one is way too vague.
13. "Suspicious people" is pretty vague, and "quite unhappy" is, too.

Exercise 10-6

1. a
4. a
7. If there is a significant genetic component to the incidence of high blood pressure, its presence in Lupe's sister and mother provides pretty good reason to think Lupe might have or develop high blood pressure, too.
9. d
12. c

Exercise 10-8

1. In order of increasing cautiousness, we'd say d, f, b, c, e, a.

Exercise 10-9

1. Insufficiently cautious
4. Overly cautious

Exercise 10-10

1. This argument is fairly strong; the conclusion exhibits a reasonable amount of caution.
4. This makes the argument weaker; a relevant difference between the previous rides and the target.
8. This makes the argument stronger. Since we don't know the terrain of the target ride, a variety of terrain among the previous rides strengthens the argument.
10. If you considered the fact that bicycling is generally easier on flat land than on hilly land, you went beyond the criteria for inductive arguments in general. This is "specialized" knowledge and is part of a different argument: "This year's ride will be on flat land, while previous rides were in hilly terrain. Bicycling is easier on flat land. Therefore, this year's ride will be easier."

Exercise 10-11

1. This supposition weakens the argument since it introduces a relevant difference between this year's crop and the ones that went before.
4. This supposition weakens the argument since it introduces a relevant difference between this year's crop and the ones that went before.
7. This supposition neither weakens nor strengthens the argument since a solar eclipse is not significant to the property in question (mildew ruining the artichoke crop).
10. This supposition weakens the argument since it introduces a relevant difference between this year's crop and the ones that went before.

Exercise 10-12

1. The two suppositions weaken the argument.
4. The supposition strengthens the argument.

Exercise 10-13

1. The six students who turned in written evaluations
4. Generalization
6. No
8. It's not very strong. The sample is small, and given that it's not random it's very likely to be

unrepresentative: The students who bothered to write have relatively strong feelings about Ludlum one way or the other, and there is no reason to think that the spread of their opinions reflects the spread among Ludlum's students in general.

Exercise 10-14

1. No. If he bet that exactly 60 percent held the belief, he would be allowing for no error margin whatsoever. If he makes that bet, take him up on it.
4. 66 percent
7. With a sample of 100, he can safely bet that no more than 70 percent share that belief, because the error margin is now ±10 percent.

Exercise 10-15

Here we want to emphasize the importance of subject-matter knowledge in the analysis of analogical arguments and inductive arguments in general. There is no substitute for wide reading, diverse friendships, life experience, and self-reflection in the development of critical thinkers.

1. The terms of the analogy are Tiger Woods and the speaker's child. The analogy is strong only if the speaker's child has other features in common with Tiger Woods, such as great powers of concentration, great physical ability, and a proper temperament for golf. It's unlikely that early lessons are as important as these traits.
4. The terms of the analogy are Senator Clinton's performance as a senator and her potential performance as president. There is a great deal more exposure as president and a great number of constituencies to serve. Still, the similarities are significant. This conclusion gets more support from its premise than many in this exercise.
7. The terms of the analogy are Bush's ratings in Georgia and his ratings in Massachusetts. Since the political scene in these two states is very different, and since they have voted very differently in recent elections, this is not a very good argument.
10. The terms of the analogy are Warren's personal appearance and his care of the Barnes's house. These terms are sufficiently dissimilar—especially as regards their motivations—as to make for a weak argument. It *may* be that Warren's personal grooming will carry over to taking care of the house, but we suspect that many neat-appearing people live in messy abodes.

Exercise 10-16

1. Biased generalization
4. Hasty generalization; quite likely biased, too
8. Hasty generalization; biased, too
10. Biased generalization
13. "Refutation" by hasty generalization

Chapter 11: Causal Arguments

Exercise 11-1

1. Causal claim
4. Causal claim
7. Causal claim, although a very vague one
10. Causal claim
13. Causal claim
16. Not a causal claim

Exercise 11-2

1. Effect: cat is not eating; cause: cat is eating mice
4. Effect: the little guy's not dehydrating; cause: giving him more water
7. Effect: that people cannot detect their own bad breath; cause: becoming used to the odor
10. Effect: a savings to the state in court expenses; cause: judges' failure to process shoplifting, trespassing, and small-claims charges

Exercise 11-3

1. a
4. b
7. a
10. b
13. a
16. b
19. a

Exercise 11-4

1. C; mowing the grass results in both fumes and grass dust.
4. C; shorter days contribute to both.
7. C; getting older can result in both conditions.
10. B; maybe smarter people eat more fish.
13. B; if there is more violence, there is likely to be more on TV.
16. A
19. A; C is also possible, since good health may have contributed both to Uncle Ted's attitude and to his longevity.
22. A; yes it could.
25. B; top executives can easily afford expensive clothes and nice cars.

Exercise 11-5

1. a

4. c

7. a

10. b

14. a

17. b

20. a

Exercise 11-9

1. There are three causal hypotheses mentioned: One is that drinking wine weekly or monthly may cause dementia; a second is that drinking wine daily probably does *not* prevent dementia; and the third is that regular beer drinking is probably a cause of dementia.

The study is cause-to-effect, but the study is largely nonexperimental because of the self-selection of the experimental group(s)—i.e., the drinkers—and the control group—the nondrinkers. Nothing is mentioned of the nature or size of either group. The description of the study is quite vague. Although the source of the study appears to be a legitimate authority, the account given here would lead us to want more details of the study before we'd give more than a very tentative acceptance of the results.

4. Causal claim: Sleeping in a room with a light until age two is a cause of nearsightedness in later years. The study is nonexperimental, cause-to-effect. No differences between the experimental groups (children who slept with lights on) and the control group (children who slept in darkness). The differences in effect were 24 percent between night light and darkness, and 45 percent between a lamp and darkness. From what is reported, no problems can be identified.

Although the study is fairly small, the results indicate it is likely that there is a causal connection between the described cause and effect—a *d* of about 11 percent would be necessary in an experimental study; the higher numbers here help compensate for the nonexperimental nature of the study.

7. Causal claim: Exercise prevents colds. The study is a controlled cause-to-effect experiment, with one experimental group and two control groups. The first control group consists of ten non-exercising volunteers; the second consists of the experimental group prior to the jogging program.

The experimental group had 25 percent fewer colds than the first control group and some non-indicated percent fewer than the second control group. We don't know enough about the groups and how they were chosen to tell if there are significant differences. Given the small size of the groups, a *d* of 40 percent is necessary to have statistical significance. The 25 percent figure is substantial and may indicate a causal connection, but it isn't enough to convince us to take up jogging.

14. Causal claim: A behavior modification program aimed at Type A individuals prevents heart attacks. The study is a controlled cause-to-effect experiment. The experimental group consisted of 592 out of 862 predominantly male victims of heart attack; they were given group counseling to ease Type A behavior. The matched control group consisted of 270 subjects who received only cardiological advice.

After three years, 7 percent of the experimental group had another heart attack, compared with 13 percent of the control group. The finding is probably statistically significant given the size of the groups and the percentages involved. Details about the length of counseling are missing and they could be important because the report implies that continuation of the program was voluntary. Also, there seems to be confusion about what the investigators were researching—the relationship between the program and heart attack rate, between an actual behavioral modification and heart attack rate, between counseling and behavioral modification, or some combination or interplay of these. The conclusion the study supports is that Type A individuals who have had one heart attack can significantly reduce their chance of a second heart attack by participating (for some unspecified amount of time) in whatever kind of counseling program was conducted in the experiment.

Exercise 11-11

Our evaluations:

1. A, A, A

6. F, C, F

10. B, C, A

Exercise 11-12

1. This explanation is full of problems. It is untestable; its relevance is questionable (we couldn't have predicted blue eyes from a previous incarnation unless we knew more about the incarnation, but the explanation is too vague to enable us to do that); it contains unnecessary assumptions; and it conflicts with well-established theory about how we get our eye color.

4. Reasonable explanation

7. Poor explanation; circular

10. Poor explanation; untestable (given the fact that subconscious desires are allowed); excessively vague; questionable relevance; conflicts with well-established theory

13. Reasonable explanation

17. Before we accepted this explanation of violence we'd want to consider alternatives: poverty, hopelessness, and discrimination, to name a few. Rap music and TV/movie violence may be reflections of violence rather than causes.

20. This poor explanation is untestable, unreliable, and extremely vague. The nondevout might add that it requires unnecessary assumptions.

Exercise 11-15

1. Explanation
4. Explanation
7. Explanation
10. Explanation used to justify or excuse behavior

Exercise 11-16

1. Explanation
4. Explanation
5. Explanation used to excuse

Exercise 11-17

Of the first three items, numbers 2 and 3 use explanations to help justify an action (or omission, in the case of 3). Item 1 does not justify any behavior.

Exercise 11-19

1. This is just an explanation of how the garage got this cluttered.
4. This is an argument that Parker is giving a test today.
8. Host gives an explanation of why he can't shave. The explanation is intended to serve as a justification.
10. The speaker is explaining why this is a great movie, and in doing so is arguing that it is a great movie.
12. This is an explanation of why the contamination is getting worse and worse, and it might be used to argue that we should change what we allow people to do.
15. This is an explanation of why you are unable to sleep.
18. The speaker explains how touching the pins can fry the logic circuits and in doing so argues that if you touch the pins, you can expect this to be the result.
21. The author is explaining why women are worse off than men economically and in doing so is arguing that women are worse off. (Don't be discouraged by the subtlety of real-life specimens.)
25. The writer is explaining what the purpose of the Humane Society is and by doing so is arguing that the Humane Society is not an animal rights organization.
26. This is an explanation used as a justification.

Exercise 11-20

1. There is no argument present.
4. This is an explanation that *might* be used to justify the Rotary's behavior, but given the behavior in question, there is certainly no need to justify it.
7. Explanation used in an argument to justify making the 445 pages of report public.
10. This is an explanation that could easily *and mistakenly* be taken as an attempt to justify a molester's behavior.

Chapter 12: Moral, Legal, and Aesthetic Reasoning

Exercise 12-1

1. Value judgment
4. Value judgment
7. Value judgment
10. Not a value judgment

Exercise 12-2

1. Not a value judgment, although it surely hints at one.
4. Value judgment
7. Not a value judgment in the ordinary sense, but since rides are often evaluated by degree of scariness, this may imply such a judgment.

Exercise 12-3

1. Not a moral value judgment
4. Moral value judgment
7. Not a moral value judgment
10. Moral value judgment

Exercise 12-4

2. People ought to keep their promises.
5. A mayor who takes bribes should resign.
7. Anyone who commits a third felony should automatically go to prison for twenty-five years.
8. Whatever is unnatural is wrong and should be avoided.

Exercise 12-5

1. Tory is being consistent in that what he is proposing for *both* sexes is that members of both should have the right to marry members of the *other* sex.
2. To avoid inconsistency, Shelley must be able to identify characteristics of art and music students, athletes, and children of alumni—for whom she believes the special admissions program is acceptable—and show that, aside from women and minority students who happen also to be in one of the listed categories, such students do not have these characteristics.

Furthermore, the characteristics she identifies must be relevant to the issue of whether an individual should be admitted into the university. It may well be possible to identify the characteristics called for. (Remember that consistency is a necessary condition for a correct position, but not a sufficient one.)

3. Marin could be consistent only if he could show that the process of abortion involves killing and capital punishment does not. Because this is impossible—capital punishment clearly does involve killing—he is inconsistent. However, Marin's inconsistency is the result of his blanket claim that *all* killing is wrong. He could make a consistent case if he were to maintain only that the killing of *innocent* people is wrong, and that abortion involves killing innocent people but capital punishment does not. There is another approach: Marin could argue that only *state-mandated* killing (which would include capital punishment but not abortion) is permissible. (Each of these last claims would require strong arguments.)

8. To avoid inconsistency, Harold would have to identify a relevant difference between the discrimination law and the marijuana law. In fact, there is one fairly obvious one to which he can appeal: The former has been declared contrary to the state constitution; the latter has not been alleged to be contrary to any constitution. So Harold may object to the failure to implement the latter even if it does conflict with federal drug laws—after all, if the law has not been found unconstitutional, shouldn't the will of the voters prevail? (It is a separate matter, of course, whether he can build a strong argument in the case of the marijuana law.)

Exercise 12-9

1. The harm principle: Shoplifting harms those from whom one steals.
2. The harm principle: Forgery tends to harm others.
4. We think the offense principle is the most relevant, because the practice in question is found highly offensive by most people (at least we believe—and hope—so). But one might also include the harm principle, because spitting in public can spread disease-causing organisms.
6. Legal moralism, because many people find adultery immoral; and, to a lesser extent, both the harm principle and legal paternalism, because adultery can increase the spread of sexually transmitted diseases.
10. The offense principle

Exercise 12-12

1. a. Principle 4
b. Principle 2
Compatible

4.a. Principle 5
b. Principle 2
Compatible

Exercise 12-13

1. Relevant on Principle 7
4. Relevant on Principle 1
7. Relevant on Principle 3

Exercise 12-14

Principle 1: June's picture does not teach us anything, for no chimp can distinguish between truth and falsity; it is a curiosity rather than a work of art.

Principle 2: By looking at June's very symbolic paintings, we are compelled to accept her vision of a world in which discourse is by sight rather than by sound.

Principle 3: Perhaps the most far-reaching impact of June's art is its revelation of the horrors of encaging chimps; surely beings who can reach these heights of sublimely abstract expression should not see the world through iron bars.

Principle 4: Dear Zookeeper: Please encourage June to keep painting, as the vibrant colors and intense brushstrokes of her canvases fill all of us with delight.

Principle 5: I never thought I would wish to feel like a monkey, but June's art made me appreciate how chimps enjoy perceiving us humans as chumps.

Principle 6: This is not art, for no monkey's product can convey the highest, most valuable, human states of mind.

Principle 7: Whether by the hand of monkey or man, that the canvases attributed to June show lovely shapes and colors is indisputable.

Principle 8: What is art is simply what pleases a person's taste, and June obviously finds painting tasty, as she tends to eat the paint.

Exercise 12-15

1. a
4. b
7. b

Photo Credits

Preface © Bill Husa/Chico Enterprise Record **Chapter 1 p. 1, 2,** © AP/Wide World Photos; **p. 5,** © Joe McBride/Getty Images/Stone; **p. 10,** © Peter Greste/Reuters/Corbis; **p. 13,** © Peter Turnley/Corbis; **p. 16L,** © Bettmann/Corbis; **p. 16R,** The Palma Collection/Getty Images **Chapter 2 p. 39, 41,** © AP/Wide World Photos; **p. 49,** © 20th Century Fox Film Corp. All rights reserved/Courtesy Everett Collection; **p. 55,** © AP/Wide World Photos **Chapter 3 p. 77,** © AP/Wide World Photos; **p. 80L,** PhotoLink/Getty Images; **p. 80R,** © Royalty-Free/Corbis; **p. 85, 86, 93,** © AP/Wide World Photos; **p. 94L,** © 20th Century Fox Film Corp. All rights reserved. Courtesy Everett Collection; **p. 94R,** Courtesy The News Hour/PBS; **p. 97, 99, 101,** © AP/Wide World Photos; **p. 102,** © 20th Century Fox Film Corp. All rights reserved. Courtesy Everett Collection **Chapter 4 p. 117,** © The New York Times; **p. 120, 124L,** © AP/Wide World Photos; **p. 124R,** © Jim Watson/Getty Images; **p. 125,** © Ahmad Al-Rubaye/AFP/Getty Images; **p. 128,** © Chung Sung-Jun/Getty Images; **p. 129,** Parody Image Copyright 2005 Registeredmedia.com **Chapter 5 p. 145,** © AP/Wide World Photos; **p. 148,** © Kayte M. Deioma/PhotoEdit; **p. 153,** Courtesy Dollsville.com; **p. 155,** © Mark Wilson/Getty Images; **p. 162,** © George DeSota/Getty Images **Chapter 6 p. 173,** © Royalty-Free/Corbis; **p. 180L,** © Poppy Berry/Corbis; **p. 180R,** Steve Cole/Getty Images; **p. 186,** C. Lee/PhotoLink/Getty Images; **p. 198,** David Haymore, courtesy April Wells-Hayes **Chapter 7 p. 215, 220,** © AP/Wide World Photos; **p. 223L,** © Royalty-Free/Corbis; **p. 223R,** © AP/Wide World Photos **Chapter 8 p. 247,** © 20th Century Fox Film Corp. All rights reserved. Courtesy Everett Collection; **p. 273,** © AP/Wide World Photos; **p. 275,** Courtesy of the authors **Chapter 9 p. 287,** © Digital Vision; **p. 305,** © Larry Downing/Reuters/Corbis **Chapter 10 p. 333,** © STR/AFP/Getty Images; **p. 336,** © The Image Works; **p. 337,** © AP/Wide World Photos; **p. 344,** © Bettmann/Corbis; **p. 348,** © Royalty-Free/Corbis **Chapter 11 p. 371,** © AP/Wide World Photos; **p. 373,** Courtesy of the authors; **p. 375,** © Walt Disney/Courtesy Everett Collection; **p. 377,** © HBO/Courtesy Everett Collection; **p. 384,** © Royalty-Free/Corbis; **p. 416,** © Norbert Schaefer/Corbis **Chapter 12 p. 419,** Photo © Erich Lessing/Art Resource, NY. © 2005 Artists Rights Society (ARS), New York / VG Bild-Kunst, Bonn; **p. 442,** © Viviane Moos/Corbis; **p. 443,** © Rachel Steiner; **p. 446,** Photo © Art Resource, NY. © 2005 Estate of Pablo Picasso/Artists Rights Society (ARS), New York; **p. 448,** © Kimimasa Mayama/Retuers/Corbis; **p. 452,** *Tilted Arc,* 1981. Weatherproof Steel, 12′×120′×2½;. Collection: General Services Administration, Washington, DC. Installed: Federal Plaza, New York. Destroyed by the Federal Government 1989. © 2005 Richard Serra/Artists Rights Society (ARS), New York. Photo courtesy of Richard Serra; **p. 453,** © Scala/Art Resource, NY **Appendix p. 484T,** McGraw-Hill Companies, Inc./Gary He, photographer; **p. 484B,** © Bill Aron/PhotoEdit; **p. 485T,** The McGraw-Hill Companies, Inc./Jill Braaten, Photographer; **p. 485B,** McGraw-Hill Companies, Inc./Gary He, photographer; **p. 499,** © Jack Plunkett/AFP/Getty Images

Index